THE

EUROPEAN

PAST

EDITED BY

SHEPARD B. CLOUGH

Professor of History

Columbia University

PETER GAY

Professor of History

Columbia University

CHARLES K. WARNER

Associate Professor of History

Middlebury College

THE
EUROPEAN
PAST

VOLUME II

REAPPRAISALS

IN HISTORY

SINCE

WATERLOO

THE MACMILLAN COMPANY, NEW YORK

Library of Congress catalog card number: 64-16049

The Macmillan Company, New York
Collier-Macmillan Canada, Ltd., Toronto, Ontario

Printed in the United States of America

DESIGNED BY RONALD FARBER

Preface

𝒥t has been the object of the editors of
this book to introduce new materials and a new approach to the study of
European history. Included in these two volumes are historical essays which
present revaluations or conflicts of interpretation centered around thirty-
two important historical topics.

¶ Sometimes controversies evolve from differences in method; sometimes
from fundamental differences in the philosophy of history; sometimes from
the selection of different data. In every case, however, the reader is introduced
to the frontiers of research in history. He is given a sense of the "sifting and
winnowing" involved in historical judgment and provided with an opportunity
to make informed judgments of his own.

¶ Controversies or reinterpretations produced by different historical
questions have, of course, been used to some degree in other books of
readings. But the typical "case study" frequently offers a hodgepodge of
primary and secondary materials in such fragmentary form as to vitiate
their meaning. The selections presented in this book aim at conveying a
sense of the depth of the subject being treated.

¶ It will be noticed that the largest part of the selections included here
have been published during the last twenty years. All come from the
current generation of scholars or their teachers. This choice has been
deliberate. The great classic controversies of the last century or the earlier
years of this one which fill the pages of some books of readings are not,
of course, without interest. But if history is a cumulative study which
permits us to know more and more about the past, is not the latest history
the best gauge of whatever consensus has been reached on a given issue?

¶ The selections presented here are either articles from scholarly journals,
most often reproduced in their original length, or they are meaningful

[v]

portions of monographs or broader studies. An innovation has been to offer, where possible, an historiographical essay as one of the selections under a particular topic. Where this has not been possible, background information is included in the topic introduction.

The editors wish to acknowledge the research assistance of James Friguglietti, the secretarial help of Patricia Cutler Warner, and the translation assistance of Cambridge Editorial Research, Inc.

S. B. C.
P. G.
C. K. W.

Contents

THE NEW STATESMEN

IMPERIALISM

EUROPE IN THE TWENTIETH CENTURY

THE
EUROPEAN
PAST

EUROPE
AND THE AFTERMATH
OF NAPOLEON

[1]

The Congress of Vienna
and the Metternich Era

$\mathcal{T}$HE TWO selections that follow cover
an event, the Congress of Vienna, which set up a system, often called the
"Metternichian system," that ordered the relations between the states of Europe
and a period 1815–1848, during which the "system" functioned.

¶ The first selection is by Henry Kissinger. Though widely known as an
analyst of contemporary international affairs, Kissinger is also the author of a
highly praised study, *A World Restored: Metternich, Castlereagh, and the
Problems of Peace 1812–1822* (1957). In his essay below, Kissinger concentrates
on the workings of the congress. At the same time he offers an interesting
combination of theory and history. He begins by defining the elements of
a practicable optimum in international settlements and concludes that
the success of the Congress of Vienna was due to circumstances which
made the achievement of such an optimum possible. Kissinger does not
discount entirely the part played by the diplomats. Although he rejects "the
myth about Talleyrand's role at the congress," he praises the abilities of
Metternich and Castlereagh and "the skill of the diplomats in *making use of
their opportunities*" (italics added). For Kissinger, "the effectiveness of
diplomacy depends on elements transcending it," and his warning against
ascribing the achievements of the Congress of Vienna "to the very process
of negotiation, to diplomatic skill, and to 'willingness to come to an
agreement' " is, in effect, a rejection of standard interpretations of the congress.

¶ The second selection, by Robert Kann, an authority on the history of
the Hapsburg Empire,[1] examines Metternich in a broader context than the

[1] R. Kann, *The Multinational Empire: Nationalism and National Reform in the Hapsburg
Monarchy, 1848–1918* (New York: Columbia, 1950); *The Hapsburg Empire: A Study in Integra-
tion and Disintegration* (New York: Praeger, 1957); *A Study in Austrian Intellectual History:
From Late Baroque to Romanticism* (New York: Praeger, 1960).

[3]

Congress of Vienna by evaluating his impact on international relations during his chancellorship and commenting on the relationship of his policies to the problems of our time. In this last respect, Kann's essay represents a qualified reappraisal of the recent rehabilitation of Metternich and his era.

The reader should remember that late nineteenth- and early twentieth-century historiography—which was in the liberal or nationalistic tradition or a combination of the two—saw the Congress of Vienna as an attempt "to turn the clock back," the Concert of Europe as an instrument to maintain the *status quo,* and the suppression of the revolutions of 1848 as thwarting the progressive forces of liberalism and nationalism. Metternich was the villain in the center of this stage, and after he fled it in 1848, his place was taken by the Emperor Francis Joseph with assistance from Tsar Nicholas I.

This is an oversimplified picture of what people believed, but in its broad outlines it was the accepted one, and it is perpetuated to some degree today in popular histories. The shift away from this point of view began after World War I with the opening of the Hapsburg and Austrian State Archives and the publication in 1925 of *Metternich,* a massive and scholarly biography by Heinrich Von Srbik, which shed new light on Metternich and his policies. But in the sense that each age rewrites history in terms of its own experience, the real rehabilitation of Metternich began after World War II.

To the generations which have seen two world wars separated by only two decades of uneasy peace, the "fifty-year peace" in Europe which followed the Congress of Vienna is impressive enough. The Crimean War, of course, ended this period and was a blow to the spirit of Metternich's system, but the Concert of Europe survived it.[2] And although the existence of the concert became increasingly precarious, the continuation of Metternich's "European conscience" has been credited with preventing the outbreak of a general European war during the hundred years between Waterloo and 1914.

The same generations which have seen two world wars have, also understandably, looked at nationalism with something less than the approbation of pre-1914 historians. From this point of view, Metternich's eighteenth-century cosmopolitanism carried into the nineteenth century has seemed more relevant than before. There have been new insights into his steadfast opposition to the unification of Germany and Italy and his determination that the Hapsburg Empire should play a leading role in Europe. In our own time, the dismember-

---

[2] All major powers were represented at the Congress of Paris (1856), which ended the Crimean War, and questions of general European concern unrelated to the war were acted on. All major powers were also represented at the Congress of Berlin (1878), which ended the Russo-Turkish War. But before then, peace settlements made between the belligerents after the Austro-Prussian War (1866) and the Franco-Prussian War (1870) had all but destroyed the concert idea. The London Conference of 1913, where the major powers dictated the peace terms of the First Balkan War to the belligerents, appears as a revival of the concert system, but it was ineffective in keeping peace either in the Balkans or Europe.

ment of that empire, so hopefully undertaken in 1919 in the name of "self-determination" (a solution to the ethnic problems of the empire that Metternich would have considered anarchic) has ended after many vicissitudes in Russian penetration of Central Europe and the Balkans. By contrast, as Kann points out, Metternich's "skillful containment of Russia" was one of his more successful policies.

Again this an oversimplified picture, but it should help the reader understand the rehabilitation of Metternich to the point where his policies seem to relate to the problems of our time.[3] As we pointed out earlier, Professor Kann's essay qualifies this assumed relationship. Although not uncritical, Kann is an admirer of Metternich and maintains that "as to the significance of his life's work for the present world . . . he surpasses most of the outstanding statesmen that came before or after him." Kann believes, however, that this significance rests on an "almost unique contribution . . . the creation of a system of international politics according to supra-national and supra-party principles and based on supposedly self-evident reason." As to the relation of Metternich's policies to our times along the lines suggested above, he has important reservations which raise interesting questions of historical causation and analogy.

THE CONGRESS OF VIENNA: A REAPPRAISAL

Henry A. Kissinger

IT IS only natural that a period anxiously seeking to wrest peace from the threat of nuclear extinction should look nostalgically to the last great successful effort to settle international disputes by means of a diplomatic conference, the Congress of Vienna. Nothing is more

[3] For a notable example of this line of thinking, see Peter Viereck, *Conservatism Revisited* (New York: Scribners, 1949; rev. ed. New York: Collier Books, 1962). In this book and in "New Views on Metternich," *The Review of Politics* (1951), pp. 211–28, Viereck also offers evidence that Metternich was more aware of the new social and political forces than most historians give him credit for, and sees him as more of a political philosopher than, for example, Kann does. Viereck's book or article can be read with profit in connection with this topic.

From *World Politics*, VIII, No. 2 (January 1956), pp. 264–80. Reprinted by permission. Copyright Princeton University Press.

tempting than to ascribe its achievements to the very process of negotiation, to diplomatic skill, and to "willingness to come to an agreement"—and nothing is more dangerous. For the effectiveness of diplomacy depends on elements transcending it; in part on the domestic structure of the states comprising the international order, in part on their power relationship.

Any international settlement represents a stage in a process by which a nation reconciles its vision of itself with the vision of it by other powers. No state can doubt its own good faith; it is the vehicle of its social cohesion. But, equally, no power can stake its survival entirely on the good faith of another; this would be an abdication of the responsibility of statesmanship. The whole domestic effort of a people exhibits an effort to transform force into obligation by means of a consensus on the nature of justice. But the international experience of a state is a challenge to the universality of its notion of justice, for the stability of the international order depends on the reconciliation of different versions of legitimacy. Could a nation achieve all its wishes, it would strive for absolute security, a world order free from the consciousness of foreign danger, and one where all problems have the manageability of domestic issues. But since absolute security for one power means absolute insecurity for all others, it is obtainable only through conquest, never as part of a legitimate settlement.

An international settlement which is accepted and not imposed will therefore always appear *somewhat* unjust to any one of its components. Paradoxically, the generality of this dissatisfaction is a condition of stability, because were any one power *totally* satisfied, all others would have to be *totally* dissatisfied and a revolutionary situation would ensue. The foundation of a stable order is the *relative* security—and therefore the *relative* insecurity—of its members. Its stability reflects, not the absence of unsatisfied claims, but the absence of a grievance of such magnitude that redress will be sought in overturning the settlement rather than through an adjustment within its framework. An order whose structure is accepted by all major powers is "legitimate." An order containing a power which considers its structure oppressive is "revolutionary." The security of a domestic order resides in the preponderant power of authority, that of an international order in the balance of forces and in its expression, the equilibrium.

But if an international order expresses the need for security and an equilibrium, it is constructed in the name of a legitimizing principle. Because a settlement transforms force into acceptance, it must attempt to translate individual demands into general advantage. It is the legitimizing principle which establishes the relative "justice" of competing claims and the mode of their adjustment. This is not to say that there need be an exact correspondence between the maxims of legitimacy and the conditions of the settlement. No major power will give up its minimum claim to security—the possibility of conducting an independent foreign policy—merely for the sake of legitimacy. But the legitimizing principle defines the marginal case. In 1919, the Austro-Hungarian Empire disintegrated not so much from the impact of the war as from the nature of the peace, because its continued existence was incompatible with national self-determination, the legitimizing principle of the new international order. It would have occurred to no one in the eighteenth century that the legitimacy of a state depended on linguistic unity. It was inconceivable to the makers of the Versailles settlement that there might be any other basis for legitimate rule. Legitimizing principles triumph by being taken for granted.

Although there never occurs an exact correspondence between the maxims of the legitimizing principle and the conditions of the settlement, stability depends on a certain commensurability. If there exists a substantial discrepancy *and* a major power which feels disadvantaged, the international order will be volatile. For the appeal by a "revolutionary" power to the legitimizing principle of the settlement creates a psychological distortion. The "natural" expression of the policy of a status-quo power is law—the definition of a continuing relationship. But against a permanently dissatisfied power appealing to the legitimizing principle of the international order, force is the only recourse. Those who have most gain from stability thus become the advocates of a revolutionary policy. Hitler's appeal to national self-determination in the Sudeten crisis in 1938 was an invocation of "justice," and thereby contributed to the indecisiveness of the resistance: it induced the Western powers to attempt to construct a "truly" legitimate order by satisfying Germany's "just" claims. Only after Hitler annexed Bohemia and Moravia was it clear that he was aiming for dominion, not legitimacy; only then did the contest become one of pure power.

The major problem of an international settlement, then, is so to relate the claims of legitimacy to the requirements of security that no power will express its dissatisfaction in a revolutionary policy, and so to arrange the balance of forces as to deter aggression produced by causes other than the conditions of the settlement. This is not a mechanical problem. If the international order could be constructed like a mathematical axiom, powers would consider themselves as factors in a balance and arrange their adjustments to achieve a perfect equilibrium between the forces of aggression and the forces of resistance. But an exact balance is impossible, and not only because of the difficulty of predicting the aggressor. It is chimerical, above all, because while powers may appear to outsiders as factors in a security arrangement, they appear domestically as expressions of a historical existence. No power will submit to a settlement, however well-balanced and however "secure," which seems totally to deny its vision of itself. There exist two kinds of equilibrium then: a general equilibrium which makes it risky for one power or group of powers to attempt to impose its will on the remainder; and a special equilibrium which defines the historical relation of certain powers among each other. The former is the deterrent against a general war; the latter the condition of smooth cooperation. An international order is therefore rarely born out of the consciousness of harmony. For even when there is an agreement about legitimacy, the conceptions of the requirements of security will differ with the geographical position and the history of the contending powers. Out of just such a conflict over the nature of the equilibrium the Congress of Vienna fashioned a settlement which lasted almost exactly a century.

For the problem at Vienna was not simply how to protect Europe against a renewed French onslaught. There was general agreement about the extent of France compatible with the peace of Europe, but this only sharpened the disagreements *within* the victorious coalition about the relative spheres of influence of Austria, Prussia, Russia, and Great Britain. And this contest was made all the more intractable because each of the protagonists meant something different by the term "equilibrium" so frequently invoked. When the British Foreign Minister, Castlereagh, spoke of the equilibrium, he meant a Europe in which hegemony was impossible; but when Metternich appealed to the equilibrium, he included a Germany in which Prussian predominance was impossible. Russia's demand for Poland threatened the equilibrium of Europe and Castlereagh could, therefore, hardly believe that any other problem was worth discussing before the Tsar's pretensions were thwarted. Prussia's insistence on Saxony merely imperiled the balance within Germany, but this was enough to absorb the full energy of Metternich. Castlereagh was interested in creating a Central Europe which would be strong enough to resist attack from both the West and the East; Metternich desired the same thing, but he was also concerned about Austria's relative position *within* Central Europe. To Castlereagh, the Continental nations were aspects of a defensive effort; but to the Continental nations the general equilibrium meant nothing if it destroyed the historical position which to them was the reason for their existence. To Castlereagh, the equilibrium was a mechanical expression of the balance of forces; to the Continental nations, a reconciliation of historical aspirations.

This led to a diplomatic stalemate, made all the more intractable because Britain and Austria had secured most of their special objectives during the war so that few bargaining weapons were left to Russia and Prussia, a stalemate which could be broken only by adding an additional weight to one side of the scales. Since the sole uncommitted major power was France, the former enemy emerged as the key to the European settlement. Thus grew up a myth about Talleyrand's role at the Congress of Vienna, of the diabolical wit who appeared on the scene and broke up a coalition of hostile powers, who then regrouped them into a pattern to his liking by invoking the magic word "legitimacy" and from an outcast emerged as the arbiter of Europe.[1] To be sure, since the Treaty of Paris had settled France's boundaries, Talleyrand could afford perhaps the most disinterested approach. His wit and caustic comments became famous, so that Gentz could say of him that he had both the laughers and the thinkers on his side. But these efforts would have availed little, had not the threat of France been eclipsed by the danger from the East, had not the differences among the Allies become greater than their common fear of France. So long as the Coalition still believed that the memory of the common wartime effort would provide the motive force of a settlement, Talleyrand was powerless. Once this illusion was shattered, the issue became one of the limits of self-restraint, whether a power would fail to add a factor to its side merely for the sake of the appearance of harmony. The logic of the situation provided the answer: France came to participate in European affairs, because they could not be settled without her.

As the plenipotentiaries were assembling in Vienna, however, the course of events seemed by no means this clear. It was still thought that the settlement would be rapid, that France would appear as but a spectator, that the rest of Europe would only be called upon to ratify an instrument drafted in relative harmony. This was reflected in the procedural scheme agreed to at preliminary conferences between Austria, Prussia, Russia, and Great Britain which placed the effective control of the Congress in the hands of the "Big Four." Talleyrand protested strenuously against the exclusion of France and the minor powers from the deliberations of the Congress, but despite his brilliance and sarcasm, he achieved only a few minor concessions. It was decided to adjourn the formal opening of the Congress until November 1, 1814, and to have the pending questions examined in the meantime by the eight signatories of the Treaty of Paris, the "Big Four" plus France, Spain, Portugal, and Sweden. The "Big Four" left no doubt, however, that they intended to continue their private discussions and to treat the "Eight" merely as a ratifying instrument or as one for settling peripheral issues.

Talleyrand's first sally failed, because a logical inconsistency is not sufficient to dissolve coalitions. Only after the claim of special righteousness, which is characteristic of coalitions, had disappeared in a conflict which indicated that the relations of the Allies among each other were simply those of contending

---

[1] It is a legend spread by those who confuse results and causes and by professional diplomats wont to ascribe to mere negotiating skill what is possible only through the exploitation of more deepseated factors. It has gained currency because Talleyrand, whose monarch had not come to Vienna, was obliged to write voluminous reports, and in order to cement his shaky domestic position, the former Foreign Minister of Napoleon tended to emphasize his indispensability. See, for example, Harold G. Nicolson, *The Congress of Vienna*, New York, 1946; Duff Cooper, *Talleyrand*, New York, 1932; Crane Brinton, *The Lives of Talleyrand*, New York, 1936; Guglielmo Ferrero, *The Reconstruction of Europe*, New York, 1941.

powers, could Talleyrand emerge as an equal partner. But first one more effort to determine whether the Tsar could be induced to limit his claims without the threat of force had to be made. So well had Castlereagh established himself as the prime contender for the European equilibrium that it was he who entered the arena to try the Tsar's resolution.

There ensued a strange and unreal series of interviews between Castlereagh and Alexander; strange, because their bitterness was accompanied by protestations of unending friendship, and unreal, because Alexander and Castlereagh could never agree on basic premises. In order to obtain a framework for negotiation, the protagonists constantly shifted positions, pretending to agree with the other's principles, but interpreting them in a manner which reduced them to absurdity. Thus Castlereagh at one stage became an avid defender of a completely independent Poland, while Alexander on another occasion defended his Polish plan as a contribution to European security. That Alexander did not propose to let protestations of Allied unity deprive him of his Polish spoils became apparent on the occasion of his first interview with Castlereagh on the day after his arrival.[2] For the first time, he avowed his Polish plans in detail. He proposed to keep all of the Duchy of Warsaw with the exception of a small portion to be ceded to Prussia. These claims, Alexander argued, were not the result of ambition, but the outgrowth of a moral duty and motivated by the sole desire of achieving the happiness of the Polish people. In short, since they were not advanced in the name of security, they could not threaten anyone. Castlereagh, in reply, urged that a Russian appendage extending deep into Central Europe would constitute a constant source of disquiet for the rest of Europe. But the Tsar left no doubt that he was unwilling to withdraw from his Polish possession. The interview between Castlereagh and Alexander had thus made evident that persuasiveness would not suffice and that the next stage of the negotiations would have to be based on force or the threat of force.[3]

While Castlereagh was negotiating with the Tsar, he made every effort to assemble such a force. As an abstract problem in diplomacy his task seemed simple. But although the equilibrium might be indivisible, it did not appear so to its components. The Tsar could not be resisted without a united front of the rest of Europe, but the powers of Europe were not at all in accord regarding the real danger. They did not wish to see the general equilibrium overturned, but they were not prepared to resist at the sacrifice of that part of it on which their historical position depended. A strong Russia might dominate Europe, but a too powerful Prussia would outstrip Austria and a united Germany might

[2] Castlereagh's report. See Charles Webster, *British Diplomacy, 1813–1815*, London, 1921, pp. 197ff., October 2, 1814.

[3] The exchange continued through October in a series of memoranda: Castlereagh to the Tsar, October 12, 1814, see Duke of Wellington, *Supplementary Despatches, Correspondence and Memoranda*, 15 vols., ed. by his son, London, 1855–1872, IX, p. 332; the Tsar's reply, October 30, p. 386; Castlereagh's reply, November 8, p. 410.

menace France. Hardenberg, the Prussian minister, was more interested in Saxony than in Poland; Talleyrand was almost as afraid that the problem of Poland would be settled *without* him as that it would be settled *against* him; and Metternich, while not indifferent to the extension of Russia into Central Europe and of Prussia into Central Germany, did not wish to resist openly since this would cause the brunt of the effort to fall on Austria, the most exposed power, while surrendering the policy of close cooperation with Prussia which Metternich considered the key to Austrian security. "I barricade myself behind time," Metternich told the Saxon envoy, "and make patience my weapon." [4]

Thus Castlereagh's effort to create a united front against Russia led to an ambiguous series of constellations, of half-hearted coalitions and tentative betrayals, of promises of unyielding support coupled with hedges against bad faith. Matters were finally brought to a head by Prussia, the power which could least afford delay. For although the treaties of Kalish, Teplitz, and Chaumont had guaranteed Prussia its territorial extent of 1805, they had never specified where Prussia might find the requisite territories, particularly if it lost its Polish possessions to Russia. The available compensations, composed of former provinces or former satellites of France, primarily in the Rhineland, where inadequate. And they were undesirable because of their geographic separation from the main part of the Prussian monarchy and the Catholic religion of their inhabitants. Thus Prussia came to look toward Saxony, coveted since the time of Frederic the Great, contiguous with its own territories and with a predominantly Protestant population. But Prussia's negotiating position was the weakest of those of the major powers. Unlike Russia, it was not in possession of its prize. Unlike Austria, it had not made its participation in the war dependent on obtaining its special conditions. If now the Polish question was settled before that of Saxony, Prussia would have paid the penalty for its total commitment; of having fought the war with so much fervor that its participation had never been negotiable, of neglecting the peace because the war, in effect, had become an end in itself. And Prussia required Austrian acquiescence in the annexation of Saxony, because the organization of Germany, the indispensable condition of Prussia's security, would become illusory if Austria emerged on the Saxon issue as the protector of the secondary German powers.

It is not surprising, therefore, that on October 9, 1814, Hardenberg submitted a memorandum agreeing to an "intermediary system based on Austria, Prussia and Britain," and directed against Russia.[5] But he made Prussia's cooperation on the Polish question dependent on Austrian agreement to the annexation of Saxony and to the provisional occupation of Saxony by Prussia as a token of good faith. In its tentative quest for allies, in its pedantic effort to achieve the advantage of every course of action, the Hardenberg memorandum merely

[4] Wilhelm Schwarz, *Die Heilige Allianz*, Stuttgart, 1935, p. 13.
[5] Comte d'Angeberg, *Le Congrès de Vienne et les Traités de 1815*, Paris, 1863–1864, II, p. 1934.

served to illustrate Prussia's dilemma: Russian support might gain it Saxony, but not legitimacy; while Austrian support might yield it Poland, but not Saxony. The Hardenberg memorandum was a plea not to leave Prussia dependent on the good will of the Tsar; to create a European order based on Austro-Prussian friendship, but also on Prussian possession of Saxony.

But this effort to combine incompatible policies provided Metternich with the means to separate the Polish and Saxon question by one of his intricate maneuvers. On October 22, he transmitted two notes to Hardenberg and Castlereagh whose tone of grudging agreement to Hardenberg's proposal obscured the fact that the moral framework which was being created to resist in Poland would prove equally effective to resist in Saxony, and that Hardenberg, in his effort to hedge his risks, had made his defeat inevitable. For Castlereagh in his overriding concern with the balance of power and Hardenberg in his obsession with Saxony overlooked two subtle and mutually inconsistent reservations in Metternich's despatches: that Prussia's annexation of Saxony should not lead to a "disproportionate aggrandizement," a condition clearly impossible of fulfillment if Prussia regained her Polish provinces,[6] and that Austria's agreement on the Saxon point was conditional on the *success* of the effort to thwart the Tsar's design on Poland [7]—which, in turn, would leave Prussia isolated in the inevitable contest over the interpretation of the first reservation.

But while Metternich was preparing the moral framework for an effort to separate Prussia and Russia, Castlereagh was looking only to Poland, as if the European equilibrium could be created with the necessity of a mathematical equation. On October 23, he finally succeeded in getting Prussia to agree to a common plan of action against Russia on the basis of Metternich's memoranda.[8] The three powers undertook to force the issue by confronting the Tsar with the threat of bringing the Polish question before the full Congress if a reasonable settlement could not be obtained by direct negotiations. They proposed three acceptable solutions: an independent Poland as it existed prior to the first partition, a rump Poland on the scale of 1791, or the return of the three partitioning powers to their former possessions.[9]

The threat of an appeal to Europe in Congress was the last effort to settle the European equilibrium by a combination *within* the anti-French coalition. When Metternich called on the Tsar to present the ultimatum on the Polish question, he was dismissed haughtily and even challenged to a duel. And when, on October 30, the three sovereigns left to visit Hungary, Alexander appealed to his brother monarchs against their ministers. He failed with the Austrian Emperor, but it did not prove too difficult to convince the stodgy and

[6] Text of note to Castlereagh, *ibid.*, II, pp. 1939ff.
[7] Text of note to Hardenberg, *ibid.*, I, pp. 316ff.
[8] Castlereagh's report, Webster, *op. cit.*, p. 212, October 29, 1814.
[9] Memorandum re procedure, *ibid.*, pp. 213ff.

unimaginative Prussian King that the secret negotiations of the three ministers were an act of bad faith. When the monarchs returned to Vienna, Hardenberg was ordered, in the presence of the Tsar, to refrain from any further separate negotiations with his Austrian and British colleagues. In this manner, on November 5, the contest over Poland ended for the time being. The effort to achieve an international order based on agreement and not on force seemed to have returned to its starting point.

But this was a mistaken impression. For if Castlereagh's failure had proved that the equilibrium could not be achieved through a demonstration of its necessity, Metternich's almost imperceptible complementary effort had created the moral framework for reopening the issue by an appeal to legitimacy. The procrastination which had proved so maddening to Castlereagh had in fact been Metternich's most effective means to overcome his dilemmas, for delay strengthened Austria's chief bargaining weapon, that legitimacy can be conferred but not exacted, that it implies agreement and not imposition. So the weeks had passed while Europe complained about the frivolity of the Austrian minister and the old school of Austrian diplomats raged that their "Rhenish" minister, whom they nicknamed Prince Scamperlin, was betraying the Empire to Prussia. But in the admiration for the famous phrase of the Prince de Ligne: "Le Congrès danse, mais il ne marche pas," it was overlooked that the Congress was dancing itself into a trap.

When Hardenberg offered Metternich his cooperation, he believed that he was clinching his gains and that he was obtaining a guarantee of Saxony, however the Polish negotiations ended. But because Metternich's reply had made Austrian agreement to the annexation of Saxony conditional on the *success* of their common measures, the effort to connect the two issues became a means to separate them. For if the Polish negotiations succeeded, Prussia would lose her moral claim to Saxony in the eyes of Europe. If Prussia regained her Polish possessions, the annexation of Saxony would represent the "disproportionate aggrandizement" against which Metternich had warned Castlereagh. But if the Polish negotiations failed, Prussia would lose her moral claim to Saxony in the eyes of Austria. Prussia's isolation was assured none the less surely, because the fact of resistance was almost as certain to alienate the Tsar as its success. Having demonstrated Austria's European concern by yielding in Saxony, intransigence could now be defended by the requirements of the European and not the German equilibrium. And Castlereagh, having obtained Austrian support in the Polish negotiations, would no longer be able to treat the Saxon issue as an internal German affair. There could be no doubt of the attitude of France or of the smaller German states. Prussia, in its effort to obtain reinsurance, had only succeeded in achieving its isolation.

When, on November 7, Hardenberg informed Metternich of the King's orders and of the difficulty of carrying out the agreed plan with respect to

Poland, Metternich finally had the moral basis for action.[10] Austria was interested in the closest relationship with Prussia, he replied, but no longer at the price of the destruction of Saxony.[11] After being forced to tolerate Russian aggrandizement in Poland, Austria could not acquiesce in Prussian aggrandizement within Germany without upsetting the equilibrium completely. Metternich suggested an alternative plan which maintained a nucleus of Saxony, while giving a large part of it to Prussia, together with other compensations in the Rhineland. But all protestations of friendship could not hide the fact that Prussia was outmaneuvered, that Metternich had lost out in Poland only to win in Saxony and then partially to restore the situation in Poland by means of Saxony.

It did not matter that, on November 8, the Russian military governor of Saxony turned over the provisional administration to Prussia, or that the Prussian military were threatening war. Russia, at the periphery of Europe, might rest its claim on Poland on the fact of possession, but a power situated in the center of the Continent could survive only as the component of a "legitimate" order both within Germany and in Europe. Thus, although by the middle of December the Congress of Vienna seemed to have reached a complete stalemate, behind the scene a fundamental transformation was preparing itself. A stalemate is not total until all the factors are engaged and France was still uncommitted. The contests during October and November had exploded the myth of Allied unity and the threat of France no longer loomed larger than that of the erstwhile ally. While Castlereagh was despairing about the Polish failure and accusing Metternich of never having really intended to resist,[12] a combination was forming on the Saxon question which was to give a new direction to the contest. For the coalition which could resist in Saxony was, by definition, also the coalition which could resist in Poland. And the claims of power defeated in one quarter would, almost necessarily, limit the assertions of arbitrariness in the other. So it was proved, after all, that the equilibrium was indivisible, although the solution did not come about through a consciousness of this. It was not in the name of Europe that Europe was saved, but in the name of Saxony.

But before this new combination could be formed, domestic pressures on Castlereagh nearly wrecked Metternich's finely spun plan. An insular power may fight its wars in the name of the European equilibrium, but it will tend to identify the threats to the equilibrium with threats to its immediate security. Because its policy is defensive and not precautionary, it will make the cause of

---

[10] D'Angeberg, op. cit., I, p. 406 (Hardenberg's note to Metternich). There is yet another indication, although no proof, that Metternich never intended the Polish negotiations as anything but a means to isolate Prussia on the Saxon question: his dismal defeat during his interview with Alexander. At no other time in his career did Metternich choose a frontal attack, negotiate so ineffectively, or surrender so easily.

[11] Text, ibid., I, p. 505.

[12] Webster, op. cit., pp. 248ff.

war depend on an overt act which "demonstrates" the danger. But the danger to the equilibrium is never demonstrated until it is already overturned, because an aggressor can always justify every step, except the crucial last one, as the manifestation of limited claims and exact acquiescence as the price of continued moderation. To be sure, Britain had entered the fray against Napoleon at an early stage and continued the contest with great persistence. But the threat to the equilibrium had become manifest through an attack on the Low Countries and a challenge to Britain's command of the seas. Now the issue was Poland, however, a "distant" country both geographically and psychologically. It was not clear until it was "proven" that the Rhine was best defended along the Vistula or that there existed any threat to peace except France. In this frame of mind the Cabinet considered the Polish dispute an irritating outgrowth of Continental rivalry, threatening a peace dearly won, and dealt with it primarily under the aspect of its impact on British domestic politics.

On October 14, Liverpool, the British Prime Minister, wrote Castlereagh that the "less Britain had to do with [Poland] . . . the better" and he transmitted a memorandum by the Chancellor of the Exchequer, Vansittart, who simply denied the reality of the Russian danger. With the petulance of mediocrity convincing itself that the easy way out is also the course of wisdom, Vansittart argued that the absorption of Poland would add an element of weakness to the Russian state while proving conducive to British commerce.[13] Finally, on November 22, the Cabinet sent its first instructions to Castlereagh since his arrival in Vienna: "It is unnecessary," wrote Bathurst, "for me to point out to you the impossibility of . . . consenting to involve this country into hostilities . . . for any of the objects which have hitherto been under discussion at Vienna." [14]

Thus, at the crucial point in the negotiations, Castlereagh was deprived of his only means of exerting pressure and at a moment when the issue was becoming one of pure power. For Prussia was being drawn by Metternich's temporizing into precipitate action. As it observed its moral and material basis slipping away, its tone became increasingly bellicose. Its military were openly speaking of war and even the more moderate Hardenberg hinted at extreme measures. But if possession without legitimacy was illusory, legitimacy through force proved chimerical. Castlereagh was merely defining Prussia's dilemma when he told Hardenberg that "he [Hardenberg] could not regard an unacknowledged claim as constituting a good title and that he never could in *conscience* or *honor* . . . make the mere refusal of a recognition a cause of war. . . ." [15] In this situation Castlereagh did not propose to follow his Cabinet's instructions. To announce British disinterest would remove the major deterrent to war and, in its effort to guarantee peace, the Cabinet would have brought about what it feared most.

[13] *Ibid.*, pp. 220ff.
[14] *Ibid.*, pp. 247ff.
[15] *Ibid.*, p. 255. December 7, 1814.

Or else, a British withdrawal from the contest would have led to an Austrian surrender and to a complete overturn of the equilibrium.

So it happened that Castlereagh and Metternich found themselves on the same side in a battle whose moral framework had been defined by the wily Austrian Minister. The more intransigent Prussia's attitude, the stronger became Metternich's position. Without the necessity for abstract discussion, Austria emerged as the protector of the secondary powers. When Metternich proposed an alliance to Bavaria and Hanover and the construction of a German League without Prussia, he was simply giving expression to a general consensus. It was at this point, when the last vestiges of the Alliance were disappearing, that Talleyrand reappeared on the scene. He emerged because Metternich put him on the stage and his eloquence was but a reflection of Metternich's desire for anonymity, for Metternich was not interested in appearing as the agent of Prussia's humiliation. It was Metternich's desire that events should come about "naturally," because that would minimize the danger of personal schisms; it was Talleyrand's effort that they should appear "caused," for that would cement his shaky domestic position.

Talleyrand was given his opportunity by Metternich, who communicated to him the Austrian note to Hardenberg and thus made clear that the Big Four had not been able to settle the issue.[16] Talleyrand replied in a trenchant memorandum, which asserted the superiority of the claims of legitimacy over the requirements of the equilibrium and denied the possibility of deposing kings, because sovereigns could not be tried, least of all by those who coveted their territories. It was not for Prussia to state what she would take, Talleyrand argued boldly, but for the "legitimate" King of Saxony to define how much he would yield.[17] It was a masterly summary of all the inconsistencies of two months of acrimony, but this was not its significance. Talleyrand had served France better by remaining "available" than by writing memoranda. The real importance of the exchange lay in the fact that France was once again part of the concert of Europe.

Only a short step separated Talleyrand from full participation in the deliberations. Castlereagh, who had hoped to avoid so drastic a step, finally agreed on December 27. When, on December 31, Castlereagh and Metternich proposed that henceforth Talleyrand participate in the meetings of the Big Four, it was clear that the special claims of the Alliance had ceased before Prussia had gained the fruit of its war effort. Even the Tsar, in Castlereagh's words, "would not advise Prussia to resist now that he has secured his own arrangement in Poland." Thus driven back on its last resources, Prussia threatened war.

But the reaction merely served to indicate Prussia's impotence. Castlereagh

16 Clemens Metternich, *Aus Metternichs Nachgelassenen Papieren*, 8 vols., ed. by Alfons von Klinkowstroem, Vienna, 1880, II, pp. 503ff.

17 *Ibid.*, pp. 510ff., December 19, 1814; D'Angeberg, *op. cit.*, pp. 546ff.

replied sharply that "such an insinuation might operate upon a power trembling for its own existence but must have the contrary effect upon all alive to their own dignity; and I added that if such a temper really prevailed, we were not deliberating in a state of independence and it was better to break up the Congress." [18] That same day, Castlereagh proposed a defensive alliance between France, Austria, and Britain. To be sure, Talleyrand was required to guarantee the Low Countries and to reaffirm the provisions of the Treaty of Paris. But Talleyrand's greatest achievement at Vienna was precisely this exhibition of self-restraint, this refusal to attempt to sell French participation in the alliance for a territorial advantage, an effort which would have united all the other powers against him. As a result he gained something more important, the end of the isolation of France and the real recognition of its equality.

If the defensive alliance provided the crisis of the Congress of Vienna, it also paved the way for its resolution. In any negotiation it is understood that force is the ultimate recourse. But it is the art of diplomacy to keep this threat potential, to keep its extent indeterminate, and to commit it only as a last resort. For once power has been made actual, negotiations in the proper sense cease. A threat to use force which proves unavailing does not return the negotiation to the point before the threat was made. It destroys the bargaining position altogether, for it is a confession not of finite power but of impotence. By bringing matters to a head, Prussia found itself confronted by three powers whose determination could not be doubted, although the treaty itself remained secret. And the Tsar proved a lukewarm ally. A series of partial settlements had isolated Prussia because "satisfied" powers will not fight for the claims of another, if an honorable alternative presents itself.

Castlereagh, therefore, took up the proposal of Metternich's memorandum of December 10 by which Prussia was to obtain part of Saxony and extensive territories in the Rhineland. It soon became apparent that Prussia would not carry out her threat of war. By January 3, 1815, after Metternich and Castlereagh had refused to negotiate without Talleyrand, Hardenberg, to save face, himself recommended Talleyrand's participation.[19] On January 5, Castlereagh could report that "the alarm of war is over." [20] The Saxon question was henceforth officially discussed by the now Big Five and was resolved largely through unofficial negotiations in which Castlereagh played the role of the intermediary between Metternich and Talleyrand on the one side and the Tsar and Hardenberg on the other.

In his endeavor to achieve a final settlement, Castlereagh had to resist an attempt by Prussia to move the King of Saxony to the left bank of the Rhine and an effort by Austria to save the Elbe fortress of Torgau for Saxony. But

[18] Webster, *op. cit.*, p. 278, January 1, 1815.
[19] *Ibid.*, p. 280.
[20] *Ibid.*, p. 282.

with the aid of the Tsar, he convinced Prussia that in the interest of the European equilibrium she would have to assume the defense of the Rhineland, and he made clear to Austria that the defensive alliance extended only to an actual attempt to overthrow the European equilibrium, not to internal German arrangements.[21] The danger of war had also made the Tsar more pliable. When Castlereagh suggested some concessions in Poland in order to make the Saxon arrangement more palatable to Prussia, Alexander agreed to return the city of Thorn to Prussia. On February 11, a final agreement was reached. In Poland, Austria retained Galicia and the district of Tarnopol, while Cracow was constituted a free city. Prussia retained the district of Posen and the city of Thorn which controlled the upper Vistula. The remainder of the Duchy of Warsaw with a population of 3.2 million became the Kingdom of Poland under the Tsar of Russia. In Germany, Prussia obtained two-fifths of Saxony, Swedish Pomerania, much of the left bank of the Rhine, and the Duchy of Westphalia. Austria had already been assured compensation in Northern Italy and predominance in all of Italy though the establishment of dependent dynasties in Parma and Tuscany.

On June 9, 1815, the final acts of Vienna were ratified by Europe assembled in congress. It was the only meeting of the Congress of Vienna.

There are two ways of constructing an international order: by will or renunciation, by force or legitimacy. For twenty-five years Europe had been convulsed by an effort to achieve order through force and to contemporaries its lesson was not its failure but its near success. Under Napoleon Europe had been unified from the Niemen to the Bay of Biscay but its cohesion was supplied by the power of the Grande Armée. It is not surprising, then, that in their effort to create an alternative the statesmen of Vienna looked back to a period which had known stability and that they identified this stability with its domestic arrangements. Nor was this assessment as ludicrous as a self-righteous historiography made it appear later on. For one of the reasons which had impelled Napoleon ever further was his often repeated conviction that the survival of his dynasty in a world of "legitimate" monarchs depended on the success of his arms. In short, Napoleon confronted Europe with a revolutionary situation because he considered the unimpaired maintenance of the other sovereign states as incompatible with his own existence.

By contrast, one of the reasons for the success of the Vienna settlement was precisely the absence of such an ideological gulf. When a power considers the domestic notion of justice of another sovereign state a mortal threat to its own survival, no basis for negotiation exists. Safety can then only be found in physical extent; diplomacy is reduced to maneuvering for position and such adjustments as do occur have but a tactical significance: to prepare the ground for the inevitable showdown. This is not to say that domestic structures must be identical

21 *Ibid.*, p. 295, January 29, 1815.

before meaningful negotiations can take place. It is enough that there exists no power which claims both exclusiveness and universality for its notion of justice. For diplomacy the art of relating powers to each other by agreement can function only when each major power accepts the legitimacy of the *existence* of the others.

In Vienna, of course, the consensus went further than this. There existed a general agreement about the nature of "just" domestic arrangements, which by limiting risks made for flexibility of relationship. The problem of relating a state's vision of itself to the vision of it by the powers, defined in the beginning as one of the key problems of an international settlement, was rarely simpler than at Vienna. This was the reason for the success—for the possibility—of "secret diplomacy," that intangibles were understood in the same manner. To be sure, the results of the Vienna Congress reflected to no small degree the skill of the diplomats in making use of their opportunity. Both Metternich and Castlereagh were extraordinary negotiators capable of shaping a conference to their ends: Castlereagh through his ability to reconcile different points of view and a singlemindedness which enabled him to keep discussions focused on essentials; Metternich through the art of defining a framework which made concessions appear, not as surrenders, but as sacrifices to the common cause. But whatever the skill of the diplomats, the second reason for the success of the Congress is no less fundamental: that in the face of all protestations of friendship and of a real measure of ideological agreement the importance of power-relationships was never lost sight of. The conviviality of the statesmen must not obscure the fact that the European order emerged from the threat of war and the formation, however temporary, of two hostile alliances. The issue was decided not only by the persuasiveness of the statesmen but by the relative strength of the opposing camps.

The settlement proved all the more lasting because the negotiators at Vienna did not confuse the atmosphere of the conference table with the elements of stability of the international system. A statesman cannot make the survival of his charge entirely dependent on the continued good will of another sovereign state; not only because he has no control over the continuation of this good will, but more importantly because the best guarantee for its remaining good is not to tempt it by too great a disproportion of power. The Vienna settlement took into account this relationship of security and legitimacy. It did not rest on unsupported good faith, which would have put too great a strain on self-limitation; nor on the efficacy of a pure evaluation of power, which would have made calculation too indeterminate. Rather, there was created a structure in which the forces were sufficiently balanced, so that self-restraint could appear as something more than self-abnegation, but which took account of the historical claims of its components, so that it met general acceptance. No power felt so dissatisfied that it did not prefer to seek its remedy *within* the framework of the Vienna settlement rather than in overturning it. Since the international order did not contain a "revolutionary" power, either ideologically or in power terms, its relations became increasingly spontaneous, based on the growing certainty that a catastrophic upheaval was unlikely. The result was a century without a major war.

METTERNICH: A REAPPRAISAL OF HIS IMPACT

ON INTERNATIONAL RELATIONS

Robert A. Kann

ONE OF the supposed truisms of history is that the test of greatness in political action is its applicability to present-day conditions. When calling the roll of the eminent Western statesmen in the field of international relations in the last centuries—from Richelieu and Kaunitz to Cavour and Bismarck, to take only a few outstanding examples—one begins to wonder if this concept is not an oversimplification. Of the many who acknowledge the great contributions of these men to the policies of their countries, only a few would claim that their methods are in any way germane to the problems of our day. It appears that historical changes during the last generations make it necessary to differentiate between great action and action applicable in the modern world.

In the case of Prince Clemens Metternich, the "coachman of Europe," from the Congress of Vienna in 1814 to his enforced abdication from power at the beginning of the revolution of 1848, the situation seems to be rather the reverse. His character appears to many to have been as controversial as that of Richelieu, Talleyrand, or Bismarck; in his domestic policies he has found fewer defenders than any one of them. His greatness is still questioned today, though probably less so than half a century ago. Yet, as to the significance of his life's work for the present world, entirely irrespective of the issue of his personal greatness, he surpasses most of the outstanding statesmen that came before or after him.

Why is this true? So sweeping an assertion must of necessity be limited in

Reprinted from *The Journal of Modern History*, XXXII, No. 4 (December 1960), pp. 333–39 by permission of the University of Chicago Press. Copyright 1960 by the University of Chicago Press.

its application. It is not to be applied to Metternich's role as the leading Austrian statesman for almost four decades, nor even to his suppression of nationalism and constitutionalism in Central Europe. Metternich's active influence on the idea of the police state, censorship, and cultural isolationism, so frequently associated with Austrian internal administration in the Restoration era, has been generally overrated. The same certainly cannot be said of the national and constitutional issues in the Germanies, the Hapsburg Empire, and Italy. Here, however, Metternich did not act very differently from many of his ministerial colleagues throughout the Restoration period, both within and outside Austria. Like him, they conceived the chief task in domestic administration to be the preservation of ancient empire structures in a fast-changing world. Whatever Metternich did in these spheres has of course become part of the flow of cause and effect in the stream of history. Yet, whether he showed greater skill or perhaps less long-range insight than others, in these respects he appears more as the tool than the free agent of history.

The significance of Metternich for our times rests on a very different and almost unique contribution, a contribution which is perhaps comparable to that of only one Western statesman after him—Woodrow Wilson. The comparison seems strange. What does Metternich, the slightly frivolous, enlightened cavalier, never fully at home in the emotional, romantic era, have in common with the austere, puritan thinker Wilson? The answer is simple: the creation of a system of international politics according to supra-national and supra-party principles and based on supposedly self-evident reason. No attempt will be made here to stress this similarity further in personal terms. Wilson in many ways the liberal, Metternich the conservative; Wilson the deep thinker and luckless manager of international relations, Metternich the conventional though not shallow writer, the brilliant operator of foreign affairs and diplomatic agencies—there is no need to dwell on these great differences in character and the even greater ones in the political environment. What stands out, however, is the fact that both men forged a program not primarily tied to the national community, a program not conceived solely as a second step to an interrelationship between the great powers, as was the case with Bismarck or Cavour. Wilson, while by no means neglecting the interests of his country, perceived them first and last within the international community, just as Metternich in more modest terms simultaneously kept in view the Concert of Europe and, as a mere part of the whole, the Hapsburg Empire.

Among the formal international agreements in the three centuries from the Westphalian peace treaty to the present, these two systems share another—in this case negative—aspect that sets them apart from most other actively promoted systems of international relations of this period: the lack of a crusading or anti-crusading idea. True enough, the Wilsonian philosophy was permeated with the ideals of a supra-national democratic humanitarianism, but this had little to do with party ideology of any kind. In the same sense one might say that, appearances notwithstanding, Metternich's anti-revolutionary, anti-national, and anti-constitutional doctrine was in fact deeply rooted in an enlightened absolutism that placed equilibrium between the powers first and recognized ideological factors only insofar as they might disturb this equilibrium. One may well rate Wilson's political ideals far higher than Metternich's, and yet one cannot help being impressed by the latter's operation of a system of clear thought, reasonably free from the stresses of day-to-day political battles and the conflicts of specific personal interests. In this respect it is significant that the man whose name has been, and in all likelihood always will be, associated with this system of political thought clearly rejected the notion that international political doctrine and strategy should be linked to a specific individual and thus be weakened in their general validity.[1]

An admission that this "system"—the term used by Metternich's friends and foes alike—was clear, dispassionate, and rational within the limits of obvious human frailties implies but faint praise. Surely the chancellor did not produce an intellectual masterpiece of political strategy comparable to Machiavelli's *Prince*. Metternich was a voluminous and facile writer, but his lengthy ruminations on the nature of politics are not distinguished by any particular originality of thought. His correspondence on current events is far superior to his theoretical memoranda. In any event, the truly brilliant writings to which the system owed its fame derive primarily from Metternich's closest collaborator in the state chancellery, Friedrich von Gentz. This should in no way detract from the significance of Metternich's life work, which is based on a rare combination of thought and action, a sublime interplay between rigidity of doctrine and flexibility of application. This point was to some extent overlooked by Metternich's eminent biographer, Heinrich von Srbik, who represented Metternich's doctrines as a powerful work of political philosophy and his diplomacy as a kind of minor skill, not quite worthy of his hero. The observer of later days may well rate the rigidity and consistency of Metternich's political thought lower while he may appraise the flexibility of its execution considerably higher.

Basically, Metternich's theories consist in the combination and interpretation of a few simple and well-established concepts.[2] He believed in a principle of legitimacy in international relations which may not be quite as broad as has been

---

[1] See "Aus Metternichs nachgelassenen Papieren," edited by his son Prince Richard Metternich-Winneburg (8 vols.; Vienna, 1880–84) (hereafter cited as *NP*), VIII, 186 and 196–97, where Metternich deplores the tendency to link an idea to a specific individual and thereby weaken its impact. This applies in particular to the political phenomenon of Louis Napoleon in December 1848. See also (*ibid.,* pp. 462 ff.) Metternich's letter of Jan. 17, 1849 to Prince Felix Schwarzenberg on the desirability of a depersonalized concept of government as he saw it practised in England. See further the biography by H. v. Srbik, *Metternich* (3 vols.; Munich, 1925–54), I, 321–26, and the following passages from *NP* referred to in it: VII, 517, 612, 639; VIII, 200, 286, 239.

[2] See in particular Srbik, I, 317–42.

claimed in a brilliant analysis by Henry Kissinger, who considers it an international order of limited conflicts always adjustable by negotiation between litigating powers.[3] It was something more than a restoration of divine right absolutism; it was a stable order determined by the consensus of the recognized great powers of the day. Here it is well to remember that after the French Revolution of 1789 and the Napoleonic wars this order was not an established one but was merely restored or manufactured. As such it required this consensus, that is, the compromise between the great powers; and thus it could never be an exact replica of the old one. It was the good fortune of Metternich that the limited ideological differences between the great powers of this period made such a compromise possible. Compromise is indeed the salient feature in the second of Metternich's great principles: equilibrium among the great powers of the European pentarchy—at that time the world pentarchy—of Austria, France, Great Britain, Prussia, and Russia. Here again the notion of equilibrium, in the sense of a balance of power as attempted by the Westphalian peace treaty and actually achieved by the treaties of Utrecht, Rastadt, and Baden after the war of the Spanish Succession, was no more a new concept than legitimacy would have been in terms of divine right theory. What was new was the application of this concept: its extension from the sphere of power politics into that of ideological differences as represented by British constitutionalism and utilitarianism; a Tsarist mixture of metaphysically inspired enlightened absolutism and imperialism; a French drive for imperial restoration in very uncertain domestic political terms; a Prussian push for supremacy in the German orbit; and an Austrian effort to maintain a mediator's position within the framework of "the unified decentralized state." [4] A mediatorship of this sort in the service of the equilibrium could function only if it were assured of two further factors, related to but not similar to those previously mentioned. These were security and stability. To Metternich, security required not only military preparedness but also a compromise between the powers. He fully realized that the absolute security of one power is in purely military terms a threat to that of others. While it is true that in an age of codified great-power dominance his concept cannot be described as collective security in the broad modern sense, it is entirely proper to refer to Metternich's security concept as based primarily on the consensus of the joint powers.

More controversial is the concept of stability, the interpretation and application of which has greatly contributed to Metternich's ill repute in the liberal camp. It is that part of his philosophy which is commonly associated more than any other with the notion of a blind restoration of the old regime and all that

[3] Henry A. Kissinger, *A world restored: Metternich, Castlereagh and the problems of peace, 1812–1822* (New York, 1957), pp. 1–3, 137, 204. See also R. A. Kann, *A study in Austrian intellectual history: from late Baroque to Romanticism* (New York, 1960), pp. 259–302.

[4] Srbik, I, 434–36; see also Metternich's memorandum of Oct. 1817, *NP*, III, 66–75.

it involves in terms of direct and indirect restrictions of human liberties, of social emancipation and freedom of opportunity. Actually, Metternich never identified stability with the status quo, nor was he opposed to the idea of slow evolutionary reform in itself. Yet, such reforms were applied primarily to the realm of international politics, where he felt at home and was thus able and willing to make concessions, and not to the social-economic sphere, where change at home as well as abroad meant to him approaching the danger zone of revolution.[5]

What has particularly exasperated his critics is the kind of verbiage which seemingly intends to obscure the fact that he thought of consensus as deriving from government power not subject to control by public opinion, and freedom of thought as pertaining to an external forum and not merely to individual conscience.[6] It is perhaps noteworthy that these later, primarily nationalist critics took rationalizations of this kind for mere hypocrisy, whereas an extremely bitter contemporary liberal opponent like Heinrich Heine in his preface to *Französische Zustände* gives Metternich credit for the fact that he never "played the demagogue . . . that one always knew where one stood with him. . . . One knew that he did not act either out of love or petty hatred but grandly in the spirit of his system. . . ."[7] Apparently Heine knew the difference between hypocrisy and flexibility. For all Metternich's outstanding diplomatic skill and perspicacity, without this flexibility his entire political theory would have been fragile indeed.

It must be remembered, of course, that Metternich was spared the difficulty of the democratic and, to a degree, even of the totalitarian governments of today —namely, the necessity of obtaining at least a measure of public support for his policy. It was perhaps not so much the reactionary character but the seeming stability of the regime in Austria as well as his personal prestige that made him more impervious to the impact of public opinion than any contemporary leading statesman, Tsar Alexander I not excluded.[8]

Lack of concern for the impact of public opinion, however, determines only one facet of diplomacy, and even that presumably only for a short period of time. Yet, by today's standards, Metternich's success was a long-range one and may

[5] See the highly illuminating memorandum of June 1853 to his successor Count Buol in *NP*, VIII, 347–50 where he readily agrees to "manipulation" in the political sphere but categorically refuses what he terms "capitulation" in the social one.

[6] See for instance the strange concoction of the terms freedom, order and tyranny, all wrapped into one, in his so-called Political Testament of 1849–55, *NP*, VII, 633–42, and especially 636–39, or his remarks addressed to Count Auersperg (Anastasius Grün) in 1838 on the identification of freedom of expression with freedom of thought. See Srbik, I, 397–98.

[7] Heinrich Heine, *Sämmtliche Werke* (12 vols.; Hamburg, 1851–65), VIII, *Französische Zustände*, Preface of 1832, pp. 19, 20.

[8] Though personally not oblivious to the effect of public opinion, Metternich conceived of it primarily as a gauge to measure the destructive forces of revolution. See, for instance, *NP*, VIII, 238–39, written in 1850.

well be measured in decades. This in spite of the fact that his disregard for
mass support did not work entirely to his advantage. After all, there was a reverse side to this problem as well; namely, the lack of such strength as could
have been drawn from such backing. It was precisely with the beginning of
Metternich's tenure of office after the peace of Schönbrunn in 1809 that Austrian
policy dismissed what Metternich considered the mere props of diplomacy. In
its stead he introduced a foreign policy that was to be put into action after he was
sure not only that Austria would not be isolated, but also that agreement existed
as to the aims of the powers with which he wanted to cooperate. Hence, Austria's late but not belated joining of the anti-Napoleonic coalition in 1813 which,
for all practical purposes, substituted a guarantee of success for the weight of
popular support in the war of 1809.[9] This cautious policy was prompted largely
by the strategic central position of Austria and the complexities of her ethnic-
historic structure, threatened in the event of defeat by complete dismemberment,
a danger to which the other key members of the great alliance, Great Britain and
Russia, were not exposed.

But such a policy, slow and perhaps hesitant in execution, did not lack daring
and imagination in planning. It should always be remembered that Metternich
was the first to perceive the opportunity for the containment of France and
was the last to agree to the destruction of Napoleon. He did so because he felt
that a Napoleon, curbed in his foreign policy, would still be strong enough to
check revolution, while his lesser successors would have to move into a power
vacuum. Whether this belief, shattered by Napoleon himself during The Hundred Days in 1815, was correct is less important than his willingness to adjust
the concept of legitimacy to stability rather than restoration.

Flexibility was demonstrated above all by the entire foreign policy of Metternich during that strange period of great-power conferences from 1815 to 1822.
Somber features in this picture are not lacking. Yet, though criticism of the
oppressive measures of the Concert of Europe against Naples and Spain may
be justified in itself, the main point should not be overlooked that in a sense this
policy was a price paid—perhaps all too willingly then—for the containment of
Russia in close collaboration with Great Britain. Here again the chief evidence
of flexible skill is the fact that Metternich cooperated sincerely and successfully
with British statesmen whose philosophy of government was much more
divergent from his own than that of Alexander I and his brother. Indeed, in
1821 it was no idle boast on Metternich's part when he wrote, "If I were not
master of making [the Russian troops] retreat just as I made them advance, do
you think I should ever have set them in motion?"[10]

It is quite true that after 1822 Metternich's grip on the European situation

9 See Metternich's reflections in regard to Austria's policy at the beginning of the Crimean
War, *ibid.*, 364–71.
10 *Ibid.*, 467; letter by Metternich to Count Stadion, quoted from Kissinger, p. 280.

relaxed, slowly at first, then at an increasing speed. The ever more obvious deficiencies of the settlement of Vienna in regard to the rising issues of constitutionalism, liberalism, and nationalism (which are outside the province of this discussion) are not solely responsible for this fact. Even in the purely diplomatic sphere it became impossible to keep two alliance systems with different *raisons d'être* permanently in line. And surely the quadruple—later quintuple—alliance, primarily concerned with the preservation of the territorial status quo, and the holy alliance, emphasizing the necessity of domestic governmental patriarchies, proved to be wholly incompatible. Metternich's policy from the Congress of Verona in 1822 to his downfall at the very beginning of the March rising in 1848 is a continuous chain of rearguard actions to delay, to cover, and to argue away the breakdown of the Concert of Europe and all it stood for.

It cannot be denied that he achieved a limited success in his relations with the Orleans monarchy in France after the great July revolution of 1830, and a more modest but perhaps more difficult one, the Münchengraetz agreement with Russia of 1833, which for a time checked further Russian advances in the disintegrating Ottoman East. Undoubtedly, these policies helped also to give a limited renewal to Austria's lease on life in the German and Italian spheres. Metternich had, after all, succeeded in maintaining the great-power position of Austria, but the glorious period from 1812 to 1822 when the Hapsburg Empire, anticipating the late Victorian position of Great Britain, acted as European mediator and arbitrator in the service of peace had passed. Austria—very much against Metternich's original intention—had been forced to shift from an overall key position in the center of Europe to a kind of Austro-Russo-Prussian entente system. Her status, deprived of the flexibility desired by the state chancellor, was thus fatally weakened, even during Metternich's lifetime, by the deterioration of her relations with Russia resulting from the Crimean war crisis. This in turn presaged and to a point predetermined the loss of her position in Italy and Germany within less than a decade.

In a sense this steady undermining of Austria's position as a great power testifies to the eminence of Metternich the statesman, since what looked for a time like the operation of an infallible system turned out to be merely the temporary success of an eminent man. As the genuine Austrian that the Rhenish aristocrat had become, he was certainly pleased by his success, but never intoxicated by victory, always cognizant that he fought a delaying battle which he could not win in the end.[11]

What does it all add up to? An evaluation of Metternich's policies and of their relationship to the problems of our times might perhaps most conveniently move from the less controversial to the more controversial. Unfortunately for Metternich's reputation, this entails stronger and wider support for the negative criticism of his policies. There have been few who have maintained seriously that

[11] See, for instance, *NP*, III, 347–48 (1820), and 472 (1821); V, 193–96 (1831).

even within the standards of his own time the prince understood the impact of the social changes brought about by the Industrial Revolution and the gradual emancipation of the peasants, the Declarations of Independence and of Rights, the continental pattern of constitutional government, the rise of liberal national- ism. While he himself naturally enough believed in the correctness of "the system," he realized better than many of his more uncritical admirers that it had not stood the test of the times. Had he gone one step farther and realized that it was not merely the upheavals of the period but something less impersonal as well that had made things go wrong, he would not have been the man he was.

In the political field the verdict is somewhat less clear than in the social one. Unquestionably, the territorial settlement of 1814-15 was in a state of dissolu- tion in the east by the end of Metternich's tenure of office. In western and central Europe the then established boundaries could still be held in a precarious kind of balance, but here the constitutional principles of the system were in rapid flux. Above all, the balance of power between east, west, and central Europe became increasingly disturbed. Here, however, it may well be argued that times like ours, subject to ever more rapid political change, might take a more tolerant view of the relative brevity of the preservation of established treaty provisions and principles.

Such comparisons of the relative similarity of historical situations should, of course, be based on complete confidence concerning the chain of historical causation itself. True enough, the bulk of evidence concerning the course of European political history from Metternich's time to ours is in. Yet before we can pass judgment on the character of the impact of his policies on our times, we would have to be very sure that he really exercised such an influence. To answer this question of causation in a fully satisfactory way is actually a far more difficult task than that of forming value judgments. Here we have to face the fact that we can assume but we cannot prove the degree to which Metternich influenced later events.

An assumption of this kind is usually based on three interrelated facts: the containment of Russia, the preservation of the Hapsburg Empire, and above all the establishment and maintenance of peace. Hardly anybody will argue that Metternich's skillful containment of Russia was successful in the long run. Still, it is sometimes asserted that his policy at this particular time might well serve as a model for policies in our day. I do not believe this to be true. If historical analogies are meaningful, we must, of course, make a generous allowance for differences in historical situations. When we come to deal with personalities as different as Alexander I and his brother, and Messrs. Stalin and Khrushchev, the allowance must be very generous indeed. If we add to these differences the more important ones in ideology, we have reached a point where historical comparisons become unprofitable. Metternich's Eastern policy may have been wise or unwise; it teaches us no specific lessons.

Anyone who, like this writer, feels that the disintegration of the Hapsburg Empire at the end of World War I was a major tragedy in international relations cannot fail to be impressed by the argument that Metternich secured the preservation of Austria and therewith the European equilibrium, so tragically destroyed in 1918. While the effect of Austria's disintegration was demonstrably one major factor, though surely not the only one, responsible for the European crises that have continued since that time, the premise that Metternich's achievements helped to secure the great-power position of Austria up to that point is far more problematical. There can be no doubt that he made an outstanding contribution to the restoration of the Hapsburg Empire from the depths of defeat in the Napoleonic wars to the key position she held for a decade after 1812 and to her continuation as a great power for some time subsequent to this. Yet restoration and preservation are by no means the same. Whether Metternich's part in establishing Austria's domestic policies and ideological alignments actually contributed to the preservation of the empire up to 1918 or, from a long-range viewpoint, possibly shortened her lease on life, is a question of extraordinary complexity. It merges with the more comprehensive question whether social and cultural change can be stopped at a certain point by governmental authority and, if so, for how long. Historians thus far have not found satisfactory answers.

The Russian and the Austrian problems are both linked to the supreme quest for the preservation of peace, the decisive test in any evaluation of Metternich. On the assumption (which, however, has not been proved) that Metternich's policies are largely responsible for the course of international relations from the Congress of Vienna to the outbreak of the war in 1914, the arguments present themselves as follows: Metternich's system secured for a full century the preservation, if not of peace, at least of an era without major war. Other schools of thought refuse to give Metternich credit at this point on the basis of the familiar and unanswerable argument that the extent of historical causation cannot be proved. More fruitful, however, is the examination of another line of thought which denies that peace was actually preserved during the century from 1815 to 1914. Here we may come close indeed to the core of the Metternich problem.

By and large, historiography prior to the first world war took an unfriendly, even hostile attitude toward Metternich's foreign policy. This, of course, was due to several factors. Established western liberalism, central European neoliberalism of the third quarter of the nineteenth century, and the German nationalism of the second empire, represented best perhaps by Treitschke's philosophy of history, rejected Metternich's doctrines and devices for obvious and specific reasons. Beyond this, however, one may well say that the people who reached manhood around 1848 and died before 1914 did not feel that they lived in an era of peace. To them the Crimean War, the Austro-Prussian War, and the Franco-Prussian War were big wars, and in view of the relative number of troops engaged and casualties suffered they had good reason to think so. Only the tragedy of two world wars has changed that picture. This, indeed, is the period when the reversal in the evaluation of Metternich, initiated by such eminent historians as Guglielmo Ferrero and Heinrich von Srbik, commences.[12]

It is psychologically quite understandable that the impact of the dark forces of our time should challenge the historian to portray Metternich in a favorable light. Undoubtedly such a shift in the frame of reference explains the motivation of those who contend that Metternich made a lasting contribution to peace. It neither proves nor disproves the contention itself. One thing only is certain. Metternich himself wanted peace, and peace not merely in terms of a Bismarck-ian saturation of power but on the basis of the status quo, adjusted by negotia-tions as he conceived them. Thus the living lesson of his work pertaining to international relations is not embedded in any particulars of political strategy but in principles which may be summarized as follows: moderation in success and perseverance in defeat, steadfastness of purpose as the intrinsic premise of compromise irrespective of conflicting ideologies, consensus based on reason and not on emotion. Surely not these principles in themselves but failure to apply them successfully is responsible for Metternich's equivocal position in history. Yet how could he have applied them successfully without linking them gradually to some kind of system of popular sovereignty? And how could he have done so without repudiating the tradition he stood for?

---

[12] Guglielmo Ferrero (Eng. trans.), *The principl-s of power* (New York, 1942) and *The re-construction of Europe* (New York, 1941). The third volume of Srbik's biography deals with the historiographical evaluation of Metternich. See also A. Wandruszka, "Der Kutscher Europas. Fürst Metternich im Urteil der Historiker von Heute," *Wort und Wahrheit*, XIV (1959), 459 ff.

[2]

1848: An Opportunity Lost?

$\mathcal{I}$n a much-quoted phrase, G. M.
Trevelyan has called the year 1848 "the turning point at which modern history
failed to turn." In 1848, liberals in France, Germany, Italy, and the Austrian
Empire carried out revolts against their authoritarian rulers and
demanded constitutions, and—in several cases or to some degree—universal
suffrage and republican governments. In Italy and Germany, the
revolutionaries aimed at national unification as well. In the Austrian
Empire, Kossuth and the Hungarians fought for an independent state. At
Prague, the Slavonic Congress asked that the empire be converted into a
federation of nations enjoying equal rights. In France, where there was
no problem of national identity, social and political considerations predominated. There the revolutionaries established the Second French Republic,
and in its provisional government, Socialists, such as Louis Blanc, held office.
By the end of 1849, however, all these revolutions had been effectively crushed.
¶ In France, the Second Republic did not formally become the authoritarian Second Empire until 1852. But in December 1848, the election of Prince
Louis Napoleon as president of the Republic gave comfort to the partisans
of order, for all that Louis Napoleon had been elected directly by universal
suffrage and had shown concern with social problems. In Italy and
Germany, the work of unification was undertaken by the "new statesmen,"
Cavour and Bismarck. Although they made concessions to moderate,
liberal opinion, *Realpolitik* rather than idealism guided their policies, and the
unification of their states was achieved largely through force of arms. In
the Austrian Empire reaction was the most complete. With the institution
of the repressive Bach system, it seemed as though the hands of the
clock had been turned back—thus Whig or liberal history's interpretation of
1848 as "an opportunity lost." Perhaps the most eloquent expression of this
point of view comes from Trevelyan.

That year as we can now see, was an ill year for the future of mankind. The failure of the Continental Liberals to establish some measure of free government and national self-expression at a time when Europe was ripe for such a change was a disaster on the grand scale. It lies at the root of many of the evils of the present day, and the year 1848 is, negatively, one of the governing dates of modern history. An opportunity was lost which did not recur. It was a moment when Parliamentary institutions and free political life might have been established on the Continent in time to become acclimatized before the social questions and class divisions of modern industrialism became unfavourably acute. If Germany had then been liberalized, it can scarcely be doubted that Russia would have reformed in time. And the new nations as Mazzini prophetically saw them, might have begun their racial life on a basis not of militarism and mutual hatred, but of complete opposition to the militant attitude of mind. The very feebleness of the military preparations of the patriots . . . illustrates the point. Conscription and government by bayonets, being at that time associated with the denial of nationalism, were unpopular with the men of '48. But owing to the failure of their efforts, national aspirations took another mold and were re-expressed in terms of military power.[1]

In 1944, Sir Lewis Namier, never one to shun historical controversy, subjected the older view of 1848 to a blistering attack in the Raleigh Lecture on History at the British Academy. In his interpretation of 1848, Namier stressed the "early manifestations of aggressive nationalisms, especially of German nationalism which derives from the much belauded Frankfort Parliament rather than from Bismarck and 'Prussianism.'" The belief that "there was something especially noble and precious and liberal minded about the collectivity of Germans at that time" is, according to Sir Lewis, "one of the legends of history. . . . With 1848 starts the Great European War of every nation against its neighbors."[2]

The two selections below, which postdate Namier's interpretation, reflect the increasing concern of historians with the nationalistic aspects of the revolutions of 1848. In the first, Hans Kohn, one of the most noted of present-day authorities on nationalism, succinctly shows the brand of nationalism professed by the liberals of Frankfort. He also concludes that in Central Europe, "No appeal was stronger than that to ethnic emotions and historical rights. The revolutionary fervor was directed toward national goals rather than liberal ones. Wherever the two conflicted nationalism prevailed." At the same time, Kohn gives an interesting account of the pacifism, idealism, and republicanism that was in the air before 1848, and offers an original analysis of the failure of the 1848 revolution in France.

[1] G. M. Trevelyan, *Manin and the Venetian Revolution of 1848* (London: Longmans, Green and Co., 1923), pp. vii–viii.
[2] L. B. Namier, *1848: The Revolution of the Intellectuals,* The Raleigh Lecture on History—1944. From the *Proceedings of the British Academy,* XXX (London: Geoffrey Cumberledge), p. 33.

The second selection, by the distinguished, German historian, Friedrich Meinecke, concentrates on the revolution of 1848 in Germany. It is, on the whole, a moderate interpretation. Meinecke admits that the nationalism of the liberals of Frankfort might have led "into the storm center of a great European war." But he points out earlier that in the revolution, the German people kept to "a comparatively high moral level" and warns against being misled by "the criminal excesses reached in our day" into "condemning the elemental national craving of the men of '48. For theirs was a genuine hunger for something indispensable."

In general, Meinecke thinks that the failure of the German revolution of 1848 was a tragedy, inevitable because of political and social factors operative at the time and because of historical factors reaching back into the German past. Meinecke's interpretation both tempers the newer, harsher view of German nationalism in 1848 and challenges, with its theme of "inevitable tragedy," the older interpretation of an "opportunity lost."

Mid-Century: The Turning Point

Hans Kohn

THE YEAR 1848 was a focal point in modern European history; it marked also the true beginning of the nineteenth century. For the first decades after 1815, life in Europe continued in the same rural and slow-moving pattern as in the eighteenth century. By 1848, industrialization and technology, railways and telegraphs had made their appearance and changed the whole tempo of life. Nor were the spiritual and moral changes from 1815 to 1848 of great depth; the leading personalities and the people preserved the eighteenth century outlook. Metternich, as well as the liberals and radicals, was a good European; like Condorcet or Herder, the liberals cherished an optimistic faith in harmony and international solidarity, in man and in the people. To Metternich's Holy Alliance of monarchs to preserve European peace, the liberals opposed a Holy Alliance of peoples to maintain European solidarity. This eighteenth century spirit animated the revolutionaries at the beginning

Reprinted with permission of The Macmillan Company from *The Twentieth Century: The Challenge to the West and Its Response* by Hans Kohn, pp. 3–18. Copyright 1949, 1957 by Hans Kohn.

of 1848; the spring of this year promised to realize all the cherished and long deferred hopes of the eighteenth century philosophers and of the orators of 1789.

Rarely has the advent of an *annus mirabilis* been greeted throughout the Continent with such identical expectations. The air was saturated with the visions of the heavenly city of eighteenth century secularized Christianity. For some years Michelet and Mickiewicz, Lamennais and Mazzini had hailed with rapturous emotional fervor the people as a new messiah, the expected revolution as a divine revelation, Paris or Rome as the new Jerusalem for a regenerated mankind, and suffering nations as the new Christ. The last two years were full of forebodings: 1846 saw the advent of a liberal Pope and the Polish uprisings in Cracow and Poznan; 1847, the civil war in Switzerland; January, 1848, the revolts in Milan and Naples. When the ice and snow of winter began melting, spring winds swept over Europe: on February 24, France was again a republic; on March 13, almost overnight, Metternich fled, and the seemingly all-powerful symbol of the recent past vanished.

The morning which followed was only a brief dawn. The dreams of the eighteenth century did not come to fruition on the Continent. The promises and hopes ended soon in bitter disillusionment. The cause of the people seemed everywhere defeated. True, the issues so bitterly fought and so miserably lost in 1848 were taken up a few decades later, and many were carried forward to apparent success. Yet this realization came in an entirely different moral and social climate, hardly familiar to Robert Blum or Herwegh, to Mazzini or Michelet. A new age had begun; and the very events of 1848 revealed, in their surprising and disappointing course, for the first time the pattern of the following century, which was dominated by the emergence and the impact of two new mass forces, of socialism and nationalism.

Both these forces predated 1848. They originated in late eighteenth century western Europe, in an atmosphere of humanitarian individualism and critical rationalism. In their youth they were animated by the prevailing hopeful outlook of general harmony which characterized the socialism of a Lamartine or Mazzini. Individual liberty and universal peace were proclaimed not only as the immediate goals, but also as the only admissible methods of socialism and nationalism. When in a brief flare-up the waves of national excitement ran high on both sides of the Rhine in 1840, Lamartine wrote his famous "Marseillaise de la Paix"; fifteen years later he still affirmed, "Homo sum, voilà ma patrie!" During the reign of Louis Philippe in France and of the Biedermeier in Germany, the tendencies of both nations were probably more peaceful than at any other time in modern history. At the same period, through men like Cobden and Bright, pacifism became a dominant creed in English political life. With the preservation of peace and the dissemination of pacifism in mind, the first proposals were then made for a close Anglo-American-French cooperation. A Western union of nations with similar traditions and aspirations was envisaged by some farsighted lovers of peace. For that purpose George M. Gibbs suggested founding in Paris, in 1842, a daily paper in French, a project warmly supported by the London Peace Society and the American Peace Society. On June 28, 1843, the first international pacifist convention was held in London, and delegates from the United States, England, and France participated. With the cooperation of Elihu Burritt, the learned blacksmith from Connecticut, and of Cobden and Bright, a League of Universal Brotherhood was founded in London and a Société d'Union des Peuples in Paris. On September 20, 1848, the first international peace congress met in Brussels. Whittier greeted it with character-istic hopes:

> Evil shall cease and Violence pass away,
> And the tired world breathe free through a long Sabbath day.[1]

More important, however, was the second peace congress which met in August, 1849, in Paris and which was officially received by Tocqueville at the French foreign office. Victor Hugo was its president, Cobden its vice president. In typical pre-1848 style, the French poet declared in his opening address, on August 21, that universal peace was a practical and inevitable goal—"this religious thought, the union of all nations by a common bond, the gospel as a supreme law, arbitration taking the place of war." Pointing to the example of the French provinces which were at war some centuries ago and had since replaced the sword by the ballot box, he predicted that the nations of Europe would similarly fuse in a higher unit while preserving their distinct individual-ities. "A day will come," he proclaimed, "when we shall see these two immense agglomerations, the United States of America and the United States of Europe, facing each other and stretching out their hands across the seas in close coopera-tion." This, Hugo was convinced, would happen very soon, for railroads and technical innovations accelerated all developments. "What do we need?" he asked, and he answered with confident simplicity and to thundering applause: "to love each other." [2] But with the ebbing of the optimism of 1848, the move-ment quickly petered out. One more congress met the next year in the St. Paul Church in Frankfort on the Main. It showed neither the participation nor the animation of the Congress of Paris. The hopes for peace and brotherly love re-ceded before the new messages of a struggle for survival and the proud realism of blood and iron. The spring of the peoples withered without blossoming forth into the hoped-for fruit; the miracle turned into a mirage.

Nor did republicanism prove the expected panacea. In 1848 the republic was greeted with mystical fervor. "In the eyes of the philosopher who contemplates a pure idea, the republic is a most perfect state, in which society which has

---

[1] The poem by John Greenleaf Whittier is called "The Peace Convention at Brussels." See his *Works* (Boston: Houghton Mifflin), seven vols., Vol. III, pp. 318–321.

[2] Victor Hugo's speech at the peace congress of 1849: *Actes et paroles, avant l'Exil, 1841–1851* (Paris: Michel Lévy, 1875), pp. 379–389.

entered the age of virile maturity, can find itself," wrote Mme. d'Agoult, who with George Sand is one of the few women who participated fully in the hopes and struggles of 1848, and who under the pen name of Daniel Stern published a well known history of the revolution of that year. "In the heart of the just and good man, the concept of the republic acquires an even higher character; it becomes the expression of the religious sentiment applied to the institutions of society." [3] The republic was seen not only as the fulfillment of the hope of the ages, but as a universal message destined for all peoples and guaranteeing the peace of mankind. The republicans throughout Europe in the spring of 1848 seemed a fraternal order above classes or nations. A typical poster calling the people of Berlin to a mass meeting on April 1, "in honor of the great European revolution," began in French and English with "Vive la République!" and "Hurrah for the Republic!" In the invitation it was announced that speeches were to be delivered in German, English, and French. The text announced the "resurrection of mankind" and proclaimed:

The hour of the last judgment has struck. Liberty rises from her tomb, and the works of Satan are swallowed up by eternal darkness. . . . Frenchmen and Poles, Italians and Swiss, Irish and English, all peoples of Europe join hands fraternally to welcome freedom with a thundering voice. German fellow-citizens, you will show that you know how to esteem liberty, and that you are ready to help to make it the common property of the whole of mankind. Long live the European Revolution! Long live the new world!

The new world which emerged, however, was very unlike that which the republicans had hoped for. It was not a world of harmony and peace, but of conflict and violence. A new Europe came into being in which the West no longer set the pace. In 1848 socialism and nationalism were transplanted from western Europe to central and eastern Europe, sections with entirely different social conditions and political traditions. There, in the precapitalistic structure of society, socialism changed its emphasis and methods. Marx's expectation that the socialist revolution would come in the highly capitalistic countries proved wrong. It did not come in Britain or in the Low Countries, in Scandinavia or in the United States, where reform took the place of revolution and Marxism never became a fighting creed, a *Weltanschauung*. These countries of the West preserved even in the nineteenth century their conservative moral climate; only in the precapitalistic or backward countries could social revolution be imposed under the banner of Marxism as the new Bible. Nor did the nation state in central and eastern Europe mean what it meant in the West, a community of free citizens based on law established in a struggle for the constitutional liberty of the individual and for the tolerance of opposition. The new nationalism

[3] The quotations from Marie Comtesse d'Agoult (1805–1876) are in Daniel Stern, *Histoire de la Révolution de 1848* (Paris: Calmann-Lévy, 1879), three vols., Vol. I, pp. 280, 288.

stressed collective power and unity far above the civil freedoms of the West: in the intermingling of ethnic groups, nationalism tended to mean independence from outside more than liberty inside; frequently, the temptations to assertion of one's own rule over ethnically disputed territory and populations were not resisted. Nationalism and socialism changed in the nineteenth century from liberal humanitarianism to aggressive exclusivism, from the emphasis on the dignity of the individual to that on the power of collectivities. What was true of the ethnic group was also true of the economic group. Both became invested with combative emotionalism. The rising era of wars of class against class and nation against nation frustrated the hopes of 1848.

The new pattern was revealed with astonishing speed in France. There the year of 1848 started with a united effort of students and artisans, bourgeois and workers, who easily overthrew the power of kingship and aristocracy. Lamartine was then the most popular man. But only four months later, at the end of June, barricades went up in Paris again, and the street fighting was infinitely more bloody and bitter than at any previous time. Yet the workers no longer fought king or noblemen; they fought the democratic republic, based upon universal suffrage, which had come into being only a short while ago with such general acclaim and hopeful expectancy. The workers had been foremost among those who welcomed the republic and general suffrage. "Political faith had found its refuge in the working class; there, it was alive and deep," Mme. d'Agoult wrote at about the beginning of the period. "The worker wished to be a citizen. On account of his ability, his sentiment of justice, and his patriotism, he had possessed for a long time the right to be a citizen. The worker in the cities desired the revolution with all his heart." His new uprising was not suppressed by king's men; it succumbed to a republican army under a republican general who himself had suffered under the monarchy for his republican convictions. These June days left an immense bitterness with the Parisian working class; and their memories are still rankling today, as does the fear in the hearts of the nonproletarian classes of a return of the chaos and terror of 1793. The brief civil war of June, 1848, left its indelible mark upon a whole century. It made itself immediately felt in the elections on December 10, 1848, when the French people for the first time elected in democratic freedom the president of the republic.

The man they chose, *l'élu du peuple,* was Louis Napoleon, who within three years put an end to the parliamentary republic in France. But he did not do it in the name of reaction; he overthrew liberty on behalf of true democracy and progress, of the will of the people which he claimed to embody and which he willingly consulted in plebiscites. The two new forces of nationalism and socialism helped him in his rise to power. He was the candidate of all those who lamented the peaceful, "anti-national" policy of Louis Philippe and who longed for the glory of the advancing armies of 1793 and of Napoleon and for revenge for Waterloo and the treaties of 1815. But the author of the book *The Extinction of Poverty* gained the broad support of the masses also by his promises of social security and economic progress. Lamartine, the poet of peace and human rights, so popular in Feburary, 1848, was in December of the same year the forgotten man. He got only 17,000 votes, less than half of one per cent of the number received by Napoleon. He was defeated by a new force, the authoritarian state backed by the masses and their emotional drives of nationalism and socialism.

The events of 1848 in France were only an adumbration of things to come later in the century. A small group of German exiles in London changed its eighteenth century name of "Bund der Gerechten" in November, 1847, to "Kommunistischer Bund" and replaced its eighteenth century slogan, "All men are brothers," in which the memories of Schiller and Beethoven lived on, with "Proletarians of all countries, unite." The emphasis shifted from the individual to the class. A few months later, in February, 1848, two young German socialists, Marx and Engels, published the *Communist Manifesto* as the program of the communist league. For it they shared the utopian hope of the early socialists of the West for a total transformation of human society, for a secularized kingdom of God here and now. But they based the expectation on entirely different methods, more in conformity with the new age which they anticipated and helped to shape. It would be as wrong to see Marx and Engels through Lenin's eyes only, as it would be to judge Frederick II or Bismarck as mere forerunners of Hitler. They were children of a different age and breathing in a very different moral climate. There was much in Marx of the German idealism and the Western humanism of the pre-1848 age. He shared their hopes. But he replaced the old methods of individual example and moral guidance by the proclamation of struggle and violence as the essence of history, the vehicle of progress, and the indispensable midwife assisting at the birth of the new humanity. He was an extremist in methods and goal. The expected revolution was to be a total revolution bringing a total salvation. As early as 1844, he wrote about Germany in terms which later seemed applicable to Russia. "The emancipation of Germany from medievalism is only possible as a simultaneous emancipation from the effects of an incomplete liberation from medievalism. It is impossible to destroy in Germany any form of slavery without destroying all its forms. Germany is too thoroughgoing to be able to make a revolution in any other way than from the very roots of society. The emancipation of Germany means the emancipation of mankind. Philosophy is the guiding impulse of this emancipation; its life blood is the proletariat." [4]

4 The quotation from Marx is from his "Zur Kritik der Hegelschen Rechtsphilosophie," Marx-Engels *Gesamtausgabs,* ed. Marx-Engels-Lenin Institute in Moscow (Frankfurt am Main, 1927), Vol. I, Pt. I, pp. 607 f.

Marx did not leave the advent of this final salvation to the uncertain moral forces of man. It was the year in which Renan wrote his *L'Avenir de la science;* science was dethroning religion and philosophy as the guiding light of mankind. With great daring, Marx and Engels made science—no longer natural science but the new social science—the unassailable basis of their apocalyptic hopes. The Old Testament prophets had also proclaimed the messianic age, the end of all suffering on earth, the coming of the full glory, as the goal of history. But they expected its advent through the inscrutable will of God and the tenuous moral improvement of man. The *Communist Manifesto* replaced these rather unpredictable factors with the infallibility of science.

The intoxication with the new age of the machine and technology filled the air and inspired the visions of the Saint-Simonists. They were the first dream of a planned society guided by experts. In his *L'Avenir de la science,* which remained unpublished until 1890 but which expressed well the growing cult of science half a century before, Renan demanded a better "exploitation of the globe." Rouget de Lisle wrote a *Marseillaise industrielle* in which he spoke of the new goddess:

> Deployant ses ailes dorées,
> L'industrie aux cent mille pas,
> Joyeuse, parcourt nos climats
> Et fertilise nos contrées.

The product of this industrial advance was the new class of factory workers. The year 1848 witnessed in the West the rise of the proletariat, which discovered itself and grew conscious of its situation and strength. Its misery aroused the sympathy of many spokesmen of other classes. Disraeli published in 1845 his novel *Sybil, or the Two Nations,* which Lord Morley called his "sincerest." In the discussion of the bill on public relief proposed by the Vicomte de Melun, Victor Hugo declared in the French Assembly on July 9, 1849: "I do not belong to those who believe that one can suppress suffering in this world; suffering is a divine law; but I belong to those who think and affirm that one can destroy poverty (la misère). Poverty is a malady of the social body as leprosy is a malady of the human body; it can disappear as leprosy disappeared." [5] Marx went a step further. He did not only proclaim the end of poverty. He gave the assurance that the suffering and humiliated proletariat was called, by the irrefutable logic of history, to overthrow the world of injustice and to establish on its ruins the reign of peace and plenty for all. The pitiless war of the proletariat against its enemies became the infallible means toward universal salvation; the adversaries of the proletariat or of Marx were by necessity the enemies of mankind's progress and hopes. Humanity, united

---

[5] Victor Hugo's speech in the Chamber, July 9th, 1849: *Actes et paroles, op. cit.,* pp. 199–212 (under the title "La Misère").

before 1848, was thus divided in the nineteenth century into two opposing battle camps. The new gospel, a heresy incredible to the eighteenth century, insisted that truth and goodness depended upon the camp to which one belonged. Man mattered less than class; the values and measures on which civilization rested became relativized; individual reality was sacrificed to a fictitious collectivity. The new social forces defeated the hopes of 1848 in France.

These social forces then played hardly a role in central Europe. The social problem there, the emancipation of the peasant, was solved, the one and only lasting achievement of the Austrian parliament in Kremsier. For eastern Europe, as backward socially and politically in relation to central Europe as the latter was to the West, the peasant problem, however, remained unsolved in 1848. Nor did the problem of nationalism in eastern Europe emerge in 1848 with the immediacy that it did in central Europe. There the Austrian parliament was unable to solve this problem. The awakening of the peoples began with a general benevolence and harmony among nationalities as among social classes. Sympathy for budding nationalities was as general and as strong as for the proletariat. But by the end of the year nationalities faced each other in bitter combat. When the incipient revolution released the Polish national leaders of 1846 from the Moabit prison in Berlin, they marched in a procession through the streets, welcomed by the German crowds, and their leader, Ludwik Mieroslawski, carrying Polish and German flags, called the Germans in French to a fraternal fight against the common enemy, Russia. But soon it became clear that the revolutions of 1848 throughout central Europe expressed less a fraternal longing for human liberty than a divisive nationalism. Though their spokesmen demanded individual liberty and constitutional guarantees after the Western model, they desired, above all, the realization of their national aspirations for collective unity and power. No appeal was stronger than that to ethnic emotions and historical rights. The revolutionary fervor was directed toward national goals rather than liberal ones. Wherever the two conflicted, nationalism prevailed.

This has been lately emphasized with regard to the German liberals who met in May, 1848, in the first German parliament in the Church of St. Paul in Frankfort on the Main. There was among them much earnest desire to end German authoritarianism, to align the nation definitely with the West, and to transform it after the model of England or France; but their passions were aroused by German demands against Denmark, Poland, and Bohemia. Not the Prussian conservatives, but liberal writers and intellectuals were the first in Germany to voice Pan-German sentiments and to put forward claims to the source and the mouth of the Rhine, to Alsace-Lorraine, and to the marches of the East with their ethnographically mixed populations and their historic ascendancy of German civilization. German liberal leaders stressed the desire for national power and unity much more than that for individual liberty. The

German-Franco-Polish fraternization of the spring of 1848 was dead four months later. German-Polish relations concerning Poznań set the new pace. "The discussion about Poland from July 24 to July 27 was one of the most important turning points in the history of the German National Assembly," its most prominent German liberal historian wrote. The Congress of Vienna gave the Grand Duchy of Poznań, the historical cradle of the Polish nation, as a sovereign country to the king of Prussia and stipulated that national institutions for the Poles should be created there. The Grand Duchy remained outside the territory of the German Confederation.

German nationalism tried to change this arrangement of the Prussian crown. The German liberals in Frankfort insisted on a division of Poznań and on the incorporation of the western part into Germany. The most impressive argument was put forward by Wilhelm Jordan, who appealed to healthy national egoism against rationalist or abstract justice, to the right of conquest by plough and sword, and called all those who saw the justice of the Polish point of view "traitors to their own people." The few voices who were opposed to the inclusion of part of Poznań into Germany, among whom Robert Blum and Arnold Ruge were prominent, could not prevail against the emotional impact of Jordan's powerful argument for a "sound patriotism." A new faith in might was proclaimed; the decision was hailed as a manifestation of patriotism; the majority of the National Assembly preferred nationalism to liberalism. At the beginning of 1848, the eighteenth century natural-right theory of equality, of the brotherhood of peoples in a universal order of justice, was still alive. By the end of 1848, it had given way to appeals based upon historical rights, the "reality" of power, and the supposed vital and strategic necessities of the nation.

The liberal German historian Dahlmann drew the consequences from the new attitude when, in his memorable speech to the Frankfort Assembly on January 23, 1849, he declared:

The road of power was the only road which could satisfy and satiate the desire for liberty which was fomenting but which had not yet understood itself. For it does not mean liberty alone, it thirsts much more for power which has so far not been granted it. Germany must at last become one of the political great powers of the Continent. That can be achieved only through Prussia; neither can Prussia recover without Germany, nor Germany without Prussia.[6]

Looking back at the events of 1848, John Stuart Mill diagnosed the new evil with unusual perspicacity in 1849. He complained that nationalism makes men

---

[6] On the German Revolution of 1848, see: Veit Valentin, *Geschichte der deutschen Revolution von 1848–49* (Berlin: Ullstein, 1931), Vol. II, p. 125; Wilhelm Jordan (1819–1904), *ibid.*, pp. 126 f.; Friedrich Christoph Dahlmann (1785–1860), Veit Valentin, *Die erste deutsche Nationalversammlung* (Munich: Oldenbourg, 1919), p. 41.

indifferent to the rights and interests "of any portion of the human species, save that which is called by the same name and speaks the same language as themselves." He characterized these feelings of exclusive nationalism and of appeals to historical rights as barbaric. He remarked bitterly that "in the backward parts of Europe and even (where better things might have been expected) in Germany, the sentiment of nationality so far outweighs the love of liberty that the people are willing to abet their rulers in crushing the liberty and independence of any people not of their race or language." [7]

This change of the character of nationalism in central and eastern Europe during 1848 was not only true of the Germans. All the other nationalities showed themselves in no way inferior in grasping and developing the new gospel of the rights of the nation. Oppressed nationalities, while appealing to the world against their own oppression, found it legitimate to oppress others when their supposed national interests seemed to demand it. Professors and writers were always at hand to produce historical and moral reasons for supporting the ambitions of their nation and to point out that their nation and its necessities represented a unique case to which the general rules did not apply. Success in war was hailed as the best proof of moral valor and historical worth. In the hopeful months which ushered in the year 1848, Pope Pius IX gained less popularity for his liberal reforms than for the words "God bless Italy," which he uttered on February 19, 1848, and for the decision to send papal troops to join the Sardinian army in the war against Austria. And many years later, Carducci, the *vates* of Italy, as he called himself, sang rapturously "the smoke of blood rising from fields of battle" [8] and the ecstasy of the brief and insignificant victory of the Sardinian army at Goito on May 30, 1848. Thus it happened that outside the West, nationalism after 1848 meant first and foremost national power and collective independence, and less and less the insistence upon individual liberty and ethnic equality. The Rumanian patriot Nicholas Bălescu emphasized in 1848 that national rights took precedence over human liberty. He wrote:

[7] See J. S. Mill, "Vindications of the French Revolution of February 1848," *Westminster Review*, April, 1849, reprinted in *Dissertations and Discussions, Political, Philosophical and Historical* (London: John W. Parker and Son, 1859), Vol. II, p. 382.

[8] From the poem "Piemonte" (1892):

> Italia, Italia!—E il popolo de' morti
> surse cantando a chiedere la guerra;
> e un re a la morte nel pallor del viso
>   sacro e nel cuore
> trasse la spada. Oh anno de' portenti,
> oh primavera de la patria, oh giorni,
> ultimi giorni del fiorente maggio,
>   Oh trionfante
> suon de la prima italica vittoria
> che mi percosse il cor fanciullo!

Poesie di Giosuè Carducci, 6th ed. (Bologna: Nicola Zanichelli, 1907), pp. 953 f.

For my part, the question of nationality is more important than liberty. Until a people can exist as a nation, it cannot make use of liberty. Liberty can easily be recovered when it is lost [an optimism which seems rather dubious a century later], but not nationality. Therefore I believe that in the present position of our country we must aim rather at the preservation of our greatly menaced nationality and seek only as much liberty as is necessary for the development of our nationality.

Each people regarded itself, with little self-criticism, as "peace-loving" and its neighbors as aggressors. Herder's remark that the Slav peasant peoples best approximated Rousseau's ideal of an idyllic and pacific rural democracy naturally found a ready response among Slav intellectuals. Czechs and Poles who felt themselves menaced by the Germans assured the world that while the Germans inclined to oppress Slavs and other peoples, the Slavs were by their very nature incapable of such designs. As soon, however, as their longings for a nation-state of their own and for national power came true, they did not hesitate to claim expansion of their national territory, either by invoking historical rights or by advancing alleged national needs. Slavs, Hungarians, and Italians were entirely equal in that respect to the Germans. It was the insistence of the Polish democrats and radicals on the Polish frontiers of 1771 which made cooperation with the Russian democrats for common revolutionary action impossible in 1861. In the welter of conflicting ethnic claims and counterclaims, national passions became overheated, historical scholarship often became subservient to nationalist aspirations, and individual liberty was lost.

Pan-Germanism quickly found its rival and equal in Pan-Slavism. Both assumed, in the second third of the twentieth century, under national-socialist and communist leadership, an official character of racial aggressiveness and exclusiveness. In 1848 and in the following decades they did not receive any official recognition. They were intellectual movements rather than national policies. The first Pan-Slavic congress met in Prague simultaneously with the German parliament in Frankfort on the Main. But under the leadership of bourgeois Czech intellectuals, the Pan-Slavism of that day differed deeply from today's brand. The Slavs then gathered in Prague desired the westernization of their peoples, whom they wished to advance as integral parts of liberal Europe. They regarded the existence of the Habsburg Empire, within which they lived, as a necessary bulwark against the danger of Russian expansion, which they dreaded as much as all other Europeans. Even more clearly than Mazzini and other non-Slav liberals, they recognized that Russia not only wished to expand westward, but aspired to world leadership.

[9] See František Palacký, *Radhost* (Collected Minor Writings) (Prague: Tempzky, 1873), Vol. III, p. 13. See on Palacký (1798–1876), *Not by Arms Alone*, pp. 64–83. On the Slav World in 1848, see H. Desprez, "La Russie et la crise européenne," *Revue des deux mondes*, March 15, 1850. Palacký's attitude changed after 1867, when he despaired of a federal solution for Austria. See Hans Kohn,

In that sense the Czech historian František Palacký,[9] the spokesman of his people and the president of the Slav congress, insisted in his letter to the German *Vorparlament* in Frankfort that Austria's preservation, integrity, and consolidation were essential not only to the Czechs, but to the security of Europe and the survival of Western civilization. He was convinced that Russian control of the Danube would constitute a threat of greatest magnitude to Europe. Only a union of the nationalities along the Danube could, in his opinion, thwart the Russian aspirations of establishing a world government and imposing the Russian way of life on all. He wrote on April 11, 1848:

You know what power it is that rules the entire huge East of our continent. You know that this power, now grown to vast dimensions, increases and expands of itself decade by decade in far greater measure than is possible for the countries of the West. You know that, secure at its own center against practically any attack, it has long become a menace to its neighbours. . . . You know too that every further step which it will take forward on this path threatens at an ever accelerated pace to establish a universal monarchy, an infinite and inexpressible evil, a misfortune without measure or bound, such as I, though body and soul a Slav, would none the less profoundly regret for the good of mankind, even though this monarchy be proclaimed a Slavic one.

The first Pan-Slavic congress in Prague in 1848 ended, as the German parliament in Frankfort did, without achieving anything. When it was dissolved in June, 1848, it found itself surrounded by an atmosphere of rapidly growing distrust separating the Czechs and Germans in Bohemia. Yet less than three months before, on March 21, the Prague writers and journalists, German as well as Czech, had unanimously and publicly proclaimed their determination to maintain a firm and permanent harmony between the two nations living in a common land. "Elated in their hearts by the feeling of liberty and unity manifested in these days among the German and Czech inhabitants of our homeland," they wrote, they would strive "that neither should Germans have preference over Czechs nor Czechs over Germans." Alas, these good intentions of the spring of 1848 were soon obliterated. The century which has since passed has brought little fruition to the hopes of liberty and harmony which blossomed in the short awakening of the peoples.

The pattern which began to manifest itself at the end of 1848 had by the end of the century imposed itself at an ever accelerated pace beyond the imagination of the most daring prophets. The teachings of Marx—in an interpreta-

Pan-Slavism, Its History and Ideology (University of Notre Dame Press 1953); Milan Prelog, *Pout' Slovanů do Moskvy roku 1867* (The Pilgrimage of the Slavs to Moscow in the Year 1867), transl. into Czech by Milada Paulová (Prague: Travaux de l'Institut Slave de Praha, 1931); Julian Klaczko, "Le Congrès de Moscou et la propagande panslaviste," *Revue des deux mondes*, September 1, 1867, pp. 132–181.

tion which Marx and Engels might perhaps not have recognized—hold sway over the minds and bodies of a quarter of the globe's population who either live under the direct or indirect control of Russia or give their supreme allegiance to her as the embodiment, or at least the assumed embodiment, of the gospel according to Marx. The democractic dictatorship which Louis Napoleon started under the acclaim of universal suffrage has been revived in forms before which the humane and civilized world of Napoleon III would have shuddered. German, Slav, and Italian nationalisms, still liberal in 1848, have since developed in an ominous way. The liberals of Frankfort and Prague would probably repudiate their offspring, the Pan-Germanism of 1938 and the Pan-Slavism of a decade later.

In the century which has passed since 1848, humanitarian hopes, the heritage of Western civilization and of the eighteenth century, have, with the growing cult of violence and of the ready and willing acceptance of class war and national conflicts, lost more and more of their restraining power. In 1848 the foundations of Western civilization—intellectual belief in the objectivity of truth and justice, ethical faith in mercy and tolerance—were still unshaken. The men who prepared the climate of 1848 believed, like Condorcet, in moral progress, in a progress of spiritual forces, no longer pointing to a realization beyond earthly existence, but here on earth, within the frame of fragile human nature. What really happened in the century since was a breathtaking progress in technical discoveries and methods and an ever growing faith in them and in the functional manipulation not only of matter, but of souls and minds. Today mankind lives among the ruins which demagogy and class war, Pan-Germanism and Pan-Slavism, exclusive and militant nationalism and socialism have produced. But history has not only its saddening lesson; its perspective may bring comfort in fighting the battles of the grim day. In the spring of 1848 mankind was full of glowing hope, but the end of 1848 dashed the hopes, and the century which 1848 inaugurated appears to have led slowly but surely to decay and disaster. Today, in its wake, mankind faces the future with dark forebodings. But it may be that in the century ahead the road may take again, unexpectedly, another turn and lead slowly but surely to the reawakening of the concern for individual liberty and humanitarian morality.

The Year 1848 in German History: Reflections on a Centenary

Friedrich Meinecke

THE POPULAR uprising of the March Days of 1848 in Berlin, superficially viewed, remained an episode, and the men who were fighting for progress along various lines failed, and were bound to fail, in their aims. The German revolution, said Friedrich Engels in his instructive articles of 1851–52 (which he published in America above the signature of Karl Marx), was a necessity, but its temporary suppression was similarly unavoidable. We shall still have to substantiate this, but must turn our gaze first upon the Berlin revolution, and upon the positive comment which it may offer for our contemporary historical situation. Yet for this too it is necessary to search somewhat deeper.

We must set before ourselves today more sharply than before, the problem of critical alternatives in the history of Germany, in order to gain a deeper insight into the infinitely complex web of her dark destiny. The natural task of Germany in the nineteenth century was not only to achieve unification, but also to transmute the existing authoritarian state (*Obrigkeitsstaat*) into commonwealth (*Gemeinschaftsstaat*). To that end, the monarchial-authoritarian structure had to be made elastic—if possible, through peaceful reform—so that the result would be an active and effective participation of all strata of society in the life of the state. This was imperatively demanded by the new configuration which was in process within the German society, and which was undermining the former aristocratic foundations of the authoritarian monarchy. An upper middle class arose, the lower middle class increased in large strides, and the beginnings of the industrial proletariat in the middle of the century gave notice of its mighty growth to come. Now, the task of reorganizing and harmonizing within a new commonwealth a people in social transition, bursting with vitality, remained largely unfulfilled, although many liberal and democratic concessions were granted by the old authorities. Which then were the decisive points in this development?' When were possibilities first seen, attempts made or frustrated, which could have brought Germany forward upon the path to the commonwealth?

From *The Review of Politics*, X, No. 1 (January 1948), pp. 475–92. Copyright, 1948, by the University of Notre Dame. Reprinted by permission.

I see, above all, three such moments. The first occurs toward the end of the Prussian era of reform, in the year 1819—the year of the Carlsbad Decrees—when with the dismissal of Wilhelm von Humboldt and Boyen, their most fruitful constitutional projects were also buried, and the authoritarian and militaristic principle triumphed in Prussia. The second crisis, when this principle once more won out in the end, was the year 1848. And the third point of decision was the Prussian era of conflict and the year 1866, which, while seeing some progress made toward satisfying the desire for national unity and strength, allowed the liberal and democratic ideas only a partial or apparent success. For it separated the way of the upsurging popular movements from the authoritarian-militaristic citadel of the entire national life.

Of these three fundamental decisions of the nineteenth century, the first was fought out in the more restricted circle of the ruling class itself, between high-minded and farsighted statesmen on the one hand and a monarch of limited understanding on the other. The third crisis developed as a duel between the liberal upper middle class and Bismarck, in which that tremendously skilful campaigner understood how to win over at last a large part of the opposition. At no time in the years before 1866, was the weapon of a revolution seriously considered by Bismarck's progressive antagonists; they were fearful of it, in accordance with the instincts of an upper bourgeoisie. The second crisis—that of 1848—offers therefore a unique, and for us today, a moving spectacle: here the whole people, not Prussians alone, but Germans of every class, stepped into the arena, and an actual revolution came about.

Revolutions, fearful as the invasion of irrational forces may be, or turn out to be, have in certain cases their deep historical justification. Such was the case in Germany, and especially in Prussia, in the year 1848. Admittedly the old order, now attacked by the revolution, was not in all aspects characterized by decay or ossification. The *Biedermeierzeit* with its lovely spiritual flowering had gone before. The Zollverein, since 1833 a work of the Prussian bureaucracy, had made secure the indispensable preconditions for the rise of modern economic forces, and thereby also for the social transformation from which the revolution itself had sprung. The psychopathic romanticist who now sat on the throne of the Hohenzollerns was himself inspired with a deep love for German civilization (*Deutschtum*), and was at some pains to bring about a German unity in its own way. But this way contradicted most sharply the urgent needs of the time. It was upon illusions that he based his attempts to reform the wretched organization of the German Bund and to fulfill the promise of a constitution (made in 1815) by the assembling of the united provincial diets in 1847. For the strongly aristocratic composition of these provincial estates, and the narrow powers which were all that the king would concede to them, were completely inadequate to satisfy the claims of popular representation which grew out of the process of social change. And in everyday life one felt everywhere the old absolutist-militarist police state, unbroken in spite of the isolated concessions to liberalism which the king, giving with one hand and rescinding with the other, might make. But behind the reaction against his personal and self-contradictory rule, and behind all individual grievances, there stood as a deepest source of discontent the feeling that the Prussian military and Junker state must be reorganized from the ground up—that the old authoritarian state must give way to a new commonwealth.

In fact this emotion, spurring on toward revolution, was not actually evoked but only powerfully stimulated, by the February revolution in France and the scattered revolts that were flaring up throughout Germany and even in Metternich's own Vienna. The remarkable circumstance that everywhere they succeeded at once, without encountering resistance, would demonstrate that the moral position of the rulers themselves was already noticeably shaken, that they no longer possessed an unquestioning and naive faith in the viability of the old order. Such a faith was necessary, if the governments were to use against the revolution the physical instrumentalities of power, still amply available to them. When later they realized that these resources were still at their disposal, the authorities did not hesitate to act accordingly, and to suppress the revolution with reaction. But as things were in March, 1848, they all, as Frederick William IV later expressed it, "lay flat on their bellies."

He, the king himself, most of all. And this in spite of the fact that he had actually launched, on the 18th of March, the physical auxiliaries of his power—his faithful army—successfully against the people's barricades in Berlin. Yet on the very next day, he permitted, through his own order, these troops—though undefeated—to abandon the inner city which they had conquered, and thereby exposed the person of the king to the severest of humiliations at the hands of the rebels. Let us leave aside entirely the tangled complexity of these events, which have been investigated time and again, and emphasize only this. So feeble and contradictory a policy could not have been conducted by any prince, who, with a pure and undiminished faith in his old world, was simply defending it against a new. This new world had already to some degree insinuated itself, secretly and unsuspected, into his own thinking, distracting and weakening his power for effective action. Sooner or later the new was bound to win out, in spite of many setbacks to come, and to replace the authoritarian state by some form of democracy.

Such an interpretation may be justified, as we look back over the whole century that separates us from the year 1848, and as we think of the task now before us—the task of casting aside all relics of the authoritarian state (of which the Third Reich was, in fact, but a malignant outgrowth), and building up a sound and vigorous democracy. The easy victory—to be sure, not a military but a political and psychological victory—by which the street-fighting in Berlin prevailed over the old military monarchy, suggested symbolically that the latter's downfall was written in the stars; that one day the sovereignty of the people would become a reality. But, at the same time, it was no more than a symbol. For the new world was as yet quite untested and immature, and the old world still possessed many unexploited resources—even the chance of remaining victorious for some time to come. Bismarck and his work, after all, had sprung from it, at once magnificent and ephemeral. But let us now mark clearly the indications of that immaturity in which the new world of democracy then continued to find itself.

First a glance at Berlin. The men on the barricades of the 18th of March certainly fought bravely and fiercely, more fiercely than the Parisians before them had fought on the 24th of February. Such was the opinion of the Frenchman Circourt, who had come to Berlin as the representative of the new republican government, and had witnessed both engagements. But was it really the whole of the Berlin populace that stood behind the fighting or accompanied it with good wishes? Pastor Bodelschwingh, son of the minister whose task it was to pass on the royal command for retreat on the 19th of March, wrote in 1902: [1] "We youngsters were running about on the streets that Sunday morning (March 19). With the uprising repelled, there reigned a joyful mood among the greater part of our population; everywhere from the houses the troops were plied with food." Of course, most of the individual bits of evidence which we possess concerning the 18th and 19th of March, are colored to some extent by the sympathies of the witness, and so this testimony of Bodelschwingh should not be taken too literally either. But even less does it deserve to be entirely discarded. And a glance at the general attitude of the German upper middle class in the years 1848–49 reveals all the more clearly that large sections of this class were still greatly desirous of tranquility, and continued to be loyal to the old authorities.

It is necessary to go more deeply into these questions, in order to explain the paradoxical fact that the German revolution of 1848 could everywhere succeed so easily at first, and then in the sequence of events be overthrown with comparatively little effort. To understand this, the character, attitudes, and moral habits of the German people as it was at that time, and those of the various social strata within it, must be taken into consideration. And our contemporary need to attain to an inner relationship with this first attempt at German democracy gives this problem all the more importance.

The German people had only just emerged from the years of thinking, writing, and striving. But the thinking and dreaming continued likewise within the framework of new achievements and new desires. This ideological groundswell is common to all parties and classes within the German people, from Frederick William IV and his devout Christian-German friends—the extremists of reaction—all the way to the extremists of revolution: the men

[1] Pastor Bodelschwingh is known as the founder of Bethel. The author wrote to him in 1902, requesting information about the revolution of 1848; the above quotation is from his reply.

whose forceful minds conceived the Communist Manifesto of 1848, Karl Marx and Engels. For did not Hegel live on with them—a Hegel in reverse and yet preserved (*aufgehoben*)? Was it not true of both these thinkers, who claimed to regard all ideologies as merely secondary efforts of fundamental economic forces, that in them there came to life something distinctly ideological—an unqualified belief in the determining power of the laws of development—set up at a time when they themselves found only a tiny handful of followers? In any case, we ought no more gainsay the strong impulse of idealism which worked in these men, than that operating in Dahlmann and Gagern—the champions of the liberal nation-state—or in the brothers Gerlach, defenders of a divinely ordained corporative state. The German revolution of 1848, admittedly, shows not only an all-pervading spirit of idealism, which often outstripped reality and became ideological. It also brought to bear what in actual effect was more powerful—the reality itself, the massive and elemental interests of individuals and social groups. And, because it *was* a revolution, it likewise saw the release of base passions, and outrages of all kinds, perpetrated by the Right as well as by the Left. But if 1848 is compared with other revolutions—and particularly with the most ignominious of all revolutions, that of 1933—it can be stated that the factor of human depravity played a comparatively insignificant role. This must not be obscured by the fact that the extremist parties took pleasure in accusing one another of disgraceful conduct. Theirs were for the most part "atrocity stories." Neither was there anything which could be termed a "brutalized soldiery," nor were the barricades and the free corps of Hecker and Struve manned by a mere "mob." The German people, considered as a whole, kept in those days to a comparatively high moral level.

It must be admitted that their level of life no longer possessed the spiritual grandeur of the age of Goethe. This decline was unavoidable in any case, since the urgent task of establishing a new political and social way of life compressed men into mass or group patterns, and made it more difficult for the individual to gather within himself the creative force from which proceeds all great culture. But what mattered now was, whether this people would prove to possess the maturity, the strength, the insight and steadfastness, that its new task demanded. Certainly, as we have noted, it was written in the stars that one day the new world would triumph over the old, popular sovereignty over the authoritarian state. But could the victory be achieved at this juncture? The fact that the revolution failed does not necessarily prove that the people were not ready; this may have been due to the coincidence of accidental factors. How bitter were the complaints, in the very midst of events, that just such a personality as Frederick William IV should have been for the revolution its "man of destiny"—a man who had actually, out of weakness, bowed before it at the outset, but who had then stubbornly resisted it; and by his refusal of the imperial office on April 3, 1849, had allowed the nation's call for the creation of the liberal nation-state to die away. Certainly another man in his place could have attempted another and possibly more propitious solution of the German problem. Then, however, the success of the attempt would once more have depended, in the last analysis, upon the world situation. This aspect of the problem we shall take up later. Suffice it now to ask again: was the German people really prepared for the task ahead?

Basic attributes and historical experiences, working together, had made the German people parochial, not only outwardly but inwardly as well, to a degree hardly equalled in any other nation of Europe. The princely territorial state, multiplied a hundredfold to the point where it exhibited absurd extremes of dwarfishness, depended everywhere upon a landed gentry which served the state and, in return, held sway over those beneath them. All this had mingled with the German bloodstream and had rendered the German people obedient and lacking in political self-reliance. In this very multiplication of authority, we see the chief means by which the mentality of the authoritarian state penetrated so deeply into the pores of German life.

One need only compare this with the development of England and France, where the royal absolutism—in England short-lived anyhow—had indeed helped to create a unified nation, but had never been able to instil so lasting and thoroughgoing a habit of obedience, as had the multiplicity of small German principalities. How far an original or native trait had helped to bring this about, can only be conjectured. Was it perhaps the spirit of fealty described by Tacitus? But the example of the Germans in Switzerland and their historical development since the Middle Ages indicates that there were other potentialities of a political nature inherent in the German character. Free of princely and therefore of rigid rule, subject only to patrician and—by the same token— more pliable authority, Switzerland was enabled to develop the native democratic tenet of her original cantons into the governing principle of her commonwealth, and thus to build upon historical foundations a modern democracy. No, the German need not submit to any fatalistic dread that because he is a German, he may for ever and ever be condemned to the habits of servility implanted by the authoritarian state. But it takes time, much time, again to tear free of it. Then too, this state has borne the German people, along with evil fruits, many and varied benefits, and thus fashioned much of ethical value that might well be carried over into the new world of the democratic commonwealth.

Good and evil alike, then, grew out of this disposition toward obedience, whose origin may well be placed primarily in the political fragmentation referred to above. Even where a larger political entity was growing up, as in Prussia, the extreme insistence upon this subservient attitude brought out in a manner especially striking the contrast between its good and evil effects. Prussia was, indeed, a state with two souls: the one austere and narrow, withdrawing into itself; the other culturally alive, striving, in Boyen's phrase, toward a threefold alliance of *"Recht, Licht and Schwert."* This Prussia, at once forbidding and attractive, now exerted her influence upon the rest of Germany. But how much was this influence again bound to confuse and distract all the aims of revolutionary Germany! The singleness of revolutionary purpose which would have been necessary for a victory over the old order, was thus rendered at the outset far more difficult to achieve. Now the German people, breaking loose from its previous subservience, did indeed reach out tumultuously for unity, power and freedom—only to find itself divided anew when it sought to determine the methods by which these were to be accomplished. How deep was the disintegrating and paralyzing effect of the Austro-German (*grossdeutsche*) problem, which implied what to some seemed an avoidable, to others an inevitable sacrifice of a portion of their fellow-countrymen (*Brudersstamm*), and the break-up of a German national community; how strongly has this problem contributed to the negative result of the revolution! It is hardly necessary, in addition, to recall the particularism of the intermediate German states. In fact, it was not merely the egotistic instincts of the princes, of their court councillors and court provisioners, but particularistic tendencies as well, conscious or unconscious, in the people themselves, which came into conflict with the new yearning for unity.

These were the factors of secular growth, going back as far as the Middle Ages, which weakened and divided in advance any unified revolutionary purpose in the German people. To these, however, were now added problems of the most modern type, arising out of the new configuration of society. It is true that the one part of the people which now broke away from the old attitudes of obedience, and rose up against the authoritarian state and against the splintering apart of the nation, was agreed upon the demand for greater unity, power and freedom; but it fell out once again over the emphasis and interpretation to be placed upon one or another of these three words. For behind the national revolution there was unfolding a social revolution, a class struggle between the old, the newer, and the newest social strata. This fact was recognized most clearly at the time by Marx and Engels, the champions of the newest class—the industrial proletariat—which had only just arisen and was still by no means very numerous. Between this youngest and (as Marx and Engels dogmatically proclaimed) potentially most important class, and that which had ruled so far— the nobility and the higher bureacracy—there lay the two clearly distinct divisions of the bourgeoisie: the upper and lower middle class. The first was of more recent origin; the other dated far back, though it was not nearly as old as the peasantry—who, together with agricultural laborers, still made up by far the preponderant majority of the people as a whole. (The committee on economic affairs of the Frankfurt Parliament estimated that they constituted virtually four-fifths of the total population at that time.) The share of the rural population in the revolution was certainly not unimportant, but created no particularly complicated issue for the fate of the revolution as a whole. Since a general land reform through the dismemberment of the large estates was not yet seriously envisioned, the agrarian problem of 1848 entailed only the casting-off of all remaining feudal encumbrances upon the peasant class and the peasant holdings. That was a comparatively simple task. Even conservative statesmen realized the necessity of solving this question at once, and when the peasants saw that steps in this direction were being taken or being planned, they calmed down again. They still shared sufficiently in the old habits of subservience, in any case. The young Bismarck could well consider using them as tools in the counter-revolution.

Side by side with the working class, the lower middle class provided most of the revolutionary energy. Craftsmen and workers formed the bulk of the fighters on the barricades. Had they not risen up, the revolution could not have achieved dynamic force at all, and all the idealists and theorists of the general movement (reaching into the upper middle class) would have remained officers without an army. There would have been no parliament in the Paulskirche, no draft for a German constitution with an hereditary Prussian emperor at its head. The craftsmen in Germany at that time were badly off. It was related in the Paulskirche that there was one small town with seventy tailors, of whom only seven were able to find employment. Some hardship was caused by guild restrictions which continued here and there. But a genuine guild spirit revived again, as is evidenced in the desperate struggle waged against the new machine by workers who were losing their livelihood, in the excesses committed by the waggoners against the railroads and by the boatsmen against the Rhine river steamers. These were all, in fact, merely symptoms of the basic feature of an age in which the machine, and the modern technology, had revolutionized the entire life of the western peoples, by creating new human masses and new, unsuspected and distressing situations among these masses.

In such a crisis, the old authoritarian state proved unable for a long time to provide effective aid. Its officialdom was vacillating between benevolence and a narrow, pedantic attitude; its police a nuisance; its army—though possessed in the militia (*Landwehr*) of a more popular aspect—aroused bitter opposition by the arrogance and drill-ground manner of the regulars and their officers. Democracy as a cure for all these sufferings was the magic word that echoed through the ranks of the lower bourgeoisie—a class so quietist by nature and so restless now. The working classes took up the same slogan, and added to it their own socialistic demands. The younger generation within the upper middle class in many places espoused the democratic cause with enthusiasm, and imbued it with the impulse of idealism. It was, to be sure, an exceedingly immature and primitive democracy of which these Germans dreamed, more a rejection of the old authoritarian state than a positive affirmation of the people's state resting upon a fully developed common spirit among all classes. The distrust and arrogance with which the various classes regarded one another, once more divided the very groups which had just made common cause against the old authorities. Let us illustrate this and other facts aforementioned, with certain experiences which the young Rudolf Virchow had in the March Days of Berlin.

Eight days before the 18th of March, he had returned from Upper Silesia, where he had been sent as a doctor to study the "hunger-typhus." He was indignant at the inability of the magistrates to take effective measures, and had long been convinced that the absolutist system of government was untenable. He assisted in the building of barricades on the 18th of March, and, armed with a pistol, placed himself at the one which blocked the Friedrichstrasse from the Taubenstrasse. Only six days later, he had to admit in a letter to his father: "Already there begins a reaction among the citizenry (Bourgeoisie) against the workers (the people). Already they are speaking of a rabble, already plans are being made for withholding equal distribution of political rights among the various groups in the nation." But, he added, the popular party would be alert and powerful, and would see to it "that no bourgeoisie should enjoy the fruits of a battle it had not waged."

One realizes here the closeness of the relationship between events in Berlin and the revolutions of 1830 and 1848 in France. But the problems of the German revolution were nevertheless much more complicated than those of the French uprisings. For the social revolution in Germany and its underlying class struggle was intertwined with the national revolution in a way which finally led to the failure of both. France no longer had need of a national revolution. She had long since achieved her unity, and her centralized power apparatus remained through one regime after another. In Germany both social equality and national consolidation were still to be achieved, with endless pains. And the need of the nation for unity and power was just as elemental and as deeply rooted in history as was the cry for domestic freedom and equality arising from those classes which the authoritarian state had so far kept down. Dahlmann in Frankfort even voiced the opinion that within the German desire for both power and freedom, the stronger impulse was now directed toward power, which had thus far been denied. The criminal excesses reached in our day by the need for power in Germany should by no means mislead us into condemning the elemental national craving of the men of '48. For theirs was a genuine hunger for something indispensable. Even Goethe had once acknowledged this fact, after the battle of Leipzig. "Art and science," he said to Luden, "are universal, and in view of these the bonds of nationality disappear. But the consolation they afford is but hollow comfort, and cannot replace the proud consciousness of belonging to a great, strong, feared and respected nation." Basically all the cravings of the year 1848 were permeated by kindred feelings and experiences. There was a general desire to leave behind the constricting and now intolerable bonds of the past, as one leaves behind a dark and airless dungeon. Just as the little man felt himself generally neglected and mistreated by the authoritarian state, so did the more cultivated German, who saw himself as a member of a great national community, and yet hemmed in by the irritating boundaries and the often ridiculous parochialism of thirty-eight greater or smaller authoritarian states. And equally neglected and thrust aside did he feel himself and his whole people to be within the entire body of European states.

All three of these desires [the liberal, the national, the European] were now, it was fondly hoped, to find their fulfillment through the Frankfurt National Assembly which, elected by universal and equal suffrage, convened on the 18th of May. Let us consider its social composition; it was noticeably different from what one might have expected as the result of the democratic suffrage imported from France. It contained no workers, only one genuine peasant, few members of the lower middle class, but many lawyers and judges—and, as is well known, many professors; nor were representatives of business and industry lacking. This indicates the still remaining respect of the lower for the upper strata of society, especially for the academically educated and in general for what is termed the upper bourgeoisie. But the same masses who now cast their votes for these people, were simultaneously in a state of unruly and turbulent commotion, which must necessarily have boded evil for the upper middle class interests and ideals. One had to rely on such an energetic thrust from below, in order to succeed at all to Frankfurt and the Paulskirche. But now it was a question, indeed, whether one could continue to employ these energies as indispensable weapons against the rulers, and yet keep them within limits, so as to guard against anarchy and the overturn of the social order.

In the last analysis, it was the danger of communism which appeared to threaten the whole bourgeoisie—not only the upper but the lower middle class as well. How real even the latter felt this threat to be, is exemplified by the bloody clash between the civil guard and the workers in Berlin on October 16, 1848. Communistic slogans and demands rang out from the enraged masses. A clearly conceived program, such as that of Marx and Engels, was in truth limited at first to the narrowest circles. But in a broader perspective, it appears that the very existence of a communist movement was perhaps decisive, or at least instrumental, in determining the course of events in 1848—and, in the first instance, the attitude and policy of the Paulskirche. For it was in view of this communist threat that the middle class and its representation in the majority parties of the Paulskirche again and again were forced over toward the Right, toward some kind of compromise with the old authorities and their military resources. The same threat was instrumental in preventing the maintenance of a unified revolutionary purpose within the whole people, to which perhaps the government might at last have been forced to submit. We use the little word "perhaps," because historical questions of this sort cannot be treated like a mere problem in mathematics; because in every case where we have to consider the historical possibility of another kind of development than that which actually took place, an unknown "X" disturbs the calculation.

In any event, the parties of the majority—right and left center—which desired to establish a liberal, constitutional nation-state with an hereditary Prussian emperor as its head, found themselves in an extremely contradictory and precarious position. They needed the resources of a revolution just as much as those of a counter-revolution. But their position did not enable them to make full and unqualified use of either, without endangering the very basis of their undertaking. In their effort, however, to pursue a middle course and to bring both revolutionary and counter-revolutionary resources simultaneously or alternately into play, they incurred the danger, in turn, of becoming powerless themselves, and of seeing their cause wrecked against the forces of the stronger contender of the two—the counter-revolution. This, viewed as a whole, was to be their fate. Let us briefly point out here only the critical stages.

From France the signal had been given in February for the revolution; from France again the signal was given for the counter-revolution in June. In a terrible, three-day street battle, Cavaignac smashed the Paris workers. To be sure, the German middle class heaved a sigh of relief; but for them the ebbing of the revolutionary wave which now followed in Germany as well, was gain and loss alike—while for the reactionary forces of the authoritarian state, this turn constituted a clear gain. With the decline of communist fortunes, those of national liberalism sank as well.

This same dynamic course of events then unfolded during September. When the Prussian government concluded with Denmark the truce of Malmö, which seriously threatened the German claim to Schleswig, the aroused majority in the Paulskirche at first rejected it outright; but shortly thereafter, in view of the impracticable consequences of a refusal, the assembly, once more grown meek, ratified the agreement. And when an uprising from the Left now led to street fighting in Frankfurt itself and endangered the assembly, it was forced to turn for help to Prussian and Austrian troops (from the federal fortress at Mainz), in order to prevent a general landslide to the Left. Once more the fortunes of the authoritarian state rose, once more those of national liberalism sank. And they dropped still lower when the governments of Austria and Prussia, in October and November respectively, put down with their own military forces the rebellious democracy in Vienna and Berlin.

Under such circumstances was born the constitutional project of the Frankfurt National Assembly, culminating in the choice of the King of Prussia as hereditary emperor on March 28, 1849. Doubtless it was a proud achievement of the noblest aspiration toward national unity and freedom. But it lacked the basis of power which would have been necessary to put it through against the particularistic and reactionary forces of the authoritarian state. It was defeated at once when Frederick William IV, on April 3, 1849, refused to accept the new crown offered to him—a crown which in his view could appear only as a product of the revolution, a Danaean gift. And when the genuine revolution now reared its head again, and the disappointment which broad masses of the people experienced over the failure of Frankfurt exploded in the May uprisings in Pfalz and Baden, the equally disillusioned middle class—in order not to be engulfed altogether by revolution and the social upheaval that might follow —was forced once more, as in September, 1848, to lean on the authoritarian state. It had now exhausted its own role as an independent power factor, and had to be satisfied with the scant dole of liberal and national concessions which the insight of those who ruled Prussia might still be willing to grant. The May uprisings, on the other hand, were easily put down by Prussian troops. The fighters of the revolution, be they idealists of the urban educated class, little people of the lower bourgeoisie, or workers, proved completely inadequate to wage a military campaign against the disciplined and dependable fighting force of the authoritarian state.

Upon these rocks was wrecked the German revolution. Only a unified revolutionary purpose, reconciling workers with bourgeoisie and upper with lower middle class, might have been able (as we have noted) to force another result and so to weaken the army's tradition of loyalty as to overthrow the old authorities. But the social transformation of the people, which brought on disruption within the entire middle class, had in fact made impossible from the first the growth of such a spirit of revolutionary unity. Without this social transformation, however—without a rising upper middle class, a lower middle class threatened with disintegration, and an aspiring working class—the revolution itself would have been impossible. Thus strangely and tragically intertwined were the inner necessity of this revolution and its inevitable failure.

We have deliberately emphasized the question whether the year 1848 could already have brought a commonwealth to the German people. For it is this very question which above all burns in our hearts in the dark situation of today. Only as a genuine and healthy commonwealth could Germany win in Europe and in the world a position strong enough to be maintained through all the crises of Europe. The Bismarckian Reich, magnificent as was its undertaking to combine the vital elements, old and new, within state and society, was yet unable to achieve that intense common spirit which is indispensable as an essential bond within the whole, and as the basis of any vigorous democracy.

There has been much talk since Ranke of a primacy of foreign policy, which is supposed to exercise a formative and dominating influence upon domestic affairs. I believe that this doctrine, while containing an indisputable kernel of truth, today requires revision and certain qualifications. The motives as well as the effects of foreign policy—and particularly whether its success is to be lasting or only temporary—depend to a considerable extent upon the inner coherence and sturdiness of the individual state; upon the type and degree of a common spirit which animates it. The Bismarckian Reich, it is true, was built up under a primary impulse of foreign policy—that is, out of the necessity to erect a strong and independent power in the center of Europe. In addition, it certainly lacked no appreciation of the fact that this power must also possess inner coherence, and rest on a sense of national community. But the synthesis which Bismarck attempted to forge between authoritarian state and commonwealth failed the test in the years of decision, when the world wars came. Too much of the authoritarian state remained in Bismarck's work.

But in what way, we must now inquire, is the year 1848 related to the primacy of foreign policy and to the world of European power politics in general? We have already seen that among the aims of the year 1848, there was also present the hope of raising Germany to the status of a great power. And this need was felt not only in the ranks of the middle class—of the party of liberal reform, the advocates of an hereditary imperial crown. More or less consciously, it inflamed also the will of many of those who wished to make of Germany "the republic one and indivisible." The Left too had its power politics —still a totally irresponsible variety—but one already spurred on in no small measure by desires and aspirations, though they were of course, assumed to advance democracy. Hence war was appraised as an instrument for winning a lasting peace among the democratically united peoples of Europe. This idea of forming an aggressive front is to be encountered often enough—for example, in the proposal of an alliance with democratic France against autocratic Russia. And was it not the Left itself in the Paulskirche—in the September crisis after the truce of Malmö—which demanded the continuation of a national war against Denmark, a war threatening to widen into a European war? It was the opinion of Karl Marx that a world war must assist his cause. Thus democrats were willing enough in such cases—though at first with merely verbal audacity— to take up the sword, the assumption being that in the future it should not be carried by the "brutalized soldiery" of an authoritarian state, but by a people's army. We realize now, that an intensification, a victory of the domestic revolution in Germany, could have led—and perhaps necessarily—into the storm center of a great European war. A realization, once more, that is deep with tragedy.

This danger of a European war, in fact, was like a lowering black storm-cloud overshadowing the whole of the revolution of 1848, and even subsequent events. All the problems of this year which were specifically national, were inflammatory in the highest degree. To gain Schleswig, a war had to be started as early as April, 1848; but it stirred immediate opposition in Russia, England, and Sweden, which eventually did bar the way to this prize. The Polish-German problem of Posen led, even in its first stage, to bloody fighting within the province itself; but it could as easily have eventuated in a Russian intervention. The great Austro-German question, the exclusion of Austria from the federative state envisioned in the Paulskirche, was most clearly burdened with the heavy mortgage of an imminent war against Russia and Austria. And France? There from the outset a common conviction prevailed that a united and powerful Germany could not be tolerated. French "security," they felt, would be endangered by such a development. Thus a new struggle over the Rhine frontier was threatening. In the French mind, offensive and defensive motives were in this case—as, perhaps, ever since then!—inextricably intertwined. But were they not also similarly present in many ways in the German mind? There was no lack here either of expansionist fantasies, though at first they were confined to individual imaginations.

Thus did the German revolution of 1848, and especially the work of the Paulskirche—the imperial constitution of 1849—contain certain warlike possibilities, which through the succeeding century became realities, and finally ended in the collapse of Germany. At that time they remained mere possibilities, because the German revolution (with the exception of the Danish war) spent itself internally; because internally it could still be held in check through the exercise of the resources of authoritarian power. But by this means were restrained not only the war-breeding impulses toward unity and power, but also the urge to freedom of the German people; the insistence upon becoming a popular, national commonwealth. Once more an inter-relationship altogether tragic—one whose significance seizes us especially today.

The fact must however be acknowledged that a large part of this fatal interaction lay in the existence of the Prussian military and authoritarian power. Only Prussia—as the party of the hereditary imperial crown at Frankfurt perceived—was able and destined to fulfill the hopes of the whole nation for unity and power; but at the cost of the nation's hope for freedom, if Prussia remained what she was. She was indeed a state with two souls; yet the Junker-militarist principle inherited from Frederick William I and Frederick the Great was stronger in her than the principle of the Prussian reform era, which had pointed toward the commonwealth. If Prussia should remain what she was, even within a Germany united under her leadership, then it was to be feared that the Junker-militarist principle would permeate the whole, in one way or another. Instead of Prussia merging into Germany, Germany would merge with Prussia—if not formally, at least in essence. This danger the sponsors of the hereditary imperial crown at Frankfurt clearly recognized— as I had occasion to point out more specifically forty years ago—and therefore they demanded that Prussia sacrifice her political unity and allow herself to be divided into provinces directly under the Empire. But this the strong and proud spirit of the Prussians rejected categorically, and thus the partisans of the hereditary imperial crown—as they cast their votes for Frederick William IV—had to comfort themselves with the uncertain hope that the force of events would some day take effect and integrate Prussia within Germany.

The force of events decided otherwise. The militaristic principle continued to dominate almost the whole of a century, until it overreached itself in hybrid form; and Prussia was not dissolved from within, but destroyed from without. The tormenting problem today is this: will *Finis Borussiae* also mean *Finis Germaniae?* To desire once more to become a great power in the traditional sense, would be to begin all over again the tragedy of the century gone by. This time let us learn at last from history! In order to avoid new catastrophies—not only for Germany, but for Europe, yes, even for the whole world—new forms of international solidarity must be discovered. And they are in fact already being sought today, with the purpose of safeguarding the morally justified and eternally valid need of a nation for strength. Goethe's phrase (from which we quoted) has indeed expressed this demand: to exist as a nation, fully respected by other nations, to whom a like respect is due. The contribution which Germans themselves have to make to the accomplishment of this infinitely difficult task, is at the same time the permanent legacy of the revolution of 1848. The weaknesses resulting from time and destiny, from which this revolution suffered and through which it failed, we have brought honestly into the open. May we succeed, as men who have been tempered by misfortune, in reaching the goal of that pure and noble yearning: national unification within a democratic commonwealth.

INTELLECTUAL CURRENTS

The Two Problems of Romanticism

Romanticism has been used as one of those convenient signposts by which historians of ideas mark off different cultural epochs such as the Renaissance, the Scientific Revolution, or the Enlightenment. Employed in this way, romanticism is generally presented as a revolt against the Enlightenment, taking place roughly in the first half of the nineteenth century and distinguished by "a reaction against scientific method," "a preference for emotion," "an exaggeration of individualism," "a return to the Middle Ages," "a movement back to nature" —to mention only some of the popularly ascribed characteristics which Jacques Barzun, in the first selection below, says are *not* romanticism.

¶ Thus the first problem romanticism presents is one of definition. Here there are difficulties; the chief ones seem to be that if romanticism is considered a movement, how can a unity be made out of its obvious diversity and contradictions, and, if it is to be fixed within chronological limits, how do we account for the "Romantics" or "Romanticists" who fall outside the agreed-on boundaries.[1] The conflicting definitions of romanticism by contemporaries and by the generations of scholars and literary critics who have succeeded them compound these difficulties.

¶ Such considerations led the late Arthur O. Lovejoy, before his death dean of American historians of ideas, to try to clear up ". . . or to diminish this confusion of terminology and of thought which has for a century been

---

[1] The obvious solution is to label them "precursors." Thus J. J. Rousseau (1712–1778) "the precursor of romanticism" falls squarely within the chronological limits of the Enlightenment.

Difficulties inherent in the "precursor" label, however, are well demonstrated by the "movement back to nature." The English nature poets wrote in the seventeenth century, and English or "natural" landscape gardening began then. The first use of the term "noble savage" has been attributed to Thomas Dryden (1631–1700). These difficulties underscore the usefulness of Jacques Barzun's distinction between "intrinsic romanticism" and "historic romanticism."

the scandal of literary history and criticism." [2] In a famous paper written in 1923, he asked scholars to abandon the idea of romanticism as a "real entity" and instead "learn to use the word 'Romanticism' in the plural" by discriminating between the various romanticisms that appeared in different countries at different times and, indeed, within the same country at different times.[3]

In another influential and controversial paper, "The Meaning of Romanticism for the Historian of Ideas," Lovejoy repeated that "there is no such thing as Romanticism . . . one may perhaps speak of—not a, but several, Romantic movements" [4] and warned that "Nothing, then, but confusion and error can result from the quest of some suppositious intrinsic nature of a hypostatized essence called 'Romanticism.' " [5] But Lovejoy did outline and sketch "a quite different sort of inquiry" which might answer the questions implicit in the title of his paper, "make for the elimination of confusion . . ., the understanding of the history of the past century and a half, and . . . the understanding of the contemporary intellectual, moral, and political situation." [6]

Its starting point is a massive historical fact which no one is likely to deny—namely, that in the last quarter of the eighteenth century, especially in the 1780's and 1790's, there were discovered, invented or revived, chiefly in Germany, a large number of ideas which had been relatively, though not always absolutely, unfamiliar or uninfluential through most of the seventeenth and eighteenth centuries; and that the total impact of what we may call, for short, the new ideas of the 1780's and 1790's (including revivals of old ideas under "new"), as they developed, ramified, and were diffused during the following decades, profoundly altered the habitual preconceptions, valuations, and ruling catchwords of an increasingly large part of the educated classes in Europe, so that there came into vogue in the course of the nineteenth century and in our own a whole series of intellectual fashions—from styles in poetry and styles in metaphysics to styles in government—which had no parallels in the preceding period.[7]

Another landmark in the continuing discussion of romanticism was the publication in 1943 of *Romanticism and the Modern Ego* by Jacques Barzun, one of America's leading intellectual historians and social critics. As its title suggests, Barzun's study of romanticism is a wide-ranging one which relates its subject to current political, cultural, and social problems. Barzun concedes

[2] Arthur O. Lovejoy, "On the Discrimination of Romanticisms" in *Essays in the History of Ideas* (Baltimore: The Johns Hopkins Press, 1948), p. 234.

[3] *Ibid.*, pp. 234–35. The original paper was delivered at the fortieth annual meeting of The Modern Language Association of America, December 27, 1923 and first published in *PMLA*, XXXIX (1924), 229–53.

[4] Arthur O. Lovejoy, "The Meaning of Romanticism for the Historian of Ideas," *Journal of the History of Ideas*, II (1941), 261.

[5] *Ibid.*, p. 260.

[6] *Ibid.*, p. 260.

[7] *Ibid.*, p. 260.

the variety and contradictions of romanticism, but he addresses himself to the problem of definition. His distinction between "historic romanticism" and "intrinsic romanticism" and his linking of all Romanticists "in the double problem of making a new world and making it in the knowledge that man is creative and limited" come as close as is likely possible to a general definition of Romanticism.[8] The first selection below, covering these points, comes from a recently revised edition of Barzun's book.

The second problem with romanticism is a more specialized one than the problem of definition and possibly a more controversial one. It is the problem of the relation of German Romantic thought to the militant German nationalism which began in the second half of the nineteenth century and culminated in the nazism of Adolf Hitler. Interestingly, the controversy over this relationship was also initiated by Arthur Lovejoy. The reader will notice in the quotations above from "The Meaning of Romanticism for the Historian of Ideas" that Lovejoy ascribed to the ideas of the 1780's and 1790's a continuing influence into the nineteenth and twentieth centuries and believed that his inquiry would bear on the contemporary situation. Thus in the second part of his paper, Lovejoy established a relationship, though expressed in reserved and highly abstract terms, between the development of three ideas of the 1780's and 1790's (diversitarianism, holism or organicism, and voluntarism or dynamism) and "the monstrous scene presented by Germany and Europe today."[9]

With the publication in 1941 of *Metapolitics: From The Romantics to Hitler* by Peter Viereck, the discussion took a more forthright turn. In the selection below, reprinted from a recent, revised edition of *Metapolitics,* Viereck, today a well-known historian, Pulitzer Prize-winning poet, and spokesman for a vital, conservative philosophy, seeks to establish "the long but unbroken chain linking Fichte's nineteenth-century theories with Hitler's twentieth-century practice." Viereck integrates an abstraction like organicism with the all-embracing quality of German Romanticism to show how even an "ivory tower" poet like Novalis—to use one of Viereck's most original examples—could become

---

[8] One is tempted to say he solves the problem of definition, but the problem of definition continues to be discussed. A noteworthy contribution is René Wellek, "The Concept of Romanticism in Literary History. I. The Term 'Romantic and Its Derivatives'; II. The Unity of European Romanticism," *Comparative Literature,* I, No. 1 (Winter 1944), 1–23; No. 2 (Spring 1949), 147–72.

Wellek argues against Lovejoy for the usefulness of the terms "pre-romanticism" and "romanticism" and seeks to demonstrate that "the major romantic movements (i.e. English, French, and German) form a unity of theories, philosophies and style, and that these, in turn, form a coherent group of ideas, each of which implicates the other."

A recent study, W. T. Jones, *The Romantic Syndrome* (The Hague: Martinus Nijhoff, 1961) is an interesting attempt to establish an empirical methodology for the study of works of art and of scientific and philosophical theory which is illustrated by a definition of the concept of "romanticism." The approach combines cultural anthropology with the history of ideas, and other "syndromes"—the Medieval, the Renaissance, and the Enlightenment, as well as the Romantic—are described.

[9] Lovejoy, "The Meaning of Romanticism . . ." pp. 270–78.

so affected by romanticism as to take a position which logically leads to some part of Nazi ideology or practice. Other examples cited by Viereck, if more obvious, are no less striking.

It was not to be expected that either Lovejoy's or Viereck's arguments would go unchallenged. No small part of Jacques Barzun's *Romanticism and the Modern Ego,* which followed closely on the publication of their views, is devoted to a refutation of the connection between romanticism and modern collectivism [10]—and there were other critics.[11] The third selection below, however, has been chosen as a more recent contribution to what has turned out to be a continuing discussion. On one hand it might be called a compromise view, for while Robert Lougee, professor of history at the University of Connecticut, its author, concedes connections between German Romantic thought and several aspects of nazism or fascism, he feels that the Fascist organization of state and a number of features associated with it "demonstrate divergencies from the very foundation of Romantic thought." On the other hand, the author concludes with the original proposition that, "In the history of political thought, romanticism as a precursor of conservatism plays a role equivalent to that of the natural rights philosophy as a precursor of liberalism. To give romanticism another part to play, is to obscure its historical significance."

WHO ARE THE ROMANTICISTS?

Jacques Barzun

* * *

WHO ARE the romanticists and what is the common bond that makes them bear a common name?

In English, the noun "Romanticism" gives two adjectives—romantic and

[10] Generally in chaps. I, II, and VIII; more specifically with respect to the German connection, *Romanticism and the Modern Ego,* pp. 44–51; *Classic Romantic and Modern,* pp. 30–35.

[11] With respect to Lovejoy's argument, see Leo Spitzer, "Geistesgeschichte vs. History of Ideas as Applied to Hitlerism," *Journal of the History of Ideas,* V, No. 2 (April 1944), 191–203. Arthur O. Lovejoy, "Reply to Professor Spitzer," is in the same issue, pp. 204–19.

romanticist. They are not commonly differentiated, but it is to be desired that they should be. We should then be able to tell apart the two distinct fields of application I have begun to distinguish: romanticism as an historical movement and romanticism as a characteristic of human beings. We should then say: "My friend X is a romantic" and "the poet Byron is a romantic*ist*." When we say *the romanticists* at large we should mean a number of men who lived at a particular time and place, and who did certain things that fixed them in the mind of posterity. However much they differ ideally or fought among themselves, Byron, Wordsworth, Shelley, Victor Hugo, Leopardi, Mickiewicz, and Schiller were romanticists. They received the name whether they liked it or not. Indeed, many romanticists vigorously disclaimed the title, like Delacroix, or accepted it for only half their work, like Goethe. In this sense, romanticism is a mere tag and not an adequate description. You cannot infer a man's personal characteristics, much less his opinions, from his correct labeling as a romanticist. What you can infer, we shall shortly see. Meantime, think of romanticist as a term comparable to "Man of the Renaissance." If someone had addressed the living Leonardo da Vinci and asked him: "Are you a typical *Renaissance-mensch?*" he would have said, "What nonsense are you talking about?" Nevertheless, in any survey of the period, there is Leonardo, "typical of his age," and there is also the very different Michelangelo, his antagonist, but no less typical. They have been caught in the chronological net and historiography has stamped them with a convenient label.

With romanticism, the problem is complicated by the fact that during the romantic period small groups of writers or thinkers appropriated the general name to themselves. In Germany, for instance, scholars distinguish between Early and Late Romantic. But in neither of these groups will you find Schiller and Goethe. They stand apart, and yet Goethe's *Faust* is a bible of Romanticism. If you wish to find another German romanticist, Heine, you must look for him among the "Young Germany" group. This is the petty politics of cultural history. In French romanticism likewise, you will at one time find Victor Hugo and Stendhal on opposite sides, each representing a different shade of literary policy. In England, no one was called a Romanticist while living. All this is of great interest to the biographer or the historian of the several arts. But to use these temporary distinctions, as some have done, in order to blur the outlines of an era is to be guilty of obscurantism through pedantry. When the educated man has a true general conception of romanticism, it will be time to refine upon its details. For our present purpose, historic romanticism can be defined as comprising those Europeans whose birth falls between 1770 and 1815, and who achieved distinction in philosophy, statecraft, and the arts during the first half of the nineteenth century.

Some of course were born outside these arbitrary limits of time, like Goethe. There are others whose fame came after the terminal date, like Blake. A few more resist classification with the main body. So long as they are few these irregularities will not disturb anyone who remembers that we are dealing with an historical grouping. History does not arrange its products in bunches; it is man who seeks to put order into the disarray of history. Hence the ragged edges, but they are the edges of something central and solid.

We have then a group of men known as romanticists and living as contemporaries between 1770 and 1850. What, besides time, binds them together? It is at this point that we pass from *historic* romanticism to what may be called *intrinsic* romanticism. I have suggested that if an attitude becomes noticeable or dominant in a given period, its elements must be latent in human beings, or in certain human beings, all the time. In individual instances we call it this or that kind of temperament. For example, it is probable that there are Puritans at all times and places; but when a great many occur at the same time and place, then we have a Puritan period. In the same manner there are heroic ages and ages of luxury, ages of classicism, of rationalism, of renaissance, of decadence —and of romanticism. Not that each of these represents a fixed type; rather it is a combination of human traits which for one reason or another happens to be stressed, valued, cultivated at a given historical moment. Why one attitude is preferred to another is something for the cultural historian to explain after the event, but *that* it is preferred is the reason for our being able to speak of a romantic period.

This distinction between *permanent* elements in human nature and their periodic emphasis in history is the first of the devices by which we can make more exact and serviceable our use of the name "romantic." If, for instance, we hear William James called a romantic, we are entitled to say: "James was not contemporary with Byron; what precisely have you in mind when you classify them under the same head?" If, as is likely, the answer given is: "I call him romantic because of his irrationalism," the field is then open to argument over the correctness of the description and over the propriety of making one belief or opinion taken at random symptomatic of a whole temperament or philosophy. The libraries are full of books, usually written in wartime, and which show that from Luther to Hitler, or from Fichte to Mussolini, or from Rousseau to Stalin "one increasing purpose runs." The demonstration is made by stringing together on one line of development all thinkers who "believe in the will" or "believe in hero worship" or "believe in the divine right of the people." In these works the intention of human ideas is disregarded for the sake of finding a collection of scapegoats.

The history of ideas cannot be written so, like an invoice of standardized goods. It is a subject requiring infinite tact. On the one hand, diversity must be reduced to clear patterns for the sake of intelligibility; on the other, the meaning of each idea must be preserved from falsification by constant reference to its place and purport in history. It is strictly meaningless to speak of someone as "a believer in a strong state"—strong for what, for whom, by what means, against whom?

The same is true of irrationalism, which is only one of the alleged symptoms of the romantic temper. Granting that the connection between romanticism and irrationalism exists, in what direction does it point? And, to begin with, what is the meaning of irrational? To hear critics wax indignant over irrationalism in such highly organized persons as James, Nietzsche, Bergson, and Freud, one would suppose that they repudiated reason and behaved like maenads. One almost expects that their writings will be ungrammatical and demented. Instead of which one finds an extraordinary concentration of thought, a great skill in raising and meeting objections, and a solicitous care for order and form.

What is true of these four moderns who are supposed to be the fountainheads of neo-romanticism is true of their predecessors of over a century ago. They were not men of one book or one idea. Hence any reduction of their thoughts or accomplishments to a single notion is inevitably belied by the facts. It is an explanation doomed to swift and complete refutation at the hands of anyone possessing even a fragment of firsthand knowledge about the subject.

At this point I may state dogmatically what I shall show in the sequel, that romanticism is not equivalent to irrationalism, nor sentimentality, nor individualism, nor collectivism, nor utopian aspirations, nor love, nor hate, nor indolence, nor feeble-mindedness. Consequently if any of these human traits particularly excite one's disapproval one must call them by their proper names, and not shirk responsibility for the judgment by terming their manifestations "romantic."

If anyone should doubt that these attributes have been made the distinguishing marks of romanticism, let him simply turn to the sampling of usage given in Chapter X, or else consult any of a dozen popular biographies of the so-called "romantic figures." For pleasure and instruction one could do far worse than to go to the conscientious work by L. and R. Stebbins on the romantic composer Carl Maria von Weber. It is the best, most scholarly, and most intelligent book on the subject; but dealing as it does with a figure from the romantic period, it accurately betrays the prevailing idea of that movement. On the jacket of the book we find the unthinking echo of what is said within: "Weber was no romantic composer, but a serious hard-working musician." In other words, a romantic composer is one who does no work, and it is a wonder how the romantic school of music managed to produce what it did.

Dip into the book itself and you come across equally bewildering generalizations, such as this concerning a German duke of obviously unbalanced mind: "He . . . was either insane or the embodiment of the nth degree of early German romanticism—which, indeed, amounts to much the same thing." Here romanticism is insanity, but in the next sentence this sweeping condemnation is mitigated: "Certainly, he exemplified the school both in aversion to effort and in a behavior which followed the impulses of his subconscious without curb." In other words, the noble duke was a rake and an idler, like thousands of other men before and since the romantic period. What was specifically romantic about him? We are never told, and an earlier definition seems to describe the movement very differently. "There was a time," we are informed, when "a man could say, godlike, 'life is thus; but thus I will not have it. Standing on the intolerable reality I recreate.' This is the essence of romanticism."

Not satisfied with this essence, however, the biographers look for another in the possible "causes" of their romantic subject, in this case, Weber: "Was he a romanticist because of his convictions, or because he was dragged about by an unpredictable father, had no proper education and was nurtured on his mother's stories of the Catholic church?" There being no reasonable answer to such questions, another, equally plausible, is put: "Schelling's romanticized teachings exerted a strong influence upon him. Would a different philosophy have shaped a classicist instead of a romantic composer?" This is followed by a still deeper muddle: Schelling and Weber have each been philosophizing, but "it was impossible to write or speak openly of liberty . . . the contemplation of eternal problems was postponed for a freer age, and romanticism provided the usual escape." Schelling, I may mention in passing, was the famed author of a work on Human Freedom.

Now for a few comments on romanticism and the affections: "Their friendship was of a romantic nature and lasted until death. . . ." "He fell in love many times," [but] "not with the easy sentimentality of his fellow romantics. . . ." And to conclude, some judgments of value about a man who is admitted on all hands to be an ornament of the romantic school: "The German romanticist proscribed labor, but there never was a man who worked harder than Weber; the German romanticist was an introvert with a subjective mind, but Weber liked society and saw his creations with an objective eye." And lastly: "One cannot lightly disregard the judgments of the great romantics, Meyerbeer and von Weber."

The juxtaposition of these sentences gives them, of course, a ludicrous air, though this is not intended, nor do I mean to discredit the biography. If the book were mere journeyman work, the authors' treatment of romanticism might matter less. But their opinions are educated opinions, and the point of singling out sentences is that they faithfully represent the usual view. Not one reader in a thousand would dwell skeptically upon them as they occur in the midst of interesting and well-documented paragraphs. These pronouncements seem to state the accepted fact; which only means that their mutual inconsistency and inherent falsity have been so often repeated that we no longer notice anything wrong.

According to this so-called educated opinion, romanticism is insanity, escape, introversion, sentimentality, and laziness; but a given romantic is objective, hard-working, steadfast in friendship, a creator of lasting works and one whose judgment is not lightly to be disregarded. I pass over the superficial psychology that makes of a shiftless father, a Roman Catholic mother, or the German philosopher Schelling the decisive factor in the production of a romanticist musician. The belief here seems to be that a man's outlook is picked up by chance or put on casually like hat and gloves. This is part and parcel of that other belief that somehow a romantic is a creature wholly different from other men, the men we know and see at work. Which makes it a matter for surprise to the biographer when his romantic subject behaves rationally, works hard, shows lasting-affection, and acts with judgment and integrity in his art.

Seeking a demonstration of widespread error in a particular book is not irrelevant to the promised definition of intrinsic romanticism. Just as in dealing with historic Romanticism it was important to show the difficulties that come from equating the upsurge against liberalism with Romanticism, so in dealing with intrinsic romanticism it is important to show the impossibility of matching up the term with the current commonplaces about irrationalism, sentimentality, and the like. I will go even further and say that none of the usual scholarly definitions, whether sympathetic or not, seems satisfactory. Romanticism is not a return to the Middle Ages, a love of the exotic, a revolt from Reason, an exaggeration of individualism, a liberation of the unconscious, a reaction against scientific method, a revival of pantheism, idealism and catholicism, a rejection of artistic conventions, a preference for emotion, a movement back to nature, or a glorification of force. Nor is it any of a dozen more generalities which have been advanced as affording the proper test. It is not any of these things for the simple reason that none of them can be found uniformly distributed among the great romanticists. Mention any such characteristic and a contrary-minded critic will name you a Romanticist who did not possess it; he may even produce one who clearly strove for the opposite. It is this truth that has led a number of critics to abandon the search—and to abuse romanticism all the more for not yielding up its secret on first inspection.

This is not to say that many of the tendencies enumerated in the textbooks were not present in the romantic age. They obviously were, and it is in romantic work that scholars have found them. But a collection of features defines nothing unless it is common to nearly all the individuals examined. The error has consisted in supposing that what unites an age are common opinions and common traits. If this were true what would become of the war of opinions which characterizes every age? If it were true, how could John Dewey and T. S. Eliot belong to one and the same culture? If it were true, how could there be any traditions handed down through time? There would be, on the contrary, blocks of unanimous people holding the stage for a century or so, followed by other solid blocks of an opposite complexion.

In other words, what we want as a definition of intrinsic romanticism is the thing that gave rise to—and that incidentally explains—all the other attitudes I have enumerated. Why did some romanticists attack Reason, why did some turn catholic, why were some liberal, others reactionary? Why did some praise the Middle Ages and others adore the Greeks? Clearly, the one thing that unifies men in a given age is not their individual philosophies but the dominant problem that these philosophies are designed to solve. In the romantic period, as will appear, this problem was to create a new world on the ruins of the old. The French Revolution and Napoleon had made a clean sweep. Even before the Revolution, which may be taken as the outward sign of an inward decay, it was no longer possible to think, act, write, or paint as if the old forms still had life. The critical philosophers of the eighteenth century had destroyed their own dwelling place. The next generation must build or perish. Whence we conclude that romanticism is first of all constructive and creative; it is what may be called a solving epoch, as against the *dis*solving eighteenth century.

Because the problem of reconstruction was visible to many men does not mean that they all proposed the same solution, or saw all its aspects in the same way. The divergences were due to differences of temperament, geographical situation, and special interest. A poet such as Wordsworth or Victor Hugo saw the emptiness of eighteenth-century diction and the need of creating a new vocabulary for poetry; a philosopher such as Schopenhauer saw the illusoriness of eighteenth-century hopes of progress and the need of recharting moral reality, with suggestions for better enduring it; a political theorist like Burke, who apprehended the wholesale destruction of the social order, had to propose an alternative means of change; a thinker like Hegel, who was at once philosopher, political theorist, and esthetician, saw creation as the result of conflict in history and in the mind, and proposed nothing less than a new logic to explain the nature of change. He then showed how to use it for rebuilding on more lasting premises.

These men clearly cannot be made into a romantic *school,* but they equally clearly partake of a romanticist *temper.* More than that, they share certain broad predilections in common, such as the admiration for energy, moral enthusiasm, and original genius. It is because an era faces one dominant problem in varying ways that certain human traits come to be held in greater esteem than they were before. The task of reconstruction manifestly does demand energy, morality, and genius, so that the new passion for them was thus not a whimsical or useless trait in the romantics, but a necessity of their position.

By the same logic, one is led to see that romanticism was far from being an escape from reality on the part of feeble spirits who could not stand it. The truth is that these spirits wanted to change the portions of reality that they did not like, and at least record their ideals when the particular piece of reality would not yield—both these being indispensable steps toward reconstruction. Our modern use of the term "escape" is unfortunately vitiated by smugness and double meanings, and one should refuse to argue its application with any-one who will not first answer this question: "Suppose a primitive man, caught in a rainstorm, who has for the first time the idea of taking shelter in a cave: is he facing reality or escaping it?" The whole history of civilization is wrapped up in this example, and a universal test for distinguishing creation from escape can be deduced from it. The mere fact that a man is seen making for a cave or heard declaring his intention to build a hut is not enough; what is he going to do *then*? What is the relation of that single act to his whole scheme of life? Applying this test to romanticism, we shall see that on the whole it was infinitely more constructive than escapist.

But, it may be said, other periods faced with the task of creation have not pro-duced cultures resembling romanticism. The very system which preceded romanticism and came to an end with the eighteenth century was created around 1650 and it took the form that we call classical. True enough; so to understand romanticism we must add to the fact of its creative mission the further fact that it conceived its mission in a certain way. It conceived it in the light of a great contradiction concerning man. I mean the contrast between man's greatness and man's wretchedness; man's power and man's misery.

It would be tedious to give citations from one romanticist after another in which this contrast is noted and commented on. But one cannot help being struck by the repetition of this independent "discovery" in the works of the romantic epoch. It obtrudes itself in many forms and contexts, whether or not one is seeking common elements in the many-sided activities of this generation of men. Moreover, there are other supporting facts outside the period that are worth remembering. Where do we find the most famous expression of this contrast in the nature of man? Surely in the *Thoughts* of Pascal, historically not a romantic, but a seventeenth-century author whose whole temper, social and religious, made him a dissenter in his own time. Whom does the classicist Voltaire most persistently attack in his own eighteenth century? It is Pascal. Voltaire wrote an *Anti-Pascal* and looked upon him as the most dangerous enemy of the Enlightenment. In much the same spirit Condorcet brought out an altered edition of the *Thoughts*. When does Pascal emerge in his full stature? and with his full meaning?—not until 1843, in the first half of the romantic nineteenth century.

The core of the conflict is Pascal's view of man's fate—the antithesis of greatness and misery—which leads him to an analysis of art and society as merely conventional and relative; justice on one side of a river, Pascal points out, becomes injustice on the other. In short, man is first of all a creature lost in the universe and he *makes* his shelter, physical, social, and intellectual. This was bound to be also the view of the later romanticists, who found themselves at odds with the remnants of the old regime, without protection from the uni-verse, and forced to build a new order.

But in a thinking reed, as Pascal terms man, the contradictory state of having powers and of feeling one's weakness is not one to be dumbly endured. Some resolution must be found even while the protective social order is being built. Indeed, many men feel that the imperfect social order is inadequate to resolve the inner conflict. Hence the search for a philosophy, a religion, a faith, which will transcend and unify the felt disharmony. Pascal himself, as we know, found this faith in ascetic Christianity. The romanticists, a hundred and fifty years after Pascal, found it in many different objects of belief—pantheism, Catholicism, socialism, vitalism, art, science, the national state. To fill out the list would be to give a catalogue of the contributions of romanticism. What matters here is the interconnection of all these faiths through their roots in the double problem of making a new world and making it in the knowledge that man is both creative and limited, a doer and a sufferer, infinite in spirit and finite in action.

* * *

ROMANTICISM AND NAZISM

Peter Viereck

* * *

WHY HAS the word "romanticism" always been so hard to pin down? Surely not because it lacks connotations. On the contrary, romanticism has too many. On hearing it, the mind is certainly conditioned to an immediate reaction. Yet what one pictures is as vague, blurred, misty in outline as those moonlit landscapes which romantic poets cherished. Such intuitive "feeling for" the meaning of romanticism is completely adequate for the romantic himself. For his critics, a concept must be found which is more precise, consistent, clear.

A precise response to the word "romantic" is impossible if only because there have been too many authoritative definitions. Romanticism has been defined

From Peter Viereck, *Metapolitics—The Roots of the Nazi Mind* (New York: Capricorn Books, 1961), pp. 17–20, 29–34, 37–40, 50–53, 68–70, 192–94. Copyright 1941, by Alfred A. Knopf, Inc. Copyright 1961, by Peter Viereck. Reprinted by permission of the author.

at great length—and differently in each case—by Goethe, the Schlegel brothers, Novalis, Heinrich Heine, Eichendorff, Victor Hugo, Stendhal, Coleridge, Carlyle, Georg Brandes, Irving Babbitt, and many others equally authoritative. They all conflict.[1] Consequently I cannot hope to avoid conflicting with much of them. But one may seek some common denominator by inquiring whether the authorities do not so much disagree as contemplate romanticism on different planes of reference.

The American philosopher Arthur Lovejoy, perhaps the most penetrating modern authority on romanticism, stresses that the word "romanticism" has become almost meaningless and speaks, instead, of many quite different "romanticisms." [2] It seems to me that these differences have two chief causes: First, the opposite creeds within the fold of German romanticism itself. (One example of such opposites is the bohemian individualism of the romantic school's earliest phase versus the totalitarian collectivism of a Fichte, Hegel, and Hitler.) Second, the differences between German romanticism and the romanticisms of France, England, and America.

Often two different romanticisms are really the same great romantic movement applied to different planes. In the case of bohemian individualism versus totalitarianism, one is on the plane of the ego and the other on that of the state. But both—and this is the point to be stressed—apply to their respective planes

---

[1] Among early nineteenth-century Germans, the two most fruitful examples of conflicting viewpoints toward romanticism are, on the one hand, the articles by A. W. Schlegel, Friedrich Schlegel, Novalis, and Schleiermacher in the periodical *Athenäum* (3 vols., Berlin, 1798–1800)—and, on the other hand, Heinrich Heine: *Die romantische Schule* (Hamburg, 1836).

Among more recent discussions of romanticism, the following books and magazine articles are suggested to the reader as the minimum of a preliminary introduction to a study of the subject. Georg Brandes: *Main Currents in Nineteenth-Century Literature* (6 vols., London, 1901–24), Vol. II, on Germany. G. A. Borgese: *Storia della Critica Romantica* (2nd ed., Milan, 1920). Hans Böhm, ed.: *Gedankendichtung der Frühromantik,* Vol. XXVII of *Kunstwart-Bücherei* (Munich, 1935); an anthology of the romantic school's new ideas. Paul Kluckhohn: *Die deutsche Romantik* (Leipzig, 1924). Richard Benz: *Die deutsche Romantik* (Leipzig, 1937). Friedrich Gundolf: *Romantiker* (2 vols., Berlin, 1930–1). L. A. Willoughby: *The Romantic Movement in Germany* (London, 1930). Ricarda Huch: *Die Romantik* (2nd ed., Leipzig, 1924). H. N. Fairchild: *The Romantic Quest* (New York, 1931). Hans Kohn: *Force or Reason* (Cambridge, Mass., 1937). Mario Praz: *The Romantic Agony* (London, 1933). Fritz Strich: *Deutsche Klassik und Romantik* (Munich, 1922). Irving Babbitt: *The New Laokoön* (Boston and New York, 1910), and *Rousseau and Romanticism* (Boston and New York, 1919). Arthur O. Lovejoy: "On the Discrimination of Romanticisms," in *Publications of the Modern Language Association,* New York and Menasha, Wisconsin, Vol. XXXIX (1924). "Romanticism: A Symposium," by J. C. Blankenagel, G. R. Havens, H. N. Fairchild, K. McKenzie, F. C. Tarr, and Elizabeth Nitchie, in *P.M.L.A.,* Vol. LV (March 1940). Jacques Barzun: ".To the Rescue of Romanticism," in *American Scholar,* New York, Spring 1940 (which I recommend as a brilliant defence of romanticism and for a viewpoint directly opposite to my own).

[2] Lovejoy, *loc. cit.* (pp. 229–53). For further aspects of romanticism, see also the following works of Lovejoy: *Bergson and Romantic Evolutionism* (Berkeley: University of California; 1913): *The Great Chain of Being* (Cambridge, Mass., Harvard University Press; 1936), lectures 10 and 11; *Optimism and Romanticism* (Baltimore: Mod. Lang. Assoc.; 1927); reprinted from *P.M.L.A.,* Vol. XLII, no. 4, December 1927, pp. 921–45.

the identical romantic philosophy of ceaseless lawless expansion and of self-justified self-worship.

The second cause for confusion we can take in our stride, for we are concerned chiefly with German romanticism. So-called romantic movements did also exist in France and England. Sometimes these did indeed stand for the same things as the original romanticism, that of Germany, but never as a widespread national movement. To a large extent I accept the following statement:

Romanticism is Germanic and reached its purest expression in those territories which are freest from Roman colonization. Everything that is regarded as an essential aspect of the romantic spirit, irrationalism, the mystic welding together of subject and object, the tendency to intermingle the arts, the longing for the far-away and the strange, the feeling for the infinite and the continuity of historic development—all these are characteristic of German romanticism and so much so that their union remains unintelligible to the Latins. What is known as romanticism in France has *only its name in common* with German romanticism.[3]

Romanticism is typically "Germanic" in its broadest versions, but never exclusively so and with many exceptions. Even further, one may treat romanticism not only as the "purest expression in those territories freest from Roman colonization" but also, and more important, as a cultural and political reaction against the Roman-French-Mediterranean spirit of clarity, rationalism, form, and universal standards. Thereby romanticism is really the nineteenth century's version of the perennial German revolt against the western heritage.

In other words, romanticism, no matter how far afield it may seem from current Nazi politics, is the most influential modern phase of Germany's old "two souls in one breast," the German cultural schizophrenia which made nazism possible.

* * *

In mankind's ordinary, Euclidean mathematics, the whole must always equal the sum of its parts. In romantic mathematics, the whole is greater than the sum of its parts. This first romantic postulate may be restated as the ideal of organic synthesis on all planes, what some philosophers call the hypothesis of "emergence" or "creative synthesis."

Let us keep in mind, throughout, the historical background of the original romantic school. The romantics were partly right in attributing the vicious side of the great French Revolution—namely, its chaos and its consequent ghastly bloodshed—to the disruptive effects of destructive rationalist analysis.

The original romantic school and modern nazism triumphed in part for the same reason. Both were welcomed by many as a synthesizing counterpoison to the alleged disintegrating effects of an aggressive rationalism. The

[3] Gustav Pauli, quoted in Vol. IV of Georg Dehio: *Geschichte der deutschen Kunst* (4 vols., Berlin, 1919–34).

French and Russian world-revolutions were the respective *bêtes noires*. The French and the Jews were the respective bogy men.

Romanticism was the most influential literary movement in German history, penetrating and transforming every single aspect of human society. It had the courage to call its aim "a universal synthesis." This synthesis was applied philosophically and religiously, scientifically, poetically, politically.

Philosophically and Religiously.—The philosophy or religion most typical of the romantic school is vitalistic pantheism. This is illustrated by the very title of the book by the influential romantic philosopher Schelling: *World-Soul* (1798). The universe is greater than the sum of all its parts and contains a vital omnipresent spirit which analysis can never find. Schelling defines the entire universe as a single indivisible "organism." [4] Romantic philosophy, especially Schelling's, was moulded by Goethe, himself only temporarily a romantic. Goethe loved to hyphenate "God-Nature" (*"Gott-Natur"*) as one unified organism. A. W. Schlegel's university lectures on vitalism helped to romanticize the youth of Germany and Austria. Today Henri Bergson's philosophy of the *élan vital* is the famous French application of Germany's old romantic tradition of vitalism.

Scientifically.—Science was told to treat nature organically rather than mechanically. Analysis has been invariably coupled with the adjective "destructive" by romantics. By dissolving the whole into its component parts, scientific analysis is accused of losing that invisible force which makes the whole greater than the total parts. Synthesis was set up for science as the counter-ideal to mechanistic analysis. This was the message of Fichte's theory of science. Its importance is shown by the fact that the German romantic school's official magazine in 1800 hailed Fichte's organic theory of science as one of the three "greatest tendencies of the age." The other two were the French Revolution (the counter-credo to romanticism) and the romantic Part One of *Wilhelm Meister* (Goethe's prose counterpart to the Part One of *Faust*).[5]

Poetically.—The repercussions of the organic view upon literary content are obvious. A simple example is the amount of space which all romantic literature devotes to deeply felt scenic beauty. Vitalistic pantheism is what makes romantic poets of all nations feel so "at one" with so-called nature. Less obvious but no less significant are the repercussions of the organic view upon technical form.

The difference between neo-classic and romantic techniques is the difference between the static and the flowing. The typical neo-classic poem is atomistic; it consists of distinctly divided lines or couplets. The romantic's typical poem is quite as organic a unit as his universe or his political society.

In our own English literature the two most familiar examples of this contrast

4 Friedrich W. Schelling: *Von der Weltseele* (2nd revised ed., Hamburg, 1806; 1st ed., 1798).
5 *Athenäum*, Vol. II, last issue.

[78] Romanticism and Nazism

are Dryden and Pope versus Shelley and Keats. Pope's famous *Essay on Man* consists of self-sufficient rhymed couplets ("heroic couplets") making perfectly good sense each by itself. The opening ten couplets can be read in reverse or mixed-up order and still remain satisfactory. In contrast, the couplets of Keats and Shelley flow into one another so that their order cannot possibly be changed: they are organically welded.

Politically.—When this organic approach was applied to state or nation or race instead of to universe or science or poem, the result was political romanticism. Without it Hitler's Third Reich is inconceivable. But the political application only followed after the æsthetic application, under the stress of the wars against France; and so our earlier attention to æsthetic and philosophic romanticism, far from being irrelevant to nazism, is its historical introduction.

Rousseau, the Swiss semi-romantic, coined the two contrasting phrases: "general will" and "will of all." These his German admirers used all too successfully to bolster up their organic view of the nation. The will of all is the mere sum of citizens' individual (atomistic) wills, what modern democracy deems synonymous with the will of the people. The general will is the indivisible state-organism's vaster will, what nazism deems synonymous with the will of the people.[6]

Living at the height of French rationalism, against which he only partly revolted, Rousseau never intended the general will as the sheer mysticism it became in Germany. The catch is that no objective criterion exists for deciding correctly what man or party is the true interpreter of the state's voice. Counting noses in elections is ruled out as mere will of all. Consequently, the general will, though never so intended by the more liberal Rousseau, became in Robespierre's French Revolution the mask for the republican Reign of Terror and became in Hitler's German Revolution the mask for limitless anti-republican despotism.

Innumerable writers of all lands have used terms treating the nation as an indivisible organism, but these were generally only useful and picturesque metaphors for the need of national unity. To German political romantics, however, the organic state was not metaphor but concrete reality. The recognized political oracle of the German romantic school was Adam Müller, just as the Schlegel brothers were the joint literary oracle. Adam Müller called the state "a vast individual enveloping all the little individuals" and called human society "solely a single noble and complete person." He wanted the state to cease being an "instrument in the hands of a person" and to become, instead, "a person itself, a freely evolving whole," to which all citizens must piously sacrifice their mere individual freedoms.[7]

[6] Jean Jacques Rousseau: *Le Contrat Social.*

[7] Friedrich Meinecke: *Weltbürgertum und Nationalstaat* (7th ed., Munich and Berlin, 1928), pp. 148–9. Reinhold Aris: *Die Staatslehre Adam Müllers in ihrem Verhältnis zur deutschen Romantik* (Tübingen, 1929) shows Müller's crucial and neglected importance in political romanticism.

Novalis is usually remembered as the greatest of romantic ivory-tower poets; but he, too, illustrates the all-embracing quality of Germany's romanticism, which applied the principles of its "universal-poesy" to all planes, including politics. Impatient foreign critics have again and again dubbed nazism "political insanity." That is praise rather than insult to many a German romantic. Novalis rhapsodized that "collective insanity," in contrast with individual insanity, "ceases to be insanity and becomes magic." Its magic is holy; he elsewhere compares it with that of God: "From each true state-citizen glows forth the soul of the state, just as in a religious community a single personal God manifests Himself as if in thousands of shapes." Novalis defines each citizen as a mere "limb" of the state organism, which is "alive and personal." [8]

More familiar examples are Hegel's evolving state organism, incarnating God's idea, and Fichte's totalitarian national-socialism. Hitler's speeches and *Mein Kampf* are a lowbrow version of political romanticism. Here the race instead of the state is the mystic whole greater than the total of its parts, welded by purity of blood. The democratic parliamentary system would atomistically divide this welded unit into separate parties. The Volk unit's general will speaks only through its oracle of the Führer.

This romantic metaphysics of race organically unites possessors of the same blood even when they live in separate states. Thus were sown in nineteenth-century thought the seeds of ceaseless future wars. In order to justify war against sovereign states with German minorities, the Nazi periodical *Rheinfront* said in 1937:

> Primarily we are not citizens of states but racial comrades. The certificate of state citizenship is an easily exchanged possession, but membership within one's Volk is something immutable, granted by God. . . . The law of blood-brotherhood . . . produces a great community of German kind which has its members in all states of the world and which finds its proud refuge and kernel in the Reich of Adolf Hitler.[9]

* * *

The State.—The organic view was valuable in unifying so loose a federation as the Germany of the eighteenth century and of the pre-Bismarck nineteenth century. Such an all too "atomistic" Germany was, we must remember, the historical context of the romantic revolt against atomism. By itself, the organic assumption, as propagated by the proto-romantics like Herder, was not aggressively nationalist nor morally and physically destructive. None of this (no revolt against external law) was in the typical quotations previously cited from Novalis and Adam Müller.

The quotations from them made the bare statement that the state is a single

---

[8] Novalis quoted in the Böhm anthology: *Gedankendichtung*, p. 71, and in Meinecke, *op. cit.*, pp. 65, 67–8.

[9] Josef Huenerfauth in *N.S.Z. Rheinfront*, quoted in *New York Times*, Sunday Magazine Section, November 21, 1937, p. 16.

superhuman individual. If we read on in these two, we watch this needed unifying force become a force of chaos at the subtle point where the mathematical fallacy passes into the repetition. Novalis goes on to say: "*All* culture springs from a man's relations with the state." [10] Adam Müller goes on to say that nothing inorganic should fetter these superhuman individuals, the states— no human law, no league of nations.

Novalis wanted a special uniform for the citizens of the state, especially for those who most fully incarnated the "state soul." The wearers of this uniform have turned out to be Hitler's Storm Troopers, a not illogical development which would have horrified Novalis and every single one of the other early romantics.

The self-justified state, like the Faustian man, must not let ethical discrimination hamper its experience of life's totality. So we are not surprised to find Adam Müller end with bloody hymns to war. The result of Hegel's state-worship, too, was that the state became the ethical end in itself in much influential German political thought. All individuals, all the external restrictions of international morality, and all the concretely existing internal parts of the state must be sacrificed to its mathematically non-existent whole, which is mystically greater than its total parts.

Volk.—Gradually this exalted organic unity of political romanticism was applied to the plane of race instead of the state. Modern nordic racism is to a surprising extent a product of nineteenth-century German romanticism. It took the Germans to revive the old Jewish concept of a Chosen People who have been defeated, dispersed, and cruelly partitioned but are messianically destined.

No romantic unity must have its organic oneness divided by external lines. The poem's unity must not be divided by classical lines nor the Volk's by class lines. No part of the Volk's totality must be despised. In the Nazi labour camps all youths, rich and poor without exception, are forced to dwell together six months in the same Spartan circumstances. The aim is to give them, in Hitler's words, "a true national community feeling . . . and above all a proper respect for manual labour." (No mention, of course, of respect for mental labour.)

Though most early romantics, unlike Fichte, still retained functional class lines, they strove successfully to wear down cultural class lines. They it is who discovered and enthroned the previously despised folk-literature. They convinced Germany that the basic and best German Kultur lay in the folksongs, epics, and symbolic myths which they collected amid the aristocratic sneers of the classicists. These writings were claimed to be not the works of individual authors but of the impersonal force of Volk, a sort of collective author. This was Herder's folksong theory. The Grimm brothers, collecting the famous *Grimm Fairy Tales,* did most to convert Germany to this theory.

All individuals, but especially educated individuals, were ruled out as the authors of folk art. Education allegedly made individuals too artificial, too

[10] Novalis (pseudonym of Friedrich von Hardenberg): *Works,* ed. Miner, II, 272.

unprimitive. Only the indivisible primeval "Volk-soul" had the required creative powers.

The mysterious dormant powers of the "common people," the mute inglorious Miltons that bloom to blush unseen, have perhaps been exaggerated. In any case, the romantic Grimm theory has been completely discredited by the most thorough later examinations. These have exposed folksongs and the quaint, apparently "native" folk-costumes as slow seepages downward from court and educated circles, as simplified borrowings from above and almost never as creations.[11]

The first romantic generation, the Jena school of the Schlegels, Tieck, Novalis, was less important in propagating Herder's ideas of folk art than was the second generation, the Heidelberg romantic school of the Grimm brothers and Arnim and Brentano. The latter two writers published the most famous German folksong collection (*The Boy's Magic Horn*) during Napoleon's rule over Germany. Later the great Prussian Minister Stein commended this single book of poems for its important part in arousing Volk patriotism to overthrow the French! So we see how close is the connection between poetry and politics in romantic Germany.[12]

Arnim and Brentano declared they had taken these folksongs down orally from the lips of the common people. Germans believed this, basing their worship of Volk to an incredible extent on this single epoch-making book and its surrounding folk-wisdom cults. Since then the book's so-called folksongs have been traced. Almost all were found copied from books of individual poets of the upper and middle classes. Some of the best and most "natural" and "primitive" of these songs, supposedly collected from the ancient lore of the race, were secretly written by the talented Brentano himself.[13]

In England the same gullible age went into ecstasies over those primitive products of the Celtic soul, Macpherson's forged *Poems of Ossian*. The worshipful attitude toward Volk gave tremendous impetus to both democracy and nationalism, the two greatest political forces of the nineteenth century, but also—via nationalism—to nazism.

* * *

Herder was the first to make German romanticists enthusiastic for the "organic, plantlike unfolding of Volk-souls." [14] This was toward the close of

[11] John Meier: *Kunstlieder im Volksmunde* (Halle an der Saale, 1906); and *Kunstlied und Volkslied in Deutschland* (Halle a. d. S., 1906). Hans Naumann: *Grundzüge der deutschen Volkskunde* (Leipzig, 1922).

[12] L. A. von Arnim and Clemens Brentano, eds.: *Des Knaben Wunderhorn* (3 vols., Heidelberg, 1808, 1819). Stein's comment cited in Johannes Janssen: *Johann Friedrich Böhmers Leben* (3 vols., Freiburg im Breisgau, 1868), I, 439.

[13] Karl Bode: *Die Bearbeitungen der Vorlagen in "Des Knaben Wunderhorn"* (Berlin, 1909; Vol. LXXVI of Palaestra series).

[14] H. O. Ziegler: *Die moderne Nation* (Tübingen, 1931).

the eighteenth century, and his words referred not merely to Germany but to all Volk-souls. Here romantic politics was still in the eighteenth-century tradition of cosmopolitan humanitarianism. This was sloughed off during the transition from books to bullets. The right to "unfold organically" became restricted to the German "Volk-soul" alone. Father Jahn, the youth leader of the Napoleonic era, best personified this transition.

The early romantics, from Herder up to the wars with the French Revolutionaries and Napoleon, saw the Volk-soul chiefly as a medium for beautiful literature, as the Rousseauist lispings of the "noble savage." But Jahn and Fichte were more interested in beating France and French thought than in art for art's sake. They, and German leaders ever after, used this folk-literature as a political medium to inculcate nationalism in the young.

Herder was the highminded founder of the Volk cults of both Germans and Slavs. He anthologized and encouraged the national literatures of every Volk impartially. His goal was the peaceful co-operation of all nationalisms. Ironically, his national anthologies later became the fountainheads of both aggressive Pan-Germanism and aggressive Pan-Slavism.

The crowning irony is Herder's theory that an age of really passionate nationalism would make war impossible forever. Past wars he explained as the products of unnational atomistic states. But an organic national state would so enjoy the fruits of its unfolding Volk-soul that it would want all other Volk-souls to have the same enjoyments and would encourage them, too, to unfold without restriction. Herder envisaged a utopia of perpetual peace in which passionate nationalisms unfolded sweetly side by side like different-coloured roses in one common garden.

This goal has all our sympathies, but we question Herder's faith in nationalism as the means. From Rousseau's untenable faith in the natural goodness of man, Herder derived his untenable faith in the goodness of nations who act "naturally." His are the romantic postulates: acting "naturally" meant unfolding organically the instincts of the national ego and being "freed" from the artificial restraints of external law. But to classicists and conservatives the essence of freedom is these traffic lights of universal external law. Without these the natural and instinctive unfolding—whether on the plane of individual or nation —means unchecked egoism and the war of all against all.

The goal of Herder's nationalism was negated when Jahn angrily denounced the "love of the German for his foreign brethren" and glorified aggressive war.[15] Yet Jahn and all later Volk nationalists through Hitler are inconceivable without Herder. That is why Nazi schoolbooks make Herder a chief hero. The Nazi and Wagnerian cult of the organic instinctive Volk could not have existed without him. Yet he would be jailed as a pacifist and internationalist if he lived in Germany today.

[15] Quoted in H. von Treitschke: *History of Germany in the 19th Century* (New York, 1919), V, 249, 244.

The trouble is the old and very human one that we cannot reach our goals without using means tough enough to be effective. And then—the means have the disconcerting habit of getting the bit in their teeth.

From a Herder to a Hitler! Was this corruption of nationalism inevitable or merely a tragic accident? Probably inevitable, but we can never really know. What we do know is that this corruption is a basic motif of the last hundred years. Not only in Germany but in all lands nationalism passed from the humane, the peaceful, and the tolerant to the war of all against all. From Herder to Hitler in Germany, from Mazzini to Mussolini in Italy, from Wordsworth to Kipling in England.

The gradual stages of this downward transition should not be slurred over as negligible nuances. The descent inside Germany appears in three distinct stages: from the literary romantics down to the active leader Jahn; from Jahn down to the racial determinism and Aryan cult of Wagner and Houston Chamberlain; from the talkers Wagner and Chamberlain down to the rock bottom of the active leader Hitler.

Each stage is accompanied by an ever broader class and mass appeal, requiring an ever lower and less educated and more demagogic common denominator. The first Volk-worshippers of the romantic school are like Marie Antoinette playing in the artificial "naturalness" of her Arcadian little shepherdess costume. Their nationalism was the sophisticated affectation of literary snobs and life-starved professors. Through them, nationalism saturated German literature and universities and history books. Through the universities, the books, the student leagues, Jahn's storm-trooper gymnasts, and the battlefields of Leipzig and Waterloo, German nationalism saturated the middle classes. Then Wagner, anticipating a more industrialized age, transferred nationalism from middle class to proletariat, from capitalism to economic socialism. With Hitler and Goebbels nationalism has reached the broadest and lowest possible common denominator.

The greatest demagogues of our age have won their proletariat—at least for the time being—to a national socialism. Until Hitler, nationalism seemed almost a class monopoly of the bourgeoisie. Hitler called "this bourgeois world . . . a class doomed by fate to decline." He shrewdly observed that the earlier "Pan-German movement was nationalistic but unfortunately *not social enough* to win the masses." [16] Therefore . . .

* * *

The gymnast Jahn and the poet Arndt were called "the popularizers of the teachings of the Volk-soul." [17] A parliamentary committee of the German Diet classified Jahn's *German Folkdom* of 1810 with Fichte's *Speeches to the German*

---

[16] Hitler: *Mein Kampf* (ed. cit.), pp. 984, 158.

[17] F. Schnabel: *Deutsche Geschichte im Neunzehnten Jahrhundert* (4 vols., Freiburg, 1929-37), I, 306.

Nation of 1808 as "the spiritual godfathers of the newer Germany." [18] Both works were written while French troops still occupied Germany; this background accounts for the fanatic bitterness of Jahn's and Fichte's nationalism.

Fichte's work was limited in its appeal by its abstruse metaphysics. Jahn's book offered a more practical program, in colorful demagogic style. General Blücher, the German co-victor at Waterloo, called Jahn's book "the Germanest verbal gun [*sic*]." [19] *German Folkdom* is halfway between scientific scholarship and demagogics—that half-way point which sounds so thrilling and convincing to the half-educated.

Jahn's credo was that the unconscious force of Volk shapes all history. To describe this force Jahn coined the word "folkdom" (*Volkstum*), today one of the most important Nazi words. Folkdom he called "that which the Volk has in common, its inner existence, its movement, its ability to propagate. Because of it, there courses through all the veins of a Volk a folkic thinking and feeling, loving and hating, intuition and faith." [20]

Cosmopolitanism Jahn spurned because "humanity appears nowhere by itself pure and simple but only as incarnated by folkdoms." [21] The Greeks and Germans are "humanity's holy people." [22] Later Hegel devoted many volumes to describing how Greeks and Germans, in turn, incarnated God's idea. "How odd of God to choose the Jews," German nationalists seem to wail, when the Germans would make a Chosen People so much superior.

Jahn attempted no new philosophic foundation. Almost all his ideas derive from the German romantics, in whom he was steeped. The romantic school's organic assumption, when applied to the plane of nation and in the context of the war with France, produced Jahn's book *Folkdom*.

Folkdom is devoted to methods for nationalizing Germany's way of life or, rather, "awakening" its allegedly innate nationalism. Without Hitler's cynicism, the book foreshadows *Mein Kampf* by its shrewd outline of propaganda techniques and educational indoctrination. So does Jahn's appeal for biological Volk purity.[23] "Animal hybrids have no genuine power of propagation, and hybrid peoples have just as little posterity." "The purer a people, the better; the more mixed, the worse." Every Volk should lead an isolated existence. The founding of a world government "is the last moment of humanity." [24]

Volk is the only true basis of a state. "A state without Volk is nothing, a soulless artifice," wrote Jahn. "A Volk without a state is nothing, a lifeless frivolous phantom like the vagabond gypsies and Jews. Only state and Volk in

18 J. Friedrich: *Jahn als Erzieher* (Munich, 1895), p. 48.
19 Jahn, *op. cit.* (Euler's introduction), I, xlvi–xlvii.
20 Euler, *op. cit.*, p. 111. Jahn, *op. cit.*, I, 154, 156.
21 Jahn, *op. cit.*, I, 158.
22 *Ibid.*, I, 162.
23 Theune, *op. cit.*, p. 124.
24 Jahn, *op. cit.*, I, 164–8.

one make a Reich. Its power of survival is its folkdom." [25] Today that sounds more trite than startling, although attempts to change the map of Europe on that basis will always mean chaos and war. Metternich, the Hapsburg Chancellor and urbane "good European," first viewed more with amusement than horror "that newfangled notion of nationality." [26] But even in his own day it became the most frightening reality of modern progress.

* * *

In the pre-Hitler past, *Realpolitik* was perhaps equally practised (tacitly) by all nations. But with frank perversity and perverse frankness, nineteenth-century Germany, like the Italy of Machiavelli, went furthest in rationalizing this deplorable practice into a glorious ideal of theory. Fichte's *Speeches to the German Nation,* during the War of Liberation, are the philosophic foundation of modern German *Realpolitik*. He preached a double moral standard: what is wicked for the individual to do becomes holy if done by the state. Unlike the individual, the state should use for victory, if needed, all possible frauds, violations of law, and violent crimes. The collective Volk-ego should be bound by no external laws or limits.

The historical background for Fichte's *Speeches* explains why so extreme a *Realpolitik* caught the German imagination at that particular time. This historical context was the coming War of Liberation against Napoleon. So great were the hates of German romantics for what they called the French tyranny, and so great seemed the odds against its overthrow, that even the most bloody and scoundrel-like means seemed justified.

The historical situation led the romantics to the extremest statements of the Germanic racial myth that had yet appeared. German nationalism and Francophobia were widespread only among the middle class, to which most romantics belonged, and even there only among a noisy minority. Both the aristocrats and the peasant masses were apathetic to the crusade Jahn and Fichte preached. The German masses realized they were in many ways better off under Napoleon's semi-liberal Jacobin rule than under their German feudal masters. Therefore the romantic-school publicists of the War of Liberation turned to a tactic which Hitler has directly borrowed from them. They preached nordic self-worship and race hatred of everything French in order to stir to white heat the apathetic public feeling against Napoleon. Moreover, unlike modern propagandists of the Goebbels school, the romantics sincerely believed the Germanic myth they preached.

Often their race hate included not only France but also the German Jews. That fact, too, appears less mysterious when viewed not in vacuo but in its

25 *Ibid.,* I, 160.
26 W. Monypenny and G. Buckle: *Life of Benjamin Disraeli* (new ed., 2 vols., New York, 1929), I, 997–1003.

historical context. Napoleon, as son of the French Revolution, made a point of freeing German Jews for the first time from their mediæval ghetto restrictions. Consequently many Jews were more loyal to Napoleon than to their native Germany and have made poor nationalists ever since. From those days on, following the tradition of Fichte and Jahn, German psychology closely links racial myth and *Realpolitik,* the former justifying the use of the latter.

Fichte in his *Speeches* says: "Between states, there is neither law nor right save the law of the strongest"; Germany, living more metaphysically than all other races, is "the Volk, metaphysically destined, which has the moral right to fulfil its destiny by *every* means of cunning and force." Starting the myth of racial purity, Fichte calls the Germans the most unmixed of all peoples and the closest to the mystic powers of nature. Their unique purity and their romantic idealism make the Germans not merely "a Volk" but "*the* Volk."

This superiority justifies "*the* Volk" in seizing whatever *Lebensraum* it needs and expelling or enslaving other Volk. In doing this, Germans must not be deterred by legality or by their own written promises, for *the* Volk is above all such scraps of paper and above such sentimental rubbish as international morality. *The* Volk must impose a German peace on Europe. This peace must be based not on treaties and written pledges but on brute force alone, a self-justified force.

These axioms of Fichte's *Realpolitik* were developed into a philosophic glorification of war by his fellow-romanticist Hegel. Thence they were carried even further by Treitschke and Houston Chamberlain and all the other philosophers and historians who form the long but unbroken chain linking Fichte's nineteenth-century theories with Hitler's twentieth-century practice.[27]

* * *

[27] J. G. Fichte: *Speeches* (*Reden an die deutsche Nation*). This and the preceding paragraph follow H. W. Steed's convenient summary of Fichte in Kolnai, *op. cit.,* pp. 8–9.

GERMAN ROMANTICISM AND POLITICAL THOUGHT

Robert W. Lougee

THE RETREAT from liberalism and the rise of fascist totalitarianisms in the interwar period occasioned widespread inquiry into the intellectual sources of the phenomenon. Writers have frequently discovered the "roots," to use the fashionable metaphor, in romanticism, particularly, German romanticism. Sharp controversies have arisen over the propriety and validity of attributing modern political lunacy ultimately to the romantic mind. A prior question may well be asked, what exactly are the elements of romantic thought which have political significance. This paper seeks to identify and analyze these elements.

Four aspects of romantic thought merit analysis for this purpose. They are the romantic epistemology, the romantic philosophy of history, the romantic notion concerning the one and the many, and the romantic spirit of protest. The term romantic is not limited here strictly to the Jena, Heidelberg, or any other literary school. It applies to those writers who, in the late eighteenth and early nineteenth centuries, represented that latter phase of the movement which brought German intellectual life to flower, who possessed a new feeling for life of extraordinary depth and richness of promise, and who stood in opposition to the Enlightenment and the concept of man as a subject only of outer sense experience.[1]

The romantic epistemology was a reaction against the rationalism of the eighteenth century. By the middle of this century reason was conceived as agent rather than as being, or as Lessing put it, the power of reason is to be found not in the possession, but in the acquisition of truth. The method of the Enlightenment was to take the positive or the given, analyze it into its elements, and then perceive how the elements were combined in the given phenomenon. The aim was to establish generally valid principles. Such a method had been used in scientific studies in the seventeenth century and now in the eighteenth century was applied to political and economic problems.

Unlike the thinkers of the Enlightenment, the romantic writers did not consider analysis an indispensable tool in discovering knowledge. This is not to say

---

[1] Paul Kluckhohn in *Deutsche Literatur*, Reihe Romantik (Leipzig, 1931), I, Introduction.

From *The Review of Politics*, XXI, No. 4 (October 1959), pp. 631–45. Copyright, 1959, by the University of Notre Dame. Reprinted by permission.

that they were unbridled irrationalists given to incessant flights of fancy, but simply that they preferred to experience deeply and directly, to feel, to emphasize, to grasp as a whole the meaning and significance of the given situation. The positive or the given as it appeared to them was their point of departure. Hence their suspicion of concepts as artificial, as nonexistential. Hence their disdain for a mechanical world view in which simple, understandable laws are used to describe and explain all nature. Hence their indifference to the logical contradiction between different elements of their thought, or, indeed, their evident pleasure in discovering and accepting as reality what to the logical, conceptual mind must appear as polar opposites.

Herder had contributed to this theory of knowledge. He had taught that

. . . every kind of human knowledge has its own characters, that is, its nature, time, place, and period of life; Greek culture, for example, grew according to the times, the place, and the circumstances and sank as these passed.[2]

Whence it follows that the uniqueness of human situations forbids the application of principles derived by the analysis of some other situation. The essence of a given situation is to be grasped by specific study and finally by *Einfühlung* —a feeling into it. His philosophy of history was that not will and reflection but given forces and circumstances engender historical change and make things happen as they do.

Why did Alexander push to India? Because he was Philip's son and, given the preparations of his father, the deeds of his nation, his age and character, and his reading of Homer, he had no other course.[3]

No one expressed the romantic sense of the inadequacy of the new knowledge of the Age of Reason better than Novalis who wrote bitingly of the

men who were restlessly engaged in eliminating poetry from nature, from the soil, from human souls and from the sciences; destroying every trace of the sacred, heaping sarcasm on all great men and events, and depriving the world of its variegated color. Light, because of its mathematical obedience and its movement, became their favorite subject. They enjoyed light more because it could be analyzed than because it could produce colors, and so they named after it their great preoccupation, the Enlightenment.[4]

Much of the spirit of German romantic irrationalism was in Burke who taught the Germans more than almost any other Englishman. He wrote of "the happy effect of following nature, which is wisdom without reflection." He abhorred "the nakedness and solitude of metaphysical abstraction" in any-

---

[2] Herder, *Ideen zur Philosophie der Geschichte der Menschheit* in *Werke,* IV, Meyers Klassiker-Ausgaben (Leipzig und Wien, n.d.), 169.

[3] *Ibid.,* 166.

[4] Novalis, *Die Christenheit oder Europa, Sämliche Werke* (München, 1924), III, 17.

thing concerning human affairs and discovered the evil genius of the *Tiers État* in 1789 in the predominate group of village lawyers, who perhaps knew their laws and regulations but not the nature of living, human reality.[5] Joseph Görres carried this spirit into later romanticism and in a clever figure ridiculed the rationalist way of thought as considering the world with a *"geschliffenen Insektenauge,"* that is, as seeing things not as wholes but as parts like the eye of an insect.[6]

The romantic theory of knowledge is explicit or implicit on nearly every page of the chief romantic political thinker, Adam Müller. The key to his *Elemente der Staatskunst* is his distinction of concept (*Begriff*) and idea (*Idee*). A concept is a word or definition which describes the state or some other institution as it appears from one viewpoint or from a given point in time. As the picture of a sunset cannot catch the subtle play and change of shape and color so does the concept fail to contain what is living and vibrant in the object. If the thought (*Gedanke*) however expands,

. . . if it moves and grows as the object moves and grows, then we name the thought not the concept but the idea of the thing, of the state, of life. Our usual theories of the state are heaps of concepts and therefore dead, useless, impractical; they are not in step with life, because they turn on the error that the state may perfectly and once and for all be conceived; these theories do not allow for movement whereas the state moves on without end.[7]

Those statesmen who have really taught us something have not taught from textbooks or from statistics, "the tiresome speculation of the study," but have based their teaching on life and movement.[8] The quintessence of the romantic view of knowledge is expressed in Müller's advice to the student of politics whom he urges to study things as they are, to get first hand experience with laws and institutions. A real feeling for these things, he says, is worth vastly more than the "watchmaker-type" of understanding, for as all higher branches of knowledge, political science is to be experienced (*erlebt*) not merely cold learned (*erlernt*).[9]

The romanticists, thus, clearly rejected analysis and speculation as the best means of acquiring ultimate knowledge. They were realists who wished to catch the flow of being first hand, so to speak, and not after it was filtered through a conceptual network. Political theorizing of any kind must be anathema to this view. Romantic thought was contemptuous of liberalism and of enlightened absolutism as well, for both represent the intervention of the rational mind into the destinies of nations. Ludwig von Gerlach and his circle,

[5] Burke, *Reflections on the Revolution in France, Works* (London, 1815–27), V, 78, 36, 90.

[6] R. Saitschick, *Joseph Görres* (Freiburg in Breisgau, 1953), 152.

[7] Adam Müller, *Die Elemente der Staatskunst* (Wien, Leipzig, 1922), I, 20.

[8] *Ibid.*, 6.

[9] *Ibid.*, 16.

the "romantic conservatives," were anti-liberal and anti-absolutist. "Right, eternal and historical, in church and state and in opposition to arbitrary action of any kind . . . in opposition to absolutism from above and from below— this was the tendency of our struggle." [10] This line of thought stood in opposition to many nineteenth century political developments—centralization and the waxing activities of a rationalistic bureaucracy, constitutions and bills of rights based on general principles of natural laws, the growth of democracy with its mechanical principle of reaching decisions by electoral divisions, and more broadly to the whole tendency of modern culture to rationalize, systematize, mechanize.

The romantic philosophy of history was complementary to the romantic epistemology. The insistence that reality must be grasped directly and not through abstractions led naturally to an interest in history which is the full play of reality in time. The romanticist did not, as the men of the Enlightenment, use history as a laboratory to test different theories, but as the means of perceiving and knowing the whole through an acquaintance with the different stages of its development and of gaining an appreciation of the various forces at work in fashioning that whole. They sought, that is, to know in the romantic sense of the word.

Their conception of history contained at least four mutually consistent but distinct idea.. In the first place, it assumed that historical change is the product of historically given circumstances and not the consequence of arbitrary intervention. To borrow the terminology of a more recent period, they held that history was the product of *Entwicklung* rather than *Entscheidung,* of gradual development rather than arbitrary decision.[11] Adam Müller made the point by rejecting the application of Archimedes' principle to political change. Archimedes had said, "Give me a fixed point outside of the earth, and I shall move the earth out of its hinges." Müller argued,

. . . do not all unfortunate errors of the French Revolution coincide in the illusion that the individual could really step out of the social contract, that he could overthrow and destroy from the outside anything that does not please him, that the individual could protest against the work of thousands of years, that he need recognize none of all the institutions he encounters, in brief, it is the illusion that there really exists a fixed point outside the state which anyone can reach and from which anyone can mark new paths for the body politic, from which he can transform an old body into a completely new one and can outline for the state in place of the old, imperfect, but well tried constitution, a new one which will be perfect at least for the next fortnight.[12]

[10] Ernst Ludwig von Gerlach, *Denkwürdigkeiten* (Schwerin, 1903), I, 234.
[11] E. Lemberg, *Geschichte des Nationalismus in Europa* (Stuttgart, 1950), 270.
[12] Müller, *Die Elemente,* 26.

By rejecting arbitrary intervention in history he did not mean to preclude historical guidance through a higher *Entscheidung,* through the immanence of the divine. Indeed, for the later theological stage of romanticism, God has had a historical role much as in the Christian philosophy of history.

Secondly, their interpretation of history was non-theological. There is no distant utopia or gradual approach to perfection. Perfection is possible at every stage and is often attained. Amid the most suitable conditions Homer produced the perfect epic, Herder believed. Later poets turned to drama and other forms and brought them to perfection. "Phidias created his mighty Jupiter and no higher Jupiter was possible." [13] Likewise, social and political forms as well as artistic come to maturity and perfection in their season and then give way to others which are not higher or better but simply different. This is what Burke meant when he wrote of "the great mysterious incorporation of the human race" which "is never old or middle-aged or young, but in a condition of unchangeable constancy, moves on through the varied tenor of perpetual decay, fall, renovation, and progression." [14] History is cyclical rather than linear, a view of enormous significance for modern conservative theory.[15]

Thirdly, romanticists emphasized the culturally and historically creative role of the simple people of the folk. The folk were idealized, spiritualized. The folk-spirit, *Volkgeist,* is the medium out of which great events and great works are precipitated. Whence came Greek culture, Herder asked.

By no master was it forced upon them; through the sound of the lyre at holy ceremonies, games, and dances, through self-discovered knowledge and skills, mostly through repeated intercourse with one another and with other peoples; by these means the people assumed now this, now that direction, custom, and law.[16]

In a magnificent passage on the Arabians in the *Ideen* Herder suggested how the origin, character and spirit of a folk is bound up with its historical destiny.

The way of life of this folk, to whom cities appeared as dungeons, its pride in its origins, in its God, in its rich and poetic speech, in its noble steeds, in sword and bow, in everything else which it possesses and believes holy—all this prepared the Arabs for a role which, when their time came, . . . they played well.[17]

Eichendorff expressed the idea succinctly.

In history nothing is arbitrary. That which is enduring is not the despotic work of the few, but rather is generated from within the folk itself.[18]

[13] Herder, *Ideen,* 169, 170.
[14] Burke, *Reflections,* 79.
[15] A. Mohler, *Die Konservative Revolution in Deutschland* (Stuttgart, 1950), 104 ff.
[16] Herder, *Ideen,* 107.
[17] *Ibid.,* 459.
[18] Eichendorff, *Über die Folgen von der Aufhebung der Landeshoheit der Bischöfe und der Klöster in Deutschland* in *Deutsche Literatur,* Reihe Romantik, X, 37.

Adam Müller held that ultimately the constitution of the state must be founded not on the will of a majority but on the "temper of a people." [19]

Fourthly, the romantic philosophy of history perceived a world order—or perhaps disorder—in which striving, creation, and recreation is constantly going on without reference to any immutable norms or principles, that is, a world order beyond the operation of natural laws valid without regard to time and place. Troeltsch found this view a principal point of distinction between Western thought and German romanticism. On the one hand he saw "an eternal, rational and divinely ordained system of Order, embracing both morality and law" and on the other "individual, living, and perpetually new incarnations of an historically creative mind," a conception of history as "an ever moving system, which throws up unique individualities as it moves and is always shaping individual structures on the basis of a law which is always new. . . ." [20]

Likewise Adam Müller wrote of the "Chimera of natural law" and utters the pungent exclamation, "A natural law which differs from the positive law!" [21]

In short, the romantic mind was a historical mind. It regarded history not as a chronicle of times past to be used for statistical or illustrative purposes, but rather as a living revelation of Spirit, the principal source of inspiration and knowledge. It was a dedication to history as a living reality, expressing itself unconditionally in each of its forms and periods. It was historicism. The coronation of history as the queen of the sciences was performed by Friedrich Schlegel in his lecture, *Über die neuere Geschichte*. Even the higher philosophy, he wrote,

> may not, without peril, neglect looking constantly to the history of the development of man and of his spiritual powers, for otherwise it unfailingly looses itself in incomprehensible things. . . . History . . . if it knows how to conceive and represent the spirit of great times and great men and events, is itself a true philosophy. . . . A sense for the excellent and highest in what is brought to us by poetry and art, comes clearly only when we know how to place ourselves in the spirit of the time out of which the art or poetry arises or which it represents.

We must turn to the past to understand the present. Only knowledge of the past will give us "a quiet and firm perspective on the present, a measure of its greatness or smallness, and a basis of judgment of it." [22]

This romantic philosophy of history has been a vital source of conservative thought. It has been an argument against sudden and basic changes in the

---

[19] Adam Müller, *Friederich der Grosse und Preussen*, in R. Kohler, ed., *Adam Müller Schriften zur Staatsphilosphie* (Munchen, n.d.), 107.

[20] From Troeltsch's essay on Natural Law and Humanity which occurs as an appendix in E. Barker, *Natural Law and the Theory of Society* (Cambridge, 1934), 204.

[21] Müller, *Die Elemente*, 40.

[22] F. Schlegel, *Über die neuere Geschichte* in *Deutsche Literatur*, Reihe Romantik, X, 30.

given social and cultural pattern. It has been directed against revolution and all movements which aim at reform or planning without regard to the historically given. It has favored those theocratic social conceptions which regard man as under divine dispensation and accordingly as well off as he ought to be in any given moment of time. It has worked against those doctrines of progress which teach that man is headed upwards from the swamp and brambles to the higher Elysian fields. Yet, the romantic philosophy of history has been equally opposed to the dogmatists of utter reaction, for history is movement and change, not stagnation. The emphasis on the creative role of the people of the nation must be considered an important source of modern nationalism.

The romantic conception of the individual and the social group—the one and the many—is distinctive and, for the Western mind, remarkable. The romanticist placed the highest value on the individual, his freedom, and his self-development and self-realization. Yet, he placed an equally high value on the group, which he considered as a living organism whose laws of organization placed the constituent individuals in a relation of mutual dependence. Unlike the Western mind which tends to set the individual and the group in opposition and assume that either the one or the other must have primacy, the romantic mind found the two completely and necessarily complementary.

Romantic individualism must be sharply distinguished from atomistic individualism. The social contract theories prevalent in the eighteenth century generally assumed that the individual in nature enjoys a position of independence from his fellows, and that he has natural rights which do not derive from any association. But to be independent is not to be unique, and these theories assumed that all individuals behave more or less in the same way and, therefore, like atoms, respond alike to general laws or forces. Romantic individualism, on the contrary, stressed the uniqueness of individuals, a uniqueness which placed them beyond conformity to any general law or principle. Schnabel has pointed out that before the romantic period all thought had assumed some point of reference outside of the individual, in God, in humanity, in classical culture, in the majority. The romanticists, in contrast, labored to individualize the world. Man became a law and measure unto himself.[23] The term *Persönlichkeit* came to be used "as a designation for a person with uniqueness and peculiarity of nature and with the implication that developing one's own individual nature is a primary objective."[24]

A *Persönlichkeit* is one who is distinct, not subordinate, cannot be counted or numbered with others. Goethe was an inspiration for this kind of individualism. Wilhelm Meister, in his long travels and involved experiences, sought to discover and to express his real self. Wilhelm writes to Werner,

[23] F. Schnabel, *Deutsche Geschichte im Neuhnzehten Jahrhundert* (Freiburg in Breigau, 1929–37), I, 243, 244.
[24] P. Kluckhohn, *Persönlichkeit und Gemeinschaft* (Halle, 1925), 2.

What good were it for me to manufacture perfect iron while my own breast is full of dross? What would it stead me to put properties of land in order, while I am at variance with myself? To speak it in a word the cultivation of my individual self, here as I am, has from my youth upwards been constantly though dimly my wish and my purpose.[25]

Kant had contributed to the freeing of the individual personality from what seemed to many of his generation as mechanistic determinism. His doctrine of the practical reason and the presence of the moral law within assured the individual of his freedom. Fichte taught in the *Wissenschaftslehre* the ultimate reality of the self-active ego which creates nature in order to realize itself. This ego may be grasped only by him who proclaims his freedom from the phenomenal world of cause and effect and perceives the universal ego through inner vision, that is, by looking within, he may more truly see all that seems to be without.

Pietism preached the "inward godly life of the individual" and thereby "brought into immediate consciousness the infinite worth of the individual human race." [26] It is scarcely surprising that one of the foremost preachers of the new individualism should have come from the pietistic Herrnhuters— Friederich Schleiermacher. The greatest Protestant theologian since Calvin elaborated a religious system which revolved around the notion of the fundamental worth of the individual's piety and religious experience. His *Monologen* repeatedly stresses the absolute quality of the inner freedom of the individual. "So freedom, art thou of all things the innermost, the first, and most fundamental. When I return into myself, in order to regard you, my gaze wanders out of the realm of time and is made free from any necessity; any heavy feeling of slavery is dissipated. . . ." [27]

The same age which displayed such striking individualism, reacted against the isolation of the individual. From the mid-1790's romantic writers more and more stress the role of the individual as a vital part of a larger organic whole. This stress did not aim at subordinating the individual to the group but rather at coordinating him with it. Still less did it aim at eliciting likeness of contribution or equality of treatment. Rather the group was thought strong according to the uniqueness and diversity of its elements. The assumption was that the individual by being completely true to himself would best represent and contribute to the character of the whole. As Schleiermacher wrote, ". . . it has become clear to me that every man ought in his own way to represent mankind." [28]

The romantic relation of the one and the many must be considered in light

---

[25] *Wilhelm Meister's Apprenticeship* (Carlyle translation, Boston, 1883), 261.

[26] Kluckhohn, *Persönlichkeit*, 5.

[27] Schleiermacher, *Monologen* in *Deutsche Literatur*, Reihe Romantik, IV, 33.

[28] *Ibid.*, 40.

of the prevailing conception of reality as a product of the tension of polar opposites. Goethe had written of the "inner totality" as consisting of the unity of "inner and outer thought and deed, necessity and freedom." Adam Müller's early work, *Die Lehre vom Gegensatz,* had expounded this thesis and his later writings applied it. In the *Elemente* the ideal society combines youth and age, the juristic (that is, the orderly) and the economic (that is, the aggressive), war interests and peace interests, progress and stability, and the like.[29] Novalis held that individuality itself arose from the assimilation and blending of diverse individualities.

In order to build himself into an individuality, one must know how to assume and assimilate other individualities unto himself, and in this way will become a substantial individuality himself.[30]

In leading the romanticists to their peculiar conception of individual and group no influence was more direct or greater than the lectures on *Die Bestimmung des Gelehrten* which Fichte held at Jena during the summer semester of 1794. There the "social impulse" is given a central place.

This impulse arises from reciprocal action, the reaction of opposites upon one another, the give and take between them, . . . not for a mere causality, which is but the activity of the one against the other; the question here is not subordination, as in the material world, but of coordination.[31]

Accordingly,

. . . the social impulse belongs among the basic impulses of man. Man is constructed to live in society; he is not perfect if he lives in isolation, indeed it is a self-contradiction.[32]

The flowering of the organic conception owed much to Schelling who published his *Ideen Zu einer Philosophie der Natur* in 1797. In this work the organic conception stands in the sharpest distinction to the mechanical, causal thought of the eighteenth century. The whole world is considered as an organism and every part related. In the *Ideen Zu einer Philosophie der Natur,* he wrote, "organization is the very essence of things, not phenomena, but object itself." [33]

The organic conception was applied to the state and society, terms not sharply distinguished in this period, by virtually every romantic writer who considered this subject. Fichte expressed it in his *Foundations of Natural Law.*

---

[29] Müller, *Die Elemente,* 98, 99.
[30] Kohler, v.vi.
[31] Fichte, *Werke* (Medicus edition, Leipzig, n.d.), I, 20.
[32] *Ibid.,* 18.
[33] J. Baxa, *Einführung in die romantische Staatswissenschaft* (Jena, 1923), 17, 28.

Just as in the product of nature every part, whatever it is, can exist only in this one union and outside of this one union would not exist—indeed outside any organic union it would not exist, for without the interaction of organic forces keeping each other in equilibrium no lasting form would exist, but an eternal struggle of being and not being would exist which we can not even imagine—similarly man obtains only in the union of the state a definite place in the chains of things, a point of rest in nature; and everyone obtains this definite place in face of others and of nature by being a part of this definite association.[34]

Müller considered the state, and by this he seems more nearly to mean society,

. . . not a mere factory, a farm, an insurance institution or mercantile society; it is the intimate association of all spiritual wealth, physical needs, of the whole of physical and spiritual wealth, of the total external and internal life of a nation in a great energetic infinitely active and living whole.[35]

In Novalis' thinking the mediaeval state or the *Ständestaat* had the character of a well-articulated, self-harmonious whole. The guilds were the limbs and strength of the state, the nobles the moral element, priests the religious, scholars the intelligence, kings the will. Görres called for a *Ständestaat* based on "the teaching, military, and food-producing classes." Similarly, Franz Baader called for an organic *Ständestaat* rather than a mechanically organized state. "Association means inequality between those bound together, because between equals only a heaping together or an aggregation takes place." [36]

The notion of the unique individual in organic harmony with the whole has been a fertile source of political and social ideas. It has been an argument against statism and leveling. It has suggested a society of self-developed individuals, but also of classes and estates with unique privileges and responsibilities, integrated into a functioning whole. This is virtually an image of the Old Regime, yet a model for modern corporate organization and even some forms of collectivism, although a modern collective consists more nearly of disciplined units than naturally associated individuals. Certainly, the organic view has been an inspiration for some lines of thought which oppose laissez-faire economic individualism. Adam Müller's guild socialism was not without influence on the *Katheder Socialisten* and has enjoyed a revival in the twentieth century.

A striking characteristic of romanticism is its penchant for *Zeitkritik*. Baxa wrote of the romanticist as "an extremely critical spirit, . . . troubled with standing doubts about the sense and purpose of his existence." [37] A critical spirit naturally accompanied the romantic temper which rejected many accepted norms. The romanticist, accordingly, had a wide latitude for criticism of existing society and culture. His conception of organic historical development was

[34] Fichte, *Werke*, II, 212.
[35] Müller, *Die Elemente*, 37.
[36] Baxa, *Einführung*, 159, 160.
[37] *Ibid.*, 7.

often a basis for critical judgment. The question was asked whether an institution, or idea, or even a whole period was a "genuine" product of historical evolution, or whether it reflected the spirit of its time, and whether it were true to itself and its innermost tendencies, rather than being an artificial excrescence on the face of time. Such a basis of judgment was, of course, not without its contradiction—perhaps the deepest contradiction in romantic political thought. For, on the romanticist's own conception of history, how can an event or development take place outside of history, that is, not be genuine? Liberalism and democracy and the modern political theory based on the concept of natural rights undoubtedly are as much rooted in the earth of historical environment and as much the product of historical forces as the rise of a feudal aristocracy in the Middle Ages and its perpetuation into modern times.

Romanticists varied widely in their specific criticisms, but there was a widespread feeling that the times were degenerate, a conviction that a pristine golden age had passed and ought to be regained. For many, the Middle Ages seemed to be such an age and hence the virtual cult of mediaevalism. As events turned more and more people away from the Revolution, romantic writers, many of whom had at first been enthusiastic admirers of what seemed to be a great movement of liberation, came to regard the Revolution and the whole background of rationalistic thought and commercial activity which had helped to produce it, as a blow at the human soul and a source of modern degeneration. Novalis, referring to the contention of the modern spirit with the old, expressed the form, if not the political substance of the romantic *Zeitkritik*. "This great inner schism . . . was a remarkable indication of the harmfulness of culture at a certain stage." [38] The romantic *Sehnsucht,* the longing for all that which is wished and that which is lost, represented a dissatisfaction and rejection of what is and as Schnabel has remarked became "the basic mood" of modern man and led to his characteristic *"Geist der Opposition."* [39]

The romantic protest was often radical and activist, manifesting not only a contempt for, but a rebellion against the status quo. Novalis wrote:

The fate which oppresses us is the sluggishness of our spirit. By enlargement and cultivation of our activity, we change ourselves into fate. Everything appears to stream in upon us, because we do not stream out. We are negative, because we choose to be so; the more positive we become, the more negative will the world around us be, until at last, there is no more negative and we are all in all. God wills gods.[40]

The admonition to stream out is at the heart of all modern radical romantic thinking, the basis of modern activism.

Müller's radicalism is somewhat more specific and almost eschatological in flavor. "I speak not of things present, but of things to come," he writes.

[38] Novalis, *Die Christenheit,* 10.
[39] Schnabel, *Deutsche Geschichte,* I, 240, 243.
[40] Novalis, *Fragmente* in *The German Classics,* ed., Kuno Francke (New York, 1913), IV, 188.

We must completely destroy this lascivious and sensuous private life, together with the cold, dried-out formality of our public life; let them die together, in common death will their atoms again be reconciled; our grandchildren will live in a new and better creation; at the least it is for us to maintain a learned interest, a philosophical lust for the general upheaval.[41]

The romanticist's interpretation of modern times as degenerate and the eschatological nature of his protest must be regarded as a powerful source of the seemingly self-contradictory movement of radical conservatism. The romantic protest was against change which seemed the product of artificial and not natural historical evolution. The revolt was not against the historically given, but against that which obscured, or blocked, or diverted the historical stream. This is the kind of revolution which has been made by modern conservatives.

What is the "responsibility" of romanticism in light of the foregoing? To be sure the idea of "revolution from the right," activism, contempt for liberal thought, the enthusiasm for the *Volk* and local color, the tendency toward corporate action, the note of irrationalism, these are certainly features which romanticism has in common with Nazism and Fascism. On the other hand, the Fascist organization of society around a dictatorial leader, and party, the ruthless demands for conformity, the nihilistic disregard for "historically" established patterns, morals, and institutions, the creation of new and strained theories and concepts—such as the doctrine of race—by which to interpret history and order society, these demonstrate the divergencies from the very foundation of romantic thought.

Romantic literature, because of its rich and multifarious nature, may, like Scripture, be a source of inspiration—and of ammunition—to the most diverse political views and arguments. Nevertheless, like Scripture, romantic thought has prevailing tendencies. Insofar as these prevailing tendencies have political significance, they clearly tend mostly to the support of a conservative view of the world—to the conservatism of principle, that is, not to a conservatism of interest. In the history of political thought, romanticism as a precursor of conservatism plays a role equivalent to that of the natural rights philosophy as a precursor of liberalism. To give romanticism another part to play, is to obscure its historical significance.

[41] Adam Müller, *Friederich der Grosse*, 100.

[4]

Social Darwinism and Darwin:
Are They Related?

$\mathcal{T}$he period from 1850 to 1870 has been called the Age of Science, not because science reached levels of discovery or application since unsurpassed, but because, for the first time, science or "natural philosophy" displaced philosophy as the prime concern of intellectuals. In the preceding half-century, scientists had been content to experiment. Now, as the century reached the halfway mark, they began to generalize and produce bold thought-provoking theories and—this is important, theories which could be understood by the educated layman. Their ideas were eagerly seized on in popular lectures by such great scientists as Clerk-Maxwell and Faraday, or in scientific best-sellers like Humboldt's *Cosmos* (1849–58).[1]

¶ In this stimulating atmosphere, Charles Darwin published *The Origin of Species* in 1859. His theory of evolution exceeded them all in its provocativeness, impact, and diffusion. As a result, a book meant for scientists and those interested in scientific ideas alarmed the churches and brought the forces of organized religion to bear against Darwin. This battle settled, evolution was taken over by the "social philosophers" and converted into "Social Darwinism," a congeries of theories and other writings which applied conclusions drawn from *The Origin of Species* to human society and made them the popular, social philosophy for a period extending into our own century.

¶ The three selections that follow, all taken from papers prepared for the centenary of *The Origin of Species,* admirably illustrate the process just described. The first, by Basil Willey, a distinguished historian of ideas, explains what was original in Darwin's theory, what Darwin meant to prove, and how he has been misunderstood on both points.

[1] For the ideas in this paragraph the editors are indebted to the excellent first chapter of Robert Binkley, *Realism and Nationalism, 1852–1871* (New York and London: Harper and Brothers, 1935).

The second selection, by Dr. Cyril Bibby, author of a definitive study of Huxley,[2] is concerned with the impact of the *Origin*. Dr. Bibby shows the popular interest in the debates Darwin's theory stirred up and how the indomitable Huxley, Darwin's advocate, crushed the opposition of the churches and the scientist Owen. But in several interesting passages, Dr. Bibby records some unique misgivings Huxley had about his victory and how, great humanist that he was, he fought racist distortions of Darwin's doctrines and broke with his friend Herbert Spencer over them. Spencer, who coined the phrase "survival of the fittest," saw in evolution justification for an extreme laissez-faire government.

While the second selection indicates the beginnings of Social Darwinism, the third selection, by anthropologist George Simpson, is devoted to a critical discussion of Social Darwinism, past and present, pro and con. Professor Simpson also addresses himself to the prickly question of whether or not Darwin was a Social Darwinist himself, a connection Basil Willey or Dr. Bibby would seem to disavow.

WHAT WAS DARWIN'S THEORY?

Basil Willey

* * *

SAMUEL BUTLER used to complain that so many Darwinians spoke of Evolution as if it were Darwin's own invention, whereas Darwin's theory was merely that evolution had come about mainly by natural selection. By now it is generally realised, I suppose, that Darwin's importance lay not in promulgating evolution itself, but in showing how it worked and making people believe in it. According to Butler, "Buffon planted, Erasmus Darwin and Lamarck watered, but it was Mr. Darwin who said 'That fruit is ripe,' and shook it into his lap." This is misleading if it is taken, as

[2] *T. H. Huxley—Scientist, Humanist, Educator* (London: Watts, 1959).

From Basil Willey, "Darwin's Place in the History of Thought," ed., Michael Banton, *Darwinism and The Study of Society—A Centenary Symposium* (London: Tavistock Publications, 1961; Chicago: Quadrangle Books, 1961), pp. 2–5. © Michael Banton, 1961. Reprinted by permission of Quadrangle Books.

Butler meant it to be taken, as an aspersion on Darwin's originality. Darwin did not arrive at his results by reading the works of his precursors, but by studying Nature herself with that infinite patience in observation, coupled with a certain visionary power, which together constitute what we call "genius." In fact, although Darwin had read his grandfather's *Zoonomia* in youth, he knew much less than many of his critics about the previous history of evolutionary thought, and was rather surprised when various "anticipations" were pointed out to him. Butler, the *advocatus diaboli* in this case, was nearer the truth when he wrote (in *Life and Habit,* 1878):

> Less than twenty years ago we never met with, or heard of, anyone who accepted evolution, . . . unless it was that someone now and again said that there was a very dreadful book going about like a rampant lion, called "Vestiges of Creation" . . . Yet now, who seriously disputes the main principles of evolution? . . . It is not he who first conceives an idea . . . but he who makes the people accept the main conclusion . . . who has done the greatest work as regards the promulgation of an opinion. And this is what Mr. Darwin has done for evolution.[1]

Although I am sure that the present audience will not need to be reminded, I should like, before sketching the earlier history of "the development idea," to remind myself of how Darwin, in the famous book whose centenary we are celebrating, summarised his own conclusions. Here are his words, which were inserted in the last chapter of the sixth edition of the *Origin of Species:*

> I have now recapitulated the facts and considerations which have thoroughly convinced me that species have been modified, during a long course of descent. This has been effected chiefly through the natural selection of numerous successive, slight, favourable variations; aided in an important manner by the inherited effects of the use and disuse of parts; and in an unimportant manner . . . by the direct action of external conditions, and by variations which seem to us in our ignorance to arise spontaneously.[2]

A simple-seeming statement: yet behind it stretch years of dogged and devoted labour, and beneath its every phrase lie the volcanic fires of controversy. "That species have been modified"—but the immutability of species, and their origin in special acts of divine creation, was so generally held by theologians and naturalists alike before 1859, that Darwin, writing to J. D. Hooker in 1844 could say: "At last gleams of light have come, and I am almost convinced (quite contrary to the opinion I started with) that species are not (it is like confessing a murder) immutable. . . . I think I have found out," he goes on, "the simple way by which species become exquisitely adapted to various ends." [3] All we need add, in order to complete this preliminary précis of Darwin's position,

---

[1] Samuel Butler, *Life and Habit,* 1924 ed., p. 276.
[2] Darwin, *Origin of Species,* World's Classic edition, 1951, pp. 549–50.
[3] Francis Darwin, *Life and Letters of Charles Darwin,* 1887, vol. II, p. 23.

are the following points: the tendency of all offspring to vary, however slightly, from the parent stock; the enormous fecundity of living creatures, leading to the Malthusian struggle for existence, and the survival of the fittest. Nature, like man when breeding domesticated animals and plants, takes advantage of the favourable variations as and when they are thrown up, and suppresses the unfavourable. Creatures that happen to put forth variations advantageous to them in the struggle, survive and perpetuate themselves; the rest dwindle or perish. Since this Conference is concerned with Darwinism and the Study of Society, I ought also perhaps to mention at this point (what is familiar to you all) that it was the reading of Malthus on Population in 1839 which gave the final shake to the slowly-forming crystal of Darwin's theory. On his return from the voyage of "The Beagle" (1831-6) he had begun systematically to arrange his observations and to collect every possible fact bearing upon the variation of creatures under domestication. He soon saw that "selection was the keynote of man's success in making useful races of animals and plants," but how selection could operate in nature remained as yet a mystery to him. Then (as he says in the *Autobiography*):

In October 1838 . . . I happened to read for amusement [an odd form of diversion, one might think] Malthus on *Population*, and being well prepared to appreciate the struggle for existence which everywhere goes on from long-continued observation of the habits of animals and plants, it at once struck me that under these circumstances favourable variations would tend to be preserved, and unfavourable ones to be destroyed. The result of this would be the formation of new species. Here then, I had at last got a theory by which to work. . . .[4]

In the Cambridge Centenary and Jubilee volume of 1909 (*Darwin and Modern Science*), J. Arthur Thomson pointed out that Malthus also furnished a clue to A. Russel Wallace, and that Herbert Spencer, before 1859, had published an article in the *Westminster Review* on the theory of population, in which he had "come within an ace of recognising that the struggle for existence was a factor in organic evolution." Thomson's comment is that Darwin, Wallace and Spencer had all been "led from a social problem to a biological theory," and that to grasp this correlation with contemporary social problems is more important than to ferret out hints and "anticipations" from older books which Darwin had mostly not read. He further quotes an interesting passage from the article "Biology" in *Chambers' Encyclopaedia,* in which the writer (P. Geddes) argues that the replacement of Paley by Darwin, as chief interpreter of the order of nature, is not just the replacement of anthropomorphism by science, but of an eighteenth century kind of anthropomorphism by a nineteenth century kind. For

"the place vacated by Paley's theological and metaphysical explanation," says Geddes, "has simply been occupied by that suggested to Darwin and Wallace by Malthus in

[4] Lady Nora Barlow (editor), *The Autobiography of C. Darwin,* London, 1958, p. 120.

terms of the prevalent severity of industrial competition, and those phenomena of the struggle for existence which the light of contemporary economic theory has enabled us to discern, have thus come to be temporarily exalted into a complete explanation of organic progress." [5]

This shows what happens when Darwin gets into the clutches of a smart intellectual. We are apt to surrender outright to such swift generalisations, yet how misleading is the suggestion that Darwin saw Nature in terms of the Industrial Revolution! Though a benevolent man, he never bothered about "the condition of England question"; his thoughts hovered over the Galapagos Islands and the coast of Peru much more than over Manchester or Birmingham. On one point only his mind was fixed: how new species are formed; and Malthus meant nothing to him save for his fruitful hint on this process. As Thomson rightly adds, moreover, Darwin at once proceeded to *verify* the formula, and its validity does not depend on what suggested it. It can be safely said, on the other hand, that any debt of Darwin's to social theory was repaid with usury, for many sociologists and others afterwards tried to interpret human history on Darwinian lines, either approving or disapproving of competition and *laissez-faire* according to their political and economic views. Opinion was divided between those who thought that, to secure the best results, the struggle between individuals, classes and nations should go on; and those who held that man, whatever his ancestry, was now an ethical being, and must transcend and control the struggle in the interests of ideal ends.

* * *

Huxley and the Reception of the "Origin"

Cyril Bibby

THE MOST important book of its century, Darwin's *Origin of Species,* catalysed a complete rearrangement of ideological patterns over a wide range of human thought. It is an interesting question why the book's impact was so immense. It was partly, no doubt, that its thesis bore

[5] J. Arthur Thomson, "Darwin's Predecessors"; Ch. II in *Darwin and Modern Science,* Cambridge 1909, p. 15.

From *Victorian Studies* (Darwin Anniversary Issue), Vol. III, No. I (September 1959), pp. 76–86. Reprinted by permission of *Victorian Studies* and the author.

so closely on vital matters of belief and speculation; partly the masterly manner in which vast numbers of facts were marshalled into overwhelming array; partly the deceptive blandness of style and simplicity of statement which allowed readers to imagine that they really understood the book. And yet theories of evolution were not new: they had cropped up repeatedly among the Greeks and Romans, and in more recent times had been proposed by both Lamarck and Darwin's own grandfather. Not even the theory of natural selection was entirely new: although Darwin was unaware of it, he had been in some measure anticipated by W. C. Wells in 1813 and in more detail by Patrick Matthew in 1831.[1] Why, then, since these earlier evolutionists had made comparatively little impression and been but little reviled, was Darwin at once so successful and so abused?

It is a fairly sound general rule that excessive indignation and unreasoning abuse arise from fear and insecurity, and, though the England of 1859 was calm on the surface, on the level of ideology she was deeply apprehensive. The European revolutions from 1789 on were not forgotten; it was not many years since England had suffered widespread riots and arson; there had recently been the Eureka Stockade revolt in Australia and the Mutiny in India; Napoleon III was at war in Italy. In 1845 Newman had seceded to Rome and given the national church a severe fright; in 1846 the English translation of Strauss's *Leben Jesu* had brought a shock from another direction; soon the Christian Socialists were actively spreading novel views; in 1850 came the "Papal Aggression"; in 1853 F. D. Maurice's *Theological Essays,* which led to his ejection from his Chair at London's King's College, gave yet another jolt; in 1858 H. L. Mansel produced his defence of orthodoxy, *The Limits of Religious Thought,* one effect of which was to remind Huxley of the man in Hogarth's election scene, sawing away his opponent's inn sign without noticing that he himself was sitting on it. There was much to indicate the need for closing the ranks of conventional thought against subversive ideas.

This may explain the virulence of some of the opposition to Darwin, but it does not explain all the opposition. To many scientists, including some very eminent ones, the evidence in favour of the transmutation of species appeared inadequate to overturn the traditional (and still scientific) view of independent creation. And today, when one usually thinks of evolution in biological terms, it is well to remember that the very word "biology" was coined only in 1813 and that in this context "scientists" must very largely mean "naturalists." For geologists, in particular, the succession of strata in the rocks, each with its characteristic fossil content, was not implausibly explained as the result of a succession of cataclysms and subsequent creations, a view held even by the master-geologist, Cuvier himself. The Pentateuchal myth, arising among a people influ-

---

[1] W. C. Wells, *Two Essays: One upon Single Vision with Two Eyes; the Other on Dew . . .* (1818); Patrick Matthew, appendix to *Naval Timber and Arboriculture* (1831).

enced by the culture of the recurrently flooded valleys of Tigris and Euphrates, could be presented quite credibly as a record (or folk-memory) of the most recent cataclysm. And, when someone as intelligent as Newman could assert that the value of Revelation was shown by the fact that without it we should never have been able to discover that Noah had preserved the animals in his ark, it is not surprising that the common view of creation was still that versed by Milton a couple of centuries earlier:

> The earth obey'd, and straight,
> Op'ning her fertile womb, teem'd at a birth
> Innumerous living creatures, perfect forms,
> Limb'd and full grown.

To the average believer, Darwin appeared to be not simply promulgating a new scientific theory, but destroying the foundations of belief; and, when a great comparative anatomist like Richard Owen asserted the theory to be untrue, it is not surprising that he and his like were greeted with open arms as scientific advisers to the Establishment.

It was fortunate for the Darwinians that Owen was a man too vain to think that he might be mistaken. Instead of admitting that Huxley was right and he was wrong in the debate about the degree of similarity between man and ape, Owen lost the opportunity to give way gracefully, and so made his position increasingly untenable by a stubborn refusal to face facts. When the fall came, it was in consequence the more resounding, and the *Punch*-reading public was treated to a series of cartoons and squibs reflecting the controversy. One, headed "The Gorrilla's Dilemma," had this touching first stanza:

> Say am I a man and a brother,
> Or only an anthropoid ape?
> Your judgment, be't one way or t'other,
> *Do* put into positive shape.
> Must I humbly take rank as quadruman
> As OWEN maintains that I ought:
> Or rise into brotherhood human,
> As HUXLEY has flatt'ringly taught?
>   (XLIII [18 Oct. 1862], 164)

Owen's defeat was reflected in another set of verses, headed "Monkeyana" and addressed from the Zoological Gardens over the signature of "Gorilla":

> Then HUXLEY and OWEN,
> With rivalry glowing,
> With pen and ink rush to the scratch;
> 'Tis Brain *versus* Brain,
> Till one of them's slain;
> By Jove! it will be a good match! . . .

> Next HUXLEY replies
> That OWEN he lies
> And garbles his Latin quotation;
> That his facts are not new,
> His mistakes not a few,
> Detrimental to his reputation.
>
> To twice slay the slain
> By dint of the Brain
> (Thus HUXLEY concludes his review),
> Is but labour in vain
> Unproductive of gain,
> And so I shall bid you "Adieu!"
>
> (XL [18 May 1861], 206)

For the lower orders, less likely to smile over *Punch* than to chortle over the vigorous burlesque pamphlets of the time, there was "A report of a SAD CASE Recently tried before the Lord Mayor, OWEN *versus* HUXLEY, In which will be found fully given the Merits of the great Recent BONE CASE" (1863), with page after page of this sort of thing:

Policeman X—"Well, your Worship, Huxley called Owen a lying Orthognathous Brachycephalic Bimanous Pithecus; and Owen told him he was nothing but a thorough Archencephalic Primate."
Lord Mayor—"Are you sure you heard this awful language?"

It is difficult today to understand the enormous interest taken by the public of the 1860's in science, when scholars and streetsweepers alike knew that Huxley had proved right and Owen wrong. As Huxley won battle after battle, he rapidly became science personified and the most influential scientist there has ever been in public affairs; his own immense personal prestige seemed like a guarantee that Darwin's theory was correct.

Yet, when powerful and varied ideological interests are defeated so quickly and so completely as in this case, there are likely to be contributory causes deep down below the surface appearance of things. It is true that Darwin's patient accumulation of evidence provided a much more powerful brief than any predecessor had prepared. (Huxley noted, "Mr. Darwin abhors mere speculation as nature abhors a vacuum. He is as greedy of cases and precedents as any constitutional lawyer."[2]), but not even the scientific world would have been so quickly convinced had it not been already in a sense awaiting conviction.

Below the public surface of geological orthodoxy, firmly based on catastrophism, there had never ceased to flow many private rivulets of doubt. On the Continent, from Fracastoro and Leonardo in the sixteenth century and Steno in the seventeenth to Desmarest in the eighteenth, there had been those who

2 "The Darwinian Hypothesis," *Collected Essays* (1893), II, 20.

suspected that the past of the earth could be explained in terms of forces presently observable. In 1785 England saw the publication of James Hutton's *Theory of the Earth,* a splendidly argued exposition of uniformitarian geology. Hutton failed to make much impression, but meanwhile more canals were being cut and before long a great burst of railway construction made it easy for Englishmen to make geological observations at home, in addition to those made during increasingly popular European travel and on long sea cruises. When the first volume of Charles Lyell's *Principles of Geology* appeared in 1830, to be discounted by most of the geological mandarins, many of the younger men were immensely impressed by its argument that the earth had slowly evolved into its present form, and the second volume dealt with plant and animal life in a manner which somehow only just failed to assert its evolution. No doubt there were many who still believed, and more who affected to believe, that old John Lightfoot of Cambridge had been correct in asserting that "Man was created by the Trinity on 23rd October, 4004 B.C., at nine o'clock in the morning," but some were beginning to think in terms of millions and hundreds of millions of years rather than in thousands. Long before the *Origin* appeared, the impregnable rock of Scripture was suffering slow erosion, ultimately as effective as the erosion which the uniformitarian geologists postulated for the earthly rocks. Geological theory, despite its firm surface, was in a flux within, and the impact of Darwin's book was sufficient to crack it wide open.

Biology, too, new as it was, was already on the verge of a fundamental reassessment. Erasmus Darwin's *Zoönomia* (1794) made as little impression on most people as it did on the young Charles Darwin, "the proportion of speculation being so large to the facts given," [3] and even Lamarck's much better based *Philosophie zoologique* (1809) was little known in England. Darwin, indeed, denied that men's minds were already prepared for his theory, asserting that he "never happened to come across a single one who seemed to doubt about the permanence of species," but he immediately followed this with the more significant remark that "innumerable well-observed facts were stored in the minds of naturalists, ready to take their proper places as soon as any theory which would receive them was sufficiently explained" (*Autobiography,* p. 124). Increasingly, with accumulating biological knowledge, the idea of independent creation had become less credible, and many, even outside the professional ranks of biology, were beginning to entertain the possibility of evolution.

This may help in part to explain the ready response which Darwin's book received among those who were not too deeply committed to orthodoxy. Even Sir Charles Lyell, "up to that time a pillar of the anti-transmutationists (who regarded him, ever afterwards, as Pallas Athene may have looked at Dian, after the Endymion affair)," [4] declared himself a Darwinian and was a tower of

---

[3] *The Autobiography of Charles Darwin,* ed. Nora Barlow (London, 1958), p. 49.
[4] *Life and Letters of Charles Darwin,* ed. Francis Darwin, 3 vols. (1887), II, 231.

strength. As for the younger men, T. H. Huxley and Alfred Newton [5] were probably not the only ones to declare their vexation at not having thought out so simple an explanation of things for themselves. Far away in New Zealand Samuel Butler received the book as a flash of illumination; at home the first edition was sold out on the day of publication and the second soon after; in Europe translations rapidly appeared in many languages and the vast literature of "Darwinismus" soon called up regular German bibliographies. People were ready for an evolutionary explanation of things and natural selection provided a credible mechanism simple enough to be understood by scientist and layman alike.

The major battle between evolution and orthodoxy, highlighted by the 1860 Oxford clash between Professor Huxley and Bishop Wilberforce, has been often enough described. What is sometimes comparatively neglected is that there were many clergy quite ready to come to terms with the new scientific outlook. Even Newman, despite his conversion to Rome, saw no especial intellectual difficulty in accepting organic evolution (with, of course, certain theological reservations about the human soul), and in the Church of England there were men who accepted the idea from the start. This was a time when, as G. M. Young has remarked, "English society was poised on a double paradox . . . Its practical ideals were at odds with its religious professions, and its religious belief was at issue with its intelligence." [6] Charles Kingsley was one of those who were anxious to bring their religion into line with their intelligence and their practice into line with their religion—once, indeed, he commented to Grant Duff, in his curious stammer, "We shall never do any good, till we have got rid of those o—dious words Re—ligion and Christi—anity." [7]

Kingsley's views come out very clearly in his fascinating correspondence [8] with Huxley. The two had first met in 1855, and four years later Kingsley wrote to express appreciation of Huxley's review of Darwin's book in *Macmillan's*. In the following year, when Huxley suffered the death of his first child Noel, the clergyman sent him a letter of consolation which evoked from Huxley a baring of the soul quite exceptional for so self-controlled a man, and thereafter they were close friends. Kingsley had no qualms whatever about accepting Darwin's theory, and Huxley wrote "it is clear to me that if that great and powerful instrument for good or evil, the Church of England, is to be saved from being shivered into fragments by the advancing tide of science—an event I should be very sorry to witness, but which will infallibly occur if men like Samuel of Oxford are to have the guidance of her destinies—it must be by the efforts of

[5] Alfred Newton (1829–1907) was appointed first professor of zoology and comparative anatomy at Cambridge in 1866.
[6] "Portrait of an Age" in *Early Victorian England* (London, 1934), II, 426.
[7] Mountstuart E. Grant Duff, *Notes from a Diary, 1886–1888* (1900), I, 170.
[8] In the muniments of the Imperial College of Science and Technology.

men, who, like yourself, see your way to the combination of the practice of the Church with the spirit of science. . . . I don't profess to understand the logic of yourself, Maurice, and the rest of your school, but I have always said I would swear by your truthfulness, and sincerity, and that good must come of your efforts" (23 Sept. 1860).

Soon, indeed, it was Huxley who was the restraining influence, and by the spring of 1863 he was warning Kingsley that there was as yet no evidence that selection could produce specific sterility: "From the first time that I wrote about Darwin's book in the *Times* and in the *Westminster* until now, it has been obvious to me that this is the weak point of Darwin's doctrine. He *has* shown that selective breeding is a *vera causa* for morphological species; he has not yet shown it a *vera causa* for physiological species" (30 Apr. 1863). It was in this year that Kingsley's satire *The Water Babies* appeared, with its suggestion that, if any water baby were ever found, it would be divided between Professors Huxley and Owen for examination (p. 44).[9] How well Kingsley kept in touch with scientific developments is indicated by his incidental reference to *Archaeopteryx* (p. 47), discovered only shortly before his fairy tale went to press. Many a nursemaid must have read to her charges the account of how Professor Ptthmllnsprts (presumably "Put-them-all-in-spirits") "got up once at the British Association, and declared that apes had hippopotamus majors in their brains as men have" (p. 94)—but perhaps few of them recognized the reference to Huxley's 1860 assertion that the brain of the ape contained a *hippocampus minor*. And, as Kingsley continued, this was a shocking thing to say, "for, if it were so, what would become of the faith, hope, and charity of immortal millions?" Even more illuminating is the account of "the great and famous nation of the Doasyoulikes," living "at the foot of the Happy-go-lucky Mountains, where flapdoodle grows wild," who by a slow process of retrogressive evolution eventually became apes. "Yes," said the fairy solemnly, "there are two sides to every question, and a downhill as well as an uphill road; and if I can turn beasts into men, I can, by the same laws of circumstance, and selection, and competition, turn men into beasts" (p. 140).

Huxley told Kingsley, "I am quite as ready to admit your doctrine that souls secrete bodies as I am the opposite one that bodies secrete souls—simply because I deny the possibility of obtaining any evidence as to the truth or falsehood of either hypothesis . . . If you tell me that an Ape differs from a Man because the latter has a soul and the ape has not, I can only say that it may be so . . . until you satisfy me as to the soundness of your method of investigation, I must adhere to what seems to my mind a simpler form of notation—*i.e.,* to suppose that all phenomena have the same substratum (if they have any), and that soul and body, or mental and physical phenomena, are merely diverse manifestations of that hypothetical substratum" (22 May 1863). As for retrogressive evolution,

9 Page references are to the Watergate Classic ed. (1948).

Huxley was in agreement that "So far from a gradual progress towards perfection forming any necessary part of the Darwinian creed, it appears to us that it is perfectly consistent with indefinite persistence in one state, or with a gradual retrogression." [10]

Nevertheless, this fallacious notion of inevitable progress towards perfection as a necessary corollary of natural selection greatly helped the acceptance of Darwinism. The validity of a scientific theory is nowise determined by its consonance or conflict with popular opinion, or by the readiness of experts to move in its direction, or by the personal characters of its proponents or opponents, or by its convenience as ideological camouflage for vested interests. All these, however, may markedly influence the speed with which a new theory gains ground, and this was conspicuously the case with Darwin's theory. Had there not been widespread readiness to accept some sort of evolutionary ideas; had not the geological work of Lyell and others prepared the minds of scientists for the idea that massive changes can be brought about by small causes granted only sufficient time; had not Darwin already established a reputation for meticulous work and earned the admiration of fellow-scientists for his conscientiousness and their affection for his modesty, and had not Huxley been so brilliant an advocate and so dauntless an agent-general; and had not the idea of "the survival of the fittest" so admirably provided a sort of pseudo-scientific sanction for the apologists of laissez-faire capitalism, there is no knowing how long the opposition to Darwin might not have maintained its strength. As things were, the worst of the abuse was spent within a decade, and after another decade what opposition remained was thoroughly respectful. Several genuine gaps in Darwin's evidence happened to be quite quickly filled—the discovery of *Archaeopteryx* provided one of the hypothecated "missing links," study of *Amphioxus* cast light upon the borderland between vertebrate and invertebrate, embryological research went apace, and the massively accumulating fossil evidence (especially in America) tended to crush opposition by its mere weight. And, with geologising become the favourite hobby of half the country clergymen, criticism was disarmed where it might most have flourished.

As early as 1863 Kingsley was writing to Maurice, "Darwin is conquering everywhere and rushing in like a flood, by the mere force of truth and fact." [11] What was really happening was that the general idea of evolution was running in like a flood, Darwin having opened the floodgates, but the flood was not pure Darwin and the force was not merely that of truth and fact. In 1861 came Maine's *Ancient Law,* in 1863 Huxley's *Man's Place in Nature* and Lyell's *Antiquity of Man,* in 1865 McLennan's *Primitive Marriage* and Tylor's *Early History of Mankind,* in 1866 Marx's *Kapital* and Bagehot's *English Constitution.*

[10] "Criticisms on 'The Origin of Species,' " *Collected Essays,* II, 90–91.

[11] *Charles Kingsley: His Letters and Memories of His Life,* ed. Mrs. Kingsley, abr. version (1883), p. 253.

Evolutionary assumptions and ways of thinking rapidly spread through anthropology, history, and theology, and in the process Darwin's own great personal contribution became obscured. "I cannot understand why you scientific people make such a fuss about Darwin," remarked Matthew Arnold to John Judd in 1871, "Why, it's all in Lucretius." [12] In the same year St. George Mivart published his *Genesis of Species* and claimed that evolution was not merely compatible with Roman Catholicism but actually approved by the Jesuit Father Suarez—a claim which at once sent Huxley to the Latin text and led him, as he said, to "come out in the new character of a defender of Catholic orthodoxy, and upset Mivart out of the mouth of his own prophet." [13] In his "Mr. Darwin's Critics" Huxley declared roundly, "If Suarez has rightly stated Catholic doctrine, then is evolution utter heresy. And such I believe it to be" (*Collected Essays*, II, 147). Huxley was quite right, but it is an interesting commentary on the trend of opinion that within twelve years of the appearance of Darwin's book he had to be *proclaiming* its heresy. Nine years later he reminded the Royal Institution that "it is the customary fate of new truths to begin as heresies and to end as superstitions; and, as matters now stand, it is hardly rash to anticipate that, in another twenty years, the new generation . . . will be in danger of accepting the main doctrines of the 'Origin of Species,' with as little reflection, and it may be with as little justification, as so many of our contemporaries, twenty years ago, rejected them." [14]

Darwin's doctrines, unfortunately, were not simply accepted, but badly distorted. The idea that natural selection led inevitably to the "survival of the fittest" appealed greatly to the "Whites," who were so evidently surviving better than the "Blacks" in the world of the nineteenth century. So, just as in earlier days the apologists of slavery were able to quote selected Bible texts, now the spokesmen of "White" supremacy were able to pick passages from Darwin. To Darwin himself the slavery system was an abomination, and Huxley urged by lecture and in print that the results of miscegenation depended upon the social setting and that there was no reason to assume that primitive peoples were incapable of advancement,[15] but pseudo-Darwinian justification of racial discrimination continued to make headway. Similarly, despite Huxley's repeated insistence that intellectual ability was not the prerogative of any one social class, that "he did not believe that if 100 men were picked out of the highest aristocracy in the land and 100 out of the lowest class there would be any difference of capacity among them," [16] that "the 'points' of a good or of a bad citizen are really far harder to discern than those of a puppy or a short-horn calf," [17] the

[12] J. W. Judd, *The Coming of Evolution* (1910), p. 3.
[13] *Life and Letters of Thomas Henry Huxley*, ed. Leonard Huxley (1900), I, 392.
[14] "The Coming of Age of 'The Origin of Species,'" *Collected Essays*, II, 229.
[15] *Birmingham Daily Post* (7–12 Oct. 1867).
[16] *Daily Chronicle* (8 June 1887).
[17] "Evolution and Ethics. Prolegomena," *Collected Essays*, IX, 23.

movement for eugenic reform developed a markedly anti-artisan bias, somewhat corrected only in the last couple of decades.

Even more crude was the distortion of Darwin to justify ruthless competitive capitalism. Men might starve, and women and children slave away for a mere pittance in the mines and mills, but all would be for the best in the end—the fittest would survive and the race thereby improve. Perhaps it is not the whole truth to call this the distortion of Darwin, for Herbert Spencer had arrived at evolutionary ideas quite independently and the phrase "survival of the fittest" was his own. As early as 1852 he had delivered to the British Association a paper "A Theory of Population, deduced from the General Law of Animal Fertility," and in the same year he developed in the *Leader* a view of evolution much on Lamarckian lines. Unfortunately, once the opposition to Darwin had been thoroughly defeated and discredited, all sorts of bastard speculation seemed legitimised; and, as a friend of Darwin and Huxley, Spencer was able to appear to the undiscriminating as a spokesman of the new knowledge. When Huxley told the Birmingham and Midland Institute, as his "Administrative Nihilism" (1871) put it, that the extreme laissez-faire view favoured "neither a monarchy, an aristocracy, nor a democracy, but an *astynomocracy, or police government*" (*Collected Essays*, I, 259), Spencer developed an attack on his friend. Seventeen years later the two were still at loggerheads on this issue, and Huxley's "Struggle for Existence in Human Society" (*Collected Essays*, IX, 195–236) led, as he had realised that it would, to a quarrel with Spencer. From the point of view of the moralist, Huxley maintained, the animal world is at about the level of a gladiators' show, and the ethical man must not fight out the struggle for existence like any other animal but devote his best energies to setting limits to the struggle. As late as 1893, in his Romanes Lecture on "Evolution and Ethics," he was still trying to combat this sort of misapplication of evolutionary theory, but the Spencers and the Nassau Seniors won. As Huxley remarked, in language worthy of Engels, "men have become absorbed in the mere accumulation of wealth; and as this is a matter in which the plainest and strongest form of self-interest is intensely concerned, science (in the shape of Political Economy) has readily demonstrated that self-interest may be safely left to find the best way of attaining its ends." [18]

The impact of the *Origin of Species* was immense, but it was not only scientific and theological orthodoxy which it shattered. Everything was put into flux, and some of the directions of flow were in an ethical and political sense reactionary. Now, a century later, we have the task of disentangling the true from the false, the applications from the misapplications, the good effects from the bad effects, and a mighty task it still is.

[18] "Administrative Nihilism," *Collected Essays*, I, 268.

Darwin and "Social Darwinism"

George E. Simpson

LIKE HOLY Writ, Darwinism is suscep-
tible to many interpretations. Aristocrats and democrats, Marxists and racists,
militarists and pacificists, social scientists and biological scientists have read and
re-read, interpreted and re-interpreted Darwin.

In *The Origin of Species* Darwin attributed the diverse forms of life and the
evolution of complex animals from simpler ones to "a Ratio of Increase so high
as to lead to a Struggle for Life, and as a consequence to Natural Selection,
entailing Divergence of Characters and the Extinction of less-improved forms."
In *The Descent of Man* he thought that the "ape-like" progenitors of man, like
other animals, must have tended to increase beyond their means of subsistence
and thus to have been involved in a struggle for existence and to the "rigid
law of natural selection." Groups composed of the largest number of individuals
possessing physical variations best adapted for gaining subsistence or for defending themselves would survive in greater numbers and produce more offspring than groups less well-endowed.

In dealing with the struggle for existence in early human tribes, Darwin
acknowledged the influence of the physical nature of the country, and he attributed some importance in this struggle to the size and stature of the men.
Greater importance, however, was given to intellectual powers (which, he said,
tend to be inherited), to superiority in the arts, and to social and moral qualities.
Such faculties as sympathy, fidelity, and courage were held to have been acquired through natural selection, "aided by inherited habit."

Kropotkin contended that Darwin's followers, including Herbert Spencer
and T. H. Huxley, "reduced the notion of struggle to its narrowest limits."
Huxley's paper on the "Struggle for Existence and Its Bearing Upon Man"
stated that among primitive men, as among animals, "the weakest and stupidest
went to the wall, while the toughest and shrewdest, those who were best fitted to
cope with their circumstances but not best in another way, survived. Life was a
continuous free fight, and beyond the limited and temporary relations of the
family, the Hobbesian war of each against all was the normal state of existence." [1]

From *Antioch Review*, XIX (Spring 1959), pp. 33–45. Reprinted by permission.

[1] Quoted in P. Kropotkin, *Mutual Aid*, New York, McClure Phillips & Co., 1902, p. 4. (Huxley's
paper was published in 1888.) George Nasmyth (*Social Progress and the Darwinian Theory*, New
York, G. P. Putnam's Sons, 1916, p. 33) points out that Huxley wrote of ethical factors and limits
to the struggle in later periods of history.

Early Social Darwinism

The application of Darwin's principle of natural selection to human society, with special emphasis on competition and struggle, became known as "Social Darwinism." This doctrine, congenial to the intellectual climate of the end of the nineteenth century, was endorsed by the advocates of unrestricted competition in private enterprise, the colonial expansionists, and the opponents of voluntary social change. Among others, Ernst Haeckel provided scientific sanction for this point of view.

The theory of selection teaches that in human life, as in animal and plant life, everywhere and at all times, only a small and chosen minority can exist and flourish, while the enormous majority starve and perish miserably and more or less prematurely. . . . The cruel and merciless struggle for existence which rages through living nature, and in the course of nature *must* rage, this unceasing and inexorable competition of all living creatures is an incontestable fact; only the picked minority of the qualified fittest is in a position to resist it successfully, while the great majority of the competitors must necessarily perish miserably. We may profoundly lament this tragical state of things, but we can neither controvert nor alter it. "Many are called, but few are chosen." This principle of selection is as far as possible from democratic; on the contrary it is aristocratic in the strictest sense of the word.[2]

Herbert Spencer and William Graham Sumner were prominent in advancing the doctrine of the social Darwinists. Despite differences in their philosophies, both saw the poor as the "unfit." Because they are the result of the operations of the laws of evolution, they cannot be assisted and efforts to help them through legislation, public charity, and social reconstruction are evil.[3] According to Spencer, "The whole effort of nature is to get rid of them, and make room for better. . . . If they are sufficiently complete to live, they *do* live, and it is well they should live. If they are not sufficiently complete to live, they die, and it is best they should die." [4]

Although Darwin pointed out that militarism and war occasion reverse selection by exposing the biologically soundest young men to early death or preventing them from marrying during the prime of life and, at the same time, by providing those with poorer constitutions with greater opportunity to marry and propogate their kind, many of the social Darwinists praised war as a means of furthering social progress. Among these, one of the most influential was Ludwig Gumplowicz, Austrian jurist and sociologist. In his doctrine,

[2] Ernst Haeckel, "Freedom in Science and Teaching," p. 93. Quoted in George Nasmyth, *op. cit.,* p. 6.

[3] John W. Bennett, review of Richard Hofstadter, *Social Darwinism in American Thought,* University of Pennsylvania Press, 1944, in *American Anthropologist* 47 (1954), p. 448.

[4] Herbert Spencer, *Social Statics,* New York, D. Appleton & Co., 1864, pp. 414–415.

social and cultural evolution was due solely to the struggle of social groups, with inter-group war functioning socially as the struggle for existence and the survival of the fittest function in the case of individuals.[5] An English scientist, Karl Pearson, wrote: "History shows me one way and one way only, in which a high state of civilization has been produced, namely the struggle of race with race, and the survival of the physically and mentally fitter race. If men want to know whether the lower races of man can evolve a higher type, I fear the only course is to leave them to fight it out among themselves."

Nineteenth century imperialists, calling upon Darwinism in defense of the subjugation of "backward" races, "could point to *The Origin of Species* which had referred in its sub-title to *The Preservation of Favored Races in the Struggle for Life*. Darwin had been talking about pigeons but they saw no reason why his theories should not apply to men, and the whole spirit of the naturalistic world-view seemed to call for a vigorous and unrelenting thoroughness in the application of biological concepts." [6] Darwinian theory was utilized to justify the conflicts of rival empires, the ententes and the alliances of the "balance of power." Bismarck in Germany, Chamberlain in England, and Theodore Roosevelt in the United States found in social Darwinism a sanction for their theories of force and expansion.

Another aspect of social Darwinism at the turn of the century was the eugenics movement. Like other early social Darwinists, the eugenicists equated the "fit" with the upper classes and the "unfit" with the poor. Believing that disease, poverty, and crime are due largely to heredity, they warned against the high reproductive rates of the lower classes. As Hofstadter shows, they differed from earlier social Darwinists in that they failed "to draw laissez-faire conclusions, and depended for a part of their own program upon state action."

Was Darwin a Social Darwinist?

Students of Darwin's work are divided on the question of whether he was a social Darwinist. Hofstadter remarks that "there was nothing in Darwinism that inevitably made it an apology for competition or force. Kropotkin's interpretation of Darwinism was as logical as Sumner's." George Nasmyth, a pacifist who popularized the work of Kropotkin and of Jacques Novicow, went further and claimed that social Darwinism was founded upon "a gross distortion of Darwin's own theory of social progress." Nasmyth contrasted Darwin's theory of society, "held together from within by the cementing power of the moral sense and social instincts," with "the philosophy of force, as represented in the sociology of Spencer, Ward, and Ratzenhofer, in which society is held together

---

[5] Howard Becker and Harry E. Barnes, *Social Thought from Lore to Science,* I, 2nd ed., Harren Press, Washington, D.C., 1952, p. 713.
[6] R. Hofstadter, *op. cit.,* pp. 146–147.

only by the external force exerted by some other society, this society having been constituted and held together in some miraculous way." Nasmyth goes so far as to say that "the inclusion of the entire human race within the bounds of the moral law—the federation of the world—becomes, therefore, in the true Darwinian theory, the ultimate goal of human evolution." He felt that Darwin had exposed the harsh reasoning of those who attributed social advance to competition, war, and opposition to reform. Asserting that Darwin had emphasized the importance of charitable actions, he added that such actions "tend to take the form in modern legislation of old age pensions, mothers' pensions, sickness and accident insurance and other social measures. . . ."

Other scholars have reached an opposite conclusion. Sweezy thinks the evidence that Darwin gave "the sanction of his great reputation to the reactionary doctrines now associated with his name under the term social Darwinism" is unmistakable.[7] As proof he cites this passage in *The Descent of Man*:

> With savages, the weak in body or mind are soon eliminated; and those that survive commonly exhibit a vigorous state of health. We civilized men, on the other hand, do our utmost to check the process of elimination; we build asylums for the imbecile, the maimed, and the sick; we institute poor-laws; and our medical men exert their utmost skill to save the life of everyone to the last moment. There is reason to believe that vaccination has preserved thousands, who from a weak constitution would formerly have succumbed to small-pox. Thus the weak members of civilized societies propagate their kind. No one who has attended to the breeding of domestic animals will doubt that this must be highly injurious to the race of man.

Bernhard Stern quoted the following passage from the same work in his claim that Darwin subscribed to the eugenic creed:

> The advancement of the welfare of mankind is a most intricate problem; all ought to refrain from marriage who cannot avoid abject poverty for their children; for poverty is not only a great evil but tends to its own increase by leading to recklessness in marriage. On the other hand, as Mr. Galton has remarked, if the prudent avoid marriage while the reckless marry, the inferior members tend to supplant the better members of society.

According to Stern, such a view applies natural selection mechanically to man, disparages the contribution of preventive medicine, and attacks the poor laws "as coddling the poverty stricken who are identified as inferior stock."[8]

While Geoffrey West thinks that Darwin himself was more elastic in his view of natural selection than most of his interpreters, "the effect of his treatment of the Struggle is infinitely more one of competition than co-operation. . . . Popular Darwinism may be a crude but it is scarcely an unfair or inaccurate presentation of the broad effect of Darwin's basic writings."[9]

---

7 P. Sweezy, "Social Darwinism," *Science and Society*, 6 (1942), p. 76.

8 Bernhard Stern, "Social Darwinism," *ibid.*, p. 76.

9 Geoffrey West, *Charles Darwin*, Yale University Press, 1938, pp. 327–328.

Although he calls attention to passages in *The Descent of Man* which empha- size the role of the co-operative spirit, Sir Arthur Keith expresses surprise that Darwin took "the action of his law of Natural Selection in bringing about the extermination of the less civilized by the more civilized peoples in such a spirit of indifference." [10]

To the present writer, Montagu's appraisal of Darwin's position seems judicious.

If it is true that the appeal to Darwinian theory for support of a social system based on ruthless competition and exploitation of colonial peoples represents a misin- terpretation of evolutionary theory, the conclusion seems inescapable that Darwin himself was the first to make this misinterpretation. The few passages in which Darwin mentions altruism and cooperation come exclusively from *The Descent of Man,* where in a book of a thousand pages they are virtually crowded out by numer- ous statements that appear to stand in direct and unequivccal contradiction to them.[11]

Social Darwinism in Recent Years

Adolf Hitler's racism and Nazism have been called perversions of Darwin- ism. Hitler's virulent doctrines were the culmination of a half-century of social Darwinistic thinking in Germany. One of his most influential immediate predecessors was General Friedrich von Bernhardi, who said of the Germans that "no nation on the face of the globe is so able to grasp and appropriate all the elements of culture, to add to them from the stores of its own spiritual en- dowment, and to give back to mankind richer gifts than it received." [12] In- spired by Heraclitus, Goethe, Treitschke, Frederick the Great, Clauss Wagner, von Schlegal, Schiller, and Clausewitz, Bernhardi glorified war as a biological necessity, as the greatest factor in the furtherance of culture and power, and claimed that the Germans could fulfill their great and urgent duty toward civilization only by the sword.

Hitler's doctrines are so well-known that extended reference to them here is unnecessary. According to *Mein Kampf,* the "Aryan" alone "furnishes the great building-stones and plans for all human progress," The Aryan had subjugated "lower races" and made them do his will, the Jew's "intellect is never construc- tive," "the mingling of blood . . . is the sole reason for the dying-out of old cultures," and hyperindividualism had cheated Germany of world domination and a peace "founded on the victorious sword of a lordly people. . . ." Hitler- ism represents the most extreme variety of social Darwinism and the one

[10] Sir Arthur Keith, *Darwin Revalued,* London, Watts & Co., 1955, p. 264.

[11] Ashley Montagu, *Darwin, Competition, and Cooperation,* Henry Schuman, 1952, p. 96. On page 132 of this work, Montagu says that Nasmyth "errs in claiming Darwin not to be a social Darwinist."

[12] F. von Bernhardi, *Germany and the Next War,* New York, Longmans, Green & Co., 1914. Originally published in 1912.

which has had the most powerful effects on the destinies of modern peoples.

Echoes of social Darwinism are found in some of E. A. Hooton's writings. During World War II he wrote:

Now if there is anything which can complete the ruin of the human animal which has been victimized by the machine, it is public charity and institutionalized care. . . . The reason why medicine has worked such biological havoc in civilized society is that it is coerced and intimidated by an imbecilic manifestation of humanitarian policy, which demands that human life be regarded as sacred. . . . The great European democracies, France and England handled this postwar anthropological situation with the same humanitarian stupidity which is a consistent policy of the United States. . . . They listened to the voices of the proletariat and allowed themselves to be weakened further by governments of socialistic and communistic incompetents who preached economic and personal equality and worshipped worthlessness. . . . We must rid ourselves of the false prophets of cultural salvation and witless preachers of human equality. . . . The future of man is dependent on biology. We must have fewer and better men, not more morons and machines.[13]

More recently, W. H. Sheldon's studies of constitutional types have included social Darwinistic views on race and war.[14]

* * *

Sheldon claims that where conditions are "both soft and unregulated, our best stock tends to be outbred by stock that is inferior to it in every respect." He urges that we adopt

the view that war is the cheapest way out of the mess we have got into. Grim, decimative war carried to the point of settling on a power basis the question of political organization of the planetary population. . . . Birth control movements, except when universally enforced by political power, constitute only another monkey trap. Since as yet a central political power has not been established for our time, any talk of birth control now is like pacifism. This is to build the second story of the house before the first.

An interesting type of social Darwinism in modern dress combines a knowledge of genetics with racism, mutualism, and a formula on race mixture. Citing the United States as "an experiment in the study of the values of races," C. D. Darlington attributes the strength of this country partly to genetic recombination between diverse races but "also, perhaps even more, to the unrecombined diversity." He contends that

from the point of view of supporting a population of human beings there can be no doubt that the white-plus-Negro society is more efficient than the Indian was or ever

---

[13] E. A. Hooton, *Why Men Behave Like Apes and Vice Versa*, Princeton University Press, 1940, pp. xvi–xix, xxv.

[14] W. H. Sheldon, E. M. Hartl, and E. McDermott, *Varieties of Delinquent Youth*, New York, Harper and Brothers, 1949, pp. 813, 836, 881.

could be. And the disparity is still increasing. Why? A white society alone would probably be little more numerous than the whites in the mixed society. A Negro society alone, even if not cut off from all intercourse with whites (to judge from the experiment in Liberia) would certainly support far fewer Negroes than there are in the mixed society. The advantage of the white-plus-Negro society is that its two racially dissimilar elements are able and willing (although only just willing) to help one another. The American Indian has been found not to be able and willing to help the other two. Their capacity and his capacity are both, of course, racial and genetic. They are determined and limited by heredity.

People, like water and vinegar, Darlington says, are different. He believes that "the future of mankind rests with those genetically diverse groups, whether races or classes, which can practice mutual help and show mutual respect. Neither of these habits can be assisted in the long run by a make-believe of equality in the physical, intellectual and cultural capacities of such groups." In his view, all races and classes have something to contribute and a plea is made for (a) "a balance . . . between the genetically differentiated elements of every nation and of all the nations of the world," and (b) "a balance . . . between inbreeding and outbreeding." [15]

Criticisms of Social Darwinism

The Russian sociologist, Jacques Novicow (1849–1912), was one of the first writers to devote himself to the refutation of the doctrine that unmitigated struggle for existence is the chief factor in human progress. In Novicow's view, the struggle for existence becomes in human society primarily an intellectual rather than a physical type of conflict. He predicted that intellectual conflict within societies would increase, be accompanied by an increase of justice and sympathy and a decrease of hatred, and bring about the survival of the best individuals.

In 1902, Petr Kropotkin wrote of the two aspects of animal life in Eastern Siberia and Northern Manchuria which had impressed him most—the severity of the struggle for existence against a formidable Nature, and the absence of the bitter struggle for existence among animals of the same species in spots where animal life was abundant. Under the former conditions, the distinctive feature was under-population rather than over-population. Wherever he observed scores of species and millions of individuals (colonies of rodents, flights of birds, a migration of fallow-deer), he saw mutual aid and mutual support which led him to conclude that this feature was highly important for the maintenance of life and the preservation and further evolution of each species. He saw further that when animals have to struggle mightily against scarcity of food (e.g., semi-wild cattle and horses, wild ruminants, squirrels), the portion

[15] C. D. Darlington, *The Facts of Life*, Macmillan, 1953, pp. 292–294.

of the species affected by the calamity "comes out of the ordeal so much impoverished in vigor and health that no progressive evolution of the species can be based on such periods of keen competition." Consequently, Kropotkin was unable to accept the view that the struggle for the means of subsistence, of every animal against all other animals of its own species, and of every man against all other men, was a natural law. Instead he was convinced that the practice of mutual aid has created the conditions of social life "in which man was enabled to develop his arts, knowledge, and intelligence."

Dobzhansky and Allen point out that natural selection in man comes about through the survival of the genetically fit, not of the genetically fittest. Calling Spencer's "survival of the fittest" an effective slogan in the campaign to get the theory of evolution accepted, they say it greatly overstated the fierceness of the struggle for existence.[16]

Ashley Montagu has called attention to the criticisms of one-sided Darwinism made by a number of outstanding modern biologists, including S. J. Holmes, Patrick Geddes, J. Arthur Thomson, George Gaylord Simpson, Theodosius Dobzhansky, Marston Bates, Warder C. Allee, William Patten, John Muirhead Macfarlane, Ralph Lillie, and Herman J. Muller. According to these scientists, co-operative forces are biologically more important and vital than struggle.[17] Attempting to resolve the competition-co-operation issue, Montagu writes:

Competition of every kind exists in the state of nature and has, of course, played an important role in the evolution of the varieties of life, but so has co-operation. In the struggle for existence one group may be competitively more successful than another because it is more co-operative. Certainly, so far as the persistence or continuation of every group is concerned, natural selection favors the *co-operative* as opposed to the *disoperative* struggling for survival.[18]

The Present Status of the Concept of Natural Selection

The view that "life is a struggle for existence in which only the fit survive, the fittest being those who have whatever it takes to survive" has been called "the Darwinian fallacy." [19] The concept of natural selection has not been discarded, but it has undergone revision. While the process of combative competition and struggle may occasionally result in one type producing a larger number of surviving progeny than another, this is not always the case. If the selection is severe, the reserves of genetic variability are soon depleted.[20]

In the evolutionary sense, fitness means that one genotype leaves more

[16] Theodosius Dobzhansky and Gordon Allen, "Does Natural Selection Continue to Operate in Modern Mankind?", *American Anthropologist*, 58 (August, 1956), p. 593.

[17] Ashley Montagu, *Darwin, Competition and Cooperation*, pp. 48–69.

[18] Ashley Montagu, *The Direction of Human Development*, New York, Harper and Brothers, 1955, p. 27.

[19] Ashley Montagu, *Darwin, Competition and Cooperation*, pp. 17–18.

[20] T. Dobzhansky and Gordon Allen, *op. cit.*, p. 593.

surviving progeny than another in the same environment. According to Dobzhansky: "The superiority may result from the fact that individuals of one genetic type are stronger and more resistant to environmental hazards, and live longer than individuals of other genetic types. Or one type may be more sexually active or more fecund than another. Individual vigor and fecundity are not necessarily correlated, and a superior fecundity may compensate or even overcompensate for deficient vigor." [21]

To J. B. S. Haldane the application of Darwinism to contemporary capitalist society would be that the poor are fitter than the rich because they leave more offspring behind them in each generation.[22] Replying to Mr. Haldane, Bernhard Stern called attention to the importance of social tradition (e.g., knowledge of birth control, influence of religious tradition, changing attitudes concerning family life) in determining family size.[23]

Darwin's opposition to birth control, on the ground that "overmultiplication was useful, since it caused a struggle for existence in which only the strongest and the ablest survived," seems outmoded. Geoffrey West remarks that now "intelligent birth control is as much a factor for survival as co-operation."

In shaping the genetic equipment of homo sapiens in the past, natural selection contributed to the development of culture. Culture has been such a successful nonbiological adaptive instrument that man has become specialized to live in man-made environments.[24] Despite the claims of the social Darwinists, social improvement seems to be due mainly to advances in technology and social organization rather than to breeding or selective elimination. Self-preservation is no longer a sufficient motive for living. Modern man determines what "the conditions and standards of a tolerable existence" are.[25]

In no human society has it been possible to breed genetic types selectively which would be adapted to different statuses. Societies change at different rates, but even during relatively stable periods social life is a complex matter. Those who show the greatest adaptability have an enormous advantage in meeting the demands of life in any type of society.[26]

While the present view of natural selection emphasizes the role of co-operation in the life of modern societies, competition is not held to be unimportant. Unmitigated competition and democracy are inconsistent, and democratic societies seek to make competition socially useful.[27]

Montagu remarks that regardless of whether competition "in its aggressive

[21] T. Dobzhansky, "Heredity, Environment, and Evolution," *Science*, vol. III (Feb. 17, 1950), pp. 164–165.

[22] J. B. S. Haldane, "Concerning Social Darwinism," *Science and Society*, 5 (1941), pp. 373–374.

[23] Bernhard Stern, "Reply on Social Darwinism," *Science and Society*, 5 (1941), pp. 275.

[24] T. Dobzhansky, "Evolution at Work," *Science*, 127 (May 9, 1958), p. 1097.

[25] David Bidney, "The Concept of Cultural Crisis," *American Anthropologist*, 40 (October, 1940), p. 546.

[26] A. Montagu, *Man's Most Dangerous Myth*, 3rd ed., Harper, 1953, p. 74.

[27] On Célestin Bouglé's criticisms of the social Darwinistic arguments against democracy, see H. Becker and H. E. Barnes, *op. cit.*, II, pp. 846–847.

combative sense, ever had any adaptive value among men, which is greatly to be doubted, it is quite clear that it has no adaptive value whatever in the modern world." Homo sapiens may not survive, but if he doesn't, extinction will be due not to Nature but to his own devices, to his inability to adjust to a cultural world of his own creation.

Conclusion

One hundred years after the publication of *The Origin of Species,* and eighty-eight years after the appearance of *The Descent of Man,* natural selection remains an important concept in biology, anthropology, sociology, even in international relations. Modern man is subject to selection, natural and artificial. If this were not so, all human genotypes would produce surviving children in the same ratio as the occurrence of these genotypes in existing populations. Today the adaptive value of co-operation is more widely acknowledged and the role of ruthless aggression as a factor in the evolution of man, society, and culture is given smaller significance. Social Darwinistic thinking has not disappeared, but increasingly the "nature, red in tooth and claw" version of natural selection is regarded as an outdated brand of Darwinism.

[5]

Marx and Marxism:
Three Recent Evaluations

$\mathcal{I}$n a short introduction it is difficult
to survey the vast literature on Marx and Marxism. The theoretical and
publicistic writings of Karl Marx and Friedrich Engels are in themselves
voluminous. But during the stormy period when Marxian socialism fought
its way to ascendancy in the Socialist movement, their writings, in turn,
engendered a whole literature of criticism and interpretation by Socialists of
all shades of opinion, some of whom claimed Marxism for their own, while
others rejected it violently. It was probably this doctrinaire struggle that led
Marx, sometime before his death in 1883, to declare that by certain
interpretations of his writings he was no Marxist.

¶ How much more might he have emphasized this declaration during
the period that begins with the triumph of Marxism-Leninism in Russia. Here
again Marxism has spawned a vast literature which, in this instance, has
transformed it into a system as all encompassing as those of an Aristotle or
an Aquinas and elevated Marx to the role of an infallible prophet. On the
other hand, the antipathy of the free world to totalitarianism and the
identification of Marxism with state communism have combined to produce
volumes of writings that only obscure the essential Marx. Therefore we must
turn to trained scholars, such as those represented in the selections that
follow, for an unemotional evaluation of Marx and Marxism. As the philosopher
Sidney Hook puts it, that "Whether one accepts or rejects Marx's ideas
they constitute a critical part of the critical tradition of the West." [1]

¶ The first two selections deal with the *Communist Manifesto,* that
powerful epitome of Marx's philosophy and program. The first of these is a
paper which Samuel Bernstein originally read before the American Historical

[1] Sidney Hook, "The Communist Manifesto One Hundred Years After," *New York Times
Magazine,* February 1, 1948, p. 38.

[123]

Association in 1948, the centennial year of the publication of the *Manifesto*. Bernstein sympathetically maintains that "after the lapse of a century, we can conclude that little of it is dated" and that it still has "a forecast and message." While acknowledging Marx's and Engel's debt to their precursors, as indeed they did themselves, Bernstein argues for the uniqueness of the *Manifesto*.

The second selection, which is a chapter from George Lichtheim's *Marxism: An Historical and Critical Study*, covers a much narrower area than Bernstein's broader synthesis. Lichtheim concentrates on the years immediately preceding the publication of the *Manifesto*, examining Marx's and Engel's writings during this period and the conditions influencing them. He deals in particular with Marx's thoughts about what form the coming revolution in Germany should take. Still, this study offers interesting contrasts with some of Bernstein's points, particularly Lichtheim's conclusion that "The *Manifesto* spells out the implications of a world-view which owed more to reminiscences of 1789–94 than its authors would have been willing to admit."

Solomon Bloom, in the third selection, deals with Marx's work in a much wider context. He examines what he calls "the representative issues of Marxism" —materialism, the state, and man. He is critical of Marx's handling of these issues, but believes that, although Marx has left us some "positive legacies," his chief significance is historical as "a passionate actor and analyst of his times."

FROM UTOPIANISM TO MARXISM

Samuel Bernstein

THE COMMUNIST Manifesto had antecedents. An example of the eighteenth century that has often been cited is Maréchal's *Manifesto of the Equals*. It was an expression of communist thinking that had its roots in eighteenth century theory and French revolutionary practice. In the first half of the 19th century there were Georg Büchner's *Der hessische Landbote* of 1834, which, in the spirit of sans-culottism, appealed to the oppressed to rise up against their oppressors, and the communist catechism of Moses Hess in 1844, which called for a society that would free man from

From *Science and Society*, XIV, No. 1 (Winter 1949–50), pp. 58–67. Reprinted by permission. Copyright 1950 by Science and Society, Incorporated.

the reign of money.[1] The previous year the leading Fourierist, Victor Considérant, published in his paper *The Manifesto of Peaceful Democracy,*[2] containing a statement of principles of the Fourierist School. These manifestoes, however, have long been relegated to obscurity. Only the *Manifesto* of Marx and Engels, published in London in February 1848, to-day commands the attention of the world.

The earlier manifestoes vigorously indicted existing conditions. But their programs were at best expressions of a hope, of a hope which depended for its realization either on an individual will or on the force of reason. The social systems, projected in them, did not grow out of the historical process, for man was placed outside of historical change. *The Communist Manifesto,* on the other hand, proclaimed a new conception of history in which the modern working class, arising out of new productive relations, held the promise of the future. Consequently, it heralded a new epoch in the socialist movement.

The *Manifesto* was written as the program of the Communist League, an international organization with its headquarters in London and nuclei in France, Belgium, Switzerland and Germany. Under the influence of Marx and Engels the League renounced Weitling's chiliastic anarchism and French egalitarianism and accepted instead the doctrines on which both men had been in agreement since 1844. In 1847 it commissioned Marx and Engels to draft a manifesto. The manuscript was sent to the printer a few weeks before the outbreak of the February Revolution in Paris.

The Manifesto of the Communist Party, to use its full title, did not at once win partisans. In fact, from 1848 to 1871, it had only a limited popularity. But it already existed during this period in English, French, Danish, Polish and Russian translations. The first English translation appeared in 1850 in the paper of George Julian Harney, the Chartist.[3] The *Manifesto* won increasing notice after the Paris Commune, which in no small way helped to publicize the names of Marx and Engels. *Woodhull & Claflin's Weekly* in New York republished the first English translation in 1871.[4]

As Marxism was made into a program by socialist parties, it became the subject of bitter controversy. Governments tried to stifle it by legislation and police measures. Intellectuals not only assailed its basic principles; they also charged that it was a paraphrase of earlier works. Thus Charles Andler contended without a shred of evidence that Engels' *Condition of the English Working Class* was a compilation out of Buret's *De la misère des classes laborieuses en Angleterre et en France.*[5] The most consistent attack has been made

---

[1] For the German text of the catechism see Auguste Cornu, *Moses Hess et la gauche hégélienne* (Paris, 1934), p. 109–18.

[2] *La démocratie pacifique,* August 1, 1843.

[3] *The Red Republican,* November 9–30, 1850.

[4] December 30, 1871.

[5] *Le Manifeste communiste: introduction historique,* p. 35 and 79.

against *The Communist Manifesto*. At least a half dozen men, notably Georg Brandes, Georges Sorel, Morris R. Cohen and Harold J. Laski, have either charged or implied that Marx and Engels had plagiarized Victor Considérant's *Manifesto of Peaceful Democracy*.[6] It can be said at the outset that no solid evidence has ever been submitted to substantiate the charge. But since it has been repeated on several occasions, a brief inquiry into it is in order.

Considérant's indictment of bourgeois society was both eloquent and arresting. In place of the old feudalism, he said, a monied aristocracy had arisen, which imposed a new type of servitude and stood as a threat both to the working and middle classes. Capital became concentrated in the hands of a few who invaded everything, and society tended to be divided into two large classes: a small number owning everything and the large number having nothing. The new feudalism henceforth formed the real government. Considérant predicted that unless a solution was found for this "social hell," as he called it, revolutions would follow.

Considérant, however, failed to reveal both the laws of change of the society he arraigned and the causes of its breakdown. The disturbing picture he drew, in his *Manifesto* as in his earlier works, strikingly resembled the portrayals of socialist contemporaries. The kind of capitalism they were all confronted with was the financial, speculative variety of the July Monarchy. Since credit was political economy's standard for valuing men, their solution of the pressing social problems, their hope of achieving their different versions of justice, depended on the organization of credit under capitalism, and not on the socialization of the means of production and distribution, as Marx and Engels contended. All the leading utopians, in common with Considérant, were alarmed at the growing power of concentrated capital, and at its perversion of the egalitarian and libertarian principles of the French Revolution. Turning their backs on the new situation born out of the technological revolution, all of them looked with confidence either to their social panaceas or to the new utopias they planned to erect.

For they did not count on the rising proletariat to lead the way to socialism. Considérant, like other socialists, to be sure, accented the existence of a class

---

[6] For example, Georg Brandes wrote in his *Ferdinand Lassalle* (English translation, New York, 1925), p. 115, that the Communist Manifesto was "almost a mere translation from Victor Considérant." Different versions of the charge have appeared from time to time. See e.g. Georges Sorel, *La décomposition du marxisme* (Paris, n.d.), p. 32; Morris R. Cohen, *The Faith of a Liberal* (New York, 1946), p. 111. The charge is also implied in Harold J. Laski, *Karl Marx; an Essay*, reprinted with *The Communist Manifesto* (New York, 1943), p. 17, by the League for Industrial Democracy. Anarchists added their strident voices to the chorus. Thus W. Tcherkesoff insisted at one time. (See *Precurseurs de l'Internationale* (Bruxelles, 1899), p. 97) that Marx and Engels had stolen their theories from Louis Blanc, and at another (See Pierre Ramus, ed., *Die Urheberschaft des Kommunistischen Manifests* (Berlin, 1906), p. 9–20) that they had filched the essential parts of their *Manifesto* from Considérant. Enrico Labriola endorsed Tcherkesoff's second conclusion. See *ibid.*, pp. 21–24.

struggle in history. In this he was not original, as we shall show later. His survey of the class conflict in fact bears a strong likeness to that of the Saint-Simonians, Bazard and Enfantin.[7] In common with them, he held that as humanity marched forward the spirit of fraternity intervened to cushion the conflict. Classes would ultimately approach one another and travel arm in arm toward the goal ahead. This conception of class relations, terminating in collaboration and harmony, rested on the belief that human history developed rationally and uninterruptedly, and it implied a confidence in the readiness of the upper classes to accept the dictates of history. Thus Considérant did not show, as Marx and Engels did, how the future emerged out of practical human activity which shaped the course of history. Having faith in the irresistible triumph of reason, Considérant set up ideal conditions for the future, whose convincing power, he believed, would inspire men to establish them.

It is important to observe, in the light of the charge of plagiarism, that, in contrast to Marx and Engels, Considérant regarded the political question as secondary to the social question. He saw no connection between economic factors and state forms, for the existing political régime did not seem to him incompatible with social progress. Democratic principles like equality before the law and the elective system of representation had already been won, he contended. It was only a matter of developing them. And who would develop them? Not the proletariat, according to Considérant, for the class struggle was not the propulsive force in his system. The principles will develop in accordance with social evolution, marked out by the progress of "the dogma of fraternity," to use Considérant's phrase. The authors of the *Manifesto* had in mind a socialist like Considérant when they said of the utopians that they "endeavor, by small experiments, necessarily doomed to failure, and by the force of example, to pave the way for the new social gospel." [8]

All indications point to the conclusion that Considérant's historical outlook was not much further advanced than that of eighteenth century perfectibilists, that he relied on an abstract principle of justice, manifesting itself in history to give rise to a cooperative order. His own blueprint of it was in line with the dreams of utopians in general. His *Manifesto of Peaceful Democracy* discloses that his view of society was a static instead of a dynamic one; that like Proudhon, his contemporary, he was at bottom a conservative in the sense that he aspired to solve existing incompatibilities by balancing interests. "Thus," wrote Engels in 1843 in an estimate of the Fourierist phalanx, "after all the beautiful theories of association and free labor; after a good deal of indignant declaration against commerce, selfishness, and competition, we have in practice, the old competitive system upon an improved plan, a poor law bastille on more liberal

---

[7] *Doctrine de Saint-Simon, Exposition, Première année,* 1829 (Paris, 1924), p. 238–39, publiée par C. Bouglé et Elie Halévy.

[8] Karl Marx, *Selected Works* (Moscow, 1935), I, p. 238.

principles." [9] It is, therefore, incomprehensible, in the light of the evidence, how students of socialist theory, who aspire to remain on the level of science, can accuse Marx and Engels of having copied Considérant.

This does not rule out their indebtedness to their precursors. In fact they were the first to acknowledge it. No one ever wrote more warmly of the great utopians than Frederick Engels; [10] and, while rejecting the remedies of economists like Simonde de Sismondi and Thomas Hodgskin, for example, Marx esteemed their penetrating judgments on capitalist production.[11] In contrast to their forerunners, Marx and Engels held that historical development could not be brought to a halt by an *a priori* social device. For the anatomy of capitalism revealed to them its laws of growth and decline. Within it were being ripened the conditions of the future and the class that would achieve it.

Now Marx and Engels did not discover the existence of a class struggle. "Long before me," wrote Marx to Weydemeyer in 1852, "bourgeois historians had described the historical development of this class struggle and bourgeois economists the economic anatomy of the classes." [12] We have seen that the class struggle was a running theme in the writings of the utopians. But the theme had already been present in eighteenth century literature. Adam Smith, in the chapter on "The Wages of Labor," described the latent and open antagonism between masters and workmen.[13] His French contemporaries, the Physiocrats, had a class theory of their own, which helped them explain the circulation of the net product.[14] Significant was their contention that the productive class alone provided the life blood of society and that a parasitic class alienated a portion of the net product. Opponents of the Physiocrats, for instance Necker and Linguet, clearly recognized an existing antagonism between capitalists and wage earners. But their class theory did not point to a solution of the antagonism.[15]

The French Revolution cast the spotlight on class distinctions. Henceforth political and economic thinkers linked the class conflict with the evolution of the forms of property. Thus, as early as 1792, Antoine Barnave approached the historical materialistic outlook and held that property relations were behind class divisions and the distribution of power.[16] Saint-Simon, who had also been influenced by the French Revolution, went beyond Barnave. Instead of considering property in general the basis of the class conflict, Saint-Simon saw it condi-

[9] Marx-Engels, *Gesamtausgabe*, Part I, Vol. II, p. 438.

[10] See e.g. *Herr Eugen Dühring's Revolution in Science* (New York [1935]), Pt. iii, ch. 1.

[11] *Histoire des doctrines économiques* (Paris, 1925), VI, p. 86–87; VII, 137–40, 149–52, 179–83, 205–207.

[12] *Selected Correspondence*, p. 57.

[13] *An Inquiry into the Nature and Causes of the Wealth of Nations*, Book 1, ch. 8.

[14] See e.g. [Quesnay], *Tableau économique avec ses explications* (1760).

[15] Necker, "Sur la législation et le commerce des grains," *Oeuvres complètes* (Paris, 1820), I, p. 126 ff. Linguet, *Théorie des loix civiles* (London, 1767), II, p. 461 ff.

[16] *Oeuvres* (Paris, 1843) I, p. 13.

tioned by property in the means of production. And he concluded that politics was the science of production.

The class struggle was also a central theme in the writings of English socialists and economists in the first half of the nineteenth century. Notable examples were Charles Hall's *The Effects of Civilization on the People in European States* (London, 1805), Thomas Hodgskin's *Labor Defended against the Claims of Capital* (London, 1825), and the numerous articles of the Chartist, James Bronterre O'Brien.[17]

The class struggle, therefore, had been regarded as a factor in social relations long before Marx and Engels. What the two did that was new was to exhibit it as a law of social change, leading to the historic moment when the proletariat won political supremacy in the nation and piloted it toward socialism.

How had the two men arrived at this conclusion? Marx reached it via a criticsm of Hegel's theory of the State and of the science of economics with its static categories, as the classical economists had conceived them; Engels, through the study of industrial and labor conditions in England. The first concluded that legal relations and state forms were not explainable by the progress of the human mind; their roots had to be sought in the material conditions of life. From his studies and observations in England the second acquired the conviction that increasing concentration of wealth and the sharpening of the class conflict would finally bring about the establishment of a system of production, founded on the collective activity of men.

The paths travelled by Marx and Engels converged and there began one of the most remarkable partnerships in history. Marx supplied his learning and his creative genius; Engels, his knowledge of labor conditions, his business experience and his skill in marking out foundations. The two closely studied classical German philosophy, English and French political economy and French and English socialism; and both devoted themselves to practical activity.

The principles they arrived at by 1848 were formulated in *The Communist Manifesto*. Though it is the statement of the Communist Party's credo, it also has the polemic quality of several of their earlier works. In the third chapter Marx and Engels took exception to the socialist and communist schools that did not represent a realistic position in relation to the general body of the proletarians. Their own view of communism, to be sure, only assimilated aspects of earlier social movements; but it also overcame their limitations; and in this respect it was qualitatively distinct from all earlier social systems. The earlier socialist and communist writings, said Marx and Engels in the *Manifesto*, "attack every principle of existing society. Hence they are full of the most valuable materials for the enlightenment of the working class." The practical measures of these writings, the two men continued, "point solely to the disappearance of class antagonisms which were, at that time, only just cropping up, and which,

[17] See e.g. *Bronterre's National Reformer*, 1837, nos. 1-11.

in these publications, are recognized in their earliest, indistinct and undefined forms only. These proposals, therefore, are of a purely utopian character." [18]

Looking at the *Manifesto* after the lapse of a century, we can conclude that little of it is dated. The program toward the end of the second chapter was written in the anticipation that the revolution, which had already begun in Milan and Palermo, would make the proletariat the political arbiter in the most advanced countries of Europe. Then there is chapter four which sketches briefly the attitude of communists towards the various opposing parties. These parts of the *Manifesto* have a bearing on the general political climate in which it was written, and can be useful for forming an estimate of the period.

The third chapter of the *Manifesto,* already referred to, reflects the theoretical controversies before 1848, and establishes the differences between the teachings of Marx and Engels and those championed by other socialists and communists at that time. Since the tenets of pre-Marxist socialists have reappeared in different versions since 1848, the third chapter can continue to serve as a basis for modern Marxist criticism. The authors of the *Manifesto* took their stand against those they characterized as reactionary socialists who today have their counterpart among elements that dream of reimposing a fixed hierarchical order of the past; they dissociated themselves from the partisans of conspiracy, "the alchemists of revolution," as Marx called them, who were detached from the working class and who counted on a small, secret group to seize power; and they could not find common ground either with a socialist reformer like Proudhon who desired to redress social grievances, "in order to secure the continued existence of bourgeois society," [19] or with socialist and communist doctrinaires, of whom Considérant and Cabet were notable examples, who appealed to philanthropists to help them set up models of the terrestrial paradise.

By contrast with these socialists and communists, Marx and Engels did not permit themselves to be distracted from reality by an apocalyptic contemplation of the future. For the social systems they rejected they substituted "the critical examination of conditions, of the advance and general results of the real social movement." [20] From their investigation of the historical process they concluded that the rise and decline of classes and institutions were subject to contradictions. The *Manifesto* lauds the great achievements of the bourgeoisie, and we are inclined to agree with a recent student that in all literature there "are probably no passages which paint the achievements of capitalism in more glowing terms than those devoted to the subject in the *Manifesto.*" [21] But it already speaks of this class as in a funeral oration. The proletariat, arising out of the new productive relations, stood ready to become its heir and successor, for

[18] Marx, *Selected Works* (Moscow, 1935), I, p. 239.

[19] *Ibid.,* p. 235.

[20] Karl Marx, *Herr Vogt* (Paris, 1927), I, p. 126.

[21] Paul M. Sweezy, "Origins of Present Day Socialism," *A Centenary of Marxism* (New York, 1948), p. 80, edited by Samuel Bernstein and the Editors of *Science and Society.*

the proletariat, in the opinion of Marx and Engels, held the promise of a vast human potential. The experience of the French and English proletariat in the thirties and forties had already taught them that. If on the eve of the revolutionary storm of 1848 they underestimated the reserve, expanding power of capitalism, if they did not foresee the growth of the world market after the decline of the economic crisis, during which the *Manifesto* was composed, if, as Engels said later, they failed to include in their calculations both Russia and the United States, they were nevertheless prophetic. In accordance with the laws of social development, as they saw them operating in history, they regarded the proletariat as the dynamic class.

The conviction was the outcome of a new conception of history, that has come to be known as historical materialism. As a guide to historical study, it is best shown in the writings of Marx and Engels on the Revolution of 1848.[22] This historical philosophy starts from the thought that men make their own history, "but in the first place," as Engels wrote, "under very definite presuppositions and conditions. Among these the economic ones are finally decisive. But the political, etc., ones, and indeed even the traditions which haunt human minds, also play a part, although not the decisive one." [23] In the letter, from which we have just cited, Engels admitted that he and Marx were "partly to blame for the fact that younger writers sometimes lay more stress on the economic side than is due to it. We had to emphasize this main principle in opposition to our adversaries, who denied it, and we had not always the time, the place or the opportunity to allow the other elements involved in the interaction to come into their rights." [24]

The historical materialistic conception pointed the way to socialism. The socialist society, instead of being a hope or conjecture, was the outcome of the tortuous turns and twists of history in which the class struggle was the moving force. Socialism as the solution of the class conflict was rational, not as the achievement of reason, but rational in the sense that it was the denouement of the historical process. Historical movement did not consist in the march from one idea to another, but in the transition from one system of production to another.

Marx and Engels explained why the transition to socialism could be made only by the proletariat. "In the conditions of the proletariat," they wrote, "those of old society at large are already virtually swamped. The proletarian is without property," [25] by which Marx and Engels meant the ownership of the means of production. Modern industry revolutionized the worker's psychology and life pattern, revealed to him the cold, cash nexus between himself and his master,

[22] Marx, *The Class Struggles in France (1848–1850)* and *The Eighteenth Brumaire;* Engels, *Germany: Revolution and Counter-Revolution.*
[23] Marx-Engels, *Selected Correspondence* (New York, 1935), p. 475–76.
[24] *Ibid.*, p. 477.
[25] *Selected Works,* I, p. 216.

and removed for him the halo surrounding existing conditions. In contrast to the classes that had previously risen to power and set up defenses for their newly acquired position, the proletariat had nothing of its own to protect. Its task was to put an end to all the safeguards of private property as the only way or getting control of the productive forces of society. Moreover, unlike all previous movements which were "movements of minorities," the movement of the proletariat, said the authors of the *Manifesto,* "is the self-conscious, independent movement of the immense majority, in the interest of the immense majority. The proletariat, the lowest stratum of our present society, cannot stir, cannot raise itself up, without the whole superincumbent strata of official society being sprung into the air." [26]

The historical perspectives in the *Manifesto,* its confidence in the workers' achievement of socialism represented a leap from the realm of fantasy, where system makers dwelt, to the realm of objective historic conditions which transformed circumstances and men. The final paragraph of chapter one in the *Manifesto,* later elaborated in the first volume of *Capital,* boldly outlines the process by which capitalist contradictions will finally lead to the triumph of the proletariat over the bourgeoisie. "In place of the old bourgeois society, with its classes and class antagonisms," said Marx and Engels in closing chapter two, "we shall have an association, in which the free development of each is the condition for the free development of all." [27] This is the forecast and message of *The Communist Manifesto.*

THE DOCTRINE OF REVOLUTION

George Lichtheim

AFTER WHAT has been said it is scarcely surprising that one should have to revert from sociology to Hegelian philosophy —and from France to Germany—in tracing the doctrine of revolution, unfolded in Marx's writings on the eve of 1848: the date of the *Communist Manifesto*

[26] *Ibid.,* I, p. 217.
[27] *Ibid.,* I, p. 228.

From George Lichtheim, *Marxism: An Historical and Critical Study* (New York: Frederick A. Praeger Inc., 1961), pp. 51–62. Reprinted by permission. Copyright George Lichtheim, 1961.

and of the abortive European democratic rising. It has become customary to treat the *Manifesto* as the theoretical expression of that "proletarian revolution" which is supposed to have triumphed in Russia in 1917 after some hopeful preparatory experiments on French soil between 1848 and 1871. More will have to be said about the link between the French and the Russian experience. For the moment the question is what "the revolution" signified for Marx (and for Engels) on the eve of 1848. And here the first point to be noted is that they were primarily concerned with Germany. This may seem obvious, seeing that they were in the forefront of the German radical movement which briefly occupied the stage in 1848-9. But it is frequently overlooked; all the more reason for emphasising it.

The only revolution possible in Germany at that stage was a "bourgeois-democratic" one, a fact quite obvious to Marx and Engels (though not to all their associates) by 1847 at the latest.[1] With the wisdom of hindsight it is easy today to perceive that in actual fact the revolution never emerged from the theoretical sphere, but in the 1840's this outcome was not easily predictable. In retrospect one can also discern a difference of emphasis on this point between Marx and Engels, the former being less inclined to hope for a successful democratic rebellion against the absolutist regime, preparatory to a normal development on Western lines. Indeed Marx never seems to have believed that such an outcome was likely on German soil, while Engels frequently insisted that it was inevitable, and moreover that it was the duty of the Communists to promote it and not let themselves be deflected by the anti-capitalist and anti-liberal tirades of those "true socialists" whose sentimental longing for a partnership between the monarchy and the working class merely served to prolong the death agony of the old regime.[2] Where both men agreed was in holding that *if* there was to be a successful revolution in Germany, it would need to mobilise the masses; but this left open the question who was to direct it. That the German middle class was quite incapable of promoting a radical break with the past did not become apparent for some years, and when it had, the theoretical and tactical differences between Marx and Engels automatically ceased to be relevant.

[1] Cf. Engels, *On the History of the Communist League*, MESW II, pp. 306-23. The urgency of such a revolution from the viewpoint of the German middle class is emphasised in Engels's "Der Status Quo in Deutschland" (MEGA I/6, pp. 231-49), written in March 1847, but not published before 1932. In view of the stress laid in this important essay on the need to promote a bourgeois revolution in Germany, for the sake of the country's national development, it is not surprising that modern Communist literature tends to be silent about it.

[2] Engels, "Der Status Quo in Deutschland," MEGA I/6, p. 231; cf. also the relevant passages in the *Communist Manifesto*, MEGA I/6, pp. 525 ff (Eng. trans. in MESW I, pp. 33 ff). A textual comparison shows that those passages which stress the progressive character of a capitalist development in Germany, and the reactionary nature of all counter-tendencies, including socialist ones, are taken over from Engels's unpublished manuscripts of 1847, including his *Grundsaetze des Kommunismus*, of which more later. For Engels's sustained animosity toward Hess, Gruen, and the "true socialists" generally, cf. MEGA I/6, pp. 33-116.

But this is to anticipate. In 1844–7, and *a fortiori* before he had formed his lifelong partnership with Engels in the autumn of 1844, Marx was occupied with the problem of fitting the imminent German revolution into the conceptual framework he had just elaborated, and here his reading of recent French history suggested a possible solution. Paradoxically, the very backwardness of Germany made it seem plausible to suppose that the Germans would not content themselves with the kind of revolution that Western Europe had undergone. True, in many respects Germany had only just reached a stage already attained in France or Britain, notably in economics.[3] But precisely because his native country was so far behind, Marx thought that the coming revolution might be all the more radical. It would then transcend the socio-political level reached in Western Europe and for the first time place the proletariat upon the stage of history:

It is not the *radical* revolution, *universal human* emancipation, which is a utopian dream for Germany, but rather the partial, merely political, revolution, which leaves the pillars of the building intact. What is the basis of a partial, merely political, revolution? Simply this: *a part of civic society* emancipates itself and attains *general* domination, a particular class, from its *particular situation,* undertakes the general emancipation of society. . . . But in Germany every class lacks not only the consistency, the incisiveness, the courage, the ruthlessness required to turn it into the negative representative of society, but also that generosity needed to identify itself, if only for a moment, with the popular mind. . . . The middle class hardly dares to conceive the idea of emancipation from its own standpoint, and already the development of social conditions, and the progress of political theory, declares this standpoint to be antiquated or at least problematical.

In France, partial emancipation is the basis of complete emancipation. In Germany, universal emancipation is the *conditio sine qua non* of any partial emancipation. In France it is the reality, in Germany the impossibility, of a step-by-step emancipation which must give birth to complete liberty. . . . Where then is there the *positive* possibility of German emancipation? In the formation of a class with *radical chains* . . . a class which is the dissolution of all classes, a sphere of society which has a universal character because its sufferings are universal, and which claims no *particular right* because the wrong committed against it is not a *particular wrong* but wrong *as such.* . . . When the proletariat declares the *dissolution of the existing social order* it does no more than proclaim the *secret of its own existence,* for it constitutes the *effective* dissolution of this order. . . . As philosophy finds its *material* weapons in the proletariat, so the proletariat discovers its *intellectual* weapons in philosophy, and once the lightning-flash of the idea has penetrated this naïve popular soil, the emancipation of the *Germans* to *manhood* will become reality. . . . The emancipation of the *German* is the emancipation of *man. Philosophy* is the *head* of this emancipation, and the *proletariat* its *heart.* Philosophy cannot realise itself without abolishing the proletariat, and the proletariat cannot emancipate itself without realising philosophy.[4]

[3] "Zur Kritik der Hegelschen Rechtsphilosophie" (1844), MEGA I/1, p. 611.
[4] *Ibid.*, pp. 617–21.

This famous passage is commonly cited as proof that in 1844 Marx was not yet a Marxist: in other words, that he had not yet developed the "materialist"outlook which after 1850—and in particular from the 1870's onward—was to become the hallmark of orthodoxy. This seems a curious way of approaching the subject. Whatever may be said about the evolution of doctrine, there is no "Marxism" apart from Marx's own writings, and the above passage is certainly one of his most characteristic early statements. Moreover, so far from being a passing aberration, it represents the very essence of his pre-1848 theorising about the coming revolution. It is true that in later years he took a less exalted view of the part which thought had to play in transforming the world, just as the concept of a social revolution which would transcend philosophy by "realising" its aims, disappeared from his writings; but it was never repudiated, nor could it have been, for it is precisely what he meant by the "union of theory and practice." Without this central idea, Marxism is just another species of materialist determinism, and this is indeed what the later socialist movement largely succeeded in making out of it. But the transformation was never complete; at the core of the system, however much it might be watered down by its own author and others to suit the positivist fashion of the later nineteenth century, there remained something resembling the original vision of a world made new by a unique event fusing thought and action, theory and practice, philosophy and the revolution, into a creative drama of human liberation. It is literally true that apart from this quasi-metaphysical *tour de force* the whole subsequent history of the Marxist movement must remain incomprehensible.

It is worth noting that while in his essay of 1844 Marx stood Hegel's conservative philosophy of the state on its head, he did so by carrying to its furthest extreme Hegel's own rationalist mode of thinking. Although the language of the lengthy passage just quoted is reminiscent of Feuerbach—notably the emphasis on the "emancipation of man"—the logic behind it is Hegelian: the present order of things stands condemned because it is irrational. Elsewhere in the same essay the existing state of affairs is declared to be "beneath the level of history" and "beneath criticism," from which it follows that its dissolution is both imminent and urgent. No more than Hegel did Marx doubt that what was irrational was also unreal. The most irrational, and consequently the least real, of all possible phenomena was a state of affairs such as that in pre-1848 Germany which, unlike the *ancien régime* of 1789, could not even claim to represent the traditional social order, but was a pure anachronism due to the backwardness of Germany and its lack of social development. To criticise this state of affairs—to lay bare its contradictions—was to demonstrate why such a condition of things could not be maintained much longer.

But in order to become effective, criticism had to abandon its purely theoretical status and turn into an instrument of revolution. If the youthful Hegel had in a general manner developed the notion that Reason must go out into the world and, as it were, work for its living in order to come to itself, Marx goes so far as to postulate a theoretical critique which makes an end of philosophy—in the traditional sense of the term—by "realising" its aims. Such a critique is indeed no longer philosophy, if by that term is meant contemplation, and on these grounds it has sometimes been said that Marx at this point ceased to be a philosopher. This suggestion fails on two counts: in the first place, Marx had never written anything but critiques, though it was only in 1844 that he extended his criticism of institutions to the point of fusing theory and practice; secondly, this fusion was no less philosophical—indeed metaphysical—for being directed against the ruling ideas of the age. To say that the coming revolution would make an end of philosophy by fulfilling its ultimate aims—liberty and equality—was to make as grandiose a claim as any that had been put forward since German Idealism was launched by Hegel and Schelling in the 1790's. Where Marx breaks away from the idealist scheme is in placing thought within a material context: philosophy by itself cannot transform the social order simply by holding up a scheme of perfection or a conceptual image of "true" reality; it needs an ally, and can find it only in a class whose existence proclaims "the effective dissolution of this order." This is a radical inversion of the idealist conception, but hardly a repudiation of philosophy as such. The "critical theory" of 1844 is still philosophical in essence; its criterion of judgment is the irrationality of religion—lengthily developed in the same essay—and the deeper irrationality reflected in the need for religious consolation. At no point is it suggested that the coming revolution is to be welcomed simply because it is inevitable. Rather its inevitability is deduced from the intolerable conflict between the demands of reason and the unreasonableness of the *status quo*.

These general considerations find their counterpart in a doctrine of revolution behind which it is not difficult to perceive the general model of Jacobinism, as modified and brought up to date to suit the theoretical requirements of the 1840's. The "critical theory" is intended as the theory of a political revolution patterned on that of 1789–94, but with this difference: instead of "the people" we now—almost for the first time—encounter "the proletariat."

The essential precondition of the hoped-for German revolution is defined as "the formation of a class with *radical chains* . . . a class which is the dissolution of all classes." Marx as good as admits that as yet no such stratum exists east of the Rhine, though it is beginning to form, thus raising backward Germany to the West European level. Its inevitable growth is expected to furnish "philosophy," i.e., the radical intellectuals, with the instrument required to overturn the existing order. That of course was substantially what had occurred in France in 1789, with the important difference that in the meantime the industrial proletariat had taken over from the traditional urban plebs. By the same token, the question why the French Revolution had in the end failed to achieve the ultimate aims of its most advanced spokesmen could now at last be answered in the light of recent socialist-communist literature: the Jacobins had been unable to transcend the framework of bourgeois society. Yet "partial emancipation" (the downfall of the *ancien régime*) had been secured, and "complete emancipation" (socialism) was sure to follow. In backward Germany, still lagging far behind, this order had to be reversed: only the revolutionary proletariat, led by the intellectual vanguard, could accomplish even the "partial emancipation" implicit in the "merely political" revolution already victorious in France; only a class whose inhuman condition proclaimed "the dissolution of the existing social order" could enable "philosophy" to realise its aims. Because that class was bound to reject the social order root and branch, "philosophy finds its material weapons in the proletariat." The coming revolution would be total because its aim was nothing less than the radical transformation of man's being in the world.

For all its utopian overtones—not to mention the strained conjunction of Hegelian and Feuerbachian concepts—Marx's essay of 1844 discloses a clear enough realisation that the German bourgeoisie would not in fact make the revolution which in his view was required to bring Germany up to the West European level. And if it failed, the task necessarily devolved upon the class which was already forming in the womb of bourgeois society, but had not yet found political expression. Hence the revolution, though "bourgeois" in origin, would have to be led by the proletariat! Three-quarters of a century later a similar mode of reasoning served to fortify Lenin in his faith that the hour had struck for Russia to proclaim the world revolution: not *although* but *because* she was the most backward of the great European nations! In so doing he was compelled to repudiate not only Social-Democratic orthodoxy, but post-1850 Marxism as well; he was not, however, being untrue to the spirit of the early Marx, though reflection might have prompted doubt whether philosophical manifestoes are meant to be taken literally and used as political guide-posts. In 1844 Marx had not yet emancipated himself from either Feuerbach or Hegel, and even the *Communist Manifesto* of 1847–8 (though written with far greater comprehension of history and economics) presents far too sweeping a synthesis of philosophy and revolutionary strategy to be of use as a political textbook. All this, however, belongs to a different chapter. In the 1840's there was no real chance of anyone in Europe—least of all in Germany—taking such formulations literally. Indeed the German proletariat so confidently invoked by Marx scarcely existed. The actual historical *locus* of revolutionary politics was Paris, and in Paris the era of proletarian insurrections in the service of bourgeois democracy was drawing to a close.[5]

---

[5] Cf. Marx, *The Class Struggles in France 1848–50* (preface by Engels), MESW I, pp. 118 ff. After the failure of the 1848–9 movement, Marx gradually relinquished his faith in historical short-cuts, but the repudiation was never quite complete and overt. Engels went further, as we shall see.

If the utopian extrapolation from Feuerbach's philosophy was to be abandoned—and by 1847, when the *Manifesto* was in preparation, Marx had already cast some of his youthful ideological baggage overboard—there arose a further difficulty: to say that the coming German revolution could only be a bourgeois one [6] was equivalent to saying that it would bring the liberals to power. This awkward conclusion could be qualified by asserting that the proletarian revolution would follow in the wake of this first upheaval; [7] but there remained the task of making these paradoxes plausible to those outside the narrow circle of the Communist leadership. Already there loomed the problem of inducing the "masses" to follow the lead of a "vanguard" which could afford to take the long view because it incorporated the science of revolution. In 1848–9 these preoccupations were to be drowned in a torrent of happenings that fell far short of accomplishing even the modest opening phase of the two-stage upheaval envisaged in the *Manifesto*. Subsequently the rise of Social-Democracy, and the virtual abandonment of the old strategy by Marx himself, served to obscure the significance of the solution with which the founders of Marxism had briefly toyed in those turbulent years. Here again it remained for the Russian Revolution to revive a dormant issue that Western socialists had long believed to be dead.

While the *Manifesto* skipped entire stages of the sacrosanct historical process in order to telescope two different revolutions into one, its authors could at least point to the example set by the French socialist and communist sects of the period. In common with them, Marx and Engels thought in terms of the revolutionary experience of 1789–94, when moderate factions were displaced by more radical ones, until the whole democratic movement had advanced far beyond its original starting-point. It was more difficult to justify the implicit assumption that European capitalism in 1847 was already outmoded and ripe for socialisation. This was to mistake the birth-pangs of the new order for its death-throes—a misunderstanding only possible in an age in which the memory of the French Revolution had accustomed people to expect the imminent collapse of the existing social order. That the latter was still largely pre-capitalist, hence in urgent need of radical *bourgeois* measures, was a circumstance not wholly lost upon Engels, who had seen enough of England to be able to correct any misconceptions Marx might have entertained on this point. Yet paradoxically it was Engels who in 1844–5 persuaded Marx to regard Britain as the laboratory of the first genuinely proletarian-socialist revolution.[8] By 1847, with

---

[6] *Manifesto of the Communist Party*, MESW I, p. 65.

[7] *Ibid.*

[8] Cf. Engels, "Umrisse zu einer Kritik der Nationaloekonomie," in *Deutsch-Franzoesische Jahrbuecher*, 1844, MEGA I/2, pp. 379 ff. It was this essay which first drew the two men together. In the following year, Engels's *Condition of the Working Class in England* presented the socialist solution as the necessary outcome of the British situation—on the grounds that a revolution was preparing which would bring the Chartists to power and thus precipitate a social transformation.

the *Manifesto* in preparation, it became urgent to formulate the theoretical grounds of this forecast, and here again it was Engels who took the lead.

He did so in a document which has not received its due share of attention, despite the fact that Marx utilised it in drafting the final text of the *Manifesto*.[9] Taken together with his earlier writings it may be said to outline a conception of history and a doctrine of revolution significantly different from that of Marx. That this is not an academic matter becomes evident when one compares these early writings with the works of the mature Engels, which from the 1870's onward became the theoretical foundation of German Social-Democracy. The internal consistency is striking; so is the persistence of certain guiding ideas which do not occur in Marx and in some respects even run counter to the general tendency of his thinking. Thus Engels makes considerable play with the "industrial revolution"—a concept which Marx had not yet begun to employ.[10] In other respects too the tenor of his argument is a good deal more technocratic than that of the *Manifesto*. At the risk of some schematisation the difference can be described as that between a socio-political concept oriented on French political experience, and a doctrine derived from the contemplation of industrial strains in early Victorian England. Thus it is plain in reading Engels that he is mainly concerned with the role of the proletariat in the "industrial revolution," and behind this theme there already looms the notion that the "proletarian revolution" is destined to set free the "productive forces" at present held back by the institutions of bourgeois society. Echoes of this technological enthusiasm recur in the *Manifesto,* as does the emphasis on the revolutionary role of capitalism in doing away with pre-industrial forms of society; but where Marx stresses the catastrophic character of the process, Engels is inclined to emphasise its liberating and progressive side: the emancipation of the productive forces already set in train by the "industrial revolution" remains incomplete under capitalism because private property stands in the way. Communism represents its consummation, and the proletarian revolution is primarily envisaged as the act whereby *the industrial revolution escapes from bourgeois control*.[11]

If this idea was destined to become a key concept of Leninism, another aspect

---

[9] Engels, "Grundsaetze des Kommunismus," MEGA I/6, pp. 503–22. The text was first published by Eduard Bernstein in 1913. Cf. also Gustav Mayer, *Friedrich Engels,* The Hague, 1934, vol. I, pp. 283–5, where it is briefly dismissed as a "casual sketch." For a thorough analysis of the document and its implications cf. H. Bollnow, "Engels' Auffassung von Revolution und Entwicklung," in *Marxismusstudien,* Tuebingen, 1954, vol. I, pp. 77–144.

[10] Engels, *loc. cit.,* p. 503; cf. also Bollnow, *loc. cit.,* p. 79.

[11] Engels, *ibid.,* pp. 510–11. The terms "Produktionskraefte" and "Produktivkraefte" are employed interchangeably by Marx and Engels in their early writings to denote the powers latent in the economy; in this they followed the example of the French economists of the period who spoke of "forces productives." Cf. Marx's use of these terms in the original French text of his *Misery of Philosophy* (1847). (*Misère de la Philosophie, Réponse à la Philosophie de la Misère de M. Proudhon;* in MEGA I/6, pp. 117–228 passim.)

of Engels's thought turns up a generation earlier in the ideology of German Social-Democracy, namely his stress upon the inevitability of the coming socio-political transformation. The latter being the necessary consequence of the industrial revolution in its relentless unfolding within the womb of bourgeois society, its tempo depended primarily upon the degree of economic development already reached under capitalism. The more industrialised a country, the more numerous its working class, and the nearer the date of socialisation, whether peaceable or violent. In 1847 Engels still thought that Britain would lead the way, with Germany far in the rear, and the backward agrarian countries waiting to be transformed by the example of the more advanced.[12] A generation later this perspective was extended to Germany, and then to Europe in general. Engels is thus in a very real sense the father both of Social-Democratic orthodoxy and of the Leninist faith in industrialisation. He could even be viewed as a distant precursor of Fabian socialism, were it not for his scepticism about the likelihood of a peaceful transition, and his dislike of the pre-1848 "socialists" who (unlike the "communists") urged measures falling short of the abolition of private property in the means of production.[13] It may be that gradualism is not a necessary consequence of determinism. The prevalence of the latter in Engels's thinking is unquestionable, and helps to explain not merely some of his more obvious divergencies from Marx, but also the fact that in the subsequent development of the socialist movement it was Engels rather than Marx who supplied guidance at the tactical level.

As against the complex dialectic of existence and essence, reality and "alienation," which Marx develops in his writings between 1843 and 1848, Engels sketches a simpler and more harmonious picture. Neither the *Condition of the Working Class* (1845) nor the fragmentary *Grundsaetze* (1847) is weighed down by philosophical ballast. In conformity with their author's life-long adherence to the optimistic world-view of the Enlightenment,[14] the emancipation of society through "communism" (i.e., through the abolition of private property in the means of production) is envisaged as a unilinear process in which modern man—man as formed by the industrial revolution and the attendant triumph of science over religious superstition—achieves complete self-realisation. In contrast to Marx, the accent falls upon the satisfaction of human needs rather than upon the transformation of (human and social) nature. The coming revolution is destined to remove the barriers to freedom and equality; its inevitability arises from the conflict between the productive forces unleashed by the new technology, and the inadequacy of the existing institutions. The Marxian *complexio oppositorum* of bourgeoisie and proletariat

---

[12] Engels, *loc. cit.*, p. 516.

[13] *Ibid.*, pp. 519–21. In the 1840's socialism was commonly regarded as a philanthropic middle-class movement; hence the preference shown by Marx and Engels for the term "communism."

[14] Cf. Gustav Mayer, *Friedrich Engels*, passim; Bollnow, *loc. cit.*, pp. 101 ff.

has no real place in this picture; although duly mentioned in passing, it is external to the real purport of Engels's argument which operates with the concepts of the Enlightenment in its most recent, positivistic, phase. In close parallel with these methodical assumptions, the role of the "subjective factor" is reduced almost to vanishing point: determination rules throughout, the active agents of progress being disembodied entities such as technology, science, or the industrial revolution as such. Other abstractions prominently displayed include society, machinery, the productive forces, capital, industry, the class struggle, and finally the new society, in which all these factors will be united in a new and superior harmony.[15]

On the eve of the 1848 upheaval, this optimistic and positivist doctrine was no more than an ingredient in the explosive theoretical mixture which Marx was preparing in the *Manifesto*. The time had not yet come for the socialist movement to step into the liberal inheritance. In 1848 most radicals commonly employed Jacobin terminology. For the tiny Communist League, then about to seize partial control of the radical stirrings in Germany, Marx's philosophy of total revolution, with its chiliastic overtones familiar to readers brought up in the Judeo-Christian tradition, was more appropriate than the hopeful anticipations entertained by Engels. Not that the two men were conscious of important differences in outlook. When it came to drafting the *Manifesto,* Engels characteristically yielded to the unquestioned authority of his senior associate. The first published document of German Communism thus bore the imprint of revolutionary French thinking, down to points of style and phrasing whose Jacobin, or Babouvist, ancestry could not possibly be mistaken. The *Manifesto* indeed is as much a French as a German document, and its incomparable rhetorical power owes more to the synthesis of these two European traditions than conventional critics have been willing to concede. For the same reason it does not translate well into English. In this seemingly external and insignificant fact it is possible to discern the latent element of a problem which was to become important when Marxism ceased to be a Continental European doctrine and tried to accommodate itself to the traditions of the English-speaking peoples. In the age of the democratic revolution, which in Western Europe climaxed in 1848, it was natural for the first generation of socialists to think of the coming transformation in terms derived from their own political experiences. On the Continent of Europe, these experiences were determined by the struggle against absolutism which ran parallel to the new conflict of classes. The birth-pangs of the industrial revolution thus aggravated a tension which had no real counterpart in Britain, let alone North America. Notwithstanding the Chartist

15 For the peculiarities of Engels's style, cf. Bollnow, *loc. cit., pp.* 105–14. That his sentence constructions disclose a distinctive manner of harmonising an optimistic world-view with a deterministic philosophy of revolution, must be apparent to anyone familiar with the original texts. It is scarcely accidental that this style (down to peculiarities of grammatical and syntactical construction) later recurs in Bernstein and Kautsky.

movement, the "social revolution" meant different things to Continental democrats still struggling to throw off the inherited deadweight of autocracy, and to English radicals not burdened with this particular problem. "Red republicanism" was confined to Europe, and within Europe it centered on France, where democracy's first battle had been fought and won on the barricades. The Communist League of 1848 was the inheritor of this tradition, and the *Manifesto* spells out the implications of a world-view which owed more to reminiscences of 1789–94 than its authors would have been willing to admit.

Man of His Century: A Reconsideration of the Historical Significance of Karl Marx

Solomon Bloom

SOME COUNTRIES may escape the stage of capitalism, and some may perhaps avoid socialism, but none has so far been able to escape a stage of "Marxism." Each great cultural area of the globe seems fated to live through an absorbing and usually bitter controversy over the merits and relevance of the doctrines of Karl Marx. The pattern of this experience has by now become tritely familiar. The controversy is usually preceded by a more or less prolonged period of neglect and indifference. At a moment of social stress the controversialists proceed to divide the nation into opposing camps, taking care to leave no articulate citizen uncommitted. The defenders, setting out from the premise that a literal acceptance of Marx's writings is somehow basic to the Socialist ideal, end up by incapacitating themselves for independent judgment; and the orthodox literature tends to oscillate between the poles of eulogy and apology. The opponents undertake to question the validity of everything he asserted and the decency of everything he desired. This is done so thoroughly that nonbelligerent critics are moved to intervene, as Thorstein Veblen did once, with the suggestion that Marx was "neither ignorant, imbecile, nor disingenuous" and that he ought to be interpreted as though he might make sense.[1] The period of "reconsidering" him anew then begins.

[1] Thorstein Veblen, *The Place of Science in Modern Civilization* (New York, 1919), p. 437 n.

Reprinted from *Journal of Political Economy*, LI, No. 6 (December 1943), pp. 494–505. Reprinted by permission of the University of Chicago Press. Copyright 1943 by the University of Chicago.

The United States has reproduced this pattern, but naturally in its own way. For a long time Marx was fairly ignored. This was, in fact, the last great country of the West to occupy itself at all seriously with his thought. Before the first World War, only a few academic people, German immigrant circles, certain Europeanized writers, and the small and uninfluential Socialist party troubled themselves about Marxism. If a few were interested, fewer still were won over. Henry Adams thought he should have been a Marxist "by rights, but some narrow trait of the New England nature seemed to blight socialism, and he tried in vain to make himself a convert." [2] In one of his less biting references to Marx, Mr. Justice Holmes wrote to Sir Frederick Pollock: "I have begun Karl Marx's book, but although he strikes me as a great man I can't imagine a combination less to my taste than Hegel and political economy." [3] This attitude was not unusual in the more enlightened American community.

The first World War forms the cultural watershed in this field, as in so many others. Specifically, it was the Bolshevik Revolution of November, 1917, that brought the United States rather suddenly face to face with Marxism; but it is interesting to reflect, by way of contrast, that if Russia had not become aware of it some two generations earlier the Revolution could hardly have taken a Marxist form. During the "normalcy" of the 1920's, however, Marxism still remained an esoteric concern, for all the febrile activity of the Communists. Great men learn from the experience of others, but great countries apparently can learn only from their own. And so it was the consequences of the crash of 1929 and their coincidence with reports of the successful operation of the First Five-Year Plan in the Soviet Union that made Americans more sensitive to the attractions of Marxism, as it also made many of them responsive to New-Dealism, industrial unionism, and Townsendism. The doctrines of Marx were suddenly "taken up" with the intensity of a fad. Publishers, journalists, teachers, labor leaders, even clubwomen, discovered an interest in the materialistic interpretation of history, the theory of the class struggle and the "withering-away" of the state. "Dialectics" almost became American idiom. But this fashion, like others, proved fickle; and presently the Russian purges, our own modest recovery, and especially the Soviet-Nazi pact of 1939 brought about a considerable revulsion of feeling. From all sides, Marxism was quite as suddenly questioned, "autopsied," revised. The wheel gradually swung full circle, and American opinion assumed an increasingly critical, and even hostile, attitude toward Marxism. That was the stage we had reached when Hitler invaded Russia. Our stake in that campaign and the extent of Russia's resistance softened that attitude but could hardly reverse it. It was too soon, for one thing. There is an unwritten law of fashion that prohibits the early return of a recent favorite.

Now, in a sense, such treatment is high tribute to Marx. For it pits his thought not against that of other men but against history itself. His significance

[2] *The Education of Henry Adams* (New York, 1918), p. 225.
[3] *Holmes-Pollock Letters* (Cambridge, 1941), I, 44.

is judged in terms of events rather than of ideas, and interest in his doctrines fluctuates with the fortunes of economic life. At bottom, however, it is the treatment accorded Christianity by King Clovis of the Franks. Pressed in battle, the King promised to be baptized if the Christian God helped him conquer. He conquered—and was converted. But the understanding of Christianity was no more advanced by the action of Clovis than the understanding of Marxism is deepened by following the shuttlecock of domestic and international affairs.

Of course, the history and cultural peculiarity of the reaction of Americans to Marx does not exhaust his relevance to their country. We sense that strongly, and hence the question of his comparative pertinence to his age and our own must remain a concern of American thought for some time to come. Perhaps it is not necessary to review and assay all the wide-ranging work of Marx in order to indicate the implied historical change. It is not proposed here to discuss his theoretical economics or to measure precisely his corrections of Hegelian "dialectics." After all, it was hardly the academic validity of any individual contribution that persuaded the rest of the Western world and eventually also the United States to reckon with him. On the economic side it was rather the occasional striking appositeness of his diagnosis and prognosis of capitalism; on the intellectual and spiritual side it was his broader reflections on the nature of society, culture, and the past and future path of historical development and, especially, the applicability of these reflections to the institutions and movements of his time.

The followers of Marx were not, however, content to look at him in this light. They did not represent his doctrines as a view of the world bearing the earmarks of a great epoch, or Marx as but another theorist and statesman. Instead, they insisted that he had propounded a method of thought so novel and revolutionary and so powerful that we could use it to control in large measure, as well as to explain, the stream of economic and political events. Marx was pictured much in the role of a Vulcan who had forged a key to unlock the social secrets of the past and pry open the door of the future. In short, the world was asked to treat and accept Marxism as an internally consistent, all-inclusive, and fully articulated philosophy of man, society, and polity.

It is interesting to re-examine this claim before employing the more customary technique of balancing contribution against limitation and fitting him into the framework of his century. As a crucial test it may be sufficient to consider some of the more important constituents of Marxism regarded as "system." Historical materialism is the speculative premise from which other aspects of the "system" are derivations and conclusions; the Marxist conception of politics represents a most vital application to practical affairs; and the Marxist view of human character must reach close to the core of a system whose chief driving force is an attempt to reorganize society fundamentally and elevate the position of humanity. These three conceptions, then—of materialism, of the state, and of man—are not only intrinsically important; they are representative issues of Marxism.

The economic interpretation of history, broadly understood, is, of course, much older than Marxism. From Swift and Mandeville to Turgot and Smith, many leaders of the Enlightenment underlined the economic factor in human affairs. So vigorous, indeed, was this current that the eighteenth century must sometime appear to be more materialistic than the nineteenth. Marx refined that interpretation, however, and—what is more to the point—employed it with great effect. He urged that the character of social and cultural life is shaped by the material forces of production. He drew a distinction between basic forces and "superstructural" ideas or institutions and, by implication, promised to explain their correlation. However, he never elaborated this view adequately, and each aspect of it has been the subject of an indecisive debate.

As closely as one may get to them, the basic forces are a mixture of technological and social factors, which it is difficult to disentangle and isolate. The "economic structure" of society consists of the "sum total" of "the relations of production" that men perforce establish in social work. That is "the real foundation" of the legal and political "superstructure." Yet that "real foundation" itself corresponds to—shall we say, rests upon?—"a definite stage of development of their material powers of production." It now appears that the "powers" of production are causally antecedent to its "relations." In fact, when these "material forces" conflict with "the relations of production," they proceed to overthrow the latter. That is what is meant by social revolution. But whatever its ultimate meaning, whether technological or social or both, "the mode of production conditions the general character of the social, political and intellectual processes of life." [4]

The "general character" turns out to be a crucial phrase, for it is by no means clear that these "processes of life" rest definitely or wholly upon the method of production. One instance will perhaps suffice. In discussing the art of the ancient Greeks, Marx acknowledged that, while there were limiting social conditions for artistic expression (mythological epics, for example, are not usually produced in an age of science), it was impossible to account for the greatness of classical art by reference to the contemporary method of production. His explanation was, indeed, as far as possible from being materialistic: the Greeks belonged to the childhood of the human race; they were normal rather than "ill bred or precocious" children; childhood has an eternal charm; Greek art will therefore always appeal powerfully to men. Under the circumstances it was natural for Marx to make this comment: "It is well known that certain golden ages of art bear no direct relation at all to the general development of society, nor to its material foundation, the skeleton structure of its organization, as it were." There is a similar remark, in the same passage, on the absence of correlation

[4] Karl Marx, *Zur Kritik der politischen Ökonomie* (Zurich, 1934), p. 5.

between production and legal relationships.[5] In later years, Friedrich Engels, indeed, admitted in a letter to a friend that he and Marx "are ourselves partly to blame for the fact that our younger disciples at times place more weight on the economic side than is due it. We had to emphasize this central factor because it was denied by our adversaries and there wasn't always time, place and opportunity to do justice to the other factors which participate in the reciprocal interaction." [6] The residue of historical materialism appears to be, strictly speaking, a conviction of the close and frequent interaction of the elements in society and a strong sense of its integral character.

The theory found an immediate application in the division of history into great stages. The inheritance from Hegel at this point takes the form of intellectual entail; Marx takes over from his philosophical predecessor not only the view that each great epoch has a unity which may be reduced to a basic element, whether it be a *Geist* or a method of production, but also the actual division and sequence of the stages. This division appears to be the result rather of historical induction than of theoretical deduction: we meet the old familiar ages of the history books.[7] But it is more revealing that Marx does not distinguish them in terms of comparable factors and does not clarify the manner of their change. The Asiatic stage rested on a communal economy but was uniquely characterized by biologic tribal bonds; moreover, it was a stagnant period (here Marx follows Hegel closely) and so belied the "dialectic" of constant social transformation.[8] The "ancient" stage rested on slavery and developed all the requisites of capitalism; it did not reach the phase of industrialism because the industrial arts failed to keep pace with the growth of commerce. There is no explanation of this interesting failure.[9] If we appeal to Marx's general theory, the famous statement in the *Critique of Political Economy* proves hardly helpful: "*No* social order *ever* disappears before *all* the productive forces, for which there is room in it, have been developed; and new higher relations of production *never* appear before the material conditions of their existence have matured in the womb of the old society [all emphases mine]." [10] The terms I have placed in italics are sharp enough, but the terms I have put in capitals are too indefinite for either proof or disproof. Instead of clarification, we get ever more assumptions; like so many forks in the road, they make us uncertain of our direction.

The next age of windmill, manor, and lord-serf relations supported Marx's purpose a good deal more cogently, especially in the manner of its death. The

[5] *Ibid.*, pp. 246–47.

[6] Karl Marx and Friedrich Engels, *Ausgewählte Briefe* (Zurich, 1934), p. 376.

[7] *Zur Kritik der politischen Ökonomie*, p. 6.

[8] Karl Marx, *Das Kapital* (Hamburg, 1921–22), I, 298, 322–23.

[9] Karl Marx, "Lettre sur le développement économique de la Russie," *Le Mouvement socialiste*, VII, 969–72. The letter was reprinted in *Ausgewählte Briefe*, pp. 289–92. See also *Das Kapital*, III¹, 311, 316–17; Karl Marx, *Der Achtzehnte Brumaire des Louis Bonaparte* (Vienna, 1927), pp. 18–19; D. Ryazanov (ed.), *The Communist Manifesto* (New York, 1930), p. 289.

[10] *Zur Kritik der politischen Ökonomie*, pp. 5–6.

transition from feudalism to industrial capitalism involved, technologically, the application of new methods of production and, socially, the rise of new classes and new conflicts. Certainly, this view is considerably supported by western European, and notably British, experience. The question, however, is whether the pattern of four or five stages can be accepted as a fair summary of history at large, beyond the West and beyond the last two or three centuries. The answer, it seems to me, must be in the negative. These stages do not appear outside of the West in anything like the prescribed order. Of this fact Marx himself was clearly aware. He expected India to pass from communalism to capitalism, leaving out feudalism and perhaps also another stage,[11] and he considered that Russia had a good "chance" of developing toward socialism without passing through capitalism.[12] We are driven to conclude that Marx regarded his theory of stages merely as a convenient statement of the "normal" sequence of societies in Western areas; certainly, we must regard it in that light.

Was that sequence "natural" and unavoidable even in those areas? This raises the much belabored issue of inevitability. We may sum up the matter briefly by saying that, while the tone and implication of the *Manifesto* and of many of the well-known passages of *Das Kapital* bespeak unqualified inevitability in the process of history and certainly in the collapse of capitalism and the rise of socialism, Marx's analyses, particularly in his political pamphlets, of specific events and movements, past and present, frequently do justice to the importance of ideas, personalities, traditions, chance events—to historical circumstance in general. These factors represent rather generous discounting of a monistic theory. Indeed, Marx in several drafts of a letter, which was never actually sent, to Russian followers, insisted that capitalism had arrived in western Europe not with the necessity of a "law" but catastrophically and drew the correct inference that no rules could be laid down for its arrival (he did not mention its departure) there or anywhere else.[13] In Marx's universe there suddenly appeared a considerable Miltonic realm where

Chaos Umpire sits

and

next him high Arbiter
Chance governs all.

Marx showed, on occasion, that he was aware of the serious implications of these reflections for his doctrines. He once denied quite specifically that he had propounded—or had meant to propound—a set of laws of the process of

---

[11] *New York Tribune*, June 25, 1853, p. 5; August 8, 1853, p. 5.

[12] Marx discussed Russia's future possibilities in the letter referred to in n. 9, above; see *Ausgewählte Briefe*, p. 290.

[13] These very significant, and largely ignored, drafts may be examined in "Vera Zazulich und Karl Marx," *Marx-Engels Archiv* (Frankfurt), I (1925), 318–40.

capitalistic growth and its "negation," laws valid for every society whatever. He would not have his outline of the origin of capitalism in western Europe (in *Das Kapital*) transformed into "an historico-philosophical theory of the general path fatally imposed upon all peoples, whatever their historical circumstances." His generalizations, he went on to insist, constituted no open sesame for unlocking social problems without considering historical differences.[14] It was, however, just such a passport that his followers thought they had inherited. Critics who rated Marx's intelligence more highly and assessed his aims more shrewdly were satisfied that here was no new philosophy, and particularly no systematic philosophy of history. Benedetto Croce was not alone in his conclusion that historical materialism was not a philosophy but a *canon* of history. It was neither "a new *a priori* notion of the philosophy of history, nor a new method of historical thought. . . ." As a canon, and one "most rich in suggestion," it recommended that "attention be directed to the so-called economic basis of society, in order that the forms and mutations may be better understood."[15] Historical materialism was also, as we shall see, a highly theoretical formulation of the "condition-of-Europe question," to paraphrase Thomas Carlyle.

If the notion that methods of production shape society is ultimately the most important in Marx's doctrine, the derivative view that it determines political forms and action is of more immediate consequence. For Marx assumed that capitalism and the material requisites of the Socialist order were fairly accomplished facts, at any rate in the countries which largely absorbed his interest. The stress must therefore be placed on the political aspect of the transition to the Socialist society.

As was his wont, he gave theoretical form to this highly practical problem. Thus arose the familiar "theory" of the state. There is a rather sudden remark in the third volume of *Capital* that the "form" in which surplus labor is squeezed from the workers determines "the political form of the relations of sovereignty and dependence, in short, the specific form of the state." Marx was quick to add that "this does not prevent the same economic basis from showing infinite variations and gradations in its [political?] appearance. This is due to innumerable outside circumstances, natural environment, race peculiarities, outside historical influences, and so forth."[16] However this précis may be construed, Marx never implemented it by stating just what forms of the state were associated with what "forms of exploitation." And where does Marx's characteristic remark that Great Britain was the "classic" economic country but France the "classic" political country[17] leave the formal relation between

---

[14] *Ausgewählte Briefe*, pp. 291–92.

[15] *Historical Materialism and the Economics of Karl Marx* (New York, 1915), pp. 77–78.

[16] *Das Kapital*, III², 324–25.

[17] *Ibid.*, I, vi, 682. Friedrich Engels once remarked that, in the *Communist Manifesto*, France had been taken as the clearest prototype of the political development of the modern nation (*Sämtliche Werke* [Marx-Engels Gesamtausgabe, Part I], VI, 527 n.).

politics and economics? This paradox throws more light on his use of "classic" than it does on political theory. The "classic" was pretty much the normal and understandable, a sort of epistemologic or pedagogic idea: British capitalism had traced a course of progress visible to the naked eye; the evolution of the French state had been drawn, particularly during the Revolution, in sensational strokes that made it eminently comprehensible. However, Marx did not suggest *economic* reasons for the difference. He seems to have thought it unnecessary to do so—a very significant circumstance; but he appears to have underestimated the zeal of his followers in building a full-panoplied philosophy of politics upon his suggestive descriptions of recent events in Western history. But then Marx, as he himself once protested, was not a Marxist.

The theory of class struggle has stood the test of events better. In the leonine rhetoric of the *Manifesto,* "the history of all society has been the history of the struggle of classes." Modern scholarship owes so much to the insight concealed in this doctrine that any brief appraisal must seem inadequate. But, like the effects, the sources of the class-struggle theory are richly varied. "Long before me," Marx acknowledged, "bourgeois historians had described the historical development of this class struggle and bourgeois economists the economic anatomy of the classes [in modern society]." [18] Indeed, the class terms and interpretations were common coinage in the eighteenth century. There was then talk of "factions" which turned out to be something much like classes. Everyone who has looked at *The Federalist* papers will remember James Madison's remarks:

. . . the most common and durable source of factions has been the various and unequal distribution of property. Those who hold and those who are without property have ever formed distinct interests in society. Those who are creditors, and those who are debtors, fall under a like discrimination. A landed interest, with many lesser interests, grow up of necessity in civilized nations, and divide them into different classes, actuated by different sentiments and views.[19]

Madison, of course, desired a constitution which would allay the pernicious and socially destructive effects of class struggles—it could not hope to repress the struggles themselves—whereas Marx would have interpreted the constitution as the inevitable expression of "factionalism" or the domination of one of the "factions."

The more technical political conclusions that Marxists have drawn from the prevalence of class conflict have been perhaps as frequently belied by events as they have been confirmed. The deterioration of his doctrine has been pronounced at this point. Proletarian developments in Germany, Great Britain, and the United States have surprised the expectations of the followers of Marx rather unpleasantly, to say the least. Yet what other countries could have

18 *Ausgewählte Briefe,* p. 48.
19 (Washington, D.C., 1937), p. 56.

provided a better testing ground for his doctrines? If modern production indicated socialism as the optimum type of political organization; if there arises a class whose stake is vitally bound up both with the exploitation of advanced methods and with the establishment of socialism—the proletarians; and if their increasing class consciousness and political drive soon push them into power—the proletarian dictatorship; then these countries should have long ago experienced revolutionary proletarian rule and should now be Socialist societies in which class distinctions have all but disappeared!

Among the more neglected aspects of historical materialism is its implied view of man. It is generally accepted that Marx defended a primarily social interpretation of human character. Yet, hidden in his thought, there are in fact *two* concepts of man, not clearly related to each other or even always distinguished, which he used in a convenient alternation. One was social and relative, the other absolute and—I almost said—divine. "Historical" man was that infinite succession of traits which are created and changed by environmental and social forces. "Generic" man, the more enduring entity, stood for the distinctively human endowments that are striving to be fulfilled: creative imagination, purposeful activity, a drive to combine mental and manual work, and, perhaps derivatively, a tendency to social grouping. Never yet completely realized, these traits are always latent. They inhere in and so define man.[20] "Scientific" socialism has as its transcendent goal their full exploitation and flowering. This concept represented the ultimate criterion of civilization, and the basis for grading societies on the scale of progress. This concept, too, formed the framework of the ethical message of *Das Kapital*. It was the rational justification of the humanitarianism of Karl Marx.

The humanitarian tendency may be allowed to speak for itself. The pertinent question is whether or not the theory of the two human facets contributes substantially toward understanding man, especially in the contemporary circumstances of social collapse, large-scale propaganda, and autocratic movements? The view that a wealth of traits are wholly conditioned by society ("historical" man), while not original with Marx or with any other thinker, has been so influential that we have come to regard it as almost axiomatic; yet so influential that it suggests a converse view that ideas play a considerable role in shaping society! Quite specifically, however, the "historical" theory would lead us to expect, after a century of continually growing industrialization in several countries, the emergence of the co-operative man. For the machine involves the most extensive scheme of socialist interaction, exchange, and interdependence that men have ever undertaken. Has this expectation been fulfilled? Certainly not conspicuously. The deepening racial hatreds of our day, the embattled and blatant chauvinisms which rend the world, hardly testify to the birth of a new social man. These phenomena seem no less the

[20] See the present author's *The World of Nations* (New York, 1941), pp. 2–4, 8–10.

product of industrialism than the attractive virtues visioned by nineteenth-century optimists. Does it not then come to this, that Marx's view of the feudal, bourgeois, or proletarian man goes further toward explaining the effect of fully formed societies at their point of maturity upon a particular group than the relations between society and man in general? The bourgeois type, for example, sums up the sharply etched tendencies impressed upon the middle class rather than the character of humanity as a whole in the era of the bourgeoisie. This limitation of the idea of "historical" man is especially apparent in a time of transition, when the old society disintegrates and the new is waiting to coagulate. If the new social man is not yet clearly recognizable, the bourgeois of our day barely resembles the liberal, progressive, and sanguine capitalist of the era of Cobden and Bright. Like Gustave Flaubert and, in a different setting much later, Sinclair Lewis, Marx painted the face not of the bourgeois in general but of the bourgeois triumphant. But neither Mme. Bovary, Babbitt, nor the bourgeois of *The Communist Manifesto* can serve adequately as subjects for an "Essay on Man," quite apart from their being somewhat dated.

The "generic" traits form together a better approximation of man as such than do the "historical." The difficulty from the point of view of a strictly materialistic philosophy is rather obvious: Marx's essential man is a *deus ex machina* thrust into the world by a socially unconditioned fiat. The notion that "history is nothing but a continuous transformation of human nature" [21] is invalidated at once by this arbitrary act. The concept itself was bequeathed to Marx by his historical background and his culture; it is a mixed product primarily of the rationalism of the Enlightenment and of the romanticism of the early decades of the nineteenth century. Although the ingredients are varied, the result errs on the side of oversimplicity. Man has latterly come to be regarded as a somewhat more complex and, at some points, even inchoate being. His potentialities seem less pointed toward definite ends; subjective and emotional factors occupy a larger place.

The fact is that the psychological side of the thought of Marx, who in this as in other matters reflected current attitudes, is strikingly weak. I do not have in mind his almost consistent failure to understand and control his closest associates and followers. More important is the fact that humanity is pictured rather stiffly in his works. This does not diminish, of course, their moral or satirical value; quite the contrary. The proletarians of *Das Kapital* are the attractive synthetic types which naturally people all tracts of social protest. Attacks against oppression and exploitation have never been based on a psychological study of the victims. It is proper also, given his aims, that Marx's bourgeois should be caricatures of themselves. *The Eighteenth Brumaire of Louis Bonaparte* and *The Civil War in France* are effective political satires

21 *Sämtliche Werke,* VI, 207.

precisely because their victims are executed in black and white. But more colors and shades are needed to depict man—the whole man who is to sustain the weight of a new social order and civilization.

A certain disillusionment attends the effort to analyze negatively a great body of thought. When we are done and the object of criticism lies on the floor strewn in a dozen pieces, we may become uneasily aware, as the mystery writers say, of "somebody" in the room. The ghost of the philosophy still hovers about. Surely there is a residual cogency in the intellectual scheme of Marx. His inquiry into the ramifications of the profit motive, his saga of the Faustian drive in capitalism, his conviction that the fate of the modern world will be decided in the West, his account of the recent course of economic progress, his overlooked attachment to the values of Western urban civilization—these and more are positive legacies. Nor can all the objections in the world erase the authentic force of his influence during the past century. A valid interpretation must jibe with that influence, while allowing for the diminishing pertinence of his doctrine, and, as a first rule of criticism, it must permit his thought to appear plausible rather than extravagant, if possible.

We may start with an assumption. Put aside the political striving of Marx; that is now a subject for historical evaluation. Look upon him not as a legislator of human destiny but, in a figurative sense, as a passionate actor and analyst of his time—of the early and middle decades of the nineteenth century. His strong sense of contemporaneity, his all-absorbing concern with a prompt revolution in western Europe, and his most characteristic traits suggest him inevitably as the voice of his immediate world. A good many contradictions, fallacies, and inadequacies which clutter up Marxism *regarded as a system* disappear from Marxism regarded as a description of the problem and promise of modern industrialism and of its historical background. The fact that Marx thought, as he seems to have done, that his views formed a whole of larger, even universal, significance itself reflected the fashion and culture of his day. It was quite natural for him to express himself in philosophical terms, to pass unconsciously from man to Man and from workaday truth to Reality; he was, after all, trained in Germany to become a professor of philosophy, and his master was Hegel. The tendency to generalize characterized many another thinker of the century. Marx's style and habit of mind need not deceive us into wrenching him from the framework of time and place, when, as a matter of fact, they help to define that very framework.

What a man takes for granted may more quickly betray his cultural heritage than what he finds it necessary to demonstrate. To those who would enlarge his economic and political views into a philosophy of society and reality, the fact that he did not concern himself directly with the problem of human nature must surely be disquieting. But others will find it illuminating that Marx expected his readers to accept without question his ambivalent view of man.

For them, as for him, that view was a *portemanteau* for many prevailing modes of thought. It reflected the theory of environmental determinism, increasingly influential in that age. Yet it also managed to preserve much of the classical view of man as a simple additon of a few well-defined traits. It made room for the evolutionary idea propounded by Hegel in philosophy and later by Darwin in biology; for the generic traits, while fixed in their essential character, would be exploited more fully as the environment was improved. There is, finally, in the "historical-generic" amalgam a clear strain of romanticism. Marx's man is cast in noble and heroic mold; his capacities are appraised with a sanguine eye; he is the core of the notion of progress. Some of the most influential ideas of the century are present here in solution. Marx's attitude toward human nature shows how avidly he absorbed and assimilated, with greater catholicity than consistency, the tendencies to which he was heir.

Historical materialism belongs in a different category from the concept of human nature. On that subject Marx thought deliberately and with the self-consciousness of the pioneer. We have already suggested some of the weaknesses of his theory. It is remarkable, however, that these weaknesses multiply directly with the geographic distance from western Europe, the socioeconomic distance from capitalism, and the temporal distance from the middle of the last century. This interesting circumstance suggests that it may be advisable to regard the theory, apart from its value as a canon for the study of history, as an account of the rise and flowering of capitalism, couched in the language dear to the heart of the Hegelian. Such an approach may be richly supported. Although Marx stated his view in ambitiously comprehensive terms, he never established the correlation at all times between particular forms of production and noneconomic forces, such as, let us say, the development of science. He hoped, of course, that scientific contributions would confirm his views, but only in the broadest possible sense. For example, he was glad to learn that Morgan had urged that the earliest human societies were communistic, since it stamped communism as not only "natural" but an actual historical fact, in the past at any rate.[22] But such scientific "confirmation" was hardly essential to his principal concern—the overthrow of capitalism. Would Marxists today abandon their social program because many modern anthropologists no longer subscribe to Morgan's interpretation of the early societies? The attempt to apply closely the theory of Marx to the field of the physical sciences and to relate closely socioeconomic and scientific developments is one of the most unfortunate aspects of recent Marxist discussions.

But, while the more formal claims of historical materialism cannot be substantiated, its special applicability to—or, perhaps better, its special derivation from—some important aspects of modern European society are visibly

[22] Lewis H. Morgan, *Ancient Society* (Chicago, n.d.), p. 537; and Engels, *The Origin of the Family, Private Property, and the State* (Chicago, 1902), pp. 9, 10.

apparent. The collapse of feudalism before the attacks of capitalism amply demonstrated the revolutionary role of commerce; the supplanting of individual handicrafts by the division of labor and the machine illustrated the superior viability of the modern productive system; the readjustment of political, ecclesiastical, and social institutions to the needs of capitalism underscored the primacy of the economic revolution in the Western world; the ever spreading wave of political revolutions in state forms, since 1776 and 1789, in the wake of economic advance, persuaded Marx and many other observers of the secondary and derivative character of politics.

His political reflections also gain in substance when placed against the background of western European practice. Whatever may be the fate of his imputed correlation between economics and politics in general, he has undoubtedly presented a convincing class interpretation of the modern history of British parliamentarianism, by pointing to connivance at the inclosure of common fields, the reactionary attitude toward social reform, and the stress on imperialistic expansion. Consider the contemporary realism of the oft quoted statement of the *Manifesto* that "the modern state authority is nothing more than a committee for the administration of the consolidated affairs of the bourgeois class as a whole." As a summary of the modern state from the fifteenth century onward, this sweeping assertion leaves much to be desired. But in 1847, when it was written, it was an apposite summary of British governance: a small propertied electorate ruled through the elective committee of the Commons, although this body shared rule with the aristocratic upper house. Nor was the implied extension of this generalization beyond Great Britain unreasonable, since its liberal, as distinguished from democratic, parliamentary forms were soon copied in many parts of the Continent.

There should be no need to insist that *Das Kapital* is more significant as a critique of modern industrialism, especially in its earlier stages, than as a treatise on the nature of society. The reader will recall Marx's insistence that the various historical "laws" set forth in *Das Kapital* were intended to outline the actual course of capitalist accumulation, expropriation, and development in western Europe, with no necessary "legal" consequences for other areas. The descriptive aspects of the book are, indeed, notable from the account of the working day, division of labor, the introduction of machinery, and the rise of the factory to the illuminating outline, widely accepted nowadays, of the process by which capitalism took hold of the British town and countryside. Indeed, in studying the history of Great Britain in the first half of the nineteenth century, it would not be safe to ignore Marx. The historical aspects of his principal work have largely stood the test of later investigations.

This analysis may be further extended. The Marxian labor theory of value has not won wide recognition in academic circles but has nevertheless played a sizable role in politics. It was an important factor in that confluence of Marxist ideology with proletarian growth that explains, probably better than anything else does, the rise of modern socialism. The significance of *Das Kapital* in general, whatever the final verdict on its scientific value, echoed powerfully, with voices like Shelley's, the cry of the modern proletarian:

> The seed ye sow, another reaps,
> The wealth ye find, another keeps,
> The robes ye weave, another wears,
> The arms ye forge, another bears.

And if, as Lord Halifax once remarked, the best qualification for a prophet is to have a good memory, Marx might feel qualified to foretell the increasing misery of the working class, for he lived in the "hungry forties." His notion that, as that class grows in numbers, its political consciousness and capacity must also grow was forcibly suggested by contemporary movements such as Chartism. It is well to recall that, in the first half of Marx's century, Great Britain possessed not only the most advanced industrial system but the most advanced, articulate proletariat as well. The expectation that the socialist revolution would occur first in the most developed countries was not fantastic in a period when the British workers frequently engaged in directly revolutionary acts.

It was, in fact, a striking pertinence to the contemporary scene that gave Marxism a pervasive and expanding influence. Marx's account of the process of industrialization was so discerning and "abstract" in a realistic sense that it bore pointedly upon the history of any country that might experience it. It is understandable, therefore, that his ideas should have struck deepest root in the areas which reproduce most nearly the conditions of western Europe a century ago and more. Present-day Russia springs to mind at once; but there are other instances as well. Indeed, a comparison with the age on which the work of Marx was a commentary constitutes the starting-point for tracing the varying fortunes of his doctrines in particular countries. Such a comparison would lead us to divide the world into several kinds of regions with distinctive lines of development, distinctive backgrounds, and hence, also, distinctive reactions and immunities to Marxism. The Western, or, perhaps, the North Atlantic, world would have to be treated as a unit. It is at once the home of Marxism and the region which has traveled the greatest distance from the early industrialism which Marx recorded. It is here that Marxism has met the steepest obstacles and has revealed the greatest limitations. The contrasts a century has worked are as striking as the powerful resemblances.

Karl Marx, then, is best understood as a classically rooted western European who functioned in a time when his area was the center of the whole world in a far greater degree than it is now; when Great Britain was the economic and political model she has now long since ceased to be; when France was a reliable catalyst of revolution; and when a predominantly agrarian society was emerging into the phase of early industrialism. His views represent an authentic aspect of the culture of his day; his political program was naturally built around its peculiar conditions. Both his influence and the uneven pattern of his latter-day relevance derive largely from the circumstance. Marx was born eighteen years after his century began, and he died seventeen years before it ended. His life-span fitted into it with a neat symmetry; his work and striving largely summed it up.

THE NEW STATESMEN

[6]

Napoleon III: Some Conflicting Verdicts

Professor Alan Spitzer, in the third selection below, has so well traced Napoleon III's varying fortunes in the hands of historians that there is no need to discuss here the details of an historical controversy that has produced so many divergent judgments on his personality and policies. Also, the three selections taken together treat nearly all of the factors that make for the differing evaluations of Louis Napoleon's reign. The enigmatic personality of the emperor, the *coup d'état* which liberals of the 1848 tradition found impossible or hard to forgive—even after Caesarism gave way to a briefly realized liberal empire —the gap between idea or ideals and performance, the economic and social programs of the empire and its foreign policy are all commented on.
   The first selection comes from the concluding chapter of Albert Guérard's sensitive and sympathetic study of Napoleon III. It reflects what Spitzer calls the "generally favorable" interpretation of the Second Empire that has prevailed in this country and England during the last two decades.
That, in the words of Spitzer, "a hostile tradition does certainly survive," is proved by the second selection. Sir Lewis Namier takes issue with some of the points made in Guérard's book and hits hard at what he considers the dictatorship of Napoleon III.
In the third selection, a model of what a critical, historiographical essay should be, Spitzer, besides reviewing the literature on Napoleon III, makes some original and trenchant judgments of his own which are a valuable contribution to the understanding of a controversial period in French history.

THE JUDGEMENT OF POSTERITY

Albert Guérard

* * *

Je me souviendrai éternellement des bontés de l'Empereur et de l'Impératrice et je resterai jusqu'à mon dernier jour fidèle à leur mémoire. . . . Malgrè les vaines et stupides clameurs de la rue et toutes les lâches défaillances de ces derniers temps, l'Empereur peut attendre avec confiance le jugement de la postérité. Son règne restera l'un des plus glorieux de notre histoire. LOUIS PASTEUR [1]

"The Emperor may await with confidence the judgment of posterity. His reign will remain among the most glorious in our history." These words written by Louis Pasteur in a glow of indignation and despair will be read by most with a pitying, melancholy smile. At the close of this study, upon which I have been engaged for thirty years, I have no hope of altering the verdict of the unthinking. Legends, it seems, are indestructible. To the end of time, people will believe that William Tell did shoot the apple; that Frederick the Great was the incarnation of the German national spirit and the hero of the Protestant faith; that Napoleon I was the crowned soldier of the Revolution, a good European, and invincible on the battlefield; that Bismarck was a flawless realist; and that Karl Marx, single-handed, transformed Socialism from vague Utopia into rigorous science. In this world of unchallenged convention, Napoleon III stands irremediably condemned.

If we pass from loose tradition to careful research, the scene changes altogether. Within the last fifty years, Napoleon III has won the respect and sympathy of practically every critical historian. The old Carlylean tone of contempt is found only in popular works or textbooks at third or fourth hand. Even the frankly biased account by the *petit bourgeois* Radical Charles Seignobos, a period piece of the Gambetta age, and that by Albert Thomas in an orthodox "Socialist" series are completely different in tone from the apocalyptic vituperations of Victor Hugo.

On the other hand, I hate the word *glorious* which Pasteur applied to the

---

[1] Letter to Marshal Vaillant, September 5, 1870; in Paul Guériot, *Napoléon III* (Paris, 1933–34), II, 322.

Reprinted by permission of the publishers from Albert Guérard, *Napoleon III* (Cambridge: Harvard University Press, 1943), pp. 281–93. Copyright, 1943, by The President and Fellows of Harvard College.

reign of Napoleon III. It is not consonant with the character of the scientist, one of the most unassuming of men; it does not stand for the best in the Second Empire. In the Napoleonic sense of martial fame, we had better forget *glory* altogether. The Crimean War was a costly blunder; Napoleon III himself was horror-stricken on the battlefields of Italy, and whatever sickly laurels he may have won fell to dust at Sedan. If *glory* evokes gorgeous display, the glittering Court, the gay uniforms, the gilded Grand Opera, behold, this also is vanity. All this tarnished splendor has acquired with the years a kind of baroque charm, futile and pathetic; but it is appealing only because it is dead.

What Pasteur had in mind, the true *glory* of Napoleon III, is that he was profoundly devoted to the cause of the masses, the inarticulate, the humble, the forgotten. This was his "democracy," his "socialism," a deeper reality than any constitutional form or any pseudo-scientific doctrine. In this he stands almost unique in the long line of French sovereigns. In comparison, the truly *glorious* rulers, Francis I, Richelieu, Louis XIV, Napoleon I, are cold and harsh; they prized France merely as their pedestal. Only three kings are remembered because there was in them a touch of tenderness for the common folk: Louis XII was called "the Father of the People," but he has become very shadowy; Louis XVI said to Turgot, "You and I alone love the people" —but his good will was a feeble reed; Henry IV is still a cherished memory, and most of all perhaps for his homely slogan, "A chicken in the pot every Sunday." In his early career, Henry of Navarre was even more of an adventurer than Louis Napoleon; when he came to power, he did not grant France any "liberties" of the Parliamentary kind; and he was no paragon of puritanical virtue. Yet to many readers, the comparison will seem absurd: Henry remains a universal favorite, the frank admirers of Napoleon III are few and apologetic. Why this difference? First of all, Henry was murdered—a great boon. Then, in those days, there were bitter factions but no organized parties; so his successors, while reversing his policies, did not find it essential to blacken his memory. And, above all, Henry had the advantage of *style*. He might be frivolous, but he was bluff and hearty. He was, in the words of the old song, "the triple-threat man, who could drink, fight, and make love," all with a delightful touch of bravado. He was "French of the French," if your ideal of France is to be found in Alexandre Dumas rather than in Alfred de Vigny. Napoleon III had no dash and very little humor; he was gentleness and silence. Yet he too was recognized by the people as their friend and their leader.

II

His faith in the people, his desire to serve the people, assumed a threefold form. In European affairs, it became *the principle of nationalities,* the right of self-determination ascertained by plebiscites. In the economic and social field, it manifested itself as *Saint-Simonian socialism:* order and prosperity, for the purpose of improving the welfare of the most numerous and poorest class. In politics, it sought realization as *direct democracy,* brushing aside those intermediate powers which invariably bolster privilege.

Upon the first two articles of his faith, we shall insist no more. He was a better European than Bismarck or Gambetta, and a better socialist than Karl Marx, because he was less narrow than they, and not poisoned with hatred and pride. The things he labored for, confusedly, haltingly, shall come to pass if this war is not to be eternal: all nationalities free and equal within a United Europe, industrial wealth for the service of the many, not for the profit of the few. These were Utopias yesterday; they are at this hour the only alternative to strife and chaos. The third part of his creed, direct democracy, is more controversial. Rightly understood, it might be his most substantial contribution to the making of modern Europe.

The ideal of Napoleon III was a national, non-partisan government. This conception is sharply opposed to the multi-party system, which is the foundation of all Parliamentary regimes; and it is even more directly antagonistic to the single-party system, which is Totalitarianism. Strictly speaking, until the fall of the Empire, Bonapartism was not a party.

The State, according to this view, represents only those interests which cannot be divided without destruction, and in which every one, whatever his private opinions may be, necessarily has a share. These can be summed up in one word, *security:* international security, which, ideally, means a just and durable peace, and, immediately, national defense; security at home, that is to say law and order. Its necessary instrument is a disciplined force, the army and the police. The head of the State, not for glory, but for service, is a man in uniform. This collective security should be above controversy: *Salus populi suprema lex esto.* The secondary task of the government is to promote *general* prosperity, through those improvements which do not exclusively serve private interests—public works, the development of natural resources. Whatever is factional or sectional is not the proper domain of the State; the government should be, not the agent of a victorious party, but the *greatest common denominator* of all private interests.

Security, order, prosperity, are strictly material ends. The government which limits itself to their service is frankly a materialistic government. These things, by definition, are Caesar's. All that we can reasonably demand of Caesar is that he should perform his restricted task honestly and well. We should not expect the police or the postal authorities to be idealistic; their sole duty is to be non-partisan and to be efficient.

Saint-Simonian socialism, generously Utopian as it appears, is yet in perfect harmony with this materialistic conception of the State. If the aim of the

State is the *common* good, if the State be indeed a *commonwealth,* leaving private interests to private initiative, then automatically it will be devoted to "the welfare of the most numerous class," which is also the poorest. Those who are above that common level do not need the State; they can take care of themselves. In concrete terms, it is the business of the State to prevent famine, but not to provide luxuries. It should "extinguish pauperism": it should not seek to create millionaires. So long as millionaires can grow richer without causing destitution, the State does not interfere with them. But if there be a connection between luxury at one end and famine at the other, then the State has the right and the duty to move. The common good, the good of the common man, must first be served.

This conception of the State as above parties is recognized to a large extent in the most orthodox of Parliamentary regimes. We deprecate partisanship even in elected office holders: a Mayor should be the Mayor of the city, not of the victorious faction. The spoils system is the natural consequence of the party spirit, for if all men must take sides, solidly, for the Blacks or the Greens, and if the other side is necessarily wrong in all things, then it is our duty to "turn the rascals out"—generals, engineers, and judges as well as governors, sheriffs, and dog-catchers. Yet we are now ashamed of the spoils system, and we are striving to eliminate it from public administration. In a crisis such as war, we have no doubt that common interests must take unquestioned precedence. Now the State should consider itself as constantly at war; not against other States—such a criminal thought never guided Napoleon III—but against disorder, disease, and want. Within that sphere, and for the duration of that eternal fight, there should be no parties.

Napoleon III was not averse to parties because he had an autocratic temperament: on the contrary, no one could be more considerate in his relations with other men, and even with dogs. He condemned parties because, in his opinion, they had irremediable faults. Even when they were perfectly honest, their squabbles paralyzed necessary action; this had been evident under Louis Philippe and the Second Republic. But could they ever be perfectly honest? Parties are inconceivable without partisanship, which is the deliberate warping of one's thought. If a man seeks to remain impartial and free, he cannot commit himself to any party organization. Worst of all, party rule, if logically carried out, is of necessity tyrannical. The party in power attempts to impose its full program upon the defeated. To be sure, the minority hopes to conquer power in its turn; party government is thus a series of wrongs offset by other wrongs, which is an extremely wasteful method of never attaining the right. These are not the excesses of the party spirit, but its very essence. The only legitimate field of government action should be the nonpartisan.

If we could afford to be as paradoxical as Einstein, we should say that this field is restricted, yet indefinitely extensible. The *greatest common denomina-*

tor may grow. We have attempted to show that Napoleon III did not believe in the "minimal State" of the philosophical anarchists. It was with him an article of faith that the government should not be defensive merely, but positive, dynamic, an instrument for the common good. In him, the policeman and the humanitarian were not at odds. The "guardian of the peace" [2] was also an agent of progress.

But, if the sphere of the government is constantly expanding, there ever remains a domain beyond: the free, boundless, teeming domain of opinions —religious, social, political, artistic. So long as a thought is merely an *opinion,* even if it be passionately held by a majority, it has no right to turn itself into a *law,* binding upon the minority. Most Americans are Christians; a majority of them are Protestants. They have steadily refused to establish a State religion, or to make their creed part of the Constitution, for, by so doing, they would be outlawing dissenters, depriving Jews, Buddhists, or agnostics of their full citizenship. *There are things that are not Caesar's.* This Napoleon III fully understood, and therein lies the radical difference between his democracy and modern dictatorships. For *they* believe in the single-party system, imposing its will upon all dwellers in the land and in every domain, the ideal as well as the material. Not only must men, under their rule, obey the same traffic regulations, but they must think and feel alike, or else they are crushed into silence.

Beyond the expanding *greatest common denominator* of security, order, prosperity, the regime of Napoleon III was definitely pluralistic. It did not matter that the Empress should be at heart a Legitimist, Morny an Orleanist, Prince Napoleon a Republican, and the Emperor himself a Socialist: if they obeyed the law and sought to promote the general welfare, they could be faithful servants of the community. Persigny, because he was a *mere* Bonapartist, was properly voted crazy. Pluralism is not identical with liberty— one might conceive of pluralistic tyrannies existing side by side—but it is the indispensable condition of liberty. The country which seeks to impose spiritual unity, by forcible or insidious means, is not free. Authority, on the other hand, is not antagonistic to liberty. The police is the protector of our innermost freedom; it makes it possible for us to differ in peace.

The Empire prohibited political meetings almost up to the end, because it was frankly committed to the suppression of factional strife. It did not abolish the liberty of the press; the blunders of a few policemen and censors should not blind us to that essential fact. Journalists were made responsible for misstatements and personal insults, but throughout the Empire there were papers which were openly Legitimist, Orleanist, Republican, anticlerical, or Ultramontane in their sympathies. Prévost-Paradol, who opposed the Empire until

[2] In French, *gardien de la paix, agent de police, sergent de ville,* and in some cases *gendarme* all mean "police officer."

1870, recognized as early as 1853 that the result of "the Tyranny" was actually to raise the intellectual and literary level of discussion. Vociferations were discouraged; incontrovertible facts stated with moderation had a chance to be heard; criticism could be sharp and even bitter, if it remained courteous. Those keen-edged weapons, allusion and irony, recovered a favor and an effectiveness they had lost since the days of Voltaire. The fearless expression of delicate thought has two enemies: the dead silence imposed by a despot, the universal tumult of full license; the second is the worst. Not merely expression, but thought itself is drowned by competitive bellowing; in the stillness of a jail, a man can at least hear himself think. The Second Empire was neither a jail nor a pandemonium; men could reflect, and talk.

More deadly to liberty than any censor are respectable conventions, unchallenged conformities. In Victorian England, wrote Hilaire Belloc, "a sort of cohesive public spirit glued and immobilized all individual expression. One could float imprisoned as in a stream of thick substance, one could not swim against it." The public spirit of the Second Empire was not cohesive, and that is why its activity was so intense and so many-sided. Never, not even in the great moments of the Renaissance and the Enlightenment, were *all* schools of thought so vigorously represented. Within the solid framework of the materialistic state, the richest spiritual anarchy prevailed; and in that domain, anarchy should be the only law. Many years ago, in *French Prophets of Yesterday,* I attempted to catalogue that unexampled surge of intellectual energy. But no critical guide can do full justice to a period in which Catholics and Protestants of all shades, Humanitarians, Freethinkers, Voltairian Rationalists, Saint-Simonians, Positivists, mystics, devil-worshippers, scientists, anarchists, socialists, believers in Art for Art's Sake, went fearlessly to the end of their thought.

"Frivolous" France under the Second Empire could be amused by fancy-dress balls, by grand reviews in dashing uniforms, by Offenbach operettas, by the sauciness of Theresa or the antics of Princess Metternich, by the light wit of Alphonse Karr, Aurélien Scholl, Albert Wolff, Arsène Houssaye, Paul de Kock, Henri Rochefort, Meilhac and Halévy. But, with the hubbub of politics almost completely hushed, she could also be stirred, as we are not, by philosophical and religious controversy. A lecture by Renan at the Collège de France was an event of national importance. His *Life of Jesus,* quiet and scholarly, gave rise at once to hundreds of passionate attacks and defenses. There were police regulations, but no taboos. No cranny of human experience was left unexplored. And under that apparent chaos, there ruled a deep and definite hierarchy of values.

Napoleon III was, to borrow Gamaliel Bradford's phrase, a "damaged soul"; and, after 1860, a damaged soul imprisoned in a damaged body. Grave, thoughtful, kind, devoted to noble causes, determined withal, fearless, and surprisingly practical, he had in him also the tortuousness of the eternal plotter, the vagueness of the Utopian, the weakened fiber of the sensualist, the fatalism of the gambler. Some characters in history are obvious in their greatness, mediocrity, or turpitude: even though our sympathies may widely differ, we feel that we can focus Washington, Victoria, Gladstone, and even Napoleon I. Napoleon III is not one of these. His elusive physiognomy changes altogether with the light that is turned upon it. At one moment, he appears impressive: the only political leader in the nineteenth century whose thought could still be a guide for us today. At other times, the caricature drawn by Kinglake and Victor Hugo seems almost convincing: the middle-aged rake in imperial trappings, sinister even in his futility. The most searching, the most persistent light of all, the one in which he was seen by every one who approached him, reveals him as gentle, not merely in speech and smile, but to the very depths of his being.

And the unique regime he fashioned was no less enigmatic: strangely attractive, not in its glitter, not even in its daring, but in its "humanity," yet damaged also, and from the very first. The Roman Expedition in 1849, the fusillade on the fourth of December 1851, were causes of confusion not wholly dispelled to this day. They inflicted upon Caesarian Democracy as Louis Napoleon conceived it wounds which at the end of twenty years still refused to heal. In addition to these tragic accidents, there were antinomies in the very structure of the Empire which made its survival precarious. The most obvious, however, was only apparent: the conflict between authority and liberty. Neither of these principles can cover the whole of life, and the Empire, more clearly than other regimes, defined their respective spheres. More dangerous was the Napoleonic heritage; a government which was modern, peace-minded, democratic, industrial, socialistic, grew out of the "Legend," which was the crude exaltation of military adventure. Napoleon III was entirely different from Napoleon I, whom he had used purely as a Promethean myth; but so long as the Bonapartes ruled, it would have been hopeless to eliminate the Napoleonic virus—as hopeless as it was for Prussia to cast off the ruthless cynicism of Frederick the Great. There are forms of ingratitude that history will not tolerate: you cannot build upon the glory of the Founder and then denounce that glory as a thing of evil.

This leads us to the fatal flaw in the Empire, the restoration of heredity. Louis Napoleon was not fully conscious of the contradiction it implied. His thought was a unique historical complex, and he sincerely believed that his blood, his tradition, his doctrine, and the will of the people were in miraculous harmony: *vox populi* and *vox Dei,* in unison, would inevitably utter the same word, *Napoleon.* This mystic delusion was at one time shared by many; but a delusion it was, and could not endure. Yet for the first twenty years of his political career, Louis Napoleon resisted the temptation. His first "Dream of a Constitution" (*Rêveries politiques*) in 1832, and the definite project he submitted to the people in 1851, provided for an elected Chief of State.

Had he given up power at the end of ten years, according to his own proposal, his term of office, although far from flawless, would have justified the highest praise. Heredity is a harmless fiction if the sovereign is but a figurehead; it becomes an absurdity if he attempts to be the active and responsible leader of the nation. Because the dynastic Empire had been restored, France had to submit, after 1861, to the rule of a man intelligent no doubt, well-meaning, experienced, but ailing, and unable to exercise for good the power he still claimed to wield. She might have been autocratically governed, in the name of a child, by a high-spirited but narrow-minded woman. She might have been exposed to the uncongenial and capricious dictatorship of Prince Napoleon. If, on the other hand, Napoleon III had yielded in time, if he had accepted in 1863–64 the offer of Adolphe Thiers and restored a Parliamentary monarchy, he would have become a mere Louis Philippe in gaudier trappings; he would have sacrificed the principle which was his *raison d'être,* Caesarian democracy.

History is not chemistry; there is no method that will enable us to analyze with irrefutable definiteness the elements of a complex situation. We have tried honestly to do so, and we are aware that the result cannot be called scientific knowledge. There entered into the making of Louis Napoleon's career accidents, a personality, and a principle; heterogeneous as they were, they remain indissolubly fused.

It is with the principle that we are chiefly concerned. That principle is *direct democracy.* The experiment failed, not because the principle could be proved wrong, but because it was not applied in its full and honest simplicity. Caesarism reverted to heredity; the opposition, of the Right and of the Left, was bent on restoring factional strife, as if that alone deserved the name of Liberty. Three forces united in raising Louis Napoleon to supreme power: the Imperial Legend, the dread of disorder, and humanitarian democracy. All three were very real, but the third was the deepest in French opinion, and in Louis Napoleon's own soul. The regime which he conceived resembles the American far more than it does British Parliamentarism on the one hand, Totalitarian Dictatorship on the other. It might be well for France, when she resumes the normal course of her destiny, to borrow her inspiration from the United States rather than from England. If she did so, the Constitution of 1852 would be for her a better starting point than the Constitution of 1875. And she would be fortunate indeed if she found again, under such a regime, a leader with the unfailing gentleness, the quiet intellectual courage, the profound generosity, of Napoleon III.

THE FIRST MOUNTEBANK DICTATOR

Sir Lewis Namier

RECURRENT SITUATIONS in history reproduce analogous forms; there is a morphology of politics. But to the basic repetition and the individual variations of organic growth an element is added peculiar to man: imitation engendered by historical memory. The modern dictatorship arises amid the ruins of an inherited social and political structure, in the desolation of shattered loyalties—it is the desperate shift of communities broken from their moorings. Disappointed, disillusioned men, uprooted and unbalanced, driven by half-conscious fears and gusts of passions, frantically seek a new rallying point and new attachments. Their dreams and cravings projected into the void gather round some figure. It is the monolatry of the political desert. The more pathological the situation the less important is the intrinsic worth of the idol. His feet may be of clay and his face may be a blank: it is the frenzy of the worshippers which imparts to him meaning and power.

Such morbid cults have by now acquired a tradition and ideology, and have evolved their own routine and political vocabulary. With Napoleon I things were serious and real—the problems of his time and his mastery of them; he raised no bogies and whipped up no passions; he aimed at restoring sanity and at consolidating the positive results of the Revolution; and if, in superposing the Empire on the Republic and in recreating a Realm of the West, he evoked the memories of Caesar and Charlemagne, the appeal was decorative rather than imitative. There would have been no occasion for his dictatorship had not the living heritage of French history been obliterated by revolution; but his system has left its own unhealthy legend, a jackal-ghost which prowls in the wake of the "Red spectre." Napoleon III and Boulanger were to be the plagiarists, shadowy and counterfeit, of Napoleon I; and Mussolini and Hitler were to be unconscious reproducers of the methods of Napoleon III. For these are inherent in plebiscitarian Caesarism, or so-called "Caesarian democracy," with its direct appeal to the masses: demagogical slogans; disregard of legality in spite of a professed guardianship of law and order; contempt of political parties and the parliamentary system, of the educated classes and their values; blandishments and vague, contradictory prom-

From Sir Lewis Namier, *Vanished Supremacies: Essays on European History 1812–1918* (London: Hamish Hamilton Ltd., 1958). Reprinted by permission. Copyright Sir Lewis Namier, 1958.

ises for all and sundry; militarism; gigantic, blatant displays and shady corruption. *Panem et circenses* once more—and at the end of the road, disaster.

The first coups of Louis-Napoleon, at Strasbourg in 1836 and at Boulogne in 1840, were miserable failures, like Hitler's Munich *Putsch* of 1923. Both men were treated with humane and neglectful forbearance, and in the enforced leisure of their comfortable prisons they composed their programmatic works —*Des Idées Napoléoniennes* and *Mein Kampf*. Not even at a later stage did the political leaders realize the full gravity of the situation—thinking in terms of their own and not in those of the masses, they could not descry either in Louis-Napoleon or in Hitler a possible ruler or dictator. Louis-Napoleon escaped from his prison at Ham in 1846, and settled in London. On the outbreak of the February Revolution he hastened to Paris, a professed supporter of the Republic; but when requested by the Provisional Government to leave the country, he complied, and the Chartist crisis of April found him acting the special constable in London. In the by-elections of 4 June he was returned to the Constituent Assembly by four *départments,* but rather than face an imbroglio, he withdrew. "When one is weak, one has to submit and await better days," he wrote to his cousin Napoleon ("Plonplon") in 1844; and on 5 June 1848: "In these moments of exaltation, I prefer to remain in the background." Re-elected in September by five constituencies, he took his seat, and read out a brief address affirming his devotion "to the defence of order and the strengthening of the Republic." "These correct words, spoken in a toneless voice, were received with perfunctory applause," writes his latest biographer, Mr. Albert Guérard.[1] He looked

disarmingly unobtrusive. His torso was long and his legs short; he moved awkwardly, with a shuffling gait; his head sat heavily on his broad and round shoulders; his countenance was pale and immobile; his eyes were small, heavy-lidded, of an undefinable grey. . . . He was not downright ludicrous; he was not exactly commonplace; he certainly was not impressive.

When the Assembly, enmeshed in constitutional doctrine and democratic dogma, decided to have the President of the Republic elected by popular vote, and not by the Legislature, the door was opened for a Bonapartist restoration. To preclude it, an amendment was moved debarring members of former ruling families.

Every eye turned towards Louis-Napoleon, for the amendment was aimed at him alone. He went up to the tribune and, in a few halting sentences, uttered with a strangely un-French accent, he protested against "the calumnies constantly hurled at his head," stammered, ended abruptly and shuffled back to his seat.

The amendment was withdrawn, its mover himself describing it, "after what we have just seen and heard," as superfluous. On 10 December 1848, in the

[1] Albert Guérard: *Napoleon III*. Harvard University Press, London: Cumberlege, 1945.

Presidential election, Louis-Napoleon received 5,400,000 votes against the 1,800,000 of his four opponents; Lamartine—poet, orator, and leader in the Provisional Government—found himself at the bottom of the poll, with a mere 17,000. "The world is a strange theatre," remarks Alexis de Tocqueville; "had Louis-Napoleon been a wise man or a genius, he would never have become President of the Republic."

"The remote lack-lustre gaze of his grey eyes, now that it was fraught with destiny, could be declared sphinx-like or prophetic," writes Guérard. And Pierre de La Gorce, historian of the Second Empire, says that the change which success produced in the public estimate of the same traits of Louis-Napoleon's character was like a picture advertising a hair-restorative: "before" and "after." Between these two appraisements, the taciturn, shadowy, impassive figure of Napoleon III has puzzled the century which has gone by, as the shrieking, convulsed, hysterical figure of Hitler will puzzle the one to come. "A sphinx without a riddle," was Bismarck's summing up of Napoleon III; "from afar something, near at hand nothing"; "a great unfathomed incapacity." And N. W. Senior reports Tocqueville having said to him in January 1852:

Louis-Napoleon is essentially a copyist. He can originate nothing; his opinions, his theories, his maxims, even his plots, all are borrowed, and from the most dangerous of models—from a man who, though he possessed genius and industry such as are not seen . . . once in a thousand years, yet ruined himself by the extravagance of his attempts.

But Napoleon III, said Grimblot to Senior in 1855, "lacked industry and capacity"—and on this point most contemporaries are agreed.

When we were together in England [continued Grimblot] I saw much of him. We have walked for hours in the Green Park. His range of ideas is narrow, and there is always one which preoccupies him . . . and shuts out the others. . . . He learns little from his own meditations, for he does not balance opposite arguments; he learns nothing from conversation, for he never listens.

And an unnamed friend of Senior's, in 1858: ". . . as he is ignorant, uninventive, and idle, you will see him flounder from one failure to another." Guizot, Thiers, Montalembert, Falloux, Duvergier de Hauranne, Victor Hugo, Ampère, Beaumont, they all despised *celui-ci*; but the opposition of the intellectuals was tolerated because, as Tocqueville put it, their writings were not read "by the soldier or by the *prolétaire*"; and "the principle of his régime was to rest on the army and the people, and to ignore the existence of the educated classes."

"Within the last fifty years," writes Guérard, "Napoleon III has won the respect and sympathy of practically every critical historian." Sympathy, perhaps; but respect is based on a man's actions, and not on his dreams and intentions.

La Gorce, summing up a life's work, wrote about Napoleon III in 1933: "Baleful (*funeste*) he was: still, hardly have I written the word than I would like to soften it, for he was good and even enlightened; but no sooner did the light break through than it was clouded." Nor does Guérard's book, the product of years of study, yield a very different result, though the story is often lyricized, especially in an attempt to represent Napoleon III as a far-sighted reformer, a "Saint-Simon on horseback" whose régime is of the most "vital importance." Moreover praise is offered of his plebiscitarian dictatorship, of "direct democracy" as contrasted with "parliamentary practices." None the less, the picture which emerges of Napoleon III is hardly fit to inspire respect in the reader.

Guérard seeks to understand Napoleon III, but finds no solution to the enigma. "His elusive physiognomy changes altogether with the light that is turned upon it." His mind was "complex, perhaps tortuous"; "perhaps un-fathomable, perhaps simply nebulous"; there was "no flash of intuition, no capacity for sudden decision." Princess Mathilde, Louis-Napoleon's cousin and at one time his betrothed, exasperated by his taciturnity, wished she could "break his head, to find out what there is in it"; and both she and her brother, Prince Napoleon, "ascribed his caution to mental hesitancy or flabbiness of will." He had grown up "in an atmosphere of elegiac resignation," writes Guérard; and in his youth he was "retarded in development, 'gently stubborn,' as his mother called him." He was a "damaged soul." But, like La Gorce, Guérard stresses Napoleon III's "profound and unaffected kindliness," his gravity, courtesy, and gentleness—"a man of '48," "a democratic humanitarian." In his own eyes Napoleon III was "a providential man," "an instrument of the Divine Purpose"; but even that faith "was 'gently obstinate,' not blatant." "I am sure that the shade of the Emperor protects and blesses me," he wrote from Ham in 1842. Even in his obsessionist ideas he lacked energy and ruthlessness. How then did such a man succeed?

By the time the Napoleonic disaster had assumed "dramatic value and epic grandeur," in the late twenties, Romanticism adopted "the Napoleonic theme," writes Guérard; and in the thirties the Emperor turned "into a hero of folk-lore." The July Monarchy, prosaic and dull, could not afford to dramatize conservatism without playing into the hands of the Legitimists, nor move to the Left, for fear of the Republicans; but they tried to surfeit France with Napoleon's glory, "retrospective, and therefore safe." As was proved by Louis-Napoleon's failure at Boulogne, this was then "but a legend . . . something to be enjoyed rather than to be believed in or acted upon . . . a sufficient motive for a pageant, but not for a revolution." How did it ever come to life? Even in the early months of the Revolution "Bonapartism was advancing . . . with a strict minimum of ideology, organization, and expenditure"—"it held it-self in reserve." But had it ever more than a minimum of ideas and resources?

To Guérard, Louis-Napoleon is not "merely the passive heir of the Legend"
—he reshaped it "in his own image" and by his pamphlets

created in the public mind that paradoxical association between Bonapartism and
humanitarian democracy which was Louis-Napoleon's special contribution to politics.
It was not exclusively the Emperor's nephew, it was also the man who had written
On the Extinction of Pauperism, who was chosen by the people in December 1848.

"The chief quality in Louis-Napoleon's style is its directness. . . . His
words are historical documents." Not many who have read those pamphlets are
likely to endorse such praise. La Gorce says that they are neither good nor
bad, but significant; turgid, contradictory, and baffling, both naive and cunning;
they develop commonplaces "with a sustained solemnity"; but occasionally,
he claims, there occurs an original idea. Some of us have failed to discover any.
In fact, had the electorate been sufficiently advanced to read Louis-Napoleon's
writings, fewer might have voted for him—but what percentage is likely
even to have heard of them?

According to Guérard, Louis-Napoleon was elected on his own program of
"authoritarian democracy," known, understood, and "freely endorsed by 5,400,-
000 votes." All political parties stood for "the privileges of some élite": with
the Legitimists the criterion was social superiority, with the Orleanists property, with the Republicans profession of their creed. Bonapartism, it is
claimed, brushed aside the "intermediate powers and special interests"—
Parliament and plutocracy—in order to realize the "unformulated doctrine" of
the people: "direct contact between sovereign and masses." This kind of
argument formed indeed the stock-in-trade of Louis-Napoleon. In his *Idées
Napoléoniennes* "the tutelary and democratic power of the plebeian hero . . .
who was the true representative of our revolution" is contrasted with the
aristocratic or oligarchic character of the British Parliamentary system; "aristocracy requires no chief, while it is in the nature of democracy to personify
itself in one man." And the Second Empire in its depreciation of *les anciens
partis,* its strictures on "sectional interests," and its bombast about the integration of all truly national interests and "the organization of modern society," is
a forerunner of the single-party totalitarianisms.

But such animadversions on Parliament call for no rebuttal. Oligarchy is
of the essence of Parliament which requires an articulated society for basis.
Elections presuppose superiorities; these may be based on birth, wealth, education, service, personal standing; or the rise may be achieved through local
bodies, party organizations, trade unions, etc. But acknowledged superiorities
there must be: and these were much impaired in the France of 1848. Three
years later their absence was adduced in justification of the *coup d'État;* Louis-
Napoleon, in a pamphlet "La Révision de la Constitution," which he sent to
the British Ambassador, Lord Normanby, naming himself as its author, de-

nounced Parliamentary Government as "totally unfit for a country like France, without aristocracy, without bodies politic, in short without any local sources of influence or power except the creatures and instruments of the Central Executive."

With such "official candidates" he himself managed in time to pack his Assemblies. But in May 1849 the electorate, which had given him an overwhelming majority half a year earlier, returned an Assembly consisting of some 300 Orleanists, 160 Legitimists, 160 Republicans, and a mere handful of Bonapartists; "partisan elections, worse confounded by local influences and local issues," writes Guérard, "were but a shattered mirror, and could not reflect the country as a whole." Obviously millions of men, politically unschooled, will in a free election put their mark against the name they happen to know. Of the five names in the Presidential election "Napoleon" alone had nation-wide currency; in Parliamentary elections a similar advantage accrued to the local notables. Louis-Napoleon's person mattered little, his pamphlets even less, and of his program only as much as could be read into his name, a greater engine of propaganda than even the modern Press and the wireless. Through the freak of a plebiscite the ghost of Napoleon entered the body politic of a sick, deeply divided community: the peasants were hostile to the big landowners and their exiled kings, and had no use for the urban bourgeois and *intelligentsia;* the Legitimists loathed the Orleanists; and everybody abhorred and feared the "Reds," so much so that even of those who knew Louis-Napoleon in the flesh and despised him—the politicians—many supported him. They thought that because he was intellectually their inferior, they would be able to run him or get rid of him; the German Conservatives—Junkers, industrialists, generals, Nationalists—thought the same about Hitler. "The elect of six millions executes, and does not betray, the will of the people," declared Louis-Napoleon, nicely rounding off the figure. But too much should not be read by historians into that verdict.

"The workmen of the great cities," writes Guérard, ". . . refused to recognize the Empire as a genuine form of democracy." Their strength and spirit were broken in the June Days of 1848, long before Louis-Napoleon appeared as the "saviour of society" (Cavaignac was his Noske). But exploiting the feeble riots of June 1849, engaged in *par acquit de conscience,* Louis-Napoleon proclaimed: "It is time that the good be reassured, and that the wicked should tremble." And after the *coup d'État* his shady associates staged their own Reichstag Fire. There had been hardly any opposition, the workers refusing to fight; but as some kind of insurrection was required to justify the coup and extensive repressions, resistance was encouraged and beaten down. Next, an accidental shot on the boulevards provoked a fusillade; the ground was strewn with dead. "These were not insurgents," writes Guérard; "it was a quiet, well-dressed crowd, which was watching the military parade as a show." And the sequel? "Mixed commissions," often of an atrocious character, condemned thousands of innocent men to death, transportation, or exile. Where was then, one may ask, Louis-Napoleon's renowned kindliness? He had written in his *Idées Napoléoniennes:* "The Imperial eagle . . . was never stained with French blood shed by French troops. Few governments can say as much about their flag!" Not he about his own any longer.

The plebiscitarian Caesar "had not grown up with the French aristocracy, the French court, the French army, the French people," writes Guérard. "He remained on the throne an enigma, an adventurer, an exile." And like Napoleon I, he "was saddled with the Bonapartes." One of them, Pierre, son of Lucien, was "a fit subject for a picaresque romance." But Louis-Napoleon himself and his favourite cousin, Napoleon, "in their exalted sphere had in them something of the Pierre Bonaparte element: they too are disquieting, they elude normal classification; they are both Caesars and *déclassés*"; while Morny, an illegitimate son of Napoleon III's mother, and Walewski, a bastard of Napoleon I, both leading Ministers of the Second Empire, were "the perfect models of aristocratic adventurers." Morny was a man of affairs—promoter, speculator, and profiteer *par excellence*—"his secret information and his great influence as a statesman were freely used to foster his private schemes." And he was not the only one of that type in the doubtful *équipe* of the Second Empire, which, says Guérard, "was free from bourgeois pettiness, but also lacked some of the bourgeois virtues." The view that it was not a régime but a racket is not altogether unfounded.

The gaudy Empire "on its glittering surface . . . was a military régime"; "the great reviews . . . were an essential part of its political strategy"; "the days of bourgeois drabness were over"; gold braid and epaulets, much martial display, conspicuous waste and maladministration. "War was made into a blend of the circus, the tournament, and the quest. There was a dash of gaiety about it all . . . the spirit of Cyrano and d'Artagnan." Louis-Napoleon "believed in the army, but not in war. . . . He believed implicitly that he was born a soldier . . . it was faith without works." His technical knowledge did not prevent him from fumbling even in peace-time manœuvres. "At Magenta . . . he was sluggish, almost paralysed. When Frossard came with the news: 'Sire, a glorious victory!' the queer 'victor' could hardly credit his luck: 'And I was going to order a retreat!'" "The Empire . . . in its warlike aspect was an imitation, and feeble at the core." Napoleon III "was unmilitary in his ineradicable gentleness. . . . A philanthropist at the head of any army is a pathetic absurdity."

A "philanthropist" and a "policeman": for the army at home was "a vast police force in reserve," "held in readiness against any possible uprising of the democratic great cities." "Napoleon III the Policeman was not in contradiction with Napoleon III the Socialist"; "racketeer, policeman, reformer . . . were mingled in that equivocal figure." In the social reformer, "the romanticist whose dreams were of the future . . . and translated themselves into terms of engineering," who realized that "modern industry is collectivistic" and through the Imperial power wanted to give it a collective sense, Guérard tries to find atonement for Napoleon III's failure in all other spheres. Still, the *éloge* is hardly convincing; Napoleon III talked the humanitarian jargon of his generation and shared its mechanic interests and hobbies, but no convincing evidence is adduced of original ideas or personal achievements. And, intermixed with vast unproven claims, appears the admission that his economic and social policies "are no less perplexing than his management of foreign affairs"—which is saying a great deal.

For Napoleon III's foreign policy was shallow and utterly confused. He believed in peace and was out to tear up the Treaty of Vienna; he believed in nationality and claimed for France her "natural frontiers"; he wanted Italy free but not united; in eighteen years he waged three major European wars and sent three expeditions overseas, without ever seeming to know what he was after. At first luck covered up, to some extent, his muddles and blunders. But after 1860 "the series of setbacks, wrong guesses, false moves on the part of the Government was unbroken"—Poland, Denmark, Sadowa, Queretaro, Mentana; the Emperor and his people were losing faith in his star. There was perplexity, aimless drift, and obscure dismay. By 1867 French hegemony was at an end; France felt intolerably humiliated, the Emperor was infinitely weary. "L'Empire a été une infatuation," writes La Gorce, "il a été l'incohérénce, il a été aussi . . . l'imprévoyance."

But here is a last attempt at justification: "Everywhere," writes Guérard, "in Paris, in provincial France, in Algeria, the true monuments of the Second Empire are its public works." (Faust, who sold his soul for power, concludes his life over public works.) "The transformation of Paris, his personal conception . . . was so nobly conceived that after half a century it was still adequate." The pulling down and rebuilding of capitals is again a recurrent feature in the history of despots and dictators, from Nero to Mussolini and Hitler. Self-expression, self-glorification, and self-commemoration are one motive. But there is also a deeper, unconscious urge, born of fear: of things lurking in the dark, narrow streets of old cities, the product of organic, uncontrolled growth. Let in light and air and suffer nothing which is not of the despot's will and making! With Napoleon III such fears found a conscious rationalization: open spaces were needed for a "whiff of grapeshot." When his empire fell not one shot was fired.

The careers of Napoleon III and Hitler have shown how far even a bare minimum of ideas and resources, when backed by a nation's reminiscences or passions, can carry a man in the political desert of "direct democracy"; and the books written about Napoleon III show how loath posterity is to accept the stark truth about such a man. And yet a careful examination of the evidence merely confirms the opinion of leading contemporaries about him: the enigma was not so much in him as in the disparity between his own spiritual stature and the weight of the ideas centred on him. Dream pictures are best projected on to a blank screen—which, however, neither fixes nor brings them to life.

How much can be safely said of Napoleon III? Biographers agree that there was something in him which defies definition and description: obviously the unstable, the shapeless, the void cannot be delineated. He was reticent, secretive, conspiratorial; at times his power of silence created the appearances of strength. Narrow and rigid in his ideas, out of touch with reality, he was a dreamer entertaining vast, nebulous schemes, but vacillating, confused, and therefore complex and ineffective in action. There was in him a streak of vulgarity. He was sensual, dissolute, undiscriminating in his love-affairs: his escapades were a form of escapism, a release. He was benign, sensitive, impressionable, suggestible, yet "gently obstinate." He talked high and vague idealism, uncorrelated to his actions. He had a fixed, superstitious, childish belief in his name and star. Risen to power, this immature weak man became a public danger. His silence was self-defence: to cover up his inadequacy and to preserve him from the impact of stronger personalities, of demands which he would have found difficult to resist, of arguments to which he had no reply; it also helped him to avoid commitments. Ampère describes him as "what is called a good-natured man" in that "he likes to please everyone he sees." Tocqueville, for a few months his Foreign Minister, and Beaumont, an ambassador, were aghast at his vast chimerical, unscrupulous, confused schemes and ideas; when argued with he would keep silent without giving in—"he abandoned nothing." He would bide his time—which with him meant inactive waiting without any approach to reality. He tumbled into situations, neither designed nor deliberately created by him. When forced to act, the day-dreamer would try to draw back: so it was before the *coup d'État,* and again in 1859—in fact in almost every crisis. But if the initiative had passed out of his hands he would drift anxiety-ridden, fumbling, wishing to call a halt, and mostly unable to do so. Under stress his personality seemed to disintegrate.

* * *

THE GOOD NAPOLEON III

Alan B. Spitzer

H.M. THE EMPEROR NAPOLEON III.—In respectful memory of a beneficent and far-sighted man, died January 9th, 1873. He has found peace; one day he will find true justice.—The Hon. Secretary of the Souvenir Napoleonien in England, Ernest Weal.—In Memoriam notice, *The Times* (London), January 9, 1962.

In the past two decades the standard interpretation of the Second Empire, in England and America at least, has become generally favorable.[1] This approach, often presented as a revision of earlier partisan judgments is based both on fresh research and on changing conceptions of what is politically right and desirable. The classic Bonapartist, republican, and socialist interpretations have been qualified or discarded, but political norms, not always articulated, continue to shape evaluations of the regime.[2]

Much of the recent literature on Napoleon III reflects the conviction that he needs to be rescued from a tendentious historiography. The very persistence of this idea is of some interest when one considers for how long and by how many historians it has been expressed. To mention a distinguished example: Pierre de La Gorce began his classic history of the Second Empire with the observation,

The reign of Napoleon III has been judged up to the present only preferentially or in hatred. It has twice undergone the trial of falsehood: the falsehood of adulation in the days of power, the falsehood of calumny in the days of misfortune. [EDITORS' TRANSLATION][3]

---

[1] The most notable recent examples of this tendency are: Albert Guérard, *Napoleon III* (Cambridge, 1943) and *Napoleon III, A Great Life in Brief* (New York, 1955); Lynn M. Case, *French Opinion on War and Diplomacy during the Second Empire* (Phila., 1954); Roger L. Williams, *Gaslight and Shadow* (New York, 1957); Theodore Zeldin, *The Political System of Napoleon III* (London, 1958); and, to some extent, J. M. Thompson, *Louis Napoleon and the Second Empire* (New York, 1955). This essay was completed before the author could obtain a copy of T.A.B. Corley *Democratic Despot. A Life of Napoleon III* (London, 1961). This work also presents a qualified favorable reinterpretation of the Second Empire, concluding, "For Napoleon the 'end' was not, as in Solon's phrase, death, but that posthumous reputation he so desired. Who shall say that this end is not well in sight?"

[2] My own approach to the Second Empire starts from the Left.

[3] Pierre de La Gorce, *Histoire du Second Empire* (7 vols.; 12th ed., Paris, 1912), I, i; *cf.*, Blanchard Jerrold, *The Life of Napoleon III* (4 vols., London, 1874–1882), III, 8; H. Thirria, *Napoléon III avant l'Empire* (2 vols., Paris, 1895), I, i–iii; Henry Berton, *L'Évolution constitution-*

From *French Historical Studies*, II, No. 3 (Spring 1962), pp. 308–29. Reprinted by permission of *French Historical Studies* and the author. Copyright 1962 by the Society for French Historical Studies. Quotations appearing in French in the original essay have been translated by the editors.

De La Gorce's attempt at an objective and critical analysis won general acclaim but it too has been challenged by his successors. F. A. Simpson in his *Napoleon and the Recovery of France* deplored a Catholic bias in de La Gorce and then developed an interpretation which has been influential in establishing the favorable image of Louis Napoleon.[4] Indeed, Albert Guérard could assert in 1943 that "within the last fifty years Napoleon III has won the respect and sympathy of practically every critical historian."[5] Nevertheless, Guérard's successors continue to break lances for the man who, in the words of Roger Williams, has been "the victim of an indifference which has been translated by most writers about him into terms of contempt."[6] In a subsequent issue of *History Today*, the journal in which Williams' remarks appeared, Theodore Zeldin wrote, "It is time, therefore, that the abuse of his enemies should be appreciated in its true light and not accepted as impartial history merely because they happened to be distinguished men."[7]

A hostile tradition does certainly survive. In a sense the unfortunate Emperor is forever represented as Victor Hugo's Napoleon the Little and his partisans as Daumier's "Ratapoil," the rakish, seedy, and sinister adventurer. These images persist in the republican historiography introduced by Taxil Delord's implacable *Histoire du Second Empire*[8] and in the socialist interpretations of Albert Thomas and his successors.[9]

---

elle du Second Empire (Paris, 1900), I, 739; Paul Guériot, *Napoleon III* (2 vols., Paris, 1933–34), II, 319–321; Hendrik N. Boon, *Rêve et réalité dans l'œuvre économique et sociale de Napoléon III* (La Haye, 1936), pp. 164–165; Octave Aubry, *The Second Empire*, trans. A. Livingston (Phila., 1940), 604; J.-B. Barbier, *Outrances sur le Second Empire* (Paris, 1946), pp. 7–9. For a somewhat dated survey of the literature on the Second Empire see Robert Schnerb, "Napoleon III and the Second French Empire," *Journal of Modern History*, VIII (September, 1936), pp. 338–355.

[4] F. A. Simpson, *Louis Napoleon and the Recovery of France, 1848–1856* (London, 1923), viii. De La Gorce has recently been damned as an apologist of the Second Empire: E. Jeloubovskaia, *La Chute du Second Empire et la Naissance de la Troisième République en France*, trans. J. Champenois (Moscow, 1959), pp. 5, 9.

[5] Guérard, *Napoleon III*, p. 282.

[6] Roger I. Williams, "Louis Napoleon. A Tragedy of Good Intentions," *History Today*, IV (April, 1954), 219.

[7] Theodore Zeldin, "The Myth of Napoleon III," *History Today*, VIII (February, 1958), 105.

[8] Taxil Delord, *Histoire du Second Empire* (6 vols.; 5th ed., Paris, 1869–1875). *Cf.* Gabriel Hanotaux, *Histoire politique*, Vol. V of *Histoire de la nation française*, ed. G. Hanotaux (Paris, 1929). For another example of a broadly unfavorable treatment see René Arnaud, *The Second Republic and Napoleon III*, trans. E. F. Buckley (London, 1939). The author claims to stand between Seignobos and de La Gorce. The attitude toward the Second Empire of the academic left (under the Third Republic) is succinctly expressed in the following comment on Bergson's eulogy of Emile Ollivier at the Académie in 1918, ". . . a philosopher for fops or dandies has dared to deliver not the eulogy, but a shameless panegyric, of M. Emile Ollivier. . . . This very Academy . . . listened without wincing to the insolent challenge to the public conscience made by M. Bergson." *Annales Révolutionnaires*, X (1918), 287–288. See also Henry Jaudon, "Émile Ollivier," *Revue bleue*, LVI (Feb., 1918), 80–84. For Bergson's speech see Henri Bergson, *Discours de Reception de M. Henri Bergson, Séance de l'Académie française du 24 Janvier 1918* (Paris, 1918).

[9] E.g., Albert Thomas, *Le Second Empire (1852–1870)*, Vol. X of *Histoire Socialiste*, ed. J. Jaurès (Paris, 1906); and Vol. XI of the same series, Jean Jaurès, *La Guerre Franco-Allemande;* Paul

Possibly the most influential republican evaluation of the reign of Louis Napoleon was engraved by Charles Seignobos on that monument to Sorbonnard historiography, the Lavisse series. He concluded his history of the Empire:

The Empire imposed on France by a military coup d'état had no other active force at its service than the army; the nation had not become imperial and only assisted the Empire through inertia; the electors voted for it because it was there. The government was nothing but a group of civil servants superimposed on the nation without becoming integrated with it; it remained an official machine without any moral authority; the great mass of the indifferent obeyed it; but where there was political life it was always opposed. With the army gone the Empire collapsed without a struggle, without opposition to the pressure of the mob. Its chiefs fled abroad, nobody tried to defend it. [EDITORS' TRANSLATION] [10]

Perhaps the gap between orthodox republican historiography and the modern revisionists can be measured by two evaluations of Seignobos. While Robert Schnerb refers to his "sufficiently objective analysis" of the Second Empire,[11] Albert Guérard describes his work as "the frankly biased account by the petit-bourgeois Radical Charles Seignobos, a period-piece of the Gambetta age." [12]

The attitudes distressing to Guérard persist, but the extent of partisan animus among contemporary French historians of the Empire can be exaggerated. The monographs of Maurain, Schnerb, Duveau, Guiral, and others probably do add up to a negative presentation of the regime, but they are scrupulously documented, fair, and balanced efforts.[13]

Unfavorable judgments never did go unchallenged in France. Aside from Bonapartist apologia, of which the most distinguished was Émile Ollivier's massive and influential justification of the Liberal Empire,[14] scholarly works

---

Louis, *Histoire du mouvement syndical en France* (2 vols., Paris, 1947), I, 41–42, 98–99; Alexandre Zévaès, "Les Candidatures ouvrières et révolutionnaires sous le Second Empire," *La Révolution de 1848*, XXIX (mars 1932-février 1933), 132–154. Jeloubovskaia, *La Chute du Second Empire*. This work is written partly as a corrective to what the author considers to be a tradition of unscientific apologetics. She presents both imperial domestic and foreign policy simply as the political manifestations of capitalist class interests.

[10] Charles Seignobos, *Le Déclin de l'Empire et l'établissement de la 3ᵉ Republique*, Vol. VII of *Histoire de France Contemporaine*, ed. E. Lavisse (Paris, 1921), p. 248.

[11] Schnerb, "Napoleon III and the Second French Empire," pp. 338–339.

[12] Guérard, *Napoleon III*, p. 282.

[13] Jean Maurain, *La Politique ecclésiastique du Second Empire de 1852 à 1869* (Paris, 1930); and *Un Bourgeois français au XIXᵉ siècle. Baroche, Ministre de Napoléon III* (Paris, 1936); Georges Duveau, *La Vie ouvrière en France sous le Second Empire* (Paris, 1949); Pierre Guiral, *Prévost-Paradol* (Paris, 1955); Jacques Droz, Lucien Genet, and Jean Vidalenc, *L'Époque Contemporaine. I. Restaurations et Révolutions* (1815–1871) ("Clio," Paris, 1953). In the *Peuples et Civilizations* series the volume by Charles Pouthas, *Démocraties et Capitalisme* (1848–1860) (Paris, 1948) shows no discernible bias; the succeeding volume, by Henry Hauser, Jean Maurain, and Pierre Benaerts, *Du libéralisme à l'Impérialisme* (Paris, 1939) presents an unfavorable picture of the later Empire.

[14] Émile Ollivier, *L'Empire libéral, études, récits, souvenirs* (17 vols., and 1 table; Paris, 1895–1915).

favorable to the Empire have appeared frequently in the twentieth century—from Lebey's treatment of the early period to Paul Guériot's well-received volumes, which characteristically concluded on the note of Louis Pasteur's eulogy of the Emperor.[15]

Louis Napoleon has enjoyed an even better press abroad. Notwithstanding occasions of great unpopularity in England and America, he has never, from the time of Bagehot's defense of his coup d'état,[16] lacked defenders—in fact, the major monographs in English have been predominantly sympathetic. A line of hostile interpretation does exist—running from Kinglake's conspiracy theory of the origins of the Crimean War [17] through H. A. L. Fisher's and G. P. Gooch's whiggish distaste for Bonapartist authoritarianism,[18] to various critiques of Louis Napoleon's diplomacy [19] and to J. Salwyn Schapiro's description of the imperial system as a harbinger of Fascism.[20]

The critical literature has been outweighed by works justifying the Empire to the foreign reader. Blanchard Jerrold's semi-official biography based upon materials in the possession of the imperial family was an early example of books exhibiting sympathy for Louis Napoleon and for his tragic Empress, who for many years continued to make documents accessible to sympathetic investigators.[21] The most influential academic reinterpretation was expressed in F. A. Simpson's two distinguished volumes, *The Rise of Louis Napoleon* and *Louis Napoleon and the Recovery of France,* first published in 1909 and 1923, respectively.[22] After Simpson, the current outside of France has continued to flow

15 André Lebey, *Louis-Napoléon Bonaparte et la Révolution de 1848* (2 vols.; Paris, 1907–08); Guériot, *Napoléon III,* II, 322.

16 Walter Bagehot, "Letters on the French Coup d'État of 1851," *Literary Studies* (2 vols.; London, 1911), Vol. I.

17 Arthur William Kinglake, *The Invasion of the Crimea: Its Origin and an account of Its Progress down to the Death of Lord Raglan* (6 vols., London, 1863–1880). For the most recent of the scholarly refutations of Kinglake, see Brison D. Gooch, "A Century of Historiography on the Origins of the Crimean War," *American Historical Review* LXII (October, 1956), 33–58.

18 H. A. L. Fisher, *Bonapartism* (Oxford, 1914), pp. 142–163, 198–200; Philip Guedalla's popular success was, if not critical, patronizing. Philip Guedalla, *The Second Empire* (London, 1922). G. P. Gooch, *The Second Empire* (London, 1960). This recent work is close in tone to a nineteenth-century liberal response to the Empire.

19 E.g., Franklin Charles Palm, *England and the Rise of Napoleon III* (Durham, 1948); A. J. P. Taylor, *The Struggle for the Mastery of Europe, 1848–1918* (Oxford, 1954), pp. 25, 133, 204 ff.; René Albrecht-Carrié, *A Diplomatic History of Europe Since the Congress of Vienna* (New York, 1958), pp. 82–83, 132–138.

20 J. Salwyn Schapiro, *Liberalism and the Challenge of Fascism* (New York, 1949), pp. 316 ff.; See also J. P. Mayer, *Political Thought in France* (London, 1943), pp. 45–69; Karl-Heinz Bremer, "Der Sozialistische Kaiser," *Die Tat,* XXIX (Juni, 1938), 160–171; and for a brief assessment of the similarities and differences with Fascism, see Frederick B. Artz, "Bonapartism and Dictatorship," *South Atlantic Quarterly,* XXXIX (Jan. 1940), 48–49.

21 The flow of works on the tragic Empress, the Gilded Beauties of the Court, and the Prince Imperial still provides a certain moisture.

22 F. A. Simpson, *The Rise of Louis Napoleon* (London, 1909); Simpson, *Louis Napoleon and the Recovery of France* (London, 1923).

strongly in Louis Napoleon's favor, swelling into the lush prose of Robert Sencourt:

. . . even in his weakness and his mistakes, he, as a Bonaparte, proved that there was in him, as in his more famous predecessor, an elasticity, a resilience, which make him a power when he seemed to have left the world branded as a failure. He completed the career of Napoleon I. Who has completed his own? [23]

The recent works of Guérard, Williams, Zeldin, Case, and (to a lesser extent) J. M. Thompson have continued the revision of an excessively critical image of the Second Empire. These works are not uncritical, but they tend to emphasize the desirable consequences of the regime and to present partial justifications for its alleged failures. The arguments most often advanced in the line of this positive revisionism might be represented in the following rather unfair pastiche:

The Second Empire has been too narrowly viewed in the light of republican or socialist predilections. A more just evaluation would recognize that the faction-ridden systems which the Second Empire replaced were only destroyed after they had failed to satisfy the national aspirations for order and unity. The new 18th of Brumaire entailed a certain amount of temporary unpleasantness, but it provided that political stability which was the indispensable context for economic and social advances scarcely possible under any alternative regime. Despite inherited disabilities the Liberal Empire was evolving towards a viable parliamentary system with the support of the vast majority of the nation. Doctrinaire critics overlook the real progress that was made in the face of complex difficulties and with that refractory human material whose last chance to be welded into a truly unified people disappeared with the Empire. Even the condemnation of Louis Napoleon's apparently disastrous foreign policy must be qualified with reference to the pressures of irresponsible political factions and of public opinion which demanded victories abroad without sacrifice at home. And one must take into account Louis Napoleon's vision of a European policy—a noble conception frustrated by the short-sighted Machiavellianism of other princes.

A full discussion of this interpretation would touch on political, economic, social, literary, religious, educational, and diplomatic history. This article will consider only certain questions of economic, political, and foreign policy evoked by the recent literature.

In judging the economic development of the Empire, although it poses the most complex problems of research and interpretation, historians are in agreement unusual in the historiography of the period. Not all would accept Sainte-Beuve's identification of Napoleon III as a "Saint-Simon on horseback," [24] but

[23] Robert Sencourt, *Napoleon III: The Modern Emperor* (London, 1933), p. 369.
[24] Guérard, *Napoleon III*, pp. 193 ff.

most admit to some real connection between imperial policies and the striking advance of the French economy. Georges Pradalié's monograph in the *Que sais-je?* series is representative of French historiography in its conclusion that, while France suffered in the long run from Louis Napoleon's foreign and domestic political policies, it owes to him a considerable legacy of national wealth and of effective economic institutions.[25]

The difficulty for a just assessment of the economic contributions of the Empire lies in the obligation to distinguish the economic consequences of government policy from the effects of other factors and to work out the relationship of short-run economic change to long. When, for example, Guérard and Pradalié commended the Second Empire for the accumulation of wealth which made possible the rapid payment of the indemnity after the Franco-Prussian war, they gave to Louis Napoleon's reign all of the credit for that viability which enabled France to make comparable efforts after 1815 and again after the World Wars of the twentieth century. Notwithstanding Guérard's disclaimers he seemed to attribute to Napoleon III the fruits of a century of French secular economic growth.[26]

One might argue that the years of the Empire happen fortuitously to coincide with a period of French, or indeed, world-wide, industrial expansion that would have occurred under any political circumstances. Similar considerations might be applied in favor of the Empire. To evaluate the break with protectionism merely by its consequences in the period 1860–1870 is to ignore the possibly beneficial long-run effects of competition on a traditionally overprotected economy.[27] Other complications arise from varying views of the economic curve of the years 1852–1870. Partisans of the Empire emphasize the burgeoning years between 1852–1857. Opponents look to the depression of 1867–1870.

Most historians have agreed, despite their different points of view, that the signs of economic growth are impressive in relation both to other periods and to other states. The years 1852–1857 particularly were an exception to a long history of relative stagnation, and the French rate of growth was unmatched by that of any other state.[28] The combined value of French exports and imports

[25] Georges Pradalié, *Le Second Empire (Que sais-je?)* (Paris, 1957), p. 124; and for the same assessment see Marcel Blanchard, *Le Second Empire* (Paris, 1950), pp. 7–8.

[26] Guérard, *Napoleon III*, p. 196.

[27] For assessments of the economic consequences of the Second Empire, see Émile Levasseur, *Histoire du commerce de la France* (2 vols.; Paris, 1911–1912); Germain Martin, *Histoire économique et financière*, Vol. X of *Histoire de la nation française*, ed. Gabriel Hanotaux (Paris, 1927), Marcel Marion, *Histoire financière de la France depuis 1715* (5 vols., Paris, 1914–1928); V. Arthur L. Dunham, *Anglo-French Treaty of Commerce of 1860 and the Progress of the Industrial Revolution in France* (Ann Arbor, 1930); Shepard B. Clough, *France: A History of National Economics, 1789–1939* (New York, 1939); Henri Sée, *Histoire économique de la France* (2d ed., 2 vols.; Paris, 1951), II.

[28] Rondo Cameron, "Economic Growth and Stagnation in France, 1815–1914," *The Journal of Modern History*, XXX (March, 1958), 1.

almost tripled between the beginning and the end of the Empire, surpassing the rate of expansion for any other European state in those years.[29] Perhaps even more impressive is the evidence of the structural changes which helped to propel France into the industrial era. The Second Empire saw the establishment of what Perroux calls the "generating industries . . . industries whose establishment was decisive for the forming of a French market," [EDITORS' TRANSLATION] and the striking growth of the railroads and the "great credit institutions." [30]

To establish the existence of these changes is not to demonstrate Louis Napoleon's responsibility for them, but significant relationships between imperial policies and constructive change are persuasively presented in such works as David Pinkney's *Napoleon III and The Rebuilding of Paris*, Louis Girard's *La Politique des Travaux Publics du Second Empire*, and Marcel Blanchard's articles on the railroad policies of the Empire.[31] At any rate, a majority of historians grant Louis Napoleon some of the credit for the unprecedented stimulus to capital formation, credit expansion, and a spirit of enterprise foreign to the crabbed, unimaginative Orleanist economic tradition, and essentially believe with Girard that France still enjoys a legacy of "the works set up by the French of the Second Empire." [EDITORS' TRANSLATION] [32]

The relevance of these conclusions to a justification of the Empire depends not so much on economic fact as on political value. Did the economic benefits outweigh the accompanying graft, favoritism, and speculation? Did the Morny who floated impressive enterprises compensate for the Morny who enjoyed a slice of Jecker's Mexican investments? Did the improved salubrious and magnificent product of Haussmann's municipal renovation cancel out the inequities, the inconveniences, and the aberrations in taste that attended the rebuilding of Paris? The answers can be founded only on individual postulates of Right and Progress.

Whatever uniformity obtains for such judgments does not extend to evaluations of Louis Napoleon's social welfare policies, perhaps because the evidence is even more difficult to assess, perhaps because the implicated values are so strongly held and so sharply conflicting.

[29] Sée, *Histoire économique*, II, 288. According to Levasseur Belgium was the only state to surpass France. Levasseur, *Histoire du commerce*, II, 331.

[30] François Perroux, "Prise de Vues sur la croissance de l'économie française, 1870–1950," *Income and Wealth*, Series V, ed. Simon Kuznets (London, 1955), p. 55.

[31] David H. Pinkney, *Napoleon III and the Rebuilding of Paris* (Princeton, 1958); cf. J. M. and Brian Chapman, *The Life and Times of Baron Haussmann* (London, 1957); Louis Girard, *La Politique des travaux publics du Second Empire* (Paris, 1952). Marcel Blanchard, "La politique ferrovaire du Second Empire," *Annales d'histoire économique et sociale VI* (Novembre, 1934), 529–545.

[32] Girard, *La Politique des travaux publics*. See also Sée, *Histoire économique*, II, 251, "If Napoleon was only a fleeting apparition from the political point of view, by contrast from the economic point of view his reign marked an epoch; it is he who opened the road for capitalism in France and from there to the whole of the continent." There are similar views in Pierre DuPont-Ferrier, *Le Marché financier de Paris sous le Second Empire* (Paris, 1925).

Louis Napoleon's sympathy for the masses has been one of his strongest claims to the affections of historians. J. M. Thompson dwelt on his sincere intention to provide the workers with "their just share of the national wealth," [33] and concluded that Louis Napoleon ". . . never ceased to clutch the inviolable shade of social equality and justice which still eludes a less corrupt and prejudiced age." [34] This interpretation, of Louis' intentions at least, is widely shared —even Karl Marx, who was scarcely charitable to "the hero Crapulinsky," granted that, "Bonaparte looks on himself as the representative of the peasants and of the people in general, against the bourgeoisie, who wants to make the lower classes of the people happy within the framework of bourgeois society." [35]

More recently, Guérard and H. N. Boon, among others, have identified Louis Napoleon as a Socialist, and in 1938 the German historian, Karl-Heinz Bremer, praised the pioneering authoritarian socialism of the Second Empire, which is not precisely what its recent admirers have in mind.[36] Admiration for Louis Napoleon's brand of socialism has, however, generally been confined to non-socialists. The hostile socialist histories of the Second Empire are analogous to the "ungrateful" electoral behavior of the contemporary French worker, which produced the paradox of "a leader . . . rejected by those whom he was most anxious to benefit." [37]

The apparent working-class preference for republican institutions in spite of the imperial benevolence is often praised, or damned, as a triumph of abstract ideological considerations over strictly material demands. Some historians have argued, however, that the intentions of the government were essentially manipulative, that occasional social reforms were only the means to authoritarian political ends, that the state remained the agency of the possessing classes, that real wages fell, and that the workers showed an increasingly mature awareness of their own material interests when they repudiated the system at the polls.[38]

How the workers actually conceived their interests and how these conceptions influenced their political behavior remain complex and difficult questions. Georges Duveau's remarkable study of working class life under the Empire delineated the "caractère équivoque" of proletarian political response in which sympathy for the Emperor might accompany hostility to the *patronat*, or resistance to the Empire be expressed not so much from the viewpoint of a worker

[33] Thompson, *Louis Napoleon and the Second Empire*, p. 103.

[34] *Ibid.*, p. 239.

[35] Karl Marx, *The Eighteenth Brumaire of Louis Bonaparte*, Vol. 35, *Marxist Library*, ed. C. P. Dutt (New York, 1936) p. 117.

[36] Guérard, *Napoleon III*, p. 198; Boon, *Rêve et réalité*, p. 154; Bremer, "Der Sozialistische Kaiser," pp. 161–164.

[37] Guérard, *Napoleon III*, p. 218.

[38] This is essentially the position of Édouard Dolléans, *Histoire du mouvement ouvrier* (4th ed., 2 vols., Paris, 1948), I, pp. 251–360; *cf.* I. Tchernoff, *Le Parti Républicain au coup d'état et sous le Second Empire* (Paris, 1906), pp. viii–ix, 404, 410, 493–494; Jeloubovskaia, *La Chute du Second Empire, passim.*

as from that of a democrat in the tradition of the old radical artisanate.[39] Duveau concluded that, in the obscurity of the contemporary industrial climate, the worker searched for his solutions "in his moral heritage and in utilizing, rather than fighting, the propaganda of the traditional parties which tried to capture his attention." [EDITORS' TRANSLATION] [40] Other historians have seen an increasing consciousness of class interests developing independently of traditional political alignments. Workers supported Louis Napoleon in 1848 precisely because he was not identified in their eyes with bourgeois interests but they eventually repudiated his paternalism, not so much for some republican ideal but because of their inchoate urge to defend their interests according to their own lights.[41]

On the basis of his findings that real wages remained stagnant during the Empire, Duveau concluded that the general progress of the French economy widened the social gap between the workers and an enriched bourgeoisie.[42] But this in itself cannot explain working-class political behavior because workers reacted not alone to this secular development but also to short-term business fluctuations, to political change, and to the government's successes and failures in international relations. Even in the years of economic depression and social conflict from 1867 to 1870 working-class behavior was variously motivated. The textile workers, for example, combined with their patrons in a campaign against imperial tariff policy,[43] yet in 1870 the alliance was shattered by strikes of unprecedented size and violence.[44]

The government's ambiguous response to the textile strikes indicates some of the complexities of an analysis of the relation between imperial policies and working-class politics. There is evidence of a certain amount of imperial sympathy for the strikers, but the strikes were ultimately met with the intervention of troops.[45] On many other occasions contradictions between Louis Napoleon's benevolence and the actual response of the government to working-class aspirations had been apparent. J. M. Thompson observes that the Emperor's sincere pursuit of social justice assumed an economic expansion essentially dependent upon bourgeois enterprise, and was "mortgaged to capitalism." The idealistic ends were sacrificed to the indispensable means. "Workers' associations and meetings might be prohibited in the name of public order, strikes broken to protect the labour market, wages kept down to stimulate production and public works. The Empire might become the victim of its own *élan vital,* the Emperor

[39] Duveau, *La Vie ouvrière,* pp. 100–103.

[40] Duveau, *La Vie ouvrière,* p. 550.

[41] Fernand L'Huillier, *La Lutte ouvrière à la fin du Second Empire* (Paris, 1957), pp. 74 ff.; Sreten Maritch, *Histoire du mouvement social sous le Second Empire à Lyon* (Paris, 1930), pp. 266–267.

[42] Duveau, *La Vie ouvrière,* pp. 385–416.

[43] Claude Fohlen, *L'Industrie textile au temps du Second Empire* (Paris, 1956), pp. 410–429.

[44] *Ibid.,* pp. 439–440; L'Huillier, *La Lutte ouvrière,* pp. 64–72.

[45] *Ibid.,* p. 70.

the prisoner of his prosperity and progress." [46] It is probable that working-class attitudes were affected more by the actual operation of the imperial system than by Louis Napoleon's conceptions of how it ought to operate.

To understand how Louis Napoleon's government qualified and perverted his most generous conceptions one must be aware of the differences between the Emperor's ideals and interests of the groups that shared power with him. The Emperor is often praised for standing above the factions and governing for the good of all, but his policies were shaped and executed by men whose values were those of the conservative, propertied minority.[47] Guérard regretted that the conservatives were able to "muscle in and to endorse a winner whose principles were the very reverse of theirs," [48] but Zeldin has shown that the imperial system continuously co-operated with local notabilities and that it recruited its parliamentary candidates "from the highest ranks of society, from the great landowners, wealthy mayors and so on." [49] This élite was scarcely enthusiastic for socialism, even of the Bonapartist brand. If the Empire, as Guérard, Williams, and Zeldin claimed, was not the instrument of the political Right, it certainly did business with and through the traditional supporters of the "party of order."

At the very peak of the imperial structure there was the court, a group which must figure in any examination of the obstacles between Louis Napoleon's good will and positive reform. The imperial entourage is often blamed for major blunders including the fatal decision for war with Prussia. J. M. Thompson is one of the few reasonably sympathetic historians of the Second Empire to point out that the political power of the imperial court was a necessary product of the imperial system. "In a government which left so little initiative to its constitutional bodies, it becomes of special importance to inquire into the relations between the Emperor and those who were his immediate associates: the Empress, his Bonaparte relations, the friends of his youth, his ministers and ambassadors." [50] The extra-constitutional influences exerted by these close associations were contradictory and inconsistent, reflecting personal and ideological cross-purposes, and from them stemmed some of the vagaries of imperial policy.

[46] Thompson, *Louis Napoleon and the Second Empire*, p. 239. Duveau, *La Vie ouvrière*, p. 549, "The Emperor wished to govern for the masses and with the aid of the masses . . . but, not without reason, he was worried over the loyalty of the working-class and finally, on the whole, he checked the workers instead of collaborating with them." [EDITORS' TRANSLATION]

[47] Duveau concedes the caesarist socialism of Louis himself, but emphasizes the fact that he surrounded himself with "civil servants still imbued with the old Orleanist spirit and, guessing the contradictions which beset the Emperor, they didn't hesitate to dictate to him frequently. Hence in the turnings of the cogwheels of the Imperial machine (there were) misses and jolts which had their repercussions in the worker's world." [EDITORS' TRANSLATION] Duveau, *La Vie ouvrière*, p. 16.

[48] Guérard, *Napoleon III*, p. 138.

[49] Persigny, quoted by Zeldin, *ibid.*, p. 11. For the view that one of the grave weaknesses of the regime was its failure to rally the established élite, see Simpson, *Louis Napoleon and the Recovery of France*, pp. 372–373, and Hanotaux, *Histoire politique*, pp. 477, 551.

[50] Thompson, *Louis Napoleon and the Second Empire*, p. 246.

Perhaps of even greater significance was the cumulative influence of the minor officials who actually executed policy. Indeed, the Empire can well be described, not as a dynastic direct democracy, but as the quintessential administrative state. According to Brian Chapman's useful survey, *The Prefects in Provincial France,* the apogee of prefectoral authority was attained under the Second Empire.[51] In a sense the prefects made the regime, for, according to Chapman, they contrived the Red Scare of 1851, which was a crucial element in Louis Napoleon's coup d'état. This interpretation is reinforced by Howard Payne's detailed analysis of the role of the bureaucracy in preparing for the coup d'état and in inviting Louis Napoleon to seize supreme power and crown the edifice of the administrative state.[52]

In another article Payne described the consolidation and reinforcement of the centralized police system and concluded that "despite the contemporary elaboration of theories of unlimited police powers they were in practice limited to an extent far removed from the totalitarian models of the twentieth century." [53] This observation does not really vitiate the cumulative force of Payne's descriptions of the increase in authority and scope of the imperial police. Louis Napoleon can be defended against rather forced comparisons with the Nazis, but the fact that nineteenth-century dictators fell short of twentieth-century totalitarians can scarcely be a conclusive answer to their liberal critics.

Napoleon III is perhaps most effectively defended against charges of authoritarianism by reference to the evolution of the Liberal Empire after 1860. The Emperor himself is the great protagonist of this transformation, not only creating new institutions but summoning up new men to operate them. Among these men Émile Ollivier was pre-eminent—the hero of those who would trade the doctrinaire insistence on republican forms for the substance of imperial liberties.[54]

The ambiguities of a constitution which stipulated ministerial responsibility

---

[51] Brian Chapman, *The Prefects and Provincial France* (London, 1955), p. 38; see also, Pierre-Henry, *Histoire des préfets* (Paris, 1950), pp. 171–194. Zeldin emphasizes the crucial electoral role of the prefects, "It was not Napoleon, nor Persigny but the prefects, who had the greatest single influence in choosing the official candidates," Zeldin, *The Political System of Napoleon III,* p. 19.

[52] Chapman, *The Prefects and Provincial France,* p. 37; Howard C. Payne, "Preparation of a Coup d'état: Administrative Centralization and Police Powers in France, 1849–1851," *Studies in Modern European History in Honor of Franklin Charles Palm,* eds., F. J. Cox, R. M. Brace, B. C. Weber and J. F. Ramsey (New York, 1956), p. 197.

[53] Howard C. Payne, "Theory and Practice of Political Police during the Second Empire in France," *Journal of Modern History,* XXX (March, 1958), 14–23.

[54] At the conclusion of a chapter devoted to Ollivier, Williams writes, ". . . recalling the despair of the Republicans after the plebiscite in 1870, is it not possible that the reforms were sufficiently promising for the reconciliation of liberty and order that the Republicans after 1870 never dared admit it?" Williams, *Gaslight and Shadow,* p. 298; cf., Berton, *L'Évolution constitutionelle du Second Empire,* pp. 381; Pierre de La Gorce, *Napoléon III et sa politique* (Paris, 1933), pp. 156 ff.; Pierre Saint Marc, *Émile Ollivier* (Paris, 1950), pp. 227 ff.; Bergson, *Discours . . . de l'Académie française.*

but did not specify its locus, which envisioned a cabinet based on a parliamentary majority but acceptable to, and presided over by, the Emperor, have been defended as necessary aspects of a difficult transition. Both Williams and Zeldin compare the constitutional progress of the Liberal Empire to the complex adjustment of executive to legislature worked out over a much longer period in seventeenth-century England.[55] It would be consistent with this analogy to argue that Louis himself had led France back into the seventeenth century. Perhaps his enemies exaggerated the "crime" of the Second of December, but it is fair to recall that the builders of the Liberal Empire had razed the parliamentary edifice of the Second Republic. The prospects of the parliamentary Empire might have been matched by those of the Republic, had it been allowed the twenty years which the Empire used to return to its point of departure. It is certainly plausible to suppose that a Republic dominated by Thiers and the "Burgraves" would have lacked the democratic ambiance of Bonapartist caesarism.[56] Still, arguments from English analogy might lead one to assume as good a chance for a fruitful evolution under a conservative parliamentary Republic before 1870 as for resolution of the contradictions of a parliamentary empire after 1870.

There is little point in pursuing this rather arid conjecture, but there is some point in examining the actual recruitment for the Liberal Empire, which did not, after all, staff itself with something very different from a reconstituted party of order. Ollivier's ministry of the Right and Left center did not include the great Orleanist paladins but did take in a range of qualified Orleanists and diluted Bonapartists who would have been perfectly at home in earlier oligarchies.[57] Some of the enemies of liberal institutions were dropped, but in the person of Rouher went a powerful partisan of free trade and with Haussmann the personification of public works, to be replaced by protectionists and scrupulous economizers. The last section of Girard's book on public works under the Empire, entitled "L'Abdication de la finance Saint-Simonienne," presents as a concomitant of liberalization the repudiation of the buccaneering and creative finance of the great period of imperial public works.[58]

[55] Williams, *Gaslight and Shadow*, p.279. Zeldin, *The Political System of Napoleon III*, p. 152. ". . . since so many people believed that France was not ripe for the institutions of nineteenth-century England, it was perhaps not as silly as it might appear to start with those of seventeenth-century England."

[56] See the characterization of Orleanist liberalism in E. Beau de Loménie, *Les Responsabilités des dynasties bourgeoises* (3 vols.; Paris, 1943), I, 171, 185, 200; and in Maurain, *Baroche*, p. 357. "The chiefs of the old party of order . . . liberal in politics because hostile to the personal government of the Emperor . . . were very conservative in social matters and refractory to the humanitarianism of Napoleon III."

[57] Zeldin, *The Political System of Napoleon III*, pp. 144–151. De La Gorce quotes one of the deputies of the Right as remarking "In the present cabinet . . . only the Duke d'Aumale in the War Ministry and the Prince de Joinville in the Navy Ministry are missing." [EDITORS' TRANSLATION] De La Gorce, *Histoire du Second Empire*, VI, 5.

[58] Girard, *La Politique des travaux publics*, pp. 359 ff.

According to Maurain the evolution of the Liberal Empire represented not only the triumph of the reconstituted party of order but also of the clergy: "The clerical party which, under the authoritarian Empire, had exercised only an indirect influence on the government, often powerful, but always limited, thus (now) took possession directly." [EDITORS' TRANSLATION] [59] Maurain's analysis of the ecclesiastical policies of the Second Empire challenged the representation of the regime as the last hope for a true political community, for he concluded that its shifts and expedients only sharpened the classic conflict between clericals and anti-clericals until, "after 1869, the dispute for power was, as in 1849, between the clerical party of order and the anti-clerical republicans." [EDITORS' TRANSLATION] [60]

An examination of these conflicts and of the social tensions attendant upon the growth and concentration of French industry reinforces the supposition that the bitter class and political struggle of 1871 must have owed something to the Empire.

Evaluations of domestic developments during the last years of the Second Empire are often affected by the knowledge that imperial foreign policy was to end in disaster. For many critics of the regime, the catastrophe of 1870 damns all of its works. The friends of the Empire, on the other hand, reject this judgment as the narrow standard of the cult of success, and some even defend those policies which led directly to the destruction of the Empire.

Historians generally agree that, notwithstanding autonomous foreign and domestic pressures which shaped imperial foreign policy, the major plans and the ultimate decisions were the Emperor's.[61] This grave responsibility has weighed heavily in the scales of his critics, but it has also served as a kind of palliation for some of his apparent blunders. His partisans emphasize his personal good will—expressed, for example, in his sincere attempt to mitigate the effects of a suicidal international *Realpolitik* by the formation of a new Congress of Europe. Binkley's volume in the Langer series coined the term *Federative Polity* to represent those tendencies which rampant nationalism was to destroy and which Louis Napoleon's foreign policy strove unsuccessfully to preserve and to extend.[62] Binkley's conviction that the Emperor was "the last good European in a position of authority" is widely shared.[63]

[59] Maurain, *La Politique ecclésiastique du Second Empire*, p. 939.

[60] *Ibid.*, p. 959.

[61] Albert Pignaud, "La Politique extérieure du Second Empire," *Revue Historique*, CLV (Sept.–Oct., 1927), 42–43; G. Pagés, "La Politique extérieure de Napoléon III," *Bulletin of the International Committee of Historical Sciences*, V (Feb., 1933), 16; Pierre Renouvin, *Le XIXᵉ Siècle, I. De 1815 à 1871*, Vol. V of *Histoire des relations internationales*, ed. P. Renouvin (Paris, 1954), pp. 269–270; Charles W. Hallberg, *Franz Joseph and Napoleon III, 1852–1864* (New York, 1955), pp. 23–24.

[62] Robert C. Binkley, *Realism and Nationalism, 1852–1871*, Vol. 16 of *The Rise of Modern Europe*, ed. W. L. Langer (New York, 1935), p. 260.

[63] E.g., Williams, "Louis Napoleon, A Tragedy of Good Intentions," p. 226; Case, *French Opinion . . . during the Second Empire*, p. vii; Simpson, *Louis Napoleon and the Recovery of*

The image of Louis Napoleon's visionary internationalism owes a great deal to hindsight. Demolished by a rival which had scarcely begun to realize its satanic strengths, imperial France may not seem terribly threatening in retrospect, but the policies she pursued were not reassuring to contemporaries, whose best evidence for the Emperor's intentions was drawn from his actions. These actions included proposals for international readjustment, often entailing some territorial bagatelle for France; two major wars before 1870, which by no stretch of even the French imagination could be considered defensive; the apparently boundless ambitions of the Mexican policy; [64] and continuous unsettling maneuvers, pronouncements, and projects which seemed to stem not from evident national requirements but from the Emperor's restless will.

Using information not readily available to Louis' contemporaries one can find a kind of consistency in his sincere belief that a revision of the unjust settlement of 1815 entailed, and without contradiction, the liberation of oppressed nationalities, the rightful extension of French territory and influence, and the reconstitution of a European polity. Most critics would now agree that the Emperor was sincere in his nationalities program, and that such policies as the weak, vulgar, and humiliating pursuit of compensations after 1866 were, in opposition to his deepest instincts, the reluctant responses to domestic pressures.[65]

To what extent Louis Napoleon's good intentions justify maladroit actions conducted under his authority is another question that can only be answered in the Emperor's favor if some force outside of the imperial establishment can be shown to have compelled the government to undertake erroneous policies. The defenders of the Empire have identified such a maleficent force in public opinion corrupted by an irresponsible opposition whose very existence depended upon Napoleon's good will.

The most thorough, effective and systematic work embodying such conclusions is Lynn Case's *French Opinion on War and Diplomacy during the Second Empire*. Case's careful analysis, based primarily on reports of the prefects and the procureurs généraux, shows that imperial policy during the springtime of the Empire's success was often carried out in spite of public opposition, but that during the last disastrous phase it was increasingly shaped by popular pressures. This was particularly striking in the case of the Emperor's program of army reform, blocked by a public which with equal zeal demanded

---

France, p. x: "Essentially he [Napoleon III] was an international figure; too good a citizen perhaps of Europe to be the ultimately successful ruler, of any one country in it." See also Luigi Salvatorelli "L'Europe de Napoléon III et l'Europe de Mazzini," *Revue historique*, CCXXIII (avril-juin, 1960), 275–286.

[64] The Mexican policy, which will not be examined here, has its defenders, *e.g.*, Sencourt, *Napoleon III: The Modern Emperor*, pp. 271–278; Guérard, *Napoleon III*, pp. 222–242; Barbier, *Outrances sur le Second Empire*, pp. 13–227.

[65] E.g., Taylor, *Struggle for Mastery in Europe*, pp. 173–177.

bellicose foreign policy and cheap defense.[66] In the light of such behavior Case has no difficulty in casting up the balance of guilt:

Thus the responsibility for the dilution of the army bill . . . falls directly upon French public opinion and its legislative representatives. This responsibility is all the heavier because at the same time that opinion was opposing the bill, it showed evidence of a universal belief in the inevitability of war with Prussia. . . . The road to Sedan, unlike that to Hell, was not even paved with good intentions. And when the tragedy of defeat finally broke upon the land, the unrepentant people loaded all the blame upon the one man who, accepting captivity to save the lives of his handicapped soldiers, had long before exerted himself more than all the others to spare them that evil day.[67]

The force of this indictment falls not only upon mass opinion but upon a political opposition that was willing to accrue factional advantage by attacking the government both for unpopular policies and for the consequences of suspending them. Still, any judgment of responsibility must take into account the nature and personnel of a watered-down caesarism. One must distinguish between the Emperor, who was eager to pursue a rational policy of acceptance of German aspirations and a prudent policy of rearmament in the face of Prussian power, and both his enemies and his supporters who were willing to accept neither. As Albert Sorel observed,

But if the projects of Marshal Niel (for army reform) miscarried, the blame should not be placed exclusively on the orators of the opposition; these orators formed only a very limited minority in the *Corps Legislatif;* they had no influence on the government, and their speeches which were destined most of the time for the public, very rarely modified the opinions of the majority. This majority was composed of government candidates and it was it, in short, which thrust aside the Marshal's reforms or amended them so as to paralyze their effect. [EDITORS' TRANSLATION] [68]

This observation has been reaffirmed by recent research.[69]

Even if the establishment had spoken with one voice on the reforms, which it did not, it could not present the public with clear alternatives because it tried to preserve an image of superior strength while soliciting remedies for relative weakness. The presentation of the official case between 1866 and 1870 scarcely contributed to a responsible and informed public evaluation of imperial programs.

These considerations do not lift the responsibility from an opposition that

---

[66] Gordon Wright, "Public Opinion and Conscription in France 1866–1870," *Journal of Modern History,* XIV (March, 1942), 26–45.

[67] Case, *French Opinion . . . during the Second Empire,* pp. 239–240.

[68] Albert Sorel, *Histoire diplomatique de la guerre Franco-Allemande* (2 vols.; Paris, 1875), I, v–vi.

[69] Cf., Zeldin, *The Political System of Napoleon III,* p. 133; Guiral, *Prévost-Paradol,* pp. 483–484; Schnerb, *Rouher,* p. 200.

was willing to seek political advantage at the expense of national security, but they indicate the flaws of a system in which supreme responsibility for foreign and military policy was concentrated in the hands of the Emperor and in which the dilution of this responsibility in part reflected the conflicts within an irresponsible entourage. There is still force in Jaurès' observation that a regime praised for ability to override the caprices of the crowd and the tumult of the forum is not also to be justified because it succumbed to public caprice and emotion.[70]

This approach was rejected in principle and in closely reasoned detail by Case, who defended even the last stumbling parade into the trap of the Hohenzollern candidacy. His research into the public response at each stage of the crisis impelled him to revise earlier estimates that public opinion was for peace in 1870.[71] These investigations suggested to Case that perhaps public opinion is inadequate to the formulation of foreign policy and that, indeed, given world realities it is problematical whether democracy can long survive in the present state system of international anarchy.[72]

This brings us back to the foundations of political value. If one does not choose to identify the concept of democracy with the momentary expression of the demos—if one conceives of democracy as a system of rules, processes and guarantees, including the right to form a meaningful opposition, then the aberrations of mass opinion in the short run do not constitute the ultimate test of democratic viability. Case praises the Empire for brushing aside political factions in order to combine authority with direct democracy, but it is precisely this caesarism which enforces an opportunism in relation to public opinion, not all of the time, for often the government flouted the public will, but only when the really difficult and embarrassing decisions had to be made. Then without the background of responsible opposition or continuous informed debate the system desperately husbands its popularity and in effect places the security of the dynasty above the health of the state.[73] In the last years, anxiety regarding public opinion was expressed in terms of the overthrow of the regime, and quite rightly, because when such a regime is repudiated it does not go out of office, it goes out of existence. There was not the margin for error afforded to the notoriously unstable Third Republic which somehow maintained a coherent foreign policy for forty years and, unlike its predecessor,

[70] Jaurès, *La Guerre franco-allemande,* p. 178.

[71] E.g., E. M. Carroll, "French Opinion on War with Prussia in 1870," *American Historical Review,* XXXI (July, 1926), 679–700.

[72] Case, *French Opinion . . . during the Second Empire,* pp. 275–277.

[73] A similar phrase is applied by Guérard to the weaknesses of imperial leadership in his monograph on Napoleon III for the Great Lives in Brief series. This book presents the same general interpretation as his earlier work but is somewhat more critical of the last phase of the regime, particularly in relation to foreign policy. Guérard, *Napoleon III, a Great Life in Brief,* pp. 148, 187–191.

found it to be politically possible to retreat upon Paris and regroup to withstand a German invasion.

It is not the cult of success which makes foreign affairs so relevant to an evaluation of the Empire, although a regime whose actions were so often justified as expedient can only justify its expediencies by success. No French statesman could have contrived a policy to stay the inexorable German advance toward economic and military hegemony but, as de La Gorce justly observes, it is particularly in the realm of foreign affairs that the characteristic weaknesses of the imperial system persist, not in the manifestations of an authoritarian will, but in the old tendencies toward *"infatuation, incohérence and imprévoyance."* [74]

Admirers of the Second Empire sometimes regret the onerous legacy it had to accept from the First. The legend of dynamic imperialism, essentially so foreign to the gentle and visionary Louis Napoleon, forced him into ventures abroad that were eventually disastrous.[75] But there is an element of the testament fabricated at St. Helena which is fully consistent with the spirit of Louis Napoleon's regime. This is the tradition of mendacity, manifested in the first Napoleon's *Memoirs* as contempt for the truth and also apparent in the absence of intellectual courage at the core of the Second Empire. In the long run the regime was not characteristically brutal, nor consistently authoritarian, but meretricious. If the imperial system anticipated any aspect of the twentieth century, it is the tendency to conduct foreign affairs as a branch of domestic public relations and to beg many difficult alternatives of policy formulation by doublethink, self-deception, and cant.

[74] De La Gorce, *Napoléon III et sa politique,* pp. 167–173.
[75] Williams, "Louis Napoleon. A Tragedy of Good Intentions," p. 220.

7

Cavour: Reluctant or Purposeful Architect of Italian Unity?

$\mathcal{I}$n popular biographies and histories, Count Camillo Benso Cavour is most often presented as the single-minded advocate and organizer of a united Italy. A frequently quoted letter written at the age of twenty-two, where he notes that he dreamt of being "Prime Minister of the King of Italy"; [1] his editorship of the prophetically named newspaper, *Il Risorgimento,* which he founded in 1847; and his early support of Daniele Manin, hero of the Venetian uprising of 1848, who from exile in Paris preached a united Italy under the House of Savoy—all have contributed to this presentation. From precisely such a viewpoint, Cavour's entire efforts at making the Kingdom of Sardinia a strong, prosperous, constitutional state, and, after the Crimean War, a voice in the Concert of Europe, were the operations of a master statesman deliberately working toward but one goal, the total independence and unification of Italy.

¶Recent historiography has been critical of interpretations that see the statesman as manipulator of events. But to be fair to Cavour, we should note that just as a number of his actions testify to a hesitancy or moderation incompatible with the image of a manipulator, so too does his correspondence show a man who did not lose himself in grand designs and for whom politics or diplomacy were, above all, "the art of the possible." Such pragmatism does not necessarily detract from Cavour's reputation.

[1] Letter to the Marchioness Barolo, quoted in Thayer, *Life and Times of Cavour,* I, 28–29. Later in this letter Cavour states, "There was so much absurdity in these illusions that I had to abandon them as soon as I was for a month together in a calmer state" (p. 28). On p. 402 of the same volume, Thayer writes, "It is time that the idle chatter as to whether Cavour desired Italian Unity should cease. There stands the letter, written in his youth in which he describes his audacious dream of 'waking up some day to find himself prime minister to the King of Italy.' From first to last he never abandoned that ideal."

Cavour's career, however, leaves the historian with a disturbing legacy. In his maneuvers against Austria, Cavour had to play from a position of relative weakness. Piedmont was no Prussia; it needed the alliance with Napoleon III, whatever the consequences. In Italy, Cavour had to play with republican and radical supporters of unification to whom, as a monarchist in the liberal, bourgeois tradition, he was opposed by temperament and conviction. These were two difficult and dangerous games at which he succeeded, but they meant that there had to be much that was equivocal in Cavour's policies and actions. True, equivocation was an accepted part of *Realpolitik*; it was a course to which Cavour readily confessed. But Cavour's relations with Napoleon III or his attitude towards Garibaldi can make him appear as something less than great.

It is on the Garibaldi problem, in particular, that some recent historians of the *Risorgimento* have concentrated.[2] And in general, since World War II, there has been an exceptional revival of interest in the *Risorgimento* on the part of scholars in and outside of Italy. This revival has been largely abetted by the publication of long-withheld documents and correspondence, particularly from the Cavour archives.[3] It is not likely that new research will ever topple Cavour from his position as the ranking leader of Italian unification. But it has thrown such a searching light on his actions and policies that reappraisals have been inevitable.

The two essays by L. C. B. Seaman, an English scholar, reprinted below, are a good example. Seaman questions the assumption that Cavour wanted Italian unification in 1858 and shows how his hand was forced in this matter by Garibaldi in 1860–61. Seaman's conclusions contradict the orthodox interpretations of the older histories and are not flattering, in the main, to Cavour.

Our first selection comes from William Roscoe Thayer's *Life and Times of Cavour,* a classic in its field. Although it was published in 1911, *The American Historical Association's Guide to Historical Literature* (1961) still calls Thayer's two-volume work "the best biography of Cavour in any language." [4] Our selection comprises a part of the conclusions reached by a historian who loved his subject. It does not touch on all of the points covered by Seaman, but a comparison of the selections by the two men show what modifications time and recent scholarship have brought to Cavour's reputation.

---

[2] Most notable and brilliant is Denis Mack Smith in *Cavour and Garibaldi 1860—A Study in Political Conflict* (Cambridge University Press, 1954). Mack Smith notes "Cavour was sometimes treacherous, often uncertain, and always more or less hostile to Garibaldi; and indeed one can say that he was *necessarily all of these things"* (pp. 438–39). Mack Smith concludes, however, that "On close inspection Cavour and Garibaldi become—probably like most people—at once greater and lesser than first appearances had suggested; and it was in their least generous and least perceptive side, namely their hostile attitude to each other, that they found one of the main springs of action with which to create a unitary state" (p. 438).

[3] For a note on falsification and mutilation of published documents from the archives and the long wait for publication of Cavour letters dealing with the annexation of southern Italy, see Mack Smith, *op. cit.,* p. x.

[4] P. 536.

PORTRAIT OF CAVOUR

William Roscoe Thayer

* * *

WHEN CAVOUR died, only the Patrimony
of St. Peter and the province of Venetia lay outside the fold. The lucky alliance
of Victor Emanuel with Prussia against Austria in 1866 served, in spite of the
defeat of the Italians at Custozza and at Lissa, to redeem the Venetians. The
French garrison having been withdrawn to give Napoleon III what help it
might in his death agony, the Italians entered Rome on September 20, 1870.
As had been asserted for over twenty years, the Pope could not, without foreign
aid, maintain his detested government against his subjects. Italy was made. The
tale which Palmerston characterized as the most extraordinary and romantic
recorded in the annals of the world was written.

But during those years of suspense, not a week passed when there was not
the consciousness of a great void. The new kingdom went on, as a steamer,
whose engines have stopped, drifts first with its own momentum, then with
the tide. The initiative was gone. Men remembered only too vividly the days
when little Piedmont, captained by Cavour, dared to break with Austria, sent
her troops to the Crimea, spoke up boldly at Paris, forced France to join her
in war, prepared the liberation of the Centre, abetted the emancipation of
the South. Although she had relied upon France, yet Piedmont never gave up
her independence: for, thanks to Cavour, the Emperor did Piedmont's bidding,
while seeming to dictate. Though Napoleon chafed, Cavour, when the time
was ripe, accepted Tuscany into the union; though Napoleon threatened, he
covertly supported the Garibaldian Expedition and boldly invaded Umbria and
the Marches.

Between 1861 and 1870, however, Italy was openly subservient to France.
Mazzini fulminated, but his fulminations now had only the quality of stale
gunpowder smoke. Garibaldi pushed his ineffectual enterprises, which involved
much peril to the country, and in return kept alive a somewhat vociferous
patriotism. Ricasoli, Minghetti and their colleagues tried loyally to continue
Cavour's victorious foreign policy. Rattazzi played the fox. In vain: Europe
perceived, and, what was worse, the Italians themselves realized, that Italy

From William Roscoe Thayer, *The Life and Times of Cavour,* 2 vols. (Boston: Houghton
Mifflin Company, 1911) II., pp. 495–97, 500–504, 507. Copyright 1911 by William Roscoe Thayer.
Reprinted by permission.

lacked the clear vision and the downright will. Happily, the foundations laid by Cavour were too staunch to give way, and Fate spared the King to be the national moderator and the symbol of unity, until unity was well consolidated. To-day, after fifty years, Italy stands upright, stronger than ever before.

It used to be contended that Cavour died opportunely for his fame. How he would have met the prosaic decades of financial and economic difficulties, how he would have warded off the undue pressure of France and opened the gates of Rome to the Italians, how he would have dealt with organized brigandage in the South or overcome the incessant feuds of the Party of Action, no one can say. But surely our best guide in such speculations is the statesman's record. To argue that Pericles, or Lincoln, or Cavour, who up to the moment of death commanded their situations, would have been unequal to cope with the confusion and panic caused by their death, is to employ a false logic.

Anyone can brandish the magician's wand; only the magician himself can conjure with it. Slowly the world has come to see that Cavour's achievement was not due to a succession of dazzling dexterities, but to the genius of the man—genius in which we must reckon temperament and natural aptitude, character, training, and an almost infallible eye for opportunity. He was a lifelong pupil of experience. He knew his time and his people through and through. Having accepted certain principles, he never betrayed them. He devoted himself to Liberty, as a divine guide against which, until mankind shall cease to advance, the blasts of tyrannies and of hierarchies cannot prevail. He understood that progress is a growth and not a manufacture; that the harvest shall be according to the seed sown; that evolution, which is a mechanical process in the brute creation, can be assisted and even hastened by man's forethought for his kind.

* * *

That in his statecraft he employed the accepted methods of diplomacy, many pages of this history have frankly shown. He could no more dispense with them than a general who hoped to win could abandon modern artillery and revert to arquebuses. No one recognized more clearly than he the conflict between private and public morals. "If we were to do for ourselves what we are doing for Italy," he remarked of the intrigues in the Two Sicilies in 1860, "we should be great rogues." He would be the first to welcome a happier era in which diplomacy as well as business and social life had the habit of perfect straightforwardness and crystalline candor.

But neither Cavour's scientific detachment, nor his readiness to sacrifice everyone, including himself, for his ideal, would have enabled him to make Italy, if he had not also possessed a vivid appreciation of the concrete. For him, persons were not abstractions, though in respect to the great design they must consent to be used or discarded as the need of the hour required. He saw his fellow-men as individuals,—compounded of flesh and blood, of passions, foibles and prejudices,—and he knew how to employ each, as the painter chooses and mixes the colors on his palette, for the special work in hand. And they, in turn, never thought of Cavour as an embodied formula or mere doctrinaire, but as the most real of human beings, energized in every nerve, who could toil like a Titan yet pause to play like a boy, who never did things by halves, yet could do many things simultaneously and do them supremely well. Objective as the chemist in his scrutiny of laws and elements, Cavour was as subjective as a woman in his human relations. It is that marriage in him of two natures commonly regarded as incompatible, that distinguishes him from the few other statesmen who are his peers.

He was a master Opportunist: but Opportunism is as futile as the veerings of a weathercock unless it be rooted in principles. How deep, how immutable, his principles were and how compelling, we have seen at every turn. They quickened his conscience; they clarified his vision; they guided his will. Whether to them or to temperament he owed his poise and his resilience, who can say? Although he had no anxiety lest Truth should die with him, yet he labored as unceasingly as if on him its existence did verily hang.

* * *

To Italians, Cavour will stand for all time as the builder of their state. Many quarried: he took the blocks, of every size and shape and quality, and made United Italy out of them. He used the material at hand, as the true architect does, uncomplaining, in default of better: and though he died before the edifice was completed, yet the walls were up, the roof was on and the general plan finished. Like Michael Angelo, he left to others to add the façade and details. If only later Italians do not spoil Cavour's Doric design or hide it beneath a Baroque exterior!

But to the world, Cavour has a still larger significance. He was one of the few statesmen whose mission it is to mediate between an era that is passing away and a new era that has not yet taken definite form. This task is of far deeper import than that of founding a dynasty or of aggrandizing a state. The rise of Prussia under Frederick the Great, for instance, simply meant that a man of very uncommon powers carved a kingdom for himself out of existing conditions: but his success marked no turning-point in civilization nor advanced civilization; it merely measured the vitality of the Old Régime, when its waning strength was wielded by a Frederick on a people as sturdy, as rigid, and politically as backward as eighteenth-century Prussians. Cavour, on the other hand, was confronted by innovations. The French Revolution destroyed; the generation that followed patched together the débris; the men who came on the scene about 1840 saw that the makeshifts and compromises could not endure. Thenceforth, their business was to construct. Democracy, a new force, which the partisans of the Old feared and hated but could not annihilate, must be grappled with. Democracy had arisen to make an end of Feudalism, which, however transformed and wearing many names and strange disguises, was still, after a thousand years, the accepted principle of official Europe. Democracy was no longer a theory, but the ideal of multitudes whose numbers swelled every day.

In such a conflict between two mutually destructive systems, the consummate statesman is he who, averting the brute shock of a bloody revolution, —which often settles nothing,—leads out of the Old into the New by steps so gradual that the clash of readjustment may be minimized. This was Cavour's method. He did not destroy the Old, merely because it was old; nor did he rush fanatically to the New, merely because it was new. But perceiving that Liberty, the ideal which underlies Democracy, is a universal principle, by properly obeying which society may be organized on a higher level than the opposing principle of Authority can ever attain, he dedicated his genius to promoting Liberty in all fields. No one knew better than he how much Liberty presupposes, and how little hitherto mankind in the mass has possessed the qualifications required for working Democracy on a high plane; but he held that it is better to fall short or to fail in striving for the highest, than to be content with the corroding prosperity of a system admittedly inferior. "Better the worst of Chambers," he said, "than the best of antechambers": and he set up reverence for Liberty as the test of man's moral nature.

* * *

It is because Cavour, by the rare blending of Reason and disciplined Emotion, guided to victory the most marvelous and difficult struggle for freedom recorded in modern times, that his name will be cherished by generations yet unborn and by races yet uncivilized. Whoever fights for liberty anywhere, fights for the uplifting of mankind everywhere. All creeds agree in making absolute freedom an attribute of the Almighty: and finite man has in no way shown his kinship with the Infinite more clearly than by his incessant craving to be free. Without Liberty, the best loses for him its savor, and even religion becomes an anodyne instead of an inspiration. Among the champions of Liberty, since the beginning, none had a nobler vision of her beauty, none confided in her more loyally, none served her more wisely than Camillo di Cavour.

NAPOLEON III AND CAVOUR

AND

CAVOUR AND GARIBALDI

L. C. B. Seaman

THE STARTING point of a rational understanding of events in Italy between 1858 and 1861 is a realization that in 1858 neither Napoleon III nor Cavour wanted or expected Italian unification. The achievement, by 1861, of an Italian kingdom comprising the whole of peninsular Italy except Rome, was something which though it happened partly because of Napoleon III and Cavour, happened to a considerable degree in spite of both of them.

The first confusion arises out of the meaning of the words "Kingdom of Italy." To all who consider the phrase after 1861 it obviously means the area ruled over by Victor Emmanuel from that year onwards, an area felt to be incomplete because it did not at that date already include either Rome or Venetia. But this is not what the phrase "Kingdom of Italy" meant before 1861. Its meaning is best elicited by examining a map of Europe either in the heyday of Napoleon I or in the time of Charlemagne. It is at once clear that the establishment of a Kingdom of Italy, so far from involving the unification of the entire peninsula under one sovereignty could, on the basis of the medieval and the Napoleonic heritage, be applied only to some variously defined part of northern Italy.

It is certain therefore that Napoleon III's phrase about "doing something for Italy" was even vaguer than it looks, for the word "Italy" was susceptible of various interpretations. It is safe to assume that the Emperor's famous words were not intended to involve anything much more than the expulsion of the Austrians from the northern part of Italy; that they involved the idea of "freedom" only in a highly qualified sense; and that they did not at all involve Italy's unification.

The creation of an Italian kingdom was, as it turned out, contrary to the interests of France. So also, as it turned out, was the creation of a German Empire. The dominating position of France in Europe in the past had depended on the weakness of both Italy and Germany. Nor was Napoleon III stupid enough to desire either of them to come into existence in the shapes they actually assumed. He seems to have wanted to do in Italy and Germany what Napoleon I had done—to create large French client states in those areas, and at the same time, though this was not essential, to acquire additional territory for France. The scheme had the additional advantage that in both areas the achievement of this policy would result in a diminution of the power and prestige of the Habsburgs who stood for the dynastic principle, of which Napoleon was Europe's chief public opponent.

It is therefore incorrect to think of Napoleon III as venturing into Italy because he was blinded by a romantic attachment to the cause of Italian nationalism. He took the action he did because he thought it was compatible with the extension of French influence in Italy. In doing something for Italy he would do something for France as well, and perhaps, if he could, something for the Bonapartes also. On the other hand it is wrong to think of his intervention as purely a matter of Machiavellian subtlety that misfired. The Man of December was far too much a product of his age not to share sincerely the contemporary dream of a free and regenerate Italy; and his entirely personal decision to take the first decisive move whence sprang the creation of an independent Italy has usually been treated with scant justice.

For in taking the step he did he was behaving in conformity both with the Napoleonic tradition and the Napoleonic legend. The voice from St. Helena told him that the first monarch to espouse the cause of the "peoples" would become the undisputed leader of Europe. That he should intervene to deliver the Italians from the Austrians was consistent with his self-chosen role as leader of the nationalities; and he clearly felt that in so doing he was placing France and himself at the head of the most powerful political force of the day. He and France, by co-operating with history, could secure the mastery of Europe's destiny by a great act of moral leadership which was also a piece of shrewd international statecraft.

Intervention was facilitated by the circumstance that it was Cavour with whom he had to deal. Alone among continental Liberals Cavour clearly understood the problem of power and that it could be solved solely by using the apparatus of power-politics, diplomacy and war. It was for this reason that he saw to it that Piedmont came to acquire this essential apparatus. He himself supplied the diplomacy, and the Piedmontese, often against their will, provided the armies and paid for their armament. But since the resources of Piedmont were small it was necessary to compensate for this fact by diplomacy of exceptional subtlety. Only by great skill would it be possible to secure the support of a Great Power and yet retain a reasonable measure of genuine independence for Piedmont; as it was, Cavour was widely accused of being Napoleon III's lackey and he was in fact far more sensitive to the need to placate the Emperor than is sometimes realized by those who are over-hasty to believe that Cavour was not merely an able man but a super-man.

Because he understood power-politics, Cavour was not a revolutionary. His spiritual home was remote indeed from the terrestrial paradise of regenerate nations linked together in brotherly love that Mazzini's mind habitually dwelt in; and Cavour hardly belonged to the same universe as Garibaldi, moving with the manly directness of a fighting pioneer from one camp fire to another. Cavour was a Liberal in the style of the July Monarchy, and had he been as French as his critics sometimes said he was, it would have been Cavour rather than Thiers or Guizot who would have guided the destinies of Orleanist France and have made a very much better job of it. Indeed there were times when his methods of managing the Parliament at Turin resembled those of Guizot more closely than those of Sir Robert Peel. As a Parliamentary Liberal, too, Cavour did not, like Mazzini and Garibaldi, believe in Italian unification. For him the idea was tainted with Radicalism, and his diplomat's sense of realities told him there were too many insurmountable obstacles in the way.

All these factors in his political character made him acceptable to Napoleon III who likewise was not planning the unification of Italy and could not prejudice his position by association with Radical insurrectionaries. In short, Cavour made the Italian movement respectable and safe. Or so it seemed.

Whatever else was planned at Plombières it was therefore not Italian unification. It appears that Napoleon III's plans were always fluid and the programme agreed on was always subject to variation in the Emperor's mind. A reasonable scheme would, he thought, involve the expulsion of Austrian influence from north and centre and the reform of the various systems of government elsewhere in Italy. Lombardy-Venetia, the Duchies and perhaps the Romagna, could be added to Sardinia to make a Kingdom of Italy large enough to be a useful French client-state but not powerful enough to resist the cession of Savoy (and Nice perhaps) or to pursue a genuinely independent policy of its own. Alternatively, Tuscany and the Romagna could form a second client state under the rule of somebody capable of substituting French for Austrian influence —perhaps the Emperor's cousin, Prince Napoleon. The Two Sicilies could perhaps be persuaded to become yet another French client state by replacing the unpopular Bourbons by Murat, yet another of the Emperor's cousins. The Pope would (somehow) be persuaded to acquiesce in the whole process by being made President of an Italian Federation to which the new Italian states would all dutifully adhere. All of the various interests concerned would then be satisfied—Italian patriots by the expulsion of the Austrians; Liberals by the abolition of ancient misgovernment; Victor Emmanuel and Cavour by the greatly increased size and prestige of Piedmont; the French clericals by the new dignity of the Pope; the French patriots by the acquisition of new territory and by the substitution of French for Austrian influence throughout the length and breadth of Italy; and the Bonapartes by the creation of new family connections in Italy.

One version of this never definitively formulated programme was offered Cavour at Plombières, another was actually agreed on there, and the last and most modest version emerged at Villafranca. Many of the variations upon it were no more than suggestions whispered into the ears of slightly bewildered ambassadors and those unofficial contact-men of all nationalities for whom the Emperor had such a great weakness.

As for what Cavour had in mind in his dealings with Napoleon III, it is probable that he was not fundamentally more precise and fixed in his objectives than the Emperor. The greatness of Cavour is like the greatness of Bismarck in this respect; it consists not in the undeviating pursuit of a ruthless master plan concocted in advance of events, but rather in the infinite suppleness with which he adapted his policy and his objectives to every changing circumstance yet at the same time remaining firmly in control. His famous sense of what was possible consisted precisely in being able to see clearly what was possible at each given moment. It is the ability to control a situation that is constantly fluid that marks the able statesman; and the success of Cavour and Bismarck is due to their possessing this ability, just as Napoleon III's inability to do so was a major cause of his failure.

All that can safely be said is that Cavour wanted to get as much as could reasonably be obtained, but no more. He certainly envisaged the acquisition of Tuscany and the Romagna, and although his great triumph at Plombières was to get Napoleon to agree to Piedmont acquiring the Romagna, he seems to have played the Emperor false about Tuscany. But his acquiescence in the proposal to cede Savoy and possibly Nice indicates how very far indeed Cavour was from being the apostle of Italian Nationalism as such. Cavour was far more concerned, and far more fitted, to play the role of an international diplomat than that of the instrument of popular Nationalism. Plombières thus only looked like a demagogic plot. In reality it was much more like an old-fashioned piece of eighteenth century diplomacy on traditional horse-dealing lines. Phrases such as "the cradle of the dynasty" or "the sacred soil of the fatherland" had no place in Cavour's vocabulary. If the Duchies and the Romagna were only to be had by giving up Savoy and Nice, then Savoy and Nice would have to be given up, and principles would have to give way to necessity.

Thus, it may well be that there was after all not much more deception involved in Cavour's treatment of Napoleon III than there was in Bismarck's treatment of the Emperor at Biarritz. And because no Italian federation resulted from Plombières, that does not mean that Cavour necessarily disliked that idea, either. True, if such a federation were to emerge, Cavour envisaged Piedmont as its effectual head rather than the Pope; but whereas a federation in Italy seemed a reasonable possibility, a unitary Italy did not, in 1858. And Cavour was not interested in the impossible. It is necessary to beware of Cavour's readiness to falsify the record after the event in the interests of his own reputation. Like Bismarck he was always at great pains to prove that everything that happened, happened because he had always wanted it to happen and because his guiding genius was in complete control of affairs from beginning to end. But that does not mean that he is to be believed when he says this, any more than Bismarck is to be believed when he says the same sort of thing about the creation of the German Empire.

The fact is that both the men of Plombières were deceived—by the Italians in general and by Garibaldi in particular. It was not merely Napoleon III's careful schemes which were swept away by Italian revolutionary zeal; Cavour's nice diplomatic calculations went the same way too. One thing about the Plombières agreement is certain; it is that neither of the two men who made it dreamed that they were inaugurating a series of events that in three years would make Victor Emmanuel king over all Italy.

As soon as the Emperor began, in his serpentine way, to prepare French and European opinion for his coming intervention in Italy, he quickly came to the conclusion that he had blundered into a trap of his own making. A man as meditative and as impressionable as he was could not fail to see how difficult it was going to be to limit and control the passions his intervention would inevitably arouse: the heady patriotism of Italian Liberals and Radicals, the justifiable fears of Catholics everywhere at this gratuitous patronage of the most belligerently anti-clerical government in Europe, and above all the furious determination of Cavour himself. Consequently it is possible to see reason in Napoleon's vacillations after Plombières. Right up to the moment of the agreement at Villafranca he devoted as much ingenuity to trying to get out of the trap he had fallen into as Cavour did in trying to keep him in it. As it was Napoleon all but succeeded in escaping; and was on the very brink of salvation when he was pushed back into the clutches of Cavour by the despatch of the fatal Austrian ultimatum. For when it arrived Cavour was about to accept the scheme for the demobilization of all the three Powers which had been proposed by the British and apparently accepted by the Austrians as well as the French. After that the Emperor had no alternative but to march into the hornets' nest, driven to it by the unscrupulousness of Cavour and the folly of the Habsburgs.

Despite the rashness of his utterances in Milan after Magenta when he appeared publicly to give "the Italians" *carte blanche* to do what they liked, Villafranca was not a real reversal of Napoleon's policy, and not, even in its failure to liberate Venetia, a betrayal of the cause of Italy, if the phrase is intended to imply the unification of the entire country, for this had never been in question. Napoleon was certainly going back on his agreement with Cavour and on his promises made in Milan. But it ill became Cavour, of all people, to complain if, after the shambles at Magenta and Solferino, and with all Europe and half France hostile to him, Napoleon felt no longer able to fight Cavour's battles for him. If the Villafranca proposals dissatisfied the Piedmontese, they secured for them more than they could have got if Napoleon had stayed at home. Piedmont obtained Lombardy and Parma. Napoleon III gained nothing; not Nice, to which he had little claim, nor even Savoy, to which he had, on national grounds at any rate, at least as good a claim as Piedmont had to Romagna and the Duchies. Indeed, the really humiliating thing about Villa-franca was that it represented failure for Cavour. Against the insistence of the Radicals that Italy should and could liberate herself by her own unaided efforts, Cavour had asserted the superiority of the orthodox methods of diplomacy and war in association with Napoleon III. And unlike Napoleon III, Cavour could resign after Villafranca, and thus appear to dissociate himself from what was after all the collapse of the policy on which he had staked his whole claim to be the leader of the Risorgimento. His rage is understandable; but in flounc-ing out of office he was not merely giving vent to his feelings. He was also pulling out on the partner he had himself chosen, leaving him to bear the stigma of treachery while preserving for himself the reputation of an outraged and bitterly disappointed patriot.

Moreover, though Cavour was out of office, Ricasoli in Tuscany, Farini in Modena and D'Azeglio in the Romagna had been, and remained, busily at work on his behalf, ensuring that in all three places the movement for annexa-tion to Piedmont should triumph over all obstacles and silence every criticism. The Villafranca proposals to return all three areas to their legitimate rulers threatened to stultify their work. Yet the fact that these regions did not so revert was as much the result of the decisions of Napoleon III as the annexation of Lombardy and Parma. Cavour in fact went on negotiating with the traitor of Villafranca, and through those negotiations got the Duchies and the Romagna after all, and, what is more, Cavour insisted that the traitor got his price—Savoy and Nice.

If the cession of Savoy and Nice lost Cavour much prestige in Italy, it was a step which cost Napoleon III a good deal more. It wrecked his own proposal for a Congress to settle the Italian problem, because no Congress would ever give him Savoy and Nice, and the change of front increased his reputation for double-dealing and made him appear greedy for territory, which in fact he was not. It made nonsense of his appeal to the principle of nationality since he had no national claim to Nice. He could claim it only on the grounds that with Savoy it helped to adjust the balance of power in the interests of France; but the popular side of his prestige was based on the assumption that he, alone among the rulers of Europe, stood, not for the balance of power, but for the principle of nationality. The annexation also prevented his obtaining the renewal of English friendship he had sought by at last openly abandoning the

Pope in the pamphlet "The Pope and the Congress"; in this he justified Piedmontese annexation of the Romagna. The clericals in France were not more
hysterical about this than were the English about the annexation of Savoy and
Nice. To the former, their Charlemagne had become a Nebuchadnezzar; to the
English the "Alexander" of the nineteenth century had been revealed in his
"true" colours as a contemptible "Annexander."

Yet if the cession of Savoy and Nice was a crime, it was a crime in which
from the beginning Cavour had been the Emperor's accomplice (as the
English realized, though they tended to plead extenuating circumstances in
Cavour's favour). It had been part of the original bargain to which Cavour
had been a freely consenting party. If it was a violation of the principle of
Italy for the Italians, it was a violation which Cavour had been willing to accept at Plombières, when he was under no constraint whatever. Neither Cavour
nor Napoleon III had ever assumed that Napoleon III was going to help Italy
for nothing. And to minimize the service the Emperor rendered to Italy is to
ignore facts and fall victim to contemporary anti-Napoleonic hysteria in England
and the sedulously cultivated prejudice against him that developed, after
Villafranca, in Italy. The work of Cavour in the north and the centre up to
April 1860 depended as completely on Napoleon III's initiative in attacking
the Habsburgs as Cavour's later work depended on Garibaldi's initiative in attacking the Bourbons in the south. In short, the contemptuous attitude usually
taken towards Napoleon III's work for Italy is one of the shoddier bits of the
mythology of nineteenth century historians. Although he doubtless repented
of it after the cession of Nice, the fairer verdict was Garibaldi's after Villafranca:
"Do not forget the gratitude we owe to Napoleon III, and to the French army,
so many of whose valiant sons have been killed or maimed for the cause of
Italy."

* * *

If Cavour had had his way there would have been no immediate sequel
in the south to the war of liberation in the north. With the absorption of
Lombardy, the Duchies, Tuscany and the Romagna, all that war and diplomacy
could achieve had been achieved. For Cavour, therefore, with his fine sense
of the possible, this was the time to stop—not as a matter of principle, but of
practical politics. Rome and Venetia could not for the moment be attained
because of the insuperable international obstacles. As for the Bourbon kingdom,
it could be acquired only by war, even if Cavour wanted it; and as an astute
politician and diplomat, he saw that an attack on the Two Sicilies was out of
the question. It is not at all certain that he was much interested in the matter.

Garibaldi was interested, however; and unlike Cavour he believed in the
impossible. He wanted Venetia, Rome and the Two Sicilies, and he wanted
them united into an Italian kingdom under the flag of the House of Savoy.

His object when he set sail with the Thousand was to get all three but he aimed chiefly at getting Rome and Venetia by a large-scale outflanking movement. It was Garibaldi and not Cavour whose policy it was to unite Italy by revolution from the south because diplomacy had made it impossible to do so from the north. Cavour said later that it was his policy. But stealing other people's slogans is a common habit among politicians. It is usual to say that Cavour encouraged Garibaldi in secret; according to some because he regarded Garibaldi as an ally, and according to others because he intended from the beginning to use Garibaldi as a catspaw. In opposing him in public, Cavour was, it is said, cleverly (and, to judge from the glee with which the story is related, rather amusingly) concealing his true aims by telling ingenious lies to confuse foreign diplomats. In other words, the expedition of the Thousand is treated as a more romantic and successful Jameson Raid, with Cavour cast for the role of a Cecil Rhodes; and a Cecil Rhodes who was not only fooling all Europe, but, according to some theories, also fooling his own particular Dr. Jameson into the bargain. It is an odd comment on the view of international morality presented to the young in the history books, that whereas Rhodes and Jameson are regarded as rather shocking, Cavour and Garibaldi are paraded as heroes.

Not only is the interpretation at fault, but so, it seems, are the facts from which it springs. Cavour's first reaction to Garibaldi's plan was the reverse of what it is usually said to be. When the expedition was being planned Cavour did his best to oppose it, but had to keep his opposition secret because he was afraid public opinion would be more on Garibaldi's side than on his. Once Garibaldi had got away, what Cavour then kept secret was his hope and expectation that Garibaldi would fail. Cavour was glad when Garibaldi attacked Sicily only in the sense that he felt it would have been much worse if he had attacked the Papal States instead.

Cavour's dislike for Garibaldi's expedition had several causes. There was first the serious possibility that Cavour would get the blame for it and be threatened with the loss of Napoleon III's support, with a renewal of war with Austria, or some sort of general European intervention. He was also convinced that Garibaldi was a stupid man who was in alliance with wild radicals who would demand a republican Italy based on a system of universal suffrage. Cavour had no more desire to see Piedmont merged into a Radical republican Italy than Bismarck had to see Prussia merged into a Liberal Germany; and if Garibaldi succeeded in Sicily it seemed likely that Radicalism would go on to sweep Naples and the Papal States and threaten to divide Italy between a Radical republican south and Liberal monarchical north. Cavour was desperately afraid of such a possibility because it would have meant civil war in Italy, and a civil war which, if it came to it, Cavour would feel compelled to fight. The third reason for his dislike arose out of the irritating arrogance which is often characteristic of the outstanding statesman; an arrogance based partly on personal conceit and partly on a justifiable sense of his own great ability. Garibaldi was so much his antithesis that Cavour could not believe that when Garibaldi said he was fighting in the cause of Victor Emmanuel that was just what he meant. Cavour could not believe that Garibaldi's break with the republican Mazzini was real. He persisted throughout 1860 in treating Garibaldi as if he were a Mazzinian republican and for that reason tried without success, but quite irrelevantly, to get Mazzini arrested. Much of this has its unworthy side. Cavour, bitterly unpopular as the man who had traitorously given Nice and Savoy to Napoleon III, could not bear the possibility of being odiously and publicly contrasted with one whom the simple people saw as their saviour. There was not room in Italy for both of these men. The fact that Garibaldi as well as Cavour realized this in the end saved much bloodshed in Italy.

Contrary to Cavour's expectations and hopes, Garibaldi succeeded in Sicily. Cavour's aim at once was to get Sicily annexed to Piedmont. Garibaldi wanted annexation too, but not before he had reached Rome. He calculated that once Sicily passed into Piedmontese control he would be unable to use it as he intended to use it, namely as the supply base for his attack on Naples and Rome. This was precisely why Cavour wanted Sicily annexed forthwith, and why Garibaldi would not agree. Another reason for delay imposed itself. Sicilians wanted to be free of the Bourbons and of Naples, but hardly any of them wanted annexation to Piedmont. Incorporation into a Kingdom of all Italy they might agree to: but that would be possible only when such a kingdom existed—after and not before Garibaldi had proclaimed it from Rome, its true capital. Another complication was that Cavour could not simply grab Sicily. It was the property of the Bourbon government in Naples; and as a diplomat Cavour realized he had to be careful. The English, true, had no objections; but Napoleon III demanded a plebiscite, so that there could be a public appeal from the law of nations to the higher principle of nationality. Yet, since hardly anybody in Sicily could read, hardly anybody wanted annexation to Piedmont, and nobody would do anything against the wishes of Garibaldi (who was already at the gates of Naples and might soon be in Rome) an early plebiscite was impossible. In an atmosphere of confusion and rather unnecessary ill-will, Cavour worked from the remote distance of Turin to get control of a situation for which he was entirely unprepared.

The problems of Naples and the Papal States, which developed simultaneously, produced an open quarrel between Cavour and Garibaldi. It was a quarrel which Cavour worked up deliberately into a public quarrel between the South and the North, and between the Liberals and the Radicals. And it was a quarrel so bitter as to make civil war the probable outcome unless it was averted by the capitulation of the South to the North, of the Radicals to the Liberals, and, above all, by the capitulation of Garibaldi to Cavour. In goading

Garibaldi into apposition to him, in diverting opinion in northern Italy from admiration of Garibaldi into detestation of him, in capturing the fruits of a Radical victory in the south for the Liberal industrialists and middle classes of the north, Cavour showed great skill, great unscrupulousness, much mean-spiritedness and at times much short-sightedness. Yet in bringing the hostility of the two main forces in Italian life into the clear light of day and in produc-ing a speedy short-term solution of them, Cavour deserved well of his country.

The questions raised by Garibaldi's arrival in Naples and the prospect of his attacking Rome were fundamental ones and had to be answered. Who was to rule Italy? Was it to be Victor Emmanuel or was it to be Garibaldi? Garibaldi always said it should be Victor Emmanuel; but if the crown of all Italy was to be given to Victor Emmanuel by the Dictator of Sicily and Naples, then the dynasty would be the prisoner of the Radicals who supported Garibaldi, and the politically and industrially more advanced North would, thanks to universal suffrage, be at the mercy of the backward and illiterate South. Nor must it be forgotten that in any constructive sense of the word the Radicals had no policy at all. With them, as with Marx, the revolution was all. Once it was achieved, policy was hardly necessary; heaven would lie all around the successful revolu-tionaries and they would need to do nothing much more strenuous than bask in the sunshine of perfected brotherhood. Cavour knew better, and on this issue of Liberalism versus Radicalism, he was right and the Radicals were wrong.

Worse still, Garibaldi would not want to stop, even at Rome. He demanded more than Piedmontese acquiescence in an invasion of Rome; immediately after that he would demand an attack on Venetia. Garibaldi's programme meant the prospect of war against all Europe. Thus, there is no doubt that the flaunting of Italian Nationalism on such a scale would produce an upsurge of German Nationalism. For though when nationality spoke with an Italian accent it said that Venetia was Italian, when it spoke with a German accent, it could say, appealing to history, that Venetia, like Lombardy, was German.

Cavour overcame Garibaldi by a series of astute moves, some more successful than others. His biggest failure was the attempt to organize a Liberal revolt in Naples to anticipate Garibaldi's arrival. In doing this, Cavour was simultane-ously trying to overthrow the Bourbons while maintaining normal diplomatic relations with them, and trying to thwart Garibaldi while keeping up an appear-ance of friendly admiration for him. The Neapolitans showed no inclination whatever to "liberate" themselves, however. To the disgust of the Piedmontese the nobility of Naples fled and the rest of the population just waited for Gari-baldi. Cavour's most famous and most successful manœuvre was the invasion of the Papal States, though here again he was irritated by the extreme difficulty of engineering even an appearance of a popular rising to justify a Piedmontese invasion. Indeed, the chief characteristic of the mass of the population in the Centre and the South in 1860 was their unwillingness to do anything to cast off the dreadful yoke of tyranny and obscurantism under which they were said to be suffering. As for union with the House of Savoy, its almost only consistent advocate, paradoxically enough, was Garibaldi himself, whose attitude to Cavour was first that he was a sympathizer and then that he was a coward whom public opinion and perhaps Victor Emmanuel would shortly sweep from office.

The Piedmontese invasion of the Papal States was not merely a wise states-man's method of minimizing the rashness of a headstrong collaborator. Cavour took this step for the purpose of taking the Risorgimento completely out of Garibaldi's hands and placing it once more under the control of Cavour and the Piedmontese. By now, indeed, the Piedmontese were beginning to be alarmed by Garibaldi's successes. He controlled as much Italian territory as did Victor Emmanuel, and it was easy to persuade them to rationalize their pique at this state of affairs by representing Garibaldi to them as a "wild beast" and a republican revolutionary. So delighted were northerners at the Piedmontese invasion of Papal territory that for one wild moment some of them believed that Cavour's object was to capture Rome ahead of Garibaldi rather than to preserve Rome intact. Cavour made no effort to disillusion them; like Bismarck he often gained much by allowing people to go misunderstanding him. For he simul-taneously gained popularity with those who did realize his real purpose; for many Piedmontese did not relish the prospect of Turin ceasing to be the capital of the Italian kingdom and therefore did not want Rome to be taken.

The invasions of the Papal States and of Naples were acts of what the twentieth century disapprovingly calls "unprovoked aggression." Moreover, they even lacked the excuse so often made for such acts, that of being inspired by the noble aim of national union or the liberation of the inhabitants of the states being violated. Not only were the inhabitants of the Papal States and Naples without any great desire to be liberated by Cavour; he had not even wanted their liberation himself. Garibaldi had forced his hand, and there is much to be said for the view that Cavour united the Italian peninsula in 1861 less to please the Italians than to spite Garibaldi. Cavour's intervention in the Papal States and Naples was as anti-revolutionary in its subtle way as the previous interventions ordered by Metternich. Yet what Cavour did was to keep the foreigner out of Italy at a highly critical moment. By saving Rome from the Italian Radicals, Cavour secured the acquiescence of Napoleon III in Pied-montese absorption of the Papal states; and by settling the matter without active assistance from the French he secured the unqualified approval of the anti-clerical government of England.

The mere news that the Piedmontese were on their way caused great confusion in Naples. Garibaldi lacked the ability or the will to organize an effective opposition to the Piedmontese and most people therefore felt that they had no alternative but to bow to the inevitable. After all, Garibaldi had always proclaimed himself the loyal servant of Victor Emmanuel. The alternative to his abdication of authority was civil war, and for Garibaldi that was unthinkable. He would not do in 1861 what in a not dissimilar situation Cromwell had done in 1647, namely accuse the nominal leaders of his cause of being false to the Truth and then summon his soldiers to turn their arms against those whose agents they had been. Yet his dreams for Italy were hardly less impracticable than Cromwell's dream of an England ruled by the Saints. His absolute control over the hearts of his followers had been greater than Cromwell's, and the effect of his generalship on the destinies of the Risorgimento were far more decisive than the effect of Cromwell's on the Great Rebellion. Garibaldi's abandonment of his authority in 1861 ought in itself to have disposed of the criticism that he was merely a wild man. He was a great soldier and an inspiring leader of men; those who opposed him had so little of these qualities themselves that they failed altogether to understand him. They saw him merely as a distorted version of themselves, as yet another politician, but one who, because he got results faster than they and secured the uncritical admiration of ordinary people, must be branded as a dangerous rival with whom no compromise was possible.

Yet the Italian politicians—Cavour and his successors—may be forgiven much of their mistrust of Garibaldi. For it was much easier to retire to Caprera with a bag of seedcorn than to have to deal with the Italian situation his zeal had created. For the plain fact was that in 1860 Italy was not ready for unification under Piedmont, and Piedmont was neither ready nor fitted for the responsibilities of governing a unified Italy. If Cavour and the Piedmontese must bear a large proportion of the blame for the disappointments that mark the early history of the Italian kingdom, Garibaldi has his responsibilities in the matter also. The revolutionary attempt to steal a march on history, to force the pace of human change in the interests of passionately held beliefs and theories, is always a mistake. The human mind is capable of just so much change and no more: it can never willingly move as fast as idealists want it to. Under the impulse of extravagant hopes and mass enthusiasm men can move very fast at revolutionary epochs; but the hopes and the enthusiasm are so much spiritual benzedrine and speedily produce a contrary reaction. The aftermath is mental disillusionment and social disarray. Garibaldi forced the pace in 1860; but it was a pace that all but killed the spirit of the Risorgimento in Italy.

The centre and south were not ready for unification, and the plebiscites in favour of annexation to the house of Savoy proved only certain negative propositions. The enormous number of voters who said "yes" to annexation by Piedmont said so because to vote against it was, in the circumstances of 1860, a vote without meaning, a vote for the impossible. It could imply nothing more than a wish to continue the prevailing confusion of an interregnum that could easily develop into anarchy and civil war. All the plebiscites really proved was that people were tired of the uncertainty that had prevailed since Garibaldi's first landing in Sicily, and therefore preferred annexation as the only visible means of getting settled government again. As to the sort of settled government they would prefer, the plebiscites gave them no chance to express an opinion about that. What is more, Cavour was determined at all costs that no chance to express an opinion should be permitted. Consequently the votes in the plebiscites represented not a rational decision in favour of anything, but a sort of emotional *te deum* proclaiming a general sense of thankfulness that the time of troubles was at an end.

Unhappily the troubles were not at an end. The real troubles of southern Italy and Sicily were not political but social and economic. Poverty, illiteracy and a great shortage of land; these were the essential facts of the situation. And since the Bourbons had not invented these facts, the departure of the Bourbons did not alter them. Worse still, the assimilation of the south to the Piedmontese system did not merely fail to settle the fundamental problems of the south; it made them worse. The most obvious immediate consequences of the Risorgimento in the south, and the creation of a Kingdom of all Italy, were conscription, higher taxation, an increased cost of living, and a brand new legal system centered upon Turin. Within a matter of weeks after the plebiscites, great tides of opinion in the south had turned against Victor Emmanuel and Piedmont; and the outstanding feature of southern Italy after 1860 was uncontrollable and widespread brigandage, combining the characteristics of a peasants' revolt and a Bourbon counter-revolution. Only if words are used in the narrowest and most legalistic sense is it permissible to say that Italy was united in 1860; for the new régime was rejected spiritually and politically by the more pious Catholics, and rejected physically to the point of open warfare by the southern peasants.

These perhaps inevitable consequences of the rapid annexation of the south by Piedmont were due to the fact that Garibaldi had forced the hand of the Piedmontese too. Cavour knew nothing of the south of Italy and did not even dare to show his face in liberated Naples. He and his agents were quite unfitted to the task of governing the south with sympathy or even intelligence. It was all very well for Garibaldi to hand his territories over to the *re galantuomo* and then go off to Caprera; but it was Cavour and his successors who were to have to manage these territories. Garibaldi had the satisfaction of doing his duty; Victor Emmanuel had the satisfaction of being the first king of all Italy. But it was Cavour who was left holding the baby; and if he and his successors did the job badly at least they have the excuse that it was Garibaldi's baby, not theirs.

Various expressions used by leading figures in Piedmont in 1860 indicate the state of mind in which the Piedmontese approached the problem of governing the south. The Neapolitans were "canaille"; they were "barbarians who cared little for liberty"; Naples was "rotten to the marrow," it was an Augean stable, and it was "not Italy, but Africa." And the Piedmontese knew so little of economic realities that they were convinced that there was great wealth in the south and that all that was wrong was the shiftless character of the Neapolitans. For the great weakness of Cavour's Liberalism, like most Liberalism (and theoretical Socialism also), was that it was cursed with an urban parochialism of mind. It neither understood nor cared for the problems of backward, rural societies: its entire philosophy reflected the needs of ambitious metropolitan man, whether he was a would-be industrialist, an aspiring member of the professional classes, or a progressively minded aristocrat who saw in an attack on the old feudal and ecclesiastical system more opportunity for the increase of his own wealth and power than he could get by defending that system. Free institutions, free trade, unrestricted opportunities for the commercial, industrial and professional middle class—these were the aims of Cavour and his allies, and these alone. Moreover, they were aims which were put in jeopardy by Garibaldi's policy of war and still more war, of revolution through the common people. Rigidly and rightly proud of their superior efficiency, pharisaically conscious of being in the van of progress, the Piedmontese Liberals were contemptuous of the people of the south for their ignorance, hostile to their religious feelings, and convinced that their low standard of living was due to their incorrigible idleness rather than to the intractability of nature. Granted that only the Piedmontese possessed adequate administrative training, and therefore had to govern the South because there were few indigenous administrators of experience, it is still unfortunate that Piedmont treated the people of the south with the arrogance of conquerors imposing alien institutions on a tribe of barbarians for their own good.

The effect of realizing that Italian unification could not have been begun without Napoleon III and would not have been completed without Garibaldi is to require a reassessment of the character of Cavour. If he is regarded as the resolute planner of Italy's unification from 1858 onwards, then the indictment against him on the grounds of his breaches of elementary political morality is a heavy one. Deliberate warmongering and calculated falsehood are characteristic of him. The fomentation of plots designed to disrupt the governments of neighboring states from within creates an alarming parallel between his treatment of the other states of Italy and Hitler's treatment of the other states of Europe. If he instigated Garibaldi's attack on Sicily he foreshadows Cecil Rhodes; if he genuinely supported Garibaldi once the expedition was making headway, then he is not altogether unlike Mussolini encouraging General Franco in Spain in the 1930's. If he is regarded as deserting Garibaldi at the end of 1860 he is open to the charge of betraying the ardour and bravery of thousands of simple men in the interests of his own narrow dynastic aims and his own narrowly based political party. And the end of it is a sorry picture of half Italy governed against its will on the only flimsily legal basis of plebiscites as unreliable as those of Napoleon III and Hitler. It is true that all these ugly facts were glossed over or explained away and that Cavour was forgiven everything and treated as a hero. To persist in applauding him as a man who sought and successfully achieved Italian unity no matter what the cost, was to reflect the fact that it was his political allies who won in Italy, and who were therefore in a position to create a myth in which he was the supreme hero. It also reflects the fact that his activities were seen in the England of his day as a praiseworthy triumph over the Whigs' two chief bogey-men, Napoleon III and Pius IX. A less trivial view is that the conventional interpretation of the facts of the years 1858–61 justifies the charge that Cavour was the first of the many who have used a claim to be acting in the interests of a nation's sacred egoism as if it were a sufficient excuse for every sort of unscrupulousness in politics. The long failure of historians to apply normal standards of morality to what they understood to be Cavour's conduct is quite shocking. When Queen Victoria, with a clairvoyant common sense that infuriated Lord John Russell, said that Sardinian activities in Naples were "morally bad and reprehensible in themselves" Lord John could reply only by talking irrelevant twaddle about William of Orange. The Queen, like everybody else, was mistaken about Cavour; but her comment came a good deal nearer to a right judgment than the verdicts either of the three wise men of her Cabinet or of those later historians who forgave Cavour everything in much the same way as the German liberals forgave Bismarck everything, merely because he appeared to have been successful.

It is therefore important to realize that, ambitious and unscrupulous though Cavour was, his original purpose was a limited one, and that whatever views may be taken of his methods up to April 1860 (and they are certainly questionable) his conduct thereafter represents a series of reactions, at first hesitant and then cool and skillful, to a situation thrust on him by Garibaldi. In this second phase, Cavour seems at first sight more sinister than in the first. Up to April 1860 he is concerned with outmanœuvring the Austrians and their hangers-on and with managing Napoleon III; and his victims in this period of his work do not perhaps deserve a great deal of sympathy. Throughout 1860, however, he was outmanœuvring Garibaldi and a considerable section of the Italian people, and doing so in a manner singularly devoid either of generosity or honesty. At first sight, one is struck by Cavour's narrowness of vision, by the indecent haste with which he sought to discredit Garibaldi and to stifle the ardour of the Radicals who had achieved by dash and bravery successes he had been too cautious even to contemplate. (Thus, the Piedmontese army, when it advanced through the Papal States towards Naples in 1860 had not even any maps of the area.) Yet, at a deeper level, Cavour was perhaps less wrong than Garibaldi. The core of Cavour's policy was not unification but freedom from Austria, coupled with the development under Piedmontese sovereignty of free institutions in those parts of Italy which were fitted for them, and which could, with the minimum of risk (though still a high risk) be assimilated by Piedmont. Garibaldi, however, like Mazzini had no rational political aims at all, except liberty and unity as such. True, Mazzini saw the achievement of nationhood as a prelude to the regeneration of the whole European society under the principles of Humanity, but this was mere mysticism; and while mysticism has an essential place in religion it has none in politics, except perhaps the dangerous function of filling people's minds with hopes that are incapable of fulfilment. And although Garibaldi had, by 1860, so far parted company with Mazzini as to believe that nationality and humanity could be served by putting all Italy under the flag of Victor Emmanuel, the fact was that he was fundamentally as empty of constructive political purpose as Mazzini, and even less clear-sighted. For even Mazzini was not fool enough to suppose that the regeneration of Europe, or Italy, or anywhere under the sun, could be achieved under the aegis of Victor Emmanuel, of all people. It is easy to blame Cavour for wanting a swift annexation of the South to Piedmont, with no questions asked, with Rome saved, the Radical revolutionaries sent packing and Garibaldi treated like discarded orange peel. Yet Garibaldi also wanted the South to go to Victor Emmanuel. His only objections were not the sensible ones that the South did not want annexation in the form they were going to get it or that Piedmont would govern harshly. What he was sorry about was solely that he had not been allowed to go on to make still further attacks on the outraged dignity of the Pope and on the equally outraged law of Europe by taking Rome and Venetia. Cavour used a great deal of sharp practice in dealing with Garibaldi in 1860; but it must not be overlooked that Garibaldi's policy was simply war unlimited, and that it was far better for Italy that he was stopped by other Italians and in Italy, and not by the inevitable European intervention that might have put all in jeopardy, and perhaps have made of Italy another such place as Hungary had become since 1849.

Thus the truth about Cavour is not that he dared all for the national ideal, never once stopping until the dream of a united Italy had been fulfilled. Cavour did not think national unity an aim that justified the contemptuous violation of all the normal rules of political and international conduct. His career does not, as it has so often seemed to, provide a precedent and an example of the notion that an appeal to the principle of nationality makes war, double-dealing and the fomentation of plots within the territories of other governments somehow highly creditable actions which ought to be applauded. Like Bismarck after him, Cavour was both an anti-revolutionary and an anti-nationalist. He saw clearly that in practice the gospel of nationality meant war without end. He was slower than Napoleon III to see it, for Napoleon realized it after Magenta and Solferino; but in the end the outstanding work of Cavour as an Italian statesman was not to achieve Italian unification in 1860, but to prevent it. That Rome and Venetia were not within the Kingdom of Italy in 1861, in flat contradiction to the declared aims of Garibaldi and the Radicals, but that what had been gained was safe from all chance of foreign interference: these are the facts on which Cavour's claim to greatness rests. And facts very like them are the basis of Bismarck's greatness also.

Otto von Bismarck:
"The Bismarck Problem"

Otto von Bismarck pushed through
Germany's unification in little more than eight years after he became
prime minister of Prussia in September 1862. His famous statement of that
month before the budget committee of the *Landtag,* "The great questions
of the time are not decided by speeches and majority resolutions
—that was the great mistake of 1848 and 1849—but by blood and iron,"
has been described as Bismarck's theory of statecraft. And, in fact, the unification of Germany was consolidated by three wars: the Danish (1864),
the Austrian or Seven Weeks War (1866), and the Franco-Prussian War
(1870–71).

¶ The speed and dimensions of Bismarck's achievement, however,
should not obscure the fact that it was accompanied by opposition. But, as the
writer of one of the selections below reminds us, "nothing succeeds like
success." After the Austrian War, the majority of the Liberals, who for
four years had forced Bismarck into the embarrassing position of
virtually governing without a parliament, were won over to his side. This
last victory, coupled with considerations arising out of the Franco-Prussian
War and its victorious conclusion, removed the last objections of the peoples
and sovereigns of the various German states to a united Germany under
Prussian leadership. It was on the motion of King Ludwig II of Bavaria,
a country that had sided with Austria in 1866, that the crown of the German
Empire was offered to William I of Prussia at Versailles in 1871.

¶ Bismarck's dazzling success is reflected in the praise bestowed on him
and William I in Heinrich von Sybel's monumental seven volume study *Die
Begründung des deutschen Reiches durch Wilhelm I* (1889–94),[1] which

---

[1] English translation: *Founding of the German Empire by William I, Based Chiefly Upon
Prussian State Documents,* 7 vols. (New York: 1890–98).

was long the authoritative work on the 1848–1870 period in German history and was a source for many minor works by lesser authors, all pro-Bismarck and nationalist in tone. As the selections below explain, reappraisal began after World War I. The opening of German archives shed new light on the ramifications of *Realpolitik*. Moreover, Germany's defeat in 1918 meant that Bismarck's Reich had been a very impermanent one indeed. But before a truly liberal reappraisal of Bismarck could develop, the Nazi regime came to power, and the new analysis of Bismarck's policies ended. It was thus not until World War II that Erich Eyck, in exile in England, published in Switzerland his *Bismarck: Leben und Werk*,[2] the first complete biography of Bismarck, and a critical appraisal of his life's work from a liberal point of view. It is, in a sense, the point of departure for each of the three selections below, which were written after it was published.

The first selection, by Professor Hans Rothfels of the University of Chicago, is a critique of Eyck's three-volume study which gives the reader a good idea of its salient points. Professor Rothfels is not so much critical of the content of Eyck's work—in fact he finds much that is good in it— as he is of the problems raised and unsolved by Eyck's liberal approach. Professor Rothfels feels that Eyck's underlying assumption, that German unity could have been attained "by other and less forceful means than those of Bismarck," overlooks some historical realities: the aggressive nationalism of German liberals (see chapter 2); the extent to which Bismarck actually "manipulated" history; the lack of Western sympathy "with the attempt at founding a 'good' German Reich, that is, on the liberal-democratic basis of 1848," and the strength of the East-West coalition threat.

The second selection by a German historian, Franz Schnabel, agrees with Rothfels' criticism of Eyck and gives us a further elaboration of the problem of liberal nationalism raised by Rothfels. Schnabel, however, advances the original conclusion that "Bismarck is the last great representative in the line of classic diplomats" beginning with the Venetian ambassadors. As such, he has little in common with the new nationalism of the nineteenth century, a point which seems proved by his lack of pan-Germanist sentiment after 1871. Bismarck, according to Schnabel, simply used nationalism, that is took it "into custody . . . subordinated it to the state conception and made it available for diplomatic craft." Schnabel does not try to excuse all of Bismarck's conduct, but by placing him in the tradition of seventeenth- and eighteenth-century state-builders, Schnabel does mitigate the criticism of Bismarck's methods found in Eyck's work.

In the third selection, Alfred von Martin, another German historian, agrees with Schnabel's emphasis on preBismarckian nationalism, but rejects his assertion

---

[2] A one vol. abridged edition has been published in English. *Bismarck and the German Empire* (London: Allen and Unwin, 1950).

that Bismarck was "the end-product of old-fashioned Cabinet diplomacy." Von Martin concurs with the writer of another German book on Bismarck who claims that Bismarck was a "revolutionary" in the Bonapartist sense of the word. A large part, however, of von Martin's short article is devoted to a warning against replacing the myth of the "good" Bismarck with that of the "bad" Bismarck. "In the final analysis," writes von Martin, "a people always has the government it deserves. . . . The examination of Bismarck ought to have led directly into necessary German self-criticism." Von Martin's essay is a good example of the intense soul-searching that German historians have carried out in the wake of World War II. And the three selections below, writing to one another or Eyck's book as they do, show the important and controversial part that "the Bismarck problem" has played in this process.

PROBLEMS OF A BISMARCK BIOGRAPHY

Hans Rothfels

FREDERICK MEINECKE in his recent book on *The German Catastrophe* [1] quotes a Danish friend and historian as saying to him during the Hitler regime: "You know that I cannot love Bismarck, but in the present situation I must say: Bismarck belonged to *our world*." It would be easy to contrast this nicely balanced statement with innumerable others which, in the last years, indulged in indictments of the founder of the German Reich as a "Nazi forefather" or threw him into the line of descent which is supposed to lead from Frederick II's attack on Silesia in 1740 to Hitler's attack on Poland in 1939. Thus the myth of the "Iron Chancellor," of the man "in high dragoon's boots" revived and, amazingly enough, the Nazi trick of appropriating "Prussianism" as epitomized in the pageantry of the so-called "day of Potsdam," was given full credit by many of their very adversaries. But there were also the voices of those who, in a more careful and responsible way, tried to find out what links may possibly connect the beginnings with the end of the Prusso-German Reich or may point ahead from 1866 and 1871 or

[1] *Die deutsche Katrastrophe* (Ed. Brockhaus, Wiesbaden, 1946), p. 27.

From *The Review of Politics,* IX, No. 3 (July 1947), pp. 362–80. Copyright, 1947, by the University of Notre Dame. Reprinted by permission.

from 1879 to the potentialities of the Hitler regime. Meinecke's treatise is one of the finest examples of such conscientious scrutiny carried out by Germans themselves.[2] From whatever angle this question is raised the towering and baffling figure of Bismarck undoubtedly has won a new actuality. And it can easily be understood that in the recent crisis of statesmanship and particularly in view of the disaster which Germany brought upon herself and the world, attention turned back to the man who stands for decisive changes in the external setup as well as in the intellectual and moral, the political and social climate of nineteenth century Europe.

The Bismarck biography in three volumes by Erich Eyck, which was published in Zurich during the war,[3] gives to all such considerations a new basis and a sharp stimulus. It is in many respects a very timely book, or rather one that was long overdue. For in spite of the host of historians, German and non-German, who concentrated on Bismarck's era, his full life story has never been told before. There were, of course, many biographical sketches and essays, some popular and some scholarly, some adulatory and some hostile. But Erich Marcks, the only author who set out to write an all-embracing biography, stopped after completing one volume of Bismarck's youth, a subject which, in fact, proved better suited for the loving pen of an impressionist than the hard, ambiguous and often unpleasant facts of a great political career. Neither the "Bismarck-orthodoxy" nor the opportunistic interpretation brought forth by the so-called *Realpolitik* nor the curious blend of both of these trends in the Wilhelmian era succeeded in producing a rounded-out biographical portrait. While the shadow thrown by the light was not neglected altogether, the general mood which prevailed among German historians of the early twentieth century was of an optimistic and harmonizing nature, little conducive to the appraisal of a "demonic" figure. Some political biographies of a limited scope were written from a more penetrating viewpoint: that by Martin Spahn (1915) from a conservative-Catholic, that by C. Grant Robertson (1919) from a liberal-English one. But like many other books they soon were dated.

This was due, in the first place, to the enormous outpouring of source material which occurred in the one and a half decades after the fall of imperial Germany. Moreover, the new sources offered ample evidence that the catchword of the "misunderstood Bismarck" had a much broader and much more fundamental meaning than O. Hammann, the aide of Bülow, who coined it, could ever have imagined. Not only an amazing number of facts appeared which were entirely new but also aspects came into the foreground which

[2] Another very impressive example of such a historiographic re-examination, though pointing in a somewhat different direction, is Gerhard Ritter's *Geschichte als Bildungsmacht* (Stuttgart, Deutsche Verlagsanstalt, 1946). As to Bismarck, see pp. 46–50.

[3] (Eugen Rentsch Verlag, Erlenbach-Zuerich) vol. I (-1864), 679 pp., 1941; vol. II (1871), 630 pp., 1943; vol. III (1898), 687 pp., 1944.

caused a change in emphasis and interpretation. While Bismarck's criticism of his bungling successors found a resounding echo and one borne out by incisive evidence, criticism turned to the basic features of his own life work. Was not the Reich of 1871 a foundation "against the ideas of the time" and therefore mortally ill from the beginning? Did not the shortcomings of the Wilhelmian era follow from the very methods of Bismarck's policy, from a will to, or a philosophy of power which first established the Reich with "blood and iron" and then arranged the balance of the constitution and the interplay of social forces essentially according to personal needs, from the suppression of independent characters and the cultivation of an autocratic spirit which denied to the Germans the opportunity of political education and deepened the submissiveness about which Bismarck himself was to complain so bitterly after 1890? These were questions, obvious from the experiences of the Western democratic world, which now entered the German way of thinking to an increasing extent.

But while the situation after 1918 forbade (or should have forbidden) any mere *laudatio temporis acti* it also became apparent that there was no better witness against all mirages of "splendid times" and all *Realpolitik* divested of any ideas—than Bismarck himself. He certainly had never been tempted to overrate what he achieved and he never indulged in the illusion that anything definite could be settled by mere power. Even in his years of revolutionary action there was the same attempt at checking irrational forces of which there is ample evidence in the documents of the years after 1871. Through the various phases of Bismarck's life, through the obvious changes in his objectives, some fundamental views could be traced which certainly stood against the "ideas of the time," particularly against the conception of the "nation-state," as prefigured in Western Europe and associated with democracy. It can be argued that his was a losing battle even in his own time. And the fact that the limited type of Bismarck's *Reich* (limited in scope, unity and intensity) eventually weathered war and defeat does not necessarily contradict such a statement. But in view of a rampant nationalism and biologism, of the emergence of the masses and many other consequences to which nineteenth century "liberalism" (rather than "Prussianism") had led, it was precisely Bismarck's nonconformity with his time upon which a good deal of attention was focussed.

These various impulses again did not succeed in bringing forth an adequate and balanced biography. Before they had been fully borne out and before the huge mass of new historical sources had been completely penetrated, there occurred the landslide of 1933. After that there was no chance of an independent and critical biography of Bismarck being written in Germany. Besides the well-known stifling effect of an official propaganda, which first "annexed" the "Iron Chancellor" and then let him linger on as a kind of larva in relation to the butterfly of the Third Reich, there was another less well known and yet very pertinent fact: eventually something like a ban was laid upon the very name and memory of Bismarck, the great "heterodox" figure of the recent German past.[4]

It was, therefore, only from outside Germany that a work could be written that had been conspicuous by absence for so long a time. And the explanation of this striking gap, while it reflects upon certain basic problems of a Bismarck biography, underlines also the highly important and significant achievement which Mr. Eyck's three volumes offer to the professional as well as to the general reader.

The book really fills the gap as far as the synthesizing of the widely dispersed fragments and sections of our knowledge is concerned. No aspect or phase has been neglected. From the viewpoint of an over-all coverage the task could not have been mastered more successfully. Likewise, the author's command of the source material is very comprehensive and in view of the difficult situation and of wartime conditions truly to be admired. So is his broad familiarity with research work previously done and with the huge monographic literature. Years of critical reading, of checking and rechecking must have gone into Mr. Eyck's book.

Of all this the author is far from making a pretentious show; references are kept to a bare minimum and placed at the end of the respective volumes. The text itself, at least in large parts, lives up to the sound traditions of narrative history, that is, the author knows how to tell the story and to tell it in an extremely interesting way. The style is smoothly flowing and colorful, sometimes it has a dramatic ring—not without descending, however, here and there into deplorable pitfalls of triviality and colloquialism.[5] This does not mean that the book tries to vie in any way with the easy belletristic type. It will hardly satisfy those needs and tastes to which Emil Ludwig has catered with such devastating effect. Instead of a cleverly got-up "psychognosis" which is so flattering to many readers, there prevails in Mr. Eyck's book a high sense of the historian's ethical responsibility, a very serious discussion of the political and social substance of Bismarck's life work as well as of its moral and philosophical implications.

It is also to the author's credit that some will like the diplomatic parts of the story best while others find them, at least in the first two volumes, too lengthy and too much loaded with detail. The wish has been expressed by one reviewer that the framework of society within which and upon which Bismarck

---

[4] Many evidences of this fact could be quoted. See, e.g., the remarks of the Princess Herbert v. Bismarck, who stated (Oct., 1938) that her father-in-law did not count for anything any more and that his name was "systematically belittled." (Ulrich v. Hassel, *Vom Anderen Deutschland* (Atlantis Verlag, Zürich, 1946), p. 23). Hassel endorses this statement and also mentions in his diaries the fact that on occasion of the 50th anniversary of the death of Bismarck's wife it was forbidden to refer to the part which religion played in the Chancellor's matrimonial life.

[5] See such examples as: I, 92 (*"nicht mit ihr zu Rande kam"*) or III, 630 (*"wie sie dem Verfasser in seinen Kram passen"*).

acted might have been submitted to closer examination,[6] but most critics would agree that Mr. Eyck, in accordance with his whole approach, has given much more than the usual attention to Bismarck's domestic (if not actually his social) policies and the class elements involved: Bismarck's clash with, and his victory over, the liberal world being in fact a main and recurrent theme of the book. The more personal parts of the biography come into their own at the beginning and the end, but also with many interspersed scenes. There is a fine sense of balance in all that.

The same can be said, to a certain extent, of the author's attitude and concepts. He has his very definite opinions, of course, even a very definite thesis: the vindication of Bismarck's liberal opponents. But he does not throw his political philosophy upon the reader on every second page. He has enough of the primary interest in what happened rather than in what might have happened or ought to happen, in other words, he has enough of the historian's lifeblood to counterbalance the temptation of an all too subjective speculation. In considerable parts of the work the reader is placed in a position to use his own judgment, he is called upon to read and to think before being faced with the author's conclusions.

This is perhaps a somewhat idealized picture of Mr. Eyck's book, to which the writer wants to pay as much tribute as he possibly can; certain reservations will have to be added. But in principle and against the background of so many examples of a different kind the author's "liberalism" stands out as genuine in as much as he makes a sincere effort to be fair before giving his verdict. There is something of a jurist's honesty in the book. As to the evaluation of Bismarck's personality we also find various viewpoints and standards applied, a procedure which avoids the danger of easy simplification. While Bismarck is repeatedly accused of brutality and cynicism, of faithlessness and of lacking a sense of justice, there is no slighting of those traits which simply do not fit the pattern of Queen Victoria's "wicked man." The author's suggestion that the German chancellor was "always peculiar and eminent in both good and bad," is at least non-partisan though obviously too smooth an explanation of his complexity. Thus in general Mr. Eyck tries to understand and to discriminate. In analyzing Bismarck's religiosity, for example (I, 43-54, 184-85, II, 503-504, III, 633-34) he shows a cautious and reverent hand. There is no trace of that enlightened arrogance which, in view of this problem, can not think of any other explanation than that of a diplomatic bargaining with God or a social mimicry. In summing up his portrait (III, 638), the author finds Bismarck one of the "great men" of world history: ". . . no figure to be loved, much less to be imitated but one to be studied—and with all critical reservations—to be admired." One

---

[6] See the interesting review by E. N. Anderson (*Journal of Central European Affairs,* April, 1946, pp. 85–90), who also finds the "moral significance of the constitutional conflict" of the sixties slighted by the author. In contrast it seems to this writer, that in the framework of a biography the moral importance of the conflict has never before been emphasized so much and so legitimately.

may say that this "dualism of values" again is typically liberal, with politico-moral and aesthetic categories falling apart from one another.[7] Something of the peculiar nineteenth century cult of the genius still lingers on; it is Bismarck's virtuosity, his resourcefulness, his creativeness, his fascinating brilliance which commands a sort of private admiration. Whether or not one agrees with such a balance sheet, it certainly does not expose the reader to any conventional pattern in black and white. Nor yet does it weaken the drive for a moral lesson which is likewise a traditional element of liberal historiography. Against the background of a broadminded appraisal of Bismarck's greatness, the thesis may appear all the more plausible that just because of his brilliant gifts he was able to turn German and European history from the right to the wrong track.

The seriousness of this thesis is not the least of the merits the book can claim. And if the accusation has a familiar ring it is derived not primarily from the usual anti-Prussian resentment, though much of it comes in, but rather from that same basic anxiety to which already two generations earlier a much profounder expression had been given by another and native historian from Switzerland. Mr. Eyck, however, does not agree with Jacob Burckhardt's verdict of the evil inherent in power as such, nor with the forebodings the wise man from Basel had about changing social conditions and the rising wave of mass civilization. The liberal historian, and this seems a decisive point, is outrightly optimistic in looking back upon the situation circa 1860. He draws his confidence obviously from certain principled views as well as from historic examples: from a great figure such as Gladstone, on whom he has written previously, and from those Prussian liberals who reconciled a sincere German patriotism, a desire for national greatness with a profound respect for justice and law, whether statutory or natural. These hopeful perspectives, however, the author sees shattered by Bismarck. His violation of the moral order was the cardinal sin which planted a poisonous germ· in the structure of the new Reich and of Europe generally; he, therefore, paved the way for the final downfall of his lifework, for the corruption of the German character by undermining the principle of *justitia fundamentum regnorum*. This is, reduced to general terms, the basic theme of the book.

Before discussing some concrete aspects, in which the problem of politics and morality appeared in Bismarck's era, the intrinsic importance of the author's approach should be stressed. It cannot be waved aside with the conventional consideration that, after all, these are the ways of the world, that none of the great states has been created or maintained without Machiavellian means and that even in the midst of, and after, the most terrible experiences of a "dehumanized" policy, these ways of the world do not seem to be mended. Even

---

[7] The same typical split appears when the *Gedanken und Erinnerungen,* first and with an untenable exaggeration, are denied any value as a historic source except that of creating a myth, and then, again with some exaggeration, are appraised as one "of the greatest masterworks of world literature." (III, 630.)

those who, with Lord Acton, find Schiller's word: *Die Weltgeschichte ist das Weltgericht,* presumptuous, will readily admit the gravity of the problem and its special applicability to Bismarck's case. That he pursued his course almost singlehandedly (as it might appear), that he certainly counteracted almost all convictions of the time, German and non-German, conservative and liberal and perhaps even his own, that he placed policy, as he put it himself, on the "only sound basis of the egotistic interests of a great state" rather than on principles, that he stretched the constitution to the breaking point and interfered with justice, that he managed to have three wars as they suited his purposes, that he used and abused men, institutions and ideas for tactical ends, or even personal ends, and that he got away with it, i.e., that he reached his aims in spite of the greatest difficulties—all this had fateful implications. It seemed to prove the fallacy of any idealistic approach or rather it proved that nothing succeeds like success. When the Junker of Schoenhausen became Prussian Prime Minister in 1862, he was thoroughly hated; four years later, after Sadowa, the liberal historian Herman Baumgarten published his pamphlet: "Liberalism criticized by itself." It was a program that abandoned principles and gratefully absorbed the new forms of German life, a program that could have but an emasculating effect. At any rate the opportunity of cooperation on an equal footing, of aligning Prussia with western standards was over and would once more elapse in the late seventies. Not that opposition was silenced altogether, but with the great liberal movement exhausted and turning away from politics, an idealistic force was waning and the human level moved on the downward grade. In 1890 William II was told that if he displaced the bulky block of the "majordomo" he would find only "flattened worms" underneath. At the same time Herman Baumgarten, in a dramatic reversal, spoke of the "great man who will bequeath to us great distress."

This is a note which strikes an even more responsive chord today than it did in the years after 1918. It concerns not only the decline in quality of German political conduct after Bismarck had gone or the self-centered and one-sided foundation of his work. More fundamentally the criticism points to the temptation to power for individuals and peoples, to the weakened sense of justice, to the arrest in civic maturity, to the glorification of expediency, to the contempt of humanitarian sentiments and moral scruples. However long and complex the way "from Bismarck to Hitler," the founder of the Reich certainly seems to stand for a "turn," or at least for legitimizing a "turn," the fateful climax of which has been only too manifest in our days.

The thesis of a disastrous "turn," however, has potentially a broader meaning than that referring in the main to moral categories. It is here, in the concrete historical matter, that the limits and some deficiencies, or even outright distortions come to the fore in the picture of "Bismarck seen by a liberal." The author, in his discussion of the sixties, does not exercise a radical criticism, such as has been sounded by other exiles in Switzerland. It is not the purpose of "national unification" as such but the Bismarckian means to this end which he rejects. In other words, he is a national liberal in the traditions of 1848 or rather of the Prussian progressive party. To him the "nation state" after the pattern of western Europe, including its democratic implications, is a natural aim for Germans just as much as for any other people. He does, therefore, not belong to the school of thought which recently and under the impact of totalitarianism has rediscovered such a man as Konstantin Frantz for the second time and sees in him (rather than in the advocates of the *Reichstaat* in Twesten, Gneist or Lasker) Bismarck's true antipode. Mr. Eyck has been blamed for this faulty perspective and half-way opposition,[8] for not realizing that the destiny of Germany and Europe was bound up with the revival (or survival) of a loose federation in the centre of the continent and that, consequently, the real aberration was the *kleindeutsche* (or *grosspreussische*) solution as such, regardless of whether the means were those of "blood and iron" or of "moral conquest." This criticism is not quite just. There can be no doubt that Mr. Eyck combines or tries to combine, a sympathy with Prussian liberalism (and, of course, an aversion to the usual scapegoats: Junkers and military men) with a good deal of pro-Austrian feeling, with an approval of Bruck's "idealistic conception" of a Greater Germany (I, 202) and the last Habsburg attempt at reforming the German Confederation in 1863 (I, 519). But it is certainly true that he is no federalist in the central-European sense of the word and that any re-examination of Bismarck's historic role is incomplete which does not take this line of approach into account.

Whatever the bearing of the federalist thesis on the Reich of 1871—and some words will have to be said in that direction—it certainly touches upon fundamental problems of German history. Before coming back to that it may simply be stated that a revisionism which questions the nineteenth century idea of the "nation state" or its applicability to central Europe altogether, helps at least to clarify the horns of the dilemma with which Mr. Eyck is faced. In all his sincere liberalism he is obviously more "centralistic" than the man who is supposed to have started Germany the wrong way. Naturally he finds Bismarck, the Prussian diplomat and "man of the state" lacking in "national motives" which he almost identifies with "ethical motives" (I, 578) though not so closely as Treitschke would have done. The author likewise seems to regret that Bismarck was not "attracted" by the idea to which E. M. Arndt in his song of the "German fatherland" had given so ringing an expression: "Good relations with the courts of Vienna and Petersburg were to him (Bismarck) more important than the fate of Austrian and Russian subjects of German tongue" (III, 29). With only a very slight change in verbal emphasis this could have been written

[8] See: Karl Thieme, *Das Schicksal der Deutschen* (Basel, Kobersche Verlagsbuchhandlung, 1945), pp. 104–107.

by a Nazi critic of Bismarck just as well. In other words, the liberal and national position is not quite outside the danger line of certain accusations either.[9] And one wonders what severe judgment would be passed upon Bismarck today, if he had ever professed the same great-Prussian and annexationist aims which some liberals held (provided that Prussia turned "western") or if he had followed the centralistic and unitary policy which the liberal Crown Prince and the men around him advocated. As a matter of fact, some of the measures for which Mr. Eyck blames Bismarck are precisely those in which he came nearest, or made concessions to, liberal demands though he differed widely in motives. One may think of the annexation of Alsace-Lorraine or of the *Kulturkampf*. And it was no less a man than Gladstone who wrote in 1874: "Bismarck's ideas and methods are not ours; they spring out of other traditions, but my sympathies though they do not go with him, are more with him than against him. I cannot but say that the present doctrines of the Roman church destroy the title of her obedient members to the enjoyment of civil rights. . . ." [10]

These few remarks may suffice to indicate that the problem of the "turn" since the sixties and seventies has a much broader dimension and is much less specifically Bismarckian than it appears in the biography. They also point to a certain difficulty which runs through Mr. Eyck's book and ends up in a good deal of misinterpretation. From the moral and legal angle he cannot help having some sympathies with Prussian conservatives such as the Gerlachs who certainly had principled views though he finds them, of course, reactionary. Among these views was the resolute rejection of the principle of nationality and its heathen consequences, a verdict which was shared in the sixties by Catholics, such as Lord Acton, and which was repeated by Konstantin Frantz in his book on federation in 1879. Mr. Eyck quotes with some approval Gerlach's thesis of 1850, that "the German nation had always ideals higher than the merely national idea" (I, 149). He finds in Bismarck nothing of these convictions but only the thought of future Prussian power. This dividing line is certainly correct though it appears overdrawn; it neglects Bismarck's turning away from a narrow Prussianism which made him a potential ally of the nationals without affecting his basic distrust of the principle of nationality. It was only along this road that Bismarck rose to statesmanship: by gradually emancipating himself from his conservative friends and accepting—with some limitations—the task which had been handed down from 1848. This, however, was a lengthy and complicated

[9] Since this was written the writer has read: L. B. Namier, *1848, the Revolution of the Intellectuals* (London, 1944). He will reply to this indictment of German liberalism in *Journal of Modern History* (September, 1947). But whatever Mr. Namier's exaggerations, he is certainly correct in stating that an aggressive nationalism "derives from the belauded Frankfort Parliament rather than from Bismarck and Prussianism." (*l. c.*, p. 33.) It can only be regretted that this insight seems to gain ground so belatedly. Not the slightest ripple of it has reached Mr. Eyck.

[10] P. Knaplund, *Letters from the Berlin Embassy (1871–85)* (Washington, 1944), p. 127. Mr. Eyck (III, 89, 163) mentions Gladstone's opposition to the Vatican decrees only in general terms.

process, more painful than the author suggests (II, 186), it implied a soul struggle very much concerned with the problems of politics and morality, of revolution and legitimism. And it was a process which did not divorce Bismarck from fundamentally conservative views even during his most revolutionary period.

There is little echo of that in Mr. Eyck's biography. In fact, it must be difficult for him to appraise a man who appropriated national ends without sharing the underlying tenets and yet continued to have opinions which were not necessarily void of principles. The author's solution is typically "liberal" in as much as it overemphasizes the sovereignty of the "titanic" individual, his ability to handle and manipulate history at will. As mentioned before he pays a sort of aesthetic admiration to this virtuosity, and he is fair enough to see the other side in Bismarck which is not sheer will power: a personal tenderness, a poetic trait, his love of nature and music, his constant desire for retirement, his aversion to court life, to the cancerous growth of bureaucracy, to the *Racker Staat,* his ultimate insight into *vanitas vanitatum*. From a detached point of view there is something tragic about the man who in his old age confessed that policy had "devoured all other carps in his pond." To the author, however, this undercurrent is in the main the self-deception of a genius who is born to rule and knows it, who wants power in the first place for himself,[11] who pretends only to be loyal to his king and in fact speaks of him in the most abusive terms, who lies whenever it suits him and uses his unusual frankness [12] for the same purpose of deception, who hates and persecutes his opponents, both dead and alive, and identifies himself with his work to the extent that he may be able to destroy what he had created himself.

No doubt many and reliable evidences are available to bear out such a picture, though some gossip has also gone into it.[13] It is not necessary to insist upon retouching any details. But regarding the central point the fact cannot be omitted that Bismarck himself, though he profoundly influenced the course of events, was not a liberal who thinks in emphatic terms about what the individual can do. Being certainly a master of surprising turns and endowed with the greatest flexibility, he confessed at the end of the Franco-German war, with a

[11] See I, 32, II, 242–43 (Sadowa was his victory; what fruits would it bear to *him?*), III, 381.

[12] The "obstinate veracity" of which John Motley spoke.

[13] Though the author does not fail to indicate the problematic character of some of his sources, the reader is constantly exposed to "the semper haeret aliquid." This is one of the reservations which has to be added to the appraisal of the fairness of the book. Also in the treatment of Bismarck's "grasping" nature, the documents regarding his double role as minister and as "subject" would be corrective and the book by Bismarck's head forester in Varzin (E. Westphal, *Bismarck als Gutsherr,* Leipzig, 1932) gives an entirely different picture. In the matter of the *Welfenfond* (II, 369–78) there is certainly every good reason for criticism, yet in fairness it may be added that it was not only used for press propaganda or for "bribing" Ludwig II (III, 553–555) but that part of the revenue went into public buildings and the improvement of the Northsea resort Nordeney, in order to continue or even increase payments formerly made by the dispossessed princes. (Bismarck, *Saemtliche Werke* VI, pp. 506, 553–554.)

ring of sincerity: *fert unda nec regitur*. Even in his stormy beginnings it did not occur to him that history could be basically manipulated; and he tended, if changes had to be made, to cut them down as far as possible. He liked to take his figures of speech from the sphere of the peasant, the fisherman and the hunter who does not move unnecessarily, who always probes the ground before taking the step and who can wait. This attitude became all the more explicit as the years went by until Bismarck eventually confessed: "The statesman cannot create the stream of time, he can only navigate on it." Or to quote another word: "The statesman must try and reach for the hem upon hearing the garment of God rustling through events."

None of these evidences has been taken into account. Of course, they are autobiographic and do not tell the full story. But they cannot simply be discarded without the slightest reference—all the less so, since Bismarck's practical policy, even in the years before 1870, corroborates them to a large extent. There are, to be sure, many documents which show an amazing gift of prophecy on his part, which outline, more or less conditionally, the course he actually did take between 1863 and 1870. And if the story is built on this ground, it naturally appeals to the sense of the dramatic while at the same time bringing out, by implication, the arbitrariness of the means resorted to. Such is Mr. Eyck's technique throughout. But there are many other evidences, particularly among the recently published documents, which prove that Bismarck was far from a "one way policy" or from an early conception of a one and only solution by the sword. In this respect a good deal had already been learned by critical historians in many countries before Mr. Eyck wrote. As Dr. G. P. Gooch expressed it fifteen years ago: "The notion of the implacable Prussian sharpening the knife for the Austrian throat . . . fades away." [14] Mr. Eyck's discussion of this problem seems a drawback and rather strained (esp. II, 15–16). Neither the plan of the so-called "peaceful dualism" before 1866 nor that of a tripartite system in the years after Sadowa are considered on the basis of their respective merits. Nor are the documents fully and impartially used. To instance only one of the major gaps, there is an instruction of February 26, 1869 which Bismarck wrote to the Prussian minister in Munich: [15] "To me also it seems likely that the German unification will have to be promoted by forceful events. But to assume the role of provoking a catastrophe and the responsibility for chosing the right moment, this is quite a different proposition. An arbitrary and merely subjective interference with the course of history has always resulted only in beating off fruits which were not ripe. It seems to me obvious that German unity is at this moment not yet a ripe fruit." Bismarck added that if the years to come would proceed

---

[14] *Studies in Modern History* (1931), p. 241. Practically the same shift in evaluation (on the basis of new sources) was acknowledged by L. D. Steefel, one of the best American experts in the field of Bismarck research. See his bibliographical article in *Journal of Modern History*, vol. II, 1930.

[15] Bismarck: *Die Gesammelten Werke* (1931), vol. VI, b., p. 2.

in the same way as they had done since the time of Frederick the Great, and particularly since 1840 "we can look to the future with tranquility and leave the rest to our descendants." Or as he says in the concluding sentence: "We can advance the clock but the time does not move more quickly for that matter."

Whatever the tactical motives implied, this instruction certainly mirrors a genuine attitude which would be borne out by many other evidences. In fact, the aversion to "arbitrary and merely subjective interference with the course of history" was given expression by Bismarck time and time again. This does not mean that he did not interfere, when the moment came, nor that some of his decisions may not seriously be questioned. A good deal of criticism can be applied to the incorporation of Schleswig-Holstein which opened the way for extending Prussia, whereas Bismarck's restraint in 1866 rather calls for admiration. That the wisdom of re-annexing Alsace-Lorraine can be questioned goes without saying and it was questioned by Bismarck himself. He took the "lost provinces," as is well known, not for national reasons of history and language, upon which almost all liberals agreed, but for reasons of military security, of protection against a nation "which for 300 years has been in the habit of invading us." Or as the American minister in Berlin, the historian Bancroft, said precisely along the same line: "The main thing now is to protect Germany by better frontiers against aggressions from the West of which there has been such a great number during the last 300 years."

This brings the discussion back to Mr. Eyck's underlying assumption that the German national unity which he himself finds natural, would have been attainable by other and less forceful means than those of Bismarck. This is a hypothesis which, of course, can neither be proved nor repudiated. It can be said, however, and in view of many "legends" it seems a matter of fairness to do so today, that there was little "western" sympathy with the attempt at founding a "good" German Reich, that is, one on the liberal-democratic basis of 1848. While Disraeli spoke of "the 50 mad professors at Frankfort," Palmerston felt alarmed by the development of a *"nation inconnu jusqu'ici au Foreign Office."* And Thiers later confessed that if he could have had his way in 1848 he would have extended the French frontiers to the Rhine and taken "the keys of Germany" into hand. When it eventually came to the half-liberal "policy of union" in 1850 it ended with a deadlock enforced by a Russo-Austrian ultimatum. Even Radowitz's very moderate aims would have to be carried out by arms. Nor was the diplomatic record of the "new era" in Prussia altogether promising. When the liberal policy of "moral conquest" was at its height in 1860, the *London Times* had this to say: [16] "Prussia is always leaning on somebody, always getting somebody to help her, never willing to help herself; always ready to deliberate, never to decide; present in Congresses, but absent in battles; speaking and writing, never for or against, but only on, the question; ready to supply any

[16] Quoted by R. J. Sontag, *Germany and England, 1848–1894* (New York, 1938), p. 33.

amount of ideals or sentiments, but shy of anything that savors of the real or the actual. She has a large army, but notoriously one in no condition for fighting. She is profuse in circulars and notes, but has generally a little to say for both sides. No one counts on her as a friend, no one dreads her as an enemy. How she became a great Power history tells us, why she remains so nobody can tell. . . . Prussia unaided could not keep the Rhine or the Vistula for a month from her ambitious neighbors."

Mr. Eyck has a rather optimistic view of these "ambitious neighbors," in particular of the French tradition of advancing to the East,[17] a view which was shared neither by the German socialists circa 1860 nor by the lauded Konstantin Frantz for that matter. It seems worthy of mentioning that the federalist thinker started from the very assumption of a double threat to *Mitteleuropa*.[18] He therefore advocated a universal system in the centre of the continent with a voluntary union of the historic states as its nucleus, a loose German and non-German federation, which Holland, Sweden, Denmark might join and England might protect. Such a system would guarantee peace by turning Russia's and France's ambitions to Asia and North Africa respectively. One may pay high tribute to this idealistic scheme and yet seriously doubt its chance of overcoming particularism by persuasion or achieving a British willingness to enter upon central European commitments and to sympathize with the economic perspectives of a great federative bloc (united by mutual preferences!). It is only in an entirely different situation, against the background of a post-Bismarckian development and with foreign powers ruling over Central Europe, that the federalist concept or rather that of a "Central European Switzerland" has gained a new meaning.

It would appear then that the consolidation of the weak centre of Europe presupposed other means than those suggested by Frantz and that the nucleus had to be created by diplomatic action rather than by a plea for sympathy or a moral appeal. Whether war was absolutely necessary may be doubted and certainly can not be demonstrated.[19] But it is definitely wrong to say that only the forceful foundation of the Reich of 1871 produced the *cauchemar des coalitions* as a sort of self-inflicted punishment. The conviction of a double threat was not of Bismarck's making. It had been widespread among the liberals of Germany around 1860 in the same sense as it was shared by Frantz. And it was the basis of Bismarck's diplomacy before 1870 just as much as afterwards it was simply a Central European fact. Only by a new distribution of power and a new security, in Bismarck's view, could the aim be reached (which he had in common with Frantz), of turning Russia's and France's ambitions "to Asia and North Africa respectively."

[17] See his discussion of the "idealism" of Napoleon III and of Ranke's "pompous" reference to Louis XIV (II, 569).

[18] Particularly in his: *Untersuchungen über das Europäische Gleichgewicht* (1859).

[19] Again this writer does not go as far as Mr. Namier does (see note 9).

This criticism of some federalist illusions, however, should not prevent us from seeing that the pre- or supra-national and anti-centralistic elements in the structure of Bismarck's Reich came nearer to a basic federalism than is ordinarily realized. On this point Mr. Eyck's book falls particularly short of the mark. The fact that Bismarck stressed the institutional links between the old German Confederation and the new Reich, that he checked the Reichstag and its universal suffrage by the "anonymous-phalanx" of the federative council, that he kept the competence of the central organs within very narrow limits, that he resisted successfully a responsible Reichsministry—all this was, in the author's view, mere tactics and only meant to concentrate the real power in Prussia and, in the last analysis, in Bismarck's hands. There is truth in this interpretation, not a new one for that matter, but it is by far not the full truth or the most substantial part of it.[20] Again all evidences are omitted which refer to some of the underlying principles. It is certainly not uninteresting and beside the point to recall today such principles as Bismarck expressed in the Reichstag (April 16, 1869): ". . . In Germanic states one should not ask . . . what can be in common, how far can the great mouth of the commonwealth swallow the apple (*hineinbeissen in den Apfel*) —but rather one should ask: what must be absolutely in common." It seems safe to say that Bismarck, quite apart from other elements of his thought, was Junker enough to be anti-totalitarian in principle. More consideration should also be given to his plans to supplement the Reichstag by *staendische* organizations. Particularly in connection with the plan for compulsory insurance against accidents, he thought of a network of professional associations to be spread over the country.[21] This again implies anti-parliamentary tactics but also an insight into the dangerous process of social atomization. While in all this there was a federalist aspect domestically, the non-centralistic setup of the Reich had a broader meaning as a pattern of transition to other federative forms beyond the frontiers: Germany with her composite character might indicate, as Bismarck pointed out, a method by the use of which "Austria could reach a reconciliation of the political and material interests which exist between the Eastern frontiers of the Russians and the Bay of Cattaro."

These potentialities are often overlooked. They are certainly not seen by Mr. Eyck and he seems to be completely and rather naively unaware of the nationalist implications of a unitary and democratic German Reich in Central Europe or of Bruck's "Greater Germany." In contrast Bismarck's national state was no "nation state" proper; it included non-Germans (about 10%) and it did not include and ought not to have included all Germans. Jokingly

---

[20] For Bismarck's system of "integration" the book of the jurist, R. Smend, *Verfassung und Verfassungsrecht* might have been consulted with usefulness.

[21] Evidences for this in the writer's, *Theodor Lohmann und die Kampf jahre der staatlichen Sozialpolitik* (1927), pp. 63–64.

Bismarck once said that, if the nine million contiguous Germans in Austria ever would try to join the Reich, he would wage war against them. In more serious words he admonished them that, instead of harking back, they should take the lead in evolving a multi-national combine in the South-East. The same restraint he observed towards the Germans in Russia, and he did so not only for diplomatic or opportunistic reasons. His so-called *étatisme* may have been a major limitation in some aspects of domestic policy; but what was opposition to democracy was at the same time opposition to nationalism. What was an attempt at checking "social atomism" was paralleled by a check on the trend towards a "national atomism" which would disintegrate Central Europe and end in a "war of races." That is why Bismarck opposed pangermanism no less than panslavism.

In this negative attitude—or rather in this conservative restraint—there was implied some positive appraisal of variety and multi-national forms of life. There was at least much more of it than liberal and federalist critics usually realize. The Crown Prince may have been thunderstruck when Bismarck, in 1870, admonished him to have his son learn the Polish language or when he added that all the Prussian rulers down to Frederick the Great had known it —and that he knew it himself. To the liberal biographer these remarks do not seem to have made any more sense than they probably made to the Crown Prince. Incidentally, Mr. Eyck does not speak of the anti-Polish "settlement law" of 1886 (*Ansiedlungsgesetz*) which ranks so high on the list of Prussian *hakatism*. As a matter of fact the settlement of German peasants in the eastern provinces was urged by the national liberals. Bismarck yielded to them but professed no sympathy with uprooting the Polish peasants or depriving them of their language. In his old age he spoke of the intermingling of peoples in the East as "riches willed by God." Whatever the shortcomings of his Polish policy he was certainly as remote from racialism and biologism as anyone could be.[22]

I do not believe that these aspects have been left out on purpose. They may appear as residua of a little known old-Prussian "policy of nationalities" and simply not interesting from a Western liberal and national angle. But these

---

[22] The above interpretation of certain federalist trends in Bismarck's policy has been worked out by the writer in his *Bismarck und der Osten, Eine Studie zum Problem des deutschen National-staats* (Leipzig, 1934). The study goes back to an address which was given in 1932 at the last pre-Nazi meeting of German historians and which ended with an attack on the "myth of the 20th century" (Rosenberg) as well as on that of the 19th century, i.e., the dogma of the "nation state." (The address is reprinted in the writer's: *Ostraum, Preussentum und Reichsgedanke* (Leipzig, 1935), pp. 65–93. If W. Roepke, *Die deutsche Frage* (2, A, 1945, p. 103 note), justly admires the courage of a German philologist who in 1940 (while writing on the Greek polis) declared the nation state to be only one political form among others, he seems to have overlooked that before, and still in the first years after 1933, there was a whole group of German writers and historians who openly assailed the general validity of the (western) dogma of the nation state and pleaded for a federative reconstruction of Central Europe with full autonomy for all the nations involved.

omissions contribute toward making the third volume the least satisfactory. True, it contains also brilliant pages, particularly in the presentation of parliamentary history. And there is no doubt that the tactical motives of Bismarck, for example, the use of foreign policy for electioneering maneuvers come out more clearly than ever before. But again, and increasingly so, the tactical interpretation, while leading to a high appraisal of Bismarck's "virtuosity," misses many important points. It misses a full appreciation of the fact (which William L. Langer very well expressed as early as 1931) that Bismarck is the rare example of a European statesman who, after amazing successes, did not succumb to intoxication or the compelling drive which leads on. And it misses the basic views and experiences which are implied in this restraint, the opposition to ideological concepts (whether liberal or anglophile or pangerman) as well as to military trends, both of which would have caused an "unnecessary" war with Russia, the distinction between "questions of life" and "questions of mere interest," the aversion to a policy of prestige and uncontrolled emotions or to engagements which would follow from economic expansion. In these respects again Mr. Eyck's biography must be characterized as a definite drawback. In his book Bismarck's foreign policy after 1871 appears mainly in its undeniable complications; it seems artificially built up because little attention is given to its underlying principles: the support of the interests of all other European powers within a given sphere, and the basic view of Germany's saturation or her disinterestedness in any aggrandizement which forms the backbone of the system. In fact documents which show Bismarck's concept as a whole (for example the *Kissinger Diktat*) are omitted, and not a few among the others are seriously misread or outright misinterpreted.[23]

But the writer does not want this article to end on a note of professional controversy. There is more at stake than that. We may criticize Bismarck for many good reasons, for paving the way to some fatal trends of our days, but while doing so we cannot very well overlook the fundamental fact that Hitler, in almost every respect, did precisely what the founder of the Reich had refused to do. Many of those who were under the heel inside or outside Germany, had an appreciation of this fact. And thus the word of the Danish historian may be taken up once more as a summary which draws the essential frontier line: Bismarck certainly "belonged to our world," that is, to the anti-Hitlerian world. That this was not generally realized is in part the fault of Germans and German historians themselves. But it may be called a kind of saving grace that revival of genuine Bismarckian thought (as different from the old Bismarck orthodoxy) was one of the forces which went into the making

[23] This applies, e.g., to the Livadia episode, to the negotiations with Britain in 79, to the so-called "bogus document" of 84, to Bismarck's letter to Salisbury of 87, and to the Reinsurance Treaty. For all these matters and many others, consult William L. Langer's *European Alliances and Alignments* (1931), rather than Mr. Eyck's book.

of the German resistance against Hitler.[24] Specifically "Prussian" elements as far as they remained alive after the landslide of 1933 were also in the anti-Nazi camp. To state this is no longer a matter of any particular importance since these forces have been radically eliminated, but it seems to be a matter of historical justice.

THE BISMARCK PROBLEM

Franz Schnabel

* * *

THE EMPIRE which Bismarck founded lasted half a century. When it fell, historians centred their interest upon the personality and life work of this man who, more than any other, put his own stamp upon the second half of the nineteenth century. What was written before 1918 on this great problem must now be considered for the most part obsolete. After the collapse of the German Empire and the monarchies in the middle and small German states, the archives were opened and a profusion of important, unknown documents brought to light. The events which took place in Germany between 1918 and 1945 were such, moreover, as to make men question what Bismarck did and said, what he was and what he wanted. Or, they made men change what he brought about. One after another, all Bismarck's opponents have risen again; once more they have borne testimony against him. The multitude of those who in his lifetime heaped praise upon him, citing the success of his endeavours, were too hasty in their conclusions. Men had to learn from experience, like those before them, that only a much later age can pass final judgment on success in history—the Empire

24 It happened by coincidence (though hardly, incidentally) that one of the leaders of the anti-Nazi conspiracy, Ulrich v. Hassell, who was designated to be the Foreign Minister of the "Other Germany" (see note 4) paid a visit to Friedrichsruhe just 10 days before the fatal attempt of 20th of July 1944, for which he was to die on the gallows. The last entry in his diaries (*l.c.,* p. 363) discusses two aspects of the problems with which this paper dealt: the distorted picture of Bismarck's "power policy" which was presented to the world and his true stature as one of the greatest and most moderate diplomats in history.

which began so brilliantly stood but for fifty years. There were times, to be sure, when Bismarck himself spoke with profound pessimism of the durability of his achievement. After his dismissal, domestic and foreign difficulties in fact continued to multiply. But dominant public opinion brushed aside any suggestion that the course along which Bismarck had directed German and European history was responsible for this state of affairs. The more painfully obvious were the shortcomings of his successors and the emperor under whom they served, the easier it seemed to bring forward the founder of the Reich in edifying contrast to them.

After the first catastrophe in 1918, however, the spiritual descendants of the earlier German liberalism and democrats took the field. They established Bismarck's responsibility for the predominance of the policy of "Blood and Iron." They voiced regret that ever since Bismarck the people and the parties had always played the role of followers or opposition, but not of participants in responsibility in the "authoritarian state" which bore the impress of the Prussian system. Bismarck was also critized for having over-estimated the vitality of the Austro-Hungarian monarchy and neglected therefore to bring about *Anschluss*. Thereafter, as cupidity increasingly took the place of concern for the state and political life as such, as the masses ceased to think of the interests of the state, which guaranteed law and order, and should have provided their rational guide to action, as nationalism and neo-romanticism, literary scribblings (*Literatentum*) and theories of the "folk" (*Volk*) gained the upper hand, Bismarck's reputation began to decline correspondingly. Though once, in an exchange of opinions with Gottfried Kinkel,[1] he drew a distinction between his soul, the "soul of a diplomat," and the heart of the patriotic leader, the heart of a poet, men at that time began to draw closer again to the patriots of the period when unification was being prepared. They were extolled because they wished to unite all "folk comrades" (*Volksgenossen*) and "bring home" the *"disjecta membra"* into the empire for which they strove, and because they wished therefore to reorganize Europe upon the basis of folk membership (*Volkstum*) and tongue. In this way, men knew, the old princely policy of territorial incorporations could be continued by a new, folkish policy of incorporations; but they did not gladly have their attention drawn to the fact that it was the doctrines of German romanticism which first really brought the nationalities of eastern Europe into movement. But, in the twentieth century, the national state conception reached a complete *reductio ad absurdum;* it brought incalculable disaster upon millions who were driven from their homes because of the language they spoke and the people to which they belonged. Not surprisingly, therefore, men found reason to re-examine critically the entire national state movement since 1815, which had

---

[1] Gottfried Kinkel (1815–82), German revolutionary poet, professor at Bonn; aided to escape (1850) from prison by Carl Schurz.

resulted in endless disorder, two world wars, and catastrophe; nor was it surprising either that they called up again those opponents of Bismarck who combated his power-permeated concept of the state, his alliance with the German national state idea, and who condemned the division of Europe into national states and demanded a European federal structure.

Thus the age of Bismarck lies today concealed in profound obscurity. We do have the documents at hand, but interpreting them is difficult because, living in devastated lands, we find it hard to attain that lofty and far-off vantage point where the historian must take his stand. In earlier ages, when historical awareness had not yet been formed, men came quickly to their own aid in explaining things. Among us, too, resentment will bring about simplification. States and empires, it is said, decline for the same reasons by which they rise. Thus an effort has been made to find a single trace that goes from Bismarck to Hitler, from the "Iron Chancellor," the man in cavalry boots, to the National-Socialist policy of violence. But this means forgetting the popular and revolutionary forces which had been at work ever since 1815. To remember where we must seek in German history for the spiritual ancestors of modern demagogy, of explosive ideologies, of the extolling of violence, we need merely read the sentences written in 1833 by Heinrich Heine in which he drew the outlines of the future German revolution. At that time Lorenz Oken,[2] the philosopher of nature who has been lauded as the "great revolutionary," tried to start a movement of revolutionary enthusiasm among the youth in Germany and was expelled from the University of Jena, on Goethe's decision, as a "Catilinarian." As always, things were expected to take place faster than they actually occurred. But, under the immediate impact of the Hambach Festival of 1832 which J. G. A. Wirth[3] organized, Heine felt so bold as to prophesy:

Kantians unwilling to hear of any piety in the phenomenal world either, ruthlessly upsetting the foundations of our European life, will make their appearance. Armed Fichteans unwilling to be hampered by aught in their fanatic wilfulness will take the stage. But most terrible of all will be the philosophers of nature, unleashing the daemonic forces of the German pantheism of yore and thus awakening that battle passion which fights not to win, but merely to fight. . . . To some extent, Christianity has mitigated that Germanic battle passion. But once the Cross is broken, then the clangour of that wildness of which the Nordic poets sing and speak so much will be heard again. . . . But when you hear such a crashing and clanging as was never before heard in the history of the world, then a drama will be played out in Germany, alongside which the French Revolution will seem but a harmless idyll. To be sure, things are still quiet among us; we do not as yet know whether the Crown Prince of Prussia

---

[2] Lorenz Oken (1779–1851), German scientist and philosopher, leading philosopher of nature of the romantic period.

[3] Johann Georg August Wirth (1798–1848), German democratic leader; organizer of the Hambach Festival of revolutionary youth, May 27, 1832.

or Dr. Wirth will come to power in Germany. But do not believe that one day to come these will appear upon the scene as the real actors. They are only the curs running about in the empty arena and snarling at each other, before the hour comes when the troop of gladiators enters who will fight for life and death. And that hour will come! The peoples will gather round Germany, as if seated upon the banks of an amphitheatre, to see the great battle-play.[4]

It must be admitted that in the procession of such antecedents there is no place for Bismarck. It is still our task to define his position in the history of Europe, and to determine what were the opportunities that were then open to him and to other, positive forces in German history, as well. These were opportunities which he hampered or destroyed. During the last war a valuable start in this task was made by Erich Eyck. His three-volume biography of Bismarck was written and published outside of Germany. It is a work of high scholarly standing. Based upon knowledge of all the German and European sources, it is well written and to the point. It is, in fact, the first large, rounded biography of Bismarck. None the less, its description of Bismarck cannot be accepted as definitive. The discussion already under way over this important work must be continued; it can become fruitful and contribute to solving the problems which we still find in understanding Bismarck, the man, and his life work. We must frankly say that Eyck was able to write an imposing and easily understood work because he examined the play of opposing forces from a fixed position. But unfortunately, in taking this position, Eyck did not rise above the times. He stayed down amidst the embattled political parties. True, the author, thanks to his great skill as a writer, was able to leave the polemics of those strife-filled decades far behind him. Only a few presently current turns of phrase hinder the flow of the narrative here and there. The personal greatness of Bismarck is recognized, and the author, when he comes up against the weaknesses of Bismarck's foes, does not keep silence about them. But Eyck is convinced that the national-liberal movement of the sixties was on the right track, that it could really have established the German national state in conformity with its own ideals. Eyck belongs among those opponents of Bismarck who may be called "German Whigs." They included persons in the highest reaches of society, including the royal family and the liberal princely courts. For the new Bismarck biographer, Gladstone is the lofty ideal of a statesman. Eyck, who lives in England, has written a fine monographic study on Gladstone. Bismarck, the great hater, held no other statesman of his time in such scorn as "the Grand Old Man" who let his policy be guided by humanitarian and even pacifist ideals, opposed the advance of imperialism, approached the Irish nationalist movement in an accommodating spirit, and extended the suffrage for the British parliament. According to Eyck, Bismarck's interference with the development of conditions

[4] Tempel ed. (Leipzig, n.d.), vii, pp. 424–26 (modified).

for the rise of a statesman like Gladstone in Prussia and Germany was the source of all the evil to come for Germany and for Europe.

By now the reader will have realized that Eyck accepts without further ado the position that the isolated national state with centralized institutions was the only correct and possible solution of the "German question," the only one corresponding to the strivings of the German people for unity. He directs his criticism just at the methods which Bismarck employed. In Eyck's opinion, if Bismarck had given more consideration to the ideals of his liberal allies, the internal structure of the new Reich would have met the needs of that day better and would have been more durable as well. Moreover, it would have been possible to found the Reich without using the violent methods which Bismarck did. Eyck voices most profound regret that the new state was born with the flaw of lawbreaking and violence, and that German liberalism developed from a party of law and order into a service group of success worshipers.

Certainly, this is not a new train of thought. There were always at least a few liberal and democratic writers in Germany, during and after Bismarck's imperial chancellorship, who held firm to ideals of freedom and humanity, deplored their loss in Germany when it came under Prussian control, and therefore remained at all times critics of Bismarck. But they produced no major historical work. They were not able to distinguish and correctly to evaluate, upon the basis of detailed research, the various streams within the liberal and democratic movement. They had no importance compared with the specialists, from Sybel down to Erich Marcks, who did the valuable scholarly service of refuting the claims which the reigning monarch [William II] made on behalf of his grandfather [William I, "the Great"]; but these erstwhile leading historians took part in the movement of liberalism into Bismarck's camp, they defended it and found it to be in conformity with the needs of modern times. Eyck is the first person who has managed to put forward the position of the liberal opponents of Bismarck in a large, well-supported analysis. Since Eyck's work is becoming known in Germany at a time when, after a lapse of almost half a century, the spiritual and political ideas of Western European liberalism are again acceptable, there is a danger that the old myth, which justified and praised Bismarck as the *"Realpolitiker"* will now be replaced by a new historical myth. All the more must our thanks go to Eyck for his analysis, which affords us a reason for examining in a fundamental way the problems of Bismarck's achievements and establishing the facts in the matter.

Hans Rothfels, now of the University of Chicago, has set down in a far-reaching critique, "Problems of a Bismarck Biography," the principal points which must be made against Eyck's approach. Not only did he carry the analysis forward, he also greatly simplified it. The assumption that the goal which Bismarck and the liberals shared—the little-German (*kleindeutsch*) national state under Prussian leadership—could have been achieved without the methods employed by Bismarck, and that Bismarck brought the *kleindeutsch* Empire into ill repute by his methods, is one which cannot be proved. All the evidence we have supports the position that the powers accepted only unwillingly the formation of a new national state in the heart of Europe. Either, like Napoleon III, they wished for "compensations," or they were surprised by Bismarck's procedure and did not have time to prepare themselves spiritually and materially to counter it. All the virtuosity of Bismarck's manipulation of the rival powers, his skill in the handling of men and his daring as well, were required to achieve the goal. It was not alone the extention of Prussian power which the other states disliked. They did see with misgivings that the traditions of Frederick the Great had been taken up again, that the old policy of rounding-off the borders of Prussia and conquering new territories which at an earlier time had been directed against Saxony, now led to the annexation of Schleswig-Holstein and the kingdom of Hanover. But the programme of establishing a national state, which at the outset had nothing to do with the Prussian drive for expansion and a Frederician policy, gave the powers no less reason for anxiety and interference. Whether or not German nationalism became an ally of Bismarck, the liberals would have come into conflict with Europe. As early as the Hambach Festival of 1832, when most of the participants were wholly under the influence of the French revolutionary spirit and of Franco-German fraternization, the speakers could not refrain from rejecting France's claim to the left bank of the Rhine, and J. G. A. Wirth dared openly to express the view that the desired unification of Germany "very probably" would also have as a result the return of Alsace-Lorraine to the ancient homeland. The executive committee of the festival then eliminated this phrase from the official minutes, "in deference to the friendly French people," and there were many who took amiss the speaker's "slip." But the *"furor teutonicus"*—as the favorite catchword of the Bismarckian period ran—burned brightly precisely after 1859, and without Bismarck's intervention. The *kleindeutsch* patriots were scarcely ready to grant compensations to Napoleon III and to renounce the left bank of the Rhine. The German variety of nationalists in St. Paul's Church [where the National Assembly met in Frankfurt in 1848] had thrashed it all out! How many times had the verse *"So weit die deutsch Zunge klingt!"* [5] ('Where'er is heard the German tongue!') been reiterated within its walls, as the basis for far-reaching claims! Amid great applause a speaker in the National Assembly at Frankfurt declared that one could not draw the sword for the Germans in Schleswig and at the same time abandon South Tyrol. It became evident at St. Paul's Church that there were *irredenta* in many parts of Europe; the courts and govern-

[5] A famous patriotic poem, *The German's Fatherland*, by Ernst Moritz Arndt.

ments of the powers agreed that to treat status as a people (*Volkstum*), nation and national state, as mutually equivalent expressions, was a "Germanism." They saw it as a great error which, as Ernest Renan expressed it in 1882, "if it came to dominate, would hurl Europe into immense wars and destroy its civilization." As a matter of fact, the governments feared the ideology of the German liberals and democrats more than the ambitions of the Prussian statesman. True, the *kleindeutsch* programme was limited to strict boundaries, but once released and given wing by its first success, the movement would necessarily develop its latent tendencies and would then be able to make use of Bismarck's power methods. We need merely to recall the great interest which was given to the question of the "Germans in the outside world" at the festivals of gymnastic, rifle, singing and Schiller societies since 1840. After 1859 this element of national ambition kept emphatically to the front; even the *Kleindeutschen* could not remain free of it. It was expected in the European courts after 1871 that a period of pan-Germanic expansion would begin, and there was astonishment and a return to calm feelings when it was seen that such plans were far indeed from Bismarck's mind.

But the movement of folk groupings was the very force which, as soon as it could attain freedom for development, had to bring disorder and war upon Europe. Among the peoples of Europe, ambitious to make their own states, the belief in humanity and the solidarity of free nations, each developing along its own lines, did not prevent an embittered struggle from breaking out at once over the frontiers of provinces and folk groupings. Though still in vain, Robert Blum,[6] together with the leaders of the nationalities of eastern Europe, had already sought to bring about the dismemberment of the Habsburg Empire, in order to split away the Germans of Austria from all the other nationalities, bringing the Germans into a centralized unified Republic. This goal was not abandoned. Yet its achievement would have brought European chaos, as Metternich and Grillparzer in Vienna, the midpoint of many nations, had predicted. In our own day, we have experienced its terrible results. The beginnings of a secular nationalist "revivalist movement" were already quite strong in 1848. Blum, it is true, did not become the "leader and arouser of the people," and no one in Germany was called upon to play the role which was enacted in Hungary by Louis Kossuth; to a remarkable degree the German movement on behalf of a national state ran an anonymous course. Then Bismarck, having brought the liberals both into alliance and into subordination, took the rudder; thereafter there was no place for a patriotic leader like Gottfried Kinkel. Bismarck held fast to the traditions of the old statecraft, and thereby placed the German movement under the command of the state-centred conception. He maintained it in the form of a constitutional monarchy,

---

[6] Robert Blum (1807–48), German political leader; head of Left at Frankfurt Assembly; executed (November 1848) by Austrians for part in Vienna uprising.

in correspondence with the relationship of forces which existed within Germany after almost all German states had received such constitutions. The wars which he waged were in their own way wars for unification. They were not organized as people's wars, but were conducted in the strict forms laid down in the armies of the kings, and with strict, wholly political aims. We must always recall to our memories the sentence which proved such breadth of vision and which has received such frightening confirmation: "What ought to be placed in that part of Europe which is at present occupied by the Austro-Hungarian monarchy? New creations in this soil could only be of a revolutionary character."

This—and just this—was the decisive course of events. Bismarck thwarted not only the beginnings of a liberal and democratic movement, but he restrained the development of [Central] European nationalism in general, which for specific, historically verifiable reasons had arisen in close relationship with the liberal and constitutionalist conception, but, where it could develop, ended in dictatorship, the centralized unitary republic, and unlimited expansion. How Louis Kossuth, Mazzini and Daniele Manin were extolled in the democratic journals of bourgeois democracy, *Didaskalia* and *Gartenlaube,* although they were certainly not liberal and constitutionalist politicians; one wished to extend Hungary to the crest of the Carpathians, the other Italy to the Brenner frontier! Even Ferdinand Lassalle had entered upon a similar path, though he started from a different point of departure; he was a fervent patriot, and he would have favoured, in fact, a *grossdeutsch* socialist centralized republic. The extent to which the liberal upper bourgeoisie could construct a barrier from its own resources is very questionable. They could not bring forth, and could not desire, an arouser of the people. Into the gap stepped the statesman who had nothing in common with the dictators of the nationalist period, but had his origin in classic diplomacy and statecraft.

For historical science it is a question of assigning to Bismarck his correct place in the historical sequence, not of justifying him or "vindicating his honour." He had naught to do with the doctrines of folk and living space (*Lebensraum*), with the old imperial idea, or with what Eichendorff [7] so ironically called "modern patrioteering" (*moderne Vaterländerei*); the patriots and national heroes, as they arose everywhere in the wake of nationalism, were of different stamp. In his old age he permitted himself to take pleasure in popularity and noisy hero-worship, which were foreign to aristocratic times. But he did not owe his successes, certainly, to the "Third Estate" or to the masses, but rather to the mastery with which he controlled the rules of the older diplomacy. Actions and transactions involving the courts and states had been developed to a high level of science and art in the chancelleries of the Italian Renaissance and the absolute monarchy of the French type.

[7] Joseph, Freiherr von Eichendorff (1788–1857), German romantic poet.

European unity was smashed to bits upon this mosaic pattern of politics, and Machiavellianism came into practice. After the kings and their counsellors had brought this to past, nationalism pushed them aside, took over and further developed their methods and works, and adapted them to the needs of the masses who were coming into prominence. The history of the rise and decline of classic diplomacy has still to be written, however rich the sources available for it; we have only fragments from the hands of experienced diplomatists. Bismarck is the last great representative in the line of classic diplomats, which begins with the famed Venetian ambassadors and the papal nuncios of the sixteenth century. He did not in any way create a new type, but rather acted out to the full an old and strong departmental tradition. Even in his time diplomacy was in the process of becoming a bureaucratized profession with a strict course of training and a caste-stratified pattern of promotion. When Junker Bismarck, then only the squire of Schönhausen, still on the lower rungs of his career as officer and jurist, entered their caste as an outsider, those who had served according to the rules were discontented. While he had deserved well of the crown in his service as a deputy, he had made his way into diplomacy by the detour of parliament. But he soon acquired the gentlemanly training of the international high society of Europe, to which stratum he belonged by origin and effort; his first assignment to Frankfurt as Prussian envoy to the Federal Diet gave him an opportunity to acquire experience and develop his abilities. His memoirs still give us today a direct impression of the way in which, in the style of the old diplomacy, he evaluated the forces at work in every situation which confronted him, and tested, and to some extent calculated through, all possible combinations one after another. Thus he was a "member of the guild" with Choiseul, Kaunitz, Talleyrand and Metternich, all of whom left us their memoirs; however different were the states and interests which they represented, politics was for each of them an exact science concerned with calculable magnitudes. We may let the question rest whether there is a difference of spiritual rank between Bismarck and his great predecessors, and it has been observed of his manner of negotiating that he had been in the habit of peddling his wool on the market square in Stettin. Talleyrand and Metternich, the bishop of the Gallican church and the Rhenish nobleman, had still absorbed the lofty intellectual culture of the *ancien régime*. But, in the last analysis, the East Elbian Junker had belonged to the exclusive student *Korps* at the University of Göttingen, educated himself in the world of society, and always maintained a French recess in his mind.

To be sure, Bismarck, as minister of a constitutional monarch, had to count no longer with potentates, courtiers and favorites. He had to play not only in the "concert of Europe," but also on the instrument of parliament as well. And here then was to be seen the limits beyond which the old classic diplomacy did not reach. The great transformation which was taking place in that period of the awakening of nationalism and its democratic concomitant, consisted precisely in the fact that it was no longer the governments which led the peoples, but the peoples which decided for the governments. Thereby an element was introduced into politics which escaped all calculation. So long as Bismarck had dealings only with the Tsar and Gorchakov, with the Empress and the ladies of the court, that is, with the great ones whom someone who knew people well could see through to some extent, his diplomatic art could hew to the old methods which earlier had been formed under the world dominance of mathematics and mechanics. But, with the rise of Panslavism, all calculations became uncertain. Bismarck took German nationalism into custody and utilized it, subordinated it to the state conception and made it available for diplomatic craft. It was a very unequal alliance which was concluded then—a true *societas leonina*, for the Prussian state received the lion's part; the nationalist movement had to permit limits to be drawn to its activity, with regard to domestic freedom as well as to "pan-German" tendencies. For the time being, Bismarck was the master; and the world in which he felt at home and moved with complete security was the grand world of the courts and aristocratic society. There he sought for the decisions, exactly as had been done in bygone times in the manner depicted in the historical writings of Ranke. Bismarck and Ranke, the contemporaries, belong together most intimately from this point of view as well, and everything, furthermore, which was common to them—the objective comprehension of reality, the conviction of the primacy of foreign policy, the doctrines of the power-state and the legitimacy of political action—came out of the school of the old diplomacy. Following the same pattern, Bismarck and Ranke both fundamentally looked upon the state from the top downwards, while the patriots saw it as their task in politics and science to judge public affairs from below, upon the basis of the rights and requirements of the people. This celebrated formulation, which fixes the difference between the enlightened-absolutist and the democratic conceptions of public life, was first coined by Arndt; Treitschke took it over from him and misunderstood it. Even in his later life Bismarck limited the labours of the statesman and the diplomat to governments and courts; he was always foreign to the newly developing diplomacy which had to devote its energies to the fatiguing tasks of directing large staffs and studying the peoples and the economic and social phenomena of distant lands. Bismarck was not equal to working in the new world of the popular forces which had come into movement—consider the fiasco of his domestic policy after 1871! In just the same way the historian Ranke did not judge correctly those parties in the past in which, alongside the diplomats and court theologians, primal forces from below forced their way. Bismarck never did learn, as Napoleon did, to flatter the crowd. He was gripped by narrow class prejudices as were other leading statesmen of his time. Hence he inaugurated his social policy principally for considerations of power politics and preferred such solutions as were, in his view, adapted to strengthening the state. Even when he desired, he was unable to negotiate with deputies and party leaders as skilfully as with ambassadors and ministers of other powers. He always looked upon Windthorst [8] as just the former minister of a defeated royal house who only sought revenge in gathering the Catholics around himself; he never even made the effort to achieve an understanding of the endeavour of the Catholic portion of the population to help shape the inner structure of the new Reich. And he made just as little effort to develop in August Bebel [9] and his party a willingness to co-operate upon the basis of even the slightest concession. There is no doubt that his narrow and unchanging horizon served to strengthen his national-liberal and conservative allies in their lack of understanding for the Christian and Social-Democratic labour movement.

Thus Bismarck is to be understood as a historical phenomenon only upon the basis of the old statecraft, with its lofty intellectuality and self-sufficiency, in which the people played no part. He created the German national state within the framework of the old state system and with the old methods; after him, it went into decline. One has to look at Hindenburg and Ludendorff and compare them to the earlier leaders of German destinies in order to realize that Germany used to live more decently. The charge has often been made, and is emphatically repeated by Eyck, that Bismarck took no care to provide for the new generation, and tolerated no independent persons of quality around him. His collaborator in St. Petersburg, Leopold von Schlözer, always called him "the Pasha." But yet it was rare for him to encounter in the government departments such fine and upstanding personalities as Schlözer himself; when he did meet them, he did not withhold his respect. Furthermore, not only in the chancelleries and governments, but in the other domains of life in the era of rising nationalism, with the entry of the masses into history, noble personalities were forced into the background behind robust and servile characters.

In the old classic diplomacy to which Bismarck belonged, it was true that the principles and methods which are included under the name of Machiavellianism had been in long use; it remains to be seen whether, in this respect, Bismarck acted without restraint to an unusual degree. Where it is required by reason of state, Machiavelli considers anything to be permissible. He recommends lying, breaking treaties, deceit, violence; one must be a lion and a fox at the same time, and success justifies the most outrageous villainy. But, on the other hand, as the sagacious and honourable Johann Jakob Moser [10] taught in the eighteenth

[8] Ludwig Windthorst (1812–91), German political leader; minister of justice in Hanover (1851–53, 1862–65), leader of Centre Party in the German Reichstag after 1870.

[9] August Bebel (1840–1913), German political leader; founder and leader of German Social-Democratic Party.

[10] Johann Jakob Moser (1701–85), German juridical scholar and teacher.

century, the small state cannot build upon force; therefore it must build upon law and justice. But it is obvious that the "minor powers," when they became involved in the affairs of the world, have been most perfidious, while the great powers maintained their strong positions and no longer had to pursue a shifty course. The Prussian state was the most recent and smallest of the powers. This is the explanation of many of the acts of treacherous behaviour which are to be found so frequently in the history of Prussian policy. But Talleyrand, too, who certainly had a great power behind him, was never squeamish, and in Bismarck's time Prussia was so great a military power that it did not need small expedients. But Bismarck always applied the methods of deceit or violence which seemed useful to him, without meditating upon them. A statesman who saw his state as incomplete, he was moved by ambition to make it larger; moreover, the increase of power by all means was a personal necessity for him. He brought about three wars with complete deliberateness, as he frankly admitted afterwards. He dragged the King of Hanover into war in order to drive him from his throne, confiscated his property in violation of an agreement, and then had parliament forbid him to make restitution. He concluded the Reinsurance treaty with Russia against Austria and carefully concealed this fact from his ally. It is not possible and not necessary to enumerate here all the misdeeds or improprieties of his foreign and domestic policy. Even at the time they were brought to light of day by those affected, and were vigorously discussed by contemporary public opinion; but when he was successful, his power became so great that all who were dependent by function or character, bowed their heads and worshipped his genius. It was an ill harbinger of things to come that these were the leading intellectuals; previously humanitarian or liberal in attitude, they wished to remain on top as time passed, whatever came to pass. Eyck has carefully brought out in the course of his narrative every instance of violation of law and justice, of violence, of unfair conduct of affairs on the part of Bismarck; we now know much more of what he did than contemporary polemists knew at the time. We possess for no other statesman, not even for Talleyrand, so elaborate a register of his sins. Bismarck had the additional misfortune of finding a historian who pursued the old sinner through every twist and turn of his career.

But, what is more, the picture of Bismarck was drawn even more unflatteringly because of his personal idiosyncrasies. Words exist to conceal ideas, went the celebrated paradox coined by Talleyrand. Such behaviour was not to Bismarck's taste. Though he was able to watch his step, he did not find it easy. He carried over into political controversy the coarse language he had used as a member of a student *Korps* at the university and as a reserve officer in the army. He never acquired the self-control which one learns in the chancellery of state or *salon* society. For him at least, parliament was not the best school at which to prepare for diplomacy. Furthermore, he tended to make his criticism too slashing. He took delight in witty conversation, which he spiced with the kind of merry tale and unexpected jest his adversaries would then turn against him. He did not scruple to speak his mind. He said openly that he would not be balked by trifles. Other cynical turns of phrase from his lips soon became public knowledge. Such cynicism, also, set his successors a bad example. His imitators mimicked his cynicism, but not his honourable traits. The time was not far off when the reigning monarch, in his overbearing arrogance, hardly cut the figure of a prince or nobleman. In a world of rapidly growing wealth and splendour, William II was more the *parvenu* than the aristocrat.

No one will deny, therefore, that Bismarck and William II introduced into politics the habit of acting harshly toward ostensible weakness, and the use of strong words, so that ever-larger sections of the German people were summarily stigmatized as enemies of the Reich. Such conduct was foreign to the despots in previous times, because they sat, lonely and silent, upon the thrones in their Escorials. To be sure, many a cynical, blunt remark ("a crime, but not a mistake") has come down to us from Napoleon, who was dependent upon the crowd. However, he too adapted very easily to the new opinions taking form among the people; what is more, he too failed. Like Hegel, the "Prussian" in philosophy, Bismarck inculcated in the German Empire the belief that one "shouldn't be squeamish" [*"Nicht viel Umstände zu machen"*]. The role which the Junkers from east of the Elbe were now called upon to perform was, perhaps, particularly appropriate to them. Every reformer, from Freiherr vom Stein down to the liberals of the pre-Bismarck period, was indeed convinced, of course, that Prussia would have to renew herself upon the basis of the forces and institutions of Rhenish and Westphalian Germany. As a matter of fact, despite Bismarck, the centre of gravity of the German national movement in the nineteenth century did lie in the West, where the Rhenish economic leaders were at home and democracy had roots in the life of the people. In northern Germany the liberal movement won influence only in the cities. In that area, the authentic Prussia of old, which was Bismarck's homeland, his methods were quickly adopted and imitated. Freiherr vom Stein and his collaborators had not worked wholly without success in Prussia; Berlin in the time of Schinkel,[11] and Königsberg in the time of Theodor von Schön, the Kantian and Prussian reformer,[12] gladly put a long distance between themselves and Frederick's Prussian system. But now, by Bismarck's example, anyone who had any power whatever to use found himself encouraged to act more abruptly. Only where constitutional courts were able to exercise effective control was there any safeguard against utter disregard of law and justice. This flouting of right under

[11] Karl Friedrich Schinkel (1781–1841), German architect and painter, particularly active in Berlin.
[12] Theodor von Schön (1772–1856), Prussian statesman; took liberal role in East Prussia in war against Napoleon.

law was frankly proclaimed at the time in the form of the right of necessity, as was done in 1914 in the invasion of Belgium.

We may be surprised, therefore, that the leaders of the Prussian-German state adopted such methods when they had ceased to be customary among legitimate monarchies after Napoleon's fall. We must ascribe to Bismarck a large individual share in promoting this development. In Prussia itself professional diplomats looked amiss at these methods. Bismarck was, after all, not only an outsider, but a man out of the ordinary, from whom one could look for a *coup d'état*; he was, therefore, of the same ilk as the men of 18th Brumaire and 2nd December. We forget too easily how deep an impression was made by the reappearance of Bonapartism at a time when the nineteenth century was becoming more and more bourgeois, in an age of liberalism and belief in progress. It was a stupendous phenomenon which aroused misgivings lest the means and resources of liberal democracy prove inadequate in the difficult and hard time just beginning. If anything encouraged Bismarck to enter upon the path of violence, it was certainly the conduct of Prince Louis Napoleon. There is reason, furthermore, to investigate more deeply the extent to which he also felt encouraged by Cavour's example; the Piedmontese was a great "realist" who also drove many princes from their thrones and yet did not become dependent upon extremism. But, beyond doubt, many aspects of Bismarck's life work trace back to the French Second Empire. That is all just history now. It would be difficult to find threads which extended from that time into the twentieth century. The general character of Caesarism or dictatorship as such, exemplified in the Renaissance and once again brought into being by Napoleon I, was such a thread. The twentieth century, on the contrary, did not find its exemplars in the great realists and proponents of reason of state, but rather in the theory and practice of violence as created by the nationalists of eastern Europe and Italy. Kossuth, Mazzini and Garibaldi mobilized the youth of their nations and led them in hosts, again and again, to destruction. They aroused men's instinctual passions. In general, they were demoniac in character for they adopted chimerical goals, used the most extreme methods, and remained relatively indifferent to success, which neither they nor their imitators met. Bismarck had no part in all their doings, not even when, in 1866, he entertained a plan to rouse up the Czechs and Magyars. Though he may have learned from Napoleon III, still we do not find in him any trace of admiration for the demoniac figure of Napoleon I. In his youth, he went through his "romantic" period; but, once the storms of youth were past, *déborder* became foreign to his nature. The traditional rules of conduct provided that in cases of extreme necessity one need not think twice about using any weapon at hand. If we wish to probe for the ultimate cause of all the processes which gave rise to Napoleon, to Bismarck and to the leaders of the nationalities, as well as to their methods and goals, we will become aware that, in general, these processes are rooted in modern humanity. It clearly was not at all the same thing when the old sovereign states used their machinery of power to define their interests, and when national sovereignty came into play. The sovereign nation, once it was swung into action, did not readily accept any limitation of its scope.

We cannot condemn these methods and accept their goals. Bismarck could attain his purposes only by such methods. How else could he have bound together the eastern and western halves of the Prussian monarchy, closing the gaps that lay between them? The King of Hanover acted cautiously and beyond criticism. He took his stand squarely on law and avoided taking any part in the conflict between the two big powers! In order to respect the rights of Hanover, Bismarck would have had to give up any hope of making the Prussian state a single territorial unit. But he wished the Prussian body politic to have one compact territory, which would enable it to prevail completely in the North German Confederation. When this was won, he turned at once to his next goal and established the German Empire. Prussia could have existed in it even if she did not have Hanover and Hesse. In any case, in spite of the federal organization of the state, which was inevitable at the time, the decisive fact remains that Bismarck did not free himself from the old political conception of the isolated, territorially-compact, state body. In this old classic policy, Machiavellianism, because it arose in fact out of the struggle of sovereign powers, was not something put in afterwards, but the principle of its very life. Though national sovereignty merely took the place of the princely sovereigns, it vastly intensified, as we know, the drive of Machiavellianism, extended it widely and made it all-inclusive.

We may correctly speak of Bismarck's being "misunderstood" nowadays in the sense that his work and activity have been viewed apart from their connexion with the previous system of states and its political conceptions. Bismarck's conduct was dictated by a line which traced back to Frederick the Great, Richelieu, Gustavus Adolphus and Maurice de Saxe. They all contributed to the destruction of Western unity, to the establishment of sovereign states, and to their mighty expansion by conquest, treaty-breaking and violence against the weak. For a long time, Bismarck merely put modern nationalism to his own uses. He was, first and foremost, the managing director of a state which played the role of a great power in the European state system of five great powers and many smaller powers; as yet, Prussia was not "saturated" within this state system. Once he said that Prussia wore too heavy armour for her small body. It is an image which corresponds to the old political thinking. Bismarck did not learn the new metaphors of nationalism. He was concerned with the interests of the state, with the state as a rational system of analysis and action. Hence he remained strange to the voluntarisms of the period of national states and democracy. The programme and slogans of nationalism—natural living space, historical borders, assimilation and national will—which derived in part from the French Revolution and for the rest from German romanticism, were widespread among the liberals in the sixties and seventies, and were already being fully acted upon among the eastern European peoples. Bismarck did not heed any of these slogans; he disregarded this programme. Even when he annexed Alsace and Lorraine, military considerations were paramount in his mind. He belonged to the system of states as it had been, when states looked out for themselves and wished to please only themselves, when the interests of the state were all that was at stake and the interests of the people were only of secondary concern. He brought two new great powers, Prussia-Germany and Sardinia-Italy into the old European state system. As a result, he transformed the "European concert." The forces which later put an axe to the entire historical state structure had been in being for a long time, and Bismarck had to reckon with them. But he still hoped to be able to bring them under control.

* * *

BISMARCK AND OURSELVES

Alfred von Martin

* * *

IN THE register of German sins there is a place for some of the history written in Germany—that produced by the Prussian school of historiography. From its inception it took a questionable attitude toward standards of objective criticism and hence toward scholarly method. As was to be expected, it did the most serious harm in works written for the general public. In this literature of edification, Bismarck, the great "folk hero" of Prussia, was apotheosized most uncritically. These works, nationalist, wholly secularist, and given over to Bismarck-worship, were put forward by a Protestantism turned political, that is, nationalist. In this literature, Bismarck's figure was placed beside that of Luther, the German, in the pantheon of that North German religion which Constantin Frantz once called "the religion of National-Liberalism."

From Hans Kohn (ed.), *German History: Some New German Views* (Boston: The Beacon Press, 1954), pp. 94–101. All rights reserved. Reprinted by permission.

The people wish to have their "great man." Their historians, too, like to say dramatically, "Men make history," but fail to ask what is the result of such history. The "great men" themselves, in rare moments of reflection, were more honest. Frederick II of Prussia once said frankly that "great men" were in the habit of making their peoples "very unhappy." On occasions Bismarck expressed wonder that "the greatest butchers of men are those most loved and admired." When Jakob Burckhardt, in his letters to Friedrich von Preen, comes to speak of Bismarck, he always calls him "the great man." Still this does not prevent Burckhardt, the humanist among historians in the German language, from remarking how "obnoxious" Bismarck's personality was to him. He knew that the morality of all "great men" in history was open to doubt. Yet not once did he carry this criticism through to its logical conclusion.

In Robert Saitschick's book,[1] we now have an impressive and informative work of Bismarck criticism, which yet is popularly written in the best sense of the word. It is the kind of book we have needed. In reading it, one gains the conviction that Bismarck's story is very much a part of the history of the German catastrophe, whose origins, therefore, go back long before Hitler. It is a worthwhile destruction of the Bismarck legend. It corrects the false picture of history upon which a good part of the German nationalist ideology was based. To be sure, this ideology is kept up to date in new guises. The most recent position of Bismarck apologetics is that his policy was an end-product of old-fashioned cabinet policy. It was an *étatist* policy "from above," in opposition to the revolutionary nationalism which forced its way up from below and served as a prelude to the power politics of the new twentieth century. They say that the old sorcerer, while using this nationalism, tamed it. According to this view, Bismarck was really sated after 1871, not just simply in the fashion of someone who wisely realizes that what has been devoured must first be digested, that renewed robbery should not be risked immediately, but because Bismarck had reached the goal he had set himself in his previous policy. He still wanted it to be state, not national, policy. And we should probably add, because he trusted none of those who would have to take over the inheritance he passed on, to be able to do more, under the most favorable circumstances, than maintain what he had created. A self-made man has every reason to take for granted that his practical genius will not be transmitted by inheritance.

Is such an attitude really "conservative"? Saitschick correctly calls Bismarck the revolutionary (he was one, as Frederick William IV, the most un-Prussian of Prussian kings, had already accurately pointed out), the adherent of a Prussian "Bonapartism" which was "older than Bonaparte" himself (Bismarck had already thus characterized himself to Leopold von Gerlach, the conservative adjutant-general of the conservative king).

[1] *Bismarck und das Schicksal des deutschen Volkes: Zur Psychologie und Geschichte der deutschen Frage* (Munich, 1948).

Even if statesmen, after 1789, and indeed after 1848, only continued the practice usual before 1789, that is, a policy—a policy of conquest, of course—which arose out of their lust for power, pure and simple, and their personal vanity, it was no longer the same. Since 1789 the voices of the people have also been heard on the European continent. The application of pure power politics in the era of the political collaboration of the nation would necessarily destroy "the forces supporting the state within the people itself," as Ludwig Bamberger, the liberal critic of Bismarck, remarked. Bamberger bears witness to the necessarily anti-conservative results of Bismarck's policy. It is playing with fire to arouse the revolutionary and nationalist passions of the people for political trickery.

Cui bono? Previously it was Frederick II who found shelter and concealment behind "service to the state." At least ideologically he was under the influence of the Enlightenment, though, in practice, to be sure, more under Machiavelli's. Meanwhile, idolatry of the state was made fashionable in intellectual society as well by Hegel, the Prussian state philosopher. But, on the other hand, Bismarck, like Frederick II before him, admitted openly, though not publicly, that vanity was the motive force of his powerful passions. He, too, sanctioned his political activity by ideological appeals to love of fatherland, but at the same time he looked upon men with cynical contempt. He was a born tyrant who wanted nothing from men but "subordination and discipline," [2] and indeed did not tolerate independent opinion, criticism or control by parliament. As a matter of fact he permitted only creatures around himself just as he could govern only with the assistance of a Press which he had made tractable by bribery. The Prussian Crown Prince and Princess, the future Emperor Frederick III and his wife, Victoria, were wholly justified when they called him an "evil" man, because he was "without principle" and was driven by a demoniacal will-to-power. Later, Bebel spoke of the pact which Bismarck made with "the devil" for the sake of contemptible political "advantage." On the eve of the war of 1866, August Reichensperger [3] meditated upon the recurring importance of arrogance in history, "from the fall of the Angel until our own day." In fact, Bismarck himself admitted to the Crown Prince at a later date, in November 1870, that he had already fixed upon his policy of war when he took office in 1862, but made no mention of it even to the king, until the "proper moment," of course. Thus he hoodwinked William I, though, to be sure, the king's sense of his Prussian political and military "honour" was always available for the *"suum cuique rapere"* (to rob each of his own), as Ludwig von Gerlach [4] realistically amplified the ideological device—*suum cuique* (to each his own)—

[2] Sidney Whitman, *Errinerungen an Bismarck,* p. 238.

[3] August Reichensperger (1808–95), Prussian art historian and political leader, founder of the Centre Party in the German Reichstag.

[4] Ernst Ludwig von Gerlach (1795–1877), German publicist and statesman, one of the founders of the Conservative Party in Prussia.

of the Prussian kings. According to the sound judgment of the Crown Prince, Bismarck's entire policy was a "frivolous game with the most sacred things." He embodied Machiavelli's *virtù,* which included *sceleratezza;* Bismarck himself felt that a Teutonic devil dwelled within him: the Germans, as a matter of fact, had not worshipped the sun, but the thunder and the lightning.

But the problem of historical guilt, properly speaking, is less concerned with individual motivations, however fascinating for the biographer, than with the objective results and consequences of political activity. It is significant, therefore, that the thoughtful, even among his faithful followers, like the historian Heinrich von Sybel, felt that Bismarck's work was very far from being a fulfilment of their wishes. Scarcely was his work ("performance," one might better say) completed in 1871 than there was a feeling of emptiness. "Now what?" they thought. Here we can already see the psychological pattern for the development out of psychic *horror vacui,* of a universally dangerous pan-Germanism. Bismarck himself in his old age caused bitter disappointment, indeed discouragement, for instance to young Count Harry Kessler, because he lacked awareness of any ultimate meaning of the universe.

Saitschick, for whom these psychological relationships do not arise, discusses in pragmatic terms, first, the seed which Bismarck sowed, and then, the harvest which inevitably grew. In this way he tries to prove that Bismarck's guilt was our "destiny." We question, in the first place, whether Bismarck was "destiny," in the sense that, had he not been there, "everything would have turned out differently." Then we doubt that we should thus thrust all our guilt upon this certainly portentous historical figure so that we ourselves appear blameless.

Viewed from without, the fateful moment of history was the year 1862. King William I was determined to abdicate on the issue of control of the army, but yielded to the persuasive power of Bismarck's energy, as he was to do so often thereafter. Had Frederick III taken over the government at that time, there would have been no "age of Bismarck." For, by then, at the time of the constitutional conflict, the Crown Prince already saw so clearly, as he wrote in 1863, the "frightfully logical" road to "disaster" in Bismarck's policy of force, which openly trampled all law and justice, that he did not shrink from a conflict with his father.

Would the policy of "Blood and Iron" have been avoided by a government of Frederick III? Or, in the sad, final analysis, even if there had been no Bismarck, could things have turned out no differently than they did? Neither the German Confederation nor the supra-national atmosphere would have endured. The restoration system of 1815 was only a provisional interruption of the age of the revolution which continued to go forward, at least covertly, from 1789. Bismarck was only the man who, in Jakob Burckhardt's fine formulation, said *"Ipse faciam"* (I myself will do it). Certainly by setting the stone into motion he defined its path and chose the moment when it began to move. But, in any case, the stone was loose and it had to start rolling.

Saitschick rightly stresses that Bismarck's establishment of the Empire was "artificial" creation, a reversal, by means of true Prussian organization of the process of organic growth. But this course of events cannot simply be charged to the person of the organizer. So individualistic—that is, one-sided and un-sociological—a method of historical analysis does not take into account that, however much one may deplore it, the development, in one way or another, from the organic and the federative, to the technically organized and centralized state of affairs, belongs to the fundamental tendencies of modern times. Finally, we must still ask just how much even so "great" a man can do if the people do not join him sooner or later. Thus the National-Liberals, the predestined Bismarckian party, so to say, were those who accepted Bismarck's principle (which also had the historiographical sanction of Ranke) of the primacy of foreign policy over domestic policy, at least in those circumstances where the geopolitical situation of a country leaves it open to unremitting pressure from without. It was the National-Liberals who betrayed freedom to "unity," that is, to power. There had long existed as a popular current a liberal and centralist nationalism, which sang "My fatherland must be greater!" and therefore created danger of "that dismemberment of the European community" which Saitschick sees as coming into existence for the first time only in Bismarck's era. Against Erich Eyck's liberal critique of Bismarck, Franz Schnabel has correctly emphasized how strong were the nationalist aspirations cherished even by the pre-Bismarckian German democratic movement. Heine already anticipated an unparalleled outburst of political radicalism as a result of the revolutionary development in Germany, first in religion, then in philosophy.

Fixing our attention upon a "great man," however grave the burden of his individual responsibility, diverts us too easily from the guilt manifestly shared by those who collectively went along with him. In the final analysis, a people always has the government it deserves. We should not, therefore, in all too simple fashion, replace previous customary glorification of the "great" man by accusations exclusively against the "evil" man. We are not divested of guilt because we have been influenced. For influence to work, someone must be open to it. Behind the endeavour to thrust all guilt upon Bismarck, and then upon Hitler, the old lack of civic consciousness and sense of responsibility, which was inculcated by the authoritarian state, none the less lies always concealed. We must ask ourselves how the German people came to give first Bismarck and then Hitler their opportunities. Indeed, how did they come to raise Bismarck and Hitler to idols? Because they have tended to worship force, because they consider every kind of inconsiderateness, especially in the military field and in domestic and foreign policy, to be proof of increased strength, so that the border-line of brutality becomes fluid; in short, because they are always impressed by the cavalryman's boot and a fist banged upon the table. The German people saw their ideal of power embodied in Bismarck. He was their great man. We ought to have a history of his fame, a history of the *Bismarck myth,* a critical history in which we would see ourselves depicted, as a mirror to hold up to ourselves, a mirror of the path of error by which we attained to ideals of such falsity. This is what we miss in Saitschick's book; he disregards this side of the problem, in the final analysis the most important one. The examination of Bismarck ought to have led directly into necessary German self-criticism.

Is it not highly suggestive that Bismarck himself felt that he was possessed of a "Teutonic" devil? Bamberger called Bismarck "the *barbare de génie.*" Straight through the soul and conscience of the Germans runs the uncertain frontier between the Christian West and barbarism, said Quariglia, the Italian anti-fascist, during the last war. What is worst is that so many among us have always been proud of our participation in barbarism, even before Hegel, then particularly after Nietzsche, and all the way down to Ernst Jünger. Barbarian or Christian? We ought to put that query to Bismarck, we must address it above all to every German. Unfortunately, Heinrich Heine was not far wrong when he expressed the opinion that Christianity had only thinly and temporarily tamed the barbarian instincts of the Germans. We must add as well the Prussian-German faculty for having simultaneously a private Christianity and a deliberately heathenish public policy which, as we saw, could call up old Thor or Donar. Ernst Troeltsch recounts that an ingenuous, but very serious Scottish pastor once declared to him, "I could not be a pastor in Germany. It just is not a Christian country." We should ask whether Bismarck's unscrupulous Machiavellianism would not have met more vigorous resistance if this had not been so.

Yet the glorification of war by Treitschke had been prepared by Hegel, and before him by the historian Luden. So we should not marvel that men of intellect, indeed jurists such as Rudolf von Ihering,[5] swarmed about the man of success and fell on their knees before him. The Prussian-German opposition to an international court of arbitration, after the period of Kant, the disqualification of desire for peace as weakness, corresponded to the fundamental defects of the German national character: the calamitous romanticism of force, and the tendency toward extreme solutions. Frederick William IV called German logical consistency the most wretched of all virtues; and Frederick III, while still a young man, said to his teacher, Ernst Curtius, that Prussian statesmen lacked the ability to give in.

Was there "another" Germany, better and wiser, besides Bismarck's Germany? There were, in any event, individual Germans who did not share his ideas and who foresaw the oncoming time of troubles, the era of destructive wars and the inevitable catastrophe. Paul de Lagarde [6] and Constantin Frantz are brought forward from time to time by Saitschick among Bismarck's con-

---

[5] Rudolf von Ibhering (1818–92), German jurist, famous for his *Geist des römischen Rechts and Der Zweck im Recht.*

[6] Paul de Lagarde (1827–91), German Orientalist and publicist.

temporaries. Ludwig von Gerlach deserves no less a place. In general, the enemies of Bismarck ought to be portrayed together by someone—it would be a
small German hall of fame. Yet they were never anything but solitary individuals, and their voices died away, almost unheard. To be sure, official policy and
semi-official historiography deliberately did their best to bury them in silence.
Thus they remained voices in the wilderness. Their warnings were in vain.
For behind these Germans, among whom Crown Prince Frederick stood not
among the last, there was no Germany they could represent. The hope of
Germany rests, in spite of all, upon the possibility that such Germans may
become representative of Germany. But no insight holds hope unless it makes
us search into our own hearts.

* * *

[9]

Disraeli and Gladstone: "Empirical Realism" versus "Righteous Passion"

Benjamin Disraeli, Earl of Beacons-
field (1804–1881), and William Ewart Gladstone (1809–1898) had parliamentary careers which lasted more than forty and sixty years, respectively.
Disraeli was *de facto* and then actual head of the Conservative party
over a period of thirty odd years; Gladstone led the Liberals for about the
same length of time. Disraeli was prime minister twice; Gladstone, four
times. As D. C. Somervell has put it, "From 1865 to 1880 British politics
was simply Disraeli versus Gladstone." [1] Somervell's remark emphasizes the
extent to which these two great men impressed their personalities and
views on their respective parties. Their record of service is extraordinary
enough, but their dominance of their parties has no subsequent parallel in
British history, nor, for that matter, does their bitter but great duel in and
out of Parliament.

¶ In spite of the animosity and differences of temperament and outlook
between them, it has been the happy fate of Disraeli and Gladstone to escape
the varied and drastic reappraisals of their policies which have been applied to
the deeds of their contemporaries on the Continent, Napoleon III, Cavour and
Bismarck. This is in large part due to the unique course of British history from
about 1850 to 1880.[2] After the Chartism of the 1830's and "hungry forties,"

---

[1] D. C. Somervell, *Disraeli and Gladstone, A. Duo-Biographical Sketch* (New York: Garden
City Publishing Company, 1926), p. 310. Eighteen sixty-five marks the death of Palmerston. Lord
John Russell succeeded him as prime minister, but Gladstone was already established as the leading
Liberal and became prime minister in 1868. In 1866 Russell resigned and his government was
succeeded by the second Derby ministry (Conservative) in which Disraeli once again became the
leader in the House of Commons.

[2] The terminal date 1880 may appear somewhat arbitrary, since Gladsone's public career continued through three more ministries until 1894. Disraeli, however, died in 1881, and the unity
and cohesiveness of English political and social life, which form the main theme of our introductory
sketch, began to break up in the 1880's and had pretty well disintegrated by the end of the 1890's.

Britain settled down to an orderly progress towards social justice which, incomplete though it may have been, had no counterpart in the political and social upheavals on the Continent. Nor was there a counterpart on the Continent to Britain's two-party system which was the agent of this progress. Rather than being locked in conflicting ideologies or class interests, both parties, loyal to the Crown and the existing economic order, sought to appeal to all classes—indeed appeared to vie with each other in sponsoring electoral and social reforms.

Thus it was the Tory Disraeli who "dished the Whigs" by doubling the electorate with the Second Reform Bill of 1867. Though Disraeli came back to power in 1874 with a program of giving Britain "a rest at home" while emphasizing the problems of British prestige and interests abroad, his second ministry (1874–1880) produced notable social legislation. It may be possible to compare the achievements of the Liberals and Conservatives in social reform and draw conclusions as to which party was most on the side of the angels, but it cannot be argued conclusively that Disraeli was any less committed to the idea of social legislation than Gladstone.

In the area of foreign affairs, however, there were real differences between the two men. Disraeli was the first, great advocate of the new imperialism. He also felt it necessary for the safeguarding of British prestige and interests that Britain should play a larger part in European affairs. His intervention in the Russo-Turkish War and his role at the Berlin Congress of 1878 were concrete examples of this determination. Gladstone, on the other hand, belonged by temperament to the "Little England" school and believed that Britain's "splendid isolation" should not go beyond support for the peaceful solution of European problems through the Concert of Europe. Yet he could become intensely preoccupied with foreign affairs, as in the matter of arbitrary despotism in the Kingdom of Naples, and would speak out with a conscience that Europe had to listen to. And when, as in the question of guaranteeing Belgian neutrality in 1870, action was needed, Gladstone could act to good effect.

During Gladstone's second ministry (1880–1885), Egypt was occupied, with misgivings, to be sure, on Gladstone's part, but occupied nonetheless. Although Gladstone was, in a sense, an "isolationist," and not an imperialist, it cannot be seriously argued that he tried to damage British prestige or interests abroad or that he tried to check in any significant way the onward surge of empire in the closing decades of the nineteenth century.

Disraeli and Gladstone were, in short, the principal actors in an age when Britain was a model of governmental and social cohesion, and when, as one

---

Disruptive forces during these last two decades were the Irish Question which became more troublesome and brought a level of demagoguery to Parliament unknown in the earlier period, more strikes, trade-unionism, the beginnings of the Labour party, and a split in the Liberal party over Irish Home Rule which made the Liberal and Conservative parties more nearly class-interest parties than they had been earlier. Also imperialism became more strident as British supremacy in world trade began to decline.

historian has described it, "Britain was the world's workshop, the world's shipbuilder, the world's carrier, the world's banker and the world's clearing house."[3] It was a period when, the Crimean War and colonial forays apart, Britain was at peace, and when, if her foreign policy of "splendid isolation" was stretched, it was most often in the direction of mediation or other measures that tried to preserve the peace of Europe.

The foregoing sketch, incomplete and oversimplified as it has to be, is perhaps the long way around to explaining the lack of controversial interpretations in histories dealing with the period of Disraeli and Gladstone. But to say that this is because both men served their country conscientiously and well in a period of greatness begs too many questions. So too, it can be argued, did Bismarck. At all events, new histories may shed more light on the personalities and policies of Disraeli and Gladstone, but latter-day historians have been in unusual agreement with earlier, favorable interpretations.[4]

Therefore, rather than present conflicting interpretations, we have selected one that records the conflict in temperament and outlook between the two men as illustrated by the bitterest and last of their many, political duels. It begins with Gladstone in presumed retirement from public life, busy with his writings on religion, after his defeat by Disraeli in the general election of 1874.

---

[3] Asa Briggs, *Victorian People* (London: Oldhams Press, 1954), p. 14.

[4] For Gladstone, there is John (Viscount) Morley, *Life of William Ewart Gladstone,* 3 vols. (1903). Morley served Gladstone, principally as Irish Secretary during the fourth ministry (1892–1894). He admits to standing too close to his subject, a deficiency corrected by Sir Philip Magnus's excellent work *Gladstone, A Biography* (1954) from which our selection is taken. By giving more details of Gladstone's private life than was customary in earlier biographies, Magnus actually adds to Gladstone's stature.

For Disraeli, there is William F. Monypenny and George E. Buckle, *Life of Benjamin Disraeli, Earl of Beaconsfield,* 6 vols. (1910 and 1920). Disraeli has not been as fortunate as Gladstone in having a good, recent biographer. Most later biographies seem superficial, possibly because of their "exotic" subject. Of Monypenny and Buckle, the American Historical Association's *Guide to Historical Literature* (1961) states: "Though a number of shorter single-volume biographies have appeared since the publication of this work, the above (Monypenny and Buckle) remains the standard life."

This review should not overlook Lytton Strachey, *Eminent Victorians* (1918) and *Queen Victoria* (1921). Strachey and other "debunkers" were immensely popular with the post-World War I generation. Strachey was witty and usually incisive, but his treatment of his subjects was superficial in the extreme. The work of Strachey and his imitators is now regarded as an interesting product of a generation which felt it had to revolt against the Victorian age.

Currently there is a popular nostalgia for the Victorian age which has produced equally superficial writing. But on the level of serious scholarship, there have been admirable attempts, in the works of such social and intellectual historians as Asa Briggs and G. M. Young, to capture the spirit of the age and penetrate the Victorian mentality. Magnus's *Gladstone,* already referred to, although a specialized work, is also a notable contribution in this direction. He, like Briggs, makes credible— one could say rehabilitates—that Victorian piety and moral earnestness which was so characteristic of Gladstone and other figures and was the principle target of the Strachey school.

TALKING TURKEY

Philip Magnus

* * *

FROM THOSE and other moody distractions, Gladstone was recalled by the extraordinary consequences of a peasants' revolt in Bosnia (part of the modern Yugoslavia) which then formed part of the Turkish Empire. The revolt which started in 1875 could not be suppressed. Aggressive Russian sympathy for the oppressed Southern Slavs clashed with British distrust of Russia and with Disraeli's desire to raise British prestige and to play a commanding rôle in Europe and the world. A great war was avoided by the narrowest of margins, and Gladstone, more furious than Achilles after the slaughter of Patroclus, returned to the political arena.

Early in 1876 it became clear that the flame of rebellion in the Balkans was spreading like a forest fire. The only political alliance on the Continent of Europe at that time was the League of the Three Emperors (Germany, Russia, and Austria) which proposed that the Turks should be coerced into granting better conditions to their Christian subjects. Disraeli rejected that proposal out of hand. He argued that it masked a conspiracy on the part of Russia and Austria to partition Turkey; and he sent a fleet to anchor off the Dardanelles as a warning to Russia. Joint intervention by the Great Powers was made difficult by that independent action; and the Turks, relying on British support as at the time of the Crimean War, were encouraged to adopt an intransigent attitude towards Russia.

The Three Emperors League was not hostile to Great Britain, but it saw no good reason why Great Britain should interfere in Eastern Europe. Disraeli, much influenced by considerations of prestige, had already, in pursuit of a colourful and active foreign and imperial policy, acquired control of the Suez Canal; and he was at that time forcing through Parliament a Bill to proclaim the Queen as Empress of India. The Queen herself was unhappily about to throw to the winds the wise restraint which she had hitherto shown. Influenced equally by distrust of Russia and dislike of Gladstone she became as violent a "Jingo" as any man or woman in the land.

In April, 1876, the Bulgarians revolted against the Sultan, and during May

---

From Philip Magnus, *Gladstone, A Biography* (London: John Murray, 1954), pp. 238–55. Reprinted by permission.

some 12,000 Bulgarian men, women, and children were massacred by Turkish irregular troops. The news gradually filtered through, and Disraeli was questioned about it in the House of Commons for the first time on 26 June. Two generations later, when the public had grown accustomed to horrors on an incomparably greater scale, British opinion might have been less deeply stirred. In 1876, however, statesmen were in a position to draw to almost any extent upon vast untapped reserves of moral indignation. Lord Derby, the Foreign Secretary, was profoundly móved by the "Bulgarian Horrors"; even the Queen was dismayed for a time by Disraeli's apparent sympathy with the Turks. Disraeli had little feeling for oppressed Christian peoples struggling to be free. He thought that the Turks would have done better to bribe than to massacre the rebels, and he was afraid lest the Russians should use the atrocities as an excuse for seizing Constantinople. From there they might have been in a position to threaten the new British naval base at Alexandria. He therefore affected to discount the atrocity stories, and he somewhat shocked public opinion by giving a flippant reply to W. E. Forster in the House on 10 July, 1876. The Prime Minister took leave to doubt whether "torture has been practised on a great scale among an oriental people who seldom, I believe, resort to torture, but generally terminate their connexion with culprits in a more expeditious manner."

Gladstone waited for nearly two months in a mood of very dangerous calm. He noted twenty years later that he had been "slow to observe the real leanings of the Prime Minister." As an ex-member of the Cabinet which had embarked upon the Crimean War in 1854, Gladstone felt a weight of personal responsibility towards the Christian minorities in the Balkans. The rights which Russia had formerly possessed to protect those minorities had been annulled after the Crimean War. The Treaty of Paris, 1856, had substituted a European guarantee of protection which the Powers had failed to enforce. Gladstone had a right, therefore, to claim that Great Britain was bound by international law to extend to the Christian minorities of the Turkish Empire the degree of succour and protection which Russia proposed to offer from motives which he optimistically held to be mainly Christian and humanitarian.

On 31 July, 1876, Gladstone asked Disraeli, in the House, to institute inquiries about the massacres. He urged that the Crimean War had substituted "a European conscience expressed by the collective guarantee and concerted action of the European Powers" for the rights which Russia had formerly possessed to intervene in Turkish affairs on behalf of the Christian minorities. He said that the only alternative to the "European Concert" was a "European convulsion." Disraeli retorted by dismissing exaggerated accounts of the atrocities as "coffeehouse babble." He said that it was futile at that late date "to enter into the politics of the Crimean War."

Thenceforward, as the crisis deepened and thrust every other issue into the shade, Disraeli's empirical realism was exposed to a constant and relentless flow of moral precepts from Gladstone. Disraeli, supported by the Queen, society, high finance, the most powerful section of the Press, and by what was left of the rough, happy, ignorant mass of merry England, took his stand on a rather narrow conception of British imperial and strategic interests. He identified those interests with the maintenance of Turkish integrity, and was only held back at the last moment from embarking on a war, which would have been as useless as the war in the Crimea, by a combination of ill-health, Cabinet dissensions, and popular discontent. When Disraeli discovered at Berlin that British prestige could be better secured by throwing over Turkish integrity, he did so without a qualm. He then received the credit for a settlement which embodied, not his ideas, but those of Lord Salisbury, Prince Bismarck, and Count Shuvalov.

Robustly opportunist as it was, Disraeli's policy throughout the crisis reflected the mood of the fashionable world. As Queen Sophie of Holland wrote on 7 September, 1876, to her intimate friend, Lady Derby: "I cannot feel any sympathy with Servians and Bulgarians, and think them as bad and cruel as their enemies." Disraeli tended to regard Turks and Christians as pawns in an exciting struggle which was being waged between Great Britain and Russia for a dominant position in the Mediterranean. To his mind, British interests were the sole test of policy, and in Gladstone's view, his interpretation of those interests excluded considerations of justice, or of humanity.

As the last round of the long duel between Gladstone and Disraeli opened, Gladstone, deriving his chief support from intellectuals, Nonconformists, and hosts of upright, God-fearing men and women many of whom had only recently been enfranchised, took his stand squarely on the moral issue. In that age his resolute insistence on that issue made his ultimate return to power inevitable. His greatest service, however, was his appreciation of the truth that the choice confronting Great Britain did not lie between support of Russia and support of Turkey. It lay between a continuance of Turkish misrule, and the adoption of the principle of national self-government in the Balkans. Gladstone constantly pointed out that the Balkan Christians were not seeking alliance with Russia, but delivery from oppression. He argued that, if Disraeli had his way, all the Christian peoples of the Near East would be driven into the arms of Russia.

Gladstone was far from being an unreserved champion of Russia. He sought to contain Russian expansion not by shoring up the decaying corpse of the Turkish Empire, but by calling into existence a string of independent Christian States from the Adriatic to the Aegean and the Black Sea. He did not want to allow Russia to become the sole champion of the principle of nationality in the Balkans; he repeatedly urged that the matter should be taken out of Russian hands and made a common European responsibility. Gladstone's approach to the problem was more realistic than Disraeli's. The future was on his side, as it had been also in the matter of the *Alabama* arbitration. Instead of identifying British interests with the integrity of Turkey, which could not, in the long run, be maintained, Gladstone identified them with the principle of nationality in the Balkans, and through that principle with the causes of Christian civilization, justice, and humanity.

Disraeli's attempt to discount the "Bulgarian Horrors" provoked an outbreak of protest meetings during the month of August, 1876, throughout Great Britain. That popular indignation gave Gladstone his opportunity to direct public opinion towards the end which he desired. He wrote calmly to Lord Granville on 7 August: "As a Party question this affords no despicable material, but there are much higher interests involved."

Gladstone was scandalized on 11 August when Disraeli, in the last speech which he made in the Commons before taking his seat in the Lords as Earl of Beaconsfield, argued that: "There is nothing to justify us in talking in such a vein of Turkey as has been, and is being, at this moment entertained. . . . What our duty is at this critical moment is to maintain the Empire of England."

Gladstone was about to talk of Turkey in a vein which succeeded in troubling momentarily, at any rate, the quietest waters of sophisticated apathy; on 29 August, after a consular report had been published which confirmed some of the worst details of the atrocities, he asked Lord Granville whether he would be shocked to hear that he proposed to write a pamphlet:

"Good ends can rarely be attained in politics without passion, and there is now, the first time for a good many years, a righteous passion."

Gladstone confided to his wife (5 September) that Granville had been lukewarm, but he added, "he could not persuade me to hold it back."

Gladstone at that moment was crippled by lumbago, but he wrote his pamphlet at white heat in four days. As he wrote, his mind was convulsed by the most violent earthquake which it had yet experienced. He laid aside a large bundle of notes, entitled *Future Retribution,* on which he had been working, labelling the wrapper: "From this I was called away to write on Bulgaria." On Monday, 4 September, 1876, his daughter Mary recorded: "Papa rushed off to London on Sunday night, pamphlet in hand, beyond anything agog over the Bulgarian horrors which pass description. The whole country is aflame—meetings all over the place."

Never had Gladstone's instinct for right-timing been more perfectly exemplified. *The Bulgarian Horrors and the Question of the East* was published by Murray on 6 September, and by the end of the month some 200,000 copies had been sold. Gladstone declared that the Turks "are, upon the whole, since the black day when they first entered Europe, the one great anti-human species of humanity." Disraeli had shamelessly condoned outrages so vile "that it passes the power of heart to conceive or of tongue and pen adequately to describe them." British and French blood and treasure, poured out like water during the

Crimean War, had served only to afford the Turks this opportunity to indulge "abominable and bestial lusts" and to enact scenes "at which Hell itself might almost blush." Women and children had been violated, roasted, and impaled; no refinement of torture had been spared; and Gladstone concluded:

"Let the Turks now carry away their abuses in the only possible manner, namely by carrying off themselves. Their Zaptiehs and their Mudirs, their Bimbashis and their Yuzbachis, their Kaimakams and their Pashas, one and all, bag and baggage, shall, I hope, clear out from the province they have desolated and profaned. This thorough riddance, this most blessed deliverance, is the only reparation we can make to the memory of those heaps on heaps of dead; to the violated purity alike of matron, of maiden, and of child. . . . There is not a criminal in a European gaol; there is not a cannibal in the South Sea Islands, whose indignation would not arise and overboil at the recital of that which has been done, which has too late been examined, but which remains unavenged; which has left behind all the foul and all the fierce passions that produced it, and which may again spring up in another murderous harvest, from the soil soaked and reeking with blood, and in the air tainted with every imaginable deed of crime and shame . . . No Government ever has so sinned; none has proved itself so incorrigible in sin or, which is the same, so impotent for reformation." He called upon the Concert of Europe, which Disraeli had done his best to disrupt, "to afford relief to the overcharged emotion of a shuddering world."

Gladstone's overcharged emotion gained only a momentary respite as a result of the publication of that fulminating pamphlet. On 9 September he addressed a great open-air meeting of his constituents at Blackheath, in pouring rain. He said that he had lived long in public life, that he had witnessed "many vivid movements of the popular mind," but that he had never witnessed "one to compare with that which during the past fortnight has taken its commencement and which has swollen with such rapidity to the dimensions of a movement truly national." He said that the question at issue had "a breadth and a height and a depth that carries it far out of the lower region of party differences, and establishes it on grounds, not of political party, not even of mere English nationality, not of Christian faith, but on the largest and broadest ground of all—the ground of our common humanity." He called upon the Russians to drive the Turks out of Bulgaria:

"I, for one, for the purposes of justice, am ready as an individual to give the right hand of friendship to Russia when her objects are just and righteous, and to say, in the name of God, 'Go on and prosper!' "

At Aylesbury, on 20 September, Disraeli accused Gladstone of using sublime sentiments for the furtherance of personal and party ends. He described him as worse than any Bulgarian horror, and was rebuked by *The Times* for bad taste. Gladstone was goaded almost beyond endurance by such language.

Disraeli was toying with the idea of occupying the Dardanelles in order to fore-stall a Russian invasion of Turkey, and at the Guildhall, on 9 November, he not only made a bitter attack on Servia and Montenegro which had declared war on Turkey; he threatened Russia openly with war if she failed to stop the flow of "volunteers" into those countries. The language which Disraeli used inspired a famous music-hall refrain:

> We don't want to fight, but by Jingo if we do,
> We've got the ships, we've got the men, we've got the money too!

Gladstone described that provocation as "almost incredible." He told the Duke of Argyll that the Jews of the East had always hated the Christians, and that he could only suppose that Disraeli was motivated by that hatred. The Duke cordially agreed. He assured Gladstone that Disraeli's "Judaic feeling" was the only genuine motive left in his mind since Lady Beaconsfield's death, and that he would be willing to sacrifice everything to it. He made Gladstone read Disraeli's favourite novel, *Tancred* (1847), in which much of the action is laid in Palestine. The theme is the corruption of Western material civilization, and the author pleads for the establishment of a new Eastern Empire, under British suzerainty, which should be guided and inspired by the mystical genius of the Hebrew race.

Gladstone always denied that he had actually loathed Disraeli, but those who knew him best were agreed that at that time his sentiment towards his rival became that of black hatred. He read in *Tancred* how the hero was advised by an Eastern potentate to "magnetize" the British Queen. Tancred was told that all he need do was to use his "beautiful voice," to whisper "fine things" into her ear. Gladstone was alarmed by the constitutional dangers which might arise as a result of the ascendancy which Disraeli had acquired over the Queen. He would have been still more alarmed if he had known the full extent to which the Queen's views had become unbalanced; before long she was urging the Cabinet to go to war, and threatening to abdicate if it ignored her outbursts.

Gladstone made no attempt to conceal his view that whatever had been objectionable in Lord Palmerston's policy had received a "tenfold development" in Disraeli. Immediately after Disraeli's death in April, 1881, Lord Acton, in a letter to Edward Burne-Jones (7 May, 1881), put Gladstone's opinion of his rival into words which "cannot be employed in public." He imagined Gladstone saying that he thought Disraeli's doctrine "false, but the man more false than his doctrine . . . that he demoralized public opinion, bargained with diseased appetites, stimulated passions, prejudices and selfish desires, that they might maintain his influence; that he weakened the Crown by approving its uncon-stitutional leanings, and the Constitution by offering any price for democratic popularity . . ." That was a moderate representation of Gladstone's opinion of Disraeli while the Eastern crisis lasted, and Disraeli reciprocated Gladstone's hatred. He gleefully told Lady Bradford (December, 1876) that the Queen really loathed Gladstone, and that she thought him mad. He told Lord Derby (October):

"Posterity will do justice to that unprincipled maniac, Gladstone—extraordinary mixture of envy, vindictiveness, hypocrisy, and superstition; and with one commanding characteristic—whether preaching, praying, speechifying, or scribbling—never a gentleman!"

It was fortunate that the Conservatives and the Liberals were both divided among themselves at that time. Lord Salisbury, Lord Derby, and Lord Carnarvon all sympathized more than Disraeli did with the aspirations of the Christian peoples in the Balkans, and they managed to exert a restraining influence over their chief's pro-Turkish policy. On the Liberal side, Lord Granville and Lord Hartington both considered that Gladstone was being much too unguarded in his encouragement of Russia, and that he did not take sufficiently into account the difficulties in the way of bringing about self-government throughout the Balkans. Lord Hartington told Lord Granville (18 December, 1876) that if Gladstone went much further, *"nothing can prevent a break-up of the Party."*

Gladstone cared little about such risks, but his family was troubled. Lady Frederick Cavendish noted in her Journal (8 October, 1876) that "Uncle William" was too headstrong. He had rebuked Lord Frederick Cavendish for meeting Turkish diplomatic representatives at dinner, and had described them as untouchable "symbols of iniquity." Gladstone complained constantly that the upper classes had betrayed their responsibility: "When did the Upper Ten Thousand ever lead the attack in the cause of humanity? Their heads are always full of class interest and the main chance."

"Of one thing," Lady Frederick recorded, "I am as certain as I have been all my life—that there is no personal ambition, or any motive but love of justice and mercy (and utter disbelief in Dizzy, I allow) in his present course."

In fashionable circles, Gladstone was now so intensely unpopular that lying stories about his rescue work in the London streets by night were freely circulated, and his family treated with contempt a spate of anonymous letters. After the breakdown of a conference at Constantinople (8 December, 1876, to 20 January, 1877), the unparalleled vehemence with which Gladstone, taking to the platform, began slowly but inexorably to arouse the indignation of the British masses against Disraeli, excited animosities which were very slow to die down. The political atmosphere remained uncomfortably heated for years, with the result that, until Gladstone's final retirement, no important issue could be debated in a dispassionate mood. The tone of moral outrage which Gladstone used with complete sincerity in talking about Turkey between 1876 and 1880 was borrowed by his opponents and often used artificially during the succeeding decade when Ireland had replaced Turkey as the principal object of Party contention.

On 24 April, 1877, after long forbearance, Russia declared war on Turkey and started an all-out drive on Constantinople. Gladstone, who had noted in his diary (15 April) that he felt it "a holy duty" to write an article in praise of Montenegro for the *Nineteenth Century,* considered that Russia had good reason for her professed resolve to discharge single-handed a duty which the European Concert had shirked. The Cabinet as a whole exercised a restraining influence over the pro-Turkish ardour of the Prime Minister and the Queen; and the Government adopted a policy of conditional neutrality for so long as no threat developed to a specified list of vital British interests.

Lord Granville and Lord Hartington set themselves the task of restraining Gladstone's pro-Russian ardour. The views of some of the Liberal rank and file were expressed in a letter from Sir William Harcourt to Sir Charles Dilke (10 October, 1876): "Gladstone and Dizzy seem to cap one another in folly and imprudence, and I don't know which has made the greatest ass of himself."

The outbreak of the Russo-Turkish War divided public opinion on an issue of foreign policy more acutely than at any period since the French Revolution, and excitement was intense when Gladstone, against the wish of all his principal colleagues, gave notice that he would move five Resolutions in the Commons on 7 May, defining his policy in the Russo-Turkish War.

The first Resolution censured Turkey for failure to fulfil her treaty obligations; the second declared that the Turks had lost all claim to British moral or material support; the third recommended self-government in the Balkans; the fourth recommended that pressure should be brought to bear on Turkey by the Great Powers; the fifth recommended the first four Resolutions to Her Majesty's Government. As soon as Gladstone's intention was known, Disraeli's Cabinet, which had been in a ferment, rallied round its chief, while Lord Granville and Lord Hartington complained that Gladstone, after formally renouncing the leadership, was threatening to split the Liberal Party and to make their position impossible. Lady Frederick Cavendish, who loved her uncle very dearly, noted in her Journal (11–17 February, 1878) that her husband had been made ill with worry on account of the tension between his brother—Lord Hartington—and Gladstone:

"They are 2 men so utterly unlike in disposition and mode of viewing things, and Uncle W. having been driven by the very nature of this great question to take a leading part (he has felt a special responsibility as the only surviving compos [1] statesman who conducted the Crimean War and was a party to the Treaty of Paris) has necessarily been prominent, though no longer leader . . . I am come round to the conviction that he should either have continued to lead the Party, or withdrawn from Parliament altogether, or taken a Peerage. It is immensely to the credit of both him and Cavendish [2] that they

---

[1] *Compos mentis,* or in possession of his faculties, Lady Frederick forgot Lord Granville and the Duke of Argyll.

[2] Lord Hartington.

have pulled together at all, and is due to the perfect honesty and sense of duty of both."

Lord Hartington made it clear to the House on 7 May, 1877, that he was not willing to support Gladstone's third and fourth Resolutions, and that he considered them inopportune. Gladstone, in speaking to the first two only, admitted frankly that the disclosure of such differences of opinion "must have had a dissipating effect on the mind of the House." He argued that "we have improperly allowed the vindication of the great cause in the East to pass into the hands of a single Power"; and he pleaded that coercion should be applied to Turkey by a united Europe after the manner in which it had been applied in the 1820s, when Greece was struggling to be free:

"But that was a policy that had no more the approval of what I may call the West End of London than the Christian cause has now. That portion of England does not express the true sentiments of England. Looking over all the great achievements that have made the last half century illustrious, not one of them would have been effected if the opinions of the West End of London had prevailed."

Gladstone rejoiced to proclaim "the knell of Turkish tyranny":

"So far as human eye can judge it is about to be destroyed. The destruction may not come in the way or by the means that we should choose; but come this boon from what hands it may, it will be a noble boon, and as a noble boon will gladly be accepted by Christendom and the world."

A future Prime Minister, Arthur James Balfour, who was then aged twenty-nine and intimate with Gladstone's family, listened to that speech from a Government back bench. The House, when Gladstone began, was hostile and impatient, and at first members streamed out of the House. Then, as reports reached them that a major eruption was in progress, they poured back until the Chamber was crowded. Balfour said that he could never erase from his memory the impression which Gladstone's speech had made on his mind. As a feat of Parliamentary eloquence, endurance, and skill, he believed that it had never been equalled. In his diary Gladstone was content to record: "Such a sense of solitary struggle I never remember . . . I rose on the main question nearly in despair . . . I spoke 2½ hours, voice lasting well. House gradually came round . . . Never did I feel weaker or more wormlike."

Replying to the debate on 14 May, Gladstone spoke with moderation. He described the Russian Emperor as "a Christian gentleman," and the Russians as a people "as capable of noble sentiments as any people in Europe." He said that if Russia succeeded, "as an Englishman I shall hide my head, but as a man I shall rejoice." Gladstone's Resolutions, which in fact constituted a plea for the coercion of Turkey, were lost by 253 to 354 votes. But for the loyalty of Lord Hartington it is likely that the figures would have been much more adverse, for contemporary estimates suggest that there were no more than sixty or seventy avowed coercionists in a House of 658.

Loyal as Lord Hartington was, he felt extremely uncomfortable. He wrote to Lord Granville (25 May, 1877):

"Mr. G. says that he has never been able to comprehend the cause of the late split, and under those circumstances it seems to me very likely that it will occur again. . . . While we remain responsible for the management of the Party in Parliament, Mr. G. cannot expect that we should entirely subordinate our own opinions and judgement to his, and unless we do, it seems inevitable that one section of the Party will follow his lead, and the other ours. . . . I think that we have some right to ask Mr. G. to look at the facts, as they exist. . . . He does not cease to be the leader of the Party by merely saying that he will not be the leader. If, as he has done since the autumn, he takes the lead, he *is* the leader, and all that he can do is to disclaim (for I do not think that he can really divest himself of it) the responsibility which naturally attends upon leadership."

Lord Granville laid that letter before Gladstone without eliciting any response, but his tact helped to ease a delicate situation. He would have been consoled a little if he had known the extent to which Disraeli's Cabinet was torn by dissensions as the Russian armies advanced. In a letter to the Queen, dated 3 November, 1877, Disraeli outlined seven distinct shades of opinion in his Cabinet, from those who wanted immediate war with Russia to one member (Lord Derby) who stood for peace at any price.

The Turks put up a brave but hopeless resistance, and early in January, 1878, the Russians, after liberating the Balkans, surged almost up to the walls of Constantinople. In that month the excitement in Great Britain was quite as intense as at the time of Napoleon's escape from Elba. A storm of anti-Russian feeling swept England south of the Trent. It was impossible in London, and difficult elsewhere, for meetings to be held in favour of peace; and Gladstone, who had his windows in Harley Street smashed by a mob, was a constant object of hostile demonstrations and a liability to the police who were responsible for his safety. He was hustled on one occasion with Mrs. Gladstone, in the streets, and even hooted (12 April, 1878) by fellow-members in the lobby of the House of Commons. He noted in his diary (11 March):

"Went to the Levée. The Princess [of Wales] for the first time received me drily. The Duke of Cambridge, black as thunder, did not even hold out his hand. Prince Christian could not but follow suit. This is not hard to bear."

Gladstone was anathematized by society, and deeply hurt on 11 January, 1878, when he was publicly described by the Duke of Sutherland, the son of his old confidante, Harriet, Duchess of Sutherland, as a Russian agent. Throughout the industrial North, however, and in Scotland, the masses had begun to hang upon every word he uttered, and to reverence him almost as a god.

On 24 January, 1878, the British Mediterranean fleet was ordered to sail through the Dardanelles to the Turkish capital. The orders were temporarily cancelled at the request of the Turks who were anxious that the Russians should be given no excuse for breaking off negotiations for an armistice; but Gladstone was stung to fury by the provocation which Disraeli offered. Speaking at Oxford on 30 January he denounced the orders to the fleet as "an act of war, a breach of international law." He admitted that he had become an agitator, and said that he had been driven to it by Disraeli:

"When you speak of the Government you mean Lord Beaconsfield. . . . Not one man in the Government has a tenth part of his tenacity of will and patient purpose . . . My purpose has been . . . to the best of my power for the last eighteen months, day and night, week by week, month by month, to counterwork as well as I could what I believe to be the purpose of Lord Beaconsfield."

Two days later, writing to Lady Bradford, Disraeli commented:

"The mask has fallen, and instead of a pious Christian, we find a vindictive fiend who confesses he has for a year and a half been dodging and manœuvring against an individual—because he was his successful rival."

On 1 February, 1878, an armistice was signed, and on 13 February orders were finally issued that the British Mediterranean fleet should sail through the Dardanelles into the Sea of Marmora. There was no opposition, but on 3 March, by the Treaty of San Stefano, which ended the Russo-Turkish War, Russia obtained far-reaching concessions from Turkey, including an outlet into the Mediterranean. Provision was made for the creation of a vast autonomous Bulgaria, which was to include Macedonia and to be under Russian tutelage. That and other provisions of the Treaty appeared unacceptable to the British Cabinet, and when the terms were made known on 22 March there was a panic on the Stock Exchange, and a shrill and prolonged public outcry.

Disraeli, who had identified his country's interests with the maintenance of Turkish integrity, was greatly concerned about prestige. Gladstone repeatedly denounced prestige as a miserable delusion, but to it, in that crisis, Disraeli appeared willing to sacrifice much. If, however, he could avoid "losing face" he was as happy to retreat from his original position and to countenance a partition of Turkey, as he would have been to comply with the Queen's hysterical desire for a useless war with Russia if he could have induced his Cabinet to agree. Disraeli wished to make Great Britain the arbiter of Europe, and on 28 March Lord Derby resigned from the Foreign Office in protest against a decision to call out the reserves, and to move Indian troops through the Suez Canal to Malta. Lord Salisbury, who succeeded Lord Derby, pressed at once for a Conference in order to resolve the deadlock between Great Britain and Russia. A deepening trade depression in Great Britain, and Russian internal unrest, provided a stimulus to agreement, and after preliminary Anglo-Russian conversations in May, a Conference opened at Berlin on 13 June, 1878, under the chairmanship of Bismarck who saw no prospect of any advantage to Germany from a European war at that moment.

Disraeli and Lord Salisbury represented Great Britain at Berlin, and by 13 July a practical compromise was ready for signature. The swollen Bulgaria of San Stefano was split into three parts, of which one—Macedonia—was returned to Turkey without any guarantee of better government. In the main, however, the settlement was based on the abandonment of the principle of Turkish territorial integrity. Many wide provinces were amputated in order to satisfy the claims of Turkey's neighbours. By a separate Anglo-Turkish convention Great Britain received the island of Cyprus, and a pledge of good government was extorted from the Turks in return for a guarantee of the future territorial integrity of Turkey in Asia.

Crippled with gout, but beaming, and leaning on Salisbury's arm, Disraeli returned to London on 16 July saying that he brought "Peace with Honour." He received an unprecedented acclaim. The Queen wanted to make him a Duke, but he would only accept the Garter. In the Gladstone family the wish was expressed that he might be made Duke of Jericho and despatched to administer his duchy; and Gladstone's first public reaction to his rival's apotheosis was silly, petulant, and ill-considered. Speaking at Southwark on 21 July, three days after Disraeli had defended the Berlin settlement in the House of Lords, Gladstone denounced it far too strongly. The country was overjoyed that the threat of imminent war had been removed, and the Treaty had much to recommend it. Gladstone's strongest abuse was reserved for the Cyprus convention, which he described as "insane . . . an act of duplicity not surpassed and rarely equalled in the history of nations."

On 27 July, Disraeli delivered a crushing retort at a fashionable banquet at which he and Lord Salisbury were entertained in the Riding School at Knightsbridge. After making the sound point that the Crimean War could have been avoided by vigorous action before its outbreak, he said that Gladstone's talk about insanity could only have proceeded from "a sophisticated rhetorician inebriated with the exuberance of his own verbosity, and gifted with an egotistical imagination that can at all times command an interminable and inconsistent series of arguments to malign an opponent and to glorify himself."

The Times scolded Disraeli mildly the next day for his "curious little burst of irritation"; Gladstone made light of it to friends, saying that he could never. "condescend" to notice Disraeli "in a personal way" because there was no "foundation of good faith" or "anything serious or sincere in any of his utterances, however vehement." Disraeli was, however, determined on that occasion to score a personal point against Gladstone, if he could. On 29 July he complained to the House of Lords that he had been described by Gladstone as "a dangerous and even a devilish character," and that Gladstone was constantly employing offensive personal expressions about his conduct and character.

Gladstone felt it necessary to write to Disraeli on 30 July to ask for details. He began his letter "Dear Lord Beaconsfield," and begged that he might be supplied with a detailed list of the times and places at which he had used the offensive and personal expressions to which Disraeli had taken exception. Disraeli was now treading on air. He had angled for that opportunity to snub Gladstone, and he replied coldly, in the third person, on the same day, that the necessary researches would take time, and that he was busy.

The matter was carried no further. As Lord Granville told the Queen (24 April, 1880):

"Lord Beaconsfield and Mr. Gladstone are men of extraordinary ability; they dislike each other more than is common among public men. Of no other politician would Lord Beaconsfield have said in public that his conduct was worse than the Bulgarian atrocities. He has a power of saying in two words that which drives a person of Mr. Gladstone's peculiar temperament into a great state of excitement."

Gladstone had learned slowly and very painfully the need for tolerance and compromise, but he was too simple, passionate, and high-minded to accept the world as it is. He never fully appreciated the limitations which are imposed by human nature upon all work that is performed by human hands, and the process of achieving a modest degree of good by reconciling a host of selfish interests was always hateful to him. Edmund Burke, in a famous passage,[3] had deified "prudence and conformity to circumstances" as "the god of this lower world." Gladstone was always himself capable of both prudence and conformity, but in his opponents, and especially in Disraeli whose personality grated on him at almost every point, he was inclined to confound those qualities with depravity, and to treat them as tokens of the Beast in *Revelation*.

Disraeli's bluff had magnificently succeeded, but Lord Salisbury admitted some twenty years later that "the wrong horse" had been backed at Berlin. The country had been led to the brink of war, and if Disraeli's gamble had failed, his fame, which is unassailable in some other fields, would have been sadly tarnished. After throwing many provinces of Turkey to the wolves as well as to the lambs, Disraeli lacked the will, and the means, to carry to its logical conclusion the policy that he had been constrained to accept in place of his own. Cyprus had been acquired ostensibly as a base from which Great Britain would be in a position to implement what was virtually a single-handed guarantee of Turkish territorial integrity in Asia against further Russian aggression, in return for a promise of better government. That promise and guarantee proved unenforceable in face of Turkish resentment at her desertion by Great Britain. Russia's ambitions received a severe check, but she retained some of her conquests in Asia and in Europe. Only a British protectorate over Asia Minor, which was impossible; large-scale money grants, which were not forthcoming; or a truly popular Turkish revolution, for which the time was not then ripe, might have availed at that period to effect the regeneration of Turkey.

[3] Letter to the Sheriffs of Bristol, 1777.

So great was the relief that war had been averted, that Disraeli's slogan, "Peace with Honour," delighted the British people. Together with the charming acquisition of Cyprus, it helped to conceal the fact that the Turkish problem in Europe had been solved to a great extent in the only possible way, by the adoption of the principle of self-government for oppressed national minorities. That was the principle which Gladstone had advocated throughout the crisis, and it was the opposite of the policy of maintaining intact the territorial integrity of Turkey which Disraeli had upheld until the last possible moment. Gladstone's hatred and distrust of Disraeli, and his delicate moral scruples about Cyprus, the acquisition of which was in many respects a brilliant coup, led him to do much less than justice to the merits of the Treaty of Berlin. It realized, at least in part, many of Gladstone's objects, and its substance was more important than the means by which it had been obtained. Gladstone had seen fit on a number of occasions to apologize publicly for his wish to make use of Russia in order to achieve his aims; his dismay at seeing those aims so unexpectedly realized by Disraeli, and the fierce language which he used, made him seem factious and inconsistent. Even the dubious arrangements about Turkey in Asia represented a fairly honest attempt in very difficult circumstances to secure reforms for which Gladstone had strongly pressed in European Turkey.

Despite the obloquy which he incurred in fashionable quarters, it is an astonishing tribute to the moral sway which Gladstone exerted over the masses whose material needs he never understood, that within eighteen months of Disraeli's apotheosis at Berlin, Gladstone should have succeeded in injecting into the minds of a majority of the British electors a potent dose of his intense, scorching conviction about the "infection" of Disraeli's personality, and the flagrant immorality of the policies which Disraeli had pursued. Thereafter, he never ceased to proclaim his faith in the political efficacy of what he called "righteous indignation," and the Queen, who thought him crazy, never forgave him. He stumped the country invoking the wrath of Heaven like some ancient Hebrew prophet; and at the General Election of 1880, when he enjoyed his finest hour, he was wafted back to Downing Street—against his innermost desire, as he was sometimes almost half inclined to believe—by the spirit of a nation which had never before been summoned from its depths by a call so heartfelt and so clear.

IMPERIALISM

[10]

The "New Imperialism": Economically or Psychologically Motivated?

$\mathcal{T}$he "new imperialism" is a term used to describe the extraordinary expansion of European rule over so-called backward peoples, which took place roughly from 1870 to the outbreak of World War I. We call it "new" because, in general, imperial systems are almost as old as history itself, and more particularly, because we can associate imperialism with the sixteenth, seventeenth, and eighteenth centuries, when some European states carved out large empires for themselves in the New World or in the East. By the early decades of the nineteenth century, most of the New World colonies had won their independence and in addition a relative indifference to colonial expansion developed in Western Europe. The old empires in the New World had been, in a sense, projections —New Spain, New England, New France—of their mother country. Colonists there had settled in uninhabited or sparsely populated lands and had brought with them the institutions or traditions of their homeland.

¶ By contrast the new imperialism was a movement in which small groups of Europeans sought to rule or to exploit relatively heavily populated areas in North Africa and Egypt, or densely populated areas in Asia, each with established institutions of their own—sovereign states, in some cases, that had entered into commercial or financial agreements with the European powers which took them over. Or, as in the case of tropical Africa and the desert regions, a whole subcontinent was divided up for what wealth or prestige it might bring without much hope of permanent European settlement.[1]

---

[1] South Africa and Algeria, with relatively extensive European settlement, could be called exceptions to the general pattern described in this paragraph. But while Britain acquired most of her South African possessions during the period of the new imperialism, she took them from

Other distinguishing features of the new imperialism were its extensiveness and the speed with which it was carried out. Not that these were intentional in the beginning. The British Empire is often described as having been created in "fits of absent mindedness." But one wheel turned another, so that by the 1890's a competitive drive for empire was on between the Western European powers.[2] It helped to sweep them into World War I, but even the war did not entirely halt the imperialist drive until France and Britain, not without some mutual recriminations and suspicion, had divided the Near Eastern parts of the defeated Ottoman Empire between them and acquired most of the former German-African colonies under the mandate system. Looking back on the course of little more than half a century, Parker T. Moon could observe in 1926 that:

Of ancient imperialism, of the empires of Alexander, of Cyrus, of Caesar, we have heard much and of Napoleon's spectacular exploits every schoolboy has read. But the realms conquered by military emperors of past ages were baubles, trifles compared with the far-flung dominions which have been won, more often with the pen than by the sword, in our own supposedly prosaic generation . . .

Little as the general public may realize the fact, imperialism is the most impressive achievement and the most momentous world-problem of our age. Perhaps this statement should be thrust home. More than half of the world's land surface, and more than a billion human beings, are included in the colonies and "backward countries," dominated by a few imperialist nations.[3]

The problem that has occupied historians and others, and one which the three selections that follow treat, is the motivation of this imperial expansion. At the time many justifications for imperialism were given—control of raw materials and new markets, sometimes called neo-mercantilism, military security, outlets for surplus population, and the civilizing mission or "white man's burden."

Under analysis and on the basis of performance, however, these justifications have had to be in large part, and in some cases entirely discarded. A first and penetrating criticism of these justifications was made by the British economist, J. A. Hobson, in 1902 in *Imperialism, A Study*. Published during the heyday of empire Hobson's book caused an immediate sensation and has had a continuing influence on subsequent writings on the subject. Hobson was one of

---

what might be called a native, white population: the Boers, descendants of seventeenth-century Dutch settlers in the Cape Colony. The conquest of Algeria began in 1830; by 1870 there were three hundred thousand European settlers and a structure for colonization established there which had no counterpart in the subsequently acquired areas of the French Empire.

[2] As will be seen in the selections that follow, the United States, Japan, and Russia were also affected by imperialism, but their efforts cannot be placed in the same category as those of the European powers.

[3] Parker Thomas Moon, *Imperialism and World Politics* (New York: The Macmillan Company, 1926), p. 1.

the first to point out that while imperialism benefited only a few interests in the nation, it burdened the collectivity with a heavy cost.

This being the case, Hobson asked what were the motive forces of imperialism. When it came to immediate causes, there were many, including such noneconomic forces as patriotism, adventure, the influence of the military, etc. Hobson also considered trade, but found it a negligible factor in comparison with the return from overseas investment. Thus he was led to conclude that investment and allied financial interests seeking an outlet outside the nation for surplus savings constituted the "economic taproot" of imperialism. The first selection below gives the essence of this interpretation and Hobson's criticism of the process.

The second selection, by William L. Langer, a distinguished diplomatic historian and authority on international relations, is a reappraisal of Hobson's *Imperialism*. Because of the influence of Hobson's economic interpretation, Langer's work is also an indirect critique of the neo-Marxian writers who took it over. But Langer also analyzes the noneconomic aspects of Hobson's thought and finds fruitful insights in them, including a precedent for Schumpeter's interpretation of imperialism as an atavism.[4] Because Langer wrote in 1935, he also relates the then-current manifestations of imperialism—Italy in Abyssinia and Japanese interference on the Chinese mainland—to his own emphasis in this article on the psychological and political factors in imperialism.

The third selection, from *The End of Empire* (1959) by John Strachey, a British writer on social and economic problems who has served in Parliament and in government, gives us a later perspective on imperialism. Strachey uses two chapters in the history of British imperialism, the acquisition of the Nile Valley and of South Africa, to illustrate his point that the economic interpretation is "the best guiding thread to an understanding of the imperialist policies of the highly developed capitalisms of the recent past." Strachey thus brings us back to an interpretation closer to Hobson's central thesis than those chronologically intervening interpretations, such as Langer's, which stress other factors.[5]

In an interesting digression, Strachey also evaluates the balance sheet of British rule in Egypt—a favorable one when Lord Cromer left in 1907, less so when British control ended. But this change was in great part due to the extraordinary rise in population which British improvements brought about. A brief discussion of the Nasser regime and some other remarks of Strachey's remind us that in our own time we have witnessed the rapid break up of colonial empires—a phenomenon as impressive in its own way as imperialism was in its. We might ponder the fact that the new imperialism reached flood tide and then ebbed away within the memory of living men.

[4] Schumpeter's interesting interpretation is now available in English. J. A. Schumpeter, *Imperialism and Social Classes* (Noonday Press: 1955); also in paperback (Meridian Books).

[5] A more extended and theoretical explanation of his position is offered by Strachey in chap. 7 of *The End of Empire*.

THE ECONOMIC ASPECTS OF IMPERIALISM

J. A. Hobson

* * *

BY FAR the most important economic factor in Imperialism is the influence relating to investments. The growing cosmopolitanism of capital has been the greatest economic change of recent generations. Every advanced industrial nation has been tending to place a larger share of its capital outside the limits of its own political area, in foreign countries, or in colonies, and to draw a growing income from this source.

No exact or even approximate estimate of the total amount of the income of the British nation derived from foreign investments is possible. We possess, however, in the income tax assessments an indirect measurement of certain large sections of investments, from which we can form some judgment as to the total size of the income from foreign and colonial sources, and the rate of its growth.

These returns give us a measure of the amount and growth of the investments effected by British citizens in foreign and colonial stocks of a public or semi-public character, including foreign and colonial public securities, railways, etc. The income from these sources is computed as follows:—

	£
1884	33,829,124
1888	46,978,371
1892	54,728,770
1896	54,901,079
1900	60,266,886
1903	63,828,715

From this table it appears that the period of energetic Imperialism coincided with a remarkable growth in the income for foreign investments.

These figures, however, only give the foreign income which can be identified as such. The closer estimates made by Sir R. Giffen and others warrant the belief that the actual income derived from foreign and colonial investments

From J. A. Hobson, *Imperialism, A Study* (London: George Allen & Unwin, Ltd., 1902), 3rd edition revised 1938, pp. 51–61, 80–93. Reprinted by permission of the publisher and The Macmillan Company, New York.

amounted to not less than £100,000,000, the capital value of the same reaching a sum of about £2,000,000,000.

Income tax returns and other statistics descriptive of the growth of these investments indicate that the total amount of British investments abroad at the end of the nineteenth century cannot be set down at a lower figure than this. Considering that Sir R. Giffen regarded as "moderate" the estimate of £1,700,000,000 in 1892, the figure here named is probably below the truth.

Now, without placing any undue reliance upon these estimates, we cannot fail to recognise that in dealing with these foreign investments we are facing the most important factor in the economics of Imperialism. Whatever figures we take, two facts are evident. First, that the income derived as interest upon foreign investments enormously exceeded that derived as profits upon ordinary export and import trade. Secondly, that while our foreign and colonial trade, and presumably the income from it, were growing but slowly, the share of our import values representing income from foreign investments was growing very rapidly.

In a former chapter I pointed out how small a proportion of our national income appeared to be derived as profits from external trade. It seemed unintelligible that the enormous costs and risks of the new Imperialism should be undertaken for such small results in the shape of increase to external trade, especially when the size and character of the new markets acquired were taken into consideration. The statistics of foreign investments, however, shed clear light upon the economic forces which dominate our policy. While the manufacturing and trading classes make little out of their new markets, paying, if they knew it, much more in taxation than they get out of them in trade, it is quite otherwise with the investor.

It is not too much to say that the modern foreign policy of Great Britain has been primarily a struggle for profitable markets of investment. To a larger extent every year Great Britain has been becoming a nation living upon tribute from abroad, and the classes who enjoy this tribute have had an ever-increasing incentive to employ the public policy, the public purse, and the public force to extend the field of their private investments, and to safeguard and improve their existing investments. This is, perhaps, the most important fact in modern politics, and the obscurity in which it is wrapped has constituted the gravest danger to our State.

What was true of Great Britain was true likewise of France, Germany, the United States, and of all countries in which modern capitalism had placed large surplus savings in the hands of a plutocracy or of a thrifty middle class. A well-recognised distinction is drawn between creditor and debtor countries. Great Britain had been for some time by far the largest creditor country, and the policy by which the investing classes used the instrument of the State for private business purposes is most richly illustrated in the history of her wars and annexations. But France, Germany, and the United States were advancing fast along the same path. The nature of these imperialist operations is thus set forth by the Italian economist Loria:

"When a country which has contracted a debt is unable, on account of the slenderness of its income, to offer sufficient guarantee for the punctual payment of interest, what happens? Sometimes an out-and-out conquest of the debtor country follows. Thus France's attempted conquest of Mexico during the second empire was undertaken solely with the view of guaranteeing the interest of French citizens holding Mexican securities. But more frequently the insufficient guarantee of an international loan gives rise to the appointment of a financial commission by the creditor countries in order to protect their rights and guard the fate of their invested capital. The appointment of such a commission literally amounts in the end, however, to a veritable conquest. We have examples of this in Egypt, which has to all practical purposes become a British province, and in Tunis, which has in like manner become a dependency of France, who supplied the greater part of the loan. The Egyptian revolt against the foreign domination issuing from the debt came to nothing, as it met with invariable opposition from capitalistic combinations, and Tel-el-Kebir's success bought with money, was the most brilliant victory wealth has ever obtained on the field of battle." [1]

But, though useful to explain certain economic facts, the terms "creditor" and "debtor," as applied to countries, obscure the most significant feature of this Imperialism. For though, as appears from the analysis given above, much, if not most, of the debts were "public," the credit was nearly always private, though sometimes, as in the case of Egypt, its owners succeeded in getting their Government to enter a most unprofitable partnership, guaranteeing the payment of the interest, but not sharing in it.

Aggressive Imperialism, which costs the taxpayer so dear, which is of so little value to the manufacturer and trader, which is fraught with such grave incalculable peril to the citizen, is a source of great gain to the investor who cannot find at home the profitable use he seeks for his capital, and insists that his Government should help him to profitable and secure investments abroad.

If, contemplating the enormous expenditure on armaments, the ruinous wars, the diplomatic audacity or knavery by which modern Governments seek to extend their territorial power, we put the plain, practical question, *Cui bono?* the first and most obvious answer is, the investor.

The annual income Great Britain derives from commissions on her whole foreign and colonial trade, import and export, was estimated by Sir R. Giffen [2] at £18,000,000 for 1899, taken at 2½ per cent., upon a turnover of £800,000,000. This is the whole that we are entitled to regard as profits on external trade. Considerable as this sum is, it cannot serve to yield an economic motive-power

---

[1] Loria, *The Economic Foundations of Politics*, p. 273 (George Allen & Unwin).
[2] *Journal of the Statistical Society*, vol. xlii, p. 9.

adequate to explain the dominance which business considerations exercise over our imperial policy. Only when we set beside it some £90,000,000 or £100,000,-000, representing pure profit upon investment, do we understand whence the economic impulse to Imperialism is derived.

Investors who have put their money in foreign lands, upon terms which take full account of risks connected with the political conditions of the country, desire to use the resources of their Government to minimise these risks, and so to enhance the capital value and the interest of their private investments. The investing and speculative classes in general have also desired that Great Britain should take other foreign areas under her flag in order to secure new areas for profitable investments and speculation.

If the special interest of the investor is liable to clash with the public interest and to induce a wrecking policy, still more dangerous is the special interest of the financier, the general dealer in investments. In large measure the rank and file of the investors are, both for business and for politics, the cat'spaws of the great financial houses, who use stocks and shares not so much as investments to yield them interest, but as material for speculation in the money market. In handling large masses of stocks and shares, in floating companies, in manipulating fluctuations of values, the magnates of the Bourse find their gain. These great businesses—banking, broking, bill discounting, loan floating, company promoting—form the central ganglion of international capitalism. United by the strongest bonds of organisation, always in closest and quickest touch with one another, situated in the very heart of the business capital of every State, controlled, so far as Europe is concerned, chiefly by men of a single and peculiar race, who have behind them many centuries of financial experience, they are in a unique position to manipulate the policy of nations. No great quick direction of capital is possible save by their consent and through their agency. Does any one seriously suppose that a great war could be undertaken by any European State, or a great State loan subscribed, if the house of Rothschild and its connexions set their face against it?

Every great political act involving a new flow of capital, or a large fluctuation in the values of existing investments, must receive the sanction and the practical aid of this little group of financial kings. These men, holding their realised wealth and their business capital, as they must, chiefly in stocks and bonds, have a double stake, first as investors, but secondly and chiefly as financial dealers. As investors, their political influence does not differ essentially from that of the smaller investors, except that they usually possess a practical control of the businesses in which they invest. As speculators or financial dealers they constitute, however, the gravest single factor in the economics of Imperialism.

To create new public debts, to float new companies, and to cause constant considerable fluctuations of values are three conditions of their profitable business. Each condition carries them into politics, and throws them on the side of Imperialism.

The public financial arrangements for the Philippine war put several millions of dollars into the pockets of Mr. Pierpont Morgan and his friends; the China-Japan war, which saddled the Celestial Empire for the first time with a public debt, and the indemnity which she will pay to her European invaders in connexion with the recent conflict, bring grist to the financial mills in Europe; every railway or mining concession wrung from some reluctant foreign potentate means profitable business in raising capital and floating companies. A policy which rouses fears of aggression in Asiatic states, and which fans the rivalry of commercial nations in Europe, evokes vast expenditure on armaments, and ever-accumulating public debts, while the doubts and risks accruing from this policy promote that constant oscillation of values of securities which is so profitable to the skilled financier. There is not a war, a revolution, an anarchist assassination, or any other public shock, which is not gainful to these men; they are harpies who suck their gains from every new forced expenditure and every sudden disturbance of public credit. To the financiers "in the know" the Jameson raid was a most advantageous coup, as may be ascertained by a comparison of the "holdings" of these men before and after that event; the terrible sufferings of England and South Africa in the war, which was a sequel of the raid, has been a source of immense profit to the big financiers who have best held out against the uncalculated waste, and have recouped themselves by profitable war contracts and by "freezing out" the smaller interests in the Transvaal. These men are the only certain gainers from the war, and most of their gains are made out of the public losses of their adopted country or the private losses of their fellow-countrymen.

The policy of these men, it is true, does not necessarily make for war; where war would bring about too great and too permanent a damage to the substantial fabric of industry, which is the ultimate and essential basis of speculation, their influence is cast for peace, as in the dangerous quarrel between Great Britain and the United States regarding Venezuela. But every increase of public expenditure, every oscillation of public credit short of this collapse, every risky enterprise in which public resources can be made the pledge of private speculations, is profitable to the big money-lender and speculator.

The wealth of these houses, the scale of their operations, and their cosmopolitan organisation make them the prime determinants of imperial policy. They have the largest definite stake in the business of Imperialism, and the amplest means of forcing their will upon the policy of nations.

In view of the part which the non-economic factors of patriotism, adventure, military enterprise, political ambition, and philanthropy play in imperial expansion, it may appear that to impute to financiers so much power is to take a too narrowly economic view of history. And it is true that the motor-power of Imperialism is not chiefly financial: finance is rather the governor of the imperial engine, directing the energy and determining its work: it does not constitute the fuel of the engine, nor does it directly generate the power. Finance manipulates the patriotic forces which politicians, soldiers, philanthropists, and traders generate; the enthusiasm for expansion which issues from these sources, though strong and genuine, is irregular and blind; the financial interest has those qualities of concentration and clear-sighted calculation which are needed to set Imperialism to work. An ambitious statesman, a frontier soldier, an over-zealous missionary, a pushing trader, may suggest or even initiate a step of imperial expansion, may assist in educating patriotic public opinion to the urgent need of some fresh advance, but the final determination rests with the financial power. The direct influence exercised by great financial houses in "high politics" is supported by the control which they exercise over the body of public opinion through the Press, which, in every "civilised" country, is becoming more and more their obedient instrument. While the specifically financial newspaper imposes "facts" and "opinions" on the business classes, the general body of the Press comes more and more under the conscious or unconscious domination of financiers. The case of the South African Press, whose agents and correspondents fanned the martial flames in this country, was one of open ownership on the part of South African financiers, and this policy of owning newspapers for the sake of manufacturing public opinion is common in the great European cities. In Berlin, Vienna, and Paris many of the influential newspapers have been held by financial houses, which used them, not primarily to make direct profits out of them, but in order to put into the public mind beliefs and sentiments which would influence public policy and thus affect the money market. In Great Britain this policy has not gone so far, but the alliance with finance grows closer every year, either by financiers purchasing a controlling share of newspapers, or by newspaper proprietors being tempted into finance. Apart from the financial Press, and financial ownership of the general Press, the City has notoriously exercised a subtle and abiding influence upon leading London newspapers, and through them upon the body of the provincial Press, while the entire dependence of the Press for its business profits upon its advertising columns has involved a peculiar reluctance to oppose the organised financial classes with whom rests the control of so much advertising business. Add to this the natural sympathy with a sensational policy which a cheap Press always manifests, and it becomes evident that the Press has been strongly biased towards Imperialism, and has lent itself with great facility to the suggestion of financial or political Imperialists who have desired to work up patriotism for some new piece of expansion.

Such is the array of distinctively economic forces making for Imperialism, a large loose group of trades and professions seeking profitable business and lucrative employment from the expansion of military and civil services, and from the expenditure on military operations, the opening up of new tracts of territory and trade with the same, and the provision of new capital which these operations require, all these finding their central guiding and directing force in the power of the general financier.

The play of these forces does not openly appear. They are essentially parasites upon patriotism, and they adapt themselves to its protecting colours. In the mouth of their representatives are noble phrases, expressive of their desire to extend the area of civilisation, to establish good government, promote Christianity, extirpate slavery, and elevate the lower races. Some of the business men who hold such language may entertain a genuine, though usually a vague, desire to accomplish these ends, but they are primarily engaged in business, and they are not unaware of the utility of the more unselfish forces in furthering their ends. Their true attitude of mind was expressed by Mr. Rhodes in his famous description of "Her Majesty's Flag" as "the greatest commercial asset in the world." [3]

* * *

. . . Overproduction in the sense of an excessive manufacturing plant, and surplus capital which could not find sound investments within the country, forced Great Britain, Germany, Holland, France to place larger and larger portions of their economic resources outside the area of their present political domain, and then stimulate a policy of political expansion so as to take in the new areas. The economic sources of this movement are laid bare by periodic trade-depressions due to an inability of producers to find adequate and profitable markets for what they can produce. The Majority Report of the Commission upon the Depression of Trade in 1885 put the matter in a nutshell. "That, owing to the nature of the times, the demand for our commodities does not increase at the same rate as formerly; that our capacity for production is consequently in excess of our requirements, and could be considerably increased at short notice; that this is due partly to the competition of the capital which is being steadily accumulated in the country." The Minority Report straightly imputed the condition of affairs to "over-production." Germany was in the early 1900's suffering severely from what is called a glut of capital and of manufacturing power: she had to have new markets; her Consuls all over the world were "hustling" for trade; trading settlements were forced upon Asia Minor; in East and West Africa, in China and elsewhere the German Empire was impelled to a policy of colonization and protectorates as outlets for German commercial energy.

Every improvement of methods of production, every concentration of ownership and control, seems to accentuate the tendency. As one nation after an-

---

[3] It will be observed that this, like not a few other words of revelation, has been doctored in the volume, *Cecil Rhodes: his Political Life and Speeches*, by "Vindex" (p. 823).

o

other enters the machine economy and adopts advanced industrial methods, it becomes more difficult for its manufacturers, merchants, and financiers to dispose profitably of their economic resources, and they are tempted more and more to use their Governments in order to secure for their particular use some distant undeveloped country by annexation and protection.

The process, we may be told, is inevitable, and so it seems upon a superficial inspection. Everywhere appear excessive powers of production, excessive capital in search of investment. It is admitted by all business men that the growth of the powers of production in their country exceeds the growth in consumption, that more goods can be produced than can be sold at a profit, and that more capital exists than can find remunerative investment.

It is this economic condition of affairs that forms the taproot of Imperialism. If the consuming public in this country·raised its standard of consumption to keep pace with every rise of productive powers, there could be no excess of goods or capital clamorous to use Imperialism in order to find markets: foreign trade would indeed exist, but there would be no difficulty in exchanging a small surplus of our manufactures for the food and raw material we annually absorbed, and all the savings that we made could find employment, if we chose, in home industries.

There is nothing inherently irrational in such a supposition. Whatever is, or can be, produced, can be consumed, for a claim upon it, as rent, profit, or wages, forms part of the real income of some member of the community, and he can consume it, or else exchange it for some other consumable with some one else who will consume it. With everything that is produced a consuming power is born. If then there are goods which cannot get consumed, or which cannot even get produced because it is evident they cannot get consumed, and if there is a quantity of capital and labour which cannot get full employment because its products cannot get consumed, the only possible explanation of this paradox is the refusal of owners of consuming power to apply that power in effective demand for commodities.

It is, of course, possible that an excess of producing power might exist in particular industries by misdirection, being engaged in certain manufactures, whereas it ought to have been engaged in agriculture or some other use. But no one can seriously contend that such misdirection explains the recurrent gluts and consequent depressions of modern industry, or that, when over-production is manifest in the leading manufactures, ample avenues are open for the surplus capital and labour in other industries. The general character of the excess of producing power is proved by the existence at such times of large bank stocks of idle money seeking any sort of profitable investment and finding none.

The root questions underlying the phenomena are clearly these: "Why is it that consumption fails to keep pace automatically in a community with power of production?" "Why does under-consumption or over-saving occur?" For it is evident that the consuming power, which, if exercised, would keep tense the reins of production, is in part withheld, or in other words is "saved" and stored up for investment. All saving for investment does not imply slackness of production; quite the contrary. Saving is economically justified, from the social standpoint, when the capital in which it takes material shape finds full employment in helping to produce commodities which, when produced, will be consumed. It is saving in excess of this amount that causes mischief, taking shape in surplus capital which is not needed to assist current consumption, and which either lies idle, or tries to oust existing capital from its employment, or else seeks speculative use abroad under the protection of the Government.

But it may be asked, "Why should there be any tendency to over-saving? Why should the owners of consuming power withhold a larger quantity for savings than can be serviceably employed?" Another way of putting the same question is this, "Why should not the pressure of present wants keep pace with every possibility of satisfying them?" The answer to these pertinent questions carries us to the broadest issue of the distribution of wealth. If a tendency to distribute income or consuming power according to needs were operative, it is evident that consumption would rise with every rise of producing power, for human needs are illimitable, and there could be no excess of saving. But it is quite otherwise in a state of economic society where distribution has no fixed relation to needs, but is determined by other conditions which assign to some people a consuming power vastly in excess of needs or possible uses, while others are destitute of consuming power enough to satisfy even the full demands of physical efficiency. The following illustration may serve to make the issue clear. "The volume of production has been constantly rising owing to the development of modern machinery. There are two main channels to carry off these products—one channel carrying off the product destined to be consumed by the workers, and the other channel carrying off the remainder to the rich. The workers' channel is in rockbound banks that cannot enlarge, owing to the competitive wage system preventing wages rising *pro rata* with increased efficiency. Wages are based upon cost of living, and not upon efficiency of labour. The miner in the poor mine gets the same wages per day as the miner in the adjoining rich mine. The owner of the rich mine gets the advantage—not his labourer. The channel which conveys the goods destined to supply the rich is itself divided into two streams. One stream carries off what the rich 'spend' on themselves for the necessities and luxuries of life. The other is simply an 'overflow' stream carrying off their 'savings.' The channel for spending, i.e. the amount wasted by the rich in luxuries, may broaden somewhat, but owing to the small number of those rich enough to indulge in whims it can never be greatly enlarged, and at any rate it bears such a small proportion to the other channel that in no event can much hope of avoiding a flood of capital be hoped for from this division. The rich will never be so ingenious as to spend enough to prevent over-production. The great safety overflow channel which has been continuously more and more widened and deepened to carry off the ever-increasing flood of new capital is that division of the stream which carried the savings of the rich, and this is not only suddenly found to be incapable of further enlargement, but actually seems to be in the process of being dammed up." [4]

Though this presentation over-accentuates the cleavage between rich and poor and over-states the weakness of the workers, it gives forcible and sound expression to a most important and ill-recognised economic truth. The "overflow" stream of savings is of course fed not exclusively from the surplus income of "the rich"; the professional and industrial middle classes, and to some slight extent the workers, contribute. But the "flooding" is distinctly due to the automatic saving of the surplus income of rich men. This is of course particularly true of America, where multi-millionaires rise quickly and find themselves in possession of incomes far exceeding the demands of any craving that is known to them. To make the metaphor complete, the overflow stream must be represented as reentering the stream of production and seeking to empty there all the "savings" that it carries. Where competition remains free, the result is a chronic congestion of productive power and of production, forcing down home prices, wasting large sums in advertising and in pushing for orders, and periodically causing a crisis followed by a collapse, during which quantities of capital and labour lie unemployed and unremunerated. The prime object of the trust or other combine is to remedy this waste and loss by substituting regulation of output for reckless over-production. In achieving this it actually narrows or even dams up the old channels of investment, limiting the overflow stream to the exact amount required to maintain the normal current of output. But this rigid limitation of trade, though required for the separate economy of each trust, does not suit the trust-maker, who is driven to compensate for strictly regulated industry at home by cutting new foreign channels as outlets for his productive power and his excessive savings. Thus we reach the conclusion that Imperialism is the endeavour of the great controllers of industry to broaden the channel for the flow of their surplus wealth by seeking foreign markets and foreign investments to take off the goods and capital they cannot sell or use at home.

The fallacy of the supposed inevitability of imperial expansion as a necessary outlet for progressive industry is now manifest. It is not industrial progress that demands the opening up of new markets and areas of investment, but mal-distribution of consuming power which prevents the absorption of commodities and capital within the country. The over-saving which is the economic root of Imperialism is found by analysis to consist of rents, monopoly profits, and other unearned or excessive elements of income, which, not being earned

[4] *The Significance of the Trust,* by H. G. Wilshire.

by labour of head or hand, have no legitimate *raison d'être*. Having no natural relation to effort of production, they impel their recipients to no corresponding satisfaction of consumption: they form a surplus wealth, which, having no proper place in the normal economy of production and consumption, tends to accumulate as excessive savings. Let any turn in the tide of politico-economic forces divert from these owners their excess of income and make it flow, either to the workers in higher wages, or to the community in taxes, so that it will be spent instead of being saved, serving in either of these ways to swell the tide of consumption—there will be no need to fight for foreign markets or foreign areas of investment.

Many have carried their analysis so far as to realise the absurdity of spending half our financial resources in fighting to secure foreign markets at times when hungry mouths, ill-clad backs, ill-furnished houses indicate countless unsatisfied material wants among our own population. If we may take the careful statistics of Mr. Rowntree[5] for our guide, we shall be aware that more than one-fourth of the population of our towns is living at a standard which is below bare physical efficiency. If, by some economic readjustment, the products which flow from the surplus saving of the rich to swell the overflow streams could be diverted so as to raise the incomes and the standard of consumption of this inefficient fourth, there would be no need for pushful Imperialism, and the cause of social reform would have won its greatest victory.

It is not inherent in the nature of things that we should spend our natural resources on militarism, war, and risky, unscrupulous diplomacy, in order to find markets for our goods and surplus capital. An intelligent progressive community, based upon substantial equality of economic and educational opportunities, will raise its standard of consumption to correspond with every increased power of production, and can find full employment for an unlimited quantity of capital and labour within the limits of the country which it occupies. Where the distribution of incomes is such as to enable all classes of the nation to convert their felt wants into an effective demand for commodities, there can be no over-production, no underemployment of capital and labour, and no necessity to fight for foreign markets.

The most convincing condemnation of the current economy is conveyed in the difficulty which producers everywhere experience in finding consumers for their products: a fact attested by the prodigious growth of classes of agents and middlemen, the multiplication of every sort of advertising, and the general increase of the distributive classes. Under a sound economy the pressure would be reversed: the growing wants of progressive societies would be a constant stimulus to the inventive and operative energies of producers, and would form a constant strain upon the powers of production. The simultaneous excess of

[5] *Poverty: A Study of Town Life.*

all the factors of production, attested by frequently recurring periods of trade depression, is a most dramatic exhibition of the false economy of distribution. It does not imply a mere miscalculation in the application of productive power, or a brief temporary excess of that power; it manifests in an acute form an economic waste which is chronic and general throughout the advanced industrial nations, a waste contained in the divorcement of the desire to consume and the power to consume.

If the apportionment of income were such as to evoke no excessive saving, full constant employment for capital and labour would be furnished at home. This, of course, does not imply that there would be no foreign trade. Goods that could not be produced at home, or produced as well or as cheaply, would still be purchased by ordinary process of international exchange, but here again the pressure would be the wholesome pressure of the consumer anxious to buy abroad what he could not buy at home, not the blind eagerness of the producer to use every force or trick of trade or politics to find markets for his "surplus" goods.

The struggle for markets, the greater eagerness of producers to sell than of consumers to buy, is the crowning proof of a false economy of distribution. Imperialism is the fruit of this false economy; "social reform" is its remedy. The primary purpose of "social reform," using the term in its economic signification, is to raise the wholesome standard of private and public consumption for a nation, so as to enable the nation to live up to its highest standard of production. Even those social reformers who aim directly at abolishing or reducing some bad form of consumption, as in the Temperance movement, generally recognise the necessity of substituting some better form of current consumption which is more educative and stimulative of other tastes, and will assist to raise the general standard of consumption.

There is no necessity to open up new foreign markets; the home markets are capable of indefinite expansion. Whatever is produced in England can be consumed in England, provided that the "income" or power to demand commodities, is properly distributed. This only appears untrue because of the unnatural and unwholesome specialisation to which this country has been subjected, based upon a bad distribution of economic resources, which has induced an overgrowth of certain manufacturing trades for the express purpose of effecting foreign sales. If the industrial revolution had taken place in an England founded upon equal access by all classes to land, education and legislation, specialisation in manufactures would not have gone so far (though more intelligent progress would have been made, by reason of a widening of the area of selection of inventive and organising talents); foreign trade would have been less important, though more steady; the standard of life for all portions of the population would have been high, and the present rate of national consumption would probably have given full, constant, remunerative employment to a far larger quantity of private and public capital than is now employed.[6] For the over-saving or wider consumption that is traced to excessive incomes of the rich is a suicidal economy, even from the exclusive standpoint of capital; for consumption alone vitalises capital and makes it capable of yielding profits. An economy that assigns to the "possessing" classes an excess of consuming power which they cannot use, and cannot convert into really serviceable capital, is a dog-in-the-manger policy. The social reforms which deprive the possessing classes of their surplus will not, therefore, inflict upon them the real injury they dread; they can only use this surplus by forcing on their country a wrecking policy of Imperialism. The only safety of nations lies in removing the unearned increments of income from the possessing classes, and adding them to the wage-income of the working classes or to the public income, in order that they may be spent in raising the standard of consumption.

Social reform bifurcates, according as reformers seek to achieve this end by raising wages or by increasing public taxation and expenditure. These courses are not essentially contradictory, but are rather complementary. Working-class movements aim, either by private co-operation or by political pressure on legislative and administrative government, at increasing the proportion of the national income which accrues to labour in the form of wages, pensions, compensation for injuries, etc. State Socialism aims at getting for the direct use of the whole society an increased share of the "social values" which arise from the closely and essentially co-operative work of an industrial society, taxing property and incomes so as to draw into the public exchequer for public expenditure the "unearned elements" of income, leaving to individual producers those incomes which are necessary to induce them to apply in the best way their economic energies, and to private enterprises those businesses which do not breed monopoly, and which the public need not or cannot undertake. These are not, indeed, the sole or perhaps the best avowed objects of social reform movements. But for the purposes of this analysis they form the kernel.

Trade Unionism and Socialism are thus the natural enemies of Imperialism, for they take away from the "imperialist" classes the surplus incomes which form the economic stimulus of Imperialism.

This does not pretend to be a final statement of the full relations of these forces. When we come to political analysis we shall perceive that the tendency of Imperialism is to crush Trade Unionism and to "nibble" at or parasitically

[6] The classical economists of England, forbidden by their theories of parsimony and of the growth of capital to entertain the notion of an indefinite expansion of home markets by reason of a constantly rising standard of national comfort, were early driven to countenance a doctrine of the necessity of finding external markets for the investment of capital. So J. S. Mill: "The expansion of capital would soon reach its ultimate boundary if the boundary itself did not continually open and leave more space" (*Political Economy*). And before him Ricardo (in a letter to Malthus): "If with every accumulation of capital we could take a piece of fresh fertile land to our island, profits would never fall."

exploit State Socialism. But, confining ourselves for the present to the narrowly economic setting, Trade Unionism and State Socialism may be regarded as complementary forces arrayed against Imperialism, in as far as, by diverting to working-class or public expenditure elements of income which would otherwise be surplus savings, they raise the general standard of home consumption and abate the pressure for foreign markets. Of course, if the increase of working-class income were wholly or chiefly "saved," not spent, or if the taxation of unearned incomes were utilised for the relief of other taxes borne by the possessing classes, no such result as we have described would follow. There is, however, no reason to anticipate this result from trade-union or socialistic measures. Though no sufficient natural stimulus exists to force the well-to-do classes to spend in further luxuries the surplus incomes which they save, every working-class family is subject to powerful stimuli of economic needs, and a reasonably governed State would regard as its prime duty the relief of the present poverty of public life by new forms of socially useful expenditure.

But we are not here concerned with what belongs to the practical issues of political and economic policy. It is the economic theory for which we claim acceptance—a theory which, if accurate, dispels the delusion that expansion of foreign trade, and therefore of empire, is a necessity of national life.

Regarded from the standpoint of economy of energy, the same "choice of life" confronts the nation as the individual. An individual may expend all his energy in acquiring external possessions, adding field to field, barn to barn, factory to factory—may "spread himself" over the widest area of property, amassing material wealth which is in some sense "himself" as containing the impress of his power and interest. He does this by specialising upon the lower acquisitive plane of interest at the cost of neglecting the cultivation of the higher qualities and interests of his nature. The antagonism is not indeed absolute. Aristotle has said, "We must first secure a livelihood and then practise virtue." Hence the pursuit of material property as a reasonable basis of physical comfort would be held true economy by the wisest men; but the absorption of time, energy, and interest upon such quantitative expansion at the necessary cost of starving the higher tastes and faculties is condemned as false economy. The same issue comes up in the business life of the individual: it is the question of intensive *versus* extensive cultivation. A rude or ignorant farmer, where land is plentiful, is apt to spread his capital and labour over a large area, taking in new tracts and cultivating them poorly. A skilled, scientific farmer will study a smaller patch of land, cultivate it thoroughly, and utilise its diverse properties, adapting it to the special needs of his most remunerative markets. The same is true of other businesses; even where the economy of large-scale production is greatest there exists some limit beyond which the wise business man will not go, aware that in doing so he will risk by enfeebled management what he seems to gain by mechanical economies of production and market.

Everywhere the issue of quantitative *versus* qualitative growth comes up. This is the entire issue of empire. A people limited in number and energy and in the land they occupy have the choice of improving to the utmost the political and economic management of their own land, confining themselves to such accessions of territory as are justified by the most economical disposition of a growing population; or they may proceed, like the slovenly farmer, to spread their power and energy over the whole earth, tempted by the speculative value or the quick profits of some new market, or else by mere greed of territorial acquisition, and ignoring the political and economic wastes and risks involved by this imperial career. It must be clearly understood that this is essentially a choice of alternatives; a full simultaneous application of intensive and extensive cultivation is impossible. A nation may either, following the example of Denmark or Switzerland, put brains into agriculture, develop a finely varied system of public education, general and technical, apply the ripest science to its special manufacturing industries, and so support in progressive comfort and character a considerable population upon a strictly limited area; or it may, like Great Britain, neglect its agriculture, allowing its lands to go out of cultivation and its population to grow up in towns, fall behind other nations in its methods of education and in the capacity of adapting to its uses the lastest scientific knowledge, in order that it may squander its pecuniary and military resources in forcing bad markets and finding speculative fields of investment in distant corners of the earth, adding millions of square miles and of unassimilable population to the area of the Empire.

The driving forces of class interest which stimulate and support this false economy we have explained. No remedy will serve which permits the future operation of these forces. It is idle to attack Imperialism or Militarism as political expedients or policies unless the axe is laid at the economic root of the tree, and the classes for whose interest Imperialism works are shorn of the surplus revenues which seek this outlet.

A Critique of Imperialism

William L. Langer

IT IS now roughly fifty years since the beginning of that great outburst of expansive activity on the part of the Great Powers of Europe which we have come to call "imperialism." And it is about a generation since J. A. Hobson published his "Imperialism: a Study," a book which has served as a starting point for most later discussions and which has proved a perennial inspiration for writers of the most diverse schools. A reappraisal of it is therefore decidedly in order. The wonder is that it has not been undertaken sooner.

Since before the outbreak of the World War the theoretical writing on imperialism has been very largely monopolized by the so-called Neo-Marxians, that is, by those who, following in the footsteps of the master, have carried on his historical analysis from the critique of capitalism to the study of this further phase, imperialism, the significance of which Marx himself did not appreciate and the very existence of which he barely adumbrated. The Neo-Marxians, beginning with Rudolf Hilferding and Rosa Luxemburg, have by this time elaborated a complete theory, which has recently been expounded in several ponderous German works. The theory hinges upon the idea of the accumulation of capital, its adherents holding that imperialism is nothing more nor less than the last stage in the development of capitalism—the stage in which the surplus capital resulting from the system of production is obliged by ever diminishing returns at home to seek new fields for investment abroad. When this surplus capital has transformed the whole world and remade even the most backward areas in the image of capitalism, the whole economic-social system will inevitably die of congestion.

That the classical writers of the socialistic school derived this basic idea from Hobson's book there can be no doubt.[1] Lenin himself admitted, in his "Imperialism, the Latest Stage of Capitalism," that Hobson gave "a very good and accurate description of the fundamental economic and political traits of

[1] I strongly suspect that Hobson, in turn, took over the idea from the very bourgeois American financial expert, Charles A. Conant, whose remarkable article, "The Economic Basis of Imperialism," in the *North American Review*, September 1898, p. 326–340, is now forgotten, but deserves recognition.

From *Foreign Affairs*, XIV (October 1935), pp. 102–19. Copyright by the Council on Foreign Relations, Inc., New York. Reprinted by permission.

imperialism," and that Hobson and Hilferding had said the essentials on the subject. This, then, has been the most fruitful contribution of Hobson's essay. When we examine his ideas on this subject we refer indirectly to the larger part of the writing on imperialism since his day.

As a matter of pure economic theory it is most difficult to break down the logic of the accumulation theory. It is a fact that since the middle of the last century certain countries—first England, then France, Germany and the United States—have exported large amounts of capital, and that the financial returns from these investments in many instances came to overshadow completely the income derived by the lending countries from foreign trade. It is also indisputable that industry embarked upon the road to concentration and monopoly, that increased efficiency in production led to larger profits and to the amassing of ever greater surpluses of capital. We must recognize further that, as a general rule, the return from investments abroad was distinctly above the return on reinvestment in home industry. In other words, the postulates of the socialist theory undoubtedly existed. There is no mentionable reason why the development of the capitalist system should not have had the results attributed to it.

But, as it happens, the actual course of history refutes the thesis. The course of British investment abroad shows that there was a very considerable export of capital before 1875, that is, during the climax of anti-imperialism in England. Between 1875 and 1895, while the tide of imperialism was coming to the full, there was a marked falling off of foreign investment. Capital export was then resumed on a large scale in the years before the war, though England was, in this period, already somewhat disillusioned by the outcome of the South African adventure and rather inclined to be skeptical about imperialism. Similar observations hold true of the United States. If the promulgation of the Monroe Doctrine was an act of imperialism, where was the export of capital which ought to have been its condition? Let us concede that the war with Spain was an imperialist episode. At that time the United States was still a debtor nation, importing rather than exporting capital. In Russia, too, the heyday of imperialism coincided with a period of heavy borrowing rather than of lending.

There is this further objection to be raised against the view of Hobson and his Neo-Marxian followers, that the export of capital seems to have little direct connection with territorial expansion. France, before the war, had plenty of capital to export, and some of her earliest and most vigorous imperialists, like Jules Ferry, declared that she required colonies in order to have adequate fields for the placement of this capital. But when France had secured colonies, she did not send her capital to them. By far the larger part of her exported funds went to Russia, Rumania, Spain and Portugal, Egypt and the Ottoman Empire. In 1902 only two or two and a half billion francs out of a total foreign investment of some 30 or 35 billion francs was placed in the colonies. In 1913 Britain had more money invested in the United States than in any colony or other foreign country. Less than half of her total export of capital had been to other parts of the Empire. The United States put more capital into the development of Canada than did England; and when, after the war, the United States became a great creditor nation, 43 percent of her investment was in Latin America, 27 percent in Canada and Newfoundland, and 22 percent in European countries. What she sent to her colonies was insignificant. Or let us take Germany, which in 1914 had about 25 billion marks placed abroad. Of this total only three percent was invested in Asia and Africa, and of that three percent only a small part in her colonies. Pre-war Russia was a great imperialist power, but Russia had to borrow from France the money invested in her Far Eastern projects. In our own day two of the most outspokenly imperialist powers, Japan and Italy, are both nations poor in capital. Whatever the urge that drives them to expansion, it cannot be the need for the export of capital.

At the height of the imperialist tide, let us say from 1885 to 1914, there was much less talk among the advocates of expansion about the need for foreign investment fields than about the need for new markets and for the safeguarding of markets from the tariff restrictions of competitors. It is certain that in the opinion of contemporaries that was the mainspring of the whole movement. But this economic explanation, like the other, has not been borne out by the actual developments. Very few colonies have done even half of their trading with the mother country and many have done less. Taken in the large it can be proved statistically that the colonial trade has always played a relatively unimportant part in the total foreign commerce of the great industrial nations. These nations have always been each other's best customers and no amount of rivalry and competition has prevented their trade from following, not the flag, but the price-list. The position of Canada within the British Empire did not prevent her from levying tariffs against British goods, nor from developing exceedingly close economic relations with the United States. In the pre-war period German commerce with the British possessions was expanding at a relatively higher rate than was Britian's.

If one must have an economic interpretation of imperialism, one will probably find its historical evolution to have been something like this: In the days of England's industrial preëminence she was, by the very nature of the case, interested in free trade. In the palmiest days of Cobdenism she exported manufactured goods to the four corners of the earth, but she exported also machinery and other producers' goods, thereby preparing the way for the industrialization of the continental nations and latterly of other regions of the world. In order to protect their infant industries from British competition, these new industrial Powers threw over the teachings of the Manchester school and began to set up tariffs. The result was that the national markets were set aside, to a large extent, for home industry. British trade was driven to seek new markets, where the process was repeated. But the introduction of protective tariffs had this further effect, that it made possible the organization of cartels and trusts, that is, the concentration of industry, the increase of production and the lowering of costs. Surplus goods and low prices caused the other industrial Powers likewise to look abroad for additional markets, and, while this development was taking place, technological improvements were making transportation and communication safer and more expeditious. The exploration of Africa at that time was probably pure coincidence, but it contributed to the movement toward trade and expansion and the growth of a world market. Fear that the newly opened areas of the world might be taken over by others and then enclosed in tariff walls led directly to the scramble for territory in Asia and Africa.

The socialist writers would have us believe that concentration in industry made for monopoly and that the banks, undergoing the same process of evolution, were, through their connection with industry, enabled to take over control of the whole capitalist system. They were the repositories of the surplus capital accumulated by a monopolistic system and they were therefore the prime movers in the drive for imperial expansion, their problem being to find fields for the investment of capital. This is an argument which does violence to the facts as they appear historically. The socialist writers almost to a man argue chiefly from the example of Germany, where cartelization came early and where the concentration of banking and the control of industry by the banks went further than in most countries. But even in Germany the movement towards overseas expansion came before the growth of monopoly and the amalgamation of the banks. In England, the imperialist country *par excellence,* there was no obvious connection between the two phenomena. The trust movement came late and never went as far as in Germany. The same was true of the consolidation of the banking system. One of the perennial complaints in England was the lack of proper coördination between the banks and industry. To a certain extent the English exported capital because the machinery for foreign investment was better than the organization for home investment. In the United States, to be sure, there was already a pronounced concentration of· industry when the great outburst of imperialism came in the last years of the past century, but in general the trust movement ran parallel to the movement for territorial expansion. In any event, it would be hard to disprove the contention that the growth of world trade and the world market brought on the tendency toward better organization and concentration in industry, rather than the reverse. It is obvious not only that one large unit can manufacture more cheaply than many small ones, but that it can act more efficiently in competition with others in the world market.

But this much is clear—that territorial control of extra-European territory solved neither the trade problem nor the question of surplus capital. The white colonies, which were the best customers, followed their own economic interests and not even tariff restrictions could prevent them from doing so. In the backward, colored, tropical colonies, which could be more easily controlled and exploited, it proved difficult to develop a market, because of the low purchasing power of the natives. The question of raw materials, of which so much has always been made, also remained open. The great industrial countries got but a fraction of their raw materials from the colonies, and the colonies themselves continued to show a tendency to sell their products in the best market. As for the export of capital, that continued to flow in an ever broader stream, not because the opportunities for investment at home were exhausted, but because the return from foreign investment was apt to be better and because, in many cases, foreign investment was the easier course. Capital flowed from the great industrial countries of Europe, but it did not flow to their colonies. The United States and Canada, Latin America (especially the Argentine) and even old countries like Austria-Hungary and Russia, got the bulk of it. The export of capital necessarily took the form of the extension of credit, which in turn implied the transfer of goods. Not infrequently the granting of loans was made conditional on trade concessions by the borrowing country. So we come back to the question of trade and tariffs. In a sense the export of capital was nothing but a device to stimulate trade and to circumvent tariff barriers, which brings us back to the coincidence of the movement for protection and the movement toward imperialism.

This may seem like an oversimplified explanation and it probably is. Some may argue that imperialism is more than a movement toward territorial expansion and that financial imperialism in particular lays the iron hand of control on many countries supposedly independent. But if you try to divorce imperialism from territorial control you will get nowhere. Practically all writers on the subject have been driven to the conclusion that the problem cannot be handled at all unless you restrict it in this way. When Hobson wrote on imperialism, he had reference to the great spectacle of a few Powers taking over tremendous areas in Africa and Asia. Imperialism is, in a sense, synonymous with the appropriation by the western nations of the largest part of the rest of the world. If you take it to be anything else, you will soon be lost in nebulous concepts and bloodless abstractions. If imperialism is to mean any vague interference of traders and bankers in the affairs of other countries, you may as well extend it to cover any form of influence. You will have to admit cultural imperialism, religious imperialism, and what not. Personally I prefer to stick by a measurable, manageable concept.

But even though Hobson's idea, that imperialism "is the endeavor of the great controllers of industry to broaden the channel for the flow of their surplus wealth by seeking foreign markets and foreign investments to take off the goods and capital they cannot sell or use at home," proved to be the most stimulating and fertile of his arguments, he had the very correct idea that imperialism was also a "medley of aims and feelings." He had many other contributory explanations of the phenomenon. For example, he was keenly aware of the relationship between democracy and imperialism. The enfranchisement of the working classes and the introduction of free education had brought the rank and file of the population into the political arena. One result of this epoch-making change was the rise of the so-called yellow press, which catered to the common man's love of excitement and sensationalism. Northcliffe was one of the first to sense the value of imperialism as a "talking point." Colonial adventure and far-away conflict satisfied the craving for excitement of the industrial and white-collar classes which had to find some outlet for their "spectatorial lust." The upper crust of the working class, as Lenin admitted, was easily converted to the teaching of imperialism and took pride in the extension of empire.

No doubt this aspect of the problem is important. The mechanization of humanity in an industrial society is a phenomenon with which we have become all too familiar, and every thoughtful person now recognizes the tremendous dangers inherent in the powers which the demagogue can exercise through the press, the motion picture and the radio. In Hobson's day propaganda was still carried on primarily through the press, but later developments were already foreshadowed in the activities of a Northcliffe or a Hearst. Hobson himself was able to show how, during the war in South Africa, the English press took its information from the South African press, which had been brought very largely under the control of Rhodes and his associates. Even at that time Hobson and others were pointing out how imperialistic capital was influencing not only the press, but the pulpit and the universities. Indeed, Hobson went so far as to claim that the great inert mass of the population, who saw the tangled maze of world movements through dim and bewildered eyes, were the inevitable dupes of able, organized interests who could lure or scare or drive them into any convenient course.

Recognizing as we do that control of the public mind involves the most urgent political problems of the day, it is nevertheless important to point out that there is nothing inexorable about the connection of propaganda and imperialism. Even if you admit that a generation ago moneyed interests believed that imperialism was to their advantage, that these interests exercised a far-reaching control over public opinion, and that they used this control to dupe the common man into support of imperial ventures, it is obvious that at some other time these same interests might have different ideas with regard to their own welfare, just as it is evident that public opinion may be controlled by some other agency—the modern dictator, for example.

But the same thing is not true of another influence upon which Hobson laid great stress, namely the biological conception of politics and international relations. During the last years of the nineteenth century the ideas of "social Darwinism," as it was called, carried everything before them. Darwin's catchwords—the struggle for existence and the survival of the fittest—which he himself always refused to apply to the social organism, were snapped up by others who were less scrupulous, and soon became an integral part of popular and even official thought on foreign affairs. It not only served to justify the ruthless treatment of the "backward" races and the carving up *in spe* of the Portuguese, Spanish, Ottoman and Chinese Empires and of other "dying nations," as Lord Salisbury called them, but it put the necessary imprimatur on the ideas of conflict between the great imperialistic Powers themselves, and supplied a divine sanction for expansion. It was currently believed, in the days of exuberant imperialism, that the world would soon be the preserve of the great states—the British, the American and the Russian—and it was deduced from this belief that survival in the struggle for existence was in itself adequate evidence of superiority and supernatural appointment. The British therefore looked upon their empire as a work of the divine will, while the Americans and Russians were filled with the idea of a manifest destiny. It will be at once apparent that glorification of war and joy in the conflict was intimately connected with the evolutionary mentality. Hobson, the most determined of anti-imperialists, was finally driven to define the whole movement as "a depraved choice of national life, imposed by self-seeking interests which appeal to the lusts of quantitative acquisitiveness and of forceful domination surviving in a nation from early centuries of animal struggle for existence."

The last phrases of this quotation will serve to lead us to the consideration of what has proved to be another fruitful thought of Hobson. He speaks, in one place, of imperialism as a sociological atavism, a remnant of the roving instinct, just as hunting and sport are left-overs of the physical struggle for existence. This idea of the roving instinct has made but little appeal to later writers, but the basic interpretation of imperialism as an atavism underlies the ingenious and highly intelligent essay of Joseph Schumpeter, "Zur Soziologie der Imperialismen," [2] the only work from the bourgeois side which has had anything like the influence exerted by the writers of the socialist school. Schumpeter, who is an eminent economist, worked out a most convincing argument to prove that imperialism has nothing to do with capitalism, and that it is certainly not a development of capitalism. Capitalism, he holds, is by nature opposed to expansion, war, armaments and professional militarism, and imperialism is nothing but an atavism, one of those elements of the social structure which cannot be explained from existing conditions, but only from

---

[2] "Zur Soziologie der Imperialismen," by Josef Schumpeter. Tübingen: Mohr, 1919, 76 p.

the conditions of the past. It is, in other words, a hang-over from a preceding economic order. Imperialism antedates capitalism, going back at least to the time of the Assyrians and Egyptians. It is, according to Schumpeter, the disposition of a state to forceful expansion without any special object and without a definable limit. Conquests are desired not so much because of their advantages, which are often questionable, but merely for the sake of conquest, success and activity.

Schumpeter's theory is in some ways extravagant, but it has served as the starting point for some very interesting speculation, especially among German scholars of the liberal persuasion. It is now fairly clear, I think, that the Neo-Marxian critics have paid far too little attention to the imponderable, psychological ingredients of imperialism. The movement may, without much exaggeration, be interpreted not only as an atavism, as a remnant of the days of absolute monarchy and mercantilism, when it was to the interest of the prince to increase his territory and the number of his subjects, but also as an aberration, to be classed with the extravagances of nationalism. Just as nationalism can drive individuals to the point of sacrificing their very lives for the purposes of the state, so imperialism has driven them to the utmost exertions and the extreme sacrifice, even though the stake might be only some little known and at bottom valueless part of Africa or Asia. In the days when communication and economic interdependence have made the world one in so many ways, men still interpret international relations in terms of the old cabinet policies, they are still swayed by out-moded, feudalistic ideas of honor and prestige.

In a sense, then, you can say that there is, in every people, a certain indefinable national energy, which may find expression in a variety of ways.

As a general rule great domestic crises and outbursts of expansion follow each other in the history of the world. In many of the continental countries of Europe, and for that matter in our own country, great internal problems were fought out in the period before 1870. The energies which, in Germany and Italy, went into the victory of the national cause, soon began to project themselves beyond the frontiers. While the continental nations were settling great issues between them, England sat "like a bloated Quaker, rubbing his hands at the roaring trade" he was carrying on. In those days the British cared very little for their empire. Many of them would have felt relieved if the colonies had broken away without a fuss. But, says Egerton, the best-known historian of British colonial policy, when the Germans and the French began to show an interest in colonial expansion, then the British began to think that there must be some value as yet undiscovered in the colonies. They not only started a movement to bind the colonies and the mother country more closely together, but they stretched out their hands for more. In the end they, who had the largest empire to begin with, got easily the lion's share of the yet unappropriated parts of the world. Some thought they were engaged in the fulfilment of a divine mission to abolish slavery, to spread the gospel, to clothe and educate the heathen. Others thought they were protecting the new markets from dangerous competitors, securing their supply of raw materials, or finding new fields for investment. But underlying the whole imperial outlook there was certainly more than a little misapprehension of economics, much self-delusion and self-righteousness, much misapplication of evolutionary teaching and above all much of the hoary tradition of honor, prestige, power and even plain combativeness. Imperialism always carries with it the connotation of the *Imperator* and of the tradition of rule. It is bound up with conscious or subconscious ideas of force, of brutality, of ruthlessness. It was these traits and tendencies that were so vividly expressed in the poetry and stories of Kipling, and it was his almost uncanny ability to sense the emotions of his time and people that made him the greatest apostle of imperialism.

We shall not go far wrong, then, if we stress the psychological and political factors in imperialism as well as its economic and intellectual elements. It was, of course, connected closely with the great changes in the social structure of the western world, but it was also a projection of nationalism beyond the boundaries of Europe, a projection on a world scale of the time-honored struggle for power and for a balance of power as it had existed on the Continent for centuries. The most casual perusal of the literature of imperialism will reveal the continued potency of these atavistic motives. In a recent number of this very journal a leading Italian diplomat, explaining the policy of the Duce, recurred again and again to the failure of the other countries to appreciate the fact that Italy is a young and active country "animated by new spiritual values." [3] By the much-decried Corfu episode of 1923, Mussolini, to give a concrete example, "called Europe's attention to the respect due to the new Italy and to the reawakened energies of the Italian people." In the present Ethiopian crisis there is not very much suggestion of economic or civilizing motives on the part of the Italians; rather the Duce holds before his followers the prospect of revenge for the defeat at Adua (reminiscent of Britian's thirst to avenge Gordon) and promises them a glorious future. Not long ago he spoke to a group of veterans among the ruins of ancient Rome and told them that every stone surrounding them should remind them that Rome once dominated the world by the wisdom of her rule and the might of her arms and that "nothing forbids us to believe that what was our destiny yesterday may again become our destiny tomorrow." [4] In much the same spirit an eminent Japanese statesman expressed himself recently in FOREIGN AFFAIRS: "As soon as the Meiji Restoration lifted the ban

[3] Dino Grandi, "The Foreign Policy of the Duce," FOREIGN AFFAIRS, July 1934, pp. 551–66.
[4] *New York Times,* June 17, 1935.

on foreign intercourse, the long-pent-up energy of our race was released, and with fresh outlook and enthusiasm the nation has made swift progress. When you know this historical background and understand this overflowing vitality of our race, you will see the impossibility of compelling us to stay still within the confines of our little island home. We are destined to grow and expand overseas." [5] It is the same emphasis given by the Italian diplomat to the need for an outlet for surplus energies.

It is, of course, true that both Italy and Japan have a serious population problem and that Japan, at any rate, has an economic argument to back her imperialistic enterprises in Manchuria and China. But it has been shown long ago that the acquisition of new territory has no direct bearing on the population problem and that emigrants go where their interest calls them, not where their governments would like to have them go. As for Japan's economic needs, it may at least be questioned whether she would not be better off if she avoided political and military commitments in China. Her cheap goods have made very extensive inroads in all the markets of the world, and her eventual conquest of the whole Chinese market is perhaps inevitable. Far from having gained much from her recent policy, she has had to face boycotts and other forms of hostility. In this case, certainly, one might debate whether the game is worth the candle.

Baron Wakatsuki, whose statement is quoted above, was careful to avoid mention of a factor in Japanese imperialism which, as every well-informed person knows, is probably the real explanation of Japanese policy. After the Meiji Restoration it was more the exuberance and bellicosity of the military caste in Japan than the enthusiasm of the country at large which determined the policy of the government. It one reads modern Japanese history aright one will find that from 1870 onward the military classes were constantly pressing upon the government for action in Korea. Only with the greatest difficulty did the civil authorities stave off this pressure. In 1894 the Tokyo government more or less rushed into the war with China in order to avoid a dangerous domestic crisis. In other words, the ideas of honor and patriotism were appealed to in order to divert attention from the parliamentary conflict which was then raging. After the Japanese victory it was the military men who, against the better judgment of men like Count Ito and Baron Mutsu, insisted on the cession of the Liaotung Peninsula, which netted Japan nothing but the intervention of Russia, Germany, and France. We need not pursue this subject in all its minute details. The point I want to make is that in the case of Japan, as in the case of many other countries, it is easier to show that the military and official classes are a driving force behind the movement for expansion than to show that a clique of nefarious bankers or industrialists is the

[5] Baron Reijiro Wakatsuki, "The Aims of Japan," Foreign Affairs, July 1935, pp. 583–94.

determining factor. Business interests may have an interest in the acquisition of territory, or they may not. But military and official classes almost always have. War is, for the soldiers, a profession, and it is no mere chance that war and imperialism are so commonly lumped together. For officials, expansion means new territories to govern and new jobs to be filled.

Hobson, with his pronouncedly economic approach to the problem, held that "the struggle for markets, the greater eagerness of producers to sell than of consumers to buy, is the crowning proof of a false economy of distribution," of which imperialism is the fruit. The remedy, he thought, lay in "social reform." "There is no necessity to open up new foreign markets," he maintained; "the home markets are capable of indefinite expansion." These contentions sound familiar enough in this day of world depression. Whether the home markets are capable of indefinite expansion is a question on which the economic internationalists and the advocates of autarchy hold different opinions. The interesting thing for us to consider, however, is the fact that movements towards autarchy should have developed at all and that so much stress should now be laid upon the problems of redistribution of wealth, of building up purchasing power, and, in general, of domestic social reform. The current of activity has shifted distinctly from expansion to revolution, peaceful or violent. Perhaps it may be argued from this that the socialist thesis regarding imperialism is now being proved; that capitalism has already transformed the backward areas to such an extent that the markets are ruined, and that the capitalist system is rapidly choking. This view might be acceptable if it were not for the fact that the colonies and backward areas are still very far from developed and if it were not for the further fact that before the depression the colonial trade with the older countries was steadily increasing. In the last five years, to be sure, international commerce has sunk to an unbelievably low point, but the difficulty has been chiefly with the trade between the great industrial Powers themselves. It is quite conceivable that the crisis is primarily due to the special situation arising from the World War and that the root of the troubles lies in the impossibility of fitting tremendous international payments into the existing framework of trade relations. The fantastic tariff barriers which have been set up on all sides have simply aggravated a situation which has been developing since the teachings of Cobdenism first began to fall into disrepute.

But whatever the true explanation of our present difficulties, very few voices are raised in favor of a solution by the methods of imperialism. Indeed, the movement toward autarchy is in a way a negation of imperialism. Economically we have been disillusioned about imperialism. We have learned that colonies do not pay. Britain's expenditure for the defense of the empire alone is enormous, yet she has never yet devised a method by which anything like a commensurate return could be secured. The French military outlay on the colonies in 1913 was more than five hundred million francs, at a time when the entire trade of France with her colonies came to hardly three times that figure. Similar statistics could be quoted for Germany, and it is a well-known fact that the colonies of both Spain and Portugal were much more of a liability than an asset.

In the same way it has turned out that foreign investments of capital are not all that they were expected to be. The higher returns from colonial investments have often been counterbalanced by the greater insecurity that went with them. European countries had more than one opportunity to learn the lesson even before the war. We need only recall the Argentine fiasco of 1890 and the wildcat Kaffir Boom in South African securities in 1895 as classical examples of what might happen. But of course all these instances are completely dwarfed by the experiences of the postwar—or perhaps better, the pre-depression decade. Foreign investments have caused acute international tensions and have resulted in phenomena like American dollar diplomacy in Latin America. The expenditure has been immense and what has been salvaged has been unimpressive enough. The nations of the world are still on the lookout for markets, as they have been for centuries, but the peoples of the world have become more or less convinced that the markets, if they can be got at all, can be got only by the offering of better and cheaper goods and not by occupation, political control or forceful exploitation. As for foreign investments, no one has any stomach for them and most of those fortunate enough to have money to invest would be glad to learn of a safe investment at home. The assurance of needed sources for raw materials is as much if not more of a problem today than it was a generation ago, but there is little sense in taking over the expensive administration of tropical or other territory to guarantee a source of raw materials, because somehow or other it usually turns out that the other fellow has the materials that you want, and it has long since become obvious that the idea of controlling sources of all the materials you may need is a snare and a delusion.

In 1919, at the Paris Peace Conference, the struggle among the victors for the colonial spoils of the vanquished reached the proportions of the epic and the heroic. It seems like a long time ago, because so much has happened since and because we have come to see that in large measure it was a case of much ado about nothing. To meet the demands for some sort of ethics in imperialism, the German colonies and large parts of the Ottoman Empire were set up as mandates under the League, the principle being wholly in consonance with the demand already put forward by Hobson that there be an "international council" which should "accredit a civilized nation with the duty of educating a lower race." But no one will deny that the mandate-seeking nations had other than purely altruistic motives. Though they should have known better, they still proceeded on the principle that some good was to be gotten out of colonies.

But the sequel has shown that, just as the more backward regions imported producers' as well as consumers' goods from Europe and thereby laid the foundation for an independent economy by no means favorable to European industrialism, so they imported from Europe the ideas of self-determination and nationalism. Since the disaster suffered by the Italians at Adua in 1896 Europe has had ample evidence of what may happen when these ideas are taken up by native populations and defended with European implements of war. The story of the last generation has been not only the story of the westernization of the world, but also the story of the revolt of Asia and Africa against the western nations. True to Hobson's prediction, the attacks of imperialism on the liberties and existence of weaker races have stimulated in them a corresponding excess of national self-consciousness. We have had much of this in India and China and we have lived to witness the rise of Mustapha Kemal and Ibn Saud, to whom, for all we know, may be added the name of Hailé Selassié. France has had her battles in Morocco and the United States has at last come to appreciate the depth of resentment and ill-feeling against her in Latin America.

That these are not matters to be trifled with has by this time penetrated not only the minds of the governing classes and of the industrial and financial magnates, but also the mind of the man in the street. Who is there in England, for example, who puts much store by the mandates? Since the war England has allowed Ireland to cut loose and she is trying, as best she can, to put India on her own. Egypt has been given her independence and the mandate over Iraq has been abandoned. It would probably not be overshooting the mark to say that the British would be glad to get out of the Palestine hornet's nest if they could, and it is whispered that they would not be averse to turning back to Germany some of the African colonies. But it is not at all clear that Hitler really wants the colonies back. There obviously are other things that he wants more and the return of the colonies is more a question of vindication and prestige than anything else. In like fashion the United States has reversed the rambunctious policy of interference and disguised control in Mexico, the Caribbean and Latin America. We are about to withdraw from the Philippines with greater haste than the Filipinos desire or than many Americans think wise or decent. Neither Britain nor America has shown much real appetite for interfering against Japan in the Far East. Public opinion would not tolerate it, and even among those who have interests at stake there seems to be a growing opinion that if the Japanese wish to make the expenditure in blood and money necessary to restore order and security in China, they ought to be given a universal blessing.

France, to be sure, has shown no inclination to give up any of her vast colonial possessions, while Italy and Japan are both on the war-path. But the case of France is a very special one. Being less industrialized than England,

Germany or the United States, she never felt to the same extent as those countries the urge for markets and sources of raw material. The imperialist movement was in France always something of an artificial and fictitious thing, fanned by a small group of enthusiasts. It takes a great and splendid colonial exposition to arouse much popular interest in the Greater France. It might be supposed, therefore, that France would be among the first nations to beat the retreat. But there is a purely military consideration that holds her back. Like England, she can draw troops from her colonies in time of crisis. In the British case this is always something of a gambling proposition. England has no choice but to defend the empire so long as it exists, but whether the dominions and colonies will support England is a question which they decide in each case as they choose. They elected to support the mother country in the Boer War and in the World War, but they did not choose to support her in the Near East when Mustapha Kemal drove the Greeks from Anatolia and appeared at the Straits in 1922.

With France the situation is different. In 1896 an eminent French statesman told Tsar Nicholas II, in reply to an inquiry, that France needed her colonies if only because they could supply her with man-power. The exploitation of that man-power reached large dimensions during the World War and it is now an important and generally recognized factor in France's military establishment. So far, so good, but the French must realize, and no doubt they do realize, that this may not go on forever. Who can say how long the "Senegalese" will be willing to pour out their blood in defense of French interests? Who can say when they will make use of the training and equipment that has been given them and turn upon their own masters? The spectacle of black troops holding down the population in the Rhineland was one which roused misgivings in the minds of many who think of western civilization in terms other than those of might and political exigency.

As for Japan and Italy, perhaps the less said the better. Japan is motivated by ideas which were current in Europe a generation ago and which are now being discarded. She has serious economic problems which have come with industrialism, and she is trying to solve them by means of territorial expansion and political control. But the peculiar thing is that, with all her progress, little headway has been made in the direction of breaking the power of the former feudal, military caste. Ideas of conquest, power and prestige are still dominant and they explain, more perhaps than economic considerations, the rampant imperialism of the present day.

The Italians, on the other hand, have involved themselves deeply in the Ethiopian affair for reasons which are hardly at all economic. If they were to conquer Abyssinia, what good would it really do them? The country is populated by some six to eight million warlike natives and it would cost a fortune in blood and treasure, poured out over a long term of years, to hold them in subjection. Can anyone seriously maintain that such an area would prove a suitable one for the settlement of very considerable numbers of Italian colonists, or that emigrants from Italy would choose Ethiopia so long as the door in Latin America is even the least bit open? It may be that there are oil reserves or gold in the country, but talk on this point is to a large extent speculation. The story of Ethiopia's wealth will, in all probability, be exploded as was the myth of Yunnan's treasure in the nineties. Taken in the large, it has been proved on many an occasion that "pegging out claims for the future" is in the long run a poor proposition. But Dino Grandi has said in so many words, in the article quoted above, that Italy's claims to empire were ignored and neglected at Paris in 1919 and that Italy must now teach the world to respect her. If that is indeed the object, Mussolini has failed to note the trend of world opinion since the war. The greatness of a nation is no longer necessarily measured by the extent of the national color on the maps of the world, and on many sides empire has come to be regarded indeed as the "white man's burden." In other words, Il Duce is behind the times. I think much of the disapproval of the Italian policy in the world at large is due to the fact that other nations have grown out of the mentality that has produced the Ethiopian crisis.

Imperialism as it existed in the last two generations will never again be possible, for the world has been definitely divided up and there are but very few unclaimed areas still to be appropriated. There may be exchanges of territory between the imperial Powers, and there will undoubtedly be aggression by one against another, but, in the large, territory has, in this age of rabid nationalism, become so sacred that its permanent transference has become more and more difficult and in many places almost impossible. The tightness of the territorial settlement in Europe long since became such that changes were possible only as the result of a great cataclysm, and the same petrifaction of the territorial *status quo* now tends to hold good of the general world settlement. If we are to give up empire, it will probably be to the natives to whom the territory originally belonged. If the tide of native resistance continues to rise, as it is likely to do, that course will become inevitable.

* * *

THE NEW IMPERIALISM

John Strachey

FROM ABOUT 1870 onwards a new wave of imperialism surged out upon the world. Two countries of Western Europe, Britain and France, led the way. But they were avidly imitated. Germany, America and Japan hastened, late but formidable, to share in the partition of the world which was taking place. Even some of the smaller states—Belgium, Holland, Portugal—managed to get or retain a share. Vast but still semi-feudal structures such as Austria-Hungary and Russia were effectively stirred.

Britain, both because she still just held the lead in industrial development and because she already possessed a nucleus of empire, essentially India (but also the West Indies), held over from the mercantile epoch, took the lion's share in this new wave of imperialism. J. A. Hobson, in his book, *Imperialism,* writing in 1902, gives the table of British territorial acquisitions in the thirty years between 1870 and 1900.

These acquisitions add up to a territory of 4,754,000 square miles with a population estimated in 1902 at 88 millions. It is important to remember that this whole "Colonial Office Empire," as it might be called, was, essentially, created only seventy or eighty years ago. Therefore its life span, since it is now in rapid dissolution, will prove to have been under a century.

It must not be thought, however, that the lion's share was the only one. On the contrary, French acquisitions in this period, principally in Africa (but also Indo-China), were territorially impressive (3,500,000 square miles but with only 26 million inhabitants). Belgium got what proved to be the rich prize of the Congo (900,000 square miles, 8½ million inhabitants). Moreover, Germany at length united, and year by year becoming the most formidable industrial power in Europe, began her colonial career in this period. She annexed, in the same 30 years, a million square miles of territory with 13 million inhabitants. Japan, which only started out on her staggeringly successful course of self-modernisation under forced draft in 1867 acquired her first colonies in this period, as a result of her wars with China at the end, and with Russia just after the end, of the century.

The United States of America also gave what appeared to be unmistakable signs of launching herself upon the imperialist course. She cleaned up fragments

From *The End of Empire*, by John Strachey. © Copyright 1959 by John Strachey. Reprinted by permission of Random House, Inc., New York and Victor Gollancz, Ltd., London.

of the empire of Spain (Cuba, Puerto Rico, the Philippines) and asserted, in a degree varying all the way from the establishment of a virtual protectorate in Panama to a mere reinterpretation of the Monroe Doctrine elsewhere, her general overlordship of the Americas. Finally, during the whole of this period Russia was pushing out her boundaries, eastward and southward over Asia. As usual, her development was a special case peculiar to herself. In particular, her acquisitions were landlocked and contiguous to her metropolitan mass, instead of maritime and scattered over the continents.

This dry catalogue of the territorial acquisitions of the imperial states in the heyday of the new imperialism, *i.e.*, in the forty years from 1870 to 1914, can convey but a faint impression of the overwhelming power of the Western drive towards the conquest of the world. Nor will it give us any clue as to the causes of this explosive phenomenon. Once again it will be best to describe some concrete examples. Let us briefly consider two cases of British expansion during the period, namely the acquisition of *de facto* sovereignty over the Nile Valley and the conquest of South Africa. It so happens that each of these acts of imperial acquisition had as one of its principal agents an exceptionally interesting, and articulate, imperialist: Cromer in Egypt, Milner in South Africa. The records of these two remarkable men may help us to identify the motives which drove forward the new imperialism.

Between 1880 and 1900 the whole of the Nile Valley, from the great lakes of Africa to the Mediterranean, passed under British control. In this remarkable episode of British expansion in its heyday, Sir Evelyn Baring, afterwards Lord Cromer, played the principal role. As Cromer (unlike Milner) wrote a history of the events which he, largely, directed, we may follow the story, in the main, as he himself tells it in his *Modern Egypt* (Macmillan, 1908).

Cromer opens his narrative with the following words: "The origin of the Egyptian Question in its present phase was financial." The public debt of Egypt (almost entirely held abroad), he continues, stood at some £3·25 m. in 1863. By 1876 it was some £94 m. £16 m. had been spent upon digging the Suez Canal. For the whole of the rest of the increase there was very little to show. Some part had been squandered, some part had been dissipated in corruption, but the largest part had been borrowed towards the end of the period in frantic and immensely costly efforts to pay the interest on that part of the debt which had already been incurred. The creditors were private persons and institutions in France, Britain and elsewhere.

When Cromer wrote that the origins of the Egyptian question were financial, he meant, as his narrative makes clear, that the *de facto* annexation of Egypt and the Soudan by Britain arose out of attempts on the part of the British and French Governments to collect the interest on the above debts on behalf of the bondholders. The process by which this happened was, however, immensely complicated. It is pointed out by Cromer, and by nearly every subsequent historian, that the British Government made persistent efforts, sometimes carried (as in the Gordon affair) to the point of opening it to charges of pusillanimity, to avoid having to take upon itself the virtual annexation of the Nile Valley. All that is quite true, *upon the assumption that, whatever else happened, the interest on the debts, or at least the greatest practicable part of it, had to be collected.* What the British Government really wanted was that somehow or other the interest should be collected without Britain having to involve herself in the complications and responsibilities of conquering Egypt. But when it became clear that that was impossible, Britain occupied and ruled Egypt and the Soudan rather than that the bondholders should lose their money. There would have been no difficulty at any time in avoiding the *de facto* annexation of the Nile Valley if the British Government had taken the view that those of their nationals who had lent their money to the Egyptian Government had done so at their own risk. But this was an attitude foreign to the imagination of the period, and Cromer does not seriously consider it in the course of his two volumes.

He does mention the issue just once. By 1878 the Egyptian Government of the Khedive was about to default on its interest payments to the bondholders. In spite of having already driven the Egyptian Government, which was as cruel as it was incompetent, to produce famine both in Egypt and the Soudan by its tax extortions, the British Government joined with the French Government in representations to the effect that there was "every reason to believe that the Khedive could pay the coupon" (*i.e.,* the interest on the bonds) "as it fell due in May if he chose to do so." In doing so, Cromer writes (*Modern Egypt,* Vol. I, p. 37), the British Government departed from "the tradition of the London Foreign Office that British subjects, who invested their money in a foreign country, must do so at their own risk." Cromer does not give any examples of this alleged tradition being observed, and the main ones which I can think of are the loans to States of the American Union and to some Latin American republics which were with impunity defaulted. But in these cases the British Government was hardly in a position to use force to collect the debts. It was simply not practical politics to make war upon the United States, or even to flout the Monroe Doctrine by intervention in South America. In any case in Egypt the money was collected from the already starving peasantry, through the agency of the Egyptian Government, by, Cromer writes, "two of the most iron-fisted Pashas who could be found."

Cromer, or Baring as he then was, was thus first sent to Egypt in this workaday role of a debt collector or bailiff's man. From 1877 to 1880 he served as "the British Commissioner of the Public Debt," that is to say, the British member of the international team which had been put in to extract order, and the bondholders' money, out of the chaos of Egyptian finances.[1] They had had

---

[1] Cromer was not appointed, like the other Commissioners, by his Government, but by Lord Goschen on behalf of the bondholders direct. But he tells us that this made little difference in practice.

some success in this endeavour when Cromer left Egypt in 1880. It was while he was absent that the decisive event took place which resulted in the British occupation. That event was one of the periodic upsurges of Egyptian nationalism, led on this occasion, as on a more recent one, by some of the younger officers of the Army, headed by a colonel called Arabi. These younger Army officers, together with some Egyptian civilians, attempted to stage what was in effect a *coup d'état* against the Government of the Khedive. The Khedive, it must be remembered, was technically merely a Viceroy or provincial Governor of the Sultan of Turkey, and Egypt was nominally a Turkish province. Here, as in the case of the Mogul Empire, we encounter the phenomenon of a decaying empire from which the provinces are not so much revolting as dropping off into a sort of quasi-independence. For several decades Turkish authority over Egypt had been nominal: on the other hand, the country was still ruled by Turkish nobles, or Pashas, of which the Khedive was merely the richest, just as Bengal in 1757 was still largely ruled by Moslem nobles.

Arabi's movement was nationalist, generally anti-foreign, anti-Turkish quite as much as anti-European. It expressed the convulsive effort of the Egyptians to regain some control of their own affairs by shaking off the double or triple layers of foreign rule to which they were subjected. As against the weak government of the Khedive Arabi's movement was successful. By the early months of 1882 Arabi had forced the Khedive to make him Minister of War and had got the country under his virtual control. If he had retained power he would no doubt have attempted to run the country on nationalist lines, as indeed Mahomet Ali, the existing Khedive's predecessor, had done fifty years before. And Arabi might have repudiated some or all of the debts. But even the possibility of this the British and, to start with, the French, Governments would not contemplate. They did not particularly want to annex Egypt, but they were determined to collect their subjects' debts come what may. The fiery M. Gambetta chanced to be the French Prime Minister for three months at the turn of 1881–2 and he persuaded the British Foreign Secretary, Lord Granville, to send a menacing joint note to the Khedive, making it pretty clear that Britain and France would not stand for a nationalist government in Egypt. This note, Cromer writes, united and galvanised the Egyptian nationalists into a real determination to achieve the independence of their country. But by the time matters came to a head in July 1882 the French Government had, as usual, changed, and was now unwilling to use force. Yet the British Government now felt committed to doing so. There was a violent anti-foreign riot in Alexandria, and British warships were sent to the port. Arabi, or the Egyptian Government, which by now hardly existed apart from him, set up batteries to defend the town. On July 11th the warships bombarded the batteries and the town, the Egyptians were driven out, and the town burnt, no one is quite certain how, probably partly by the bombardment and partly by Arabi's disorderly troops. A British expeditionary force was sent and the Egyptian Army under Arabi was routed at Tel-el-Kebir on September 13th (1882). The British occupation of Egypt, which was to last until 1956, had begun.

Writing in 1959, it is impossible not to compare the Arabi movement of the last century with that of Nasser in our own time. Naturally the Egypt of seventy-five years ago was a much less developed place than the Egypt of to-day. Yet the similarities between the two movements are striking. Nor does Cromer himself lightly dismiss the possibility of Arabi having been able to set up an effective nationalist government, had he been allowed to do so. Cromer wrote:

It was more than a mere military mutiny. It partook in some degree of the nature of a *bona-fide* national movement. It was not solely, or, indeed, mainly directed against Europeans and European interference in Egyptian affairs, although anti-European prejudice exercised a considerable influence on the minds of the leaders of the movement. It was, in a great degree, a movement of the Egyptians against Turkish rule. Although previous to the issue of the Joint Note some hope might have been entertained of guiding the movement, and although I am distinctly of opinion that an effort to guide it should have been made, it must be admitted that the chances of failure predominated over those of success (Vol. I, p. 324).

Cromer goes on to discuss the question of whether Arabi could have succeeded in running a government on the basis of "Egypt for the Egyptians" and comes to the conclusion that he probably could not have done so. But this is because Cromer assumes that Arabi would have physically driven out of Egypt not only the Europeans, but also the Turkish Pashas (in whom, "in spite of many defects, the habits and traditions of a governing class still lingered"), the Syrians and Armenians, and all other foreigners. From what Cromer himself tells us of Arabi this seems unlikely. Nevertheless, it must readily be agreed that a nationalist Egyptian Government in the eighteen-eighties would have been not only an exceedingly rough-and-ready, but also, very likely, an unstable affair, which might well have collapsed after a shorter or longer period of rule. Cromer, writing in 1907, naturally concludes that some kind of foreign occupation and government of Egypt was probably indispensable and beneficial, and, equally naturally, that, if so, a British occupation was by far the best. That may or may not be so. The question is really only a special case of the far broader question of whether a period of widespread capitalist imperialism was or was not indispensable for the development of the world.

On the narrower issue of the balance-sheet of the seventy-five-year period of British imperialism in the Nile Valley we may make the following observations. In the first place, no one should doubt the remarkable character of the British constructive achievement in Egypt, and later in the Soudan. In September 1883 Cromer was recalled to Egypt, but this time as "British Agent and Consul-General." This modest title ineffectively concealed the fact that he was the absolute ruler of the country and remained so for twenty-four years, till his departure in May 1907. There is no doubt that in this quarter of a century of (disguised) colonial status the material condition of Egypt was (in some respects) transformed. And this in spite of very serious difficulties. The very first thing which Cromer had to face in his new pro-consulship was the loss of the whole of the Soudan. Maddened by the rapacity of the Egyptian Government's efforts to collect money "to pay the coupon," the Soudanese rose, in 1883, under the leadership of the Mahdi, or Moslem saviour, drove out or surrounded the feeble Egyptian garrisons, slaughtered the Egyptian expeditionary force (under a British General, Hicks) sent to reconquer them, and for some time acutely menaced Egypt's southern frontier. This led to the Gordon affair, in which an attempt was made (against the wishes of Cromer and the British Government) to reconquer the Soudan on the cheap. Gordon got himself killed at Khartoum, and it was not till 1898 (thirteen years later) that the Soudan was methodically reconquered by Kitchener.[2]

All this put a heavy strain on the new Egyptian Government, working under close British direction. Nevertheless, a very great deal was accomplished. Egypt as Cromer found it in 1883 must have been one of the most miserable countries

[2] Cromer claims, no doubt justly, that one of the major services which Britain rendered to Egypt was to force the Egyptian Government temporarily to "cut its loss" and abandon the Soudan for the first years of the British occupation. It is in this connection that he gives a delightful thumbnail sketch of Lord Granville, Gladstone's Foreign Secretary from 1880 to 1885. Cromer had to deal with this great, bland Whig grandee throughout the first critical years of his pro-consulship. When, Cromer writes, he put to his Foreign Secretary the necessity of preventing the Egyptians from attempting a reconquest of their lost province of the Soudan, Granville concurred in the following characteristic language, which it is irresistible to quote in full:

"It takes away," he said, "somewhat of the position of a man to sell his racers and hunters, but if he cannot afford to keep them, the sooner they go to Tattersall's the better." I have a large number of private letters from Lord Granville. Some of them are very interesting. His light touches on serious questions were inimitable, and his good humour and kindness of heart come out in every line he wrote. It was possible to disagree with him, but it was impossible to be angry with him. It was also impossible to get him to give a definite answer to a definite question when he wished not to commit himself. His power of eluding the main point at issue was quite extraordinary. Often did I think that he was on the horns of a dilemma, and that he was in a position from which no escape was possible without the expression of a definite opinion. I was generally mistaken. With a smile and a quick little epigrammatic phrase, Lord Granville would elude one's grasp and be off without giving any opinion at all. I remember on one occasion pressing him to say what he wished me to do about one of the numerous offshoots of the general tangle, which formed the Egyptian question. The matter was one of considerable importance. All I could extract from him was the Delphic saying that my "presence in London would be a good excuse for a dawdle."

I remember once comparing notes with Lord Goschen on this subject. He told me that on one occasion, when he was at Constantinople, after many unsuccessful endeavours to obtain definite answers to certain important questions which he had addressed to Lord Granville, he wrote a very lengthy and very strong private letter, intimating that unless clear answers were sent, he would resign. The only reply he received from Lord Granville was as follows: "My dear Goschen—Thank you a thousand times for expressing your views so frankly to your old colleagues" (*Modern Egypt*, pp. 392–3).

which have ever existed. As he left her in 1907 she had become not only solvent and easily able to pay her creditors (which was undoubtedly the original object of the exercise), but also on the road at least to modern development. Competent, honest, although alien, government had been able greatly to reduce taxation on the peasants, while raising far more revenue. During the period of Cromer's rule direct taxation was reduced by £2 m. a year; the salt tax, the octroi duties, the bridge and lock dues on the Nile, and the taxes on river and fishing boats were abolished. Many other indirect taxes were greatly reduced. Good administration at the same time raised the revenue from just under £E.9 m. in 1883 to £E.15 m. in 1906 (see *Modern Egypt,* Vol. II, pp. 447-9). Above all perhaps, the irrigation upon which Egypt's life depends had been salvaged and extended. The mediaevalisms of "the Courbash" (the rhinoceros hide whip universally used to chastise the peasant) and "the corvée," or unpaid forced labour for the annual clearance of the irrigation ditches, had gone. Justice, hygiene and education had begun. A fairly competent army had been formed. The peasant was, relatively, prosperous. The middle class was rapidly growing. Cromer could not unreasonably look forward to steady further improvement in the conditions and standard of life of the Egyptian people, if British rule were continued.

In the event, that rule was continued, although in a decreasingly direct form, for nearly fifty years more. And yet in the end, when the British did actually leave, in 1956, the final balance-sheet was not nearly so favourable as Cromer in 1907 might legitimately have hoped and expected that it would be. Egypt had been fairly effectively modernised. (It is this which enables her to lead the Arab Nationalist Movement to-day.) But it is doubtful if the standard of life of the Egyptian people, still overwhelmingly peasant, had improved nearly as much as might have been expected, as compared with 1882, or had improved at all as compared with 1907. This, no doubt, was above all due to the new menace which had arisen, in spite of—indeed precisely because of—all the civilising improvements introduced by British rule—namely, the now inordinate rate of the growth of the population. Cromer says that the population was given as 6·3 million in 1882 (although this may have been an underestimate) and 11·2 million in 1907. To-day (1959) it is over 24 million. Within the limits of the type of pre-industrial development of the British period, such an increase in population is no doubt prohibitive of any marked raising of the standard of life. At any rate, in my experience, a visitor to the Egyptian village of 1954 would find it hard indeed to imagine what conditions must have been like if and when they were even worse.

To some extent no doubt we ought to judge our success or failure in Egypt by the virtues or defects of the nationalist régime of Colonel Nasser which has succeeded it. (At any rate we are quick to take credit for the virtues of the

Indian successor régime in the parallel case.) It is of course much too early to know what the verdict of history upon the Nasser régime will be. One great virtue that régime possesses: it aims at national development: at industrialisation: at the abolition of the abysmal poverty of its people. How far that constructive side is being overlaid by an appetite for larger territorial expansion and by the feud with Israel is still doubtful. But at least the spark of constructive desire is there. Moreover, criticism of the defects of the new régime must be regarded, after seventy-five years of British rule, quite as much as criticism of Britain as criticism of the Egyptians. The strict limits of the benefits which even the best form of alien rule can confer upon a people are apparent. Not materially, of course, but psychologically, the Egyptians under Nasser seem to be beginning again where they were compelled by outside power to leave off under Arabi. Once again the only form of self-government which they can produce is the no doubt appropriate but not very evolved form of an army dictatorship led by middle-rank or junior officers. Once more zenophobia has to be the main binding force which holds them together.

But the differences as well as the similarities between Arabi's movement and Nasser's are marked. This time it is clear that the attempt to create an "Egypt for the Egyptians" will not be arrested from the outside. The bombardment of Port Said in 1956 did not lead on to occupation, as did the bombardment of Alexandria in 1882. Now, as then, the only real alternatives, as Cromer so clearly saw, were to let the nationalist Egyptian movement have its way or to occupy the country and rule it. Now, as then, it was argued that the interests of "the powers" made it impossible to allow the nationalists to retain power. In 1882 it was fear that the interest on the bonds would not be paid; in 1956 it was fear that the Egyptians could not, or would not, work the Suez Canal. But this time the matter has been put to the test, and it appears that the Egyptians are experiencing no difficulty at all in this respect.

In fact, however unpleasant it may be for many people in Britain to realise, the Nasser Government is clearly quite capable of governing Egypt without foreign tutelage. Whether it will govern it ill or well is, of course, another matter. But surely there can be no doubt that once a people is capable of ruling itself at all, it must be allowed to do so. What is sad is that the historical development has been such that now that, for the first time, almost literally since the Pharaohs, Egypt became genuinely self-governing, she has become for a time the leader of anti-British feeling in the whole of her region of the world. But can we sincerely deny that the main fault for that lies with Britain, not Egypt? And yet, if we had had the statesmanship to end our period of rule in Egypt in even approximately the same way in which we ended it in India, the new Egypt might have become a most valuable friend, for our real interests do not conflict. Our record of achievement on behalf of the Egyptian people during the period in which we were responsible for their welfare is better, not worse, than our record in India, since it is not marred by an initial period of pillage. But the end spoilt everything.

An interesting passage in the conclusion of Cromer's book invites us to speculate as to what his attitude would have been to the events of the present day. Writing, let us recall, at the peak point of British imperial success, when, as we shall note, imperialism seemed even to its strongest opponent to be irresistible, he concludes his book as follows:

Although, however, I will not venture to predict the goal which will eventually be reached, I have no hesitation in expressing an opinion as to which we should seek to attain. So far as can at present be judged, only two alternative courses are possible. Egypt must eventually either become autonomous, or it must be incorporated into the British Empire. Personally, I am decidedly in favour of moving in the direction of the former of these alternatives.

It is true that Cromer was also convinced that Britain could not withdraw from Egypt for some time to come. In fact, she did not do so for half a century after he wrote. We may easily suppose, therefore, that Cromer, faced in 1956 by the clear alternatives of once again suppressing Egyptian nationalism or of permitting Egypt to become genuinely autonomous, would have chosen the second. Instead, the British Government of 1956 half-heartedly attempted to repeat the actions which had led, in 1882, to the occupation. In the world of the mid-twentieth century they merely led to fiasco. It is unlikely that Cromer, the sanest, best-balanced and most fair-minded of the great British pro-consuls of the imperial heyday, would have approved of policies which have undone much of his lifework.

Our business, however, is to assess the motives which led Britain to annex the Nile Valley in the second half of the nineteenth century, in order to see if they throw light on the more general question of the motives which led both her and the other powers to annex in the same period much of the rest of the habitable globe. We have seen that Cromer, the man who did the job, had no doubts about the matter. The motives were "financial": it was a matter of debt-collecting. What happened was that British (and French) private citizens had lent to, or invested in, Egypt: when the Egyptian Government would not or could not "pay the coupon" an Egyptian Government which would pay had to be put in its place.

No more terse statement of the economic motives for imperial expansion has ever been made than Cromer's. But we must not accept it as conclusive just because he was the man on the spot. Cromer may have been oversimplifying the Egyptian case: or the motives for other acquisitions may have been different. And in fact it is obvious enough that motives other than the directly economic played their part, not so much perhaps in the original acquisition of

Egypt as in the retention of British *de facto* sovereignty there for so long. Those motives are clearly what are often called "strategic." We held on to Egypt not so much in order to continue to "collect the coupon" as because through Egypt lay the water route and the electric telegraph to India and to the Far East. This is the "life-line of empire" argument, which was to dominate British thinking on the Middle East.

All this has led some observers to conclude that strategic considerations are more important than economic as the motivation behind empire-building. And it is quite true that in a particular case at a particular time, as in this case of the retention of Egypt, those strategic reasons may be decisive. No doubt we kept Egypt above all because we wanted to secure ourselves in India. But this fact does no more than illuminate a principle, namely that strategic reasons, however important, cannot be regarded as the primary motive behind imperial expansion. For why, in this case, did we want to secure ourselves in India? Because we had taken India. And, as we have seen, we had taken India from economic motives in a rather simple sense—because the conquest enormously enriched a very limited number of people. The strategic motive is essentially secondary. Strategy is a means to an end not an end in itself. The end is the conquest of other peoples or the avoidance of conquest by them. Therefore, however high we rate the strategic motive for particular imperial actions— and it has often been decisive—we are still left with the basic question of why people wish to conquer and to avoid being conquered.

It would be to anticipate the whole of the argument of the rest of this book to try to answer that question here. But clearly one answer would be to say that people wish to conquer rather than to be conquered because, in our epoch of history, the conquerors have usually found means of making the conquered work for them to a greater or lesser extent. And it is very much nicer to be worked for by, than to work for, other people. We shall ultimately conclude that this is an inadequate answer, both in the sense that there have been periods of human existence when it has been impracticable to make other people work for one with advantage, and that there are some signs that mankind may be about to re-enter such a period, and also in the sense that there have always been, and are, other biological and deep seated, propensities to conquest and domination. Still, it will pay us to consider this concept as an hypothesis as to the main motivation of the new imperialism of the late nineteenth and early twentieth centuries.

* * *

Let us turn to another example of British imperial expansion in the above period: the annexation of South Africa. And for a protagonist of this event, we may follow the actions and words of Milner in South Africa in the same way that we have followed those of Cromer at the other end of the continent in Egypt. It is of course more or less arbitrary to choose Milner as the key figure in this enterprise. Joseph Chamberlain or Cecil Rhodes might equally be held typical. Milner, however, was the most intellectual and the most interesting of them. Moreover it was Milner's will power, above all, which carried through, in the face of no small obstacles, the annexation of the two Boer republics of the Orange Free State and the Transvaal.

The history of the Boer War, its origins, its course, its results, both immediate and as they are becoming apparent in the nineteen-fifties, are too well known to require re-telling here. But who can really doubt that the simple issue on which the war was fought was whether or not independent Boer sovereignty was to be cleared out of the way of the British entrepreneurs and investors who wanted to make their fortunes out of mining the diamonds and the gold which, it had been discovered, underlay the fields which the Boers were tilling? For the Boer régimes, while they did not prohibit the exploitation of these precious minerals, did hamper it, refused civil rights and citizenship to the incoming British entrepreneurs and their staffs, taxed them arbitrarily, and generally stood in the way of the full exploitation of what was turning out to be one of the most attractive of all the fields for the overseas investment of the flood of British capital which was being generated at home.

Moreover, the mines of Kimberley and the Rand were likely, it was felt, to be immensely profitable, not only because of their diamonds and their gold, but also because there was available on the spot a supply of ultra-cheap labour. This was provided by the "Kaffirs" or native African tribesmen who had been recently subdued and could be made to work for subsistence or less. The question of who should use this labour and benefit from the surpluses which it produced, the British in mining or the Boers in farming, could, it turned out, only be decided by war. That this was in truth the issue is well commemorated by the terminology in use to this day in the City of London in regard to the matter. The City has always been, and still is, in the coining of its slang at least, delightfully frank. How apt it is that South African goldmining shares are known as "Kaffirs"! Thus in a single word the underlying fact is revealed that what is really being exploited in South Africa is not only the gold of the Rand nor the diamonds of Kimberley, but the exceptionally cheap labour of the Africans, or Kaffirs, conveniently embodied in the mined gold or diamonds. Indeed, that the particular product in which the surplus created by this labour is embodied is a secondary question is illustrated by the fact that of late it has been found just as profitable to embody it in copper (from Rhodesia) or in uranium. We shall note the limits to which the exploitation of this cheap labour in fact benefits the national accounts. But there was not and is not any doubt at all of the remarkable extent to which it benefited the accounts of the particular entrepreneurs engaged in exploiting it.

How much the supply of cheap labour mattered is illustrated by one of

Milner's last, and most politically disastrous, acts. When, after the dislocation caused by the war, the African labour supply proved temporarily inadequate, Milner arranged to import Chinese indentured labourers. It is characteristic of the man that he was genuinely astonished that anyone in England found anything objectionable in his doing so. It would, he felt, have been very queer to have crushed Boer independence in three bloody years of war, fought primarily in order to get satisfactory conditions for working the mines, and then to let anything stand in the way of working them. But what he had failed to notice was that the great sleepy British public, which had of course never faced the fact that this was what the war had been about, could not "take" the importation of rather thinly disguised serf-labour to carry out the imperial purpose, especially when Milner, as he naïvely writes (*Milner Papers,* Vol. III, p. 559), had not thought twice about giving a British official authority to flog that labour without any legal process.

On the other hand it is not to-day possible to accept the somewhat naïve views of the "pro-Boer" minority of the British public. The fathers and grandfathers of the Boer farmers who are now practising *apartheid,* and who then held the same view of the Africans, cannot be held up as innocent victims of the British imperialists. The truth is that there were at the end of the nineteenth century two distinct layers of imperialism in South Africa. There was an in-rushing tide of British mining and land-speculating imperialism, determined to exploit "Kaffir" labour in the new and incomparably more profitable way of gold- and diamond-mining instead of in farming. But in possession was a previous layer of somewhat home-spun Boer imperialism, content to exploit African labour on a relatively small scale upon its farms. The Boer War was essentially a conflict between these two layers, or forms, of imperialism. In a sense, no doubt, the British were much the greater, more up-to-date, more powerful, imperialists. But both sides were Europeans intent upon the exploitation of the labour of far more primitive societies, either in agriculture or in the extraction of raw materials, such as gold and diamonds, for their own benefit. Thus all the generous views of the British "pro-Boers" of the turn of the century must to-day seem a little beside the point. If we accept the basic premises of up-to-date imperialism, Chamberlain, Rhodes, Milner and the British generally were in the right. The Boer republics had become an anachronism standing in the way of the effective exploitation of irresistibly attractive wealth. On the other hand, if we accept the premise of an earlier imperialism, the Boers had a right to continue to exploit "their" natives in their own primitive (but rather ruthless) way, since they had got there first. The rights, if any, of the Africans did not arise in anybody's mind, except occasionally as a talking point to throw at the other side.

Of course neither Milner, Rhodes nor Chamberlain publicly admitted what the war was about. They spoke rather of the British imperial mission. And it is quite true that for Milner the longer-term issue was whether Southern Africa was to take its place as a part of a vast super-state called the British Empire which he was utterly convinced that he and a chosen few, both of collaborators and of young disciples, had a mission to create. He gave what is in some ways the definitive expression to his imperial vision in his Johannesburg speech upon leaving South Africa in 1905.

When we who call ourselves Imperialists talk of the British Empire, we think of a group of states, all independent in their local concerns, but all united for the defence of their own common interests and the development of a common civilization; united, not in an alliance—for alliances can be made and unmade, and are never more than nominally lasting—but in a permanent organic union. Of such a union the dominions of our Sovereign as they exist to-day are, we fully admit, only the raw material. Our ideal is still distant, but we deny that it is either visionary or unattainable. And see how such a consummation would solve, and, indeed, can alone solve, the most difficult and the most persistent of the problems of South Africa; how it would unite its white races as nothing else can (*The Milner Papers*, Vol. II, p. 547).

The sting of Milner's remarks is in the tail. What he was concerned with, now that the war was won, was to unite the white races in order to establish a secure white hegemony. The curious thing, however, about this vision of empire is its vagueness. On the one hand the above passage suggests that Milner had in mind something not unlike the Commonwealth as we hope to develop that association to-day. There is to be a free association of self-governing nations. On the other hand, the association must be united in "a permanent organic union," whatever that may be. Probably Milner, like Seeley before him, had taken care never to think through his imperial conception, for if he had done so its contradictions could not have escaped him. What he was actually concerned in building up, after all, was the very opposite of a free association of independent nations. On the contrary, he had just succeeded in coercing the two Boer republics into becoming parts of the British Empire, crushing, in the end, their passionate determination to remain outside it. The trouble with Milner, and the whole school of contemporary British imperialists of which he was the intellectual leader, was that they were determined to force a large part of the world voluntarily to associate with them. And that is rather a difficult thing to do.

As we have just noted, the Empire had become, by 1905, when the Johannesburg speech was delivered, above all an enormous aggregation of newly acquired colonies, together with India, which had no self-government, let alone independence, and which Milner was the first to say must not be given any in the proximate future. In a word, when Milner exulted, as he did, in his task of empire-building he was really engaged in creating an empire of the normal, old-fashioned kind, consisting of one central sovereign state, ruling and, if it so desired, exploiting a number of colonies. True, there were also "the white Dominions" and they really did enjoy an ever increasing degree of freedom and independence. But for that very reason there was every year less and less chance of them accepting any "permanent organic union," which phrase was no doubt meant to hint at some sort of super-imperial Council or Parliament with some such overriding powers in Foreign Affairs, Finance and inter-imperial commerce as those possessed by the Federal Government of the United States.

How can a man of Milner's first-rate intelligence have supposed that an imperial ideal shot through and through with such insuperable contradictions as these could ever have been realised? Perhaps a sufficiently resolute and ruthless policy of force might have kept together an orthodox type of empire for some time longer than was actually done, although certainly at the cost of ruining any possibility of the development of a voluntary commonwealth. But to think that such a policy of force could somehow be reconciled with the progressive grant of independence to "the white Dominions," and, at the same time, that the whole imperial structure could be somehow turned into a voluntary association, was a strange delusion to be entertained by, I repeat, a highly intelligent man.

Almost certainly the best chance of something constructive coming out of the two-layered South African imperialism which we have defined above was that taken by the Liberal Government which came into office in 1906, and at once gave South Africa full self-government. By hindsight we can now see that the Liberals ought to have made far-reaching guarantees for equality before the law, and for political rights, for the African population, a condition for the grant of self-government. Indeed their failure to do so makes it doubtful if, in the second half of the twentieth century South Africa will be willing to continue indefinitely to participate in an association of nations which must come increasingly to number Asiatic and African states in its membership. But to ask the Liberal statesmen of over half a century ago to have foreseen the tragedy of *apartheid* is to ask much. And certainly to have failed to apply some form of self-government to South Africa would have been to lose even the chance of a solution. Yet Milner violently opposed the Liberal attempt to apply in practice the voluntary principle to which he paid lip service.

And yet Milner was probably not a conscious hypocrite. He was rather an extremely finished product of a very special period and, in particular, of a very special form of education. He had carried all before him at Oxford. In the fabulous Balliol of Jowett, with Asquith, Gore and the elder Toynbee to compete with, he was perhaps the outstanding scholar, winning the Hertford, the Eldon and the Derby scholarships, and only missing the Ireland because he would not show up a copy of Greek verses with which he was dissatisfied. What a comment it is upon Oxford education as it then was that splendid human material such as Milner should be sent out into the late nineteenth-century world without really knowing anything about it at all. What other result could you expect if you gave all the highest, and, to a poor boy like Milner, indispensable, rewards for an ability to write verses in two of the languages of a previous civilization? [3]

We have now sketched two of the principal incidents of the process of headlong imperialist expansion undertaken by Britain and, to the utmost of their powers, by all the other highly developed capitalisms between 1870 and 1914. We have seen that the acquisition of Southern Africa and of the Nile Valley occurred from distinct, although closely related, motives. The Boer republics were overthrown and annexed because their existence hampered the exploitation of Kaffir labour in the mining of gold and diamonds by British capital. The power of the State was called in on behalf of adventurous British entrepreneurs like Rhodes investing their capital in overseas enterprises. In Egypt, on the other hand, the power of the State was used to protect bond-holders, *i.e.*, persons who had lent their money at a fixed rate of interest to a foreign government. What is common to both cases is that it was found that if the investment of British capital overseas was to be adequately promoted and protected, large slices of the world must be, in fact or in form, annexed.

On the other hand, the two examples of South Africa and Egypt provide, by themselves, quite inadequate evidence for the view that economic motives were the mainspring of the new wave of imperialism which engulfed the world after about 1870. Moreover, we should find, if we examined the other examples of imperialist acquisition in this period, that some of them fit less well with the explanation that force was being used essentially in order to promote or to protect the investments or loans of the major capital-generating powers. We should find examples of annexations of territories which had much less obvious attraction for risk capital than the Rand: and subversions of incompetent governments to which much less money had been lent than to that of the Khedive in Egypt. Evidently other powerful, if perhaps secondary, motives, such as the strategic motive suggested above, were at work. Rather unpromising parts of the map, such as the Sahara, for instance, were annexed by powers such as France which had by no means so great a capacity for generating capital surpluses as had late-nineteenth-century Britain. Perhaps a sheer spirit of emulation, as well as military strategy, played a part in these instances.

Again, we should find that "the flag" did not invariably come to the rescue

---

[3] Not that, in my opinion, Milner and his contemporaries ought to have been taught technology: that would have made them still more ignorant of contemporary social relations: nor am I suggesting that knowledge of the social relations of the ancient world, derived by reading, say, Thucydides and Plato, in English (as we read the Bible) would have been irrelevant. What I am saying is that the concentration on mere linguistic feats produced a disastrous type of ignorance. The above note on Milner is indebted not only to Professor Headlam's two comprehensive volumes of *The Milner Papers,* but also to Mr. Edward Crankshaw's recent (1950) study, *The Forsaken Idea* (Longmans, 1950).

of the pound, the dollar, the franc or the mark, even when foreign investments or loans were endangered by "native" incompetence or recalcitrance. The British investors, we noted, lost a good many millions in both South America and in the southern states of North America without the British Government intervening to rescue them in the way in which it did in both Egypt and South Africa. Evidently these were situations in which it was too difficult or too dangerous to protect the foreign investor, at least by force of arms. For such an intervention would have encountered not the feeble Egyptian Government, or the small Boer republics, but the resistance of another well-developed society, in this case the United States.

Such considerations should warn us at the outset that any mechanical application of an economic interpretation of the new imperialism will not do. Still, the example of Egypt and South Africa, in which that explanation is especially clear, would, obviously, not have been chosen unless I had considered that this interpretation is the best guiding thread to an understanding of the imperialist policies of the highly developed capitalisms of the recent past.

* * *

EUROPE IN THE
TWENTIETH CENTURY

The Origins of World War I:
An Older and a Newer View

$\mathcal{T}$he writing of the history of the
causes of World War I begins with the war itself. The parallel development
of nationalism and democracy during the second half of the nineteenth
century meant, among other things, that now entire peoples instead of heads
of state waged war. Thus within months of the outbreak of war in
August 1914, the governments of all belligerents had placed before their
parliaments and people and, not incidentally, the court of world opinion,
collections of diplomatic documents so arranged as to show the perfidy of
their enemies and the rightness of their cause.[1] As the war dragged on and
costs and casualties soared, the unprecedented emphasis on the righteousness
of this war was followed by an exceptional preoccupation with the question
of "war guilt,"—a preoccupation that found its logical—or should we say
illogical?—expression in the famous Clause 231 of the Treaty of Versailles:

The Allied and Associated Governments affirm, and Germany accepts, the
responsibility of Germany and her allies for causing all the loss and damage to
which the Allied and Associated Governments and their nationals have been
subjected as a consequence of the war imposed upon them by the aggression of
Germany and her allies.

¶ The reaction of Germany to the Versailles Treaty and the war-guilt
clause in particular are too well known to require elaboration. The point made
here is that Socialist governments in Germany and Austria, exposed to the
odium of signing the peace treaties, published in 1919 complete collections
of documents from secret archives bearing on the crisis of July 1914. The

---

[1] These were the *German White Book* (August 3), *British Blue Book* (August 6), *Russian
Orange Book* (August 7), *Belgian Gray Book* (October), *Serbian Blue Book* (November), *French
Yellow Book* (December), *Austrian Red Book* (February 1915).

Soviets had anticipated them in this. In 1917 they had begun to publish the secret treaties and other diplomatic documents of the Tsarist regime. The idea was to discredit the "imperialist" governments the Socialists had displaced, and whether or not they succeeded in this, they did succeed in showing that the question of war guilt was not the black and white one the Versailles Treaty had made it out to be.

The various collections of documents were widely read by interested parties in both the defeated and victorious nations. The German documents were, in fact, translated into English in this country by the Carnegie Endowment for International Peace. The result, particularly in face of reticence on the part of France and Britain to make similar disclosures, was a flood of popular "revisionist" histories in which German responsibility for the outbreak of the war was minimized, chiefly at the expense of France and Russia.[2]

Scholars bided their time a little longer, however, until in 1926 the British government published all their documents relative to the July crisis. As a result, Sidney B. Fay was able to complete his masterful, two-volume study, *The Origins of the World War,* in 1928, just ten years after the war had ended. It subsequently went through numerous reprintings and a revision and still stands as one of the most important works in its field, testimony alike to Professor Fay's scholarship and the unprecedented early flow of archival material just described.[3] The selections from it below give, first, Professor Fay's summary of the underlying causes of the war, and second, his conclusions about the roles of the various belligerents during the July crisis.

Since the publication of Professor Fay's book, a great deal of additional evidence has appeared in the form of memoirs, collections of private papers, and new archival material. The French began publishing their diplomatic documents for the period 1871–1914 in 1929; the Italians theirs for the period 1863–1914 in 1952; and "the complete files for the crisis of 1914 are said to have been published." [4] Thus the second selection below, from one of the best of recent books that treats the long-range and immediate causes of World War I, has the benefit of additional sources not available to earlier writers. In "The Outbreak of War in Europe, 1914" from A. J. P. Taylor's *The Struggle for*

---

[2] Probably the best written and most popular of these in this country was Harry Elmer Barnes, *Genesis of the World War: An Introduction to the Problem of War Guilt* (1926). Also enjoying a wide circulation was Frederick Bausman, *Let France Explain* (1922). Extremely influential here and abroad was Count Maximilian von Montgelas, *Case for the Central Powers: An Impeachment of the Versailles Verdict* (1925). Montgelas served on the commission that opened up the German archives in 1919. Revisionist books also appeared in France.

[3] Mention should also be made of Bernadotte E. Schmitt, *The Coming of the War,* 2 vols. (1930), an excellent and equally well-documented study. From France there is Pierre Renouvin, *Les origines immédiates de la guerre, 28 juin—4 août 1914* (1925), English translation: *Immediate Origins of the War, 28th June—4th August, 1914* (1928), another scholarly and objective study.

[4] Bernadotte E. Schmitt, *The Origins of the First World War* (London: Published for the Historical Association by Routledge and Kegan Paul, 1958), p. 2.

Mastery in Europe, the reader will find an interpretative narration of developments prior to the outbreak of hostilities in August 1914 that complements Professor Fay's more general conclusions for the same period. By comparing the two the reader can determine how well Professor Fay's conclusions have stood up and the modifications that recent research has brought to them.

The Underlying and Immediate Causes of

World War I

Sidney B. Fay

* * *

THOUGH IT is now possible, in a single volume, to treat in detail and somewhat definitively the immediate causes of the War, this is by no means true in the case of the underlying causes. These are so complex and reach so far back into the past that any attempt to describe them adequately would involve nothing less than the writing of the whole diplomatic history of Europe since 1870, or rather from 1789; some questions go back to the age of Louis XIV, and even to that of Charlemagne. It would also involve the difficult technical study of the military and naval forces of the various countries, their plans of campaign, the relation of the military to the civilian authorities in each country, the psychology of fear, and all the other factors which go to make up the somewhat vague conceptions of "militarism" and "navalism" as causes of war. No less important would be the analysis of that complex force which first began to be a powerful, disruptive agency during the French Revolution, and which steadily gathered strength for a century and a quarter, which we call "nationalism." This in turn is closely bound up with psychological and political questions of race, religion, democracy, education, and popular prejudice. Still more important, in many minds, as underlying causes of the War are the intricate political and economic problems which have arisen from the transformation of society during the past hundred years

Reprinted with permission of the publisher from *The Origins of the World War* by Sidney B. Fay, 2nd ed.; rev. 2 vols. in one (New York: The Macmillan Company, 1930), I, pp. 32–35, 38–49; II, pp. 547–58. Copyright 1928, 1930 by The Macmillan Company.

by the modern industrial system which began in England and subsequently penetrated more or less all the great countries of the world—problems of excess population, food supply, foreign markets and raw materials, colonial possessions, and the accumulation of capital seeking investment abroad. Finally, the influence of the newspaper press is a factor much greater than commonly supposed in causing the World War. For decades it fed the constant undercurrents of irritation of one country against another, and by its clamor and misrepresentations often made difficult or impossible the peaceful settlement of sources of conflict. How far government officials controlled newspaper opinion, and how far they themselves were hampered in their freedom of action by it, is a subject which greatly needs further careful historical investigation. Obviously, no single volume can hope to deal thoroughly with all these complex and interrelated factors which constitute the underlying causes of the World War. They may be conveniently grouped under five heads: (a) the system of secret alliances; (b) militarism; (c) nationalism; (d) economic imperialism; and (e) the newspaper press.

(a) The System of Secret Alliances

The greatest single underlying cause of the War was the system of secret alliances which developed after the Franco-Prussian War. It gradually divided Europe into two hostile groups of Powers who were increasingly suspicious of one another and who steadily built up greater and greater armies and navies. Though this system of alliances in one sense tended to preserve peace, inasmuch as the members within one group often held their friends or allies in restraint for fear of becoming involved in war themselves, the system also made it inevitable that if war did come, it would involve all the Great Powers of Europe. The members of each group felt bound to support each other, even in matters where they had no direct interest, because failure to give support would have weakened the solidarity of the group. Thus, Germany often felt bound to back up Austria-Hungary in her Balkan policies, because otherwise Germany feared to lose her only thoroughly dependable ally. Similarly, France had no direct political (only financial) interests in the Balkans, but felt bound to back up Russia, because otherwise the existence of the Dual Alliance would have been threatened, the balance of power destroyed, and the best guarantee of French safety from a German attack would have been lost. Likewise, the officials of the British Foreign Office became increasingly convinced that England must support France and Russia in order to preserve the solidarity of the Triple Entente as a check to the Triple Alliance. In the crisis of July, 1914, it was not merely a question of Austria, Serbia and the Balkans; it was a question of the solidarity and prestige of the two groups of Powers into which Europe had become divided. As one reads the new *British Documents,* one is struck by the emphasis on this necessity of preserving the solidarity of the Triple Entente. As Sir Eyre Crowe noted in a "minute" early in the crisis: "It is clear that France and Russia are decided to accept the challenge thrown out to them. Whatever we may think of the merits of the Austrian charges against Serbia, France and Russia consider that these are the pretexts, and that the bigger cause of Triple Alliance versus Triple Entente is definitely engaged. I think it would be impolitic, not to say dangerous, for England to attempt to controvert this opinion, or to endeavour to obscure the plain issue, by any representation at St. Petersburg and Paris. . . . Our interests are tied up with those of France and Russia in this struggle, which is not for the possession of Serbia, but one between Germany aiming at a political dictatorship in Europe and the Powers who desire to retain individual freedom." It was stated more bluntly by Herr Zimmermann to the British Ambassador in Berlin on August 1, when he saw with excited regret that Germany, France, and perhaps England, would be drawn into a war which none of them wanted: "It all came from this d———d system of alliances, which was the curse of modern times."

* * *

(b) Militarism

A second underlying cause of the War, closely connected with the system of secret alliances, was militarism. The word is often used vaguely. But usually it includes at least two definite conceptions. First, the dangerous and burdensome mechanism of great standing armies and large navies, with the attendant evils of espionage, suspicion, fear, and hatred. Second, the existence of a powerful class of military and naval officers, headed by the General Staff, who tend to dominate, especially at a time of political crisis, over the civilian authorities.

The system of great armies, embracing the larger part of the male population capable of bearing arms, began with the French during the Revolution and under Napoleon. It was extended and efficiently developed by the Prussians in the War of Liberation. As a result of its success in the victories of Moltke and Bismarck in the Wars of 1864, '66 and '70, it came to be esteemed and imitated in the rest of Continental Europe. From the Franco-Prussian War onwards the military and naval armaments of all the Great Powers tended to grow larger and larger, and the financial burden became heavier and heavier. Armaments were alleged to be for defense and in the interests of peace, according to the fallacious maxim, *si vis pacem, para bellum.* They were intended to produce a sense of security. That was the argument used in getting from legislatures the necessary grants of money. What they really did produce was universal suspicion, fear, and hatred between nations. If one country increased its army, built strategic railways, and constructed new battleships, its fearful neighbors were straightway frightened into doing likewise. So the mad competition in armaments went on in a vicious circle. This was especially the case during and after the Balkan Wars of 1912–1913, when it seemed that the Great Powers might be involved. It was also accentuated by the system of alliances. Germany and Austria, uncertain of Italy's loyalty, believed they must increase their armaments to secure their own safety. France urged Russia to increase her army and build strategic railways against Germany, and readily loaned her half a billion francs on condition that it be spent for these purposes. Russia urged France to extend the term of French military service from two to three years. "Russia is ready; France must be also," declared the Russian Minister of War in an alarming newspaper article early in 1914. So armaments were increased, not only to give security to an individual country, but also to strengthen the alliance to which it belonged.

Militarism implied also the existence of an influential body of military and naval officers, whose whole psychological outlook was naturally colored by the possibility, if not the "inevitability," of an early war. To these professional fighters war held out the prospect of quick promotion and great distinction. It would, however, be a grave injustice to them to imply that they urged war for selfish motives of personal advancement. Nevertheless, the opportunity to put into practice the results of the work of preparation for war to which their lives were devoted cannot have failed to have its psychological effect. Quite aside from any personal motives, the military officers in all countries had a high sense of national honor and patriotic duty, as they understood it. It was their supreme duty to be ready at any moment to protect the state by force of arms. It was the constant preoccupation, day and night, of the General Staff in every country to be ready to make or meet an attack in the shortest possible time. To this end every General Staff drew up or revised every year the most minute and complete plans for mobilization and march to the frontier to satisfy all possible contingent situations. Military officers generally held to the theory that it was advantageous to take the offensive. This meant striking the foe before his mobilization was complete—at the moment, therefore, when the enemy country was in the most vulnerable process of transforming itself from a peace to a war footing. It meant also that the war, with all its frightful economic devastation and demoralizing political and psychological effects, would be carried on in the enemy's country instead of within one's own frontiers. In a political crisis, therefore, the military leaders were always quick to conclude that war was "inevitable," and exerted all their influence to persuade the ruling civilian authorities to consent to an order for general mobilization at the earliest possible moment, in order to gain the advantage of the offensive. But a general mobilization, according to prevailing military opinion, actually did make war inevitable. It was a process virtually impossible to halt when once begun. This was one of the greatest evils of militarism. It is always at a crisis, precisely when it is most difficult for diplomats to keep their heads clear and their hands free, that militarist leaders exert their influence to hasten decisions for war, or get the upper hand altogether.

Another evil of militarism was the fact that the plans of the General Staff were technical and were worked out and guarded in such absolute secrecy. Not only were they unknown to Parliament and the public; they were often not even known to the Minister of Foreign Affairs, or at least their details and significance were not grasped by him. Sir Edward Grey says that between 1906 and 1911 he knew nothing of the plans which the English and French military authorities were working out for Anglo-French military cooperation in Northern France. As to the negotiations between the Anglo-Russian naval authorities in the spring of 1914, he likewise writes: "I never enquired at the Admiralty afterwards, but I imagine the practical result of the consultations between the two naval authorities was not great. . . . [In the Siebert documents they] are constantly referred to as 'conventions.' How the military and naval authorities themselves described them, I do not know." Similarly, in Russia, it is clear that M. Sazonov did not at first grasp the fact that the plans of the militarists made a "partial mobilization" against Austria a piece of folly, if not a downright impossibility. And in Germany Herr von Bethmann-Hollweg never envisaged clearly the implications of the Schlieffen-Moltke plan to attack France through Belgium, although he was probably aware of it, according to Ludendorff, as early as 1912.

This then was another evil of militarism. The General Staffs worked out in absolute secrecy the plans which they calculated to be best adapted to bring military victory, regardless of the political implications which they might thereby impose on the civilian authorities. And when war became "inevitable," there was tremendous pressure upon the civilians to accept the arrangements which the militarists had long planned in secret. The militarist mind was much the same in all the countries, but there was a difference as to the extent to which the military and civilian authorities exercised control. General Joffre, in 1912, precisely like the German strategists, urged the strategic necessity of disregarding Belgian neutrality; but while Moltke was allowed to build his whole plan of campaign upon this violation of a treaty which Bethmann was helpless to avert if war came, M. Poincaré was strong enough and shrewd enough to veto General Joffre's views. He realized the bad effect it would have on public opinion in England, and the danger that it might cause the British Government to make use of its stipulated freedom to withhold armed aid.

Closely akin to this influence of military and naval officers was the pressure exerted on civilian authorities by munition makers and "big business."

Some militarists believed in "preventive" war—the waging of a war upon a neighbor while he was still weak, in order to prevent him growing stronger later on. So it is often alleged that Germany wanted war in 1914, in order to have a final reckoning with Slavdom before Russia should have completed her "Great Program" of military reorganization in 1916 or 1917. M. Poincaré and his associates are alleged to have wanted war in 1914 before Germany grew any stronger by reason of her rapidly increasing population, wealth, and naval force, and also before French Socialists, revolting against the burden of French military expenditure, should repeal the recently voted three-year term of service. For the same reasons Russian militarists are said to have wanted war sooner rather than later. England even is often said to have been glad of the opportunity to crush the growing German navy before it should become a greater menace to that of England. Though here and there some individual military and naval officers in most countries may have held such views, the present writer does not think that the militarist doctrine of preventive war was a decisive factor in causing the World War. Only in Austria-Hungary did it exercise a strong influence on state policy; here it was generally felt that a conflict with Serbia must come sooner or later, and, as Baron Conrad repeatedly urged, the sooner the better. The murder of the Heir to the Throne was eagerly seized upon as a good excuse for trampling upon the Greater Serbia danger.

Nor is there any more substantial truth in the common assertion that the German authorities welcomed war as a means of crushing the rising tide of socialism, than there is in the similar assertion that Russia welcomed war as a good way of putting an end to workingmen's strikes and revolutionary unrest.

Generally speaking, it may be said that this aspect of militarism—the influence of the military upon the civilian authorities—was a serious matter in the three eastern monarchies of Germany, Austria, and Russia. It was much less in France, and virtually non-existent in England, where civilian ministers were ordinarily in charge of the army and navy.[1]

We shall have something more to say about militarism and navalism in connection with the system of alliances.

(c) Nationalism

Nationalism, whose essence and development have recently been so admirably analyzed by a distinguished American historian,[2] must be accounted

---

[1] On these aspects of militarism, cf. H. N. Brailsford, *The War of Steel and Gold,* London, 1914; Karl Liebknecht, *Militarism,* New York, 1917; Munroe Smith, *Militarism and Statecraft,* New York, 1918; [F. C. Endres], *Die Tragödie Deutschlands,* 3rd ed., with abundant bibliographies, Stuttgart, 1924; and the admirable volume of G. L. Dickinson, *The International Anarchy, 1904–1914,* London, 1926.

[2] C. J. Hayes, *Essays on Nationalism,* New York, 1926; and "Contributions of Herder to the Doctrine of Nationalism," in *Am. Hist. Rev.,* XXXII, 719–736 (July, 1927).

one of the major underlying causes of the War. In its chronic form of Pan-Germanism, Pan-Slavism and *revanche,* it nourished hatred between Germany and her two neighbors on the East and West. It worked in curious and devious ways. It had contributed happily to the unification of Germany and Italy. On the other hand, it had disrupted the Ottoman Empire and threatened to disrupt the Hapsburg Monarchy. In its virulent form, it had contributed for a century to a series of wars for national liberation and unity in the Balkans. It was such an important factor in the Balkan situation and led so directly to the immediate occasion of the World War that some account of it in this corner of Europe will be given below in the chapter on Balkan Problems.

(d) Economic Imperialism

Economic imperialism embraces a series of international rivalries which resulted in large part from the Industrial Revolution in England and its subsequent introduction into the other great countries of the world.[3] It led to quantity production of goods which in turn involved the struggle for new markets and new sources of raw materials. It resulted in a great increase of population, part of which sought to emigrate to the still unoccupied regions of the world, thereby sharpening the colonial rivalry of the Great Powers. It brought about the accumulation of capital which sought investment abroad, thus leading to economic exploitation and political competition. In consequence of these and other factors, the Great Powers began to partition Africa among themselves, to secure territory or exclusive spheres of influence in China, and to build railroads in Turkey and elsewhere. This struggle for markets, raw materials, and colonies became more acute during the last quarter of the nineteenth and the beginning of the twentieth century, owing to the fact that Germany and Italy entered the competition. Hitherto politically weak and divided, they had now secured national unity and wished to come forward to share with the other Powers in the partitioning of the world. It can hardly be said that any one of the Great Powers was more responsible than another for the international jealousies and friction which arose out of this economic imperialism. By 1914, all the Great European Powers had secured slices of Africa. In China, Italy only had failed to gain something for herself. In the matter of railway construction, which was one of the most important forms of economic imperialism because it involved political as well as economic interests, one sees the English building the Cape-to-Cairo railway, the Russians the Trans-Siberian, and the Germans the so-called Bagdad Railway. The first of these came into conflict with German, Belgian and French ambitions; the second

[3] For an excellent recent discussion of this whole subject, see Parker T. Moon, *Imperialism and World Politics,* New York, 1926; and A. Lumbroso, *Le origini economichi e diplomatichi della guerra mondiale,* Milano, 1927.

was partly responsible for the Russo-Japanese War; the third caused endless suspicions and friction between Germany and the Triple Entente.

Protective tariffs which usually accompanied the modern industrial system, except in England, were another form of economic imperialism. "Tariff wars" and retaliatory measures caused irritation between countries, especially in the mind of the man in the street and in newspaper discussion. There was always the danger that great merchants and industrialists would use official government support to secure economic advantages for themselves. This tended to bring governments into conflict with one another.

Generally speaking, however, this economic imperialism is usually exaggerated as one of the underlying causes of the War. It is often said, for instance, that the industrial development of Germany, and the jealousy with which it was regarded by England, made a war between these two countries "inevitable" sooner or later. This, however, is an unsound view. It arises from the fact that economic rivalry tends to become exaggerated in the mind of the public, because it is a subject which touches the pockets of wide classes, and is more generally discussed and perhaps understood than other questions like secret treaties, militarism, or nationalism. It often happens that great merchants or industrialists own or control newspapers which are selfishly interested in contributing to the exaggeration of these economic questions. But if one reads the diplomatic correspondence of the years before the War, one is struck by the relatively slight importance which is given to these economic rivalries which haunt so largely the mind of the average business man and newspaper editor. It is not so much questions of economic rivalry as those of prestige, boundaries, armies and navies, the Balance of Power, and possible shiftings in the system of alliances, which provoke reams of diplomatic correspondence and raise the temperature in Foreign Offices to the danger point.

(e) The Newspaper Press

Another underlying cause of the War was the poisoning of public opinion by the newspaper press in all of the great countries. This is a subject which is only beginning to receive the careful investigation which it deserves.[4]

Too often newspapers in all lands were inclined to inflame nationalistic feelings, misrepresent the situation in foreign countries, and suppress factors

---

[4] *Cf.* E. M. Carroll, "French Public Opinion in the War of 1870," in *Amer. Hist. Rev.*, XXXI, 679–700, July, 1926; J. F. Scott, *Five Weeks: a Study of the Surge of Public Opinion on the Eve of the Great War*, New York, 1927; I. C. Willis, *How We Went into the War*, London, 1918; L. M. Salmon, *The Newspaper and Authority* (N. Y., 1923), chs. xii–xiv; F. R. Flournoy, *Parliament and War—The Relation of the British Parliament to the Administration of Foreign Policy in Connection with the Initiation of War*, London, 1927.

in favor of peace. In the diplomatic correspondence of the forty years before the War there were innumerable cases in which Governments were eager to establish better relations and secure friendly arrangements, but were hampered by the jingoistic attitude of the newspapers in their respective countries. Ambassadors and Cabinet Ministers frequently admitted the senseless attitude of the leading newspapers in their own country, apologized for it and promised to exert themselves to restrain it, if only the other Government would do the same toward its press. These were often quite genuine efforts and may frequently be seen in Anglo-German relations in the quarter of a century before the War. At other times, however, Ministers sought to score an advantage or to defend their attitude by alleging that their freedom of action was restricted because of the press and public opinion—that if they yielded the point under dispute there would be such a howl from the newspapers and the public that they would be turned out of office. Such allegations are sometimes true, but more often they are not, particularly in the countries of Central and Eastern Europe, where the Government was generally able to exercise a greater control over the press than in England. It is, nevertheless, true that the newspapers of two countries often took up some point of dispute, exaggerated it, and made attacks and counter-attacks, until a regular newspaper war was engendered, which thoroughly poisoned public opinion, and so offered a fertile soil in which the seeds of real war might easily germinate. A particularly good example of this is to be seen in the press feud carried on between Austria and Serbia in the weeks following the murder of the Archduke Ferdinand. Here was a case in which the Governments of both countries, instead of apologizing for their press or trying to restrain it, deliberately allowed the newspapers to incite public opinion and fire it to an indignation and enthusiasm for war. It would, perhaps, be too much to say that, had it not been for this Austro-Serbian newspaper feud, the War might have been averted. But it is true that the violence of the Serbian press was one of the determining factors which led Count Tisza to change his opinion and to accept war with Serbia, whereas at first he had been stubbornly opposed to it; and without his consent Count Berchtold and the militarists could not have made war on Serbia.

There is a vast literature on freedom of the press, censorship of the press, slander and libel, and the professional aspects of journalism, but there is very little sound writing on the relations of the press to governmental control and on its influence in fomenting national hatreds and war. Yet there is abundant material for the study of this in the newspapers themselves; in *Die Grosse Politik,* and other diplomatic documents; and in the writings and biographies of men like W. T. Stead, Wickham Steed, Spender, and Northcliffe; of Busch, Hammann, and Theodor Wolff; of Lauzanne, Gauvin, and Tardieu; of Blowitz and Suvorin; and of Godkin, Ogden, Villard, and Lippmann. It is to be hoped that some careful scholars will turn their attention to this problem of the influence of the newspaper press as one of the underlying causes of the War. Bismarck's oft-quoted remark is even more true for the generation immediately preceding the World War than for his own: "Every country is held at some time to account for the windows broken by its press; the bill is presented, some day or other, in the shape of hostile sentiment in the other country."

* * *

None of the Powers wanted a European War. Their governing rulers and ministers, with very few exceptions, all foresaw that it must be a frightful struggle, in which the political results were not absolutely certain, but in which the loss of life, suffering, and economic consequences were bound to be terrible. This is true, in a greater or less degree, of Pashitch, Berchtold, Bethmann, Sazonov, Poincaré, San Giuliano and Sir Edward Grey. Yet none of them, not even Sir Edward Grey, could have foreseen that the political results were to be so stupendous, and the other consequences so terrible, as was actually the case.

For many of the Powers, to be sure, a European War might seem to hold out the possibility of achieving various desired advantages: for Serbia, the achievement of national unity for all Serbs; for Austria, the revival of her waning prestige as a Great Power, and the checking of nationalistic tendencies which threatened her very existence; for Russia, the accomplishment of her historic mission of controlling Constantinople and the Straits; for Germany, new economic advantages and the restoration of the European balance which had changed with the weakening of the Triple Alliance and the tightening of the Triple Entente; for France, the recovery of Alsace-Lorraine and the ending of the German menace; and for England, the destruction of the German naval danger and of Prussian militarism. All these advantages, and many others, were feverishly striven and intrigued for, on all sides, the moment the War actually broke out, but this is no good proof that any of the statesmen mentioned deliberately aimed to bring about a war to secure these advantages. One cannot judge the motives which actuated men before the War, by what they did in an absolutely new situation which arose as soon as they were overtaken by a conflagration they had sought to avert. And in fact, in the case of the two Powers between whom the immediate conflict arose, the postponement or avoidance of a European War would have facilitated the accomplishment of the ultimate advantages aimed at: Pashitch knew that there was a better chance for Serbian national unity after he had consolidated Serbian gains in the Balkan Wars, and after Russia had completed her military and naval armaments as planned for 1917; and Berchtold knew that he had a better chance of crushing the Greater Serbia danger and strengthening Austria, if he could avoid Russian intervention and a general European War.

It is also true, likewise, that the moment war was declared, it was hailed with varying demonstrations of enthusiasm on the part of the people in every country—with considerable in Serbia, Austria, Russia and Germany, with less in France, and with almost none in England. But this does not mean that the peoples wanted war or exerted a decisive influence to bring it about. It is a curious psychological phenomenon that as soon as a country engages in war, there develops or is created among the masses a frenzy of patriotic excitement which is no index of their pre-war desires. And in the countries where the demonstrations of enthusiasm were greatest, the political influence of the people on the Government was least.

Nevertheless, a European War broke out. Why? Because in each country political and military leaders did certain things, which led to mobilizations and declarations of war, or failed to do certain things which might have prevented them. In this sense, all the European countries, in a greater or less degree, were responsible. One must abandon the dictum of the Versailles Treaty that Germany and her allies were solely responsible. It was a dictum exacted by victors from vanquished, under the influence of the blindness, ignorance, hatred, and the propagandist misconceptions to which war had given rise. It was based on evidence which was incomplete and not always sound.[5] It is generally recognized by the best historical scholars in all countries to be no longer tenable or defensible. They are agreed that the responsibility for the War is a divided responsibility. But they still disagree very much as to the relative part of this responsibility that falls on each country and on each individual political or military leader.

Some writers like to fix positively in some precise mathematical fashion the exact responsibility for the war. This was done in one way by the framers of Article 231 of the Treaty of Versailles. It has been done in other ways by those who would fix the responsibility in some relative fashion, as, for instance, Austria first, then Russia, France and Germany and England. But the present writer deprecates such efforts to assess by a precise formula a very complicated question, which is after all more a matter of delicate shading than of definite white and black. Oversimplification, as Napoleon once said in framing his Code, is the enemy of precision. Moreover, even supposing that a general consensus of opinion might be reached as to the relative responsibility of any individual country or man for immediate causes connected with the July crisis of 1914, it is by no means necessarily true that the same relative responsibility would hold for the underlying causes, which for years had been tending toward the creation of a dangerous situation.

[5] For a recent analysis of the evidence laid before the Commission on Responsibility for the War at the Paris Peace Conference, and the untenability of the conclusions based upon it, see A. von Wegerer, "Die Wiederlegung der Versailles Kriegsschuldthese," in *Die Kriegsschuldfrage*, VI, 1–77, Jan., 1928; also his article, with replies to it, in *Current History*, Aug., 1928, pp. 810–828.

One may, however, sum up very briefly the most salient facts in regard to each country.

Serbia felt a natural and justifiable impulse to do what so many other countries had done in the nineteenth century—to bring under one national Government all the discontented Serb people. She had liberated those under Turkish rule; the next step was to liberate those under Hapsburg rule. She looked to Russia for assistance, and had been encouraged to expect that she would receive it. After the assassination, Mr. Pashitch took no steps to discover and bring to justice Serbians in Belgrade who had been implicated in the plot. One of them, Ciganovitch, was even assisted to disappear. Mr. Pashitch waited to see what evidence the Austrian authorities could find. When Austria demanded coöperation of Serbian officials in discovering, though not in trying, implicated Serbians, the Serbian Government made a very conciliatory but negative reply. They expected that the reply would not be regarded as satisfactory, and, even before it was given, ordered the mobilization of the Serbian army. Serbia did not want war, but believed it would be forced upon her. That Mr. Pashitch was aware of the plot three weeks before it was executed, failed to take effective steps to prevent the assassins from crossing over from Serbia to Bosnia, and then failed to give Austria any warning or information which might have averted the fatal crime, were facts unknown to Austria in July, 1914; they cannot therefore be regarded as in any way justifying Austria's conduct; but they are part of Serbia's responsibility, and a very serious part.

Austria was more responsible for the immediate origin of the war than any other Power. Yet from her own point of view she was acting in self-defence—not against an immediate military attack, but against the corroding Greater Serbia and Jugoslav agitation which her leaders believed threatened her very existence. No State can be expected to sit with folded arms and await dismemberment at the hands of its neighbors. Russia was believed to be intriguing with Serbia and Rumania against the Dual Monarchy. The assassination of the heir to the throne, as a result of a plot prepared in Belgrade, demanded severe retribution; otherwise Austria would be regarded as incapable of action, "worm-eaten" as the Serbian Press expressed it, would sink in prestige, and hasten her own downfall. To avert this Berchtold determined to crush Serbia with war. He deliberately framed the ultimatum with the expectation and hope that it would be rejected. He hurriedly declared war against Serbia in order to forestall all efforts at mediation. He refused even to answer his own ally's urgent requests to come to an understanding with Russia, on the basis of a military occupation of Belgrade as a pledge that Serbia would carry out the promises in her reply to the ultimatum. Berchtold gambled on a "local" war with Serbia only, believing that he could rattle the German sword; but rather than abandon his war with Serbia, he was ready to drag the rest of Europe into war.

It is very questionable whether Berchtold's obstinate determination to diminish Serbia and destroy her as a Balkan factor was, after all, the right method, even if he had succeeded in keeping the war "localized" and in temporarily strengthening the Dual Monarchy. Supposing that Russia in 1914, because of military unpreparedness or lack of support, had been ready to tolerate the execution of Berchtold's designs, it is quite certain that she would have aimed within the next two or three years at wiping out this second humiliation, which was so much more damaging to her prestige than that of 1908–09. In two or three years, when her great program of military reform was finally completed, Russia would certainly have found a pretext to reverse the balance in the Balkans in her own favor again. A further consequence of Berchtold's policy, even if successful, would have been the still closer consolidation of the Triple Entente, with the possible addition of Italy. And, finally, a partially dismembered Serbia would have become a still greater source of unrest and danger to the peace of Europe than heretofore. Serbian nationalism, like Polish nationalism, would have been intensified by partition. Austrian power and prestige would not have been so greatly increased as to be able to meet these new dangers. Berchtold's plan was a mere temporary improvement, but could not be a final solution of the Austro-Serbian antagonism. Franz Ferdinand and many others recognized this, and so long as he lived, no step in this fatal direction had been taken. It was the tragic fate of Austria that the only man who might have had the power and ability to develop Austria along sound lines became the innocent victim of the crime which was the occasion of the World War and so of her ultimate disruption.

Germany did not plot a European War, did not want one, and made genuine, though too belated efforts, to avert one. She was the victim of her alliance with Austria and of her own folly. Austria was her only dependable ally, Italy and Rumania having become nothing but allies in name. She could not throw her over, as otherwise she would stand isolated between Russia, where Panslavism and armaments were growing stronger every year, and France, where Alsace-Lorraine, Delcassé's fall, and Agadir were not forgotten. Therefore, Bethmann felt bound to accede to Berchtold's request for support and gave him a free hand to deal with Serbia; he also hoped and expected to "localize" the Austro-Serbian conflict. Germany then gave grounds to the Entente for suspecting the sincerity of her peaceful intentions by her denial of any foreknowledge of the ultimatum, by her support and justification of it when it was published, and by her refusal of Sir Edward Grey's conference proposal. However, Germany by no means had Austria so completely under her thumb as the Entente Powers and many writers have assumed. It is true that Berchtold would hardly have embarked on his gambler's policy unless he had been assured that Germany would fulfil the obligations of the alliance, and to this extent Germany must share the great responsibility of

Austria. But when Bethmann realized that Russia was likely to intervene, that England might not remain neutral, and that there was danger of a world war of which Germany and Austria would appear to be the instigators, he tried to call a halt on Austria, but it was too late. He pressed mediation proposals on Vienna, but Berchtold was insensible to the pressure, and the Entente Powers did not believe in the sincerity of his pressure, especially as they produced no results.

Germany's geographical position between France and Russia, and her inferiority in number of troops, had made necessary the plan of crushing the French army quickly at first and then turning against Russia. This was only possible, in the opinion of her strategists, by marching through Belgium, as it was generally anticipated by military men that she would do in case of a European War. On July 29, after Austria had declared war on Serbia, and after the Tsar had assented to general mobilization in Russia (though this was not known in Berlin and was later postponed for a day owing to the Kaiser's telegram to the Tsar), Bethmann took the precaution of sending to the German Minister in Brussels a sealed envelope. The Minister was not to open it except on further instructions. It contained the later demand for the passage of the German army through Belgium. This does not mean, however, that Germany had decided for war. In fact, Bethmann was one of the last of the statesmen to abandon hope of peace and to consent to the mobilization of his country's army. General mobilization of the continental armies took place in the following order: Serbia, Russia, Austria, France and Germany. General mobilization by a Great Power was commonly interpreted by military men in every country, though perhaps not by Sir Edward Grey, the Tsar, and some civilian officials, as meaning that the country was on the point of making war —that the military machine had begun to move and would not be stopped. Hence, when Germany learned of the Russian general mobilization, she sent ultimatums to St. Petersburg and Paris, warning that German mobilization would follow unless Russia suspended hers within twelve hours, and asking what would be the attitude of France. The answers being unsatisfactory, Germany then mobilized and declared war. It was the hasty Russian general mobilization, assented to on July 29 and ordered on July 30, while Germany, was still trying to bring Austria to accept mediation proposals, which finally rendered the European War inevitable.

Russia was partly responsible for the Austro-Serbian conflict because of the frequent encouragment which she had given at Belgrade—that Serbian national unity would be ultimately achieved with Russian assistance at Austrian expense. This had led the Belgrade Cabinet to hope for Russian support in case of a war with Austria, and the hope did not prove vain in July, 1914. Before this, to be sure, in the Bosnian Crisis and during the Balkan Wars, Russia had put restraint upon Serbia, because Russia, exhausted by the effects of the Russo-Japanese War, was not yet ready for a European struggle with the Teutonic Powers. But in 1914 her armaments, though not yet completed, had made such progress that the militarists were confident of success, if they had French and British support. In the spring of 1914, the Minister of War, Sukhomlinov, had published an article in a Russian newspaper, though without signing his name, to the effect, "Russia is ready, France must be ready also." Austria was convinced that Russia would ultimately aid Serbia, unless the Serbian danger were dealt with energetically after the Archduke's murder; she knew that Russia was growing stronger every year; but she doubted whether the Tsar's armaments had yet reached the point at which Russia would dare to intervene; she would therefore run less risk of Russian intervention and a European War if she used the Archduke's assassination as an excuse for weakening Serbia, than if she should postpone action until the future.

Russia's responsibility lay also in the secret preparatory military measures which she was making at the same time that she was carrying on diplomatic negotiations. These alarmed Germany and Austria. But it was primarily Russia's general mobilization, made when Germany was trying to bring Austria to a settlement, which precipitated the final catastrophe, causing Germany to mobilize and declare war.

The part of France is less clear than that of the other Great Powers, because she has not yet made a full publication of her documents. To be sure, M. Poincaré, in the fourth volume of his memoirs, has made a skilful and elaborate plea, to prove *"La France innocente."* But he is not convincing. It is quite clear that on his visit to Russia he assured the Tsar's Government that France would support her as an ally in preventing Austria from humiliating or crushing Serbia. Paléologue renewed these assurances in a way to encourage Russia to take a strong hand. He did not attempt to restrain Russia from military measures which he knew would call forth German counter-measures and cause war. Nor did he keep his Government promptly and fully informed of the military steps which were being taken at St. Petersburg. President Poincaré, upon his return to France, made efforts for peace, but his great preoccupation was to minimize French and Russian preparatory measures and emphasize those of Germany, in order to secure the certainty of British support in a struggle which he now regarded as inevitable.

Sir Edward Grey made many sincere proposals for preserving peace; they all failed owing partly, but not exclusively, to Germany's attitude. Sir Edward could probably have prevented war if he had done either of two things. If, early in the crisis, he had acceded to the urging of France and Russia and given a strong warning to Germany that, in a European War, England would take the side of the Franco-Russian Alliance, this would probably have led Bethmann to exert an earlier and more effective pressure on Austria; and it would perhaps thereby have prevented the Austrian declaration of war on

Serbia, and brought to a successful issue the "direct conversations" between Vienna and St. Petersburg. Or, if Sir Edward Grey had listened to German urging, and warned France and Russia early in the crisis, that if they became involved in war, England would remain neutral, probably Russia would have hesitated with her mobilizations, and France would probably have exerted a restraining influence at St. Petersburg. But Sir Edward Grey could not say that England would take the side of France and Russia, because he had a Cabinet nearly evenly divided, and he was not sure, early in the crisis, that public opinion in England would back him up in war against Germany. He could resign, and he says in his memoirs that he would have resigned, but that would have been no comfort or aid to France, who had come confidently to count upon British support. He was determined to say and do nothing which might encourage her with a hope which he could not fulfil. Therefore, in spite of the pleadings of the French, he refused to give them definite assurances until the probable German determination to go through Belgium made it clear that the Cabinet, and Parliament, and British public opinion would follow his lead in war on Germany. On the other hand, he was unwilling to heed the German pleadings that he exercise restraint at Paris and St. Petersburg, because he did not wish to endanger the Anglo-Russian Entente and the solidarity of the Triple Entente, because he felt a moral obligation to France, growing out of the Anglo-French military and naval conversations of the past years, and because he suspected that Germany was backing Austria up in an unjustifiable course and that Prussian militarists had taken the direction of affairs at Berlin out of the hands of Herr von Bethmann-Hollweg and the civilian authorities.

Italy exerted relatively little influence on the crisis in either direction.

Belgium had done nothing in any way to justify the demand which Germany made upon her. With commendable prudence, at the very first news of the ominous Austrian ultimatum, she had foreseen the danger to which she might be exposed. She had accordingly instructed her representatives abroad as to the statements which they were to make in case Belgium should decide very suddenly to mobilize to protect her neutrality. On July 29, she placed her army upon "a strengthened war footing," but did not order complete mobilization until two days later, when Austria, Russia, and Germany had already done so, and war appeared inevitable. Even after being confronted with the terrible German ultimatum, at 7 P.M. on August 2, she did not at once invite the assistance of English and French troops to aid her in the defense of her soil and her neutrality against a certain German assault; it was not until German troops had actually violated her territory, on August 4, that she appealed for the assistance of the Powers which had guaranteed her neutrality. Belgium was the innocent victim of German strategic necessity. Though the German violation of Belgium was of enormous influence in forming public opinion as to the responsibility for the War after hostilities began, it was not a cause of the War, except in so far as it made it easier for Sir Edward Grey to bring England into it.

In the forty years following the Franco-Prussian War, as we have seen, there developed a system of alliances which divided Europe into two hostile groups. This hostility was accentuated by the increase of armaments, economic rivalry, nationalist ambitions and antagonisms, and newspaper incitement. But it is very doubtful whether all these dangerous tendencies would have actually led to war, had it not been for the assassination of Franz Ferdinand. That was the factor which consolidated the elements of hostility and started the rapid and complicated succession of events which culminated in a World War, and for that factor Serbian nationalism was primarily responsible.

But the verdict of the Versailles Treaty that Germany and her allies were responsible for the War, in view of the evidence now available, is historically unsound. It should therefore be revised. However, because of the popular feeling widespread in some of the Entente countries, it is doubtful whether a formal and legal revision is as yet practicable. There must first come a further revision by historical scholars, and through them of public opinion.

The Outbreak of War in Europe, 1914

A. J. P. Taylor

THE NEW antagonism between Germany and Russia which had been brought out by the Liman von Sanders affair dominated European relations in the spring of 1914. Both sought to strengthen their diplomatic position. But there was a basic difference of aim. The Russians wanted to create an alliance with Great Britain and France so strong that Germany would shrink from war; the Germans wanted to challenge Russia before the opposing alliance was consolidated and while they still had a military lead. Sazonov wrote to Benckendorff on 19 February: "The peace of the world will be secure only when the Triple Entente . . . is transformed into a defensive alliance without secret clauses. Then the danger of a German

From A. J. P. Taylor, *The Struggle for Mastery in Europe, 1848–1918* (Oxford: The Clarendon Press, 1954), pp. 511–31. By permission of the Clarendon Press, Oxford.

hegemony will be finally ended, and each of us can devote himself to his own affairs: the English can seek a solution of their social problems, the French can get rich, protected from any external threat, and we can consolidate ourselves and work on our economic reorganization." [1] Benckendorff replied, "If Grey could, he would do it to-morrow." [2] This was an exaggeration. Though the permanent officials at the foreign office advocated an alliance with Russia —as much to keep her favour as to restrain Germany—Grey would have none of it. He sheltered behind the excuse of public opinion; and any proposal for alliance with Russia would certainly have broken up the liberal government. But the policy of keeping a free hand represented Grey's own outlook. He wished to be on good terms with Russia; and he would undoubtedly urge support of France if she were attacked by Germany. Beyond this he would not go. He could not understand an alliance as a security for peace; like most Englishmen, he regarded all alliances as a commitment to war. Besides, though he welcomed Russia's weight in the Balance of Power, he was not convinced that her interests in the Near East were a vital concern for Great Britain— perhaps it would be better if Russia and Germany fought things out there and exhausted each other. In April he accompanied George V to Paris—his first visit to the Continent as foreign secretary—and, while there, defined his attitude to the French:

If there were a really aggressive and menacing attack made by Germany upon France, it was possible that public feeling in Great Britain would justify the Government in helping France. But it was not likely that Germany would make an aggressive and menacing attack upon Russia; and, even if she did, people in Great Britain would be inclined to say that, though Germany might have successes at first, Russia's resources were so great that, in the long run, Germany would be exhausted without our helping Russia.[3]

The French did not welcome this reply. They felt themselves to be a hostage towards Germany for both Great Britain and Russia; and were more anxious to bring the two together than at any time since Delcassé first launched the project of a Triple Entente in the days before the Russo-Japanese war.

Grey made some concession, more to please the French than the Russians: he agreed to Anglo-Russian naval talks on the model of the 1912 discussions with France.[4] This was not a serious project: the two fleets could not cooperate anywhere. As Grey wrote later, it was useful "for the purpose of keeping Russia in good disposition, and of not offending her by refusing." [5] The

[1] Sazonov to Benckendorff, 19 Feb. 1914. *Mezhdunarodnye otnosheniya,* third series, i, no. 232.
[2] Benckendorff to Sazonov, 25 Feb. 1914. *Ibid.,* no. 328.
[3] Grey to Bertie, 1 May 1914. *British Documents,* x (ii), no. 541.
[4] This time Grey took the precaution of securing the approval of the cabinet from the start.
[5] Grey, *Twenty-Five Years,* i. 284.

British cabinet held that they were not committed by the naval agreement with France; therefore they authorized similar talks with the Russians. These, on the other hand, exaggerated the extent to which Great Britain was committed to France; and therefore supposed that they were getting something of value. Grey exacted a price even for this concession. He repeated his old demand that Russia must behave better in Persia if she wanted the entente to become more effective; and this time the Russians did something to meet him. Sazonov tried to restrain his agents in Persia. Moreover, he offered to surrender the neutral zone to the British [6] and even to give them a guarantee of India, for what that was worth, if only the naval agreement could be settled.[7] These negotiations were still hanging fire at the end of June: there was no Anglo-Russian alliance, nor even any certainty that their disputes in Persia would be smoothed over.[8]

Russia had not improved her diplomatic position against Germany. On the contrary, the Germans learnt of the proposed naval talks through the treachery of a member of the Russian embassy in London, who kept them regularly supplied with Benckendorff's correspondence; and they published the story in a German newspaper. The outcry which followed in England made it impossible for Grey to go on with the talks for the moment. What is more, radical members of the government still believed that relations with Germany were improving. Churchill imagined that a meeting between himself and Tirpitz "might do good, and could not possibly do any harm." [9] Lloyd George went further. On 23 July he spoke in the House of Commons and said of Germany: "Our relations are very much better than they were a few years ago. . . . The two great Empires begin to realize they can co-operate for common ends, and that the points of co-operation are greater and more numerous and more important than the points of possible controversy." [10] A general election was now approaching in Great Britain; [11] and, though a historian should never deal in speculations about what did not happen, it is difficult to resist the surmise that Lloyd George was planning to fight this election as leader of a radical-labour coalition. Reconciliation with Germany, and resistance to Russia in Persia, must have been part of the coalition's programme. In France, too, opinion was changing. There a general election in April returned a majority against the three-year service; and in June Poincaré had to appoint a

[6] Sazonov to Benckendorff, 24 June 1914. *Mezhdunarodnye otnosheniya,* third series, iii, no. 343.

[7] Sazonov to Benckendorff, 25 June 1914. *Ibid.,* no. 361.

[8] The last letter written by George V to Nicholas II in peace-time (16 June 1914) was an appeal to improve relations in Persia. *British Documents,* x (ii), no. 549.

[9] Memorandum by Churchill, 20 May 1914. *Ibid.,* no. 511.

[10] *Hansard,* fifth series, lxv. 727.

[11] By the terms of the Parliament Act of 1911, a general election must have taken place before December 1915; practice made it more likely in the autumn of 1914 or, at latest, the spring of 1915.

left-wing government under Viviani, much against his will. Only a sordid private scandal [12] enabled him to escape Caillaux, supported by Jaurès and the socialists, with a programme of full Franco-German reconciliation. In fact, a coalition of the three advanced western Powers against the Russian colossus seemed just round the corner.

Bethmann, at least, recognized that the situation was changing in Germany's favour. He wrote on 16 June: "Whether a European conflagration comes depends solely on the attitude of Germany and England. If we both stand together as guarantors of European peace, which is not prevented by the engagements of either the Triple Alliance or the entente, *provided we pursue this aim on a common plan from the start,* war can be avoided." [13] Nor had the Germans any illusion about Austria-Hungary. Tschirschky, the ambassador at Vienna, wrote in May: "How often do I consider whether it is really worth while to unite ourselves so closely to this state-structure which is cracking at every joint and to continue the laborious task of dragging her along." [14] The Germans could have escaped this task, if security was their only object, by accepting the friendship of British and French pacific radicalism; but a genuine alliance for peace was not to their taste. The Germans were bent on going forward in the world; and Austria-Hungary was essential to them if they were to gain control of the Near East. The Austro-Hungarian ambassador at Constantinople posed the choice before the Germans with bitter satisfaction: "Either the abandonment of the Bosphorus and of Germany's position in the Near East or marching on the side of Austria through thick and thin." [15] As often happens, Germany's ambitions made her the captive of her weaker partner. The Germans set out to refloat Austria-Hungary as a Great Power; her ambitions had to be encouraged, her resources bolstered up for the conflict. On 12 May Conrad met Moltke at Karlsbad (Kárlovy Vary). Previously Moltke had urged Conrad to keep the peace until a more favourable opportunity. Now he declared that it was hopeless to wait for a promise of neutrality from Great Britain which she would never give: "Any delay means a lessening of our chances; we cannot compete with Russia in man-power." [16] The conclusion was obvious: Germany and Austria-Hungary must strike before the expansion of the Russian army got under way.

The two central Powers were still far from an agreed programme. The Germans had neither sympathy nor understanding for the national problems

---

[12] Caillaux's second wife killed the editor of a Paris newspaper, to prevent the publication of love-letters which her husband had written to her before their marriage. This made Caillaux impossible as prime minister for the time being.

[13] Bethmann to Lichnowsky, 16 June 1914. *Grosse Politik,* xxxix, no. 15883.

[14] Tschirschky to Jagow, 22 May 1914. *Ibid.,* no. 15734.

[15] Pallavicini to Berchtold, 6 July 1914. *Österreich-Ungarns Aussenpolitik,* viii, no. 10083.

[16] Conrad, *Aus meiner Dienstzeit,* iii. 670.

of the Habsburg monarchy. Certainly they wanted to preserve it as a Great Power; and they even recognized that Hungary was its core. William II said to Tisza in March: "A *German* Austria and a *Hungarian* Hungary were the two firm pillars of the Monarchy." [17] But they thought that this was compatible with a policy which would win both Serbia and Rumania to their side. They never considered how this could be done with Serbia, except for vague talk "of the dependence of the lesser upon the greater as in the planetary system." [18] Rumania seemed to them to hold the key to the Balkans: if she were loyal to her alliance of 1883 she could force Serbia on the same course. This policy was antiquated. Rumania had once sought security against Russia; now, as a great wheat-exporting country, she had a common interest with her in the free passage of the Straits. Even more decisive, her national aspirations had been stirred by the victory of the Balkan states. Unlike theirs, these could not be achieved against Turkey. They could succeed only by liberating the 2,000,000 Rumanians of Transylvania who were under Hungarian rule. This was a more dangerous challenge to the Habsburg monarchy than even the South Slav movement. A South Slav, or at any rate a Croat, kingdom might have been set up if Francis Ferdinand had come to the throne. The rulers of Hungary would never surrender Transylvania, where lay their richest estates and where lived nearly a million Magyars.

William II preached "a *Hungarian* Hungary"; yet he also advocated a conciliation of the Rumanians, which must have caused a head-on struggle with the Magyars. Only Francis Ferdinand was ready for this; and even he dared not air it to William II. The party of the heir-apparent made some feeble efforts to achieve their policy. In the autumn of 1913 Czernin, one of this group, went as minister to Bucarest. He soon reported: "the treaty of alliance is not worth the paper and ink with which it is written." [19] He proposed that Berchtold should put matters right by offering Rumania and Serbia a "guarantee" [20]—as though this would have satisfied either of them. The guarantee could have operated only against Bulgaria; and Berchtold was always dreaming of an alliance with her, so far as he had a policy at all. Czernin also urged some concessions to the Rumanians in Transylvania. Tisza, the Hungarian prime minister, brushed these aside; the German alliance should be used to force Rumania back into line.[21] The Germans wanted Hungary to make concessions to Rumania and Serbia in order to strengthen the Austro-German alliance; Tisza answered that this alliance made concessions

---

[17] Treutler to foreign ministry, 24 Mar. 1914. *Grosse Politik*, xxxix, no. 15716.

[18] Memorandum by Berchtold, 28 Oct. 1913. *Österreich-Ungarns Aussenpolitik*, vii,' no. 8934.

[19] Czernin to Berchtold, 7 Dec. 1913. *Österreich-Ungarns Aussenpolitik*, vii, no. 9062.

[20] Czernin to Berchtold, 23 Apr. 1914. *Ibid.*, no. 9600.

[21] Memorandum by Tisza, 15 Mar. 1914. *Ibid.*, no. 9482.

unnecessary. He got his way. No one in Vienna could control him; and the Germans were dazzled by his resoluteness. William II found him "a truly great statesman." [22]

On 13 June Francis Ferdinand met William II, for the last time, at Konopischt.[23] He nerved himself to denounce Tisza as the cause of all their troubles. William II only replied that he would instruct his ambassador to repeat to Tisza: "Lord, remember the Rumanians." [24] The Magyars were free to continue on their intransigent course; in the last resort, they dominated the Habsburg monarchy and so Germany, and could drag both Powers along with them. On 24 June Berchtold completed a memorandum on Austro-Hungarian policy, which had originated with Tisza. It advocated alliance with Bulgaria against both Serbia and Rumania. This was nothing new—it had been urged ineffectively by Berchtold since the beginning of the Balkan wars. But the Russian spectre was now brought in to make the proposal more attractive to the Germans: "the open endeavours of Russia to encircle the Monarchy have the ultimate aim of making it impossible for the German Empire to oppose Russia's distant aims of gaining political and economic supremacy." [25]

The Austrians had been raising the cry for thirty years that Russia was aiming directly at their destruction. The Germans had always been able to reply that Austria-Hungary was in no danger, so long as she kept clear of aggressive action in the Balkans; and this reply was often given. It was truer now than it had ever been. The Russians had no interest in the aggrandizement of either Serbia or Rumania; they merely wanted to keep these two countries as independent barriers between Germany and the Straits. But the Austrians could now argue that the real Russian challenge was to Germany and that she must therefore support Austria-Hungary's Balkan plans for her own sake. The Germans, like the Russians, had no Balkan interests. Their route to Constantinople was predominantly by sea through the Channel to the Mediterranean. They, too, wanted to keep Serbia and Rumania independent, though, of course, they hoped to keep them friendly by concessions at Austria-Hungary's expense. Instead they were dragged into these Balkan disputes in order to keep their only reliable ally afloat. The greater includes the less, as William II said on another occasion. The Germans anticipated a struggle for the mastery of Europe and the Middle East; the Austrians merely wished to end the nationalist agitation of two Balkan states with whom Germany had no quarrel. The

---

[22] Treutler to foreign ministry, 27 Mar. 1914. *Grosse Politik,* xxxix, no. 15720.

[23] This was the meeting at which the two were supposed to have planned a European war. In reality, they discussed only the question of Rumania. In any case, it is difficult to see how Francis Ferdinand could have planned a war which was to begin with his assassination.

[24] Treutler to Zimmermann, 15 June 1914. *Ibid.,* no. 15736.

[25] Memorandum by Berchtold, 24 June 1914. *Österreich-Ungarns Aussenpolitik,* viii, no. 9984.

only point of agreement between them was in believing that both problems could be settled by war.

The Austrians were right on the question of fact: both Serbia and Rumania were lost to the central Powers. That had been obvious with Serbia for long enough; though the Austrians exaggerated the Serb danger in order to excuse their own helpless incompetence in dealing with the South Slavs. The defection of Rumania was a more dramatic blow; it symbolized the ending of the precarious balance which had existed on the lower Danube since the Crimean war. On 14 June Nicholas II and Sazonov visited the king of Rumania, at Constantsa. Sazonov, on a motor-tour, crossed the Hungarian frontier into Transylvania. This somewhat tactless sign of approval for Rumanian irredentism was rewarded by assurances of neutrality, though not of armed support, in an Austro-Russian war. Sazonov noted: "Rumania will try to go with the side that turns out to be the stronger and can offer her the greater gains." [26] Sazonov had no serious intention of offering these gains unless war actually broke out. His policy was encirclement, not aggression, so far as the Balkans were concerned; or, to use a more respectable modern term, it was containment. Exactly the same was true of Great Britain in the west. No Power of the Triple Entente wanted a European upheaval; [27] all three would have liked to turn their backs on Europe and to pursue their imperial expansion in Asia and Africa. Germany, on the other hand, had come to feel that she could expand her overseas empire only after she had destroyed the European Balance of Power; and Austria-Hungary wanted a Balkan war in order to survive at all.

Yet it would be wrong to exaggerate the rigidity of the system of alliances or to regard the European war as inevitable. No war is inevitable until it breaks out. The existing alliances were all precarious. Italy was only the extreme example—renewing the Triple Alliance and making exaggerated promises of military support to Germany on one side; seeking to negotiate a Mediterranean agreement with France and Great Britain on the other. In France the Russian alliance was increasingly unpopular; it was threatened by a coalition between Caillaux the radical and Jaurès the socialist, which in the summer of 1914 seemed inevitable. Both men were anti-Russian, or at least anti-tsarist; both were friendly to Germany. In England the crisis over Home Rule was reaching its height. If it had exploded, there must have followed either a radical government, which would have been friendly to Germany, or—less likely—a conservative government, so weak as to be debarred from having a

[26] Sazonov to Nicholas II, 24 June 1914. *Mezhdunarodnye otnosheniya*, third series, iii, no. 339.

[27] It is often said that the French projected war in order to recover Alsace and Lorraine. There is not a scrap of evidence for this. The French knew that they would be hard put to it to maintain their independence against Germany if it came to a war, let alone make gains. Of course they demanded Alsace and Lorraine when war broke out, just as the British demanded the destruction of the German navy and the Russians demanded Constantinople. But these demands did not cause the war; they were caused by it.

foreign policy. Moreover, in June 1914, the British government at last reached agreement with Germany over the Bagdad railway; and the French had already done so in February. Both seemed to be taking sides with Germany against Russia in the great question of Turkey-in-Asia. The Russians had every reason to be dissatisfied with their position. The conservatives at court disliked both the estrangement from Germany and the demagogic patronage of Serbia. Imperialists were offended by British policy in Persia, especially its pursuit of oil-concessions.[28] They would gladly have swung on to an anti-British course, if Germany had given them security at the Straits.[29] Some Russians, more daring still, thought of an alliance with Turkey against the three western "capitalist" Powers; and in May 1914 a Turkish delegation visited Nicholas II at Livadia. If this revival of Unkiar Skelessi had been achieved, a diplomatic revolution must certainly have followed. As it was, alliance between Russia and Turkey had to wait until 1921.

Plenty of Germans knew that the ring round them was not solid. Bethmann and the foreign ministry counted rightly that Great Britain would turn away from Russia and towards them, if France were left alone. The great capitalists were winning the mastery of Europe without war: the industries of southern Russia, the iron-fields of Lorraine and Normandy were already largely under their control. Each group in Germany had a single enemy and would have liked to make peace with the others. But Germany lacked a directing hand to insist on priorities. It was easier to acquiesce in all the aggressive impulses and to drift with events. Germany lay in the centre of Europe. She could use this position to play off her neighbours against each other, as Bismarck had done and as Hitler was to do; or she could abuse her position to unite her neighbours against her, not from policy, but by having none. Tirpitz and his capitalist supporters wanted a naval conflict with Great Britain and deplored the hostility to France and Russia; the professional soldiers and their capitalist supporters wanted a continental war, especially against France, and deplored the naval rivalry with Great Britain; the mass parties—the social democrats and the Roman Catholic Centre—were friendly to both Great Britain and France and could be won only for the old radical programme of war against Russia. It is futile to discuss whether the great navy, the Bagdad railway, or the bid for continental supremacy was the decisive factor in German policy. But the bid for continental supremacy was certainly decisive in bringing on the European war. If Germany destroyed France as an independent Power, she could then pursue her imperial rivalries against Russia and Great Britain with some chance of

[28] In the spring of 1914 the Anglo-Persian Oil company, which was controlled by the Admiralty, made a compact with German interests in order to exclude their Russian and American competitors.

[29] This was always Nicolson's fear, and also that of Buchanan, ambassador at St. Petersburg. "Russia may strike a bargain with Germany and then resume her liberty of action in Turkey and Persia. Our position then would be a parlous one." Buchanan to Nicolson, 26 Apr. 1914. *British Documents*, x (ii), no. 588.

success. Both Powers had recognized this by supporting the independence of France long before either the German navy or the Bagdad railway existed. Nevertheless, they would not have been so ready to co-operate with France, and not ready at all to co-operate with each other, if Germany had not also challenged them directly. German policy, or rather lack of it, made the Triple Entente a reality. The feeble rulers of Germany, William II and Bethmann, preferred a ring of foreign enemies to trouble at home.

It has been strongly argued that the Germans deliberately timed war for August 1914.[30] There is little evidence for this, and a decisive argument against it. Bethmann and William II were incapable of consistent policy; Moltke, the chief-of-staff, could not conduct a campaign, let alone make a war. The Germans were involved in war by Austria-Hungary, but they went with her willingly. It was easy to co-operate with her; it would have needed a statesman to refuse. On 28 June Francis Ferdinand was assassinated at Sarejevo, the capital of Bosnia, by a Bosnian Serb.[31] Berchtold was weary of being jeered at by Conrad as irresolute and feeble. Moreover, when Turkey-in-Asia took the place of the Balkans as the centre of international rivalry, Austria-Hungary was pushed aside too; and the Germans had rejected with impatience Berchtold's claim to be allotted a "sphere" in Asia Minor.[32] The murder at Sarejevo revived the Balkan question and enabled Austria-Hungary to reappear misleadingly as a Great Power. This time she could only hold the centre of the stage if she actually provoked a war. The German talk of writing off Austria-Hungary and of somehow restoring good relations with Russia at her expense had not escaped Austrian attention: and the Habsburg monarchy brought on its mortal crisis to prove that it was still alive.

Berchtold determined to force war on Serbia, though he had no proofs of Serbian complicity and never found any.[33] Tisza, the Hungarian prime minister, opposed him. Berchtold wanted to restore the prestige of the monarchy; Tisza cared only for great Hungary. Like Kossuth before him, he looked to Germany,

[30] For instance by R. C. K. Ensor, *England 1870–1914*, pp. 469–70, 482.

[31] Much ink has been spilled over the question whether the Serbian government knew of the plot. A certain Ljuba Jovanovich claimed to have been told of it by Pashich, the Serb prime minister, in May. It later turned out that he also claimed to have been told of the plot to assassinate King Alexander in 1903. He was evidently an accomplished crystal-gazer. The Serbian government was unprepared for war, which could not have come at a less welcome time, when the army had not been remodelled after the Balkan wars. They certainly thought that it was likely Francis Ferdinand would be assassinated, if he provoked nationalist feeling by going to Sarajevo; and they warned Bilinski, the Austro-Hungarian minister of finance who was in charge of Bosnia, against the visit early in June. But, of course, the visit was meant to provoke nationalist feeling or, rather, to challenge it. It was deliberately timed for Serbia's national day, the anniversary of Kossovo. If a British royalty had visited Dublin on St. Patrick's day at the height of the Troubles, he, too, might have expected to be shot at.

[32] Jagow to Tschirschky, 25 Jan. 1914. *Grosse Politik,* xxxvii (ii), no. 15100.

[33] This is agreed by all authorities. The later evidence of Serbian complicity, even if accepted, is therefore irrelevant to the judgment of Berchtold's policy.

not to Vienna, as Hungary's ally and would not have much regretted the collapse of the Dual Monarchy, so long as great Hungary survived.[34] Berchtold turned Tisza's opposition by appealing to Germany for support; Tisza could not hold out if Berlin, not Vienna, urged war. Berchtold took out his memorandum of 24 June, which had urged alliance with Bulgaria; added a postscript blaming Serbia for the assassination; and accompanied this with a letter from Francis Joseph to William II, which managed to blame Russian Panslavism as well. The conclusion: "Serbia must be eliminated as a political factor in the Balkans . . . friendly settlement is no longer to be thought of." These two documents were presented to William II on 5 July.

At Berlin there was no serious consultation. William II invited the Austro-Hungarian ambassador to lunch at Potsdam. At first he said that he must wait for Bethmann's opinion; then changed his mind after lunch and committed himself. Szögyény, the Austrian ambassador, reported: "Action against Serbia should not be delayed. . . . Even if it should come to a war between Austria and Russia, we could be convinced that Germany would stand by our side with her accustomed faithfulness as an ally." [35] Bethmann arrived in the afternoon, went for a walk in the park with William II, and approved of what he had said. The next day he gave Szögyény official confirmation: "Austria must judge what is to be done to clear up her relations with Serbia; but whatever Austria's decision, she could count with certainty upon it, that Germany will stand behind her as an ally." [36] Berchtold's plan of partitioning Serbia with Bulgaria was explained to Bethmann. He approved of it and added: "If war must break out, better now than in one or two years' time when the Entente will be stronger."

William II and Bethmann did more than give Austria-Hungary a free hand; they encouraged her to start a war against Serbia and to risk the greater consequences. They had grown used to Berchtold's irresolution during the Balkan wars and were determined not to be blamed for it. The most probable outcome of all the stir, they expected, would be an Austro-Hungarian alliance with Bulgaria. Further, both of them thought that Russia was not ready for war and that she would allow the humiliation of Serbia after some ineffective protest; then their position would be all the stronger to strike a bargain with Russia later. On the other hand, if it came to war, they were confident of winning it now and less confident of winning it later. They did not decide on war; but they did decide on 5 July to use their superior power either to win a war or to achieve a striking success. Bethmann had always said that Germany

---

[34] Tisza also disliked Francis Ferdinand personally, for his favouring the South Slavs and Rumanians. He said on the news of his death: "The Lord God has willed it so, and we must be grateful to the Lord God for everything."

[35] Szögyény to Berchtold, 5 July 1914. Österreich-Ungarns Aussenpolitik, viii, no. 10058.

[36] Szögyény to Berchtold, 6 July 1914. Österreich-Ungarns Aussenpolitik, viii, no. 10076.

and Great Britain should co-operate to keep the peace. If he had wanted a peaceful solution of the present crisis, he would have approached the British at once. Instead he did nothing. He did not wish to alarm them. His aim, so far as he had one, was to keep them neutral in a continental war, not to enlist their support for a general peace.

The German reply gave Berchtold what he wanted: it enabled him to convert Tisza. He could now argue that Germany was urging them to war. On 14 July Tisza gave way: great Hungary had to keep German favour. He laid down one condition: Austria-Hungary should not acquire any Serbian territory. Though Berchtold accepted this condition, he meant to cheat Tisza, once Serbia had been crushed: her southern territories would be partitioned between Albania and Bulgaria, and the rest would become a dependency of the monarchy, even if it were not directly annexed.[37] The one chance of success for Austria-Hungary would have been rapid action. Instead Berchtold dawdled, in the usual Viennese fashion. The ultimatum to Serbia was sent on 23 July, when all Europe had forgotten its first indignation at the archduke's murder. The Serbs replied on 25 July, accepting Berchtold's conditions much more nearly than had been expected. It made no difference. The Austrians were determined on war; and the Germans encouraged them to action. On 28 July Austria-Hungary declared war on Serbia. Military reasons were not the motive: the Austro-Hungarian army could not be ready even against Serbia until 12 August. But, as Berchtold said: "The diplomatic situation will not last as long as that." He needed a declaration of war in order to reject all attempts at mediation or a peaceful solution: they had now been "outstripped by events."

The Austro-Hungarian declaration of war on Serbia was the decisive act; everything else followed from it. Diplomacy had been silent between the assassination of Francis Ferdinand on 28 June and the Austro-Hungarian note of 23 July; there was nothing it could do until the Austro-Hungarian demands were known. Then the statesmen tried to avert the crisis. The Russians advised Serbia not to resist, but to trust to the Great Powers;[38] Grey offered to mediate between Serbia and Austria-Hungary. But the Russians had repeatedly declared that they would not allow Serbia to be crushed; they could do no other if they were to maintain the buffer of independent Balkan states. Poincaré and Viviani were in St. Petersburg just before the Austro-Hungarian note to Serbia was sent off. They emphasized again French loyalty to the alliance; but there is no evidence that they encouraged Russia to provoke a war, if a peaceful settlement could be found. When Austria-Hungary declared war on

---

[37] This plan of partition, never carried out during the First World war, was put into operation by the Germans (many of them Austrian) in 1941, when Bulgaria received Macedonia, and Albania the plain of Kossovo.

[38] Russian council of ministers, 24 July 1914. *Mezhdunarodnye otnosheniya*, third series, v, no. 19.

Serbia, the Russians attempted to mobilize against her alone, although they had no plans except for total mobilization. They were, in fact, still acting in terms of diplomacy; they were raising their bid, not preparing for war. The Germans now entered the field. They had assured the Austrians that they would keep Russia out of things, and they set out to do so. On 29 July they warned Sazonov that "further continuation of Russian mobilization would force us to mobilize also." [39]

This time the Russians were determined not to retreat; they raised their bid still higher. On 30 July they resolved on general mobilization. This, too, was a diplomatic move; the Russian armies could not be ready for many weeks. But, in Jagow's words, "the German asset was speed." Their only military plan was to defeat France in six weeks and then to turn against Russia before she was fully prepared. Therefore they had to precipitate events and to force a rupture on both Russia and France. William II might still carry on a private telegraphic correspondence with Nicholas II, which was prolonged even after the declaration of war; Bethmann might still seek an impossible diplomatic success. They were both swept aside by the generals; and they had no answer to the military argument that immediate war was necessary for Germany's security. Yet even the generals did not want war; they wanted victory. When Bethmann urged caution at Vienna and Moltke at the same time urged speedier action, Berchtold exclaimed: "What a joke! Who rules at Berlin?" The answer was: nobody. German statesmen and generals alike succumbed to the demands of technique.

On 31 July the Germans took the preliminary step towards general mobilization on their side. [40] From this moment, diplomacy ceased so far as the continental Powers were concerned. The only German concern was to get the war going as soon as possible. On 31 July they demanded from Russia the arrest of all war measures; when this was refused, a declaration of war followed on 1 August. The French were asked for a promise of neutrality in a Russo-German war; if they had agreed, they would also have been told to surrender their principal fortresses on the frontier, Toul and Verdun, as pledge of their neutrality. Viviani merely replied: "France will act in accordance with her interests." The Germans had no plausible excuse for war against France. They therefore trumped up some false stories of French violation of German territory; and with these decked out a declaration of war on 3 August.

Negotiations between Germany and Great Britain were more prolonged. Their object, on the German side, was to secure British neutrality, not to avert a continental war. All along, Bethmann had urged Berchtold to appear conciliatory in order to impress the British, not in order to find a compromise. On

---

[39] Bethmann to Pourtalès, 29 July 1914. *Deutsche Dokumente,* p. 342.

[40] The Austrians also decided on general mobilization on 31 July, as the result of German prompting, and before learning of the Russian mobilization.

29 July he offered not to annex any French territory if Great Britain remained neutral; the offer did not extend to the French colonies. As well, Germany would respect the integrity of Belgium after the war, provided that "she did not take sides against Germany." [41] Grey stuck to his line of policy to the end. He made repeated attempts to settle the original Austro-Serb dispute by negotiation; later he tried to assemble a conference of the Great Powers. He warned the Germans not to count on British neutrality; equally he warned the French and Russians not to count on her support.

It is sometimes said that Grey could have averted the war if he had defined his policy one way or the other. This is not so. The German general staff had long planned to invade France through Belgium and would not have been deterred by any British threat. Indeed they had always assumed that Great Britain would enter the war; they did not take her military weight seriously, and naval questions did not interest them. Bethmann had wanted a British declaration of neutrality in order to discourage France and Russia; once it was clear that they would go to war in any case, British policy ceased to interest him. Emotionally he deplored the breach with Great Britain; but he did nothing to avert it and, in any case, was impotent to influence the German generals. On the other side, France and Russia decided on war without counting firmly on British support; the French believed that they could defeat Germany, and the Russians could not risk their own diplomatic defeat. A British declaration of neutrality would not have influenced their policy. Besides, Grey was resolved that they should decide their policy without encouragement from him; war must spring from their independent resolve.

Those who urged a clear British line did so from contradictory motives. Nicolson feared that Russia and France would win a complete victory and that the British empire would then be at their mercy. Eyre Crowe, more representative of official opinion, feared that France would be defeated and that Great Britain would then be at the mercy of Germany. In any case it was impossible for Grey to make any clear declaration; public opinion would not have allowed it. If there is a criticism of Grey, it must be that he had not educated the British public enough in the previous years. No doubt he had shrunk from increasing the tension in Europe; but, as well, the unity of the liberal party and the survival of the liberal government had ranked higher in his mind than a decisive foreign policy. It was common form to regret discussion of foreign issues. Eyre Crowe, for instance, "deplored all public speeches on foreign affairs"; [42] and Grey agreed with him. As a result, in July 1914, the cabinet overruled any commitment. On 27 July Lloyd George said: "There could be

[41] Goschen to Grey, 29 July 1914. *British Documents*, xi, no. 293.

[42] Paul Cambon to Pichon, 21 Oct. 1913. *Documents diplomatiques français*, third series, viii, no. 367.

no question of our taking part in any war in the first instance. He knew of no Minister who would be in favour of it." [43]

Moreover, Grey supposed that British intervention would not carry much weight. He thought solely of naval action; it seemed impossible to him to send even an expeditionary force to France,[44] and he certainly never imagined military intervention on a continental scale. On 2 August the cabinet authorized him to warn the Germans that their fleet would not be allowed to attack France in the Channel. Even this condition was not decisive; the Germans would have gladly agreed to it, in exchange for British neutrality. But on 3 August they sent an ultimatum to Belgium, demanding free passage to invade France; the British answered on 4 August demanding that Belgian neutrality be respected. Here again Grey has been criticised for not acting earlier; he should, it is said, have made British neutrality conditional on respect for Belgium. It would have made no difference. The German ultimatum to Belgium was drafted on 26 July, that is, even before the Austro-Hungarian declaration of war on Serbia; invasion of Belgium was an essential, indeed the essential, part of their plans. Only a French surrender could have held them from it. If Grey had acted earlier he would have achieved nothing, except perhaps the break-up of the liberal government; if he had delayed longer he would not have saved Belgium and he would have lost the inestimable value of moral superiority.

On 4 August the long Bismarckian peace ended. It had lasted more than a generation. Men had come to regard peace as normal; when it ended, they looked for some profound cause. Yet the immediate cause was a good deal simpler than on other occasions. Where, for instance, lay the precise responsibility for the Crimean war, and when did that war become inevitable? In 1914 there could be no doubt. Austria-Hungary had failed to solve her national problems. She blamed Serbia for the South Slav discontent; it would be far truer to say that this discontent involved Serbia, against her will, in Habsburg affairs. In July 1914 the Habsburg statesmen took the easy course of violence against Serbia, as their predecessors had taken it (though with more justification) against Sardinia in 1859. Berchtold launched war in 1914, as consciously as Buol launched it in 1859 or Gramont in 1870. There was this difference. Buol counted on support from Prussia and Great Britain; Gramont on support from Austria-Hungary. They were wrong. Berchtold counted rightly on support from Germany; he would not have persisted in a resolute line if it had not been for the repeated encouragements which came from Berlin. The Germans did not fix on war for August 1914, but they welcomed it when the occasion offered. They could win it now; they were more doubtful later. Hence they surrendered easily to the dictates of a military time-table. Austria-Hungary was growing

---

[43] Memorandum by Scott, 27 July 1914. Hammond, *C. P. Scott*, p. 177.

[44] So he told Benckendorff on 2 Aug. (to Sazonov, 2 Aug. 1914. (*Mezhdunarodnye otnosheniya,* third series, v, no. 456) and Cambon on 4 Aug. (to Doumergue, 4 Aug. 1914. *Documents diplomatiques français,* third series, xi, no. 754).

weaker; Germany believed herself at the height of her strength. They decided on war from opposite motives; and the two decisions together caused a general European war.

The Powers of the Triple Entente all entered the war to defend themselves. The Russians fought to preserve the free passage of the Straits, on which their economic life depended; France for the sake of the Triple Entente, which she believed, rightly, alone guaranteed her survival as a Great Power. The British fought for the independence of sovereign states and, more remotely, to prevent a German domination of the Continent. It is sometimes said that the war was caused by the system of alliances or, more vaguely, by the Balance of Power. This is a generalization without reality. None of the Powers acted according to the letter of their commitments, though no doubt they might have done so if they had not anticipated them. Germany was pledged to go to war if Russia attacked Austria-Hungary. Instead, she declared war before Russia took any action; and Austria-Hungary only broke with Russia, grudgingly enough, a week afterwards. France was pledged to attack Germany, if the latter attacked Russia. Instead she was faced with a German demand for unconditional neutrality and would have had to accept war even had there been no Franco-Russian alliance, unless she was prepared to abdicate as a Great Power. Great Britain had a moral obligation to stand by France and a rather stronger one to defend her Channel coast. But she went to war for the sake of Belgium and would have done so, even if there had been no Anglo-French entente and no exchange of letters between Grey and Cambon in November 1912. Only then, the British intervention would have been even less effective than it was.

As to the Balance of Power, it would be truer to say that the war was caused by its breakdown rather than by its existence. There had been a real European Balance in the first decade of the Franco-Russian alliance; and peace had followed from it. The Balance broke down when Russia was weakened by the war with Japan; and Germany got in the habit of trying to get her way by threats. This ended with the Agadir crisis. Russia began to recover her strength, France her nerve. Both insisted on being treated as equals, as they had been in Bismarck's time. The Germans resented this and resolved to end it by war, if they could end it no other way. They feared that the Balance was being re-created. Their fears were exaggerated. Certainly, Russia would have been a more formidable Power by 1917, if her military plans had been carried through and if she had escaped internal disturbance—two formidable hypotheses. But it is unlikely that the three-year service would have been maintained in France; and, in any case, the Russians might well have used their strength against Great Britain in Asia rather than to attack Germany, if they had been left alone. In fact, peace must have brought Germany the mastery of Europe within a few years. This was prevented by the habit of her diplomacy and, still more, by the mental outlook of her people. They had trained themselves psychologically for aggression.

The German military plans played a vital part. The other Great Powers thought in terms of defending themselves. No Frenchman thought seriously of recovering Alsace and Lorraine; and the struggle of Slav and Teuton in the Balkans was very great nonsense so far as most Russians were concerned. The German generals wanted a decisive victory for its own sake. Though they complained of "encirclement," it was German policy that had created this encirclement. Absurdly enough, the Germans created their own problem when they annexed Alsace and Lorraine in 1871.[45] They wanted an impregnable frontier; and they got one, as was shown in August 1914, when a small German force held its own there against the bulk of the French army. After 1871 the Germans could easily have fought Russia and stood on the defensive in the west; this was indeed the strategical plan of the elder Moltke. It was not a strategy which guaranteed final, decisive, victory; and Schlieffen therefore rejected it. In 1892 he insisted that France must be defeated first; ten years later he drew the further inevitable conclusion that the German armies must go through Belgium. If the strategy of the elder Moltke had been adhered to with all its political consequences, it would have been very difficult to persuade French and British opinion to go to the assistance of Russia; instead, it appeared in 1914 that Russia was coming to the assistance of France and even of Great Britain. Schlieffen first created the Franco-Russian alliance; and then ensured that Great Britain would enter the war as well. The Germans complained that the war could not be "localized" in 1914; Schlieffen's strategy prevented it. He would be content with nothing less than total victory; therefore he exposed Germany to total defeat.

There is a deeper explanation still. No one in 1914 took the dangers of war seriously except on a purely military plane. Though all, except a few fighting men, abhorred its bloodshed, none expected a social catastrophe. In the days of Metternich, and even afterwards, statesmen had feared that war would produce "revolution"—and revolutionaries had sometimes advocated it for that very reason. Now they were inclined to think that war would stave off their social and political problems. In France it produced the "sacred union"; in Germany William II was able to say: "I do not see parties any more; I see only Germans." All thought that war could be fitted into the existing framework of civilization, as the wars of 1866 and 1870 had been. Indeed, these wars had been followed by stabler currencies, freer trade, and more constitutional governments. War was expected to interrupt the even tenor of civilian life only while it lasted. Grey expressed this outlook in extreme form, when he said in the house of commons on 3 August: "If we are engaged in war, we shall suffer but little more than we

---

[45] This was, of course, also true politically. Though France would have had an interest in maintaining Russia as a Great Power even if she had not lost Alsace and Lorraine, her public opinion would have been less deeply committed; and the Germans would not have assumed that France would inevitably attack them in case they were at war with Russia.

shall suffer if we stand aside"; [46] and by suffering he meant only the interruption of British trade with the continent of Europe. No country made serious economic preparations for war. In England the cry was raised of "business as usual" to mitigate the unemployment which war was expected to cause. The Germans so little understood the implications of total war that they abstained from invading Holland in August 1914, so as to be able to trade freely with the rest of the world.

The Balkan wars had taught a deceptive lesson. Everyone supposed that decisive battles would be fought at once, and a dictated peace would follow. The Germans expected to take Paris; the French expected to break through in Lorraine. The Russian "steam-roller" would reach Berlin; more important, from the Russian point of view, their armies would cross the Carpathians and take Budapest. Even the Austrians expected to "crush" Serbia. The British expected to destroy the German fleet in an immediate naval engagement and then to establish a close blockade of the German coast; apart from that, they had no military plans, except to applaud the victories of their allies and perhaps to profit from them.

None of these things happened. The French armies failed to make headway in Lorraine and suffered enormous casualties. The Germans marched through Belgium and saw from afar the Eiffel Tower. On 6 September they were halted on the Marne and driven back in defeat. But though the French won the battle of the Marne, they could not exploit their victory; the Germans were neither destroyed nor even expelled from French soil. By November there was a line of trenches running from Switzerland to the sea. The Russians invaded east Prussia; they were catastrophically defeated at Tannenberg [47] on 27 August, and their armies in Galicia failed to reach the Carpathians. The Austrians occupied Belgrade, from which the Serbs had withdrawn; they were driven out again in November, and Serbian forces entered southern Hungary. The German fleet remained in harbour; and the British fleet was similarly imprisoned in order to balance it. Everywhere siege warfare superseded decisive battles. The machine-gun and the spade changed the course of European history. Policy had been silenced by the first great clash; but in the autumn of 1914 diplomacy was renewed. All the Powers sought to consolidate their alliances; to enlist new allies; and, more feebly, to shake the opposing coalition.

[46] Grey, *Twenty-Five Years*, ii, 306.

[47] The Russian advance led Moltke to send two army corps to east Prussia from the western front. In this sense the Franco-Russian alliance justified itself, and the Russians helped to win the battle of the Marne. But this was only a minor cause of the German defeat. The principal causes were the blunders of German leadership and the strategical recovery of Joffre, the French commander-in-chief. Of course, Germany would have had more forces available for the western front if the Franco-Russian alliance had not existed; but in that case France and Germany would not have been at war.

[12]

The Treaty of Versailles:
A Carthaginian Peace?

*W*hereas the revisionism outlined in
Chapter 11 was directed at the Versailles Treaty's war-guilt clause, John
Maynard Keynes's *The Economic Consequences of the Peace* (1919) condemned
the peace settlement in general and its economic clauses in particular.
According to Keynes, the Peace Conference at Paris was a "morass"
where a "Carthaginian peace" prevailed over Wilson's idealistic Fourteen
Points. The reparations that the treaty called for were beyond Germany's
capacity to pay and insured a troubled economic, political, and social
future for Europe.

¶ Although his *General Theory* was yet to be written, John Maynard
Keynes (later Baron Keynes of Tilton) was already an economist widely
known in academic circles when the war broke out. Except for a brief period
of public service in the India Office, he had been lecturer in economics at
King's College, Cambridge, where he had assumed an important position
as editor of *The Economic Journal* in 1913. In 1915 he was attached
to the British Treasury. In 1918, he was chairman of the International
Financial Delegates in armistice negotiations with Germany; in 1919, deputy
for the chancellor of the exchequer on the Supreme Economic Council
and official representative of the British Treasury at the Paris Peace Conference.
He resigned from these last two posts on June 7, 1919 and, in a few months,
wrote *The Economic Consequences of the Peace*.

¶ The sincerity implicit in Keynes's resignation, the moral passion and
brilliance with which he denounced the treaty, and the authority of his
position as economist and representative at the Peace Conference gained
the widest possible audience for his book. It was, of course, the subject of
immediate controversy. Keynes's biting descriptions of the conference and its
leaders angered some; others criticized the book's political chapters or

else found it politically inopportune. But very few challenged Keynes's prophecies or conclusions about the economic aspects of the treaty, and as postwar developments seemed to confirm them, the earlier criticism was silenced.

R. F. Harrod, Keynes's biographer, has answered the often-made charge that *The Economic Consequences of the Peace* bolstered American isolationism. He replies that, in such a case, one would have "to specify precisely how but for the book, the situation would have developed differently." [1] The same answer could be made to the additional charge that the book encouraged Allied disunity and apathy in the enforcement of the Peace Treaty. But to the extent that writings influence public attitudes, it must be admitted that *The Economic Consequences of the Peace* played a most important part in shaping public opinion about the Versailles Treaty. [2]

At all events, it was not until 1946 and another world war that Keynes's book found a serious challenge in *The Carthaginian Peace or The Economic Consequences of Mr. Keynes,* by Étienne Mantoux. Mantoux's work had the advantage of historical perspective, but although his book contains moving passages, it is not polemical. It is a scholarly book which hits hard at Keynes's arguments. At the same time, as its author intended, there are no blows "aimed below the belt."

Étienne Mantoux, after graduating from the University of Paris and the *École des Sciences Politiques,* attended the London School of Economics in 1935–36, where he attracted the attention and friendship of such figures as Harold Laski and Friedrich Hayek. The *Carthaginian Peace* was written in English on a Rockefeller fellowship at the Institute for Advanced Study in Princeton. On its completion early in 1943, the young author joined the Free French Forces in England. In the last weeks of the war Étienne Mantoux died in action in Germany. A brilliant career was thus ended prematurely.

The first selection below, from the *Economic Consequences of the Peace,* gives the essential points of Keynes's position. Although Mantoux's *Carthaginian Peace* attempts a point by point rebuttal of Keynes, our second selection from it concentrates on the reparations question which is at the core of the argument and forms an important chapter in the economic history of Germany between World Wars I and II.

---

[1] R. F. Harrod, *The Life of John Maynard Keynes* (London: Macmillan & Co., Ltd., 1951), p. 282. It was the actual "course of events culminating in the fiasco of the Ruhr invasion that swayed America. . . . The book did little more than give pleasure to them (the Americans) by confirming their worst suspicions."

[2] "By 1924 the book had been translated into eleven languages and its various editions had run into some 140,000 copies. . . . It had been read, in the opinion of Sir William Beveridge, 'by—at a moderate computation—half a million people who never read an economic work before and probably will not read one again.' " Étienne Mantoux, *The Carthaginian Peace* (London: Oxford University Press, 1946), p. 6.

THE CASE AGAINST THE VERSAILLES TREATY

John Maynard Keynes

*　*　*

IN THOSE parts of the Treaty with which
I am here concerned, the lead was taken by the French, in the sense that it
was generally they who made in the first instance the most definite and the
most extreme proposals. This was partly a matter of tactics. When the final
result is expected to be a compromise, it is often prudent to start from an extreme position; and the French anticipated at the outset—like most other
persons—a double process of compromise, first of all to suit the ideas of their
allies and associates, and secondly in the course of the Peace Conference proper
with the Germans themselves. These tactics were justified by the event. Clemenceau gained a reputation for moderation with his colleagues in Council by
sometimes throwing over with an air of intellectual impartiality the more extreme proposals of his ministers; and much went through where the American
and British critics were naturally a little ignorant of the true point at issue, or
where too persistent criticism by France's allies put them in a position which
they felt as invidious, of always appearing to take the enemy's part and to
argue his case. Where, therefore, British and American interests were not
seriously involved their criticism grew slack, and some provisions were thus
passed which the French themselves did not take very seriously, and for which
the eleventh-hour decision to allow no discussion with the Germans removed
the opportunity of remedy.

But, apart from tactics, the French had a policy. Although Clemenceau
might curtly abandon the claims of a Klotz or a Loucheur, or close his eyes
with an air of fatigue when French interests were no longer involved in the
discussion, he knew which points were vital, and these he abated little. In so
far as the main economic lines of the Treaty represent an intellectual idea, it is
the idea of France and of Clemenceau.

*　*　*

He felt about France what Pericles felt of Athens—unique value in her, nothing else mattering; but his theory of politics was Bismarck's. He had one illusion—France; and one disillusion—mankind, including Frenchmen, and his colleagues not least. His principles for the peace can be expressed simply. In the first place, he was a foremost believer in the view of German psychology that the German understands and can understand nothing but intimidation, that he is without generosity or remorse in negotiation, that there is no advantage he will not take of you, and no extent to which he will not demean himself for profit, that he is without honor, pride, or mercy. Therefore you must never negotiate with a German or conciliate him; you must dictate to him. On no other terms will he respect you, or will you prevent him from cheating you. But it is doubtful how far he thought these characteristics peculiar to Germany, or whether his candid view of some other nations was fundamentally different. His philosophy had, therefore, no place for "sentimentality" in international relations. Nations are real things, of whom you love one and feel for the rest indifference —or hatred. The glory of the nation you love is a desirable end—but generally to be obtained at your neighbor's expense. The politics of power are inevitable, and there is nothing very new to learn about this war or the end it was fought for; England had destroyed, as in each preceding century, a trade rival; a mighty chapter had been closed in the secular struggle between the glories of Germany and of France. Prudence required some measure of lip service to the "ideals" of foolish Americans and hypocritical Englishmen; but it would be stupid to believe that there is much room in the world, as it really is, for such affairs as the League of Nations, or any sense in the principle of self-determination except as an ingenious formula for rearranging the balance of power in one's own interests.

* * *

According to this vision of the future, European history is to be a perpetual prizefight, of which France has won this round, but of which this round is certainly not the last. From the belief that essentially the old order does not change, being based on human nature which is always the same, and from a consequent skepticism of all that class of doctrine which the League of Nations stands for, the policy of France and of Clemenceau followed logically. For a Peace of magnanimity or of fair and equal treatment, based on such "ideology" as the Fourteen Points of the President [Wilson], could only have the effect of shortening the interval of Germany's recovery and hastening the day when she will once again hurl at France her greater numbers and her superior resources and technical skill. Hence the necessity of "guarantees"; and each guarantee that was taken, by increasing irritation and thus the probability of a subsequent *Revanche* by Germany, made necessary yet further provisions to crush. Thus, as soon as this view of the world is adopted and the other discarded, a demand for a Carthaginian Peace is inevitable, to the full extent of the momentary power to impose it. For Clemenceau made no pretense of considering himself bound by the Fourteen Points and left chiefly to others such concoctions as were necessary from time to time to save the scruples or the face of the President.

* * *

Two rival schemes for the future polity of the world took the field,—the Fourteen Points of the President, and the Carthaginian Peace of M. Clemenceau. Yet only one of these was entitled to take the field; for the enemy had not surrendered unconditionally, but on agreed terms as to the general character of the Peace.

This aspect of what happened cannot, unfortunately, be passed over with a word, for in the minds of many Englishmen at least it has been a subject of very great misapprehension. Many persons believe that the Armistice Terms constituted the first Contract concluded between the Allied and Associated Powers and the German Government, and that we entered the Conference with our hands free, except so far as these Armistice Terms might bind us. This was not the case. To make the position plain, it is necessary briefly to review the history of the negotiations which began with the German Note of October 5, 1918, and concluded with President Wilson's Note of November 5, 1918.

On October 5, 1918, the German Government addressed a brief Note to the President accepting the Fourteen Points and asking for Peace negotiations. The President's reply of October 8 asked if he was to understand definitely that the German Government accepted "the terms laid down" in the Fourteen Points and in subsequent Addresses and "that its object in entering into discussion would be only to agree upon the practical details of their application." He added that the evacuation of invaded territory must be a prior condition of an Armistice. On October 12 the German Government returned an unconditional affirmative to these questions;—"its object in entering into discussions would be only to agree upon practical details of the application of these terms." On October 14, having received this affirmative answer, the President made a further communication to make clear the points: (1) that the details of the Armistice would have to be left to the military advisers of the United States and the Allies, and must provide absolutely against the possibility of Germany's resuming hostilities; (2) that submarine warfare must cease if these conversations were to continue; and (3) that he required further guarantees of the representative character of the Government with which he was dealing. On October 20 Germany accepted points (1) and (2), and pointed out, as regards (3), that she now had a Constitution and a Government dependent for its authority on the Reichstag. On October 23 the President announced that, "having received the solemn and explicit assurance of the German Government that it unreservedly accepts the terms of peace laid down in his Address to the Congress of the United States on January 8, 1918 (the Fourteen Points), and the principles of settlement enunciated in his subsequent Addresses, particularly the Address of September 27,[1] and that it is ready to discuss the details of their application," he has communicated the above correspondence to the Governments of the Allied Powers "with the suggestion that, if these Governments are disposed to effect peace upon the terms and principles indicated," they will ask their military advisers to draw up Armistice Terms of such a character as to "ensure to the Associated Governments the unrestricted power to safeguard and enforce the details of the peace to which the German Government has agreed." At the end of this Note the President hinted more openly than in that of October 14 at the abdication of the Kaiser. This completes the preliminary negotiations to which the President alone was a party, acting without the Governments of the Allied Powers.

On November 5, 1918, the President transmitted to Germany the reply he had received from the Governments associated with him, and added that Marshal Foch had been authorized to communicate the terms of an armistice to properly accredited representatives. In this reply the Allied Governments, "subject to the qualifications which follow, declare their willingness to make peace with the Government of Germany on the terms of peace laid down in the President's Address to Congress of January 8, 1918, and the principles of settlement enunciated in his subsequent Addresses." The qualifications in question were two in number. The first related to the Freedom of the Seas, as to which they "reserved to themselves complete freedom." The second related to Reparation and ran as follows:—"Further, in the conditions of peace laid down in his Address to Congress on the 8th January, 1918, the President declared that invaded territories must be restored as well as evacuated and made free. The Allied Governments feel that no doubt ought to be allowed to exist as to what this provision implies. By it they understand that compensation will be made by Germany for all damage done to the civilian population of the Allies and to their property by the aggression of Germany by land, by sea, and from the air."

The nature of the Contract between Germany and the Allies resulting from this exchange of documents is plain and unequivocal. The terms of the peace are to be in accordance with the Addresses of the President, and the purpose of the Peace Conference is "to discuss the details of their application." The circumstances of the Contract were of an unusually solemn and binding character;

---

[1] Perhaps the most important points made in these Addresses which serve Keynes's argument and which he quotes along with others are: February 11, 1918 before Congress, "There shall be no annexations, no contributions, no punitive damages"; September 27, 1918 in New York City, "The impartial justice meted out must involve no discrimination between those to whom we wish to be just and those to whom we do not wish to be just. . . . No special or separate interest of any single nation or group of nations can be made the basis of any part of the settlement which is not consistent with the common interest of all." [EDITORS' NOTE.]

for one of the conditions of it was that Germany should agree to Armistice Terms which were to be such as would leave her helpless. Germany having rendered herself helpless in reliance on the Contract, the honor of the Allies was peculiarly involved in fulfilling their part and, if there were ambiguities, in not using their position to take advantage of them.

* * *

This wise and magnanimous program for the world had passed on November 5, 1918, beyond the region of idealism and aspiration, and had become part of a solemn contract to which all the Great Powers of the world had put their signature. But it was lost, nevertheless, in the morass of Paris;—the spirit of it altogether, the letter in parts ignored and in other parts distorted.

* * *

The categories of damage in respect of which the Allies were entitled to ask for Reparation are governed by the relevant passages in President Wilson's Fourteen Points of January 8, 1918, as modified by the Allied Governments in their qualifying Note, the text of which the President formally communicated to the German Government as the basis of peace on November 5, 1918. These passages have been quoted in full at the beginning of Chapter IV. That is to say, "compensation will be made by Germany for all damage done to the civilian population of the Allies and to their property by the aggression of Germany by land, by sea, and from the air." The limiting quality of this sentence is reinforced by the passage in the President's speech before Congress on February 11, 1918 (the terms of this speech being an express part of the contract with the enemy), that there shall be "no contributions" and "no punitive damages."

It has sometimes been argued that the preamble to paragraph 19 [2] of the Armistice Terms, to the effect "that any future claims and demands of the Allies and the United States of America remain unaffected," wiped out all precedent conditions, and left the Allies free to make whatever demands they chose. But it is not possible to maintain that this casual protective phrase, to which no one at the time attached any particular importance, did away with all the formal communications which passed between the President and the

---

[2] "With reservation that any future claims and demands of the Allies and the United States of America remain unaffected, the following financial conditions are required: Reparation for damage done. Whilst Armistice lasts, no public securities shall be removed by the enemy which can serve as a pledge to the Allies for recovery or reparation of war losses. Immediate restitution of cash deposit in National Bank of Belgium, and, in general, immediate return of all documents, of specie, stock, shares, paper money, together with plant for issue thereof, touching public or private interests in invaded countries. Restitution of Russian and Roumanian gold yielded to Germany or taken by that Power. This gold to be delivered in trust to the Allies until signature of peace."

German Government as to the basis of the Terms of Peace during the days preceding the Armistice, abolished the Fourteen Points, and converted the German acceptance of the Armistice Terms into unconditional surrender, so far as it affects the Financial Clauses. It is merely the usual phrase of the draftsman, who, about to rehearse a list of certain claims, wishes to guard himself from the implication that such list is exhaustive. In any case, this contention is disposed of by the Allied reply to the German observations on the first draft of the Treaty, where it is admitted that the terms of the Reparation Chapter must be governed by the President's Note of November 5.

Assuming then that the terms of this Note are binding, we are left to elucidate the precise force of the phrase—"all damage done to the civilian population of the Allies and to their property by the aggression of Germany by land, by sea, and from the air." Few sentences in history have given so much work to the sophists and the lawyers, as we shall see in the next section of this chapter, as this apparently simple and unambiguous statement. Some have not scrupled to argue that it covers the entire cost of the war; for, they point out, the entire cost of the war has to be met by taxation, and such taxation is "damaging to the civilian population." They admit that the phrase is cumbrous, and that it would have been simpler to have said "all loss and expenditure of whatever description"; and they allow that the apparent emphasis on damage to the persons and property of *civilians* is unfortunate; but errors of draftsmanship should not, in their opinion, shut off the Allies from the rights inherent in victors.

But there are not only the limitations of the phrase in its natural meaning and the emphasis on civilian damages as distinct from military expenditure generally; it must also be remembered that the context of the term is in elucidation of the meaning of the term "restoration" in the President's Fourteen Points. The Fourteen Points provide for damage in invaded territory—Belgium, France, Roumania, Serbia, and Montenegro (Italy being unaccountably omitted)—but they do not cover losses at sea by submarine, bombardments from the sea (as at Scarborough), or damage done by air raids. It was to repair these omissions, which involved losses to the life and property of civilians not really distinguishable in kind from those effected in occupied territory, that the Supreme Council of the Allies in Paris proposed to President Wilson their qualifications. At that time—the last days of October, 1918—I do not believe that any responsible statesman had in mind the exaction from Germany of an indemnity for the general costs of the war. They sought only to make it clear (a point of considerable importance to Great Britain) that reparation for damage done to non-combatants and their property was not limited to invaded territory (as it would have been by the Fourteen Points unqualified), but applied equally to *all* such damage, whether "by land, by sea, or from the air." It was only at a later stage that a general popular demand for an indemnity, covering the full costs of the war, made it politically desirable to practice dishonesty and to try to discover in the written word what was not there.

What damages, then, can be claimed from the enemy on a strict interpretation of our engagements?

* * *

We are finally left with the following—

Belgium	$ 2,500,000,000 [3]
France	4,000,000,000
Great Britain	2,850,000,000
Other Allies	1,250,000,000
Total	$10,600,000,000

I need not impress on the reader that there is much guesswork in the above, and the figure for France in particular is likely to be criticized. But I feel some confidence that the *general magnitude,* as distinct from the precise figures, is not hopelessly erroneous; and this may be expressed by the statement that a claim against Germany, based on the interpretation of the pre-Armistice engagements of the Allied Powers which is adopted above, would assuredly be found to exceed $8,000,000,000 and to fall short of $15,000,000,000.

This is the amount of the claim which we were entitled to present to the enemy. For reasons which will appear more fully later on, I believe that it would have been a wise and just act to have asked the German Government at the Peace Negotiations to agree to a sum of $10,000,000,000 in final settlement, without further examination of particulars. This would have provided an immediate and certain solution, and would have required from Germany a sum which, if she were granted certain indulgences, it might not have proved entirely impossible for her to pay. This sum should have been divided up amongst the Allies themselves on a basis of need and general equity.

But the question was not settled on its merits.

* * *

I cannot here describe the endless controversy and intrigue between the Allies themselves, which at last after some months culminated in the presentation to Germany of the Reparation Chapter in its final form. There can have been few negotiations in history so contorted, so miserable, so utterly unsatisfactory to all parties. I doubt if any one who took much part in that debate can

[3] Assuming that in her case $1,250,000,000 are included for the general expenses of the war defrayed out of loans made to Belgium by her allies.

look back on it without shame. I must be content with an analysis of the elements of the final compromise which is known to all the world.

The main point to be settled was, of course, that of the items for which Germany could fairly be asked to make payment. Mr. Lloyd George's election pledge to the effect that the Allies were *entitled* to demand from Germany the entire costs of the war was from the outset clearly untenable; or rather, to put it more impartially, it was clear that to persuade the President of the conformity of this demand with our pre-Armistice engagements was beyond the powers of the most plausible. The actual compromise finally reached is to be read as follows in the paragraphs of the Treaty as it has been published to the world.

Article 231 reads: "The Allied and Associated Governments affirm and Germany accepts the responsibility of Germany and her allies for causing all the loss and damage to which the Allied and Associated Governments and their nationals have been subjected as a consequence of the war imposed upon them by the aggression of Germany and her allies." This is a well and carefully drafted Article; for the President could read it as statement of admission on Germany's part of *moral* responsibility for bringing about the war, while the Prime Minister could explain it as an admission of *financial* liability for the general costs of the war. Article 232 continues: "The Allied and Associated Governments recognize that the resources of Germany are not adequate, after taking into account permanent diminutions of such resources which will result from other provisions of the present Treaty, to make complete reparation for all such loss and damage." The President could comfort himself that this was no more than a statement of undouted fact, and that to recognize that Germany *cannot* pay a certain claim does not imply that she is *liable* to pay the claim; but the Prime Minister could point out that in the context it emphasizes to the reader the assumption of Germany's theoretic liability asserted in the preceding Article. Article 232 proceeds: "The Allied and Associated Governments, however, require, and Germany undertakes, that *she will make compensation for all damage done to the civilian population of the Allied and Associated Powers and to their property* during the period of the belligerency of each as an Allied or Associated Power against Germany *by such aggression by land, by sea, and from the air,* and in general all damage as defined in Annex I. hereto." [4] The words italicized being practically a quotation from the pre-Armistice conditions, satisfied the scruples of the President, while the addition of the words "and in general all damage as defined in Annex I. hereto" gave the Prime Minister a chance in Annex I.

So far, however, all this is only a matter of words, of virtuosity in draftsmanship, which does no one any harm, and which probably seemed much

---

[4] A further paragraph claims the war costs of Belgium "in accordance with Germany's pledges, already given, as to complete restoration for Belgium."

more important at the time than it ever will again between now and Judgment Day. For substance we must turn to Annex I.

A great part of Annex I. is in strict conformity with the pre-Armistice conditions, or, at any rate, does not strain them beyond what is fairly arguable. Paragraph 1 claims damage done for injury to the persons of civilians, or, in the case of death, to their dependents, as a direct consequence of acts of war; Paragraph 2, for acts of cruelty, violence, or maltreatment on the part of the enemy towards civilian victims; Paragraph 3, for enemy acts injurious to health or capacity to work or to honor towards civilians in occupied or invaded territory; Paragraph 8, for forced labor exacted by the enemy from civilians; Paragraph 9, for damage done to property "with the exception of naval and military works or materials" as a direct consequence of hostilities; and Paragraph 10, for fines and levies imposed by the enemy upon the civilian population. All these demands are just and in conformity with the Allies' rights.

Paragraph 4, which claims for "damage caused by any kind of maltreatment of prisoners of war," is more doubtful on the strict letter, but may be justifiable under the Hague Convention and involves a very small sum.

In Paragraphs 5, 6, and 7, however, an issue of immensely greater significance is involved. These paragraphs assert a claim for the amount of the Separation and similar Allowances granted during the war by the Allied Governments to the families of mobilized persons, and for the amount of the pensions and compensations in respect of the injury or death of combatants payable by these Governments now and hereafter. Financially this adds to the Bill, as we shall see below, a very large amount, indeed about twice as much again as all the other claims added together.

The reader will readily apprehend what a plausible case can be made out for the inclusion of these items of damage, if only on sentimental grounds. It can be pointed out, first of all, that from the point of view of general fairness it is monstrous that a woman whose house is destroyed should be entitled to claim from the enemy whilst a woman whose husband is killed on the field of battle should not be so entitled; or that a farmer deprived of his farm should claim but that a woman deprived of the earning power of her husband should not claim. In fact the case for including Pensions and Separation Allowances largely depends on exploiting the rather *arbitrary* character of the criterion laid down in the pre-Armistice conditions. Of all the losses caused by war some bear more heavily on individuals and some are more evenly distributed over the community as a whole; but by means of compensations granted by the Government many of the former are in fact converted into the latter. The most logical criterion for a limited claim, falling short of the entire costs of the war, would have been in respect of enemy acts contrary to International engagements or the recognized practices of warfare. But this also would have been very difficult to apply and unduly unfavorable to French interests as compared with Belgium (whose neutrality Germany had guaranteed) and Great Britain (the chief sufferer from illicit acts of submarines).

In any case the appeals to sentiment and fairness outlined above are hollow; for it makes no difference to the recipient of a separation allowance or a pension whether the State which pays them receives compensation on this or on another head, and a recovery by the State out of indemnity receipts is just as much in relief of the general taxpayer as a contribution towards the general costs of the war would have been. But the main consideration is that it was too late to consider whether the pre-Armistice conditions were prefectly judicious and logical or to amend them; the only question at issue was whether these conditions were not in fact limited to such classes of direct damage to civilians and their property as are set forth in Paragraphs 1, 2, 3, 8, 9, and 10 of Annex I. If words have any meaning, or engagements any force, we had no more right to claim for those war expenses of the State, which arose out of Pensions and Separation Allowances, than for any other of the general costs of the war. And who is prepared to argue in detail that we were entitled to demand the latter?

What had really happened was a compromise between the Prime Minister's pledge to the British electorate to claim the entire costs of the war, and the pledge to the contrary which the Allies had given to Germany at the Armistice. The Prime Minister could claim that although he had not secured the entire costs of the war, he had nevertheless secured an important contribution towards them, that he had always qualified his promises by the limiting condition of Germany's capacity to pay, and that the bill as now presented more than exhausted this capacity as estimated by the more sober authorities. The President, on the other hand, had secured a formula, which was not too obvious a breach of faith, and had avoided a quarrel with his Associates on an issue where the appeals to sentiment and passion would all have been against him, in the event of its being made a matter of open popular controversy. In view of the Prime Minister's election pledges, the President could hardly hope to get him to abandon them in their entirety without a struggle in public; and the cry of pensions would have had an overwhelming popular appeal in all countries. Once more the Prime Minister had shown himself a political tactician of a high order.

A further point of great difficulty may be readily perceived between the lines of the Treaty. It fixes no definite sum as representing Germany's liability. This feature has been the subject of very general criticism,—that it is equally inconvenient to Germany and to the Allies themselves that she should not know what she has to pay or they what they are to receive. The method, apparently contemplated by the Treaty, of arriving at the final result over a period of many months by an addition of hundreds of thousands of individual claims for damage to land, farm buildings, and chickens, is evidently impracticable; and the reasonable course would have been for both parties to compound for a round sum without examination of details. If this round sum had been named in the Treaty, the settlement would have been placed on a more business-like basis.

But this was impossible for two reasons. Two different kinds of false statements had been widely promulgated, one as to Germany's capacity to pay, the other as to the amount of the Allies' just claims in respect of the devastated areas. The fixing of either of these figures presented a dilemma. A figure for Germany's prospective capacity to pay, not too much in excess of the estimates of most candid and well-informed authorities, would have fallen hopelessly far short of popular expectations both in England and in France. On the other hand, a definitive figure for damage done which would not disastrously disappoint the expectations which had been raised in France and Belgium might have been incapable of substantiation under challenge,[5] and open to damaging criticism on the part of the Germans, who were believed to have been prudent enough to accumulate considerable evidence as to the extent of their own misdoings.

By far the safest course for the politicians was, therefore, to mention no figure at all; and from this necessity a great deal of the complication of the Reparation Chapter essentially springs.

The reader may be interested, however, to have my estimate of the claim which can in fact be substantiated under Annex I. of the Reparation Chapter. In the first section of this chapter I have already guessed the claims other than those for Pensions and Separation Allowances at $15,000,000,000 (to take the extreme upper limit of my estimate). The claim for Pensions and Separation Allowances under Annex I. is not to be based on the *actual* cost of these compensations to the Governments concerned, but is to be a computed figure calculated on the basis of the scales in force in France at the date of the Treaty's coming into operation. This method avoids the invidious course of valuing an American or a British life at a higher figure than a French or an Italian. The French rate for Pensions and Allowances is at an intermediate rate, not so high as the American or British, but above the Italian, the Belgian, or the Serbian. The only data required for the calculation are the actual French rates and the numbers of men mobilized and of the casualties in each class of the various Allied Armies. None of these figures are available in detail, but enough is known of the general level of allowances, of the numbers involved, and of the casualties suffered to allow of an estimate which may not be *very wide* of the mark. My guess as to the amount to be added in respect of Pensions and Allowances is as follows:

5 The challenge of the other Allies, as well as of the enemy, had to be met; for in view of the limited resources of the latter, the other Allies had perhaps a greater interest than the enemy in seeing that no one of their number established an excessive claim.

British Empire	$ 7,000,000,000 [6]
France	12,000,000,000 [6]
Italy	2,500,000,000
Others (including United States)	3,500,000,000
Total	$25,000,000,000

I feel much more confidence in the approximate accuracy of the total figure [7] than in its division between the different claimants. The reader will observe that in any case the addition of Pensions and Allowances enormously increases the aggregate claim, raising it indeed by nearly double. Adding this figure to the estimate under other heads, we have a total claim against Germany of $40,000,000,000.[8] I believe that this figure is fully high enough, and that the actual result may fall somewhat short of it.[9]

* * *

On the 13th May, 1919, Count Brockdorff-Rantzau addressed to the Peace Conference of the Allied and Associated Powers the Report of the German Economic Commission charged with the study of the effect of the conditions of Peace on the situation of the German population. "In the course of the last two generations," they reported, "Germany has become transformed from an agricultural State to an industrial State. So long as she was an agricultural State, Germany could feed forty million inhabitants. As an industrial State she could insure the means of subsistence for a population of sixty-seven millions; and in 1913 the importation of foodstuffs amounted, in round figures, to twelve million tons. Before the war a total of fifteen million persons in Germany provided for their existence by foreign trade, navigation, and the use, directly or indirectly, of foreign raw material." After rehearsing the main relevant provisions of the Peace Treaty the report continues: "After this diminution of her products, after the economic depression resulting from the loss of her colonies,

[6] M. Klotz has estimated the French claims on this head at $15,000,000,000 (75 milliard francs, made up of 13 milliard for allowances, 60 for pensions, and 2 for widows). If this figure is correct, the others should probably be scaled up also.

[7] That is to say, I claim for the aggregate figure an accuracy within 25 per cent.

[8] In his speech of September 5, 1919, addressed to the French Chamber, M. Klotz estimated the total Allied claims against Germany under the Treaty at $75,000,000,000, which would accumulate at interest until 1921, and be paid off thereafter by 34 annual instalments of about $5,000,000,000 each, of which France would receive about $2,750,000,000 annually. "The general effect of the statement (that France would receive from Germany this annual payment) proved," it is reported, "appreciably encouraging to the country as a whole, and was immediately reflected in the improved tone on the Bourse and throughout the business world in France." So long as such statements can be accepted in Paris without protest, there can be no financial or economic future for France, and a catastrophe of disillusion is not far distant.

[9] As a matter of subjective judgment, I estimate for this figure an accuracy of 10 per cent in deficiency and 20 per cent in excess, i.e., that the result will lie between $32,000,000,000 and $44,000,000,000.

her merchant fleet and her foreign investments, Germany will not be in a position to import from abroad an adequate quantity of raw material. An enormous part of German industry will, therefore, be condemned inevitably to destruction. The need of importing foodstuffs will increase considerably at the same time that the possibility of satisfying this demand is as greatly diminished. In a very short time, therefore, Germany will not be in a position to give bread and work to her numerous millions of inhabitants, who are prevented from earning their livelihood by navigation and trade. These persons should emigrate, but this is a material impossibility, all the more because many countries and the most important ones will oppose any German immigration. To put the Peace conditions into execution would logically involve, therefore, the loss of several millions of persons in Germany. This catastrophe would not be long in coming about, seeing that the health of the population has been broken down during the War by the Blockade, and during the Armistice by the aggravation of the Blockade of famine. No help, however great, or over however long a period it were continued, could prevent these deaths *en masse.*" "We do not know, and indeed we doubt," the report concludes, "whether the Delegates of the Allied and Associated Powers realize the inevitable consequences which will take place if Germany, an industrial State, very thickly populated, closely bound up with the economic system of the world, and under the necessity of importing enormous quantities of raw material and foodstuffs, suddenly finds herself pushed back to the phase of her development, which corresponds to her economic condition and the numbers of her population as they were half a century ago. Those who sign this Treaty will sign the death sentence of many millions of German men, women and children."

I know of no adequate answer to these words. The indictment is at least as true of the Austrian, as of the German, settlement. This is the fundamental problem in front of us, before which questions of territorial adjustment and the balance of European power are insignificant. Some of the catastrophes of past history, which have thrown back human progress for centuries, have been due to the reactions following on the sudden termination, whether in the course of nature or by the act of man, of temporarily favorable conditions which have permitted the growth of population beyond what could be provided for when the favorable conditions were at an end.

* * *

In proposing a modification of the Reparation terms, I have considered them so far only in relation to Germany. But fairness requires that so great a reduction in the amount should be accompanied by a readjustment of its apportionment between the Allies themselves. The professions which our statesmen made on every platform during the war, as well as other considerations, surely require that the areas damaged by the enemy's invasion should receive a priority of compensation. While this was one of the ultimate objects for which we said we were fighting, we never included the recovery of separation allowances amongst our war aims. I suggest, therefore, that we should by our acts prove ourselves sincere and trustworthy, and that accordingly Great Britain should waive altogether her claims for cash payment in favor of Belgium, Serbia, and France. The whole of the payments made by Germany would then be subject to the prior charge of repairing the material injury done to those countries and provinces which suffered actual invasion by the enemy; and I believe that the sum of $7,500,000,000 thus available would be adequate to cover entirely the actual costs of restoration. Further, it is only by a complete subordination of her own claims for cash compensation that Great Britain can ask with clean hands for a revision of the Treaty and clear her honor from the breach of faith for which she bears the main responsibility, as a result of the policy to which the General Election of 1918 pledged her representatives.

With the Reparation problem thus cleared up it would be possible to bring forward with a better grace and more hope of success two other financial proposals, each of which involves an appeal to the generosity of the United States.

The first is for the entire cancellation of Inter-Ally indebtedness (that is to say, indebtedness between the Governments of the Allied and Associated countries) incurred for the purposes of the war. This proposal, which has been put forward already in certain quarters, is one which I believe to be absolutely essential to the future prosperity of the world. It would be an act of far-seeing statesmanship for the United Kingdom and the United States, the two Powers chiefly concerned, to adopt it.

* * *

Failing such a settlement as is now proposed, the war will have ended with a network of heavy tribute payable from one Ally to another. The total amount of this tribute is even likely to exceed the amount obtainable from the enemy; and the war will have ended with the intolerable result of the Allies paying indemnities to one another instead of receiving them from the enemy.

For this reason the question of Inter-Allied indebtedness is closely bound up with the intense popular feeling amongst the European Allies on the question of indemnities,—a feeling which is based, not on any reasonable calculation of what Germany can, in fact, pay, but on a well-founded appreciation of the unbearable financial situation in which these countries will find themselves unless she pays. Take Italy as an extreme example. If Italy can reasonably be expected to pay $4,000,000,000, surely Germany can and ought to pay an immeasurably higher figure. Or if it is decided (as it must be) that Austria can pay next to nothing, is it not an intolerable conclusion that Italy should be loaded with a crushing tribute, while Austria escapes? Or, to put it slightly differently, how can Italy be expected to submit to payment of this great sum and see Czecho-Slovakia pay little or nothing? At the other end of the scale there is the United Kingdom. Here the financial position is different, since to ask us to pay $4,000,000,000 is a very different proposition from asking Italy to pay it. But the sentiment is much the same. If we have to be satisfied without full compensation from Germany, how bitter will be the protests against paying it to the United States. We, it will be said, have to be content with a claim against the bankrupt estates of Germany, France, Italy, and Russia, whereas the United States has secured a first mortgage upon us. The case of France is at least as overwhelming. She can barely secure from Germany the full measure of the destruction of her countryside. Yet victorious France must pay her friends and Allies more than four times the indemnity which in the defeat of 1870 she paid Germany. The hand of Bismarck was light compared with that of an Ally or of an Associate. A settlement of Inter-Ally indebtedness is, therefore, an indispensable preliminary to the peoples of the Allied countries facing, with other than a maddened and exasperated heart, the inevitable truth about the prospects of an indemnity from the enemy.

It might be an exaggeration to say that it is impossible for the European Allies to pay the capital and interest due from them on these debts, but to make them do so would certainly be to impose a crushing burden. They may be expected, therefore, to make constant attempts to evade or escape payment, and these attempts will be a constant source of international friction and ill-will for many years to come. A debtor nation does not love its creditor, and it is fruitless to expect feelings of goodwill from France, Italy, and Russia towards this country or towards America, if their future development is stifled for many years to come by the annual tribute which they must pay us. There will be a great incentive to them to seek their friends in other directions, and any future rupture of peaceable relations will always carry with it the enormous advantage of escaping the payment of external debts. If, on the other hand, these great debts are forgiven, a stimulus will be given to the solidarity and true friendliness of the nations lately associated.

The existence of the great war debts is a menace to financial stability everywhere. There is no European country in which repudiation may not soon become an important political issue. In the case of internal debt, however, there are interested parties on both sides, and the question is one of the internal distribution of wealth. With external debts this is not so, and the creditor nations may soon find their interest inconveniently bound up with the maintenance of a particular type of government or economic organization in the debtor countries. Entangling alliances or entangling leagues are nothing to the entanglements of cash owing.

The final consideration influencing the reader's attitude to this proposal must, however, depend on his view as to the future place in the world's progress of the vast paper entanglements which are our legacy from war finance both at home and abroad. The war has ended with every one owing everyone else immense sums of money. Germany owes a large sum to the Allies; the Allies owe a large sum to Great Britain; and Great Britain owes a large sum to the United States. The holders of war loan in every country are owed a large sum by the State; and the State in its turn is owed a large sum by these and other taxpayers. The whole position is in the highest degree artificial, misleading, and vexatious. We shall never be able to move again, unless we can free our limbs from these paper shackles. A general bonfire is so great a necessity that unless we can make of it an orderly and good-tempered affair in which no serious injustice is done to any one, it will, when it comes at last, grow into a conflagration that may destroy much else as well.

* * *

The Question of Reparations

Étienne Mantoux

* * *

WHY, THEN, it will now be asked, was it so difficult to secure the enforcement of Reparations? Did not the following years confirm the prediction that "the claims against Germany were impossible of payment," and that "the economic solidarity of Europe was so close that to enforce these terms might ruin every one"?

A brief reconsideration of Reparation payments should supply the answer.[1] The history of Reparations divides itself into three distinct chapters. From 1920 to 1924, the execution of the Treaty was in the hands of the Reparation

[1] The facts of the Reparation story are entirely of a public character and ought to be known to the whole world. But the merit belongs to Mr. G. Borsky and to Lord Vansittart for having recently rescued them from a limbo of uneasy silence. (*The Greatest Swindle in the World*, New Europe Publishing Company, London, 1942. See also Lord Vansittart: *Lessons of My Life*, London, 1943.)

From Étienne Mantoux, *The Carthaginian Peace or The Economic Consequences of Mr. Keynes* (London: Oxford University Press, 1946; New York: Charles Scribner's Sons, 1952). Reprinted by permission of Mme. Paul Mantoux.

Commission. From 1924 to 1930, Reparations were governed by the Dawes Plan. From 1930 to 1931 they were governed by the Young Plan, then suspended, and finally cancelled altogether in 1932.

1. *The Reparation Commission.* The Treaty had prescribed that a Commission would fix the total amount of the Reparation debt. It was then to draw up a schedule of payments and to control its execution over a period of thirty years, which could be prolonged if necessary.

The German delegation protested vehemently against this scheme. "German democracy is thus annihilated at the very moment when the German people were about to build it up after a severe struggle. . . . The Commission, which is to have its permanent headquarters outside Germany, will possess incomparably greater rights than the German Emperor ever possessed; the German people under its regime would remain for decades shorn of all rights, and deprived, to a far greater extent than any people in the days of absolutism, of any independence of action, of any individual aspiration in its economic or even in its ethical progress. These comments," added Mr. Keynes, after having analysed at length the functions of the Commission, "were hardly an exaggeration." [2]

Yet the Allied Reply had had little difficulty in doing justice to them. "The observations of the German delegation," said the Note of 16 June, "present a view of this Commission so distorted and so inexact that it is difficult to believe that the clauses of the Treaty have been calmly or carefully examined. It is not an engine of oppression or a device for interfering with German sovereignty. It has no forces at its command. It has no executive powers within the territory of Germany; it cannot, as is suggested, direct or control the educational or other systems of the country. Its business is to ask what is to be paid; to satisfy itself that Germany can pay; and to report to the Powers, whose delegation it is, in case Germany makes default. . . ." "This," wrote Mr. Keynes, "is not a candid statement of the scope and authority of the Reparation Commission." And he went on to explain how the terms of the Treaty could open the way to an interpretation much wider than that assumed in the Allied Reply. What he omitted to say was that in a reply by the Conference's Committee on Reparation to a request from the German delegation for further elucidation, it had been stated that the Allied Reply of 16 June would have binding force as interpretative of the Articles on Reparation.[3] Candid or not candid, the interpretation given in the Note was therefore an authoritative one, and was invoked as such before the Commission later on.[4]

---

[2] *E.C.P.*, p. 201. [Economic Consequence of the Peace: London and New York, 1920—EDITORS' NOTE]

[3] This reply had been approved by the Council of Four. (Miller, vol. xix, p. 287.)

[4] Let it be added that the discussions which had taken place in the Council of Four over the drafting of that section confirm this restrictive interpretation of the Commission's powers. Thus Mr.

Now if it were true that the Commission "was to possess incomparably greater rights than the German Emperor ever possessed," etc., etc., how strange that Mr. Keynes, when he came to demonstrate that Germany could not meet the coal demands of the Treaty, should have suggested that the powers of the German Government would probably be inadequate to restore the length of the working day in the mining industry to its former figure of eight hours! [5] If the German Government could not, surely the Commission, with its exorbitant powers, could? Thus on the one hand we were told that the Commission would be "in many different particulars the arbiter of Germany's economic life"; [6] but on the other we were warned not to expect that the German miners could work more than seven hours a day.

The truth is that time and again the Commission had been instructed to spare the social, economic, and financial structure of Germany. It was to return to Germany out of her payments before 1921 the sums necessary to meet "such supplies of food and raw materials as may be judged by the Governments of the Allied and Associated Powers to be essential to enable her to meet her obligations." (Article 235.) In considering the Allied claims, it was to give the German Government a just opportunity to be heard, though not to take part in the Commission's decisions. (Annex II, part 10.) It was required to hear, if the German Government so desired, evidence and arguments on the part of Germany on any question connected with her capacity to pay. And in periodically estimating this capacity, the Commission was to satisfy itself that in general, the German scheme of taxation was "fully as heavy proportionately as that of any of the Powers represented on the Commission." [7] In other words, the charges supported by Germany were to be *at least* equal to those supported by the Allies—but it was not specified that they should be greater. So *this* was the measure of the burden imposed upon Germany! *This* was "the policy of

---

Lloyd George thought that the original drafting of the paragraph that enabled the Commission to demand payment "in the form of properties, chattels, commodities, business rights," etc., etc., was "too stiff." "It would give the Commission power practically to take any property or material to which it took a fancy." President Wilson agreed. "What he wanted was to avoid even the appearance of a forced Brest-Litovsk Treaty." So the provision was modified accordingly. (Burnett, op. cit., vol. I, pp. 1000 ff.) Such instances could be multiplied. If my guess is right, this particular meeting (27 April) must have been precisely the one described by Mr. Keynes in his famous second chapter. Perhaps his mind was too deeply engaged in a contemplation of Clemenceau's shoe-buckles to pay attention to such details.

[5] *E.C.P.,* p. 83.

[6] *E.C.P.,* p. 200.

[7] The discussion of this clause by the Council of Four on 23 April shows that their intention was to enable the Commission to relieve Germany, if it was thought proper, once it was established that taxation was proportionately as heavy as in the most heavily taxed country represented on the Commission, but not before. This principle was so obviously just that it was embodied five years later in the Dawes Plan, which Mr. Keynes, as we shall see, described at first as "an honourable document."

reducing Germany to servitude for a generation"! Let us now see how it was actually carried into effect.

The period which starts with the coming into force of the Treaty and ends with the adoption of the Dawes Plan subdivides itself into three intervals. The first ends with the acceptance by Germany of the Schedule of Payments of May 1921. The second with the occupation of the Ruhr in January 1923. The third with the application of the Dawes Plan in 1924.

In January 1920 the Reparation Commission entered upon its tasks. Its first mission was to secure, in execution of Article 235, a payment of 20 milliard marks before 1 May 1921. "The payment," said this Article, "should be made in such instalments and in such manner (whether in gold, commodities, ships or otherwise) as the Commission may fix." In order to show how the Treaty gave to the Commission "dictatorial powers over all German property of every description whatever," [8] Mr. Keynes had placed upon it the most extreme interpretation. "They can under this Article," he wrote, "point to any specific business, enterprise, or property, whether within or outside Germany, and demand its surrender. . . . For example, they could pick out— as presumably they will as soon as they are established—the fine and powerful German enterprise in South America known as the *Deutsch Ueberseeische Elektrizitätsgesellschaft* (the D.U.E.G.), and dispose of it to the Allied interests. The clause is unequivocal and all-embracing." [9]

One of the first acts of the Commission was to ascertain the extent of its own powers under Article 235. There is no indication that it even considered the possibility of disposing of all kinds of German property whatsoever. All it did was to debate whether the foreign securities in the possession of German nationals (apart from those that were already specifically affected by the Treaty) could be demanded. Four legal experts answered in the affirmative. The American expert, Mr. Hugh A. Bayne, entered a dissenting opinion. One of the most convincing arguments adduced in its support was a reference to a passage in the Allied Reply of 16 June 1919. "Outside the Empire," said the Note, "the Allied and Associated Powers have abstained from claiming the transfer of German property and interests in the neutral countries." This, wrote Mr. Bayne, settled the meaning of the Treaty, and would render it improper to contend that "under Article 235 the Reparation Commission has the power to compel the surrender of German interests in neutral countries." [10]

"The difference of opinion disclosed in the legal service," adds the Commission's report, "was reproduced in the Commission itself." And as under

[8] *E.C.P.*, p. 71.

[9] *E.C.P.*, pp. 71–2.

[10] Reparation Commission, V, *Report on the Work of the Reparations Commission from 1920 to 1922*, p. 187.

the Treaty unanimity was necessary for interpretation of the Treaty's text, the Commission could not demand these securities.[11]

So the fate of the D.U.E.G., which had inspired Mr. Keynes with such doleful forebodings, was undisturbed. And it happened, incidentally, that the use to which its assets were put did not turn out to be exactly in furtherance of Allied interests. The company was thoroughly reorganized in 1920; its most important installations in South America were transferred to a new firm, the Hispano-American Electric Company, founded by a certain number of Spanish banks. The preferred stock and all the bonds were then refunded to the holders in paper marks; and 120,000 new shares were attributed, as a commission, to the founders of the new company. Their value, amounting to more than 120 million gold marks, represented so much capital exported from Germany under the nose of her creditors.

To return to the Commission: all that it could do was to inform Germany that it was necessary for her to use all "neutral securities" in the possession of the Government or of her nationals in payment for the indispensable food supplies and raw materials to which Article 235 entitled her; and to declare that it would consent to no sum of money being deducted from the 20 milliard gold marks to pay for these supplies unless the German Government was immediately to take all steps necessary to acquire the securities in question and apply them to meeting Germany's requirements.[12] As for the rest of the 20 milliards, Germany was left literally to raise the money in her own way. All that the Commission did was to address a letter to the German Government requesting to be informed as soon as possible of how it proposed to carry out Article 235.

There is no record, in the published documents of the Commission, of any reply to this letter. Meanwhile, Germany had not yet paid to the Commission one single cent in cash.[13] But in January 1921 the German Government submitted to the Commission a memorandum purporting to demonstrate that the value of deliveries in kind effected since the Armistice amounted already to more than 20 milliard marks. The Commission replied that a number of the items involved were not liquid or capable of being made liquid in the near future; that it made all reservations on the evaluation of the other items; and that the final account under Article 235 could not, in these conditions,

---

[11] *Ibid.*, p. 13.

[12] Reparation Commission, IV, *Statement of Germany's Obligations*, p. 14. Even though these securities were not delivered, yet 3.8 milliard marks were deducted from the 20 milliard debt in order to pay for Germany's food and raw material supplies.

[13] Apart from the 3.8 milliards spent by Germany for her own supplies. The only cash payments made to the Commission prior to May 1921 amounted to some 84 million marks (£4.2 million) and came not from Germany, but from France and Denmark, as credits for the value of property ceded under the Treaty. (Reparation Commission, IV, *Statement of Germany's Obligations*, pp. 5 ff.)

fail to reveal a deficit of at least 12 milliard marks. On 14 March the German Government answered, maintaining its former position. The Commission persisted. It reminded Germany that she had to pay the balance before 1 May; and that she must pay before 25 March *at the latest without fail* (things had come to a point where the Reparation Commission did not refrain even from the use of italics!) a first instalment of one milliard gold marks. After a further exchange of letters, unbrightened by any cash payments, the poor Commission found that "there was nothing left but to notify the Allied Governments formally that Germany was in default in respect of her obligations under Article 235 of the Treaty to the extent of at least 12 milliard gold marks." [14]

Thus did the first task of the Commission come to an end.

It met with more success in the second, which was the fixing of Germany's total obligations. On 27 April 1921 the Commission made it known, as we have seen, that the total liability came to 132 milliard marks,[15,16] in accordance with Mr. Keynes's calculations; and the Supreme Council of the Allies worked out a Schedule of Payments which was accepted a few days later by Germany, after an ultimatum including the threat to occupy the Ruhr valley had been sent by the Supreme Council.

The provisions of the Schedule of Payments fell into three parts: (1) a delivery of bonds in three portions, A, B, and C, the details of which are now of little interest as they were never carried into any practical effect (it would be unfair not to mention Mr. Keynes's remark at the time, that these details were "not likely . . . to be operative, and need not be taken very seriously" [17]); (2) the constitution for the supervision of Germany's payments of a Committee of Guarantees to which were assigned, said Mr. Keynes, "the various wide and indefinite powers accorded by the Treaty of Peace to the Reparation Commission"; [18] Germany's payments were, in addition, regulated by special provisions. She was to pay each year 2 milliard marks plus a sum equivalent to 26 per cent of the value of her exports, or alternatively an equivalent amount as fixed in accordance with any other index proposed by Germany and accepted by the Commission. Payments were to be made by quarterly instalments, but one milliard was to be paid within the first 25 days. "The probable burden of the new settlement in the near future," wrote Mr. Keynes, "is

[14] Reparation Commission, IV, *Statement of Germany's Obligations,* p. 23.

[15] In the course of the discussions, the German Government had submitted estimates of 7.3 milliards for damages to France and 2 millards to Belguim.

[16] $33,000,000,000. [EDITORS' NOTE]

[17] *R.T.,* p. 60. [Revision of the Treaty, Being a Sequel to the Economic Consequences of the Peace: London, 1922—EDITORS' NOTE]

[18] *R.T.,* p. 62; this comment was made in spite of the express provision to the effect that the Committee was "not authorised to interfere in German administration."

probably not much more than half that of the Treaty." [19] But although it provided a transition from "foolish expectations," it could not be more than "a temporising measure" which was "bound to need amendment." [20] "Some time between February and August 1922 Germany will succumb to an inevitable default. This is the maximum extent of our breathing space." [21]

The reader shall be spared a detailed account of the harassing epistolary tournament that followed between the imploring Reparation Commission and the dodging German Government. With the aid of short-term foreign credits, the first milliard prescribed by the Schedule was duly paid in August 1921. (This was the first *cash* payment made for Reparation since the Treaty had come into force.) The Committee of Guarantees, after a visit to Berlin, found little that was encouraging to report. Although the German Government complained that the difficulty was to collect foreign bills for the external payments, the exportation of private capital continued practically unchecked. Public expenditure and budget deficits were increasing. Germany's "food policy, which could be justified immediately after the raising of the blockade, has been continued on a large scale and still figures in the budget for several milliards." [22] And the Committee expressed fears that the German Government might declare that it was unable to make the next payments.

Nevertheless, in November 1921, Germany paid another instalment of 500 million marks. But the following month, in reply to a letter from the Commission entreating them to take the necessary steps for the next instalment, the German Government declared that it would be unable to pay it, and, for the first time, officially requested a moratorium.

Greatly annoyed, the Commission expressed "its surprise" that the German Government should not even have mentioned a time limit to the extension requested, or an indication of the security proposed in the meantime; nevertheless, a provisional postponement was soon granted. This was confirmed a little later, after the Conference of Cannes had reduced Germany's obligations for 1922 to a total of some 2.2 milliard marks. As a condition of the postponement, Germany was asked to undertake a thorough reorganization of her finances, under the supervision of the Commission.

This decision was greeted in Germany with an outburst of indignation. The principle of supervision, claimed Chancellor Wirth in a bitter speech, was incompatible with the right of self-determination or with the honour of a nation. A reply to this effect was accordingly dispatched to the Commission.[23]

[19] R.T., p. 65.
[20] R.T., p. 67.
[21] R.T., p. 71.
[22] Reparation Commission, III, *Official Documents*, p. 38.
[23] See Carl Bergmann: *The History of Reparations*, 1927, p. 121. According to this authority, the speech in question had been drafted by Rathenau.

The Commission noted "with surprise and regret" that its proposals were rejected. But while it still insisted on the necessity of increased taxation, it hastened to reassure the German Government that as far as supervision was concerned, its disquietude was quite unjustified. The German Government accepted the Commission's apology and noted with satisfaction that there existed no intention of trespassing upon Germany's sovereignty. And so monetary inflation, tax evasion, public expenditure, and capital flight continued as fast as ever; and in July 1922 the German Government asked for a complete postponement for the rest of the year, adding, by the way, that the Allies had better not expect any payments in 1923, or in 1924 either.

Thus Mr. Keynes's prediction of "inevitable default" was, in a way, verified.

On 31 August the unhappy Commission saved its face. It announced that it would accept German Treasury bills for the next instalments, and Germany was thus freed of all cash payments for the rest of the year.

Greatly encouraged, the German Government now decided that the time had come for positive demands. In November 1922 it insisted that Germany should be relieved of all Reparation payments for the next three or four years, with a view to stabilizing the mark; in return, it declared itself ready to issue internal and foreign loans, as soon as an improvement in the mark exchange should have restored Germany's credit.

M. Poincaré, the French Premier, who, as is well known, had no sense of humour, was not amused. At a Conference held in London, he announced his intention to occupy the Ruhr if the German defaults were to continue. On 26 December the Commission was asked by its chairman, M. Barthou, on behalf of the French delegation, to declare Germany in default on deliveries of timber. Sir John Bradbury admitted that the delivery had not been made, but he questioned whether this delay constituted a "default" as contemplated by paragraph 17 of Annex II. "Since," he concluded, "in the tenth year of the war, Troy fell to the stratagem of the wooden horse, history recorded no similar use of timber. The situation was at present somewhat different; it was the fifth year of the peace, and the city under attack was not Troy, but Essen." [24] By a vote of three to one, Germany was declared in default of her obligations under the Treaty.

Another Conference met at Paris. Mr. Bonar Law, the British Prime Minister, proposed a plan whereby Germany's debt would be reduced to 50 milliard marks; M. Poincaré declared that this scheme would destroy the Treaty of Versailles. Mr. Bonar Law answered that to insist upon the application of the Treaty was destroying Germany's credit. No agreement could be reached. On 4 January the Conference ajourned. On 9 January the Reparation Commission, by a vote of three to one, declared Germany in voluntary default

24 Reparation Commission, v, *The History of Reparations*, 1927, p. 253.

in respect to coal deliveries. On 11 January French and Belgian troops occupied the Ruhr district, and Germany ceased all Reparation deliveries.

The occupation of the Ruhr met with sharp disapproval in Great Britain, where the general belief was that no useful purpose could be served by applying military coercion to enforce demands which were economically "impossible." In France, while there was a good deal of opposition to M. Poincaré's venture, it was still generally believed that Germany was not incapable, but unwilling to pay. The deadlock continued throughout the year, in spite of active diplomatic correspondence between the two Governments.

In Germany, wrath was naturally widespread. A policy of "passive resistance," marked by strikes and sabotage, was actively organized by the industrialists and the Government. This attitude brought a series of conflicts with the occupying authorities, and led to coercive measures, including the expulsion of a large number of recalcitrants into non-occupied Germany. Economic life in the Ruhr district was disorganized until a Franco-Belgian engineering mission (the "MICUM") took over control of transport and production. In September 1923 the German Government abandoned the policy of passive resistance, and came to an agreement with the MICUM for the resumption of production and of certain deliveries in kind.

The limited material yield that was brought by the occupation of the Ruhr has often been taken as the proof that "force can settle nothing" in economic affairs. The experience of Europe after 1939 has perhaps taught us differently; for it is irrelevant to argue that the German "New Order" "failed" in the face of the resistance of the peoples of Europe. It it true that if these peoples had not resisted, Germany's task would have been easier; but when the "New Order" failed it was because Germany was met by superior force, and the severity of the efforts necessary to bring about this defeat is the measure of the success with which Germany used force to "settle" her dominion over Europe. If the occupation of the Ruhr was only partly successful, it was because the coercive policy carried out by France was, compared to Germany's "New Order," an evidently half-hearted one, and also because no unity between the Allies had been achieved. Had this unity existed, not even the *application* of force would have been necessary.

It is also generally alleged that the occupation of the Ruhr, as the culmination of a period of reckless efforts to enforce the Treaty of Versailles, precipitated the final annihilation of the mark and the "collapse" of the German economy. This afforded complete proof, in the eyes of the public, of Mr. Keynes's claim that the Reparation demands were impracticable, and that any attempt to enforce them would end in ruining Germany and the whole of Europe.

The depreciation of the German mark has often been ascribed to the adverse affect of Reparation payments upon Germany's exchanges. It cannot be denied that even in the absence of internal inflation, the strain placed upon the balance of payments by the remittance of large sums abroad would, under a paper standard, have affected the exchange rate. But in the first place, this external depreciation would not in itself have depressed the internal purchasing power of the mark, if a continuous increase in the volume of the currency had not been taking place simultaneously, and it would have stopped after a new position of equilibrium had been reached. External depreciation could have gone far, no doubt, if the payments had been large; yet it cannot be seriously maintained that the payment of *less than 2 milliard marks,* which was all that Germany ever paid in cash between 1919 and the end of 1923, could have had this effect.[25]

The Reparation charges added to the budgetary deficit which it was the purpose of inflation to cover; in this sense, Reparations did contribute to the German inflation. But compared to other expenses, the Reparation charges were small. Before the signing of the Treaty, the deficit amounted already to some 10 milliard gold marks; from 1920 to 1923, the deficits totalled some 18·7 milliards; while all expenses under the Treaty represented 6·5 milliards.[26] As was the case in all belligerent countries, monetary inflation had started during the war; in October 1918 the volume of fiduciary circulation was nearly four and a half times as large as in 1914. After 1919 the mark depreciated continuously. When all Reparation cash payments ceased in July 1922, the rate was about 500 to the dollar. It was after that period, and particularly in 1923, when the German Government was financing "passive resistance" by a massive issue of notes, that the mark depreciated until in November 1923 the rate was 4,200,000,000,000 to the dollar. The currency was then stabilized at the rate of 1,000,000,000,000 paper marks for 1 "rentenmark." Thus, the German inflation, which had started before Reparation payments had begun, reached its wildest proportions after they had ceased.

⸰ The depreciation of the mark was essentially due to inflation, a malady from which all countries in Europe suffered as a consequence of the War, and the evil effects of which had been brilliantly exposed by Mr. Keynes.[27] The victors were not immune from it; the value of the German mark was reduced by more than 99·9 per cent, but the value of the French franc was finally reduced by more than 80 per cent. Thus inflation could take place even in the absence of Reparations. If, on the other hand, Reparations had been paid to the full, inflation could still have been avoided. After 1933 Germany

[25] Deliveries in kind, being unpaid-for exports, no doubt also affected the balance of payments, even though they involved no foreign exchange operations; but if the balance of payments was then heavily passive, it was because imports into Germany continued unchecked—which would not have happened if the ordinary effects of transfer depreciation had alone operated and which shows that Germany's needs in foodstuffs and raw materials were not denied satisfaction.

[26] See C. Bresciani-Turroni: *The Economics of Inflation,* London, 1937, p. 93.

[27] *E.C.P.,* pp. 220 ff.

was able to finance a much heavier public expenditure without any considerable depreciation of her currency, by means of an energetic policy of taxation,
forced loans, and exchange control. Similar measures could have prevented
inflation in Germany after 1919. The stabilization of the mark was achieved
with great success in 1923, *during the period of the Ruhr occupation*. It could
have been achieved no less easily before that time if the German Government
had been ready to put a stop to the issue of notes.

This being said, the annihilation of the mark was undoubtedly a catastrophe;
the German middle classes were beggared, and the resulting social instability
had much to do with the success of National Socialism in later years. But
while inflation affected the distribution of wealth, it did not destroy national
wealth as a whole. Even if it is reckoned that, in spite of the increase in capital
represented by the progress of industrial equipment during that period, the
capital structure of Germany was put out of equilibrium, it is clear that Germany was not seriously impoverished by inflation. We often hear of the
"collapse" of the German economy. What is meant by a "collapse" is at best
questionable. The collapse of a bank, of a commercial firm, even of the finances
of a state—all these have a very definite significance, as the holders of German
bonds found to their own cost. But as long as the physical resources of a nation
are not impaired, it is idle, even in the case of the gravest disturbances of economic life, to speak of the "collapse" of the national economy. One year after
the extinction of the mark, the real income of the German people was already
97 per cent of what it had been in 1913, and the value of their savings was
about three times as large as Mr. Keynes's maximum estimate of their capacity
to pay. To what particular category of "collapse," then, belongs that which is
followed by immediate prosperity?

2. *The Dawes Plan.* In December 1922, Secretary of State Hughes had suggested that if statesmen could not agree, the task of working out a solution
should be given to financial experts of different countries, and that he did not
doubt that Americans would be willing to serve on such a commission. The
proposal was renewed by President Coolidge in October 1923. And in November the Reparation Commission announced that it had decided to create
two Committees of experts, "in order to consider, in accordance with the provisions of Article 234 of the Treaty of Versailles, the resources and capacity of
Germany." One would examine "the means of balancing the budget and the
measures taken to stabilize the currency"; the other, "the means of estimating
the amount of exported capital and of bringing it back to Germany."

The two Committees submitted their reports in April 1924. The first Committee, constituted under the genial chairmanship of General Charles G. Dawes,
proposed that the German currency be stabilized on a gold basis, and made
known the amount of the charges which it considered compatible with the
balancing of the budget. In the first two years, the annuities should be respec-

tively of 1,000 million and 1,220 million marks; in a transitional period, they were to rise to 1,200 and 1,750 millions; in the fifth year there would be a "standard" payment of 2,500 millions, and thereafter the payments could be increased according to an index reflecting the variations of Germany's prosperity. The plan, as we have seen, retained the principle that Germany's fiscal charges should be commensurate with those of her creditors. Its execution was to be supervised by an organization of trustees (for the German railways, for certain industrial debentures, and certain controlled revenues), under the authority of an Agent General for Reparation Payments.

The most original feature of the plan was the solution given to the transfer problem. "There is," said the report, "an important difference between Germany's capacity to pay taxes, and Germany's capacity to transfer wealth abroad." Accordingly, a transfer committee was to obviate the dangers to currency stability arising from excessive remittances; the annuities were to be paid in marks by the German Government to the Agent General's account at the Reichsbank, and the Committee, composed of "five persons skilled in matters relating to foreign exchange and finance," was to decide how much could be transferred without endangering the currency. The Dawes Committee also recommended that a loan of 800 million marks be granted to Germany for the purpose of establishing the Bank of Issue and the currency system on a new basis.

The Dawes Report has generally been considered as a remarkable document, and such, at first, was the opinion of Mr. Keynes. "Germany," he wrote, "can scarcely expect better terms than these. . . . If the plan is worked with skill and good faith, it seems to protect Germany from the dangers of oppression and ruin. . . . The Report is the finest contribution hitherto to this impossible problem. It breathes a new spirit and is conceived in a new vein. . . . Though it compromises with the impossible and even contemplates the impossible, it never prescribes the impossible. This façade and these designs may never be realized in an edifice raised up in the light of day. But it is an honourable document and opens a new chapter." [28] The merit of the plan, in his eyes, was that even if the demands made upon Germany were to reveal themselves as excessive, the necessary safeguards were provided within the plan itself "in the event of optimistic forecasts going wrong."

The proposals of the Dawes Report were embodied in the agreements signed a few months later between Germany and her creditors. This time Germany was acting under no ultimatum and the agreement was freely concluded. But in the meantime, for some unexplained reason, the opinion of Mr. Keynes had changed. In the first place, the plan did not, in spite of the loan, allow Germany

[28] "The Experts' Reports. I. The Dawes Report," *The Nation and Athenaeum*, 12 April 1924, pp. 40–1.

the respite she needed for the replenishment of her working capital. In the second place, "the Dawes plan pretends to erect a system which is not compatible with civilization or with human nature. It sets up foreign control over the Banking, the Transport, and the Fiscal Systems of Germany, the object of which will be to extract from the German people the last drop of sweat. . . . No reparations will ever be obtained from Germany except such moderate sums, well within her powers, as she will voluntarily pay. The Dawes Scheme pretends to attempt more than this. Therefore it will fail." [29]

The Dawes Plan worked to perfection. During the following five years, the annuities were paid regularly and transferred to the creditors without any difficulty. But then a new factor had come into play: Germany's massive and continuous foreign borrowings.

As soon as the mark had definitely been stabilized in 1924 foreign capital began to pour into Germany. Between 1924 and 1930, the importation of long-term capital amounted to more than 9 milliard Reichsmarks, and the short-term credits to some 12 milliards. To these sums must be added direct investments in real property, German securities, etc. It was reported in December 1931 that according to the figures submitted by the German authorities, the total foreign capital in Germany amounted to nearly 30 milliard marks.[30] This sum, however, does not represent the *net* inflow of capital, as a certain amount of capital was also exported out of Germany at the same time. It was calculated in August 1931 that the net influx between 1924 and 1930 amounted to some 18 milliards.[31] This corresponds fairly closely to the estimate which has been given above [32] of the total debits of the German balance of payments during that period; it explains why this balance, at a time when Germany was paying Reparations, was constantly *passive*. In other words, the net importation of foreign capital by Germany during the period of the Dawes Plan was more than twice the amount of her Reparation payments, and the gross importation was more than three times that amount.

It is for this reason that the transfer safeguards provided by the Dawes Plan were never put into operation; there was always a considerable excess of foreign exchange at the disposal of the German Government, and the stability of the mark was never endangered. But, at the same time, the effect of the borrowings

[29] "The Dawes Scheme and the German Loan," *The Nation and Athenaeum*, 4 October 1924. Mr. Keynes did not believe that the machinery of control had been conceived in a spirit of oppression, but rather to perfect the demonstration that "when the breakdown comes, every possible precaution had been taken, and that the breakdown was, therefore, due to nothing else but the inherent impossibility of the task which had been set."

[30] Report of the Young Plan Advisory Committee. (See *The Economist*, Supplement, 2 January 1932.)

[31] See C. R. S. Harris: *Germany's Foreign Indebtedness*, London, 1935, pp. 8–9.

[32] *Supra*, p. 119.

meant that the ultimate problem of German payments was being postponed. Reparations were being paid, literally, with the money of foreign investors, not with the savings and taxes of the German people.

It is not surprising, therefore, that Germany showed such signs of prosperity during that period. We have already noted the progress of her national income. The relative charge represented by Reparation payments is given below:

Year	National Income (Milliards)	Reparation Payments (Milliards)	Per cent
1925	59.9	1.1	1.8
1926	62.6	1.3	2.1
1927	70.7	1.8	2.5
1928	75.4	1.8	2.4
1929	75.9	2.5	3.3
1930	70.2	1.6	2.3

Thus, the heaviest burden imposed upon Germany by the Dawes Plan represented 3·3 per cent of her national income. Such was the scheme that was "to extract from the German people the last drop of sweat."

It is unnecessary to dwell at any length on the increase of Germany's wealth during that period. The signs were obvious to every visitor, and they persisted even after the depression of 1929–33.[33] It was estimated in 1930 that the total value of new building in Germany since 1924 amounted to more than 40 milliard marks—more than five times the amount of Reparations paid during that period.[34] At the same time, consumption increased continuously, and by 1926 Mr. Keynes was of the opinion that the German worker had already "very nearly recovered his pre-war real wages." [35]

That the real problem was thus being postponed was repeatedly stressed by Mr. Keynes. "Reparations and Interallied Debts," he wrote in 1926, "are being mainly settled in paper and not in goods. The United States lends money to Germany, Germany transfers its equivalent to the Allies, the Allies pay it back to the United States Government. Nothing real passes—no one is a penny the worse." [36] But what would happen when the foreign loans ceased? That

[33] "You could search far and wide through Berlin's sea of houses or Hamburg's huge harbour district, but you could never find a slum or anything approaching one," wrote an American journalist, relating the impressions of his arrival in 1936. (Howard K. Smith: *Last Train from Berlin*, New York, 1942, p. 9.) This could not have been due to the housing policy of the National Socialists, who had been there for only three years, but to a legacy from the palmy days of the Weimar Republic—that is from the Versailles period.

[34] Estimate of the Institut für Konjunkturforschung. See *Report of the Agent General for Reparation Payments*, 21 May 1930, p. 284.

[35] "Germany's Coming Problem: The Prospect of the Second Dawes Year," *The Nation and Athenaeum*, 6 February, 1926, p. 636.

[36] *The Nation and Athenaeum*, 11 September 1926.

was the question; and, for this reason, it is true that the German payments under the Dawes Plan were not in themselves a proof that the system was workable. But it is enough, as we have already observed, to consider the net amount of capital imports *into* Germany during that period to see that large transfers could be effected without injury either to the capital-exporting or to the capital-importing country; for Germany did not, during that period, complain that the inflow of capital might "disturb" the balance of her economy. On the contrary: when the long-term loans ceased in 1929, she continued to borrow at short term and throughout the following crisis she was constantly asking for more.

3. *The Young Plan and the End of Reparations.* The Dawes Plan had been conceived as a provisional settlement. It had left untouched the question of Germany's total liability, which remained in principle that fixed by the Schedule of 1921, a total which the Dawes annuities would never have been sufficient to discharge. In 1929 the creditors assembled again, and after a series of negotiations that led to agreements at The Hague, adopted the plan of a new Committee of Experts presided over by Mr. Owen D. Young.

The Young Plan was to be the final solution of the Reparation problem. Germany's obligations were again considerably reduced. Although the plan provided only for annual payments and did not expressly fix the capital value of the debt, the present value of the fifty-nine annuities provided for was about 37 milliard marks; the annuities, which were to be paid until 1938, varied in amount with time, and totalled 121 milliards. Another original feature of the plan was that the system of transfer protection was modified: Germany was to find the foreign exchange herself, but a fraction of the annuity (the "conditional" fraction) could be postponed if circumstances required it. On the other hand, a new German loan was to be issued, this time of 1,200 million marks. The Reparation Commission, which had faded into oblivion since 1924, was finally suppressed, and all payments were to be made through the new Bank of International Settlements, to which were assigned the administration and the "commercialization" of Germany's debt in future.

The Young Plan was short-lived. While it was being discussed, the Great Depression had already begun. It grew in violence in 1930 and 1931. Prices fell, production slowed down, unemployment increased throughout the whole world. In Germany these effects were particularly severe. By the end of 1931 the index of industrial production had fallen from 100 to 66—in other words one-third of the industrial life of Germany had stopped. Unemployment (including part-time) rose to a figure of 5 million. In May 1931 the financial crisis had been precipitated by the failure of the Austrian Credit Anstalt. The withdrawal of foreign credits took alarming proportions, and in 1931 the balance of payments was suddenly reversed, showing a net surplus of 2·3 milliard marks.

By June, the Reichsbank was facing withdrawals at the rate of 200 million a week, and the Stock Exchange deteriorated rapidly. On 29 June President Hoover issued his proposal for a one-year moratorium of all Reparations and inter-Allied debts. After somewhat difficult negotiations (for France, who had been told, after so many successive abatements, that the Young Plan was *positively* the last settlement, and that the unconditional part of the annuity could never be postponed, would not easily consent to a new revision which boded ill for the future) the moratorium was accepted by all parties. Reparation payments were suspended. They were never resumed.

It appeared, therefore, that once Germany ceased to receive foreign loans, the crisis became inevitable. The reversal of the balance of payments certainly did not point to any "stickiness"; but although this process was by no means *impossible,* it was so violent as to provoke a catastrophe to Germany's national economy—and even to the whole financial world; so that in the eyes of the public, the forebodings of Mr. Keynes were once again "confirmed."

There is no doubt that, in view of the gravity of the financial crisis, the postponement of Reparation payments could be justified. Yet the notion that the crisis of 1931 was caused mainly by Reparation payments, or that it indicated that such payments would be *impossible* in future, will hardly bear examination.

The crisis of 1931 was essentially a "run" on the German banks, and to a large extent a run away from them. The strain brought upon the financial system and the balance of payments was not only due to the withdrawal of foreign credits, but also to the massive flight of German private capital. In August 1931 the amount of German assets abroad was estimated at more than 9 milliards,[37] and additional exports of short-term capital had taken place on a large scale in the course of the crisis. Compared with this figure, or even with a fraction of it, the 800 million paid for Reparations in the first half of 1931 do not suggest that they were the major factor of the crisis. If a strict exchange control had been established by the German Government, the strain on the balance of payments would not have been so heavy. But the measures taken at that time—even the increase in the bank rate—were quite insufficient. German capital was allowed to flee abroad, and it found there a refuge from whence it was later safely repatriated (at least in part), for no obstacles were placed by the countries of refuge to their return. On the other hand, all foreign credits in Germany were "frozen"; no more withdrawals could take place, and the stability of the mark was thus assured. Taken earlier, such measures would have stopped the flight of capital. Exchange control was used with some success after 1933 to build up Germany's war economy; but the German Government's

[37] Estimate of the Wiggin Committee.

reluctance to use this method merely to allow the payment of Reparations to continue was entirely understandable.

That the financial system was, for a short time, brought to a standstill was no evidence of the economic "collapse" of the country. Financial crises have been known to all times, and the moratorium of 1931 was hardly different in kind, if not in degree, from the methods used by the City of London to surmount the periodical crises of the nineteenth century. It was hardly different from the measures taken in the United States in March 1933, when all the banks were closed by Governmental order, and the gold standard suspended. Economic recovery followed more or less quickly in all cases. The Young Plan's Special Advisory Committee, which had been summoned in December 1931 to recommend the measures to be taken, had been well inspired when it had observed that "notwithstanding the exceptional character of the present crisis, there is no instance in economic history of a crisis, no matter how great, which was not followed by periods of stability and prosperity. . . . In past years, Germany has built up an immense and powerful economic equipment, capable of yielding a great return. The restriction of markets and the fall of prices have prevented her from utilizing this equipment to the full. The activity of her factories is now necessarily reduced,—but although it is impossible to fix a date for the recovery of stability which is still threatened to-day, it is none the less certain that this stability will ultimately be restored with the help of the measures suggested. . . ."

To argue from the crisis to the final impossibility of Reparation payments, therefore, would be "the humbug of finance" at its best.

It is unnecessary to describe here the negotiations which led, in July 1932, to the Lausanne agreements. Reparations were finally cancelled. Germany agreed to deliver to the Bank of International Settlements bonds for a total of 3 milliard marks, not to be issued before three years; any amount remaining unsold to be cancelled after fifteen years. Should any of my readers be interested in this type of investment, I feel confident that the Bank will be pleased to sell him—while there is still time—as many bonds as he desires, up to 3 milliard marks, with the special compliments of Dr. Hjalmar Schacht.

Thus did Reparations come to an end. An examination of how much Germany did actually pay will constitute a fitting epilogue to their melancholy story.

4. *The Reparation Account.* According to the books of the Reparation Commission, the total of Germany's payments, from 1918 to 1931, amounted to some 21 milliard marks; the German Government, on the other hand, asserted in a communiqué of 1932 that Germany had paid some 68 milliards. The details of these accounts can be conveniently summarized as follows: [38]

[38] For further details, see *Le Temps*, 13 February 1932; M. Antonucci: *Le Bilan des Réparations et la Crise Mondiale*, Paris, 1935, pp. 424 ff.; Borsky, op. cit., p. 45.

	Reparation Commission	German Government
	(Million Marks)	
I. Payments made between 11 November 1918 and 31 August 1924	9,637.8	42,059.0
II. Payments under the Dawes Plan	7,553.2	7,993.0
III. Payments under the Young Plan	2,800.0	3,103.0
IV. Other Payments	778.9	14,608.0
Total	20,769.9	67,763.0[39]

Germany therefore claimed that she paid more than three times the amount credited to her in the books of the Reparation Commission. How can such a fantastic divergence be explained? Was it not evident, it was argued, that even after taking into account a certain amount of exaggeration on the part of Germany, the Reparation Commission, which represented Allied creditors and could not be a really impartial body, erred on the side of its own interests?

Let us examine the nature of these divergences. In the case of payments made under the Dawes and Young Plans, the difference is small, but deserves special mention: it represents the value of the service on the Dawes and Young loans. In other words, the German Government, after having first used the proceeds of the loans for the initial Reparation payments (or for the stabilization of its currency) entered again the interest on these loans as Reparation charges.

The main difference is accounted for by the other payments. In the first place, the German Government entered a certain number of items which the Reparation Commission did not even retain. Thus, it entered as a Reparation delivery the value of German ships seized during the War. It entered under "destruction of war material" a sum of 8·5 milliards, which included the scuttling of the fleet at Scapa Flow. It entered 1·2 milliards, the value of the work performed by German prisoners of war—but did not enter on the debit side the work done by many more Allied prisoners and by civilians deported into Germany during the War. The cost of "industrial disarmament"(?) was also entered as 3·5 milliards. It is only to be wondered that the whole of Germany's War costs were not included as Reparation payments.

The remaining and most important divergence is found in the payments made between the Armistice and the coming into force of the Dawes Plan. As these were made almost exclusively in kind (there is no substantial divergence over cash payments, which amounted in all to some 1·7 milliards), there arose a difficult problem of valuation. The endless disputes to which this problem gave birth provide, in the writer's opinion, one of the strongest possible arguments against the system of payments in kind, and they rank among the best

[39] The totals represent approximately $5,250,000,000 and $17,000,000,000, respectively. [EDITORS' NOTE]

examples of the dangers attending any system of exchange which attempts to do without the lubricant of money. It is possible and even probable that the real value of these deliveries to the Allies was in several cases inferior to the sacrifice they represented to the German economy, and we have already concurred, in that respect, with the criticisms addressed by Mr. Keynes to the clauses of the Treaty dealing with German private property. But even when this factor is taken into account, the facts of Germany's exaggeration are still patent.

Thus, the value of the merchant fleet was estimated by the Reparation Commission at 711·5 million marks, and by the German Government at 3,436 millions. It would appear that even the Commission's figure was an over-estimate; for Helfferich had valued the entire merchant fleet before 1914 at one milliard marks, and only half of this tonnage was delivered under Versailles. It may be added that the German Government paid as compensation to shipowners in Germany a sum even smaller (550 million marks) than the credit given by the Reparation Commission. This did not prevent the German merchant fleet increasing by 2,800,000 tons in the next two years.

Again, the item of public property in the ceded territories was valued by the German Government at more than three times the estimate of the Reparation Commission (9,670 against 2,780 millions). The case of the Saar mines is particularly interesting. They had been estimated by Helfferich at 300 million marks before the War; the Commission entered the same estimate, the German Government a figure of 1,018 millions; but after the Saar plebiscite, the German Government, which, under the Treaty, was to pay back in gold the value of the mines to the French Government, offered a sum of 900 million francs—or about 150 million marks—and this sum was, of course, accepted. Such examples could be multiplied.[40] In the absence of any further proof to the contrary, we are therefore, I believe, justified in adopting Mr. Borsky's conclusion that the statement of the Reparation Commission was on the whole an accurate one, and that the German estimates "were not merely characteristic exaggeration, but also an attempt to render the whole scheme ridiculous in the eyes of the world and thus to hoodwink its critical faculty." [41] This attempt was entirely successful.

[40] They will be found, with many instructive details, in Mr. Borsky's study, quoted above. See also, M. Antonucci, op. cit., pp. 424 ff. For a German source, see Heinecke: *No More Reparations*, 1932, pp. 23–6.

[41] Borsky, op. cit., p. 53. H. G. Moulton and C. E. McGuire, who made in 1923 an interesting analysis of the valuation problem, came to the conclusion that the Reparation Commission's estimates were too low (though not so low as the German Government pretended) and that the value of Germany's losses (as distinct from the value to the Allies of Germany's payments) between 1918 and 1923 amounted to 25,791 million marks. (See their *Germany's Capacity to Pay*, New York, 1923.) This figure was adopted by Mr. Keynes at that period. ("How Much has Germany Paid?" *The Nation and Athenaeum*, 27 October 1923.) In the absence of detailed justification from the accounts concerned for every item, however, there is no reason to accept this figure rather than that of the Commission.

It is therefore interesting to consider what was the real burden supported by Germany during this period. We have already seen that, after 1924, Germany borrowed some 30 milliard marks abroad. But this is not all. Before 1923, a vast quantity of German bank notes and balances were bought by foreigners, at a time when the German exchange was rapidly deteriorating, in the ingenuous expectation that the mark would some day recover to par. It was estimated in 1924 that Germany had profited by the sale of mark credits and notes by an amount of from 7·6 to 8·7 milliard marks. "What Germany has appeared to pay in Reparations," observed Mr. Keynes at the time, "is nearly equal to what the foreign world has subscribed in return for worthless marks. . . . A million foreigners, we are told, have acquired bank balances in Germany, and each of these accounts has cost its owner on the average about £400. It is these lively gentlemen who have paid the bill so far." [42] Not a single cent, therefore, had really been paid by Germany before 1924. There remain the loans made to Germany after that date. The quasi-totality of these investments was lost in consequence of German defaults, more or less propped up by bank moratoria, standstill agreements, exchange clearings, and other such contrivances, all powerfully assisted by the running accompaniment of Dr. Schacht's suave exhortations: [43]

> "I weep for you," the doctor said,
> "I deeply sympathize."

But Germany swallowed up "those of the largest size," and interest was paid in shells, bombs, bullets, torpedoes—and other "sinking" funds.

Thus a total of some 35 to 38 milliard marks had been received by Germany from abroad between 1920 and 1931, as against the 21 milliards she had paid for Reparation.[44] Such was Germany's burden after the Treaty of Versailles.

The Politics of Reparation

Mr. Keynes had predicted that the Reparation clauses could never be carried out. They never were. This outcome has earned him the glory of a prophet. It is perhaps fair that others should have some share of these laurels. Foch, for instance, had expressed his own opinion to M. Klotz in no equivocal terms:

[42] "The Experts' Reports. II. The McKenna Report"; *The Nation and Athenaeum,* 19 April 1924, p. 77.

[43] "I have the greatest compassion," said Dr. Schacht on 29 October 1934, "for the foreign holders of German bonds who, believing what they were told in their countries, thought they were making a good investment by subscribing to German loans, and are now compelled to forgo interest. Nevertheless, I cannot see any way to help them, except by telling them: one can pay one's debts only when one is making money."

[44] If we adopt the figure of Moulton and McGuire for the 1918–23 period, the total paid would come to a little more than 37 milliards.

"With the Treaty you have just signed, sir," he said, "you can expect with certainty to be paid in monkey tricks." Neither was Foch alone, in France or elsewhere, in harbouring such misgivings.

Following events, as we have seen, confirmed several of the Marshal's presentiments. It would appear there here, too, his apprehensions were correct. Reparations were not outside the range of economic *possibility*. Had they been literally enforced, they would no doubt have put the screw on Germany up to the topmost pitch. For having suggested that Germany be *squeezed till the pips squeaked,* Sir Eric Geddes was exposed by Mr. Keynes to the superciliousness of a pharisaical posterity; it is too often forgotten that the man whose efficiency and drive had overcome, in the face of administrative prejudice, some of the deadliest "bottlenecks" of the war, and who himself had made Britain's own pips squeak in the process, was probably entitled to view the limits of financial possibility in a more sanguine light than many others. In fact, a large part of what appeared to increase the burden to such heavy proportions consisted in the provisions relating to interest, and the Treaty had given sufficient powers to the Commission to reduce the rate according to circumstances; Clemenceau himself had conceded that the Allies might have to forgo interest altogether. Reparations were not paid because Germany, as was quite natural, did not want to pay them, and—which was perhaps not *quite* so natural—the Allies showed themselves incapable or unwilling to take jointly the necessary measures which could have made Germany pay.

The whole question, therefore, boiled down to political expediency.

Now expediency, political or otherwise, is not a negligible factor in human affairs, and there would have been nothing dishonourable in taking account of it squarely in the making of the Peace. Thus, when the Draft Treaty came up for final reconsideration, it was to expediency that Mr. Lloyd George, at the meeting of the Imperial Cabinet, had explicitly drawn the attention of his colleagues. The terms imposed, he said, "must be expedient as well as just. Justice was a question which the Germans were at liberty to raise, but expediency was a matter for the Allies to consider and not the Germans. . . ." [45] And almost at the same time, Mr. Hoover was raising the question at the meeting of the American delegation.

"*Mr. Hoover:* Apart from all questions of justice, how far does the question of expediency come in?"

"*President Wilson:* In order to get them to sign, do you mean?"

"*Mr. Hoover:* In order to get them to sign. It strikes me that that is a more important thing than the question of justice or injustice, because the weighing of justice and injustice in these times is pretty difficult.

"*President Wilson:* Yes, nobody can be sure they have made a just decision.

[45] Lloyd George: *The Truth about the Peace Treaties*, vol. I, p. 701.

But don't you think that if we regard the treaty as just, the argument of expediency ought not to govern, because, after all we must not give up what we fought for? We might have to fight for it again.

"*Mr. Hoover:* But we look at expediency in many lights. It may be necessary to change the terms of the reparation in view of getting something, rather than to lose all. And it is not a question of justice; justice would require, as I see it, that they pay everything they have got or hope to get. But in order to obtain something, it may be expedient to do this, that and the other." [46]

Expediency, therefore, could have been understood as requiring that Reparation demands should not be too heavy. In such a case, Mr. Keynes had shown a strong sense of political expediency in 1919. Yet, strangely enough, the criticism most frequently levelled against his book in early days was that it lacked all sense of political necessity. But, later on, it was his critics who were to be chaffed for their subservience to political opportunism and their disregard of economic laws. "One may," wrote Lord Stamp, several years afterwards, "distinguish political from economic wisdom by saying that the latter will and must ultimately prevail, but that it is too hard and unpalatable for a world that will not 'come off' its wishes until relentlessly pulled by the force of events. It may be political 'wisdom' to flatter the public mind with slightly weaker and weaker doses of what it likes and slightly stronger and stronger doses of what it will have to get used to. . . . If that be the sense of political wisdom, then Keynes's book wholly lacked it." [47] Clearly "political necessity" could have more than one meaning.

I have endeavoured, for my part, to show that the demands of the Treaty of Versailles were not economically impossible. Whether they were *politically practicable* is of course another question. It could be contended that the economic and financial achievements of wartime were no longer obtainable in peacetime; that it was *politically impossible* for the Allies to enforce these demands upon the German people. We have seen, for instance, that Mr. Keynes did not believe that the German Government would have the power to increase the length of the working day. He feared, in 1919, that excessive demands might provoke revolution in Central Europe. He explicitly declared that there were cases where "particular claims, however well founded in sentiment or in justice, must yield to sovereign expediency." [48] And he claimed, a few years later, that neither the collection of War Debts nor the enforcement of Reparations was "serious politics" in the long run. [49]

The Economic Consequences of the Peace, therefore, did not "wholly lack"

[46] Baker, vol. III, p. 501.

[47] Sir Josiah Stamp: "The Economic Consequences of the Peace," *Foreign Affairs,* October 1934, p. 106.

[48] *E.C.P.,* p. 89.

[49] *R.T.,* p. 165.

a sense of "political wisdom." It was probably impolitic to run the risk of incurring Germany's resentment if one was not prepared to take the consequences. It was certainly impolitic to overlook the indisputable fact that Germany's nuisance value was greater than that of her victims. But then it is hard to see how this political wisdom on the international plane was very different, in moral essence, from (say) the subservience of politicians to the wrath of their electorates. It was only much later that "realism" was frankly invoked to justify the "appeasement" of Germany. But then Mr. Keynes protested that it was "to fraternize with what is vile."

In 1919, the Allied and Associated Powers, rightly or wrongly, had not believed that to compromise with justice would be an act of political wisdom. "Justice," they said in their Reply to the German delegation, "is the only possible basis for the settlement of the account of this terrible war. Justice is what the German delegation asks for and says that Germany has been promised. Justice is what Germany shall have. But it must be justice for all. There must be justice for the dead and wounded and for those who have been orphaned and bereaved that Europe might be freed from Prussian despotism. There must be justice for the peoples who now stagger under war debts which exceed £30,000,000,000 that liberty might be saved. There must be justice for those millions whose homes and land, ships and property German savagery has spoliated and destroyed.

"That is why the Allied and Associated Powers have insisted as a cardinal feature of the Treaty that Germany must undertake to make reparation to the very uttermost of her power; for reparation for wrongs inflicted is of the essence of justice. . . . Somebody must suffer for the consequences of the war. Is it to be Germany, or only the peoples she has wronged?

"Not to do justice to all concerned would only leave the world open to fresh calamities. If the German people themselves, or any other nation, are to be deterred from following the footsteps of Prussia, if mankind is to be lifted out of the belief that war for selfish ends is legitimate to any State, if the old era is to be left behind and nations as well as individuals are to be brought beneath the reign of law, even if there is to be an early reconciliation and *appeasement*,[50] it will be because those responsible for concluding the war have had the courage to see that justice is not deflected for the sake of convenient peace."

But Mr. Keynes was not satisfied. "I cannot," he wrote, "leave this subject as though its just treatment wholly depended either on our own pledges or on economic facts. The policy of reducing Germany to servitude for a generation, of degrading the lives of millions of human beings, and of depriving a whole nation of happiness should be abhorrent and detestable—abhorrent and detest-

---

[50] Italics mine.

able, even if it were possible, even if it enriched ourselves, even if it did not sow the decay of the whole civilised life of Europe. Some preach it in the name of Justice. In the great events of man's history, in the unwinding of the complex fate of nations Justice is not so simple. And if it were, nations are not authorised, by religion or by natural morals, to visit on the children of their enemies the misdoings of parents or of rulers." [51] Amen. But what was to be *the alternative*? Could Mr. Keynes tell us *how* the innocent was to be saved? *Delicta majorum immeritus lues*. . . . What happened was that the misdoings of a nation were visited on the children of its victims.

* * *

As the years went by, Mr. Keynes was able to follow in some detail the fulfilment of his own prophecies, and to draw, from time to time, the attention of the public to the process. "So far," he wrote in 1921, "the forecasts, which I was rash enough to make 18 months ago, have been borne out by the event." First, the claims against Germany had been evaluated by the Reparation Commission at a total lying between the two limits of his own estimates. Second, "the Treaty provided for certain specific deliveries from Germany prior to May 1, 1921, and these were estimated in Paris at a prospective value of £1,000 million. I criticized this," continued Mr. Keynes, "and put the value at a maximum between 330 and 430 million; this was exclusive of current deliveries of coal," which now proved broadly correct. Thirdly, he had predicted that Germany's total output of coal would fall at least as low as 100,000,000 tons; this was exactly the figure for the year 1920. Lastly, the prediction that there would be a two-thirds majority for Germany in Upper Silesia was also confirmed by the plebiscite.[52]

We have already had occasion to acknowledge the correctness of Mr. Keynes's estimate of Germany's final liability. So far, so good. The next item calls for some reservations. Article 235 of the Treaty, as we have seen, had prescribed a payment of 20 milliard marks (£1,000 million) before 1 May 1921. The Treaty had also, quite independently, provided for certain specific deliveries, the value of which was to be credited to Germany in the discharge of that initial sum. But nowhere was it provided that these deliveries would cover it completely; on the contrary, one of the very features to which Mr. Keynes had taken the strongest exception was that the payment of the 20 milliard marks could be requested by the Reparation Commission "in such manner as they may fix, whether in gold, ships, securities or otherwise," implying thereby that the specific deliveries mentioned elsewhere would probably not be sufficient to cover that initial payment. As we have seen, the Commission did not even take the necessary steps to secure this payment;

[51] *E.C.P.*, pp. 209–10.
[52] Letter to *The Times*, London, 2 May 1921.

thus the foreign securities of Germany, for instance, which ranked at £100 to £250 million in Mr. Keynes's 1919 estimate of £330 to £430 million [53] were not even demanded. It was therefore most irrelevant to take the figure of £400 million published by the Commission in 1921, which represented the value of *all* the deliveries made by Germany up to that date, as comparable with the £330–430 million calculated in 1919 by Mr. Keynes of certain assets, some of which were never delivered.

The third forecast was not so very accurate either. The figure of 100 million tons mentioned in 1919 related to output exclusive of lost territory and of consumption at the mines.[54] The 100 million tons produced in 1920 were, as Mr. Keynes had indicated, inclusive of consumption at the mines; but he did not indicate so clearly that they were exclusive of *all* Upper Silesian territory. Now in 1920 partition had not yet taken place, and Germany's total coal output was then 131 million tons. But even if the loss of Polish Upper Silesia was reckoned, the total output, exclusive of lost territories, was not 100, but 107·5 millions, since a substantial part of Upper Silesia was to be retained by Germany in the end. Perhaps I labour the point; but if Mr. Keynes had thought it worth while to draw the public's notice to this particular piece of prophecy, he might at least have got his figures right, the more so as his fourth forecast related to the Upper Silesian plebiscite, the result of which was to leave part of the district to Germany. While this prediction, again, was correct, it was not one that pointed to any economic impossibility in the enforcement of the Treaty, but to a possibility which the Treaty, in the very provision for the plebiscite, had precisely taken into account—while Mr. Keynes's argument about this part of the Treaty had assumed that the whole of Upper Silesia would be lost, and indicated that to the extent that this assumption proved erroneous, "the conclusions must be modified." [55]

"All my other forecasts," Mr. Keynes had added, "still lie in the future." The future having now receded into past, we are to-day in a position to verify the full extent of their fulfilment.

In *The Economic Consequences of the Peace,* Mr. Keynes predicted that the Treaty, if it was carried into effect, "must impair yet further, when it might have restored, the delicate, complicated organisation, already shaken and broken by war, through which alone the European peoples can employ themselves and live." [56] Europe would be threatened with "a long, silent process of semi-starvation, and of a gradual, steady lowering of the standards of life and comfort." [57] Ten years after the Treaty, European production was well above

[53] *E.C.P.*, pp. 168, 171.
[54] *E.C.P.*, p. 83.
[55] *E.C.P.*, p. 78 n.
[56] *E.C.P.*, pp. 1–2.
[57] *E.C.P.*, p. 277.

its pre-war level, and European standards of living had never been higher.[58]

He predicted that the iron output of Europe would decline as a consequence of the Treaty.[59] In the ten years that followed the Treaty, the iron output of Europe, which had fallen considerably during the War, increased almost continuously.[60] In 1929, Europe produced 10 per cent more iron than in the record year 1913, and would no doubt have produced still more had not the producers combined to restrict output for fear of injuring prices by overproduction.

He predicted that the iron and steel output of Germany would diminish.[61] By 1927, Germany produced nearly 30 per cent more iron and 38 per cent more steel than in the record year 1913, within the same territorial limits.[62]

He predicted that the efficiency of the German coal-mining industry lowered by the War, would remain low as a consequence of the Peace.[63] By 1925, the efficiency of labour, which had dropped seriously in the meantime, was already higher, in the Ruhr coal industries, than in 1913; in 1927 it was higher by nearly 20 per cent; and in 1929 by more than 30 per cent.[64]

He predicted that a pre-war level of output could not be expected in the German coal industry.[65] In 1920, 1921, and 1922, coal output was well above the average level of the five years preceding the war, within the same territorial limits. It fell sharply in 1923, and was slightly below pre-war average in 1924. It was above that average in 1925; and in 1926, it was already higher than in the record year 1913.[66]

He predicted that Germany "cannot export coal in the near future, . . . if she is to continue as an industrial nation." [67] In the first year following the Treaty, Germany exported (net) 15 million tons of coal; and in 1926 she exported (net) 35 million tons, or *twice* the amount of the average (1909–13) pre-war exports of *all* her pre-war territories.[68]

He predicted that the German mercantile marine "cannot be restored for

---

[58] The general index of European production compiled by the Berlin Institut für Konjunkturforschung (Sonderheft No. 31, 1933, p. 66) shows that European production (U.S.S.R. excluded) had regained its pre-war level around 1925 and was above that level by 20 per cent in 1929.

[59] *E.C.P.*, p. 91.

[60] With one exception, in 1921. The output of pig-iron and ferro-alloys in Europe (U.S.S.R. excluded) was as follows (000,000 tons):

1909–13	1913	1920	1921	1922	1923	1924	1925	1926	1927	1928	1929
39.2	45.7	22.5	18.7	25.9	25.9	33.2	36.5	35.2	45.6	45.4	50.3

[61] *E.C.P.*, pp. 89–92.

[62] See Reichs-Kredit-Gesellschaft, *Germany's Economic Development in the Second Half of the Year 1930*, Berlin, 1931, p. 6.

[63] *E.C.P.*, p. 92.

[64] Reichs-Kredit-Gesellschaft, op. cit., p. 15. Output per underground labourer was 1,161 kilogr. in 1931; in 1920 (after a reduction in working hours from 8 or 9 to 7 or 7½) output was 830 kilogr.; in 1921, 809 kilogr., and increased constantly after 1924, reaching 1,558 kilogr. in 1929.

[65] *E.C.P.*, p. 83.

[66] *Supra*, p. 86.

[67] *E.C.P.*, p. 84.

[68] *Supra*, p. 86.

many years to come on a scale adequate to meet the requirements of her own commerce." [69] The total German tonnage was a little above 5 millions in 1913. It was reduced in 1920 to 673,000; but in 1924 it already approached 3 million tons; in 1930 it was well above 4 million, and German liners were the wonder of the transatlantic world.

He predicted that "after what she has suffered in the war and by the Peace," Germany's annual savings would "fall far short of what they were before." [70] The monthly increase in German savings bank deposits was 84 million in 1913; in 1925 it had become 103 million; and in 1928 it was nearly 210 million.[71]

He predicted that Germany's annual surplus would be reduced to less than 2 milliard marks.[72] In 1925, the net accumulation of domestic capital was estimated at 6·4 milliards, and in 1927 at 7·6 milliards.[73]

He predicted that in the next thirty years, Germany could not possibly be expected to pay more than 2 milliard marks a year in Reparation. In the six years preceding September 1939, Germany, by Hitler's showing, had spent each year on rearmament alone about seven times as much.[74]

Here, if not before, the reader's patience comes to an end. What point can there be in all this pedantic splitting of statistical hairs? Will any amount of figures detract from the broad fact that the German people were thrown by the Treaty of Versailles into misery and despair, and that Mr. Keynes's apprehensions were very much more than confirmed?

In 1919 Mr. Keynes had quoted at length a Note addressed by Count Brockdorff-Rantzau to the Supreme Council, in which the Consequences of the Peace were duly outlined. After the diminution of products due to territorial losses, "after the economic depression resulting from the loss of her colonies, her merchant fleet and her foreign investments, Germany will not be in a position to import from abroad an adequate quantity of raw material. An enormous part of German industry will, therefore, be condemned inevitably to destruction. The need of importing foodstuffs will increase considerably at the same time that the possibility of satisfying this demand is as greatly diminished. In a very short time, therefore, Germany will not be in a position to give bread and work to her numerous millions of inhabitants, who are prevented from earning their livelihood by navigation and trade. These persons should emigrate, but this is a material impossibility, all the more because many countries and

---

[69] E.C.P., p. 61.

[70] E.C.P., p. 191.

[71] Reichs-Kredit-Gesellschaft, *Germany's Economic Development in the First Half of the Year 1931*, p. 27.

[72] E.C.P., p. 192.

[73] *Supra*, p. 116.

[74] There is, of course, nothing new about these facts. Several of them were pointed out by a witty and clairvoyant observer, R. C. Long (*The Mythology of Reparations*, London, 1928, pp. 103–4).

the most important ones will oppose any German immigration. To put the Peace conditions into execution would logically involve, therefore, the loss of several millions of persons in Germany. . . . No help, however great, or over however long a period it were continued, could prevent these deaths *en masse*. . . . Those who sign this Treaty will sign the death sentence of many millions of German men, women and children." "I know," added Mr. Keynes, "of no adequate answer to these words." [75]

Yet there *had* been an answer. It had been sent, a few days later, by Clemenceau in the name of the Supreme Council. "This report," it said, "appears . . . to contain a very inadequate presentation of the facts of the case, to be marked in parts by great exaggeration, and to ignore the fundamental considerations arising both out of the incidence and the results of the War, which explain and justify the terms that it is sought to impose." The total population of Germany, the note went on, would be reduced by about six million persons in the non-German territories which it was proposed to transfer. "It is the needs of this reduced aggregate that we are called upon to consider." The note insisted that there was nothing in the Treaty to prevent either the continued production of commodities in the areas lost by Germany or their importation into Germany as before. "On the contrary, the free admission of the products of the Eastern districts is provided for during a period of three years. . . ." [76] The German Note complained repeatedly of the necessity to import certain products from abroad in future. "It is not understood why Germany should be supposed to suffer from conditions to which other countries contentedly submit. It would appear a fundamental fallacy that the political control of a country is necessary in order to procure a reasonable share of its products. Such a proposition finds no foundation in economic law or in history. . . . There is not the slightest reason to believe that a population is destined to be permanently disabled because it will be called upon in future to trade across its frontiers instead of producing what it requires from within. A country can both become and continue to be a great manufacturing country without producing the raw materials of its main industries. . . . There is no reason whatever why Germany, under the new conditions, should not build up for herself a position both of stability and prosperity in the European world." [77]

But perhaps Mr. Keynes did not think this was an *adequate* answer.

[75] *E.C.P.*, pp. 214–15.

[76] This part of the Note referred to the Eastern districts, but the same could, as we have seen, have been said of the other lost territories.

[77] Full text of the Note in Burnett, vol. II, Doc. 366, pp. 27–31. Curiously enough, this opinion was being shared, and expressed, almost at the same moment, by General Groener, then Head of the German Army. "The aim we must now, in my opinion, set before ourselves," he told a meeting of officers, "is to hold the 60 million Germans firmly together in one single State, as far as possible a centralized State. . . . When we have attained this, a great deal will have been gained. And if we then go on steadily working, . . . then I do not see why we should not forge ahead again, especially in the economic field. . . ." (Quoted in K. F. Nowak, *Versailles*, London, 1928, pp. 280–1.)

Twenty-one years later, the German Army was entering Paris. With steady stride they came, the sturdy youths, marching along the streets of the half-deserted city to the tunes that had carried them across Europe. "Erika . . . Heidi, heido . . . Wir fahren gegen England." . . . Here were the "starved and crippled" children of 1919. They would soon be scouring across the steppes of Russia, the sands of Libya, the skies of London and of Crete, the waters of the broad Atlantic. . . . At the sight of them, the Parisian housewives broke out in angry stupefaction: "And we were told they were starving!"

Who knows an adequate answer to *these* words?

* * *

The Nature of Totalitarianism:
A Theoretical Discussion

$\mathcal{J}$n an introductory chapter to the book from which the selections below are taken, Carl Friedrich notes that:

In the general studies concerned with man and society totalitarianism is the most perplexing problem of our time. It has burst upon mankind more or less unexpected and unannounced. There are antecedents, to be sure, both in thought and in action, but they do not add up to the reality with which the mid-twentieth century finds itself confronted and by which it finds itself persistently challenged.[1]

Professor Friedrich's remarks anticipate both the difficulty of defining totalitarianism in general terms and the difference between his attempt at definition and Nicholas Timasheff's.

¶ In the first selection, Professor Timasheff, a political sociologist, offers two definitions of totalitarianism: one, a type of society, and two, a trait that can appear in different societies at different times. He excludes totalitarianism from consideration as a unique phenomenon and chooses to explore the second definition.

¶ By contrast, in the second selection, Professor Friedrich, political scientist and historian, stresses the uniqueness of totalitarianism as a contemporary phenomenon and defines "five factors or aspects which basically are shared by all totalitarian societies of our time."

¶ Professors Timasheff's and Friedrich's papers were read at a conference on totalitarianism held by the American Academy of Arts and Sciences in Boston in March 1953 and the third selection below presents some discussion of their papers by colleagues at the conference. It brings additional considerations to bear on the challenging and urgent task of probing the nature of totalitarianism.

[1] Carl J. Friedrich (ed.), *Totalitarianism* (Cambridge, 1954), p. 1.

Totalitarianism, Despotism, Dictatorship

N. S. Timasheff

THE TERM "totalitarian society" is applied in two closely related but nevertheless distinct meanings. In the first meaning it connotes a *type* of society characterized by a number of traits such as concentration of power in the hands of a few; the absence of rights ascribed to the individuals *vs.* the collectivity; and an unlimited extension of the functions of the state making the state almost tantamount with society. Other combinations of traits are possible; for example, the addition of the ideocratic nature of the state, of imperialism, of the organization of atomized men.[1] In another meaning the term connotes one definite *trait,* namely the unlimited extension of state functions; then, the term designates not a concrete type of society, but a trait isolated by means of abstraction and apt to appear in societies of various types.

Definitions, as is well known, cannot be proved to be right or wrong. They are verbal equations equalizing the term with a combination of attributes; the formula is: N is that which possesses traits or properties A, B, C. These verbal equations can be tested from the point of view of their adequacy. The test of adequacy must establish (1) whether the traits chosen coincide with clusters of traits observable in reality; (2) whether the meaning ascribed to the term approximately coincides with common speech and etymology; (3) whether the definition is a satisfactory tool for scientific inquiry.[2]

Since this is an exploratory paper, no assertion is made that one of the two definitions is more adequate than the other. But the position is hypothetically taken that the second definition, identifying totalitarianism with one definite trait appearing in society rather than identifying it with a type of society, is at least plausible and fruitful.

Let us begin by establishing a few differences which obtain depending on the definition chosen. If the first definition is chosen, totalitarian society may

[1] The last two traits form the central core of Hannah Arendt's conception of totalitarianism (*The Origins of Totalitarianism*, 1951).

[2] See my paper, "Definitions in the Social Sciences," *American Journal of Sociology*, LIII, 201–209.

be considered as a unique phenomenon having appeared in our day, though this is subject to doubt. G. Ferrero applies the term "totalitarian" to the Consulate and Empire [3] while Pitirim Sorokin points to totalitarian periods in the history of Ancient Egypt, the late Roman Empire (since Diocletian), China, and the state of the Incas.[4]

If the second definition is chosen, the term "totalitarian" my be applied to a society which differs significantly from the concrete totalitarian societies of our day, Communist, Fascist, and National Socialist. One could then combine the term "totalitarian" with the term "democratic," which is obviously impossible if Definition 1 is chosen. There recently appeared a book, by Professor J. L. Talmon, entitled *The Rise of Totalitarian Democracy*.[5] This combination of terms is used to designate the type of society which was being created in France under the Jacobins. Finally, if Definition 2 is chosen, correlations of isolated traits may be studied, while under the first definition, comparative study of total social configurations is the adequate approach.

Definition 2, to be explored in this paper, is logically connected with the requirements of a multidimensional analysis of the political phase of social life. This multidimensional analysis must be logically embedded in the essen ial properties of the structure and functions of the state.

The organization of the state presents enormous variations. For our purposes, these variations may be reduced to a formula expressing the basis of the political status of those in power, in other words, answering the question: why are these men and not other ones in power, while the other ones obey orders issued by the former? [6] The foundation of the political status of those in power may be, first, explicit and periodically checked consent of the governed; then, the government is democratic. Second, the foundation of the political status of those in power may be implicit but unchecked consent of the ruled, derived from the fact that obedience to those in power and their predecessors is consecrated by tradition; then, the government is traditional. Or, third, the political status of those in power may be based upon the seizure of power by the rulers and their ability to maintain it against attempts to dislodge them. Then, the government is dictatorial.

It is obvious that the three types are ideal or pure types. In concrete situations, there may be mixtures of two or even all the three. The government of this country is primarily democratic, but secondarily traditional since the rules of the democratic game have been received into America's culture tradition. The government of the Soviet Union is dictatorial, but it makes attempts

---

[3] *The Reconstruction of Europe* (1941), p. 51.

[4] *Social and Cultural Dynamics* (1937), III, 188–192; see also II, 575.

[5] Published in 1952.

[6] The classification offered in the text follows the lines of those offered by Ferrero, pp. 53–54, and R. MacIver, *The Web of Government* (1947), pp. 147ff. Both obviously develop ideas expressed by Max Weber in *Wirtschaft und Gesellschaft* (1925).

to invoke, in its favor, both the results of elections and the millennial tradition of Russia. The government of Napoleon also was dictatorial; but it made attempts to restore in its favor the tradition of the *ancien régime* and to strengthen itself by democratic consent in the form of plebiscites.

Other lines of analysis must be related to the three main divisions of the functions of the state. Two of them cover the state's essential functions, i.e., functions without which the state cannot exist.

The first of them is self-assertion in the framework of the greater society consisting of bodies politic in interaction. The second is maintenance of law and order which is manifested mainly in criminal and civil justice and is a substitute for conflict solution by means of violence; later on, it will be called protective. The two functions, by inner necessity, must be carried on by one organization or, eventually, a system of organizations forming a hierarchy. This is so because each function can be adequately performed only by one organization possessing overwhelming power—that is, power sufficient to break the resistance of reluctant individuals. It is obvious that, in a given area, there cannot be two overwhelmingly strong organizations, for each of them would be deprived of this attribute by the very existence of the other.

The third division of the state's functions is residual. It covers all functions which are not ramifications of the self-assertive and protective functions. These functions which can be called auxiliary arise on the background of the principle of the heterogeny of ends. An organization exists and is endowed with overwhelming power. It is there primarily for self-assertion and maintenance of law and order. Then, under most diversified conditions, part of its energy is diverted to achieve other ends. This happens if their achievement receives positive social evaluation, and the possibility and/or desirability of their achievement in nonpolitical ways is questioned.

Depending on the scope and modalities of the exertion of the three types of functions, the politically organized societies may be distributed along continua, each, in principle, independent of the others.[7]

With respect to the self-assertive function, the states may be distributed along a continuum beginning with peace-loving societies and finishing by warlike, highly aggressive, morbidly nationalistic or imperialistic societies. This position of the individual units (states) can be measured. Such a measurement has been carried out, with interesting results, by L. T. Hobhouse and associates relating to primitive societies,[8] and by Pitirim Sorokin[9] and Q.

---

[7] This is well understood by Sorokin (III, 182ff.), who identifies the dimension liberalism-totalitarianism with the *number of relationships* (activities) controlled by the state and the dimension legalism-despotism (though he does not use the terms) with the *intensity* of the measures of control.

[8] *The Material Culture and the Social Institutions of Simpler Peoples* (1915).

[9] Sorokin, III, 289ff.

Wright [10] relating to advanced societies. The latter measurement could be refined if the individual wars counted in the two works were divided into defensive and aggressive ones.

Concerning the protective function of the state, units can be distributed along a continuum beginning with that which, in German, is called *Rechtsstaat* and, in English, is covered by the phrase, "due process of law," and ending by the despotic state. A society is despotic if, in the relationship between the state and the citizens, the state ascribes to itself all the rights and imposes on its citizens a heavy burden of duties. A society is legalistic (let us use tentatively this term), if the opposite is the case. The position of the individual states can be indirectly measured by comparing the average intensity of the criminal sanctions they use.[11]

Concerning the auxiliary functions of the state, the units can be distributed along a continuum beginning with liberal society and finishing with totalitarian society. A society is totalitarian if the number of the auxiliary functions of the state is so high that almost all human activities are regulated by it. A society is liberal if the number of the auxiliary functions is so small that the state's activities are almost confined to its logical minimum. The contradistinction between the two extreme positions on the continuum can be best illustrated by two quotations, one from Jefferson, another from Mussolini. Jefferson advocates a government "which shall restrain men from injuring one another, which shall leave them otherwise free to regulate their own pursuits of industry and improvement." Mussolini declares that everything must be done within the nation (in the meaning of the state), nothing against the nation or outside the nation; the individuals are related to each other through the medium of the whole, or of one of its spheres (political, economic, and so on).

It is noteworthy that the exertion of the auxiliary functions of the state can appear in at least three forms: (1) state regulation of activities of individuals or corporations carrying out a function; (2) licensing of individuals or corporations desirous to perform a function; or (3) absorption of the function, manifested in the annexation of the corresponding organizations by the bureaucratic machinery of the state.

This is a continuum relating to which indirect measurement is possible. The auxiliary functions of the state must be enforced, and the main instrument of enforcement is, of course, criminal law. Consequently, the larger the

[10] *A Study of War* (1942), I, 218ff.

[11] The present writer had the opportunity to carry out such a computation relating to five advanced societies and seven epochs beginning with the early Middle Ages and finishing with our day. The results were incorporated, with Sorokin's interpretations, into his *Social and Cultural Dynamics,* II, chap. xv.

scope of the auxiliary functions, the larger is the number of types of conduct punished by criminal law.[12]

The scientific problem which arises when confronting and correlating the distribution of the units (i.e., states) among the classes or positions in the four-dimensional space just traced is this: are, or are not, the positions of the units in the four dimensions related in such a way that, from the position along one of the dimensions, positions along the other dimensions can be predicted? This is of course an enormous problem, the solution of which would require years of team work. At this place only a tentative answer can be given: There are incompatible locations; there are, on the other hand, frequent and naturally recurring combinations; there is, however, also a significant area of freedom characterized by the appearance of diverse combinations.

We observe, or have recently observed, a number of political units whose position on the four coördinates must be termed as dictatorial, highly aggressive, despotic, and totalitarian (in the meaning of Definition 2), and we are inclined to construct, to cover them, an historical, or concrete, type (totalitarian in the meaning of Definition 1). Such are, or have been, Communist Russia, now also Communist China, National Socialist Germany, Fascist Italy, perhaps also Franco's Spain.[13] But relating to the Western satellites, the classification would not be exactly the same. These societies are dictatorial and despotic, but they cannot be aggressive (since they are themselves victims of aggression), and they have not yet reached the climax of totalitarianism. Salazar's Portugal is a dictatorship; it is far advanced toward totalitarianism (but without reaching the limit); it is not aggressive and is not so much despotic as authoritarian, a position midway between legalism and despotism. In the twenties, thirties, and early forties, there were in Europe many semifascist societies, such as Spain under Primo de Rivera, Poland under Pilsudski and his successors, Lithuania under Waldemaras and his successors, Latvia under Ulmanis, Rumania under Carol II and Antonescu, Bulgaria under K. Gueorguiev and his successors, Greece under Metaxas, Vichy France. They all were dictatorships, close to despotism, inclined to aggression (*vide* Lithuania *vs.* the Memelland, Poland *vs.* Lithuania and Teschen, Hungary *vs.* the provinces lost in 1918, Rumania *vs.* Bessarabia and a vast area East of it, Bulgaria *vs.* the lands granted her by the treaty of San Stefano, but lost through the treaty of Berlin). They were also inclined to totalitarianism without going, however, more than halfway.[14]

[12] Such a computation has been carried out simultaneously with the one mentioned in the preceding footnote. Other computations pertinent to the subject of this paper appear in chapters, iv, vi, and vii of vol. III of Sorokin's work.

[13] H. Arendt, in the *Origins of Totalitarianism,* narrows down the concept of totalitarian society to cover only Hitler's Germany and Stalin's (not Lenin's) Russia.

[14] On the scope of the functions of the state in these societies see N. S. Timasheff, *Three Worlds* (Milwaukee, 1949), pp. 76–101.

As a contrast to these combinations, let us mention the combination of democracy, legalism, and liberalism in the United States, Belgium, and Switzerland, and the combination of democracy, legalism, and significant expansion of the functions of the state toward totalitarianism in Great Britain, Australia, New Zealand, France, Italy, and many other, formerly liberal countries.

If we leave the contemporary European scene, we find other combinations. France, under the Jacobins, was a combination of democracy (the Convention having been elected by universal suffrage!), aggressiveness, despotism, and far-advanced totalitarianism (tendency to regulate everything, including religion). The mercantilistic states of continental Europe in the seventeenth and eighteenth centuries were also well advanced toward the totalitarian regulation of life (especially, economic life); they were however traditional in their organization, but despotic as to the relations between the state and the individuals, with a few striking exceptions: Frederick the Great's Prussia approximated the ideal of legalism. At the same time England was a traditional body politic with incipient concessions toward democracy, as inclined to totalitarianism as the continental nations, but, like Prussia, approximating legalism. Some of the English colonies in America presented peculiar combinations of democracy, legalism, and quasi-totalitarianism, especially relative to religion and the connected regulations of everyday life.

Russia under Nicholas I was traditional, despotic, aggressive, and inclined to totalitarianism, as were the Western states fifty years earlier. Under Nicholas II, Russia was traditional, but with significant concessions to democracy; closer to legalism than to despotism; aggressive, but closer to the liberal than to the totalitarian position on the fourth continuum.

The Latin American dictatorships are commonly despotic (sometimes only authoritarian), but little inclined to totalitarianism: life is politically regulated only so far as it is relevant for the maintenance in power of those who hold it. But Paraguay under the Jesuits was close to totalitarianism; Peron's Argentina is midway between the liberal and totalitarian positions.

The Ancient World presents instances of combinations closely resembling totalitarian society (Definition 1) of our day, but also combinations of democracy with despotism and inclination toward totalitarianism.[15]

It is worth while to conclude this survey by comparing the lists of actions considered criminal in the Middle Ages, the climax of liberalism (from the French Revolution up to the last quarter of the nineteenth century), and the postliberal period characterized by the rise of modern totalitarianism (Definition 1). This comparison shows that (1) there is a hard core of such actions perpetuated from period to period and approximately corresponding to the "maintenance of law and order" function of the state; (2) in the Middle Ages, and well into the eighteenth century, such actions appeared punishable as

[15] See J. Bryce, *Modern Democracies* (1921), I, 166ff.

apostasy, heresy, schism, conversion to another religion, sorcery, nonperformance of the rites of the official religion, contact with Jews, fornication, sodomy, wearing of prohibited apparel (thus violating the symbolic separation of the social classes), infringement of government regulations concerning the production of specified commodities; (3) in the postliberal period, many subtle types of sexual abuse and many complex modalities of the violation of the order of production and exchange made their appearance, even in nontotalitarian societies. But even the totalitarian societies do not penalize many of the actions enumerated above, thus testifying to the fact that they are not interested in the corresponding activities; of course, they punish deviations from their secular ideologies and the principles of action derived therefrom.[16] The number of types of action punishable in modern totalitarian societies and in typical medieval societies is perhaps not very much different.[17]

Of course, this survey is very superficial. It proves, however, that the extreme positions along the four dimensions discussed above do not necessarily go together. In the survey, some of the theoretically possible combinations are conspicuous by their absence. No traditional society has been simultaneously despotic *and* liberal; no democratic society either; no dictatorial society has been legalistic. But this is not sufficient evidence in favor of the proposition that such combinations are impossible.

For further study of totalitarian society as of an historical type these conclusions may be drawn: (1) it is worth while analyzing it into elements; (2) it is desirable to establish, throughout history, the fluctuations of concrete societies along the types of organization and the continua corresponding to the three divisions of the functions of the state, applying, whenever possible, quantitative methods; (3) it is desirable to find out the conditions directing societies toward the choice of dictatorship and of extreme positions on each of the continua; (4) it is desirable to reach, by case study, the understanding of conditions favorable to the *simultaneous* movement of a society in the directions just stated. This is, perhaps, the most promising way to understand the compound which is totalitarian society (Definition 1), and eventually to control movements conducive to its emergence and expansion.

[16] The statements above condense material appearing in Sorokin, II, chap. xv.

[17] The idea that the totalitarianism is a unique, purely modern phenomenon is probably generated by the fact that it emerged after a long period of liberalism.

THE UNIQUE CHARACTER OF TOTALITARIAN SOCIETY

Carl J. Friedrich

IT IS the contention of this paper that (*a*) fascist and Communist totalitarian society are basically alike, that is to say are more nearly alike to each other than to any other systems of government and society, and (*b*) totalitarian society is historically unique and *sui generis*. These two theses are closely linked and must be examined together. At the outset, it should be stated that these contentions do not presuppose that our understanding of totalitarian society is complete or even adequate; these theses are based upon what we at present know reasonably surely about them. Nor do the two theses presuppose that totalitarian societies are fixed and static entities—on the contrary, it is being assumed that they have undergone and continue to undergo a steady evolution; presumably involving both growth and deterioration.[1] The debate about these causes or origins of

---

[1] Mr. George Kennan, in his discussion, stresses this point. As for the problem of uniqueness, existing literature varies widely, as it does on the question whether fascist and Communist totalitarianism are basically alike or not. Sigmund Neumann, in *Permanent Revolution* (1942), treats them as basically alike; indeed his is the first comprehensive treatment of the general problems of totalitarian dictatorship. Franz Neumann, in *Behemoth* (1942 and later), on the other hand, deals with the Hitler dictatorship as something quite distinctive, essentially the creation if not the creature of big business, the bureaucracy, and the army. Among earlier works, Alfred Cobban's *Dictatorship, Its History and Theory* (1939) on the one hand definitely links modern dictatorship with enlightened despotism, Bonapartism, and other tyrannical systems of the past, while on the other definitely treating fascist and Communist dictatorship as alike. His book also undertakes to suggest the derivation of totalitarian dictatorship from Hobbes, Rousseau, and the French Revolution's doctrine of popular sovereignty; this theme has lately been developed brilliantly, though unconvincingly, by J. L. Talmon in *Totalitarian Democracy* (1952). Two other volumes also stressed the connection between fascist and Communist dictatorship: *Dictatorship in the Modern World* (edited by Guy Stanton Ford, 1935 and 1939), and Hans Kohn's *Revolutions and Dictatorships* (1939). Among the books emphasizing either explicitly or by implication the distinctness of fascism, mention might be made of E. B. Ashton (pseudonym), *The Fascist—His State and His Mind* (1937); Herbert W. Schneider, *Making the Fascist State* (1928); G. A. Borgese, *Goliath, the March of Fascism* (1937); Max Ascoli and Arthur Feiler, *Fascism for Whom?* (1938); and several books on Nazi Germany, including Frederick L. Schumann, *The Nazi Dictatorship* (1935 and later); Fritz Morstein Marx, *Government in the Third Reich* (1936 and later); Karl Loewenstein, *Hitler's Germany* (1939 and later). Konrad Heiden's *Der Führer—Hitler's Rise to Power* (1944), like the recent work by Alan Bullock, *Hitler—A Study in Tyranny* (1952), brings out the personal side of totalitarian dictatorship; this approach, while important, tends to obscure the uniqueness of totalitarianism. Bertram Wolfe's

---

Reprinted by permission of the publishers from Carl J. Friedrich (ed.), *Totalitarianism: Proceedings of a Conference Held at the American Academy of Arts and Sciences, March 1953*. Cambridge, Mass.: Harvard University Press, Copyright, 1954, by The President and Fellows of Harvard College.

totalitarianism, and more especially of fascism, has run all the way from a primitive bad-man theory to the "moral crisis of our time" kind of argument. A detailed inspection of the available evidence would seem to suggest that virtually everyone of the factors which has been stressed as offering by itself an explanation of the origin of totalitarianism has played its role. For example, in the German case, Hitler's moral and personal defects, weaknesses in the German constitutional tradition, certain traits involved in the German "national character," the Versailles Treaty and its aftermath, the economic crisis and the "contradictions" of an aging capitalism, the "threat" of Communism, the decline of Christianity and other spiritual moorings, and so forth have all played a role in the total configuration of factors contributing to the over-all result. As in the case of other broad developments in history, only a multiple-factor analysis will do. In keeping with his general philosophical methodological position, the author is presupposing that *ta politika* are decisive for the patterning of any society.[2]

The argument of historical uniqueness of any configuration does not mean that it is "wholly" unique; for nothing is. All historical phenomena belong to broad classes of analytical objects. When we say that the Greek *polis* was historically unique, we do not mean that there were never any cities, or city-states, but we do mean that the Greek and more particularly the Athenian *polis* had so many and such striking traits peculiar to it that it deserves to be considered "historically unique." History is primarily concerned with individualities, whether these be persons, things, or events, and a sufficiently variegated pattern of distinctive elements therefore constitutes historical uniqueness.[3] In passing, one should perhaps safeguard oneself against the objection that everything historically considered is "historically unique." This objection, while often made, is not actually correct. A great many events (as well as persons and things) are so nearly alike that they lack that distinctive quality

---

Three Who Made a Revolution (1938), and other works on Stalin, serve the same good purpose. The most searching study on the level where the impact of ideas upon political practice occurs is Hannah Arendt's *The Origins of Totalitarianism* (1951); it bears a certain resemblance to Herrmann Rauschning's *The Revolution of Nihilism* (1939), and to Borgese's book cited above, but it develops the important thesis that totalitarianism is an outgrowth of the establishment of dictatorship under modern conditions.

[2] See *Constitutional Government and Democracy* (1941 ed.), chap. xxv. The understanding of these political relationships is the most important aspect of societies with which the student must be concerned; in the words of Aristotle, political science is the highest or most important science. See also footnote 28.

[3] This distinction was elaborated by Heinrich Rickert, *Kulturwissenschaft und Naturwissenschaft* (1898, 1910, and later), building upon studies of Wilhelm Dilthey, especially his *Einleitung in die Geisteswissenschaften* (1883). The point was central to the famous argument between Eduard Meyer and Max Weber, of which Max Weber's part is found in *Gesammelte Aufsaetze zur Wissenschaftslehre* (1922), "Kritische Studien auf dem Gebiet der kulturwissenschaftlichen Logik," pp. 215–290.

which constitutes historical uniqueness; but it is true that when taken in sufficiently large "classes" and broad enough perspective, their uniqueness often appears. Thus the monarchy in this or that German territory in the eighteenth century is not in any sense historically unique, but the monarchical paternalism of all these and a number of related societies in the seventeenth and eighteenth centuries does indeed constitute what we may call a "historically unique" configuration.

Why do we say that fascist and Communist totalitarian society and government are *basically alike?* In the first instance, the qualifying adverb "basically" is intended to indicate that they are *not wholly alike*. Popular and journalistic interpretation has oscillated between these two extremes of proclaiming the two societies as wholly alike or as not at all basically alike. The latter was the prevailing mood during the popular front days in Europe, and in "liberal" circles in the United States; it was even more popular during the Second World War, and more especially among Allied propagandists. It is, of course, the insistently promoted official Soviet and Hitler party line. The proposition that they are wholly alike is presently favored in the United States and Western Europe, and hence it may seem unnecessary to labor the point. But there is, in the first place, a lingering doubt remaining from former days, and there is secondly and perhaps more importantly the problem of the range of alikeness, or to put it another way, the question of what makes them "basically" alike. For it is obvious that they are not alike in intention. The sharply divergent content of their ideologies proves it.[4] So do the historical facts which show the fascist movements to arise in reaction to the Communist challenge and to offer themselves to a frightened bourgeoisie as saviors from the Communist threat. These facts are so familiar that they do not require documentation. The well-known frauds involved in the argument are part of the pattern of psychic antagonism and combative projection.

It is equally obvious that more of the preceding liberal and constitutional society survives in the fascist than in the Communist society; but this is in part due to the fact that no liberal, constitutional society preceded Soviet Communism. It is conceivable that at least for a considerable initial period, the situation in this respect would be sharply different in, say, Great Britain or the United States. This tendency of isolated fragments of the preceding state of society to survive has been a most potent source of misinterpretation of the fascist totalitarian society. In the twenties, Italian totalitarianism was very commonly misinterpreted as being "merely" this and that, with the "trains on time" and "the beggars off the street" thrown in for symbolic measure.[5] In the

---

[4] Mr. Inkeles' paper rightly comments, on the other hand, that totalitarian dictatorships are alike in having such ideology.

[5] Borgese, *Goliath,* sarcastically comments upon this very symptomatic escapism of the Western liberal. A striking instance of it, as far as the Soviet Union is concerned, is found in Maurice Hindus' *Mother Russia* (1942), but there are many others.

thirties, various authors, some Marxist, others of Marxist antecedents, still others just befuddled, undertook to interpret German totalitarianism as either "the end phase of capitalism" [6] or of "militarist imperialism" (in the manner of Veblen).[7] It is not generally appreciated, even by scholars, how profound a shock to Marxist orthodoxy the rise of German fascism turned out to be. Men of the dogmatic acumen of Hilferding were so struck by it that they felt a complete reassessment of Marxist doctrine was called for.[8] For there was no trace in Marx and Engels of this eventuality emerging. To be sure, Marx was not unaware (how could he be?) that a frightened bourgeoisie might rally behind a rider on horseback, such as Napoleon III, but this kind of amiable *opera bouffe* of mid-nineteenth-century politics is a far cry indeed from the totalitarian society of our time. All one has to do is to look at the intellectual life of France in that period to sense the difference. It was a natural escape for such Marxist and Veblenian interpreters to try and depict the totalitarian society Hitler and Himmler were building as nothing but a capitalist one, totally at variance with the socialist society which was being formed in the Soviet Union. Blinded by the dichotomy of capitalism and socialism of the Marxian heritage, and afflicted by its preoccupation with the economic as contrasted with the governmental and political aspects of society, they did not see that the "planned," that is to say the thoroughly coördinated and governmentally controlled, economy of the Nazi state was different from that of the Soviet state only by the degree of thoroughness with which the coördination and subordination of the "managerial" as well as "labor" elements had been carried forward; this process was advancing apace and given another ten to twenty years would probably have become as nearly complete as in the Soviet Union.[9] Characteristically, however (to mention only one common feature), strikes are completely barred, as criminal sabotage of the "workers' state" in both totalitarian societies. Having said this much, one has at the same time indicated once more some significant divergences between the two totalitarian societies as well: they do not advance toward the totality of their economic controls either by the same stages, or at the same tempo. (It might, as an amusing variant of this line of reasoning, be recalled that Sidney and Beatrice Webb in *The Truth about Soviet Russia* (1942) argued that Stalin was no dictator at all, but had brought not only political but economic democracy to Russia, whereas the real dictator appeared to them to be the American president, Franklin D. Roosevelt.)

Other attempts at differentiating sharply between the Soviet Communist and the fascist regimes turn upon such items as the content of their divergent

[6] See Neumann, *Permanent Revolution;* Maxine B. Sweezey, *The Structure of the Nazi Economy* (1941); and R. A. Brady, *The Spiritual Structure of German Fascism* (1937).

[7] Karl Loewenstein, *Hitler's Germany* (1940), and W. Ebenstein, *The Nazi State* (1943).

[8] R. Hilferding, "State Capitalism or Totalitarian Economy," in *Modern Review* I, 266–271.

[9] James Burnham, *The Managerial Revolution* (1941).

ideologies, the national characters of the peoples within which they arise, the stage of respective economic development, and the like. It would be tedious to refute these various lines of reasoning, especially as their positions will by implication be denied through a more positive analysis of the basic features which, according to general agreement, they have in common. These same features do at the same time constitute the ground for asserting that these totalitarian societies are historically unique.

The factors or aspects which basically are shared by all totalitarian societies of our time are five, or can be grouped around five closely linked clusters of characteristic features. These societies all possess:

1. An official ideology, consisting of an official body of doctrine covering all vital aspects of man's existence, to which everyone living in that society is supposed to adhere at least passively; this ideology is characteristically focused in terms of chiliastic claims as to the "perfect" final society of mankind.[10]

2. A single mass party consisting of a relatively small percentage of the total population (up to 10 per cent) of men and women passionately and unquestioningly dedicated to the ideology and prepared to assist in every way in promoting its general acceptance, such party being organized in strictly hierarchical, oligarchical manner, usually under a single leader and typically either superior to or completely commingled with the bureaucratic governmental organization.

3. A technologically conditioned near-complete monopoly of control (in the hands of the party and its subservient cadres, such as the bureaucracy and the armed forces) of all means of effective armed combat.

4. A similarly technologically conditioned near-complete monopoly of control (in the same hands) of all means of effective mass communication, such as the press, radio, motion pictures, and so on.

5. A system of terroristic police control, depending for its effectiveness upon points 3 and 4 and characteristically directed not only against demonstrable "enemies" of the regime, but against arbitrarily selected classes of the population; such arbitrary selection turning upon exigencies of the regime's survival, as well as ideological "implications," and systematically exploiting scientific psychology.

The suggestion that to these five clusters of basic traits there should be added that of the secret police gaining ascendancy over the army,[11] seems unacceptable, because both of these factors are controversial, whereas the five which have been delineated are quite generally admitted to be factually established features of these regimes. In the nature of the case, it is very difficult to deter-

---

[10] The role of ideology is penetratingly discussed by Arendt, *Origins,* and in the article cited below, footnote 28.

[11] See the remarks by Hannah Arendt below.

mine whether, when, and to what extent the secret police gained ascendancy over the army; another difficulty arises from the fact that in so far as the police is a branch of the civilian government, it is in the ascendancy in constitutional states as well.

The argument that total subversion is another distinctive feature of totalitarian systems has merit, but it is arguable whether this aspect of totalitarianism constitutes a sufficiently separate item. It would seem to me that it is comprehended under the first of the five characteristics, where we state that the official ideology is one "to which everyone living in that society is supposed to adhere." The five main clusters of traits, for the sake of clarity, ought not to be unnecessarily expanded.

Within this broad similarity, there are many significant variations, both in time and in place, as already mentioned. For instance, the party appears to play less of a role in the Soviet Union today than earlier; [12] the ideology of the Soviet Union is more rigid, because of its Marxist bible, than that of Italian or German fascism, where ideology was formulated by the leader of the party; [13] and—to give a third illustration at random—Hitler's extermination

[12] This was written at the time Stalin was still living; there are some indications, such as the appointment of Khrushchev instead of Malenkov to be general secretary of the party, that this may be less true in the future. But the searching inquiries of Merle Fainsod definitely point in this direction. See his "Controls and Tensions in the Soviet System," *American Political Science Review*, xliv, 266–282, and "The Komsomols—A Study of Youth under Dictatorship," *ibid.*, xlv, 18–40, as well as his forthcoming *How Russia Is Ruled*, which I have been privileged to catch glimpses of in seminar discussions and conversations.

[13] There have been considerable controversies on the question of the degree of rigidity of Soviet ideology. During the war it was customary among all those who wished to soft-pedal the potential conflict between the Soviet Union and the West to claim that ideology had become unimportant, in spite of the fact that Stalin and others repeatedly stressed it. For an indication of the "line," see as representative Robert E. Sherwood, *Roosevelt and Hopkins* (1948), especially pp. 301–308. However, not only those who wished to play it soft, but also the self-styled "realist" school, denying the real significance of ideas and talking in terms of geographical and other kinds of "real" interest, have tended to take the line that Stalin was pursuing the policy of the Tsars of Russia and that ideology was little more than camouflage. Very interesting in this connection is Walter Lippmann's *U.S. Foreign Policy: Shield of the Republic* (1943), in which the two tendencies are combined. Lippmann, after demonstrating that the United States has never been willing to permit a power in continental Europe to become predominant, and then clearly recognizing that Russia will be the dominant power after the war (p. 149), fails to draw the inevitable conclusion, except by way of insisting that the alliance must be maintained. He has some shrewd things to say about what will happen, if it is not (note the remark on p. 148 on the conflict over territorial settlements), but characteristically Lippmann discusses the matter in terms of Russia rather than the Soviet Union, just as he speaks of Germany and the "German war" rather than Hitler and the Nazi state, thereby displaying his desire to minimize the ideological factor in terms of which this first world revolutionary war was actually fought. Barrington Moore, Jr., in *Soviet Politics—The Dilemma of Power* (1950), gives a discriminating discussion of the role of the ideology, to which he assigns a central role in the analysis of Soviet politics, while Julian Towster, in *Political Power in the U.S.S.R.* (1948), rightly started his discussion of Soviet government with a sketch of the underlying ideology. He speaks of it as "avowed theory" and comments at the outset that "an understanding of its [the USSR's] operative constitutional order would lack coherence without due attention to avowed theory." That the USSR's government is no "constitutional order" in terms of our analysis is obvious.

of the Jews was ideologically motivated and contrary to the apparent immediate needs of the regime, whereas Stalin's recent Jewish purges appear to be taking place in response to exigencies of the international situation, rather than to ideology, hence the vigorous denial of anti-Semitism.[14]

It is submitted that every one of these factors to a large extent, and all of them in combination, are certainly lacking from all historically known despotic, let alone authoritarian, societies of the past. It might be mentioned in passing that many authoritarian societies of the past should in point of fact be sharply differentiated from autocratic societies. The medieval and early modern distinction of monarchy and tyranny was in many ways sounder than our common differentiation of "democratic" and "autocratic." [15] Neither the oriental despotisms of the more remote past nor the absolute monarchies of modern Europe, neither the tyrannies of the ancient Greek *polis* nor the imperial establishment of Rome, nor yet the tyrannies of the city-states of the Italian Rennaissance exhibit any one of these factors to any marked extent. Attempts, such as Thornton Wilder's *The Ides of March* (in which he tries to show Caesar to have been a totalitarian dictator in the making) or more learned efforts along similar lines,[16] collapse when subjected to a more detailed scrutiny in terms of these five factors. To be sure, there have often been made efforts to organize some kind of secret police, but they are not even horse-and-buggy affairs compared to the enterprises of a Himmler or a Beria. Similarly, there have been in the past both military and propagandistic concentrations of power and control, but as in the previous case, the limits of technology prevented any thorough-going development along totalitarian lines. Rather than elaborate this point, which is obvious enough, once one has faced up to it, it seems more urgent to stress the common reason for the uniqueness of factors 3, 4, and 5, and thus to turn back to the other side of the general thesis.

This common cause appears to be our advanced technology. Without the inventions of the last few generations, none of these features could have been created, no matter how glad Peter or Frederick the Great might have been to do so. This technological aspect of totalitarianism is, of course, particularly striking in the matter of arms and communications. The constitution of the United States guarantees to every citizen the "right to bear arms." In the days of

---

[14] Recent developments suggest that the Soviet Union is abandoning this line again. As for Hitler's anti-Semitism, the damage done to his foreign policy, as well as the weakening of his domestic support are obvious. The problem has been explored in its ramifications by Hannah Arendt, *Origins of Totalitarianism,* chaps. vi–ix. However, her tendency is to overrate this aspect of fascist ideology. Even early in the regime, mass support for Hitler was primarily based upon other factors, and anti-Semitism tended to weaken rather than strengthen Hitler's appeal with many, as was shown very convincingly on the basis of numerous psychological interviews by Theodore Abel, *Why Hitler Came into Power* (1938).

[15] See Harold D. Lasswell, *Power and Society,* § 6.5.

[16] See Alfred Cobban, *Dictatorship—Its History and Theory* (1939); Carl Schmitt, *Die Diktatur von den Anfaengen des modernen Souveraenitaetsgedankens bis zum proletarischen Klassenkampf* (2nd ed., 1928).

the Minutemen this was a very important right, and the freedom of the citizen was indeed symbolized by the gun over the hearth, as it is in Switzerland to this day. But who can "bear" such arms as a tank, a bomber, or a flame-thrower, let alone an atom bomb? The citizen as an individual, and indeed in larger groups, is simply defenseless against the overwhelming technological superiority of those who can centralize in their hands the means wherewith to wield these modern arms and thereby physically to coerce. Similar observations readily apply concerning the press, the radio, and so forth. "Freedom" does not have the same intrinsic value, resting upon individual effort and exertion, which it had a hundred and fifty years ago. The trend of technological advance carries with it, with relatively few exceptions, the trend toward greater and greater size of organization. Thus, totalitarian societies appear in this respect to be merely exaggerations, but nonetheless logical exaggerations, of inherent implications of the technological state in which we find ourselves.[17]

The situation is rather different with respect to the first two distinctive features of totalitarian societies. Neither ideology nor party have any significant relation to the state of technology.[18] But they do have a vital relation to another common feature of all contemporary societies, namely, the increasing amount of general literacy.[19] To this literacy must be added (in Russia, Italy, Germany, and other countries where totalitarian societies have arisen within the context of the Christian tradition) the fact that Christianity has tended to establish a broad predilection for convictional certainty.[20] But probably more important than either is the "democratic" antecedents of these totalitarian societies. Marx and Engels saw themselves as constituting the vanguard of the democratic movement of their day, and Stalin talked of the Soviet totalitarian society as the "perfect democracy" with evident conviction.[21] However, not only Marx and Engels, but Mussolini and Hitler organized parties with a

[17] The role of technology in the development of modern politics has received inadequate attention. Charles A. Beard, following Thorstein Veblen, occasionally lays stress upon it. James Burnham's *The Managerial Revolution* (1941) is built upon it, but the conclusions go beyond the evidence.

[18] This is not strictly true, since the mass conversion continually attempted by totalitarian propaganda through the effective use of its monopoly of communications (factor 4) could not be carried through without it. This in turn affects the party and its dynamics.

[19] In this connection the rate of literacy in Japan as contrasted with China used to seem significant, but would not seem to be similarly striking now. However, in our view the question as to whether China actually is a totalitarian dictatorship cannot be answered satisfactorily at the present time. No doubt the Chinese Communists are a totalitarian movement; but whether they will succeed in organizing China along totalitarian lines remains to be seen. If they do, the effect will probably entail the rapid reduction of illiteracy, as has happened in the Soviet Union in conjunction with the forward march of totalitarianism.

[20] The objection that China does not fit this pattern—should not only be considered in the light of what is said in the previous footnote, but also in relation to the fact that the totalitarian developments in China are closely associated with the reception of these Western ideas. Sun Yat Sen's *Three Principles of the People,* probably the most influential book of modern China, provides ample evidence for this aspect of the matter.

[21] See especially Stalin's great speech in the election of February 1946.

program intended for mass appeal, designed to win as many adherents as possible.[22] It would never have occurred to the absolute monarchs of seventeenth- and eighteenth-century Europe to stoop so low, nor would the Roman Emperors have considered such an undertaking as politically significant. They appealed to the masses against senatorial privilege from time to time, but an organized and ideologically homogeneous party was "inconceivable." There was, to be sure, a party of the Medicis in Florence,[23] but this was in the days of flourishing factions contesting for power with each other—in other words, during a period resembling in some limited ways democratic conditions. But the carefully organized single mass party, complete with program and ideology, is a distinct peculiarity of the totalitarian societies of our time. The tie to its Christian and democratic antecedents may gradually weaken—there are signs that both the ideology and the party in Soviet totalitarian society are declining in importance [24]—but there is some room for doubt as to whether a totalitarian society could survive their destruction.

The foregoing may lend itself to the misinterpretation that democracy, Christianity, or technology had, in the author's view, "caused" totalitarianism. No proposition of the kind is intended. All that is meant is that it could only have arisen in the kind of context created by Christianity, democracy, and modern technology. But it seems basically unsound to pick out of past intellectual history some one or several exponents or supposed exponents of some aspect of totalitarian views—for instance, of an authoritarian society, be it Plato or Thomas Aquinas, Hobbes or Rousseau, Hegel or Carlyle—and hold him "responsible" for the totalitarian movements or societies by claiming that he was a totalitarian. None of those mentioned were, because none of them could be: the historically unique features of the totalitarian society were unknown to them.[25] Usually, it is quite easy to show that the particular thinker would, on his own terms, have turned with disgust and indignation upon these latter-day totalitarians, for a variety of reasons inherent in his system. The peculiar moral obtuseness of contemporary totalitarian societies which has been stressed as *the* distinguishing feature of these societies (we think, wrongly),[26] manifesting itself in violence on an unprecedented scale, is

---

[22] Konrad Heiden, in *Der Führer,* has given the most elaborate account to date, to which Alan Bullock's *Hitler* adds little. Very revealing, even as a title, is the book by E. Czech-Jochberg, entitled *Hitler—Eine Deutsche Bewegung* (1930).

[23] From this our modern word state is in part derived, as the Medici party was called *il stato.* In the north, the estate of the king provided another source.

[24] See, regarding this aspect, footnote 11 above.

[25] See J. L. Talmon, *Totalitarian Democracy;* W. M. McGovern, *From Luther to Hitler* (1941); and Aurel Kolnai, *The War Against the West* (1938).

[26] It is not a distinguishing feature of these totalitarian societies, because such moral obtuseness has been recurrent in the history of human government. As far as amorality is concerned, Nero and Cesare Borgia yield little to contemporary dictators; indeed, their amorality seems more thoroughgoing, since they do not camouflage it by relating it to a presumably moral end, such as the Communist world society.

demonstrably entirely alien to the thinkers we have named. They are all ardent rationalists, if not moralists, whereas the totalitarians of today are indifferent to such considerations because theirs is essentially an engineering approach to society. They solve problems in a manner which they believe to be "scientific," while at the same time denying the importance of freedom and more especially freedom of inquiry, of teaching and learning, the essential conditions of scientific truth.

Closely related to these issues of novelty and conceptual distinctiveness is the as yet unresolved problem of succession in totalitarian regimes. This issue has recently been high-lighted by the death of Stalin. Most of the comments revealed as in a flash the hopeless noncomprehension of the totalitarian reality, as men gravely disputed about the successor to Stalin as if he had been occupying a legally or traditionally defined office, such as the King of France, or even the Tsars of Russia. In fact, the problem of succession in government has to date not been solved in any totalitarian society. This is a most important shortcoming, in view of the millennial importance of succession. Constitutional democracy and hereditary monarchy, oriental despotism with its deification of the ruler as well as its ancient tribal antecedents—they all revolve around this issue of succession. Tyranny has perennially been weak on this score, as Aristotle noted, and as the history of the two Napoleons suggests. Maybe, totalitarian societies will discover a means to cope with the problem. The vast array of documentary evidence we now have about fascism does not contain any really viable scheme for succession. The obstacles to evolving one are formidable. The building up of concentrated veneration for the one "father of the people" or "leader," which approximates and at times exceeds what the deifiers of kings used to do, obviously must create a vacuum the moment this unique person has gone "the way of all flesh." How the then controller of the machinery of communication can be brought to shift, and shift dramatically, to a new man who only yesterday was his equal and maybe competitor seems perplexing. Equally puzzling appears the question of what will be done by him who controls the terror apparatus.[27]

The sharp delineation of what distinguishes the past from the present in thought as well as action should not be mistaken, of course, for a denial of significant links. One does not have to mistake Hobbes for a totalitarian in order to recognize the connection between his failure to understand the vital role of religion and of intermediary groups in a well-ordered commonwealth and the totalitarians' comparable blindness in these matters. The road of Western thought runs from Luther to Lincoln, as it does from Luther to Hitler; the seamless web of history is woven of many intertwined strands,

---

[27] It may be recalled in this connection that Bodin, even though he seeks to give the sovereign very broad authority, declares the laws of succession inviolable. While it is incorrect to call these "constitutional laws," as has at times been done, it is clear that Bodin assumed that such a succession would be regulated by law. In a totalitarian dictatorship, such regulation is inconceivable.

and totalitarianism, for all its uniqueness, does not spring from the head of any ideologue or demagogue without antecedents. But these antecedents did not "cause" the phenomenon, and there was nothing inevitable about Hitler or Stalin. The totalitarian societies are basically alike, and they are historically unique; but why they are what they are we do not know.[28] Like everything genuinely novel in history, whether good or bad, whether beautiful or ugly, totalitarianism remains wrapped in the womb of creation. Hence only the genuinely creative answer will do effective service in supplanting and superseding it. The future, if there is one, will be a future beyond Communism and fascism, not some neo-ism of recent or more ancient prescription.

DISCUSSION

Bertram Wolfe, George Denicke, Hannah Arendt,

Albert Lauterbach, George F. Kennan

Mr. Bertram Wolfe: We have heard two sharply different approaches to the phenomenon with which our Conference is to deal. Mr. Friedrich insists upon the uniqueness of the totalitarian syndrome, whereas Mr. Timasheff urges us to view totalitarianism as a variant upon the older phenomena of despotism and dictatorship.

This problem, of course, is basic to all historiography; the historian must

[28] That is why the dispute over the origins of totalitarianism is at once so sharp and so inconclusive; e.g., between Eric Voegelin, "The Origins of Totalitarianism" and Hannah Arendt's reply, *The Review of Politics*, xv, 68ff. Miss Arendt wisely remarks that her book is not really a study of the origins, but when she says that it "gives an historical account of the elements which crystallized into totalitarianism," she overstates the case for her remarkable book; for it deals only with *some* of the elements, and they did not "crystallize," but were molded and used by the creators of totalitarianism. In her recent contribution to *Offener Horizont—Festschrift fuer Karl Jaspers* (1953), entitled "Ideologie und Terror," she rightly stresses the novelty and the creative aspect. In this connection, the observation may be in order that it is a Bergsonian and romantic prejudice to view all creation as somehow "good," and hence to overlook the "procreation in sin" and the possibility of fashioning the ugly which is wholly new. Man finds himself in a situation and he brings to his response such creative resources as are in him, both for good and evil.

Reprinted by permission of the publishers from Carl J. Friedrich (ed.), *Totalitarianism: Proceedings of a Conference Held at the American Academy of Arts and Sciences, March 1953* Cambridge, Mass.: Harvard University Press, Copyright, 1954, by The President and Fellows of Harvard College.

assume both continuity and uniqueness. But one can admit, from case to case, differing degrees of emphasis upon the one or the other, and in the present context I side with Mr. Friedrich.

Aristotle once asserted discrimination is the beginning of all wisdom. That which distinguishes totalitarianism, it seems to me, is rooted in the word *total*. All cultures have had their ideologies, but the ideology in a totalitarian society is deliberately total—that is, it embraces and prescribes for every aspect of human life. Similarly, every modern society has involved a "state," but the totalitarian state is designedly total, in that it becomes coëxtensive with the society itself.

This totality is unique to our age. Luckily for us all, only a few societies have "gone totalitarian" in the total sense, but we must recognize that a latent tendency to totalitarianism exists in all modern states, not excepting the United States today. This is the distinguishing characteristic of our age.

* * *

Mr. George Denicke: The issue between Mr. Friedrich and Mr. Timasheff I was privileged to discuss with Rudolf Hilferding in Paris in 1938–39. He held (and I agree) that totalitarianism is *sui generis*. Each occurrence can be described, but no adequate general concept can be defined.

I would, however, point to one common feature of all three members—Russia, Italy, and Germany—of the species. It happens that I was a witness to the early stages of all three systems, and I was struck each time by the element of extreme *voluntarism*. Goebbels once averred that *"Nationalsozialismus ist keine Weltanschauung, sondern eine Willensrichtung."* And Mussolini, in the early days of the Fascist movement, announced *"Ich will regieren. Das ist mein Programm."* This trait, I should argue, should be added to Mr. Friedrich's list of five: the totalitarian movement is a voluntaristic movement. From the very first there is a compelling and controlling will to power.

* * *

Miss Hannah Arendt: My agreement with almost all of Mr. Friedrich's statements comes, I believe, from a more general and fundamental agreement with his "presupposition that *ta politika* are decisive for the patterning of any society" and "that . . . political science is the highest or most important science." Seen in the light of political science, his thesis that "totalitarian society is historically unique and *sui generis"* can only mean that totalitarian domination constitutes a novel form of government. This conclusion seems inevitable; yet it is extremely daring. For throughout our history there have been few forms of government, all of them already known to and described by the ancients. It seems so unlikely that we of all people should be confronted with a novel form of government.

This doubt, which certainly is legitimate, has given rise to certain descriptions of totalitarianism, usually couched in psychological or sociological terms, in which totalitarian government appears as some more radical form of something already well known. It is indeed true that the novelty of totalitarian government reveals itself clearly only if one considers its political institutions and modes of action. I would therefore be a little reluctant to use the term "totalitarian society" as freely as Mr. Friedrich. Totalitarian domination, if fully developed, is destructive of "society" strictly speaking, from its higher forms in interest groups down to its elementary level of family units.

I agree with Mr. Friedrich that we can understand the essence of this new form of government only by an analysis which insists on making distinctions. To the distinctive traits contained in his paper I should like to add two more: *First,* it seems to be a general feature of both Bolshevik and Nazi government that the army loses its position as the chief executive arm of government, and all the honors which went with it, to the police. This is an important shift of power, which was curiously foreshadowed perhaps in the eclipse of the army in the modern republics, particularly in the Third Republic which for more than thirty years expected a *coup d'état* from the side of the violently anti-Republican general staff of the French army, which never materialized. Only a similar loss of "will to power" can explain how in Germany the attempted military dictatorship of General Schleicher, backed by the presidency of a field marshal, lasted exactly four weeks. It is interesting that from the beginning Hitler was not so much interested in winning the Reichswehr and securing the monopoly of the means of violence as he was intent on building up the police and police troops (the SS) under a nonmilitary commander (Himmler). The eclipse of Roehm, the organizer of the SA and a military man, in favor of Himmler had already begun in 1929. The development, as we all know, ended in the forties when Himmler as chief of the SS and the police, was virtually the commander in chief of the armed forces. The trial of Tukhachevsky marked the same development in Soviet Russia; the Red Army then lost its position within the government's power machine and was put under the surveillance and virtually the command of the police.

My *second* point bears on a distinction between totalitarian governments and the movements, Communist, Nazi, or Fascist, which lead up to them. If we say that these movements are totalitarian, we credit them, to a certain degree, with the wisdom of hindsight; they never can be fully totalitarian in the pre-power stage. In this stage, they still share many characteristics with revolutionary movements and with those "above-parties groups" which were so significant for Continental party politics between the two wars. Some of them, for instance the Fascist movements of Italy and Spain, never developed into totalitarian government, but became one-party dictatorships. When it comes to judging the present different Communist parties or violent leftist or rightest movements throughout the world, one may find it useful to distinguish between those which are fully totalitarian, for instance completely under the control of Moscow, and those which are not.

One of the chief distinctions between totalitarian movements and groups which aim at the overthrow of government in some other fashion seems to be the following: revolutionary groups have a long tradition of constituting themselves as secret societies and using conspiratory methods. They do not pretend, however, that the government they want to overthrow is itself such a conspiracy. The totalitarian movements act in a different manner: they establish themselves openly and pretend that their opponents are members of a conspiracy. In order to combat this conspiracy, they pretend, they must use conspiratory methods. They establish a counterconspiracy in broad daylight. The conspiratory methods which they introduce are the methods of the secret police whose close connection with the methods of secret societies has often been demonstrated. The danger is that precisely because they function in broad daylight they are in a position to introduce these methods into society at large. They act in exactly the same manner as the secret police all through the nineteenth and the beginning of the twentieth century since they start from the same assumption and justify their existence with the existence of a secret conspiracy. That these methods of the secret police, as well as the organizational structure of secret societies, can be used by mass movements (and without keeping anything secret) is one of the most revealing aspects of modern politics. In brief, I should like to propose to call every movement totalitarian that pretends to fight, not the enemies of a class or a nation or the policies of a government, but a conspiracy such as the Elders of Zion, the Trotskyites, Wall Street, and so forth. Typical totalitarian thinking creeps into a free society, as when, for instance, the old fight against the New and Fair Deals by the Republican Party was perverted by certain people who pretended that a conspiratory clique existed within the United States government with power to influence United States policy.

I wish to respond finally to Mr. Friedrich's strictures, at the end of his paper, on those who stress totalitarianism's "peculiar moral obtuseness" as a distinguishing feature of totalitarian domination. His remarks may well have been addressed to me and my writings, yet I do not believe that I am wrong in finding this is one of those basic distinctions with which we both are concerned. The point, however, is not the use of violence per se, not even on an unprecedented scale, but that "totalitarian indifference" to moral considerations is actually based upon a reversal of all our legal and moral concepts, which ultimately rest on the commandment, "Thou shalt not kill." Against this, totalitarian "morals" preaches almost openly the precept: Thou shalt kill! The assumption, which can be seen very clearly in Himmler's speeches to the SS generals in Eastern Occupied Territories, is that this precept is as difficult to follow as its opposite. In other words, the peculiarity of totalitarian crimes is that they are committed for different reasons and in a different framework which has a "morality" of its own. The morality is contained in the ideology, or rather in what totalitarianism has made of the respective ideologies which it inherited from the past. I therefore would not agree with Mr. Friedrich that "both the ideology and the party in Soviet totalitarian society are declining in importance."

* * *

Mr. Albert Lauterbach: I too agree in general with Mr. Friedrich, but I think he narrows his case too much. Both he and Mr. Timasheff concentrate entirely on political institutions and relationships. Once one turns (as our Conference will at a later session) to the psychological aspects of totalitarianism, the case for an assumption of uniqueness becomes far more conclusive. These systems differ from all others in imposing upon society, as a matter of public policy, a standardized perceptual scheme and a favored personality type.

These considerations lead me to a further remark. Mr. Friedrich writes in his paper of the "Communist challenge" as an essential element in the rise of fascist movements, and Miss Arendt has just spoken of the "counterconspiracy" aspect. One must beware of mistaking images for reality here: the point is not necessarily that there *is* a conspiracy to be countered, but rather that people are induced to *perceive* one, and to fear it. The Communists in the Germany of 1932 were probably not a genuine danger, but they were widely believed to be one.

In Europe today, similarly, the popularity of the Communism in Italy and France is perhaps based on a perceived and feared, but not necessarily a real, danger of resurgent fascism. Conversely, the Gaullist movement in France may be feeding on an unrealistic fear of Communism.

We have much to learn about the psychological aspects of totalitarianism. Are the Nazi and Soviet cases closely similar in these respects, or are there significant differences? Can we apply their similarities (or their differences) to the analysis of any attitudes in the United States today? Is there an American version of the totalitarian state of mind? All these are important questions to explore.

* * *

Mr. George F. Kennan: I should like to add a few remarks to Miss Arendt's reflections on the place of the secret police. I agree that their significance is seldom appreciated.

One fact is worth notice. In Russia, both before the Revolution and since, and in Germany both before and after the Nazis came to power, the secret police (in Germany, the Nazi precursors) were in close alliance with the criminal underworld. Or perhaps more accurately, there was coöperation between the secret police and a demi-world not quite criminal in its complexion. The rulers in totalitarian societies, at least in the first generation, are themselves products of this demi-world; they have had intimate connections with it, and they continue to rely upon it.

In general, I would ask the Conference members not to concentrate too heavily on what totalitarianism in some abstract sense *is,* to the exclusion of concern with what it is *becoming*. Totalitarianism is dynamic: it does not stand still. Let me advance some illustrations of my meaning.

Once the movement has seized power, the nature and the function of the party is changed. The rank-and-file members fade out as politically relevant strata; the party as a whole becomes a glorified *Beamtenbund*. It is an organized means of getting a job, not an inspirational force.

Again, I would revert to Miss Arendt's remarks on the secret police. They gain ascendancy not merely over the army, but over the party too. The totalitarian "state"—if there is such a thing—seems to me to consist in the top party clique plus the secret police apparatus.

The central policy question, of course, is the future, Where is all this leading? I see signs, in Soviet Russia, of a rigidifying of the regime. Stalin in the thirties deliberately tried to prevent the formation of stable loyalty-groups by constantly moving personnel around. Hence also the purges. Since 1947, however, the higher echelons have been highly stable, the terror has slackened off relative to the 1930's or to the years of World War II, and the higher strata seem to be able to give their children a distinctive sort of up-bringing and education. The explanation for all this lies, I think, in Stalin's anticipation of the problem of succession, which has become real with today's newspaper headlines. If these tendencies should survive whatever difficulties Stalin's death may entail, I think we may see a stable regime of wealth and privilege which may move in the direction of oligarchical despotism and may, perhaps, lose some of its totalitarian aspects.

* * *

[14]

Totalitarianism in Historical Perspective

One of the early classics in the growing field of literature on totalitarianism is *Dictatorship, Its History and Theory* (1939) by the distinguished, British historian, Alfred Cobban. As its title indicates, Cobban's book does not neglect theory.[1] However, in the selection from it reprinted below, although he makes some significant comparisons, Cobban does not attempt a general definition of what he describes. Instead he takes up in succession the three, great, modern, European dictatorships and with remarkable economy analyzes the social philosophies that inspired them, the political conditions that gave them their start, and the most important phases of their subsequent evolution. This selection is an indispensable complement to the more abstract and theoretical considerations of totalitarianism presented in the preceding section.

[1] For the theoretical orientation of Cobban's book see fn. 1 of Carl Friedrich's article in chap. 13.

The Dictatorship of the Proletariat, Fascism, and National Socialism

Alfred Cobban

The Dictatorship of the Proletariat

From the standpoint of the early twentieth-century Bonapartism appeared a strange aberration, a flying in the face of the secular trend of modern history. All over the world parliaments were springing up like mushrooms. The fall of the surviving autocratic dynasties, Hapsburgs, Hohenzollerns and Romanovs, during and after the World War, seemed to put the seal on the triumph of democracy. It was not noticed, or at least was not regarded as significant, that the victory was only won by investing individuals—Woodrow Wilson, Clemenceau, and Lloyd George—with an authority which practically amounted to a dictatorship in the Roman sense of the term. Nor was it realized how fleeting the triumph would be. Already, two years after the Armistice, one of the most acute observers of politics, Lord Bryce, had pointed out the many weaknesses in the parliamentary system as it was being worked,[1] and within a few years, from left and from right the rule of parliamentary democracy was being challenged.

The opposition to it first took concrete form in Russia, where the revolutionary social democratic government, based on Western liberal ideas, was overthrown by the bolsheviks, and what was called the dictatorship of the proletariat was set up. With this a new factor enters the history of dictatorship. Bonapartism, early and late, had been a practical response to circumstances. Any special theory of dictatorship behind it—and there was little—was an attempt to justify it after the event. But with the twentieth century definite dictatorial theories appeared, and challenged the supremacy of liberal, parliamentary doctrine. With Marxian socialism, or communism, as a general theory we are not concerned, but it must be mentioned here because it has the credit of introducing the new theories of dictatorship into practical politics: in a sense all European dictators of the present day are the children of the *Communist Manifesto*.

[1] J. Bryce, *Modern Democracies,* 1921, Part III, chs. lviii, lix.

From Alfred Cobban, *Dictatorship, Its History and Theory* (London: Jonathan Cape Limited, 1939), pp. 111–44. Reprinted by permission.

Das Kapital is a long book and a difficult one, and can only have been read by comparatively few, and understood by a still smaller and more select company; but the *Communist Manifesto* is short, concise, eloquent, full of brilliant and memorable phrases, and a great part of it is patently true. It effected a revolution in the attitude of large numbers to politics, because it swept away the old conception of the state as a power directed towards the common welfare and above all the struggling individuals and groups comprised within it. Marx and Engels were the political heirs, not of Robespierre, but of Marat. "Political power," they said, "is the organized use of force by one class in order to keep another class in subjection." [2] Bentham had made exactly the same discovery, but he believed that the sublime machinery of universal suffrage— one man, one vote—would remedy this state of affairs. Marx had the advantage of having seen a more or less reformed Parliament in operation and to him it seemed if anything merely a more efficient instrument of class government. Economic power, he believed, was the real force behind the façade of politics. Parliament, as he saw it, was merely "an administrative committee of the bourgeoisie"; its rule "open, unashamed, direct and brutal exploitation." [3] Times have changed—at least, we manage things differently to-day—but it is hard to deny some truth to this as a description of Parliament in the age of the Chartists.

The conclusion that Marx draws is that the rule of force can only be overthrown by force, and that the dictatorship of the possessing classes can only be replaced by a dictatorship of the proletariat. It is clear that the term "dictatorship" is here used not as we have defined it, but in the sense of a government based on the forceful suppression of one section of the community by another . section. The experience of 1848 and 1871, however, showed that the proletarian masses were not ready to seize power. Hence arises the belief in the necessity for the leadership of a class-conscious minority in the proletariat, who will stir the masses to revolt when the critical moment appears, and subsequently exercise political power on their behalf.

One group of revolutionary socialists held that the revolution must be made by the revolutionary minority itself. This group, of which Auguste Blanqui was the leading representative, was influential in Paris during the early days of the revolution of 1848, and played a large part in the commune of 1871. According to Blanqui and his disciples revolution was a skilled art, not to be entrusted to the masses, but to be practised by a small, carefully organized cadre of determined men, who would occupy the technical and administrative centres of authority by a sudden attack, and thus seize control of the machinery of the state. What the Blanquists dreamed of was in fact a *coup d'état* rather than a revolution; their tactics were put to good use by would-be dictators, but

[2] *The Communist Manifesto.*
[3] *The Communist Manifesto.*

were inapplicable to the conditions of a social revolution. Their teachings were specifically repudiated by the first successful social revolutionaries, the bolsheviks. Trotsky, who made very effective use of Blanquist methods during the October revolution, quotes Lenin, who had expressly said, "We are not Blanquists, not advocates of the seizure of power by a minority." [4] The bolsheviks only struck when they believed that they had the support of the masses in Russia for their immediate programme. But after the revolution, as had happened in 1848, the peasant majority, which had supported the workers of the towns in the initial stages, began to show signs of breaking away. Such a development had been Lenin's greatest fear, and faced with this, to save the revolution, the minority must now, as a matter not merely of fact, but of right, seize control of the machinery of state. In this way, to the belief that the political system in all existing states is based on force and not on consent, was added a claim on behalf of a minority to the right of exercising that force.

This minority, the class-conscious proletariat, is in effect the Communist Party. Stalin has thus explained the relationship between the party and the people: "No important political or organizational problem is ever decided by our soviets or other mass organizations, without directives from the party. *In this sense,* we may say that the dictatorship of the proletariat is substantially the dictatorship of its vanguard, the 'dictatorship' of the party, as the force which guides the proletariat." [5] He proceeds to quote from Lenin the definition of the party as "the directly managing vanguard of the proletariat; it is the leader." [6] In the following pages this idea of leadership is reiterated again and again. An English apologist has pointed out the difference between the parliamentary conception of a party and the party in the U.S.S.R., which he defines as "the organized political leadership of the people." [7] This conception of dictatorship—or leadership—by a party, from which it seems only one step further to the Führer-principle, is a new element in theory, though the rule of the Jacobins during the French Revolution approximated to it in practice.

The communist dictatorship, if not exactly dictatorship in our sense of the word, shares certain of the characteristics which have already emerged from our study of Bonapartism. It is a government set up and maintained by force. On principle it repudiates the rule of law. Like the Jacobins, it governs by means of terror, which it justifies in theory as "a weapon utilized against a class, doomed to destruction, which does not wish to perish." [8] Thus the communists took up the tradition of 1871 and 1793; but the authority of Lenin depended more on his personal superiority in intellect and character than on

---

[4] L. Trotsky, *A History of the Russian Revolution,* trans. N. Eastman, 1932, vol. III, p. 128.
[5] Stalin, *Leninism,* 1928, vol. I, p. 33.
[6] *Id.,* p. 36.
[7] P. Sloan, *Soviet Democracy,* 1937, p. 210.
[8] Trotsky, cited in H. J. Laski, *Communism,* 1927, p. 142.

the execution of opponents or rivals within the ranks of the revolutionaries, and at no stage can he really be regarded as a dictator.

It must be added, moreover, that in communist theory this dictatorship of the proletariat was only a transitional phase, necessary while the war against capitalism was still being carried on, but destined to give way in the end to a true communistic democracy, which in turn would "wither away," as the repressive machinery of the state became less and less necessary, until the political millennium aimed at was reached. The actual historical evolution of revolutionary Russia has deviated—to use the fashionable term—from this hypothetical line. First, the most important element in the state apparatus, a standing army, had to be built up at the very beginning: it was destined to become, internally and externally, an essential bulwark of the regime.

In the second place, we must note the remarkable reaction that took place against the soviet principle in government and administration. When Lenin was struck down by illness, supreme power passed into the hands of a group of party leaders, and for some time it seemed as though government by committees or soviets was to be the peculiar characteristic of the communist political system. No feature has received higher praise: it was through the method of government by soviets, above all, that the feudal and bourgeois state was to be destroyed, because it put an end to the existence of a ruling class, distinct from the nation.[9] Trained observers, such as the Webbs, remarked on it and apparently had no suspicion that "government by committee" would not prove permanent.[10] But the Russian Revolution contained inconsistent elements and the interest in the Union of Socialist Soviet Republics was to see whether the committee system or the dictatorial tendency would prove the stronger. By 1934, in the report of the Congress of the Communist Party, the reaction against the system of collegiate instead of individual responsibility had become plain, with the demand for "the splitting up of the commissariats," "the abolition of depersonalization in work," "the abolition of the functional system, increasing personal responsibility and taking the line towards liquidating collegiates." [11]

This tendency to substitute personal for committee rule went with a great increase in the importance of the bureaucracy, and determined the constitutional evolution of the U.S.S.R. It is not necessary to trace its development from the assumption of power after Lenin's stroke by a triumvirate of Zinoviev, Kamenev and Stalin, aiming at the exclusion of Trotsky, through the gradual stages by which Stalin undermined and destroyed his enemies of the right and the left, to the trial and execution of the sixteen old bolsheviks in 1936, which proved the opening phase in the systematic destruction of all the old communist leaders,

9 A. Rosenberg, *A History of Bolshevism*, 1934, p. 87.
10 S. and B. Webb, *Soviet Communism*, 1937, vol. I, p. 436.
11 *A Handbook of Marxism*, ed. E. Burns, 1935, pp. 949–50.

both local and national, who were unwilling to accept the supreme authority of the party secretary. It is worthy of note that this last stage went with the introduction of a nominally more democratic constitution, including such features as direct election, secret ballot, and a fairer representation of the rural districts. Not for the first or last time democracy and dictatorship appear hand in hand. The introduction of the new constitution has been interpreted as a method of "dissolving" the proletariat in the nation,[12] but the proletariat is after all a conception of doubtful scientific value: the party presents a more concrete objective. It is not a wild surmise to suggest that the new Russian constitution was needed not to free the people from the rule of a dictator, but to emancipate the dictator from control by the Communist Party, by making him, instead of the party, the embodiment of the dictatorship of the proletariat, the incarnation of the *vox populi,* which is also *vox dei.*

Thus up to the present it would seem as if the political implications of dictatorship, even of the proletariat, were proving more powerful than the ideology of the Communist Party. The state, which according to Marxist theory should at least have commenced to wither away with the extinction of the capitalist classes in Russia, has on the contrary swollen and become all powerful. The evolution of government in Russia has patently been following national rather than Marxist principles. Nationalism, a useful instrument in the early stages of the revolutionary struggle, a force which a communist might use against capitalist imperialism, but which those who sang the *Internationale* could never fall victims to themselves, has gone from strength to strength, until it seems as though the appeal of the government in Russia is far more to national patriotism than to the communist fervour of the masses.

The evolution of the bolshevik regime is to be explained, according to one of its founders, by the triumph of bureaucracy. There would be nothing strange in this, for national traditions are strong and bureaucracy has been the established government of Russia for centuries. But the bureaucracy could not function without a head—"an inviolable super-arbiter, a first consul if not an emperor." [13] Hence what Trotsky calls Soviet Bonapartism. We should prefer to suggest that with the re-birth of a new Holy Russia may be coming the reappearance of a Little Father of all the Russians, terrible in his wrath to the enemies of his country, yet at heart benevolent and kind, the protector of his adoring subjects, the head of a great bureaucracy, an all-powerful state machine, supported by a mighty army and a dreaded secret police, the autocrat of all the Russias, Stalin—a true heir to the Czars in all except the non-hereditary nature of his power. If this interpretation of the development of revolutionary Russia be correct—and, while not put forward in any over-confident spirit, it at least appears to afford a reasonable explanation of the facts that now and

---

[12] L. Trotsky, *The Revolution Betrayed,* 1937, p. 261.
[13] L. Trotsky, *The Revolution Betrayed,* 1937, p. 277.

then percolate to the outside world from Russia—then the third great modern revolution had at last produced its dictator.

Fascism

The communist revolution thus had unforeseen developments; but if it produced a Stalin, had not the French Revolution produced a Bonaparte? Revolutions have their own logic, and even a Lenin, whose inflexibility of purpose controls the beginning, may not predict the end. But he who sows dragon's teeth should know what harvest to expect, and socialists, who come to bring revolution, should at least not be surprised when revolutions appear.

The 1917 revolution in Russia was in its beginnings the kind of revolution socialism had expected, and throughout Europe in the period immediately following the conclusion of the European War, the revolutionary socialistic movement was spreading, though it came to fruition nowhere outside Russia. The establishment of parliamentary and generally republican systems in place of the defunct monarchies in the defeated countries and the successor states, indicates the failure, rather than the success, of the revolutionary socialist movement. The next truly revolutionary regime to be established was of an unexpected type. Italian fascism borrowed a good deal from the technique of communism, but it found its intellectual origins in a different brand of socialist theory, and it proved that the revolutionary urge might assume forms unanticipated by those who provided its first impetus.

The doctrine from which fascism took its basic ideas was syndicalism, a branch of socialist theory which was widespread in France and Italy before 1914. Its chief prophet, Georges Sorel, wrote his *Reflections on Violence* in 1908. His justification of force as a political weapon attracted considerable attention because of the manner in which it was stated, but went no farther in this direction than orthodox Marxian Socialism. The particular contribution of Sorel to the development of socialist theory was his emphasis on the emotional elements in politics. Socialists as a whole had accepted the belief of the early democrats in the rationality of man as a political animal. Sorel, at the end of a century's experience of democracy, or attempts at democracy, drew another conclusion, and taught the syndicalists to use other methods than the mere appeal to reason, to self-interest, or to a humanitarian idealism. He revived the Platonic idea of the myth as the ruling influence in politics, in the form of the General Strike, which he defined as "the passage from capitalism to socialism conceived as a catastrophe." Literally a myth and a catastrophe it has proved in practice; but for Sorel, through the General Strike and physical violence in other forms, the mystical or emotional forces in the life of the people were to be released and used to establish a condition in which the state would be reduced to a federation of self-governing industries, termed corporations or syndicates, and the ideal condition of society thus achieved.

A wave of revolutionary strikes followed the rise of syndicalism in Italian labour politics, but the influence which was to have a more permanent importance lay in another direction. The syndicalists, believing in the use of violence and of emotional forces in politics, were emancipated from the humanitarian, liberal ideology that the orthodox social democratic parties had inherited; and when the modern imperialist movement in Italy took form with the war for the conquest of Tripoli in 1911, more than a few of them drifted into the nationalist camp. One of their chief leaders, Labriola, who had broken away from the Socialist Party as early as 1906, wrote, "Revolutionary syndicalism has well been called a form of workers' imperialism, since it reveals the same tendencies of energy and conquest as appear in capitalist imperialism, the same distrust for sentimental and humanitarian democracy." [14] The transition from syndicalism to imperialism was less difficult than might have been supposed. Professor E. Barker has pointed out that the syndicalist belief in the real personality of groups is only a defence against the state if it is assumed not to apply to states.[15] Syndicalism, applied to the state, becomes absolutism, and so it has proved in the history of Italian politics.

The syndicalists who abandoned the internationalism of socialist theory were able to translate their new nationalist ideas into socialist phraseology without much difficulty. Transferring the idea of the class war into the international field, they began to talk of "proletarian nations" and "capitalist nations"; and just as, internally, for the communist, an aggression by the capitalist class was a monstrous piece of tyranny, while the use of force on the proletarian side was the mere exercise of a natural right, so in external relations, for the "have-not" nations—to use a current term—imperialism was a sacred and irresistible duty, imposed by the dialectic of history.[16]

Along with the introduction of the idea of imperialism under a new guise into left-wing ideology went a new development in the conception of political society, with the idea of a natural aristocracy, to replace the effete hereditary one. An Italian thinker, whose kinship with Labriola and Sorel is evident, Vilfredo Pareto, expresses this belief thus—"The use of force is indispensable to society; and when the higher classes are averse to the use of force . . . it becomes necessary, if society is to subsist and prosper, that the governing class be replaced by another which is willing and able to use force. Roman society

[14] Quoted in H. W. Schneider, *Making the Fascist State*, 1928, p. 140. The notes to this section will show my indebtedness to this excellent survey of Italian Fascism.

[15] E. Barker, introduction to Gierke, *Natural Law and the Theory of Society*, trans. 1934, p. lxxxiv.

[16] L. Villari, *The Economics of Fascism*, in G. S. Counts, L. Villari, etc., *Bolshevism, Fascism and Capitalism*, 1932, p. 68.

was saved from ruin by the legions of Caesar and Octavius. And it may happen that our society will one day be saved from decadence by the heirs of the syndicalists and anarchists of our day." [17]

A minor figure in the syndicalist movement at this time was the young socialist, Benito Mussolini, who headed a general strike at Forli in 1911 as a protest against the nationalist war in Tripoli, and subsequently became the founder of a journal, the *Popolo d'Italia,* started for the purpose of bringing Italy into the World War on the side of the Allies. Like many others he had adopted nationalist aims without abandoning his syndicalist ideas. In 1919 he was proclaiming that "Imperialism is the eternal and immutable law of life." [18] In 1921, internationalism has become for him "an article of luxury, good for the aristocracies of art, banking, industry, and a snobbish imbecility; in short, for the bourgeoisie of capitalism and of socialism; but at bottom internationalism is an absurd fable; the great masses do not escape, nor can they, and it is the best of fortune they cannot escape, the insuppressible datum of race and nation. 'Go home to your own country!' This is the formula that sums up the workers' internationalism." [19]

After the war, in March 1919, Mussolini founded the first fascist groups. Fascism was still, of course, a revolutionary and socialist movement, hostile to the monarchy, to finance, and to parliamentary government, demanding social reform and workers' control, but separated from the other branches of the socialist movement by its intense nationalism. The extreme left-wing socialist and communist movements that had threatened—or promised—to introduce social revolution in Italy immediately after the war, had collapsed by 1920, and the resulting disorder and disillusionment left the field open for rival parties. The nationalist section of the syndicalist movement now had its opportunity; it began to grow in importance, nor were the nationalists unaware of the strength syndicalism brought them, as d'Annunzio showed when he gave a corporative system to the independent government he temporarily set up in Fiume. The nationalist syndicalists were strong enough by January 1922 to hold a congress at which they declared their alliance with the new Fascist Party.

With this exception, fascism—revolutionary national socialism, as it might well have been called—found itself at enmity with all the existing political parties, and in particular it directed its attack against the parliamentary institutions through which they ruled. It has been suggested that fascism took up the attack on parliamentary democracy because it needed an objective and therefore had to create a "villain of the piece" to denounce as the source of all the woes of Italy. This view rather under-estimates the importance of the fundamentally

---

[17] V. Pareto, *The Mind and Society* (*Trattato del Sociologia generale*), trans. and ed. A. Livingston, 1935, vol. III, pp. 1292–3.

[18] Schneider, *op. cit.,* p. 273.

[19] *Id.,* p. 275.

anti-democratic pre-suppositions of fascism, but it must be admitted that a more suitable or a more unpopular enemy could hardly have been chosen for attack. Parliamentary government was a new institution, which the greater part of Italy had only known since its union with Piedmont; and while Cavour had managed to conduct parliamentary government successfully in Piedmont, when the rest of the country, lacking any aristocracy with political training, and illiterate and backward in almost every respect, was added, the system experienced a strain under which it broke down. The fault was not exactly excess of democracy, except in relation to the political capacities of the people; indeed, parliamentarism in Italy has sometimes been accused of being little better than a euphemism for government by corruption. In this it did not differ conspicuously from the despotic regimes which it replaced, but the newest generation was not to know that.

By 1919 the really active forces in Italian politics were thus revolutionary and anti-parliamentary. Italy emerged from the war with the psychology of a defeated rather than a victorious country. She had deserted her allies and thrown in her lot with the Western Powers, who had promised her great territorial gains, but disappointment with the terms of the treaty of peace, the burden of the war, the humiliating defeat of Caporetto, and economic distress, had put a strain on the Italian political structure which it could not stand. Parliamentary liberals and socialists still controlled the majority in parliament, but those who were willing to vote were not willing to fight for them.

The new factor that was to be the determining one in the situation was the appearance of rival revolutionary parties, each appealing to force and proclaiming the need for dictatorship, but the one on a national and the other on an international basis, the one relying on the spirit of the class war, the other on national loyalties and jealousies. For a brief period the communist movement seemed to be sweeping to victory: its very success was fatal, for alarm seized the possessing classes, from the peasantry upwards. The existing parliamentary parties seemed too effete to offer a solid resistance to communism, and hence much support was given openly or secretly to the fascists.

This half-hearted backing, as the lesser of two evils, would not have been adequate to carry the fascists to victory, however, without the use of methods borrowed from their opponents. The similarities between bolshevism and fascism in their rise are striking. They both arose out of military defeat and civil strife and came to the front because they were united, closely organized, well disciplined and rigidly centralized parties, with a single pre-eminent leader, whereas their opponents were divided and practically leaderless and the government weak. Neither had any scruples about letting loose the dogs of civil war, and using revolutionary methods to undermine constitutional government. On the other hand, whereas it was fifteen years or more before the dictatorial method of government introduced in Russia brought its natural fruits in a nationalist dictatorship of one man, the fascist regime in Italy was this from the beginning; for Caesarism was a tradition which had not died out in Italy with the fall of the Roman Empire. It renewed its vitality with the Renaissance tyrants and might easily have emerged again in the *Risorgimento*. Before Mussolini became famous the career of d'Annunzio had shown that Italy was ready for a leader.

With the triumph of the Fascist Party the whole Parliamentary structure of government in Italy crumbled like a stucco façade. From top to bottom of the political system nomination by authority replaced election. The powers of the prefects were greatly enlarged, and for the elected mayors of the communes were substituted appointed officials. The country ceased to be ruled by the ordinary process of legislation, until finally in a law of 1936 decrees were given the force of law, with the rider that they must be published in the official gazette and submitted to "Parliament," if one can call it such, within two years. It is doubtful if even these fairly simple rules have been observed.[20] During the four years 1922 to 1926 a complete dictatorial regime was gradually set up in Italy. This was a true revolution. What were its fruits?

The national, imperialist and dictatorial elements in fascism, along with the gospel of force, are manifest throughout its rise; so too is the derivation of its power from the sovereignty of the people. In the elections of 1924 fascism obtained—not without the assistance of the usual Italian electoral methods—the support of nearly five million voters, more than twice those voting for the numerous opposition parties. The plebiscite of 1929 produced an overwhelming vote in favour of the fascist list of candidates to the national Grand Council. There were, of course, no other candidates, and the authorities provided printed ballot papers, the patriotic affirmative ballot being decorated with the Italian tricolour, which was naturally absent from the negative ballot, while the envelope provided was transparent, so that those who voted against Signor Mussolini should not be able to conceal their light under a bushel. It is interesting to compare a speech of Signor Mussolini—"This plebiscite will take place under absolute tranquillity. We will exercise neither trickery nor pressure"—with a circular from a provincial fascist administration—"All provincial organizers shall inform the voters verbally that, on the basis of a revision of the registers of every ward, we can easily learn who has failed to fulfil his duty as an Italian, as a public official, and as a free adherent of a fascist association." [21]

In spite of such devices, which do not wholly reflect a democratic spirit, and although fascism prides itself on the creation of a new aristocracy, its plebiscitary origins, the constant appeals to public opinion, and the omnipresent and unceasing stream of propaganda it emits, are proof that it is conscious of its dependence on the popular will. Appropriately enough, its *Duce* was first and foremost a

[20] *New Governments in Europe,* ed. R. L. Buell, 1934, p. 65.
[21] C. Haider, *Capital and Labour under Fascism,* 1930, pp. 257, 259.

great journalist, and fascism has been described as "government by journalism." Mussolini has often been compared to Napoleon Bonaparte, not unjustly, and of Napoleon Vandal writes, "He was a journalist in his very soul." [22]

The socialist or syndicalist element cannot at first be traced in the policy of the new governments so clearly as the democratic. Fascism only conquered power by degrees and extensive economic changes were not possible in the early stages of the process. The affiliation between socialism and fascism was rather theoretical than practical; and principles have generally been the handmaid of practical politics in Italy. "Fascism," writes Schneider, "was carried along on its career by the force of events and not by any inner aims. The essence of the movement lay not in its programmes, which were subject to change without notice, nor in its ideas, which shiftily followed its shifting fortunes, but in its growing power." [23]

Moreover, fascism had been backed by the great industrialists: their reward seemed to have come when Mussolini appointed De Stefani, a rigid *laissez-faire* individualist, as his first finance minister. De Stefani abolished death duties, reduced direct taxation on the wealthy classes, imposed additional indirect taxation on the poor, repealed such socialistic laws as existed in Italy, abolished the Ministry of Labour, and in fact seemed to be turning Italy into a paradise of the classical economy.

But the original tendencies of the movement were too strong to be permanently suppressed. After the first few years, syndicalist leaders entered the government, and by decree after decree the unwieldy machinery of the Corporative State was slowly hoisted into position. A vast and expensive bureaucracy, through which their deserved reward was given to thousands of loyal party men, was set up to man the new machinery of economic control, as it already manned the political structure. Before a decade was out the capitalists and financiers woke up to find that instead of a servant they had created a master. The new fascist *condottieri*, at first regarded as the mercenary troops of capitalism, having won the victory, revolted against their employers,[24] and a new phase began in the economic life of the country.

The syndicalist organization which was established on paper, does not appear as yet to have functioned effectively; indeed one might suppose that a dictatorial government was by its very nature hardly likely to be able to give the Corporations any real power.

But the fascists had to persuade the masses that something was being done for them; moreover, the leader and some at least of his followers, came from the working classes or the peasantry and had socialist antecedents; so, measures of minor or local importance were sometimes taken in favour of the employed

[22] Vandal, *L'avènement de Bonaparte,* vol. II, p. 388.
[23] Schneider, *op. cit.,* p. 111.
[24] G. Salvemini, *Under the Axe of Fascism,* 1936, p. 120.

and against the employing classes. Further, Mussolini, like Napoleon, required the support of the peasantry, and therefore their interests had to be considered, as well as those of the wealthier landowners. Through the *Dopo Lavoro* organization "games" were provided for the poor, even if bread was short. Nor should one under-estimate the positive achievements of fascism in the field of administration, not the least of which was the destruction of the Mafia in Sicily and the Camorra in Naples, secret societies which had too long ruled whole districts tyrannically and corruptly. There was no room for these rival organizations and for fascism in the same community.

Such reforms were not irreconcilable with the existing capitalist structure of society. But the decisive factor in shaping the economic development of fascist Italy was the political nature of the regime. In the end the dictatorship proved incompatible with liberal economics. Fascism meant glory, and glory is the most exigent of national gods to serve. Glory demanded great public works, *autostrada,* draining marshes—all dictators insist on draining marshes—constant and expensive public celebrations, the old Roman "bread and games," a great multiplication of officials, a large army and navy, and finally—most costly of all—war.

Even De Stefani had found that the *lire* needed discipline. His modest attempt at this had induced Mussolini, under pressure from the bankers, to abandon him in 1925; but the fascist government was to be driven to far more extreme measures of economic control than its first finance minister had dreamed of. "Italy," Mussolini could claim by 1933, "is not a capitalist country in the meaning now currently given to that term." [25] Under the stress of war in Africa and Spain, the government had gradually to take control of one branch after another of the nation's economic life, until the dictatorship was as complete in the economic sphere as in the political. The apparent contradiction here evident between origins and end must not prevent us from realizing the facts. Even as Marxian socialism had given birth to a Stalin, and the humanitarian and reforming ardour of eighteenth-century France produced a Bonaparte, so the syndicalist dream of a state which was to be a free federation of guilds led up to Mussolini's Italy, and the second great dictatorship of the contemporary world.

National Socialism

While Italian fascism has syndicalist antecedents, the German National Socialist Movement proclaims both in title and in policy its affiliations with the older state socialism. It is notable that each of the three great dictatorships of to-day can be traced to socialist origins. In Germany liberalism had never been

[25] Address to the National Corporative Council, November 14th, 1933; in B. Mussolini, *Fascism, doctrine and institutions*, 1935, p. 53.

a very strong growth: the body of the German people has always looked to the state for authoritative leadership. Moreover the Bismarckian state had been no merely political or military machine. Its essays in state socialism, as well as episodes such as the *Kulturkampf,* are proof of its innate tendency to assert its power in the religious and economic spheres of life. But the absolutist police-state theory of the Hohenzollerns had fallen in ruins in 1918, and for Germans, to whom a theory of the state was the first condition of its existence, the various brands of socialism seemed the only ones that remained available. Hence they practically monopolized German political thought in the post-war period, the newer forms, such as National Socialism and Communism, naturally attracting the more vigorous spirits. The great advantage these had was that they did not leave souls to wander in the wilderness of liberalism, to find their own political salvation: they each offered an infallible dogma and an authoritarian leadership such as a defeated and disorientated people naturally craved. One might have guessed, even in 1919, that some form or other of dictatorship was inevitable in Germany.

Stresemann, perhaps the only great statesman Germany has produced since Bismarck, wore himself out in vain in the attempt to create a stable political system in his country. While he was labouring to restore Germany to its rightful place in Europe, and rebuild the German economic system, his political support was gradually vanishing beneath his feet. The People's Party had sunk to insignificance before its Chancellor was dead. The blockade, Versailles, the inflation, above all the occupation of the Ruhr, were not forgotten—even though the years 1925 to 1929 were years of economic recovery—and they were to bring their nemesis when the economic slump, which began with the crash of October 1929, in Wall Street, reached Germany. In September 1930, Dr. Brüning and Dr. Schacht began the policy of deflation, which destroyed the home market, lost all the gains of the period of recovery and earned them the title of the starvation government. Unemployment grew to huge numbers. Desperate men became prepared for desperate remedies. Economic disaster completed the ruin of the middle parties in Germany; but in truth they had only continued so long in nominal authority because the forces of dictatorship were divided between the extreme right and the extreme left.

That German politics had become by 1930 a race between Communism and National Socialism is well known; it is not so commonly realized that even the Weimar Republic had strong dictatorial elements in its constitution. The men who drew up the Weimar Constitution in 1919 could no more than any other constitution makers dissociate themselves from their own past. They had abandoned the Kaiser—or he had abandoned them—but merely to put the President in his place. Modern Germany, it must be remembered, was used to a strong hand. Bismarck had established a tradition from which it was found difficult to depart. In Germany in 1919, as in France in 1848, it was believed that in face

of the menace from the "reds" the executive must retain its strength and independence, and that it could only do this in a democratic state if its power
were derived directly from the people. This was the view of the principal
theorist of the new Constitution, Hugo Preuss,[26] and it was accepted by the
Weimar Coalition of the Catholic Centre, Democrats, and Social Democrats.
The middle parties, afraid above all of the communist menace, aimed at obtaining a strong Presidency, the chief duty of which would be to nominate the
Chancellor and the other ministers, who would thus by way of the President
derive their authority from the people, and so be in a sense independent of the
Reichstag. Subsequently the Social Democrats realized the dangers involved
in the position of the President, but their partners in the Coalition upheld the
famous Article 48.

The political system constituted by Hugo Preuss has been called "parliamentary caesarism." [27] In theory both elements in the Constitution derived their
authority from the people, but in a disagreement Caesar was likely to count for
more than Parliament in a country with Germany's traditions. The German
President, elected by the whole people, re-eligible for office, the head of the
executive government, and Commander-in-Chief of the army, was from the
beginning a dictator in embryo. Enshrined in the terms of the republican constitution was a provision which made him in emergency a real dictator, the
already mentioned Article 48, which demands quotation: "If a state fails to
carry out the duties imposed on it by the national constitution or national laws,
the President of the Reich may compel performance with the aid of armed
force. If public safety or order be seriously disturbed or threatened within the
German Reich, the President of the Reich may take the necessary measures
. . . if necessary with the aid of armed force. For this purpose he may
temporarily suspend in whole or in part the fundamental rights enumerated
in Articles . . ." Nor was this Article a dead letter. If the period of comparative prosperity, from 1925 to 1930, saw it invoked only nineteen times, it had
been used 135 times between 1919 and 1925; while 1931 was to see it applied
in 42 cases and 1932 in 59. It remained only to unite the offices of President
and Chancellor, generalize Article 48, and dictatorship would be complete.

The interesting problem then is not why Germany became a dictatorship,
but why her dictatorship took the particular form it did. The early history
of the Nazi Party, in so far as one can disentangle it from the prejudice of
hostile accounts and the hagiography of its disciples, presents nothing very
remarkable. It did not seem a very important occasion when in July 1919,
Corporal Hitler, who had been engaged in nationalist propaganda among
the troops after the Armistice, became the seventh member of the German

[26] E. Gordon, *Les nouvelles constitutions européennes et le rôle du chef de l'état*, 1932, p. 86.
[27] *Id.*, p. 257.

Workers' Party, but this was a critical moment in the history of modern Europe.

The civil engineer, Gottfried Feder, provided this party with a programme of Twenty-five Points in February 1920. These are worth pausing over. Nationalism takes pride of place in the first Article, along with the demand for equal treatment for Germany, for the abolition of the Treaties of Versailles and St. Germain (2), and the granting of land and colonies to cope with surplus population (3). Then follows racialism (4 to 8), and equality for all citizens (9 and 10), and with these we may link the demand for a people's army (22). A series of articles embodies an extensive programme of state socialism: measures are to be taken against war profiteers and financiers (12), trusts are to be nationalized (13), and unearned income is to be abolished (11), for work is the first duty of every German (10). The government is to be strong and centralized (25) and is to assert its might in every field of national activity, including the press, art and literature (23); it is to promote health (21) and a reformed education (20); old age pensions are to be introduced (15); agrarian reform is proposed at the expense of the great proprietors, who are threatened with expropriation without compensation (17). Religions are given a warning, for they are promised freedom only "so far as they do not endanger the state or oppose the customs and morals of the German race" (24). Finally, one freak clause—the old German common law is to replace Roman law (19), and one which was to be instrumental in winning the Nazi Party much support—small shopkeepers are to be protected from the competition of great multiple shops and department stores (16). The significance of many of these points will emerge in due course, but already we may note that nationalism is becoming "racialism," that the socialist elements come only next in importance to the nationalist, and that the whole programme is built up on the conception of an immensely powerful and omni-competent state.

Captain Ernst Röhm brought the little party which had accepted this programme into association with the Reichswehr and with the volunteer corps, which had sprung up in Germany during the period of anarchy and had been of service in crushing the Spartacist revolt. But despite its ambitious programme the party seemed in no way important, and its ignominious collapse on the occasion of the Beer-house *Putsch* of November 1923 in Munich set the seal on its insignificance.

In 1925 Hitler reorganized the party; in 1926 he founded the S S; by 1928 he had twelve deputies in the German Reichstag. In September 1930 the number leaped to 107; in March, 1932, Hitler obtained 13,400,000 votes at the second ballot in the presidential election, and in February 1933, 17,200,000 votes.

The peculiar interest of post-war German history for us lies in the reasons for the rise of Hitler to supreme power. Germany, we have said, was almost bound to have a dictatorship, and it was bound to be a dictatorship based on some kind of socialist theory. But why, out of various possibilities, should National Socialism have been chosen? The first point in answer to this question is clearly that the party had at its head a potential dictator, a man with the personality requisite for making a leader of the people. As Napoleon had the intellectual power, the military genius and the dramatic qualities that appealed to eighteenth-century France, Louis Napoleon the romanticism of the mid-nineteenth century, and Mussolini the ruthlessness and the efficiency of the Machiavellian prince, so in Hitler it is not difficult to detect the semi-religious fervour, the mysticism, the emotionality necessary to win the affections of the land of Luther and Beethoven, along with the sentimentality of a Heine or a Mendelssohn, and the brutality of the robber barons. Above all Hitler possessed the power of oratory, and in a supreme degree that hypnotic element in his personality which is necessary to all great demagogic leaders. For, and this is the second point, although force was an element in the rise of Hitler, as of Napoleon or Mussolini, the popular will was a far more important factor. The para-military formations of the Nazi Party, the S A and the S S, the martial parades, the assassinations, the street warfare with the communists, all give the superficial impression of a conquest of power by force; but in fact it was by winning the support of the people, and through the ballot box and not the machine-gun, that Hitler was called to his high office.

Probably he did not even need to falsify the election returns. The Nazi mastery of the instrument of propaganda was an irresistible weapon. "Propaganda," he had written in *Mein Kampf*, "is not science. . . . The more modest its scientific ballast, and the more exclusively it addresses itself to the emotions of the masses, the more decisive will be its success. . . ." "The more narrow-minded their ideas were," he said of the Marxists, "the more easily were they taken up and assimilated by the masses, whose spiritual level corresponded well with the pasture it was offered." [28] Through a long and untiring agitation the Nazi Party carried on its propaganda, at mass meetings in the great towns and small gatherings in the villages throughout the countryside, whither political agitation had never penetrated before. With fortified headquarters, armed, drilled and more or less disciplined troops, great parades to "show the flag," especially through opposition quarters, like the march through the communist section of Altona-Hamburg in July 1932, when fifteen were killed and seventy injured, the appearance and a good deal of the reality of a civil war was created; because under war conditions the particular appeal of the party was more likely to succeed.

[28] *Mein Kampf*, (ed. of 1935) 1. 6, 12, pp. 196–8, 376.

Different classes aligned themselves behind the Führer for different reasons. In the beginning he had those who desired to see a socialistic reorganization of society, but who rejected the theoretical internationalism, and the actual subservience to Russian interests of the Communist Party, as well as a fair sprinkling of mere adventurers. The socialistic elements in the party creed continued to provide sufficient attraction to proletarian recruits to enable the Nazis to compete seriously for working-class allegiance with the communists. Into one or other of these parties the youth of Germany was flocking; whereas the average age of the Social Democrats in the Reichstag of 1930 was 51, that of the Communists and the Nazis was each about 37.[29] But while the Communists could offer world revolution and a new and somewhat speculative order of things to the poor and the disinherited youth of Germany, the Nazis made more concrete promises, appealing to the interests and passions of more varied sections. Above all they appealed to what Continental thinkers call the "petty bourgeoisie," with its bitter memories of the inflation, resentful of a Social Democratic legislation which had seemed to protect the interests of the industrial workers at the expense of other classes, feeling themselves menaced with utter ruin by the development of great capitalist enterprises, and traditionally looking to the state for guidance and salvation. Pareto has some hard things to say about the German middle classes. He quotes from *Vorwärts* that "Force and struggle are two words that are not to be found in the dictionary of the German middle classes," and adds in comment, "These classes are the most docile of all classes. Respectful, timid, they like nothing better than to be led blindfold." [30] But the War and the inflation had ruined the German middle classes. If a bourgeois is, in the French definition, *"quelqu'un qui a des reserves,"* the German bourgeoisie had lost this natural ballast; it had become a new proletariat, a new revolutionary class, destined to accomplish a new kind of revolution.

On the other hand, it should be remembered that the middle classes are also those in which above all nationalist, patriotic emotions are to be found. The aristocracy and the proletariat may be internationally minded. But nationalist sentiment and the middle classes rose side by side at the beginning of modern history, and nationalism became a dominant force when the middle classes achieved political supremacy in the nineteenth century. Thus the German middle classes were ready to support a movement which was at the same time nationalistic, and hostile to the great financial interests as well as to the older socialistic movements. The Nazi Party was ideally fitted to supply a response to their demands.

The importance to the Nazi movement of the support of the big industrialists and capitalists has perhaps received undue attention. Not, of course, that

---

[29] The exact figures are given in Buell, *op. cit.*
[30] Pareto, *op. cit.*, vol. IV, p. 1487 *n.*

one should forget, though in the nature of the case their existence is hardly susceptible of proof, the heavy subsidies said to have been paid to the party by the big industrialists, anxious to overthrow the yoke of social democracy, fearing even more the onset of communism, and hoping through the rearmament of Germany to bring back prosperity to the heavy industries. Between 1928 and 1932 it is said that the annual Nazi budget was over 250 million marks. Certainly the expenses of maintaining the party, with its huge private army and its costly publicity campaigns, must have been colossal. It was not from altruistic motives that Hitler, when he came to power, made Thyssen, the greatest of the Ruhr iron-masters, supreme state authority for Western Germany, and returned for the time to private hands the control of the great steel trusts, which Brüning had seized during the economic crisis. But to infer from these facts any permanent and essential alliance between the dictatorship and that classic economic individualism which has led in the end to the modern capitalist system, would be as much a mistake in Germany as in Italy. German capitalists were to find in the Nazi Party, even more than the Italians in the Fascist, a hard task-master. If private ownership of capital was allowed to survive in Germany it was only on terms of absolute subjection to the will of the state, and to a state dominated not by the economic interests of the great capitalists but by the ideology of the National Socialist Party.

A parallel may be found in the support given at a later date to Hitler by some sections of the older landed aristocracy. The suggestion has been made that it was the pressure from the coterie of East Prussian junkers, alienated by a proposal to appropriate some of their lands for small-holdings, upon the younger Hindenburg, which induced the wooden colossus, the President, in the end to abandon Brüning. But the candidate of the junkers was not Hitler, but the ineffable von Papen; and the whole policy of the Nazis, since achieving power in Germany, as later in Austria, has been bitterly hostile to the old aristocracy and its claims. The three great dictators of present day Europe all arose from the masses: towards the *ci-devants,* contempt, mixed with a little fear, has been their natural attitude. The German and Italian dictators have been willing to use them, as Napoleon used the royalists, but only for their own ends.

A third body of supporters for the Nazi coup was found in the Army. More careful, with more political wisdom, possibly, than any other element in German politics possessed, the great German General Staff had preserved its traditions and survived during a period of socialism, pacifism and compulsory disarmament, by carefully cultivating a policy of apparent political neutrality. When a general with political ambitions, like von Schleicher, became Chancellor, after the fall of von Papen, and attempted to steal the Nazi thunder by wooing left and right at the same time, the General Staff as a whole remained discreetly aloof: hence it was uncompromised by the miserable collapse of the von Schleicher clique after only a two months' struggle. The neutrality of the Army allowed Hitler to come to power, but he was not their candidate, and on more than a few occasions since he became Chancellor the Army and the Party have been in conflict. On the whole, one may say that the German Army authorities have tended to confine themselves to professional interests and have only occasionally had an important influence over government policy. The downfall of its strongest man, the Commander-in-Chief, von Fritsch, himself, showed that the General Staff was not likely to regain under Hitler that commanding influence over high policy which it formerly exercised under Wilhelm II.

A further factor in the rise to power of the National Socialists can be dismissed very briefly. Anti-Semitism undoubtedly was one of the strongest cards in their hand; "Down with the Jews" provided a more effective rallying cry than any other. It formed the really substantial element in the racial theory: it provided a scapegoat—such as was necessary if the national pride was to be restored—for the military defeats and the financial disasters that had befallen Germany, and it revived the very old German pastime of Jew-baiting. That Germany has only been partially affected by the great movements of thought which began with the Renaissance in Western Europe, is shown in nothing so clearly as in this survival of the more barbarous side of medievalism. Indeed, anti-Semitism is such a simple and crude relic of an earlier stage in European civilization that, cleverly as it has been used by the Nazi leaders, it hardly seems to demand any more detailed analysis, except in so far as the "racialism" of which it is a manifestation represents a further development of nationalism: but this point will require special treatment later.

Thus nationalism and socialism, even though they made use of incongruous allies, remained the two essential forces in the formation of the German dictatorship. But one of these had to come first, one had to be the end and the other merely the means. Their conflict had begun in the early days of the Nazi movement: it was continued on the bloody night of June 30th, 1934, when the Führer became for a day "the high court of the German people" in person. Did he scorn to add to his judicial functions the role of public executioner? In the miscellaneous killings of those twenty-four hours, the fate of the leaders of the left wing showed that the aims of the socialistic members of the party, if they were realized at all, would only be realized in the train of nationalism, and that the magnification of the power of the nation was to be the real end of the German revolution.

The law of March 1933, co-ordinating the states and the Reich and abolishing in effect the federal system in Germany, and the Civil Service law of April 1933, putting all judges and other legal officers, police, municipal officials, teachers in schools and universities, workers in public enterprises, and all public officials of any kind, under the same centralized control and unified discipline—these were merely the completion of a task left unfinished by Bismarck. More characteristic of the new form of government was the law making the Nazi Party the "Bearer" of the government, a corollary of the process by which its leader had become the Head of the State. And since the Nation is the State, and the State is the Party, and the Party is the Leader, in German National Socialism the power of the modern dictator has reached its apogee.

* * *

The Origins of World War II:
A Controversial Interpretation

$\mathcal{I}$n 1961, A. J. P. Taylor, one of the
leading British historians, published *The Origins of the Second World War*.
In the first chapter of his book, he referred to his subject as a "forgotten
problem," pointing out that the important work on the origins of
World War II was done soon after the war ended,[1] and that it echoed
views held during the war or even before it had begun. Now, more
than twenty years later, Taylor notes that these same views are generally held
as an explanation of the events leading up to September 1939, a
marked contrast to the revisionism which followed the end of World
War I (see Chapter 11).

¶ Taylor admits there are reasons for this, but adds that "it seems
unlikely that historians a hundred years hence will look at these events exactly
as men did in 1939."[2] The task that Taylor sets himself is "to tell the
story as it may appear to some future historian working from the
records."

The result may be to demonstrate how much historians miss or misunderstand.
We must go on writing history all the same. Like my imaginary successor, I have
often had to confess ignorance. I have also found that the record, considered in detachment, often pushed me towards interpretations different from those which men
(including myself) gave at the time. This has not weighed with me one way or the
other. I am concerned to understand what happened, not to vindicate or condemn.
I was an anti-appeaser from the day that Hitler came to power; and no doubt should
be again under similar circumstances. But the point has no relevance in the writing

---

[1] Works by authors named by Taylor are Maurice Baumont, *La faillite de la paix, 1918–1939*,
3rd ed. (1950); Sir Lewis B. Namier, *Diplomatic Prelude, 1938–1939* (1948); John W. Wheeler-
Bennett, *Munich: Prologue to Tragedy* (1948); Elizabeth Wiskemann, *The Rome-Berlin Axis: A
History of the Relations Between Hitler and Mussolini* (1949).

[2] A. I. P. Taylor, *The Origins of the Second World War*, p. 9.

of history. In retrospect though many were guilty, none was innocent. The purpose of political activity is to provide peace and prosperity; and in this every statesman failed, for whatever reason. This is a story without heroes; and perhaps even without villains.[3]

The main points of Taylor's thesis may be described as follows. The war that broke out in 1939 was not premeditated. It was the result of diplomatic blunders on both sides. Although Hitler changed much in Germany to the point of destroying freedom and the law, his foreign policy was simply that of his predecessors since 1919—freeing Germany from the restrictions of the Versailles Treaty and making her the greatest power in Europe from her "natural weight." Hitler's foreign policy was not systematic.[4] He waited for opportunities rather than initiating them, as was the case with Austria and Czechoslovakia. He carried on a war of nerves—bluff, violent talk and threats to use force. But the foreign policy of France and Britain also rested ultimately on force, although they hoped not to have to use it.

Hitler had no territorial grievances against France and Britain; he accepted the Versailles settlement in the West. He did have territorial and other grievances in the East; specifically Danzig, and more generally a restoration of the Brest-Litovsk settlement which Versailles had undone.[5] To quote Taylor, "Hitler probably intended a great war of conquest against Soviet Russia so far as he had any conscious design; it is unlikely that he intended the actual war against Great Britain and France which broke out in 1939."[6] But "the statesmen of western Europe moved in a moral and intellectual fog —sometimes deceived by the dictators, sometimes deceiving themselves, often deceiving their own public,"[7] and so Great Britain and France dithering between resistance and appeasement "helped to make war more likely."[8]

The above summary does not do full justice to Taylor's account of events, but it should, at least, give the reader an idea of how far Taylor's interpretation departs from the more orthodox explanations. Taylor's views have not gone unchallenged. In fact, they have started the most spectacular controversy in recent British historiography, where Taylor's foremost opponent has been

[3] Ibid., pp. 16–17.

[4] It is a cardinal point with Taylor that "systems are created by historians. . . . Statesmen are too absorbed by events to follow a pre-conceived plan" p. 69.

[5] Such a restoration need not have affected the sovereignty of Poland or the Baltic states although it would have drawn them in the German orbit. If it meant carrying out the Treaty to the letter, however, it would have made a German satellite out of the Ukraine, an obvious act of aggression against the Soviet Union.

[6] Taylor, op. cit., p. 103. "He was as much dismayed on 3 September 1939 as Bethmann had been on 4 August 1914."

According to the much-quoted Hossbach Memorandum, 1943 was the date for Hitler's war. Taylor tends to discount the Hossbach Memorandum as a real statement of Hitler's plans. It was featured as an important piece of evidence at the Nuremberg Trials.

[7] Ibid., p. 107.

[8] Preface to American edition, p. ix.

Hugh Trevor-Roper, another distinguished British historian.[9] The two men have exchanged criticism, some of it quite bitter, in *Encounter* magazine and in a television debate.[10] Other historians have joined in, and the last word has probably not yet been had.

The character of Hitler has dogged Taylor's interpretation; many critics are offended by the detachment with which Taylor views Hitler as a diplomatist. Can foreign policy be so dissociated from domestic policy and the character of its author? Here Taylor stands fast on the validity of his method. He has professed many times over his abhorrence of Hitler's wicked deeds, but he feels they are not related to—indeed, consideration of them would obscure—a study of the negotiations that went on in the chancelleries of Europe. If these negotiations were not in large part gentlemanly, they were at least conducted according to "the textbooks of diplomacy."

A more specific criticism of Taylor is his tendency to discount Hitler's ambitions for world conquest as expressed in *Mein Kampf* and other documents. Taylor makes the point several times in *The Origins of the Second World War* that when Hitler talked it was often for effects quite different than those which, from his words, would seem to be the apparent ones. Taylor writes, "It is an elementary part of historical discipline to ask of a document not only what is in it, but why it came into existence." [11] Whether one can impute too much from such a method is perhaps an open question, if one considers the alternative as accepting documents at their face value. But it is, nevertheless, a question that Taylor's critics have pointedly asked.

Another question revolves around what may be called Taylor's philosophy of history. We have noted his contention that the war was a mistake, "the result of diplomatic blunders on both sides," and that his story is one "without heroes" or "perhaps even without villains." If one reads Taylor right, statesmen are dominated by circumstances rather than vice versa. Their field of action is restricted by the realities of the situation. The realities of the situation after World War I were that the war had left Germany defeated and exhausted, but that Versailles had left her united and, potentially, in terms of manpower and resources, the strongest state on the continent. Thus the area in which German diplomacy inevitably moved was the realization of this potential; that of Great Britain and France, the conciliation of Germany. The two allied powers saw, of course, a *cordon sanitaire* against German expansion in Czechoslovakia and Poland. But these creations of Versailles, as it turned out, were poor substitutes for the dismembered Austro-Hungarian Empire and a Russia now forced out of a European role. French and British diplomacy was only further restricted by the circumstances of its alliance with the eastern buffer states.

Trevor-Roper has thus been led to interpret Taylor's philosophy as one where "the real determinants of history . . . are objective situations and human blunders."

> Objective situations consist of the realities of power; human intelligence is best employed in recognizing these realities and allowing events to conform with them; but as human intelligence seldom prevails in politics, the realities have to assert themselves, at greater human cost, through the mess caused by human blunders. . . . Do statesmen really never make history? [12]

Such then are the important questions raised by *The Origins of the Second World War*. From the selection that follows, the reader may be able to answer some of them to his own satisfaction. "War for Danzig," the last chapter of Taylor's interesting and provocative study, is a masterfully written account of the dilemmas of the statesmen and the tortuous negotiations that preceded the German attack on Poland on September 1, 1939 and the declaration of war on Germany by Great Britain and France two days later.

WAR FOR DANZIG

A. J. P. Taylor

THE CRISIS of August 1939 which led to the second World war was, ostensibly at any rate, a dispute over Danzig. This dispute was formulated in the last days of March, when Germany made demands concerning Danzig and the Corridor, and the Poles rejected them. From that moment everyone expected Danzig to be the next great topic of international conflict. Yet, in strange contrast to earlier crises, there were no negotiations over Danzig, no attempts to discover a solution; not even

---

[12] Trevor-Roper, *Encounter* (July 1961), p. 90.

---

attempts to screw up the tension. This paradoxical calm was partly caused by the local situation at Danzig. Here both Germany and Poland had an impregnable position so long as they did not move; a step by either would start the avalanche. Hence there could be none of the manoeuvres and bargaining which had marked the Czechoslovak crisis. The Sudeten Nazis, like the Austrians before them, built up the tension gradually without guidance from Hitler. In Danzig the tension was already complete; and Hitler, so far as he did anything, held the local Nazis back. They had already won Danzig internally; the Senate of the Free City was firmly under control. But Hitler could not take advantage of this situation. If the Danzig Nazis openly defied the treaty-settlement by voting for incorporation into Germany, the Poles would be free to intervene with the approval of their Western allies; and this intervention would be effective. For Danzig was cut off from East Prussia, the only neighbouring German territory, by the unbridged Vistula; while the Poles controlled three railways and seven roads leading into it. There could be no half-hearted German aid to Danzig, only a full-blown war; and Hitler would be ready for such a war only when his military preparations matured at the end of August.

Until then Danzig lay at Poland's mercy. But the Poles, too, could not turn this position to their advantage. Though they had alliances with Great Britain and France, they had failed to secure any firm promise of support over Danzig itself; indeed they knew that both their allies sympathised with the German case. They could retain the favour of their allies only by hanging back and waiting for the "clear threat" to Polish independence. It had to appear that action was forced on them; and in Danzig it never was. Under similar circumstances, Hitler's previous antagonists, Schuschnigg and Benes, had sought desperately for a way of escape, endlessly devising compromises which might avert the threatened crisis. The Poles faced the approaching crisis imperturbably, confident that Hitler would be exposed as an aggressor and that the justified grievances of Danzig would then be forgotten. They would not respond to Nazi provocation; but equally they ignored the pleas for concession which came to them from the West.

On the larger field of grand policy also, both Hitler and the Poles held rigid positions in the war of nerves. After 26 March Hitler did not again formulate demands concerning Danzig until the day before war broke out. This was not surprising; it was his usual method. So he had waited for offers from Schuschnigg over Austria; so he had waited for offers from Benes, from Chamberlain, finally from the conference at Munich over Czechoslovakia. Then he did not wait in vain. Did he appreciate that this time no offer would come from the Poles? It seems so from the record. On 3 April he issued instructions that preparations for an attack on Poland "must be made in such a way that the operation can be carried out at any time as from 1 September

1939." [1] But a further directive a week later explained that these preparations were purely precautionary, "should Poland change her policy . . . and adopt a threatening attitude towards Germany." [2] On 23 May, however, he spoke with less reserve to a gathering of generals: "There will be war. Our task is to isolate Poland. . . . It must not come to a simultaneous showdown with the West." [3] This sounds clear enough. But Hitler's real plans are not so easily detected. He had talked just as bravely about war against Czechoslovakia in 1938; yet then, almost certainly, he was playing for victory in the war of nerves. Now, too, preparations had to be made for war whether he were planning to win by war or diplomacy. When Hitler talked to his generals, he talked for effect, not to reveal the workings of his mind. He knew that the generals disliked and distrusted him; he knew that some of them had planned to overthrow him in September 1938; probably he knew that they were constantly sounding the alarm at the British and French embassies. He wanted to impress the generals and, at the same time, to frighten them. Hence on 23 May he talked not only of war against Poland, which he may have seriously intended; but even of a great war against the Western Powers, which was undoubtedly not part of his plan. Hitler's calculation worked: no sooner was the conference of 23 May ended than the generals, from Goering downward, were imploring the Western Powers to bring Poland to reason while there was still time.

Hitler's later behaviour suggests that he had not made up his mind as decisively as he indicated on 23 May. To the very last minute he was battering away for the Polish offer which never came. Maybe he did not expect the Polish nerve to break of itself; but he expected the Western Powers to do the breaking for him, as they had done predominantly with Benes in 1938. He did not foresee exactly how the nerve of the Western Powers would crumble or precisely what effect this would have on the Poles. Nor was it of much moment to him whether the Poles then gave way without war or were left to be destroyed in isolation; the results would be the same either way. On the larger point—the crumbling of Western nerve—he never doubted. There are also indications that, as the summer wore on, he began to foresee how this would come about. A collapse of the Anglo-Franco-Soviet negotiations would, he thought, do the trick. Hitler's confidence that these negotiations would fail is an extraordinary feature even in this extraordinary story. How could he be so sure? Why did he make little effort to approach Russia and assert that the Russians would come over to his side of themselves? Had he secret means of information, never to be traced by historians—some agent in Whitehall or at the Kremlin, perhaps a direct line to Stalin himself? Was it profound social

---

[1] Directive by Keitel, 3 April 1939. *German Foreign Policy*, series D. vi. No. 149.

[2] Directive by Hitler, 11 April 1939. *Ibid*. No. 185.

[3] Minutes of conference, 23 May 1939. *Ibid*. No. 433.

analysis—a realisation that *bourgeois* statesmen and Communists would not find terms of mutual understanding? Maybe; we have no means of knowing. Probably it was simply the gambler's invariable conviction that his hunch must be right—otherwise, after all, he would not play. A casual phrase reveals more of Hitler's policy than all the grandiloquent talk to generals. On 29 August, Goering, anxious for a compromise, said: "It is time to stop this *va banque.*" Hitler replied: "It is the only call I ever make." [4]

It was Hitler's misfortune (and not his alone) to encounter in the Poles political gamblers of the same school. *Va banque* was not merely the only call they made; it was the only call they could possibly make if they were to maintain their illusory position as an independent Great Power. Sober statesmen would have surrendered at discretion when they contemplated the dangers threatening Poland and the inadequacy of her means. Germany, powerful and aggressive, was on one side; Soviet Russia, potentially hostile on the other; and in the distance, two unwilling allies, eager to compromise with Hitler and geographically unable to give effective aid. The Poles had to depend on such resources as they possessed themselves; and had not even developed these efficiently. Less than half the men of military age had received military training; fewer still could hope for equipment. Czechoslovakia, the year before, with not much more than a third of Poland's population, had a larger trained manpower; and the Czechs were armed with modern weapons into the bargain. Of these the Poles had virtually none: some 250 first-line aeroplanes of antiquated type, one tank battalion also not up to date. Under such circumstances what could the Poles do except dismiss Hitler's threats as bluff? It was obvious that any move by them must involve concession; therefore they made none. After all, standing still is the best policy for anyone who favours the *status quo,* perhaps the only one. Poland's Western allies were of course an additional reason for her diplomatic immobility; it was obvious that Great Britain and France would give way over Danzig, if the Poles once opened the door to negotiation. Therefore they kept it closed. "Munich" cast a long shadow. Hitler waited for it to happen again; Beck took warning from the fate of Benes.

Germany and Poland held rigid positions. The three Western Powers—Italy, as well as Great Britain and France—shrank from raising the question of Danzig for the opposite reason: because their positions were so soft. All three were convinced that Danzig was not worth a war; all three were agreed that it should return to Germany, with safeguards for Polish trade. But all three recognised that Poland would not give way without a fight and that Hitler would not postpone Danzig until a more peaceful moment. Italy was committed to Germany by the Pact of Steel, Great Britain and France were committed to Poland. None of the three wanted to fight over Danzig; neither of

[4] Weizsäcker, *Erinnerungen,* 258.

the two principals would yield. The only course therefore was to ignore the question of Danzig and to hope that the others would ignore it also. The three Western Powers did their best to wish Danzig out of existence:

> *As I was going up the stair,*
> *I met a man who wasn't there.*
> *He wasn't there again today.*
> *I do so wish he'd go away.*

This was the spirit of European diplomacy in the summer of 1939. Danzig was not there; and if all the Powers wished hard enough it would go away.

When August arrived, it became clear that Danzig had not gone away. The local Nazis stepped up their provocations to the Poles; the Poles responded with challenging firmness. Reports of German troop movements grew stronger; and this time the rumours were well founded. Hitler, it was expected, would act soon. But how? and, still more important, when? This was the vital question in both the Czech and Polish crises. On each occasion the Western Powers assumed that Hitler would explode the crisis in public, at the Nazi party rally in Nuremberg. On each occasion this assumption was mistaken; but in the Czech crisis the Western Powers erred on the right side, in the Polish crisis on the wrong one. In 1938 the party rally was held on 12 September; Hitler's military plans were set only for 1 October, and therefore "appeasement" had an unexpected fortnight in which to operate. In 1939 the party rally was fixed for the first week in September; this time Hitler had decided to achieve success beforehand. At the "Rally of Peace," he would announce victory, not prepare for it. No one could have guessed that the German military plans were timed for 1 September. The date—like 1 October in the previous year —was not chosen on any rational ground, meteorological or other, despite assertions to the contrary by most later writers; it was arrived at, as such dates usually are, by sticking a pin in the calendar. The margin for negotiation was narrow in any case; the diplomatic plans of the Western Powers misfired partly because the margin was about a week narrower than they thought.

At the beginning of August, the Western Powers were still marking time, in the hope that their undefined relations with the Soviet Union would deter Hitler. Others were less confident. A procession of visitors to Berchtesgaden tried to gauge Hitler's intentions. Perhaps the probings first made him decide what these were. The Hungarians led the field. On 24 July Teleki, the Hungarian prime minister, wrote two letters to Hitler. In one he promised "that in the event of a general conflict Hungary will make her policy conform to the policy of the Axis"; but in the other, "Hungary could not, on moral grounds, be in a position to take armed action against Poland." [5] On 8 August Csáky, the Hungarian foreign minister, received at Berchtesgaden a

---

[5] Memorandum by Weizsäcker, 24 July 1939. *German Foreign Policy*, series D. vi. No. 712.

ruthless answer. Hitler did not want Hungarian assistance. But "Poland presents no military problem to us. . . . It is to be hoped that Poland will still see reason at the last minute. . . . Otherwise not only the Polish army but also the Polish state will be destroyed. . . . France and Britain will not be able to prevent us from doing this." Csáky stammered, apologised, and withdrew Teleki's letters, "as unfortunately, they had apparently been misunderstood." [6]

Three days later it was the turn of Burckhardt, the League High Commissioner at Danzig. Hitler was again bellicose: "I shall strike like lightning with the full force of a mechanised army, of which the Poles have no conception." But he also showed signs of conciliation: "if the Poles leave Danzig absolutely calm . . . then I can wait." He made it clear what he would wait for. He would still be content with the terms which he demanded on 26 March—"unfortunately that is definitely ruled out by the Poles." Then, more generally, "I want nothing from the West . . . But I must have a free hand in the East. . . . I want to live in peace with England and to conclude a definite pact; to guarantee all the English possessions in the world and to collaborate." [7] With both Csáky and Burckhardt, Hitler was clearly talking for effect—bellicose at one moment, conciliatory at the next. It was exactly the tactic of the previous year. Why not now? If his talk of peace was play-acting, so also was his talk of war. Which would become real depended on events, not on any resolution taken by Hitler beforehand.

On 12 August a more important visitor appeared: Ciano, the Italian foreign minister. The Italians had been full of fight so long as war seemed a long way off; they grew anxious when reports accumulated that war was approaching. Italy was exhausted by her prolonged intervention in Spain—perhaps the only significant effect of the Spanish civil war. Her reserves of gold and raw materials were run down; her rearmament with modern weapons had hardly begun. She could be ready for war only in 1942; and even this was an imaginary date which merely meant "in some distant future." On 7 July Mussolini said to the British ambassador: "Tell Chamberlain that if England fought on the Polish side over Danzig, Italy would fight on that of Germany." [8] A fortnight later he swung round, and asked for a meeting with Hitler on the Brenner. He proposed to insist that war must be avoided, and that Hitler could get all he wanted at an international conference. The Germans first waved the meeting away; then said that one should be held solely to discuss the coming attack on Poland. Maybe Mussolini distrusted his ability to stand up to Hitler; at any rate he decided to send Ciano instead. Mussolini's instructions were clear: "We must avoid a conflict with Poland, since it will be impossible to

[6] Memorandum by Erdmannsdorff, 8 Aug. 1939. *Ibid*. No. 784.
[7] Minute by Makins, 14 Aug. 1939. *British Foreign Policy*, third series. vi. No. 659.
[8] Loraine to Halifax, 7 July 1939. *Ibid*. No. 261.

localise it, and a general war would be disastrous for everybody." [9] Ciano spoke up firmly when he met Hitler on 12 August, but his remarks were swept aside. Hitler announced that he proposed to attack Poland unless he got complete satisfaction by the end of August; "He was absolutely certain that the Western democracies . . . would shrink from a general war"; the whole operation would be over by 15 October. This was more precise than any previous statement by Hitler; yet doubt remains. He knew that anything he said to the Italians would be passed on to the Western Powers; and he was concerned to shake their nerve, not to reveal his real plans to Mussolini.

An odd little episode showed what these plans were. While Ciano was talking to Hitler, "the Führer was handed a telegram from Moscow." Ciano was told what was in it: "The Russians agreed to a German political negotiator being sent to Moscow." According to Ciano, "The Russians asked for the sending to Moscow of a German plenipotentiary who would negotiate a pact of friendship." [10] No such telegram has been found in the German archives; and none can ever have existed. For the Russians agreed to the sending of a German negotiator only on 19 August, not on 12 August.[11] Of course Stalin may have communicated his decision to Hitler, by some hidden means, a week before he made it. But this is a fantastic hypothesis, for which all evidence is lacking. It is far more probable that the telegram was a fabrication, designed to impress Ciano and to quieten his doubts. Yet, though a fabrication, it was not without foundation. This foundation was Hitler's "hunch"—his conviction that what he wanted to happen would happen. His second sight had never failed him so far. This time he was staking everything on it, certain in advance that the Anglo-Franco-Soviet negotiations would break down and that then the Western Powers would collapse also.

On 12 August the Anglo-Franco-Soviet negotiations had not broken down. They were actually being resumed. The British and French military missions had at last arrived in Moscow. The French had been told by Daladier to get a military convention as quickly as possible. The British, on the other hand, were instructed to "go very slowly" until a political agreement was reached (though discussions for this had been suspended on 27 July until a military convention was made): "Agreement on the many points raised may take

[9] *Ciano's Diary 1939–1943*, p. 123.

[10] Conversation between Hitler and Ciano, 12 Aug. 1939. *German Foreign Policy*, series D. vii. No. 43; *I documenti diplomatici italiani*, eighth series. xiii. No. 4.

[11] It is now universally admitted that there was no telegram from Moscow on 12 August. But it is often suggested that agreement to the visit of a German negotiator was given by the agency of Astakov, the Soviet chargé d'affaires in Berlin. This also is untrue. Astakov merely said that "the Soviets were interested in a discussion of individual questions." He did not mention a pact of friendship; and "he left the matter open as to who was expected in Moscow to conduct the conversations, whether the Ambassador or someone else." *German Foreign Policy*, series D. vii. No. 50. Astakov was probably acting on his own initiative, as he had often done before. In any case, there is no evidence that the information was passed on to Hitler.

months to achieve." [12] The British government, in fact, were not interested in solid military cooperation with Soviet Russia; they merely wanted to chalk a Red bogey on the wall, in the hope that this would keep Hitler quiet. But, when the talks started, the British spokesmen soon found themselves being bustled by the French and by Voroshilov, the Soviet leader, into serious discussion. British and French plans for war were described in detail; the resources of the two countries somewhat generously catalogued. On 14 August the Soviet turn came. Voroshilov then asked, "Can the Red Army move across North Poland . . . and across Galicia in order to make contact with the enemy? Will Soviet troops be allowed to cross Rumanian territory." [13] It was the decisive question. The British and French could not answer. The talks ran to a standstill; on 17 August they were adjourned, never to be seriously resumed.

Why did the Russians ask this question so ruthlessly and so abruptly? Was it merely to have an excuse for negotiating with Hitler? Perhaps. But the question was a real one which had to be asked—and answered. Poland and Rumania had presented insuperable obstacles against any Soviet action in 1938. These obstacles had to be overcome if Soviet Russia were to act now as an equal partner; and only the Western Powers could overcome them. The question raised the old dispute of principle in a new form. The Western Powers wanted the Soviet Union as a convenient auxiliary; the Russians were determined to be recognised as principals. There was also a difference of strategical outlook which has been less noticed. Great Britain and France still thought in terms of the Western front during the first World war. They therefore exaggerated the strength of defensive positions. The military mission had been told: if Germany attacked in the West, even through Holland and Belgium, "sooner or later, this front would be stabilised." In the East, Poland and Rumania would slow down a German advance; with Russian supplies they might stop it altogether.[14] In any case the Red Army would have plenty of time to build up lines of defence after the war had started. Then everyone would remain securely entrenched until Germany collapsed under pressure of a blockade. Holding these views, the Western Powers could see in the Russian demand to advance through Poland only a political manoeuvre; the Russians, they thought, wished to humiliate Poland or perhaps even to destroy her political independence.

No one can tell whether the Russians had such designs. But it is clear that they had different strategical conceptions which were enough in themselves to explain their demands. The Russians started from their experiences in the

[12] Instructions to the British Military Mission, Aug. 1939. *British Foreign Policy,* third series. vi. Appendix v.

[13] Minutes of meeting, 14 Aug. 1939. *Ibid.* vii. Appendix ii.

[14] Instructions to Military Mission, Aug. 1939. *British Foreign Policy,* third series. vi. Appendix v, para. 83.

civil wars and wars of intervention, not from the preceding World war. Here cavalry offensives had everywhere carried the day. Moreover, as Communists, they automatically favoured a strategical doctrine more dynamic and revolutionary than that held in the decadent capitalist West. The Russians held that cavalry offensives, now in mechanised form, were irresistible, or rather they could be resisted only by similar offensives at some other part of the front. It was their intention, in case of war, to fling armoured columns into Germany, regardless of German attacks elsewhere. This remained their intention even in 1941; and they were prevented from putting it into operation only by the fact that Hitler attacked them before they were ready. Their doctrine was, in fact, mistaken, though not more so than that of the Western Powers; and in 1941 Hitler's surprise attack saved them from a disaster which might have been beyond remedy. These later experiences are irrelevant to the diplomacy of 1939. Then the Russians asked to go through Poland because they believed, however mistakenly, that this was the only way to win a war. Political aims may have existed as well; but they were subordinate to genuine military needs.

The British and French governments did not appreciate these Soviet calculations; but they realised that the unwelcome question would have to be answered, now that it had been asked. Both turned, though without much hope, to Warsaw. The British still used political arguments: "Agreement with the Soviet Union would be calculated to deter Hitler from war." If negotiations broke down, "Russia might either share the spoils with Germany . . . or constitute the chief menace when the war was over." [15] Beck gave an equally political answer: agreement to the passage of Russian troops across Poland, far from deterring Hitler, "would lead to an immediate declaration of war on the part of Germany." [16] Both political arguments made sense; both were irrelevant to the military situation. The French thought in more practical terms. They were only concerned to get the Red Army involved in conflict with Hitler, and did not mind if this were done at the expense of Poland. Left to themselves they would gladly have jettisoned Poland if they could have won Soviet co-operation in exchange. London forbade any such threat; therefore the French had still to attempt persuasion. Bonnet thought he saw a way out. The Russians insisted on an agreement for military collaboration with the Poles before war started; the Poles would accept Soviet aid only when the war had begun. Hence Bonnet argued that a moment had arrived which still seemed like peace to the Russians but like war to the Poles. The manoeuvre failed. Beck was obdurate: "It is a new partition of Poland that we are being asked to sign." On 21 August the French lost patience. They decided to ignore the Polish refusal and to go ahead,

[15] Halifax to Kennard, 17 Aug., 20 Aug. 1939. *British Foreign Policy,* third series. vii. No. 38, 39, 91.
[16] Kennard to Halifax, 18 Aug. 1939. *Ibid.* No. 52.

hoping to commit the Poles willy-nilly. Doumenc, the head of the military mission in Moscow, was instructed to give "an affirmative answer in principle" to the Russian question; and he was to "negotiate and sign whatever arrangement might best serve the common interest, subject to the final approval of the French Government." The British refused to be associated with this move, though they did not protest against it.

In any case, the chance of a Soviet alliance, if it ever existed, had now been lost. On 14 August, a few hours after Voroshilov had raised his fateful question, Ribbentrop drafted a telegram to Schulenberg, his ambassador in Moscow: "There exist no real conflicts of interests between Germany and Russia. . . . There is no question between the Baltic Sea and the Black Sea which cannot be settled to the complete satisfaction of both parties." Ribbentrop was prepared to come to Moscow, there "to lay the foundations for a final settlement of German-Russian relations." [17] This message was the first real move in German-Soviet relations. Until then they had been stagnant; the discussions between subordinates, of which so much was to be made later by Western writers, were no more than soundings, inspired by regrets for the vanished intimacy of Rapallo. Now Hitler was at last taking the initiative. Why did he do so at this precise moment? Was it supreme political skill, a second sight which told him that the military talks would reach deadlock two days after they started? Was the coincidence of Voroshilov's question and Ribbentrop's approach arranged secretly between Stalin and Hitler in advance? Did some unknown agent in the Kremlin tell Hitler that the right moment had arrived? Or was the coincidence pure chance? Hitler had first blurted out his plan of breaking Anglo-French nerve by an agreement with Soviet Russia when he boasted untruly to Ciano of an invitation from Moscow on 12 August, and so stilled Italian fears. Perhaps Hitler only devised this strategy consciously at the moment of boasting. After all, he was always the man of daring improvisations; he made lightning decisions, and then presented them as the result of long-term policy. Ribbentrop remained at Berchtesgaden until 13 August. He returned to Berlin on 14 August. This was therefore the first day when the message to Moscow could have been sent. Probably chance is the correct answer; but this is one of the problems which we shall never be able to solve.

Schulenberg delivered Ribbentrop's message on 15 August. Molotov refused to be hurried. Though he received the message "with greatest interest," he thought negotiations would take some time. He asked: "How were the German Government disposed towards the idea of a non-aggression pact with the Soviet Union?" [18] The answer came back within less than twenty-four hours: Germany offered not only a non-aggression pact, but a joint guarantee of the Baltic States and mediation between Soviet Russia and Japan. The essential thing was

[17] Ribbentrop to Schulenberg, 14 Aug. 1939. *German Foreign Policy,* series D. vii. No. 56.
[18] Schulenberg to Ribbentrop, 16 Aug. 1939. *Ibid.* No. 70.

the visit by Ribbentrop.[19] The Russians still kept the way open on both sides. On 17 August Voroshilov told the British and French military missions that there was no point in a further meeting until they could answer his question about Poland; however, after some prodding, he agreed to meet again on 21 August. At almost exactly the same time Molotov told Schulenberg that the improvement in Soviet-German relations would be a long business. First there must be a commercial agreement; next a pact of non-aggression. Then perhaps they could think about a visit from Ribbentrop; but the Soviet government "preferred to do practical work without fuss." [20]

On 18 August Ribbentrop knocked harder than ever at the Soviet door. Relations must be clarified at once "so as not to be taken by surprise by the outbreak of a German-Polish conflict." [21] Once more Molotov hesitated. Ribbentrop's visit "could not be fixed even approximately." Within half an hour, Schulenberg was called back to the Kremlin; Ribbentrop, he was told, could come a week later.[22] There is no means of knowing what brought this sudden decision. Schulenberg thought that Stalin had intervened personally; but this was a guess, like all others made later. The Soviet invitation was not soon enough for Hitler; he wanted Ribbentrop to be received at once. This may have been simply the impatience which always followed his prolonged hesitations. Perhaps there is a deeper explanation. 26 August would be soon enough if Hitler merely aimed to clear the way for an attack on Poland on 1 September. It was not soon enough to give him time for two operations: first breaking the nerve of the Western Powers by an agreement with Soviet Russia; then breaking the nerve of the Poles with the assistance of the Western Powers. Hence Hitler's urgency strongly suggests that he was aiming at another "Munich," not at war.

At any rate, Hitler now acted without a diplomatic intermediary. On 20 August he sent a personal message to Stalin, agreeing to all the Soviet demands and asking that Ribbentrop should be received at once.[23] The message was a milestone in world history; it marked the moment when Soviet Russia returned to Europe as a Great Power. No European statesman had ever addressed Stalin directly before. Western leaders had treated him as though he were a remote, and ineffectual, Bey of Bokhara. Now Hitler recognised him as the ruler of a great state. Stalin is supposed to have been immune to personal feelings; Hitler's approach must have flattered him all the same. The moment of decision had arrived. On 20 August the commercial treaty between Soviet Russia and Germany was settled; the first Soviet condition had been fulfilled. On the morning of 21 August Voroshilov met the two military missions. They had nothing

[19] Ribbentrop to Schulenberg, 16 Aug. 1939. *German Foreign Policy*, series D. vii. No. 75.
[20] Schulenberg to Ribbentrop, 18 Aug. 1939. *Ibid*. No. 105.
[21] Ribbentrop to Schulenberg, 18 Aug. 1939. *Ibid*. No. 113.
[22] Schulenberg to Ribbentrop, 19 Aug. 1939. *Ibid*. No. 132.
[23] Ribbentrop to Schulenberg, 20 Aug. 1939. *German Foreign Policy*, series D. vii. No. 142.

to report; and the meeting adjourned *sine die*. At 5 p.m. Stalin agreed that Ribbentrop could come to Moscow at once—on 23 August. The news was announced that same night in Berlin, and on the following day in Moscow. The French still tried to save something. On 22 August Doumenc saw Voroshilov on his own. On Daladier's instructions, he offered to agree to the Soviet demand without waiting for a reply from the Poles. Voroshilov rejected the offer: "We do not want Poland to boast that she has refused our aid—which we have no intention of forcing her to accept." [24] The Anglo-Franco-Soviet negotiations were at an end. On the following day, 23 August, the French finally wheedled out of the Poles a grudging formula. The French might say to the Russians: "We have acquired the certainty that in the event of common action against a German aggression collaboration between Poland and the U.S.S.R. is not excluded (or: is possible)." [25] The formula was never placed before the Russians. In any case it was fraudulent. Beck agreed to it only when he knew that Ribbentrop was in Moscow and that there was no danger of Soviet aid to Poland. Nor did this dismay him. He still believed that an independent Poland had more chance of reaching agreement with Hitler. Soviet Russia, he thought, was withdrawing from Europe; and that was good news for the Poles. "It is now Ribbentrop's turn," he said complacently, "to experience Soviet bad faith." [26]

Ribbentrop did not think so. He came to Moscow to reach agreement; and he succeeded immediately. The public Pact, signed on 23 August, provided for mutual non-aggression. A secret protocol excluded Germany from the Baltic states and from the eastern parts of Poland—the territory east of the Curzon line which was inhabited by Ukrainians and White Russians. This was, after all, what the Russians had sought to obtain from the Western Powers. The Nazi-Soviet pact was only another way of doing it: not so good a way, but better than none. The settlement of Brest-Litovsk was at last undone, with the consent of Germany, instead of with the backing of the Western Powers. It was no doubt disgraceful that Soviet Russia should make any agreement with the leading Fascist state; but this reproach came ill from the statesmen who went to Munich and who were then sustained in their own countries by great majorities. The Russians, in fact, did only what the Western statesmen had hoped to do; and Western bitterness was the bitterness of disappointment, mixed with anger that professions of Communism were no more sincere than their own professions of democracy. The pact contained none of the fulsome expressions of friendship which Chamberlain had put into the Anglo-German declaration on the day after the Munich conference. Indeed Stalin rejected any such expressions: "The Soviet Government could not suddenly present to the public German-

---

[24] Conversation between Voroshilov and Doumenc, 22 Aug. 1939. *British Foreign Policy*, third series. vii. Appendix ii. No. 10.

[25] Kennard to Halifax, 23 Aug. 1939. *Ibid*. No. 176.

[26] Noël, *L'agression allemande*, 424.

Soviet assurances of friendship after they had been covered with buckets of filth by the Nazi Government for six years."

The pact was neither an alliance nor an agreement for the partition of Poland. Munich had been a true alliance for partition: the British and French dictated partition to the Czechs. The Soviet government undertook no such action against the Poles. They merely promised to remain neutral, which is what the Poles had always asked them to do and which Western policy implied also. More than this, the agreement was in the last resort anti-German: it limited the German advance eastwards in case of war, as Winston Churchill emphasised in a speech at Manchester immediately after the end of the Polish campaign. In August the Russians were not thinking in terms of war. They assumed, like Hitler, that the Western Powers would not fight without a Soviet alliance. Poland would be compelled to yield; and, with the Polish obstacle out of the way, defensive alliance with the West might then be achieved on more equal terms. Alternatively, if the Poles remained defiant, they would fight alone; and in that case they would be driven to accept Soviet assistance after all. These calculations were falsified by the actual outcome: a war in which both Poland and the Western Powers took part. Even this was a success for the Soviet leaders: it warded off what they had most dreaded—a united capitalist attack on Soviet Russia. But it was not the intention of Soviet policy; the events of 1 September and 3 September could not be foreseen on 23 August. Both Hitler and Stalin imagined that they had prevented war, not brought it on. Hitler thought that he would score another Munich over Poland; Stalin that he had at any rate escaped an unequal war in the present, and perhaps even avoided it altogether.

However one spins the crystal and tries to look into the future from the point of view of 23 August 1939, it is difficult to see what other course Soviet Russia could have followed. The Soviet apprehensions of a European alliance against Russia were exaggerated, though not groundless. But, quite apart from this—given the Polish refusal of Soviet aid, given too the British policy of drawing out negotiations in Moscow without seriously striving for a conclusion—neutrality, with or without a formal pact, was the most that Soviet diplomacy could attain; and limitation of German gains in Poland and the Baltic was the inducement which made a formal pact attractive. The policy was right according to the textbooks of diplomacy. It contained all the same a grave blunder: by concluding a written agreement, the Soviet statesmen, like Western statesmen before them, slipped into the delusion that Hitler would keep his word. Stalin obviously had doubts. At the moment of parting with Ribbentrop he said: "The Soviet Government take the new Pact very seriously. He could guarantee on his word of honour that the Soviet Union would not betray its partner." There was a clear implication: "Do thou likewise." All the same Stalin obviously thought that the pact had value, not only as an immediate manoeuvre, but over a long period. This is curious, but not unusual. Men, themselves without scruple, often complain when they are cheated by others.

At any rate the bomb had exploded. Hitler was radiant, confident that he had pulled off the decisive stroke. On 22 August he entertained his leading generals to the wildest of his speeches: "Close your hearts to pity. Act brutally." This rigmarole was not a serious directive for action—no formal record was kept. Hitler was glorying in his own skill. Tucked away in the speech was a hard core: "Now the probability is great that the West will not intervene." [27] As well, Hitler was talking for effect. A report of the speech reached the British embassy almost at once; [28] whether intentionally or not, the so-called German "resistance" did Hitler's work for him. On 23 August Hitler took a further step. He fixed the attack on Poland for 4.40 a.m. on 26 August. This, too, was play-acting to impress the generals and, through them, the Western Powers. The German time-table could operate only from 1 September. Before then an attack on Poland was possible only if she had already surrendered. But technical considerations no longer seemed to matter: the Nazi-Soviet pact was assumed to have cleared the way for a diplomatic collapse on the part of the Western Powers.

The French almost came up to Hitler's expectations—or down to them. Bonnet had always been eager to desert the Poles. He resented the way in which they had behaved during the Czech crisis; he accepted the German case over Danzig; he had no faith in the Polish army. The Russians, Bonnet argued, claimed that they could not fight against Germany without a common frontier; a German conquest of Poland would provide one, and the Franco-Soviet Pact could then be revived to real effect. On 23 August, when Ribbentrop's journey to Moscow became known, Bonnet asked Daladier to summon the Committee of National Defence. There he hinted at his policy: "Should we blindly apply our alliance with Poland? Would it be better, on the contrary, to push Warsaw into a compromise? We could thus gain time to complete our equipment, increase our military strength, and improve our diplomatic position, so as to be able to resist Germany more effectively if she turned against France later." But Bonnet was no fighter, even for peace. He left the decision to others. The generals would not confess France's military weakness, for which they were responsible; perhaps they did not even appreciate it. Gamelin declared that the French army was "ready" (whatever that might mean); he further said that Poland would hold out until the spring and that by then the Western front would be impregnable.[29] No one raised the question whether it was possible actually to aid the Poles. Obviously those present all assumed that the French

---

[27] Memorandum of speech by Hitler, 22 Aug. 1939. *German Foreign Policy*, series D. vii. No. 192 and 193.

[28] Ogilvie-Forbes to Kirkpatrick, 25 Aug. 1939. *British Foreign Policy*, third series, vii. No. 314.

[29] Bonnet, *Fin d'une Europe*, 303–4.

army would merely man the Maginot line, despite Gamelin's promise to the Poles of an offensive. There was no discussion of policy, no proposal to warn the Poles of their danger. The Poles were left free to resist Hitler or to compromise with him, just as they chose. Even more remarkable, there was no approach to the British, no Anglo-French meeting of ministers such as had marked the Czech crisis. The British, too, were left free to resist Hitler or to compromise, without any information as to French wishes or French strength. Yet the British decision would commit France. The French would either abdicate finally in eastern Europe or would carry, almost alone, the burden of a great European war, entirely according to which London preferred. There was silence towards the British, silence towards the Poles, almost silence towards the Germans. Daladier sent a letter of warning to Hitler. Otherwise French statesmen did nothing throughout the week which determined, for many years, the fate of France.

This was a strange passivity, but no stranger than the French policy during previous years. The French did not know which way to turn. They would not deliberately abandon the settlement of 1919; and yet sensed that they were incapable of maintaining it. They had behaved like this over German rearmament. They refused to allow it, yet could find no way of preventing it. It was the same over Austria: "No" was repeated until the Anschluss happened. Czechoslovakia would have seen the same story again, had it not been for British prompting. Then the British urged surrender, and the French acquiesced. Now no word come from the British; and Daladier, the most representative of French politicians, relapsed into sullen resistance. The French cared no more for Danzig than they had done for the German-speaking territories of Czechoslovakia; but they would not themselves destroy what they once had made. They wanted to make an end one way or the other. "Il faut en finir" was the universal French mood in 1939. They had no idea what the end would be. Hardly any Frenchmen foresaw military defeat; victory over Germany seemed equally remote. There is some slight evidence that the French secret service exaggerated the opposition inside Germany. But there was no rational calculation behind the decision of 23 August. The French were at a loss what to do; they therefore decided to let things happen.

Decision thus rested exclusively with the British government. Their policy, too, seemed in ruins; the Anglo-Soviet alliance was gone beyond recall. This was a basic misunderstanding of the British position—indeed a misunderstanding which did as much as anything else to cause the second World war. Alliance with Soviet Russia was the policy of the Opposition—the policy of Labour, of Winston Churchill, and of Lloyd George. It was they who insisted that resistance to Hitler was possible only if Soviet Russia were on the Allied side. The government did not share this view. They never attached practical value to the

Soviet alliance; and they drifted into negotiations unwillingly, driven on by agitation in Parliament and in the country. They were relieved when negotiations broke down; delighted to be able to say, "We told you so," to their critics; and freed from an embarrassment. The Conservative back-benchers went further. Many of them had favoured Hitler as a bulwark against Bolshevism; now he became, in their eyes, a traitor to the cause of Western civilisation. At the same time as the Conservatives swung against Hitler, Labour turned, with almost equal bitterness, against Stalin; resolved to show that they, at any rate, were sincere in their anti-Fascism, even if it meant supporting Chamberlain. On any rational calculation, the Nazi-Soviet Pact ought to have discouraged the British people. Lloyd George was almost alone in making this calculation. Otherwise the Pact produced a resolution such as the British had not shown for twenty years. On 22 August, to universal applause, the Cabinet determined to stand by their obligation to Poland.

There was no discussion how this obligation could be fulfilled; indeed there was no way of fulfilling it. Military advisers were not called in except to consider the civil defences of London. The British government still thought in terms of policy, not of action. Their policy remained unchanged: on the one hand, firm warnings to Hitler that he would face general war if he attacked Poland; on the other, equally steady assurances that he would receive concessions if he acted peacefully. They were resolved on this policy. Hence they did not consult the French whether war were practicable, nor enquire of the Poles what concessions could be made. Indeed they were determined on concessions over the Poles' heads, if Hitler were reasonable. The British government still agreed with Hitler in regard to Danzig. But even now the question of Danzig was not formally raised. Hitler waited for offers which could be screwed up; the British waited for claims which could be scaled down. Whichever made the first move would lose; hence neither made it. The British government found a middle way: they would warn Hitler against war and, at the same time, hint at the rewards which peace would bring him. Their original intention had been to send a special emissary—not Chamberlain this time, but perhaps Field Marshal Lord Ironside. In the hurry consequent on the Nazi-Soviet pact, this was impossible. The message had to be delivered by the ambassador, Nevile Henderson, who flew to Berchtesgaden on 23 August.

It was an unfortunate choice. Henderson no doubt tried to speak firmly, but his heart was not in it. With consistency worthy of a better cause, he remained convinced that the Poles were in the wrong. He wanted them to be forced to give way, as the Czechs had been forced to give way the year before. A few days previously he wrote to a friend in the Foreign Office: "History will judge the Press generally to have been the principal cause of the war. . . . Of all Germans, believe it or not, Hitler is the most moderate so far as Danzig and the Corridor are concerned. . . . We could not say Boo to Benes last year till we were on the abyss of war. And we can't say Boo to Beck now." [30] He certainly failed to say Boo to Hitler. Though he loyally delivered the British message, he still paraded British conciliation. He told Hitler, quite truly: "The proof of Chamberlain's friendship was to be found in the fact that he had refused to have Churchill in the Cabinet"; and he said further that the hostile attitude in Great Britain was the work of Jews and enemies of the Nazis, which was exactly what Hitler thought himself.[31] Faced with such a half-hearted opponent, Hitler bullied and stormed. When Henderson left the room, Hitler slapped his thigh and said: "Chamberlain will not survive that conversation; his Cabinet will fall to-night." [32] Henderson responded as Hitler intended. Immediately on his return to Berlin, he wrote to Halifax: "I have held from the beginning that the Poles were utterly foolish and unwise"; and again: "I personally no longer see any hope of avoiding war unless the Polish Ambassador is instructed to apply today or at the latest tomorrow for personal interview with Hitler." [33]

In England, however, events did not come up to Hitler's expectation. Quite the reverse. Parliament met on 24 August, and unanimously applauded what it supposed to be the government's firm stand. Hitler began to have doubts: evidently more was needed to extract from the British government the concessions on which he still counted. On 24 August Hitler flew to Berlin. On his instructions, Goering called in the Swede Dahlerus, and sent him off to London with an unofficial appeal for British mediation. This was an ingenious trap: if the British refused, Hitler could claim that he had never made a move; if they yielded, they would be compelled to put pressure on Poland. The same evening Hitler held a meeting with Goering, Ribbentrop, and the principal generals. Should they go on with the attack on Poland, now due to begin within thirty-six hours? Hitler declared that he would make a further attempt to detach the Western Powers from their Polish allies. The attempt took the form of a "last offer," communicated to Henderson shortly after noon on 25 August. Germany, Hitler declared, was determined "to abolish the Macedonian conditions on her eastern frontier." The problems of Danzig and the Corridor must be solved— though he still did not say how. Once these problems were out of the way, Germany would make "a large, comprehensive offer"; she would guarantee the British Empire, accept an agreed limitation of armaments, and renew the assurance that her frontier in the west was final.[34] Henderson was impressed, as usual. Hitler, he reported, spoke "with great earnestness and apparent sincerity." [35] Later writers have all dismissed Hitler's offer as fraudulent; and so in

---

[30] Henderson to Strang, 16 Aug. 1939. *British Foreign Policy*, third series. vii. No. 37.
[31] Memorandum by Loesch, 24 Aug. 1939. *German Foreign Policy*, series D. vii. No. 200.
[32] Weizsäcker, *Erinnerungen*, 252.
[33] Henderson to Halifax, 24 Aug. 1939. *British Foreign Policy*, third series. vii. No. 257 and 241.
[34] Henderson to Halifax, 25 Aug. 1939. *Ibid*. No. 283.
[35] Henderson to Halifax, 25 Aug. 1939. *Ibid*. No. 284.

a sense it was. The immediate object was to isolate Poland. Yet the offer also represented Hitler's permanent policy: though he wanted a free hand to destroy conditions in the east which enlightened Western opinion had also pronounced intolerable, he had no ambitions directed against Great Britain and France.

But what could Hitler hope to achieve by this offer in the circumstances of the moment? Henderson promised to fly to London on the morning of 26 August; and by then the attack on Poland presumably would have begun. Was Hitler merely talking for the record—to clear himself in the eyes of posterity or even of his own conscience? Or had he forgotten his time-table, unable to realise that orders, once given, will be ultimately carried out? The latter seems the more likely explanation. Throughout the afternoon of 25 August, Hitler raged round the Chancellery, uncertain what to do. At 3 p.m. he ordered that the attack on Poland should be carried out. Three hours later Attolico, the Italian ambassador, arrived with a message from Mussolini: though Italy stood by Germany unconditionally, she could not "intervene militarily," unless Germany at once supplied all her needs in war material; and these, when the list came, were—in Ciano's words—"enough to kill a bull if a bull could read." Mussolini had acted the strong man till the last moment; now, with war apparently imminent, he ran away. Immediately after this blow came another. Ribbentrop reported that the formal alliance between Great Britain and Poland had just been signed in London. Hitler summoned Keitel, his chief-of-staff: "Stop everything at once, fetch Brauchitsch [the commander-in-chief] immediately. I need time for negotiations." The new orders went out shortly after 7 p.m. The premature offensive was as precipitately cancelled.

Here was another mysterious episode. Why did Hitler pull back at the last moment? Did he lose his nerve? Did the two events of Mussolini's neutrality and the Anglo-Polish alliance really take him by surprise? He himself, with the normal propensity of statesmen to put the blame on others, at once complained that it was all the fault of Mussolini: news of the Italian decision not to fight had stiffened the British just when they were on the point of surrender. This was nonsense. The British did not know of Mussolini's decision when they signed the alliance with Poland, though they could make a good guess at it. Nor was the alliance timed for its effect at that particular moment. Its conclusion had been held up during the negotiations with Soviet Russia; once these failed, there was no reason for further postponement, and the British signed it as soon as formalities could be completed. They were unaware that Hitler had fixed on 25 August as the day of crisis. They were thinking in terms of the first week in September; just as Hitler had long thought in terms of 1 September. Probably this is the explanation of his apparent hesitation on 25 August. Advancing the offensive to that date was a "try-on," an extra call rather like his exaggerated obstinacy at Godesberg the previous year. Quite apart from the diplomatic events of 25 August, there were good military reasons for reverting to the original date. On 25 August the Western frontier of Germany was still virtually undefended. Perhaps thereafter Hitler faced the fact that some sort of war with the Western Powers was in the offing. But it is more likely that he spoke the truth to Keitel: he needed time for negotiation.

The British, too, were intent on negotiation. The signing of the Anglo-Polish alliance was a preliminary to this, not a firm decision for war. There is clear evidence that the British did not take the alliance all that seriously. Their draft had been designed to fit in with an Anglo-Soviet alliance, now vanished. In the hugger-mugger which followed the Nazi-Soviet pact, clauses from a Polish draft were included as well; and one of these contained the pledge which the British had hitherto evaded—a full extension of the alliance to cover Danzig. Yet almost at the moment of signing the alliance, a member of the foreign office drafted "possible counter-proposals to Herr Hitler" which postulated that Danzig should have "the right to determine its political allegiance," subject to the recognition of Poland's economic rights; [36] and Halifax himself told the Polish ambassador that "the Polish Government would make a great mistake if they sought to adopt a position in which discussion of peaceful modifications of the status of Danzig was ruled out." [37] Thus the British government and Hitler were close to agreement on how the crisis should end; and the Poles were out of step. The problem however was not how negotiations should end, but how they should begin; and for this no solution was found.

Preliminaries for a negotiation proceeded furiously between 26 August and 29 August: the British hinting at what they would offer, Hitler at what he would demand. Both sides hesitated to go over the brink into actual negotiations. There was further confusion in that these soundings were conducted on two levels. Nevile Henderson acted as official intermediary; Dahlerus shuttled between Berlin and London even more assiduously. He flew to London on 25 August and back to Berlin on 26 August; to London and back on 27 August; and the same again on 30 August. In Berlin he saw Goering and sometimes Hitler; in London he was received with every precaution of secrecy, and saw Chamberlain and Halifax. The British might insist that their remarks to Dahlerus were "off the record"; Hitler was bound to feel all the same that a second Munich was being prepared for him. He may have been genuinely taken aback by the signature of the Anglo-Polish alliance; this effect was lost as Henderson and Dahlerus multiplied their exertions. Yet at the same time the British, listening to Dahlerus, imagined that their position was improving. A member of the foreign office commented on the activities of Dahlerus: "This shows that the German Government are wobbling. . . . Whilst we may and should be conciliatory in form, we should be absolutely firm in substance. . . . The latest indications are that we have an unexpectedly strong hand." This

---

[36] Memorandum by Makins, 25 Aug. 1939. *British Foreign Policy,* third series. vii. No. 307.
[37] Halifax to Kennard, 25 Aug. 1939. *Ibid.* No. 309.

minute bears the further comment: "Seen by S. of S. who says he quite agrees with it." [38] With extreme ingenuity Halifax even believed that a second Munich would discredit Hitler, not the British government. He wrote: "When we speak of Munich we must remember the change that has supervened since then in the attitude and strength of this country, and in many other directions—Italy—and let us hope Japan—etc. And if Hitler is led to accept a moderate solution now, it is perhaps not altogether wishful thinking to believe that his position will suffer a certain diminution within Germany." [39]

Thus the two sides circled round each other like wrestlers seeking advantage before the clinch. The British offered to arrange direct negotiations between Germany and Poland if Hitler would promise to behave peacefully; Hitler replied that there would be no war if he got his way over Danzig. Later writers have argued that Hitler's reply was dishonest; that he was concerned to isolate Poland, not to avoid war. This may well be true. But the offer by the British government was dishonest also: there was no chance of extracting concessions from the Poles once the danger of war was removed, and the British knew it. In the previous year Benes had appealed for British support. They had implied that he might secure it if he were conciliatory enough; and he had swallowed the bait. Now the British were already committed—their hands tied not so much by their formal alliance with Poland, as by the resolution of British public opinion. They could not dictate concessions to the Poles; they could not allow Hitler to dictate them. Yet there would be no concessions unless someone did the dictating. On 23 August Sir Horace Wilson, acting on Chamberlain's behalf, saw Kennedy, the American ambassador. After the conversation, Kennedy telephoned the State Department: "The British wanted one thing of us and one thing only, namely that we put pressure on the Poles. They felt that they could not, given their obligations, do anything of this sort but that we could." [40] President Roosevelt rejected this idea out of hand. Chamberlain—again according to Kennedy—then lost all hope: "He says the futility of it all is the thing that is frightful; after all, they cannot save the Poles; they can merely carry on a war of revenge that will mean the destruction of all Europe." [41]

The deadlock lasted until 29 August. Then it was broken by Hitler. He was in the weaker position, though the British did not know it. There was not much time left before 1 September for him to pull off diplomatic success. At 7.15 p.m. he made to Henderson a formal offer and a formal demand: he would negotiate directly with Poland if a Polish plenipotentiary arrived in Berlin the following day. This was a retreat from the position Hitler had rigorously asserted since

[38] Minute to Kirkpatrick, 27 Aug. 1939. *British Foreign Policy*, third series, vii. No. 397.
[39] Minute by Halifax on Henderson to Halifax, 29 Aug. 1939. *Ibid.* No. 455.
[40] *Moffat Papers 1919–43* (1956), 253. Cordell Hull supplies Wilson's name. *Memoirs*, i. 662.
[41] Kennedy to Hull, 23 Aug. 1939. *Foreign Relations of the United States*, 1939. Vol. I. General.

26 March—that he would never again deal directly with the Poles. Though Henderson complained that the demand was perilously near an ultimatum, he was eager to accept it; it constituted in his opinion the "sole chance of preventing war." Henderson pressed the demand on his own government; he urged the French government to advise an immediate visit by Beck; he was most insistent of all with the Polish ambassador Lipski.[42] Lipski took no notice—apparently he did not even report Hitler's demand to Warsaw. The French government responded as clearly in the opposite direction—they told Beck to go to Berlin at once. But the decision rested with the British government. Here was the proposal which they had always wanted and which they had repeatedly hinted at to Hitler: direct negotiations between Poland and Germany. Hitler had now done his part; but they could not do theirs. They had the gravest doubt whether the Poles would thus present themselves in Berlin at Hitler's behest. Kennedy reported Chamberlain's feeling to Washington: "Frankly he is more worried about getting the Poles to be reasonable than the Germans." [43] The British gnawed over the problem throughout 30 August. Finally they hit on a sort of solution. They passed Hitler's demand on to Warsaw at 12.25 a.m. on 31 August—that is to say, twenty-five minutes after the German ultimatum, if such it were, had expired. The British had been correct in their apprehension of Polish obstinacy. Beck, when informed of Hitler's demand, at once replied: "If invited to Berlin he would of course not go, as he had no intention of being treated like President Hacha." [44] Thus the British, by acting too late, could still claim that they had offered something which they knew they could not deliver: a Polish plenipotentiary in Berlin.

Hitler had not anticipated this. He had expected that negotiations would start; and he then intended them to break down on Polish obstinacy. On his instructions detailed demands were at last prepared. These were principally the immediate return of Danzig, and a plebiscite in the Corridor [45]—the very terms which the British and French governments had themselves long favoured. But, failing a Polish plenipotentiary, the Germans had difficulty in making their terms known. At midnight on 30 August Henderson brought to Ribbentrop the news that a Polish plenipotentiary was not coming that day. Ribbentrop had only the rough draft of the proposed German terms, scribbled over with Hitler's emendations. It was not in a condition to be shown to Henderson; and Ribbentrop had instructions from Hitler not to do so. He therefore read the terms over slowly. Later a myth grew up that he had "gabbled" them, deliberately cheating Henderson with terms that were only for show. In fact Henderson got the gist clearly, and was impressed. Taken at their face value, he thought, they were "not

---

[42] Henderson to Halifax, 29 Aug., 30 Aug. 1939. *British Foreign Policy*, third series, vii. No. 493, 510.

[43] Kennedy to Hull, 30 Aug. 1939. *Foreign Relations of the United States*, 1939. Vol. I. General.

[44] Kennard to Halifax, 31 Aug. 1939. *British Foreign Policy*, third series. vii. No. 575.

[45] Schmidt, circular dispatch, 30 Aug. 1939. *German Foreign Policy*, series D. vii. No. 458.

unreasonable." On his return to the British embassy, he summoned Lipski at 2 a.m., and urged him to seek an interview with Ribbentrop at once. Lipski took no notice, and went back to bed.

The Germans were now anxious that their terms had not gone properly on record with Henderson. They once more employed Dahlerus as an allegedly unofficial emissary. Goering, claiming to be acting in defiance of Hitler, showed the terms to Dahlerus, who in turn telephoned them to the British embassy about 4 a.m. Since Goering knew that all telephone conversations were monitored by at least three government agencies (one of them his own), his defiance of Hitler was of course a fiction. The next morning Goering abandoned it. Dahlerus was given a copy of the German terms, and took it round to the British embassy. Henderson again summoned Lipski, who refused to come. Dahlerus and Ogilvie-Forbes, the British counsellor of embassy, were dispatched to see Lipski. He remained unmoved. He refused to look at the German terms. When Dahlerus was out of the room, Lipski protested against introducing this intermediary, and said: "He would stake his reputation that German morale was breaking and that the present régime would soon crack. . . . This German offer was a trap. It was also a sign of weakness on the part of the Germans." [46] In a further effort to break through the crust of obstinacy, Dahlerus telephoned to Horace Wilson in London. The German terms, he said, were "extremely liberal"; it was " 'obvious to us' [Dahlerus? Goering? Henderson?] that the Poles were obstructing the possibilities of a negotiation." Wilson realised that the Germans were listening-in; he told Dahlerus to shut up and put down the receiver.[47]

The precaution came too late. Every move of the last few hours had been as public as if it had been announced in the newspapers. The telephone calls between Henderson and Lipski, and between Dahlerus and Henderson, the comings and goings between the British and Polish embassies—all these were known to the Germans. They were undoubtedly known to Hitler. What conclusion could he possibly draw? Only the conclusion that he had succeeded in driving a wedge between Poland and her Western allies. This was true in regard to the French government. It was true in regard to Henderson. He wrote late on 31 August: "On German offer war would be completely unjustifiable. . . . Polish Government should announce tomorrow, in the light of German proposals which have now been made public, their intention to send a Plenipotentiary to discuss in general terms these proposals." [48] Hitler was not to know that Henderson no longer carried the weight in London which he had carried the year before. But even the British government were losing patience with the Poles. Late on the night of 31 August Halifax telegraphed to Warsaw: "I do

---

[46] Henderson to Halifax, 31 Aug. 1939. *British Foreign Policy*, third series. vii. No. 597.
[47] Minute by Cadogan, 31 Aug. 1939. *British Foreign Policy*, third series. vii. No. 589.
[48] Henderson to Halifax, 1 Sept. 1939. *Ibid*. No. 631.

not see why the Polish Government should feel difficulty about authorising Polish Ambassador to accept a document from the German Government." [49] Given another twenty-four hours, and the breach would be wide open. But Hitler had not got the twenty-four hours. He was the prisoner of his own time-table. With his generals watching sceptically, he could not again call off the attack of Poland unless he had something solid to show; and this was still denied him by the Poles. The breach between Poland and her allies gave him a chance. He had to gamble on it.

At 12.40 p.m. on 31 August Hitler decided that the attack should proceed. At 1 p.m. Lipski telephoned, asking for an interview with Ribbentrop. The Germans, who had intercepted his instructions, knew that he had been told not to enter into "any concrete negotiations." At 3 p.m. Weizsäcker telephoned Lipski to ask whether he was coming as a plenipotentiary. Lipski replied: "No, in his capacity as an ambassador." This was enough for Hitler. The Poles, it seemed, were remaining obstinate; he could go forward to the gamble of isolating them in war. At 4 p.m. the orders for war were confirmed. At 6.30 p.m. Lipski at last saw Ribbentrop. Lipski said that his government were "favourably considering" the British proposal for direct Polish-German negotiations. Ribbentrop asked whether he was a plenipotentiary. Lipski again answered No. Ribbentrop did not communicate the German terms; if he had tried to do so, Lipski would have refused to receive them. Thus ended the only direct contact between Germany and Poland since 26 March. The Poles had kept their nerve unbroken to the last moment. At 4.45 a.m. on the following morning the German attack on Poland began. At 6 a.m. German aeroplanes bombed Warsaw.

Here was a clear *casus foederis* for both Great Britain and France. Their ally had been wantonly attacked; it only remained for them to declare war on the aggressor. Nothing of the kind happened. Both governments addressed a pained remonstrance to Hitler, warning him that they would have to go to war unless he desisted. Meanwhile they waited for something to turn up; and something did. On 31 August Mussolini, carefully following the precedent of the previous year, proposed a European conference: it should meet on 5 September and should survey all causes of European conflict, with the precondition that Danzig should return to Germany in advance. The two Western governments were favourable to the proposal when it first reached them. But Mussolini had got his timing wrong. In 1938 he had three days in which to avert war; in 1939 less than twenty-four hours, and this was not enough. By 1 September, when the Western governments replied to Mussolini, they had to postulate that fighting must first stop in Poland. Nor was this all. While Bonnet was enthusiastic for Mussolini's proposal, in Great Britain public opinion took charge. The House of Commons was restive when Chamberlain explained that Germany had merely been "warned"; it expected something more solid next day. Halifax,

[49] Halifax to Kennard, 1 Sept. 1939. *Ibid*. No. 632.

swinging as usual with the national mood, insisted that the conference could he held only if Germany withdrew from all Polish territory. The Italians knew that it was hopeless to place such a demand before Hitler; they dropped the conference without further effort.

Yet both the British and French governments, the French especially, went on believing in a conference which had vanished before it was born. Hitler had initially replied to Mussolini that, if invited to a conference, he would give his answer at mid-day on 3 September. Therefore Bonnet, and Chamberlain with him, strove desperately to postpone a declaration of war until after that time, even though the Italians no longer intended to invite Hitler or anyone else. Bonnet conjured up the excuse that the French military wanted the delay in order to carry through mobilisation, undisturbed by German air attack (which, they knew, would not occur anyway—the German air force was fully employed in Poland). Chamberlain conjured up no excuse except that the French wanted delay and that it was always difficult to work with allies. In the evening of 2 September he was still entertaining the House of Commons with hypothetical negotiations: "If the German Government should agree to withdraw their forces then His Majesty's Government would be willing to regard the position as being the same as it was before the German forces crossed the Polish frontier. That is to say, the way would be open to discussion between the German and Polish Governments on the matters at issue." This was too much even for loyal Conservatives. Leo Amery called to Arthur Greenwood, acting leader of the Opposition: "Speak for England," a task of which Chamberlain was incapable. Ministers, led by Halifax, warned Chamberlain that the government would fall unless it sent an ultimatum to Hitler before the House met again. Chamberlain gave way. The objections of the French were overruled. The British ultimatum was delivered to the Germans at 9 a.m. on 3 September. It expired at 11 a.m., and a state of war followed. When Bonnet learnt that the British were going to war in any case, his overriding anxiety was to catch up with them. The time of the French ultimatum was advanced, despite the supposed objections of the General Staff: it was delivered at noon on 3 September and expired at 5 p.m. In this curious way the French who had preached resistance to Germany for twenty years appeared to be dragged into war by the British who had for twenty years preached conciliation. Both countries went to war for that part of the peace settlement which they had long regarded as least defensible. Hitler may have projected a great war all along; yet it seems from the record that he became involved in war through launching on 29 August a diplomatic manoeuvre which he ought to have launched on 28 August.

Such were the origins of the second World war, or rather of the war between the three Western Powers over the settlement of Versailles; a war which had been implicit since the moment when the first war ended. Men will long debate whether this renewed war could have been averted by greater firmness or by

greater conciliation; and no answer will be found to these hypothetical speculations. Maybe either would have succeeded, if consistently followed; the mixture
of the two, practised by the British government, was the most likely to fail.
These questions now seem infinitely remote. Though Hitler blundered in supposing that the two Western Powers would not go to war at all, his expectation
that they would not go to war seriously turned out to be correct. Great Britain
and France did nothing to help the Poles, and little to help themselves. The
European struggle which began in 1918 when the German armistice delegates
presented themselves before Foch in the railway-carriage at Rethondes, ended
in 1940 when the French armistice delegates presented themselves before Hitler
in the same carriage. There was a "new order" in Europe; it was dominated
by Germany.

The British people resolved to defy Hitler, though they lacked the strer.gth
to undo his work. He himself came to their aid. His success depended on the
isolation of Europe from the rest of the world. He gratuitously destroyed the
source of this success. In 1941 he attacked Soviet Russia and declared war on the
United States, two World Powers who asked only to be left alone. In this way
a real World war began. We still live in its shadow. The war which broke out
in 1939 has become a matter of historical curiosity.

[16]

Social Solutions at Mid-Century

The three selections below may be said to represent three different views of economic planning. The first, from Friedrich Hayek's *The Road to Serfdom,* is against economic planning on the grounds that planning is incompatible with democracy and leads to dictatorship and the destruction of personal freedom. The second, from Barbara Wooton's *Freedom Under Planning,* assumes the necessity of planning and maintains that "A happy and fruitful marriage between freedom and planning can . . . be arranged." The third selection, from Barbara Ward's *Five Ideas That Change the World,* describes a totally planned society where the liberty of the individual has been subordinated to the economic direction of the state.

¶ The three selections may be said to suggest three different paths. The first, beginning with the laissez faire, liberal economics of Adam Smith in the eighteenth century, has led through various turnings to the system we call capitalism today. The second, originating in some of the non-Marxist socialisms of the late nineteenth and early twentieth centuries, leads to the programs of the Labour Party in Great Britain and the democratic socialist parties of Western Europe. The third path started with Marx and has ended in the totalitarian communist state.

¶ Helpful as the preceding description and analogy may be in understanding the material that follows, they should not obscure the fact that on another level we have, in the first two selections, a closely reasoned debate on how coextensive the state and society should be. The debate focuses on economic planning because Western society has as one of its basic values a guaranteed minimum standard of living, freedom from want, without which another basic value, the freedom of the individual from arbitrary power, can become meaningless.[1]

[1] For a further discussion of Western values see Shepard B. Clough, *Basic Values of Western Civilization* (New York: Columbia University Press, 1960). A chapter is reprinted under the last topic.

Professor Hayek, author of many works in economics, economic theory, and social philosophy, obviously realizes that the regulatory powers of the state over activities affecting the public welfare have necessarily increased from what they were even a generation ago. As John Chamberlain pointed out in the foreword to the American edition of *Road to Serfdom,* "Hayek is no devotee of laissez faire; he believes in a design for an enterprise system. Design is compatible with minimum-wage standards, health standards, and a minimum amount of compulsory social insurance. It is even compatible with certain types of government investment." [2] But beyond this point, Hayek believes, the state should not go. And Barbara Wooton, who has had a distinguished career in university and public life,[3] just as firmly believes it should. In the best tradition of scholarly dispute, Professor Hayek permitted Miss Wooton an early view of *Road to Serfdom,* and her book is a direct answer to his. Our selections have been arranged to match the central points of their argument as closely as possible.

Barbara Ward, an authority on the relations of the West with the rest of the world [4] and well-known university lecturer in the United States and in her native England, roundly criticizes Communist doctrine and Soviet practices, and in her remarks about the market economy and bureaucratic planning, seems closer to Professor Hayek's position than Miss Wooton's. But she adds to the dimensions of their argument by touching on the achievement, remarkable in its way, of a state where state and society have become coextensive and by describing the appeal of this achievement to the underdeveloped nations of the world.

[2] Friedrich A. Hayek, *The Road to Serfdom* (Chicago: University of Chicago Press, 1944) p. iv.

[3] Some of Miss Wooton's recent publications include *Testament for Social Science* (London: Allen & Unwin, 1950), *The Social Foundations of Wage Policy* (New York: Norton, 1955), *Social Science and Social Pathology* (New York: Macmillan, 1959).

[4] *The West at Bay* (New York: Norton, 1948), *Policy for the West* (New York: Norton, 1951), *Interplay of East and West* (New York: Norton, 1957), *The Rich Nations and the Poor Nations* (New York: Norton, 1962).

PLANNING AND DEMOCRACY

Friedrich A. Hayek

* * *

THE COMMON features of all collectivist systems may be described, in a phrase ever dear to socialists of all schools, as the deliberate organization of the labors of society for a definite social goal. That our present society lacks such "conscious" direction toward a single aim, that its activities are guided by the whims and fancies of irresponsible individuals, has always been one of the main complaints of its socialist critics.

In many ways this puts the basic issue very clearly. And it directs us at once to the point where the conflict arises between individual freedom and collectivism. The various kinds of collectivism, communism, fascism, etc., differ among themselves in the nature of the goal toward which they want to direct the efforts of society. But they all differ from liberalism and individualism in wanting to organize the whole of society and all its resources for this unitary end and in refusing to recognize autonomous spheres in which the ends of the individuals are supreme. In short, they are totalitarian in the true sense of this new word which we have adopted to describe the unexpected but nevertheless inseparable manifestations of what in theory we call collectivism.

The "social goal," or "common purpose," for which society is to be organized is usually vaguely described as the "common good," the "general welfare," or the "general interest." It does not need much reflection to see that these terms have no sufficiently definite meaning to determine a particular course of action. The welfare and the happiness of millions cannot be measured on a single scale of less and more. The welfare of a people, like the happiness of a man, depends on a great many things that can be provided in an infinite variety of combinations. It cannot be adequately expressed as a single end, but only as a hierarchy of ends, a comprehensive scale of values in which every need of every person is given its place. To direct all our activities according to a single plan presupposes that every one of our needs is given its rank in an order of values which must be complete enough to make it possible to decide among all the different courses which the planner has to choose. It presupposes, in short, the

Reprinted from *The Road to Serfdom* by Friedrich A. Hayek by permission of The University of Chicago Press. Copyright 1944 by the University of Chicago. All rights reserved. Reprinted by permission of Routledge & Kegan Paul Ltd., London.

existence of a complete ethical code in which all the different human values are allotted their due place.

The conception of a complete ethical code is unfamiliar, and it requires some effort of imagination to see what it involves. We are not in the habit of thinking of moral codes as more or less complete. The fact that we are constantly choosing between different values without a social code prescribing how we ought to choose does not surprise us and does not suggest to us that our moral code is incomplete. In our society there is neither occasion nor reason why people should develop common views about what should be done in such situations. But where all the means to be used are the property of society and are to be used in the name of society according to a unitary plan, a "social" view about what ought to be done must guide all decisions. In such a world we should soon find that our moral code is full of gaps.

We are not concerned here with the question whether it would be desirable to have such a complete ethical code. It may merely be pointed out that up to the present the growth of civilization has been accompanied by a steady diminution of the sphere in which individual actions are bound by fixed rules. The rules of which our common moral code consists have progressively become fewer and more general in character. From the primitive man, who was bound by an elaborate ritual in almost every one of his daily activities, who was limited by innumerable taboos, and who could scarcely conceive of doing things in a way different from his fellows, morals have more and more tended to become merely limits circumscribing the sphere within which the individual could behave as he liked. The adoption of a common ethical code comprehensive enough to determine a unitary economic plan would mean a complete reversal of this tendency.

The essential point for us is that no such complete ethical code exists. The attempt to direct all economic activity according to a single plan would raise innumerable questions to which the answer could be provided only by a moral rule, but to which existing morals have no answer and where there exists no agreed view on what ought to be done. People will have either no definite views or conflicting views on such questions, because in the free society in which we have lived there has been no occasion to think about them and still less to form common opinions about them.

Not only do we not possess such an all-inclusive scale of values: it would be impossible for any mind to comprehend the infinite variety of different needs of different people which compete for the available resources and to attach a definite weight to each. For our problem it is of minor importance whether the ends for which any person cares comprehend only his own individual needs, or whether they include the needs of his closer or even those of his more distant fellows—that is, whether he is egoistic or altruistic in the ordinary senses of these words. The point which is so important is the basic fact that it is impossible for any man to survey more than a limited field, to be aware of the urgency of more than a limited number of needs. Whether his interests center round his own physical needs, or whether he takes a warm interest in the welfare of every human being he knows, the ends about which he can be concerned will always be only an infinitesimal fraction of the needs of all men.

This is the fundamental fact on which the whole philosophy of individualism is based. It does not assume, as is often asserted, that man is egoistic or selfish or ought to be. It merely starts from the indisputable fact that the limits of our powers of imagination make it impossible to include in our scale of values more than a sector of the needs of the whole society, and that, since, strictly speaking, scales of value can exist only in individual minds, nothing but partial scales of values exist—scales which are inevitably different and often inconsistent with each other. From this the individualist concludes that the individuals should be allowed, within defined limits, to follow their own values and preferences rather than somebody else's; that within these spheres the individual's system of ends should be supreme and not subject to any dictation by others. It is this recognition of the individual as the ultimate judge of his ends, the belief that as far as possible his own views ought to govern his actions, that forms the essence of the individualist position.

This view does not, of course, exclude the recognition of social ends, or rather of a coincidence of individual ends which makes it advisable for men to combine for their pursuit. But it limits such common action to the instances where individual views coincide; what are called "social ends" are for it merely identical ends of many individuals—or ends to the achievement of which individuals are willing to contribute in return for the assistance they receive in the satisfaction of their own desires. Common action is thus limited to the fields where people agree on common ends. Very frequently these common ends will not be ultimate ends to the individuals but means which different persons can use for different purposes. In fact, people are most likely to agree on common action where the common end is not an ultimate end to them but a means capable of serving a great variety of purposes.

When individuals combine in a joint effort to realize ends they have in common, the organizations, like the state, that they form for this purpose are given their own system of ends and their own means. But any organization thus formed remains one "person" among others, in the case of the state much more powerful than any of the others, it is true, yet still with its separate and limited sphere in which alone its ends are supreme. The limits of this sphere are determined by the extent to which the individuals agree on particular ends; and the probability that they will agree on a particular course of action necessarily decreases as the scope of such action extends. There are certain functions of the state on the exercise of which there will be practical unanimity among its citizens; there will be others on which there will be agreement of a substantial majority; and so on, until we come to fields where, although each individual might wish the state to act in some way, there will be almost as many views about what the government should do as there are different people.

We can rely on voluntary agreement to guide the action of the state only so long as it is confined to spheres where agreement exists. But not only when the state undertakes direct control in fields where there is no such agreement is it bound to suppress individual freedom. We can unfortunately not indefinitely extend the sphere of common action and still leave the individual free in his own sphere. Once the communal sector, in which the state controls all the means, exceeds a certain proportion of the whole, the effects of its actions dominate the whole system. Although the state controls directly the use of only a large part of the available resources, the effects of its decisions on the remaining part of the economic system become so great that indirectly it controls almost everything. Where, as was, for example, true in Germany as early as 1928, the central and local authorities directly control the use of more than half the national income (according to an official German estimate then, 53 per cent), they control indirectly almost the whole economic life of the nation. There is, then, scarcely an individual end which is not dependent for its achievement on the action of the state, and the "social scale of values" which guides the state's action must embrace practically all individual ends.

It is not difficult to see what must be the consequences when democracy embarks upon a course of planning which in its execution requires more agreement than in fact exists. The people may have agreed on adopting a system of directed economy because they have been convinced that it will produce great prosperity. In the discussions leading to the decision, the goal of planning will have been described by some such term as "common welfare," which only conceals the absence of real agreement on the ends of planning. Agreement will in fact exist only on the mechanism to be used. But it is a mechanism which can be used only for a common end; and the question of the precise goal toward which all activity is to be directed will arise as soon as the executive power has to translate the demand for a single plan into a particular plan. Then it will appear that the agreement on the desirability of planning is not supported by agreement on the ends the plan is to serve. The effect of the people's agreeing that there must be central planning, without agreeing on the ends, will be rather as if a group of people were to commit themselves to take a journey together without agreeing where they want to go: with the result that they may all have to make a journey which most of them do not want at all. That planning creates a situation in which it is necessary for us to agree on a much larger number of topics than we have been used to, and that in a planned system we cannot confine collective action to the tasks on which we can agree but are forced to produce agreement on everything in order that any action can be taken at all, is one of the features which contributes more than most to determining the character of a planned system.

It may be the unanimously expressed will of the people that its parliament should prepare a comprehensive economic plan, yet neither the people nor its representatives need therefore be able to agree on any particular plan. The inability of democratic assemblies to carry out what seems to be a clear mandate of the people will inevitably cause dissatisfaction with democratic institutions. Parliaments come to be regarded as ineffective "talking shops," unable or incompetent to carry out the tasks for which they have been chosen. The conviction grows that if efficient planning is to be done, the direction must be "taken out of politics" and placed in the hands of experts—permanent officials or independent autonomous bodies.

The difficulty is well known to socialists. It will soon be half a century since the Webbs began to complain of "the increased incapacity of the House of Commons to cope with its work." [1] More recently, Professor Laski has elaborated the argument:

"It is common ground that the present parliamentary machine is quite unsuited to pass rapidly a great body of complicated legislation. The National Government, indeed, has in substance admitted this by implementing its economy and tariff measures not by detailed debate in the House of Commons but by a wholesale system of delegated legislation. A Labour Government would, I presume, build upon the amplitude of this precedent. It would confine the House of Commons to the two functions it can properly perform: the ventilation of grievances and the discussion of general principles of its measures. Its Bills would take the form of general formulae conferring wide powers on the appropriate government departments; and those powers would be exercised by Order in Council which could, if desired, be attacked in the House by means of a vote of no confidence. The necessity and value of delegated legislation has recently been strongly reaffirmed by the Donoughmore Committee; and its extension is inevitable if the process of socialisation is not to be wrecked by the normal methods of obstruction which existing parliamentary procedure sanctions."

And to make it quite clear that a socialist government must not allow itself to be too much fettered by democratic procedure, Professor Laski at the end of the same article raised the question "whether in a period of transition to Socialism, a Labour Government can risk the overthrow of its measures as a result of the next general election"—and left it significantly unanswered.[2]

---

[1] Sidney and Beatrice Webb, *Industrial Democracy* (1897), p. 800 n.

[2] H. J. Laski, "Labour and the Constitution," *New Statesman and Nation*, No. 81 (new ser.), September 10, 1932, p. 277. In a book (*Democracy in Crisis* [1933], particularly p. 87) in which Professor Laski later elaborated these ideas, his determination that parliamentary democracy must

It is important clearly to see the causes of this admitted ineffectiveness of parliaments when it comes to a detailed administration of the economic affairs of a nation. The fault is neither with the individual representatives nor with parliamentary institutions as such but with the contradictions inherent in the task with which they are charged. They are not asked to act where they can agree, but to produce agreement on everything—the whole direction of the resources of the nation. For such a task the system of majority decision is, however, not suited. Majorities will be found where it is a choice between limited alternatives; but it is a superstition to believe that there must be a majority view on everything. There is no reason why there should be a majority in favor of any one of the different possible courses of positive action if their number is legion. Every member of the legislative assembly might prefer some particular plan for the direction of economic activity to no plan, yet no one plan may appear preferable to a majority to no plan at all.

Nor can a coherent plan be achieved by breaking it up into parts and voting on particular issues. A democratic assembly voting and amending a comprehensive economic plan clause by clause, as it deliberates on an ordinary bill, makes nonsense. An economic plan, to deserve the name, must have a unitary conception. Even if a parliament could, proceeding step by step, agree on some scheme, it would certainly in the end satisfy nobody. A complex whole in which all the parts must be most carefully adjusted to each other cannot be achieved through a compromise between conflicting views. To draw up an economic plan in this fashion is even less possible than, for example, successfully to plan a military campaign by democratic procedure. As in strategy it would become inevitable to delegate the task to the experts.

Yet the difference is that, while the general who is put in charge of a campaign is given a single end to which, for the duration of the campaign, all the means under his control have to be exclusively devoted, there can be no such single goal given to the economic planner, and no similar limitation of the means imposed upon him. The general has not got to balance different independent aims against each other; there is for him only one supreme goal. But the ends of an economic plan, or of any part of it, cannot be defined apart from the particular plan. It is the essence of the economic problem that the making of an economic plan involves the choice between conflicting or

---

not be allowed to form an obstacle to the realization of socialism is even more plainly expressed: not only would a socialist government "take vast powers and legislate under them by ordinance and decree" and "suspend the classic formulae of normal opposition" but the "continuance of parliamentary government would depend on its [i.e., the Labour government's] possession of guarantees from the Conservative Party that its work of transformation would not be disrupted by repeal in the event of its defeat at the polls"!

As Professor Laski invokes the authority of the Donoughmore Committee, it may be worth recalling that Professor Laski was a member of that committee and presumably one of the authors of its report.

competing ends—different needs of different people. But which ends do so conflict, which will have to be sacrificed if we want to achieve certain others, in short, which are the alternatives between which we must choose, can only be known to those who know all the facts; and only they, the experts, are in a position to decide which of the different ends are to be given preference. It is inevitable that they should impose their scale of preferences on the community for which they plan.

This is not always clearly recognized, and delegation is usually justified by the technical character of the task. But this does not mean that only the technical detail is delegated, or even that the inability of parliaments to understand the technical detail is the root of the difficulty.[3] Alterations in the structure of civil law are no less technical and no more difficult to appreciate in all their implications; yet nobody has yet seriously suggested that legislation there should be delegated to a body of experts. The fact is that in these fields legislation does not go beyond general rules on which true majority agreement can be achieved, while in the direction of economic activity the interests to be reconciled are so divergent that no true agreement is likely to be reached in a democratic assembly.

It should be recognized, however, that it is not the delegation of lawmaking power as such which is so objectionable. To oppose delegation as such is to oppose a symptom instead of the cause and, as it may be a necessary result of other causes, to weaken the case. So long as the power that is delegated is merely the power to make general rules, there may be very good reasons why such rules should be laid down by local rather than by the central authority. The objectionable feature is that delegation is so often resorted to because the matter in hand cannot be regulated by general rules but only

[3] It is instructive in this connection briefly to refer to the government document in which in recent years these problems have been discussed. As long as thirteen years ago, that is before England finally abandoned economic liberalism, the process of delegating legislative powers had already been carried to a point where it was felt necessary to appoint a committee to investigate "what safeguards are desirable or necessary to secure the sovereignty of Law." In its report the Donoughmore Committee (*Report of the [Lord Chancellor's] Committee in Minister's Powers*, Cmd. 4060 [1932]) showed that even at that date Parliament had resorted "to the practice of wholesale and indiscriminate delegation" but regarded this (it was before we had really glanced into the totalitarian abyss!) as an inevitably and relatively innocuous development. And it is probably true that delegation as such need not be a danger to freedom. The interesting point is why delegation had become necessary on such a scale. First place among the causes enumerated in the report is given to the fact that "Parliament nowadays passes so many laws every year" and that "much of the detail is so technical as to be unsuitable for Parliamentary discussion." But if this were all there would be no reason why the detail should not be worked out *before* rather than after Parliament passes a law. What is probably in many cases a much more important reason why, "if Parliament were not willing to delegate law-making power, Parliament would be unable to pass the kind and quantity of legislation which public opinion requires" is innocently revealed in the little sentence that "many of the laws affect people's lives so closely that elasticity is essential"! What does this mean if not conferment of arbitrary power—power limited by no fixed principles and which in the opinion of Parliament cannot be limited by definite and unambiguous rules?

by the exercise of discretion in the decision of particular cases. In these instances delegation means that some authority is given power to make with the force of law what to all intents and purposes are arbitrary decisions (usually described as "judging the case on its merits").

The delegation of particular technical tasks to separate bodies, while a regular feature, is yet only the first step in the process whereby a democracy which embarks on planning progressively relinquishes its powers. The expedient of delegation cannot really remove the causes which make all the advocates of comprehensive planning so impatient with the impotence of democracy. The delegation of particular powers to separate agencies creates a new obstacle to the achievement of a single co-ordinated plan. Even if, by this expedient, a democracy should succeed in planning every sector of economic activity, it would still have to face the problem of integrating these separate plans into a unitary whole. Many separate plans do not make a planned whole—in fact, as the planners ought to be the first to admit, they may be worse than no plan. But the democratic legislature will long hesitate to relinquish the decisions on really vital issues, and so long as it does so it makes it impossible for anyone else to provide the comprehensive plan. Yet agreement that planning is necessary, together with the inability of democratic assemblies to produce a plan, will evoke stronger and stronger demands that the government or some single individual should be given powers to act on their own responsibility. The belief is becoming more and more widespread that, if things are to get done, the responsible authorities must be freed from the fetters of democratic procedure.

The cry for an economic dictator is a characteristic stage in the movement toward planning. It is now several years since one of the most acute of foreign students of England, the late Élie Halévy, suggested that, "if you take a composite photograph of Lord Eustace Percy, Sir Oswald Mosley, and Sir Stafford Cripps, I think you would find this common feature—you would find them all agreeing to say: 'We are living in economic chaos and we cannot get out of it except under some kind of dictatorial leadership.' " [4] The number of influential public men whose inclusion would not materially alter the features of the "composite photograph" has since grown considerably.

In Germany, even before Hitler came into power, the movement had already progressed much further. It is important to remember that, for some time before 1933, Germany had reached a stage in which it had, in effect, had to be governed dictatorially. Nobody could then doubt that for the time being democracy had broken down and that sincere democrats like Brüning were no more able to govern democratically than Schleicher or von Papen. Hitler did not have to destroy democracy; he merely took advantage of the decay of democracy and at the critical moment obtained the support of many to

---

[4] "Socialism and the Problems of Democratic Parliamentarism," *International Affairs*, XIII, 501.

whom, though they detested Hitler, he yet seemed the only man strong enough to get things done.

The argument by which the planners usually try to reconcile us with this development is that, so long as democracy retains ultimate control, the essentials of democracy are not affected. Thus Karl Mannheim writes:

"The only [sic] way in which a planned society differs from that of the nineteenth century is that more and more spheres of social life, and ultimately each and all of them, are subjected to state control. But if a few controls can be held in check by parliamentary sovereignty, so can many. . . . In a democratic state sovereignty can be boundlessly strengthened by plenary powers without renouncing democratic control." [5]

This belief overlooks a vital distinction. Parliament can, of course, control the execution of tasks where it can give definite directions, where it has first agreed on the aim and merely delegates the working-out of the detail. The situation is entirely different when the reason for the delegation is that there is no real agreement on the ends, when the body charged with the planning has to choose between ends of whose conflict parliament is not even aware, and when the most that can be done is to present to it a plan which has to be accepted or rejected as a whole. There may and probably will be criticism; but as no majority can agree on an alternative plan, and the parts objected to can almost always be represented as essential parts of the whole, it will remain quite ineffective. Parliamentary discussion may be retained as a useful safety valve and even more as a convenient medium through which the official answers to complaints are disseminated. It may even prevent some flagrant abuses and successfully insist on particular shortcomings being remedied. But it cannot direct. It will at best be reduced to choosing the persons who are to have practically absolute power. The whole system will tend toward that plebiscitarian dictatorship in which the head of the government is from time to time confirmed in his position by popular vote, but where he has all the powers at his command to make certain that the vote will go in the direction he desires.

It is the price of democracy that the possibilities of conscious control are restricted to the fields where true agreement exists and that in some fields things must be left to chance. But in a society which for its functioning depends on central planning this control cannot be made dependent on a majority's being able to agree; it will often be necessary that the will of a small minority be imposed upon the people, because this minority will be the largest group able to agree among themselves on the question at issue. Democratic government has worked successfully where, and so long as, the functions of government were, by a widely accepted creed, restricted to fields where agreement among a majority could be achieved by free discussion; and it is the great

[5] *Man and Society in an Age of Reconstruction* (1940), p. 340.

merit of the liberal creed that it reduced the range of subjects on which agreement was necessary to one on which it was likely to exist in a society of free men. It is now often said that democracy will not tolerate "capitalism." If "capitalism" means here a competitive system based on free disposal over private property, it is far more important to realize that only within this system is democracy possible. When it becomes dominated by a collectivist creed, democracy will inevitably destroy itself.

We have no intention, however, of making a fetish of democracy. It may well be true that our generation talks and thinks too much of democracy and too little of the values which it serves. It cannot be said of democracy, as Lord Acton truly said of liberty, that it "is not a means to a higher political end. It is itself the highest political end. It is not for the sake of a good public administration that it is required, but for the security in the pursuit of the highest objects of civil society, and of private life." Democracy is essentially a means, a utilitarian device for safeguarding internal peace and individual freedom. As such it is by no means infallible or certain. Nor must we forget that there has often been much more cultural and spiritual freedom under an autocratic rule than under some democracies—and it is at least conceivable that under the government of a very homogeneous and doctrinaire majority democratic government might be as oppressive as the worst dictatorship. Our point, however, is not that dictatorship must inevitably extirpate freedom but rather that planning leads to dictatorship because dictatorship is the most effective instrument of coercion and the enforcement of ideals and, as such, essential if central planning on a large scale is to be possible. The clash between planning and democracy arises simply from the fact that the latter is an obstacle to the suppression of freedom which the direction of economic activity requires. But in so far as democracy ceases to be a guaranty of individual freedom, it may well persist in some form under a totalitarian regime. A true "dictatorship of the proletariat," even if democratic in form, if it undertook centrally to direct the economic system, would probably destroy personal freedom as completely as any autocracy has ever done.

The fashionable concentration on democracy as the main value threatened is not without danger. It is largely responsible for the misleading and unfounded belief that, so long as the ultimate source of power is the will of the majority, the power cannot be arbitary. The false assurance which many people derive from this belief is an important cause of the general unawareness of the dangers which we face. There is no justification for the belief that, so long as power is conferred by democratic procedure, it cannot be arbitrary; the contrast suggested by this statement is altogether false: it is not the source but the limitation of power which prevents it from being arbitrary. Democratic control *may* prevent power from becoming arbitrary, but it does not do so by its mere existence. If democracy resolves on a task which necessarily involves the use of power which cannot be guided by fixed rules, it must become arbitrary power.

* * *

The power of the planner over our private lives would be no less complete if he chose not to exercise it by direct control of our consumption. Although a planned society would probably to some extent employ rationing and similar devices, the power of the planner over our private lives does not depend on this and would be hardly less effective if the consumer were nominally free to spend his income as he pleased. The source of this power over all consumption which in a planned society the authority would possess would be its control over production.

Our freedom of choice in a competitive society rests on the fact that, if one person refuses to satisfy our wishes, we can turn to another. But if we face a monopolist we are at his mercy. And an authority directing the whole economic system would be the most powerful monopolist conceivable. While we need probably not be afraid that such an authority would exploit this power in the manner in which a private monopolist would do so, while its purpose would presumably not be the extortion of maximum financial gain, it would have complete power to decide what we are to be given and on what terms. It would not only decide what commodities and services were to be available and in what quantities; it would be able to direct their distribution between districts and groups and could, if it wished, discriminate between persons to any degree it liked. If we remember why planning is advocated by most people, can there be much doubt that this power would be used for the ends of which the authority approves and to prevent the pursuits of ends which it disapproves?

The power conferred by the control of production and prices is almost unlimited. In a competitive society the prices we have to pay for a thing, the rate at which we can get one thing for another, depend on the quantities of other things of which by taking one, we deprive the other members of society. This price is not determined by the conscious will of anybody. And if one way of achieving our ends proves too expensive for us, we are free to try other ways. The obstacles in our path are not due to someone's disapproving of our ends but to the fact that the same means are also wanted elsewhere. In a directed economy, where the authority watches over the ends pursued, it is certain that it would use its powers to assist some ends and to prevent the realization of others. Not our own view, but somebody else's, of what we ought to like or dislike would determine what we should get. And since the authority would have the power to thwart any efforts to elude its guidance, it would control what we consume almost as effectively as if it directly told us how to spend our income.

* * *

CULTURAL AND CIVIL FREEDOMS

Barbara Wooton

IN THE background of any discussion of the compatibility of economic planning and cultural freedom, there lurks a fundamental philosophic issue. Is it in fact possible to plan for indeterminate cultural ends? For real cultural freedom demands not merely variety, but actual indeterminacy, of cultural ends. Such freedom is not achieved, unless economic planning sets people free to do and say things of their own choosing —things which are not known beforehand to, much less decided by, the planners. That would imply a fundamental difference between the political state and all other forms of association which involve organised action. The political state, where there is real cultural freedom, is no more than a convenient instrument for promoting the joint and several purposes of its members, and has no specific, determinate purpose of its own beyond this. A trade union exists to create better conditions of employment for its members, a church to promote the worship of God, a dramatic society to produce, if not to appreciate, drama; but the state exists—for what? To make it possible for men and women to live their own lives in their own way.

In the past, however, these states—groups of human beings organised politically in geographical units—have, on the one hand, found a determinate purpose in the defence of each against armed aggression by the others (or in the conduct of such armed aggression) and in activities incidental to this purpose, such as the cultivation of an imperialist and martial spirit; while, on the other hand, they have been content in large measure to leave other social ends to look after themselves. Things are changing, however, in more ways than one. In the first place, civilised people do not now take pride and pleasure in warfare, and find it increasingly difficult to defend military prowess as the proper and primary social purpose of political groups. In the second place, as our way of life grows more complicated, individuals within the state find it increasingly difficult to pursue their own ends satisfactorily without a great deal of help from the state itself. The second change leads to a demand for state planning; while the first creates a vacuum in the place of some determinate end for which to plan.

The right way to meet this situation is not, I think, to cast about for some

From Barbara Wooton, *Freedom Under Planning* (London: George Allen & Unwin Ltd., 1945), pp. 26–40, 139–44. All rights reserved. Reprinted by permission.

new social purpose with which to fill that vacuum. It is certainly tempting to do so, and many of the attempts to achieve integration through religious revivals or quasi-religious syntheses [1] (when they have any concrete meaning at all) are illustrations of the force of this temptation. Nevertheless this is, I submit, the wrong end at which to begin. It is wrong because of the two peculiarities which distinguish the state from all other forms of association—the fact that membership is compulsory, and the fact that the rules made by the state are backed up by physical force. An association with both these peculiarities cannot, by definition, both respect cultural freedom and pursue specific cultural ends. It cannot do both these things because minorities who reject these ends can neither defy the law nor resign their membership of the state by which that law is enforced: they therefore lose their cultural freedom. For instance, if Parliament should decide that the proper cultural purpose of this country is to exalt the Christian religion and to exterminate atheistic practices, it would be necessary to suppress all agnostic societies and publications, and to take steps to see that every child was taught the Christian doctrine and that every adult took his part in Christian worship. This is not cultural freedom for non-Christians. (If in the two preceding sentences the word "Marxist" is substituted for "Christian" we have a scarcely exaggerated description of the policy of the Soviet government in the early years of the Revolution.) There is, moreover, no parallel to this power in any form of association other than the political state; for no other society which adopted policies or principles of which even a minority of its members disapproved could prevent those members from resigning their membership, or compel their compliance by law. I think it is still true in this country, though not perhaps as securely true as might be wished, that this incompatibility of freedom with the pursuit of specific ends by the political state is appreciated, so far as religious freedom is concerned. The power of the state is not therefore used, as it was for instance used at one time in Russia, to compel compliance with official doctrine. What we have to do is to accept this as a *general* truth, applicable to cultural

---

[1] A good example is to be found in Mr. J. B. Coates' book *A Common Faith*. Mr. Coates seems to have got into a proper muddle. On p. 53 he believes that "the liberal *states* will find themselves obliged, by the necessities of the objective situation if by no other reason, to *plan the cultural* and *psychological* as well as the political and economic aspects of their *national* life." They will in consequence "need to bring under a unified control the two functions performed in the past by Church and state." I take this to mean that the liberal state will have to adopt a definite system of moral and cultural values—the "new synthesis" which Mr. Coates is concerned to create in our divided societies. But on p. 55 we read "The danger of the wrong kind of social control being set up over the minds of men everywhere is a very grave one, for *a cultural synthesis imposed by the state* will always tend to be contrary to man's truest insight." (Italics mine throughout).

Which is it to be? We cannot have it both ways. Either the state, which is a force-controlling organization, imposes a synthesis (in the sense of a system of moral and cultural values) or it doesn't. If it does, there is no cultural freedom. Mr. Coates and all the would-be democrats who sigh after the glories of totalitarian achievement overlook the fundamental distinction that while conformity can be imposed, agreement cannot.

freedoms *generally*. Voluntary societies can and should commit themselves to specific cultural ends: compulsory societies should not.

The problem of planning for freedom thus resolves itself into the problem of determinate planning for indeterminate cultural ends. Stated thus it sounds insoluble. Once again, however, a problem which is theoretically insoluble in the limiting case, turns out to be quite tractable in the concrete form in which it is likely to crop up in practice. We need not despair of the possibility of combining useful planning and cultural freedom, provided that certain conditions are observed.

The first condition is the obvious one that such planning must know where to stop. There are few, if any, cultural freedoms which can be enjoyed in such a vacuum that their exercise makes no demands whatever on the productive resources of the community. It follows that determination of economic priorities, carried to the ultimate limit, would prohibit cultural freedom. Freedom of speech, for example, is not the same thing as freedom of soliloquy. If speech is to be more than soliloquy, there must be an audience to hear what is said, or read what is written. That means a building in which an audience can be gathered, or a microphone to reach them in their own homes, or paper on which to write what they can read. Similarly, even the most austere forms of religious worship usually require a building in which they may be conducted, while many rituals demand organs, books, censers, candles, altar cloths. It follows that any government with absolute power to plan the use of the community's resources down to the last detail can make *effective* freedom of speech or of worship impossible for any body, person, or society, of whom it disapproves, merely by withholding such essential materials.

"Can," however, is not in this context, and must not be, the same word as "will." Admittedly it is possible for a state authority responsible for planning the output of the building industry to assign halls to the League of the Godless and to refuse them to the churches; or *vice versa*. But it is equally possible to make suitable buildings available for all denominations on the same terms. As Dr. Mannheim has remarked, it is possible to "co-ordinate the time tables of the different railway lines without controlling the topics of conversation inside the carriages." [2]

No one can lay down, in general terms, the exact limitation on the scope of economic planning which the preservation of cultural freedom demands. But the examples just given illustrate the kind of distinction which would need to be drawn in practice; and they serve to show the fallacy of the assumption that extensive economic planning is *inherently* synonymous with uncompromising cultural conformity. As a matter of fact, the policy of the Soviet Union in regard to religious freedom has actually undergone important changes since the early days of the Revolution. Religious freedom has been

[2] *Diagnosis of Our Time*, p. 103.

increased without relaxation of state determination of economic priorities. This at least proves that alternative courses are possible.

It is therefore not enough for Professor Hayek to assert (quite correctly) that "the power of the planner over our private lives" rests on his power over production.[3] It does. But power can be exercised in different ways and in different degrees. All extensions of power involve certain risks: some offer advantages also. If the advantages did not sometimes outweigh the risks, complete anarchy would be preferable to any government. In any particular instance it is necessary to weigh the risks against the possible advantages and to decide in the light of this balance. The argument is not advanced by prejudging the issue in favour of the risks. To condemn all economic planning on the ground that if carried to extremes it *can* be used to nullify all freedom of expression is of a piece with forbidding innocent activities on the ground that in certain circumstances they would be anti-social. I have heard it argued, for example, that it is, in all circumstances, wrong to play tennis or golf on Sundays, since, in certain conditions, to do so might disturb a neighbour's devotions, or deprive the caddy of his Sabbath rest. It would be safer to say that Sunday games are wrong because they offend against the will of God: for this argument has at least the advantage of being incapable of disproof. In terms of any rational utilitarian ethic, these all-or-nothing arguments are equally indefensible, whether applied to economic planning or to Sabbatarian principles.

Somewhat similar is the argument which contends that cultural freedom and economic planning are incompatible since an economic plan and a cultural pattern are, for practical purposes, identical. If the term "cultural" is defined sufficiently widely, this is certainly true in part; but there is no reason why it should be wholly true, unless we perversely wish to make it so. Moreover, the points at which cultural freedom is unavoidably restricted by an economic plan are also the points at which it would be restricted in the absence of any such plan. If cultural liberty means individual freedom to determine the whole way of life, we are bound to admit that this freedom must be in great measure foregone in any large and complex society. An example should make the point clear. The size of cities has an important influence on the average citizen's ability to spend life as he pleases. In very large cities (arranged as such cities are now) it is, to mention only one thing, necessary for many to spend much time in travelling. But if you happen to be one of those who wishes, say, that London were a smaller city, you are individually powerless to bring this about. You *may* be able to go and live in a smaller place, Letchworth for example: but living in Letchworth is not the same thing as living in a smaller London. The degree of urbanisation of the community, with all the limitations on one's

[3] *The Road to Serfdom*, p. 69.

personal freedom which that implies, has for practical purposes to be accepted by the ordinary individual.

It is important, however, to repeat that this restriction has nothing to do with economic planning. The size and shape of most of our present cities are, at present, only in a very small degree the result of the conscious determination of economic priorities. London and Liverpool have not been made: they have happened. But the individual is not, on that account, the more able to modify them to suit his own taste. All that he can do to that end is himself to live out-side their boundaries. In that way, by lowering the demand for urban accom-modation he casts his vote, for what it is worth (in what Professor Mises has called the ballot-box of the market place), against the growth of cities. But it is at best a vote in a very large and undemocratic constituency. Similarly, in cases where the size of towns is consciously determined as a matter of deliberate policy he can, in a democratic society, exercise some tiny weight of opinion. It is a mat-ter for argument, in the light of the particular circumstances of particular cases, whether planning increases or diminishes the freedom of the individual to shape his own cultural pattern in such matters as this. Whichever way the argument goes, however, two things are clear. First, so long as we live in large and complex communities, this freedom is unavoidably very narrowly restricted, whatever method is used for determining economic priorities. And second, none of this alters the fact that there is a world of difference between a society in which people are allowed to say what they please and one in which they are not, even though the externals of life in both cases may be much the same, people living in the same sort of cities and following even much the same daily routine. Moscow, Berlin, New York, Mexico City and London begin to look remarkably alike: the quality of life to be lived in each of them remains different.

It is, therefore, nonsense to assert that comprehensive economic planning *cannot* stop short of the point at which it destroys all cultural freedom. The critical issue is this business of knowing where to stop. While, as has been said, there can be no general answer to this question, there are one or two things that are worth remembering in this context. For instance, the temptation to exact unnecessary cultural uniformity is always likely to be strong amongst those men and women who are personally responsible for making the decisions which constitute economic planning. It will be strong because it is, generally speaking, easier to plan for uniformity than for diversity. It will be strong because people who arrive at positions of power are, inevitably, people who enjoy the exercise of power. This is, of course, as true of the powerful whose intentions are good as of those whose designs are evil. Both are likely to find it more satisfying that people should do what those in authority want them to do or think that they should do, rather than what they themselves want to do.

In practice this means that the lengths to which economic planning can safely be carried depend on a number of intangibles such as the quality of the planners (a matter to be dealt with in Chapter X), and the general social conditions of the community in which it is conducted. The critical fields are those of the press, broadcasting, education and any other powerful determinants of public opinion. In the case of education, for example, British and Scandinavian experience at least has already demonstrated that a considerable degree of cultural diversity is possible within a system in which most of the schools are owned, and the teachers paid, by public bodies. The same experience has also shown that this freedom has its limits; but there is no reason to suppose that these limits are fixed for all time, and they are certainly not the same in all countries. It is in the light of considerations like this that one must decide on merits in each instance whether it is expedient to retain a privately-owned press, privately-owned schools, or to permit a public monopoly in broadcasting. These are not so much questions of principle as of expediency. They are also specialist questions which need much fuller discussion than I can give them here. I would only hazard the opinions that it is doubtful whether the time has come in this country when educational freedom is sufficiently secure for a complete state monopoly (which would involve, among other things, the abolition or transfer to public ownership of all the present "progressive schools") to be enthusiastically advocated; and that the evils of a privately-owned press could be greatly diminished by control of profits and advertising revenue.

The second condition of successful economic planning for indeterminate cultural ends is that the planners should show a nice discrimination in their methods. There has been some muddled thinking here amongst democrats who have wistfully observed the success of totalitarian régimes in putting over totalitarian ideologies; and who long to enlist some of the same techniques in the cause of democracy. The answer is that many of these techniques are simply not applicable to the promotion of indeterminate ends. The hysterical dramatisation of politics, in which the Nazis have specialised, is a terrifyingly powerful instrument for the creation of a mass mind bent on uniformity. Similar methods cannot, in the nature of things, be employed in the service of diversity and freedom. The progressive political parties in this country seem to be in a great state of conflict about all this. Covetous of the success of their enemies, they are tempted to dabble in emotional propaganda appealing to motives that are both irrational and irrelevant to the issues to be decided. Their experiments in this field range from the use of party colours to well-staged processions and pageants. On the whole, however, the Left, in this country, does these things badly. It does them badly because it does them half-heartedly; and it is half-hearted because it is more than half aware of their fundamental incompatibility with the very freedoms in whose cause they are enlisted. This, and not only lack of money, is the reason why the Left in this country is generally speaking less efficient at this sort of game than the Right. Irrational propaganda can, within limits, be used to create opinion in favour of ends chosen by the propagandists: it cannot, in the nature of things, be successful in the service of ends to be selected by those to whom the propaganda is directed. The nineteenth century thinkers, whom it is now fashionable to decry, were consistent and right in their assumption that political democracy implies a rational approach to politics. They were wrong only in exaggerating the actual rationalism of the actual electorate. If it should unhappily prove true that men and women generally cannot ever attain the degree of rationality which political democracy demands, the answer would not be that an up-to-date democracy should treat them as the irrational creatures that they are. The answer would be that a free democratic society is impossible. There are no short cuts to freedom.

Of all our liberties those that are least likely to be threatened by economic planning are the civil rights concerned with the method of enforcement of the law, and the position of the actual or supposed lawbreaker. Even Professor Hayek does not specifically suggest that these are in danger. Of course any large extension of the functions of government necessarily multiplies the number of possible offences against laws and regulations. Everybody is well aware of this from wartime experience: indeed there must be few, even of the most conscientious citizens, who have not, advertently or inadvertently, been guilty of breaking some war-time regulation. This multiplication of the possible occasions of offence is, however, a quite different matter from the procedure adopted to ensure that the law is kept, or the methods of dealing with offenders. There is no logical connection between state regulation of the output of mining or agriculture or any or all industries on the one hand, and the abolition of *habeas corpus* or of trial by jury, or the establishment of a gestapo, on the other. Here again, war-time experience in Britain is, on the whole, comforting. It is true that a serious breach in these civil rights has been made by the Home Secretary's power under Defence Regulation 18b to imprison without charge or trial persons who, in his personal opinion, ought to be incarcerated: but it is also true, both that this power has been sparingly exercised, and that in the stresses of war there may be occasions for suspicion which have nothing whatever to do with state control of economic priorities. I am not arguing that, even so, the public safety might not have been adequately safeguarded without use of these powers. But even the undoubted wrong inflicted on a certain number of entirely harmless and innocent individuals does not alter the fact that such treatment is still quite exceptional. The vast bulk of offences against all the new, as well as the old, laws are dealt with through the ordinary courts and with such protections as these afford. These protections are not perhaps in practice in every case as complete as they appear on paper. Nevertheless they are real. Under our present war-time laws a man can be imprisoned for inciting others to strike (outside a Trade Union meeting), for bad timekeeping on essential work, or for dealing on the black market. For these and for the hundreds of other offences like them the machinery of 18b is not employed, any more than it is used for dealing with thieves and motoring offenders or persons suspected of other pre-war crimes. And it is still true in this country that a man cannot disappear overnight, without any charge being preferred against him, and never be heard of again. Words like totalitarian and Fascism are loosely used: such use should not be allowed to obscure the fact that we are not, in this sense, totalitarian. And we have established as a matter of experienced fact that, even under the stresses of war, comprehensive economic planning is possible without recourse to such totalitarianisms.

This experience is the more remarkable since the multiplication of offences due to economic planning, or to other war-time exigencies (such as blackout) creates an undoubted temptation to short-circuit the slow and cumbrous methods of British justice. A certain amount of nibbling at the edges of civil freedom has certainly taken place as a result of this temptation. It has, for instance, been argued that witnesses who may be engaged on war work ought not to be brought to court in cases where it is anticipated that a plea of guilty will probably make their attendance unnecessary. This means that if, in fact, a plea of not guilty is entered, a case must be adjourned for these witnesses to be called. The mere fact that such an adjournment will be necessary is in itself an inducement to many defendants to plead guilty; when you are before the courts (especially on charges that are not very serious) the desire to be over and done with it often prevails over everything else. This is certainly a danger with young people; and the practice in some juvenile courts of not calling witnesses for the prosecution at a first hearing in war-time has been a matter of concern to magistrates. Such modifications of judicial practice are a warning; but not more. Police and other public officials are always open to temptation to save their own time and trouble at the expense of other people's freedom. A part, though by no means all, of the law's delays are justified as safeguards against this temptation. If economic planning increases the pressure on the courts, as it well may, the remedy is twofold. First, we should provide judicial machinery adequate to meet any demands made upon it without sacrificing the established defences of freedom; and, second, we should watch and, if necessary, strengthen those defences. The inference here from war to peace conditions is, as often, invalid, for the reason that in war the value of time is disproportionately high.

State economic planning does not, in short, alter the fact that power will be used by cruel and tyrannous people in one way, and by the humane and the lovers of liberty in another. We are thus brought back to the distinction between "can" and "will." Just as the power of the state *can* be used to destroy all cultural freedom, so also it *can* be directed against every kind of civil freedom. Whether it *will* be used in either or both of these ways depends on how far political power is in practice absolute, and what kind of people exercise that power for what kind of ends. The judicial species of civil freedom in particular—that is, fundamentally, freedom from arbitrary punishment—is only *necessarily* threatened by economic planning if it is true that a government which takes responsibility for economic decisions is for some reason *necessarily* composed of more dictatorial people than one which leaves these matters alone. In a chapter which carries the question-begging title: *Why the Worst Get on Top,* Professor Hayek has attempted to establish that this is probable. Since this is essentially a question of the quality of plans and planners his argument is dealt with in Chapter X.[4]

The whole question of the impact of economic planning upon both cultural and civil freedoms has been greatly confused by ill-considered inferences from the experience of the U.S.S.R. That country offers the one and only example of really comprehensive economic planning in time of peace which the world has yet seen. Throughout this experiment the degree of both civil and cultural freedom permitted to Soviet citizens has been intolerably low by the standards which the British uphold for themselves (though not everywhere for their Empire). The Soviet plans, have, however, from the beginning, been avowedly devoted to promotion of specific cultural ends: first, the promulgation of Marxist-Leninist doctrine, then, in later years, the increase in the military strength and prestige of the Soviet people. There have indeed been changes from time to time: the expulsion of Trotsky from the ranks of the elect, for instance, involved certain revisions in official doctrine. Down to 1927 the Soviet citizen was free to speak of Trotsky in terms of the highest admiration, but enjoyed no corresponding freedom to denounce him: after that date these freedoms and unfreedoms changed places. Again, there have been changes, to which reference has already been made, in the degree of religious freedom permitted. There seems also to have been a decided shift of emphasis, no doubt associated with the growing importance attached to military considerations, away from traditional socialist internationalism towards a much more conventional type of nationalistic patriotism. But throughout the twenty-seven years since the revolution there have always been plenty of opinions which no Soviet citizen could safely express. The retort commonly offered by fanatical Soviet admirers, that no Soviet citizen ever wishes to say anything but what the law permits, is a poor defence either of freedom or of the Soviet authorities. It is clear that up till now the Soviet government does not conceive its task as a matter of economic planning for indeterminate ends. That being so, one cannot reasonably expect that Soviet experience will throw any great light on the practicability of such a project.

As for civil liberties, let us remember the background. The Soviet system was begotten and born in the violence of revolution and civil war. It was the child, on the one side, of the Tsarist Empire, and on the other of an expressly anti-democratic Marxist policy. In a country accustomed to secret police, political

---

[4] Of course if Professor Hayek's thesis is right, this distinction between the technique of planning and the contents of particular plans loses all significance. If all plans are necessarily made by bad people for bad ends, then any discussion of the impact of good plans upon personal freedoms must be ludicrously academic. In other words the first nine chapters of this book become irrelevant, and Chapter X wrong.

imprisonment and assassination, the new Government openly set out to establish a particular type of dictatorship. In these conditions, civil liberties, as we understand them, could not be destroyed by the revolution, since they were not there to destroy. Between the introduction of the revised constitution of 1936 and the German invasion of Russia there was indeed a good deal of talk about relaxation of some of the rigours of the dictatorship, especially in the direction of greater political freedom. No one, however, who reads the Soviet authorities' own enthusiastic accounts of the work of their political prisoners, or who has personally known men and women whose relatives disappeared overnight in the great purges, or who has read press summaries of the Moscow trials of the nineteen-thirties, with their fervent denunciations of the treachery of defendants whose cases were still *sub judice*—no one who has given a moment's attention to any of this evidence can pretend that the Soviet range of civil liberties is comparable with that to which we are accustomed in this country. Equally, however, in the light of the declared objectives of the Soviet government, no one can conclude in the light of this experience that the attempt to combine civil liberty and economic planning has been tried and has failed.

Inferences from the Soviet experiment are likely to crop up repeatedly, whatever the particular liberties that may be under discussion. Just as the Soviet plans have been carried out against a certain civil and cultural background, so also their execution has made use of certain economic compulsions, or restrictions on economic liberties which are highly prized elsewhere. It may be useful, therefore, to summarise here what would appear in every case to be the limits of safe inference from Russian practice. In the first place, Soviet experience can be illuminating when there have from time to time been changes in the quantity or quality of liberty allowed under that régime. In such cases we learn, at the least, that it is *possible* to do things in more ways than one, and we may, in addition, have material for instructive comparisons. Second, Soviet experience is useful in so far as it gives positive evidence of the compatibility of planning with particular freedoms. Positive evidence proves that a thing can be done: negative evidence not that it cannot, but that it has not. Thus positive evidence from the U.S.S.R. has established that it is possible to plan at least up to the Soviet level of efficiency in time of peace without recourse to universal industrial conscription. Negative evidence, such as the fact that there are no legal opposition parties in the U.S.S.R., proves nothing except that there are no legal opposition parties in the U.S.S.R.

* * *

. . . I have tried to show that there is nothing in the conscious planning of economic priorities which is inherently incompatible with the freedoms which mean most to the contemporary Englishman or American. Civil liberties are quite unaffected. We can, if we wish, deliberately plan so as to give the fullest possible scope for the pursuit by individuals and social groups of cultural ends which are in no way state determined. The consumer can enjoy the pleasure of comparing prices and qualities, and spending money that is freely available to the limit of his income, just as and when he thinks fit. Industrial direction and industrial conscription are unnecessary. Planning need not even be the death-warrant of all private enterprise; and it is certainly not the passport of political dictatorship. It is true (and indeed obvious) that the *same* part of the economic pattern cannot both be deliberately planned, and left to emerge as the result of the unco-ordinated actions of thousands of consumers. But consumers' sovereignty, in any meaningful and defensible sense, seems to be quite unattainable and certainly never to have been attained outside the covers of an academic textbook; and there is the less cause for tears on this account, inasmuch as no ordinary consumer would be conscious whether he enjoyed that sovereignty or not. It is true also that the preservation of free choice of employment under planning would be impossible if wages were to be settled by a private tug-of-war between employers and employed, in which each party exploited its full economic strength. But against this must be set the fact that free choice of employment will never be a reality without planning, since legal freedom of choice is a mockery if economic pressure compels the chooser to accept the first available job. The right of effective choice of employment is the one great freedom which the pre-war Englishman, or American, or Continental European outside Russia, has never enjoyed. Planning could give it to him.

A happy and fruitful marriage between freedom and planning can, in short, be arranged. That leaves us with the problem (which we have so far taken as solved) of translating "can" into "will." This is a problem of social and political psychology. Success or failure turns on the behaviour of the actual men and women who have the responsibility of planning: on the measure in which positions of power are filled by men and women who care for the freedom of others and (what is not less important) in whom this love of liberty is not subsequently stifled by the habit of authority. Here, of course, there can be no secure guarantee. All the old clichés are just as true as ever they were—power still corrupts, absolute power still corrupts absolutely, and eternal vigilance is just as much the price of liberty as ever it was. The prospect for freedom is indeed bright only where these truths are fully appreciated and constantly in mind. The practical question is how best to apply these age-long lessons of experience to the modern world.

If we are to accept Professor Hayek's view that economic planning inevitably brings the worst to the top, we may as well throw up the sponge altogether. His arguments in support of this thesis are, however, happily inconclusive and unconvincing. Three main reasons are given for his fears. The first rests on the argument that "in general the higher the education and intelligence of individuals becomes, the more their views and tastes are differentiated and the less likely they are to agree on a particular hierarchy of values." From this proposition derives the corollary that a "high degree of uniformity and similarity of outlook" will only be found in "the regions of lower moral and intellectual standards." Any group strong enough to impose their values on all the rest will, accordingly, never consist of "those with highly differentiated and developed tastes." In the second place, the number of those whose "uncomplicated and primitive instincts happen to be very similar" is unlikely to be sufficient to give a "potential dictator" all the support that he needs. It therefore becomes necessary for the dictator to convert others to the "same simple creed"; and his readiest converts will be found amongst "the docile and the gullible" who have no strong convictions of their own and whose "passions and emotions are readily aroused." [5]

The force of both these arguments is clearly contingent on the validity of Professor Hayek's further thesis that economic planning necessarily implies cultural uniformity and political dictatorship. They are framed all along in terms of the methods by which a *dictator* must win support in order to impose a uniform cultural pattern. If, however (as has been argued in Chapters II and IX of this book) it is perfectly possible for a free democracy to plan for cultural diversity, then these particular fears are irrelevant to the only society in which we are interested. Even that, however, is not the only answer. For it is by no means certain that what we have called the "area of common agreement" necessarily relates only to the "lower moral values." There seems to be a double confusion in Professor Hayek's statement that "the largest group of people whose values are very similar are the people with low standards." On the one hand high moral value appears to be here confused with intellectual complexity. Obviously, more people will agree to intellectually simple propositions than to those which can only be grasped by sustained mental effort; but this has nothing to do with morals. On the other hand, moral values that are "low" in the sense that they are *elementary* seem to be confused with those that are low in the sense that they are *base*. Agreement on certain *elementary* moral values, *e.g.* (apart from the special circumstances of war), on respect for human life generally and for the lives of children in particular—is unquestionably widespread. Is this to be dismissed as a "low" moral standard? A public duty to protect men and women from unnecessary danger (as by factory legislation [6]), and to promote the health of mothers and children (as by a service of infant welfare clinics) is no longer disputed. Admittedly, the prevailing ethic in these and other matters falls short of that set for themselves by the most morally sensitive and unselfish members of the community. But this is no argument against giving practical effect to the more elementary moral standards attained by more ordinary folk. To suggest otherwise is to imply that private virtue cannot surpass

[5] *The Road to Serfdom*, pp. 102, 103.
[6] Professor Hayek himself does not quarrel with factory legislation. *The Road to Serfdom*, p. 60.

the prevailing level of public duty. That is evident nonsense. The obligation to comply with minimal factory legislation has never prevented public-spirited employers from providing amenities far beyond the requirements of any Act of Parliament. Nor have exceptional men and women ceased to lead lives of outstanding kindliness and generosity merely because we are all now compelled to contribute something to the support of the sick, the unemployed and the aged. If the many cannot reach the standards of the few, there is no inherent law of planning by which the few *must* be dragged to the level of the many. In this country the standard of public morality has been slowly rising for at least three generations, as the higher standards of the few have become the accepted values of the many. In Nazi Germany the worst got to the top all right. The one experience is just as valid as the other.

Professor Hayek's third reason for expecting the scum to come to the top is that "it seems to be almost a law of human nature that it is easier for people to agree on a negative programme, on the hatred of an enemy, on the envy of those better off, than on any positive task ... The enemy, whether he be internal like the Jew or the Kulak, or external, seems to be an indispensable requisite in the armoury of a totalitarian leader." [7] The last sentence needs no further commentary, since it again implies the identification of planning and totalitarianism which this book is concerned throughout to dispute; though even so, we might question the logic which argues that the worst must come to the top from the way in which they behave, after they have got there.

The main substance of this final argument contains a useful caution, but is not itself conclusive. Certainly it is a common experience, not confined to totalitarian régimes, that people exert themselves more willingly, and co-operate better, in response to appeals to fight an enemy rather than in simply helping one another. It may be prudent for the constructive planner to make some concessions on this account—to march under the banner of war on want, for instance, rather than to sing the praises of a world of plenty. But these are relatively minor issues. The root of the matter is that mere demonstration that the negative and destructive appeal is easy is no proof either that it is the only appeal possible, or that it must in all circumstances prevail. At the most the defeatist can prophesy that time will show that destruction always wins. Time has not shown this yet. But there is a challenge here that the constructive planner would do well to meet with care and courage.

If this is all the evidence, there seems hardly better case for taking for granted that planning will bring the worst to the top than for the opposite assumption that the seats of office will be filled with angels. Our rulers are a mixed lot. Hitler, Chiang Kai-Shek, Roosevelt, Churchill, Stalin, Mustapha Kemal, Hansson, Alcazar, Cardenas, Blum, are all men who have held high political office in recent years. No obvious correlation is apparent between their

[7] *The Road to Serfdom*, p. 103.

merits (or those of their colleagues) as rulers, and the degree of economic planning for which their Governments were responsible. In these conditions the rational person will treat the problem as an open one, capable of better or worse solution according as we are successful, or unsuccessful, in creating the conditions which favour the rise to power of the wise and public-spirited and the preservation of their wisdom and public spirit against the corruptions of office.

* * *

THE APPEAL OF COMMUNISM

Barbara Ward

* * *

COMMUNISM, IN short, is the tragedy of ideas working free from the reasonable restraint of fact. In Marx's own day, its entire analysis and strategy were based upon the first phase of capitalist accumulation—a grim period in any society. In the Leninist aftermath, its doctrines were fashioned in the last phase of Western colonialism. Today, both phases are a matter of history. Western capitalism has evolved far beyond its painful beginnings. Western imperialism is being liquidated more rapidly—and on the whole more peacefully—than any comparable dominion in the human record. But Communism keeps pounding along, repeating the same slogans and proclaiming the same myths as though the whole march of events had been arrested at the moment at which Marx and then Lenin turned a baleful eye on Western society. The gap between ideology and fact thus grows wider every hour, and like all demonstrations of unreality, it grows more dangerous. Unanchored in anything save power, fear, ambition, and fantasy, who can say to what risks and follies it may not seduce the leaders of the Communist world?

How, then, has an order of ideas, a doctrine, an ideology patently at variance with the facts contrived to become one of the greatest revolutionary forces ever known to man? The answer, I believe, has very little to do with Communist orthodoxy but everything to do with the concrete experience of the Soviet

Reprinted from *Five Ideas that Change the World* by Barbara Ward. By permission of W. W. Norton & Company, Inc. Copyright © 1959 by W. W. Norton & Company, Inc.

state. In 1914, Russia was about to go through the "sound barrier" of modern capitalism. The fearsome privations and turmoil of early industrialism still lay heavily on the country, and the degree of capital accumulation was not yet sufficient to transform industrialization from an iron penance for all save the few to a means of greater prosperity for everyone.

The First World War ruined what had been begun. By 1917, the whole fragile structure of Czarist Russia, caught between a dying and an unborn order of society, collapsed. The universal confusion gave Lenin and his determined Bolshevik minority the opportunity to seize power. Then they found themselves in charge of a vast country but with no doctrines that seemed to apply. Marx had expected revolution to occur only when a full-scale industrial apparatus, created by the bourgeoisie, was already in being. None existed in Russia in 1918. The Bolsheviks tried pure Communism for a time, putting workers in charge of factories. It did not work. To keep some feeble pulse stirring in the country Lenin had to restore a measure of free enterprise under his New Economic Policy, and I think one can safely say that if Russian policy had advanced no further than the confusions of its first decade, we should have heard little of Communism as a worldwide force.

Stalin's contribution was the forced-draft industrialization of Russia. He combined two traditions—the industrial experience and techniques worked out under private enterprise in the West and the traditional "Asian method of production" based upon centralized control, state planning, and a vast bureaucracy. Under such stringent political control, there seemed no limit to the amount of saving that could be shorn from the people. The thirties were a time of bloody oppression and misery for millions of Russians. But the basis of a vast industrial apparatus was laid—and laid in time to resist the Nazi invasion.

Nor was it simply a physical achievement. Communism provided the element of zeal, discipline, and almost Puritanical fervor which had distinguished the earlier Calvinist attitude toward the creation of wealth. In the great drive to modernize the country, no resources—either human or material—were neglected. Education was made universal, the curriculum redesigned for modern scientific society; able children were forced forward up the ladder of learning, the university became the entry to the new elite.

For thousands of workers, for the ignorant peasants coming in from the countryside, for the bewildered tribesmen of Uzbekistan or Khirgizia, the new industrial world was as alien and hideous as the worst slum in Glascow or Pittsburgh. According to one estimate, as many workers were killed in the building of Magnitogorsk as in the Battle of the Marne. But for their children there was the chance for a new existence, and by clearing away the old aristocratic Czarist superstructure, the Communist leaders had thrown open these chances to more people than had any previous way of life.

The appeal of Communism is not so much its dialectic or its metaphysics— save to a minute group of intellectuals in search of a new faith—but its ability to carry backward countries speedily through the tremendous crisis of modernization. It offers a successful pattern of industrial saving and it provides the drive and discipline without which saving, particularly in poor countries, cannot be achieved. It also promises that the fruits of the transformation will ultimately be enjoyed "by each according to his need."

This last promise cannot yet be judged. Those who control the means of production—whether they are capitalists or bureaucrats—tend to reward themselves rather more handsomely than the mass of the people. Certainly, the gap between the Commissar and the day laborer in Russia is greater than between the average American manager and trade unionist. But compared with the gulf between rich and poor customary in preindustrial society, the results of Communism already show it to be an instrument of radical justice as well as of technical innovation. We should not forget that Marx, for all his scientific jargon, was a prophet in the great Hebrew tradition, putting down the mighty from their seats and exalting them of low degree. In the misery and confusion of our present worldwide economic revolution, there are millions who will listen to his prophetic promises of justice who never heard of the dialectic and would not recognize a synthesis if they saw one.

It is not, therefore, difficult to grasp the appeal of Communism to backward areas of the world, to lands still living in misery and economic stagnation, plagued by ambitions toward a better lot, restrained by the traditions of preindustrial society and the authority of older modes of leadership. In China, as we have seen, the wreck of the old Manchu system was followed by forty years of almost continuous war, during which the industrial transformation of society could hardly be carried through under middle-class leadership on the Western model, weakened as it was by inflation and by its association with "colonial" foreign capital. Communism was therefore able to repeat the Bolshevik tactic. It based itself on peasant discontent in a country sickened with war and destruction and, once in power, began to thrust through, with comparable rigor, the total modernization of the economy.

Must we, then, assume that the driving vigors and simplicities of Communism offer the future pattern of modernization and that, at least outside the older industrial West, we face in Communism "the wave of the future"? There are, I believe, solid grounds for believing that the future is not so rigidly determined. Russia and China are great powers, the greatest powers in numbers and soon perhaps in resources that the world has seen. Communism in their powerful system does not entail being subjugated to anyone else, does not, in short, entail imperialism. But the fate of Eastern Europe suggests that Communism for smaller powers carries no such guarantee of independence and elbow room.

I do not myself believe that imperialism at this late day is going to become more attractive simply by calling itself "international proletarian solidarity." Hungary stands as the tragic proof that national independence and international Communism are not yet compatible. I suggest that this lesson is not lost on the nationalist leaders around the world who are supposed to be preparing Communism's advance.

Again, I do not believe that Communism as a system has yet shown us that it can do more than drive societies at breakneck speed through the "sound barrier" of modernization. But out on the other side, a thousand problems remain—above all, the problem of an economy flexible enough and sensitive enough to provide ordinary people with the things they really want. For this, the market economy is a much better instrument than bureaucratic planning. Yet one may question whether the Communists will dare risk the step of making the consumer supreme, for this change might also enhance his position as a voter. How much choice can you admit economically without awkward questions of political choice arising too?

And here we touch on what, surely, remains the greatest failure and potential weakness of Communism. It is politically inflexible. It enshrines the principle of despotic authority in a world now shot through with the dreams, hopes, and experiences of free government. You cannot cancel this pressure and this ferment, any more than you can turn imperialism into something else by inventing new names for it. And this failure to confront the realities of politics has been, I believe, the fundamental flaw in Marx's thought from the very first hour.

He dismissed as irrelevant trappings the political traditions of Western life— the rule of law, constitutional practice, the vote, supremacy of parliament, the hard-won rights and liberties of the individual. But these were the means whereby Western industrial society eased itself through the crises of early industrialism, sloughed off its colonial past and began, by trial and error and innovation and experiment, to turn industrialism into an instrument of well-being for more and more of its citizens while leaving them to enjoy the supreme good of individual rights and ordered liberty.

Communism misunderstands totally the central problem of power. By relying on such puerile fantasies as the "withering away of the state," it has allowed a concentration of political and economic power to come about in the Communist state which goes even beyond the oriental tyrannies that are its model. Power still corrupts; absolute power still corrupts absolutely, and Khrushchev's recital of Stalin's iniquities at the 20th Party Congress was only one more dreary record of the despot's traditional cruelties and crimes.

Nor is it only the domestic community which bears the terrible risks and penalties of unfettered power. The Government which respects no limits on its internal authority tends to be equally lawless in its external relations. The Soviet and Chinese governments, for all their internationalist protestations, stand firm on the principle of unlimited sovereignty and state power. And they do so in the atomic age when the unbridled right of all states to do exactly what they wish can lead inexorably to the holocaust that destroys them all.

The Cold War: Questioning the Obvious Approaches to an Understanding

Since the Potsdam Conference of 1945 and the indefinite postponement of a peace treaty with Germany at the Paris Peace Conference of 1946, the West and Russia have been in a "cold war." Its main battle line has been the divided city of Berlin, but it has spread to every part of the world where a revolutionary situation or a power vacuum exists. It has produced its share of "freezes" in such forms as the notorious Berlin wall, the presence of Soviet missiles and military forces in Cuba, and the United States blockade of that island.

On the other hand, there have been "thaws," such as an increase in cultural exchanges between Russia and the West and visits by groups of ordinary citizens. Back of these is the more relaxed attitude towards relations with the West that seems to characterize the Khrushchev regime. But only the most sanguine observer would predict an early end to the cold war.

¶ George Kennan, a former ambassador to Russia and a scholar with wide experience in Russian affairs, is definitely not such an optimist. In the selection below, he describes how, in the West, "an over-simplified and over-militarized view of the cold war contrived to settle down quite comfortably, in many minds, beside a highly utopian concept of the ways in which this cold war could be brought to an end." The utopian ways, according to Kennan, are the ones we have become most accustomed to think of as the best means of ending the cold war—summit meetings, the United Nations, and disarmament agreements among others. Kennan believes that in the light of certain Soviet attitudes, the latter are impracticable and offers an alternative. Kennan's alternative will no doubt dismay those who seek a quick and easy solution to the cold war, but as he phrases it himself, he is afraid it is "a comfortless message" that he brings.

SOVIET MIND AND WORLD REALITIES

George F. Kennan

* * *

WE ARE all familiar with the posture of irreconcilable hostility, ostensibly only towards the Western governments but in effect towards the Western peoples as well, which has at all times animated the Soviet leaders. We have learned to expect at their hands an unremitting effort to undermine our world position, to disrupt our relations with those who have formerly been our friends, to destroy our confidence in ourselves and the confidence of others in us—to reduce us, in short, to a state of isolation, helplessness, and impotence in the affairs of the world.

Now what is it that could bring men to take so intolerant and unpromising an attitude, one so out of accord with the obvious needs of our time, and so sure to produce tensions and dangers, inconveniences for themselves as well as for everyone else? I think one must clarify one's answer to this question before one can think usefully about the Western response.

The rationale for this posture on the part of the Soviet Government has, as we all know, invariably been expressed in ideological terms—in the characteristic jargon, that is, of Marxist-Leninist thought. There has been a common tendency here in the West in recent years to dismiss this ideological posture as mere window-dressing, to ignore its political content and implications, and to see behind it nothing more than a primitive lust for military conquest—usually envisaged as a determination to overrun Western Europe, in particular, by force of arms, as soon as military conditions might prove favourable.

I personally feel that this is a dangerously inaccurate view of what we are up against, and I believe many others who have known Russian Communism at first hand would feel the same. The hostility has been there, certainly; and it has been a deadly hostility, aimed at a destruction of all that we most intimately cherish—a destruction no less sweeping, no less final, than that which would be occasioned by an outright war. But the threat has not been one of all-out military attack. It has been a combined political and military threat, but more political than military—a threat intimately associated with the weaknesses of our Western civilization itself—looking to these weaknesses, in fact, rather than to the strength of the Soviet arms, to constitute the main instruments of our undoing. The Soviet design has consisted, in other words, primarily of a determination to exploit every element of disunity, of confusion, of short-sightedness in our society, with a view to causing us to eliminate ourselves as rivals to Soviet power and influence everywhere.

Now in connection with this design, armed force has, to be sure, been cultivated on a major scale by the Soviet Government. It has been cultivated partly as a precaution, partly as a psychological weapon, partly because it was always envisaged that the Soviet armed forces might some day be called upon to play a subsidiary role in the final phases of the demise of Western capitalism. But it has never—at least not until very recently—never been looked to as the major instrument by which our undoing was to be accomplished.

One of the most serious evils of this over-militarization of thinking in the West on the nature of the Soviet threat has been that it has confused people badly about the question of what could be done to meet this threat. Assuming that the ideological foundation for Soviet policy was simply disingenuous, many people have tended to suppose either that the Soviet leaders were genuinely suspicious of Western purposes, and that this was the real cause of their hostility; or that they were simply evil men, who wanted power for its own sake and believed that they could outpace us in the military competition to a point where we could safely be attacked and disposed of. And taking one or the other of these views, people assumed that if only we could prove ourselves strong enough to discourage military aggression, or, correspondingly, if we could lay to rest the Soviet suspicions about our motives, this whole situation could be suddenly cleared up—an entirely new outlook could suddenly be induced in the Soviet mind—and the cold war would be terminated at a stroke; and, as the culmination of this happy process, people usually envisaged some sort of a summit meeting, at which the last misunderstandings would be removed and agreements would be arrived at for a peaceful collaboration in the future.

In this manner, as you see, an over-simplified and over-militarized view of the cold war contrived to settle down quite comfortably, in many minds, beside a highly utopian concept of the ways in which this cold war could be brought to an end.

These tendencies naturally received a certain fillip in recent years from the death of Stalin. His successors appeared to be men of greater moderation and good-will and even humanity; and in some respects they really were —and are. Stalin, of course, also talked peace in his day, as Khrushchev does now; but he accompanied that talk with policies so harsh, so forbidding, so obviously imbued with a total enmity towards the Western world that even the most sanguine of us here in the West found it hard, in the end, to believe in the possibility of any amicable settlement. Stalin's successors, and especially Mr. Khrushchev, have talked peace with a greater show of warmth and earnestness; and they even accompanied this talk, initially, with just enough in the way of normalization of the atmosphere of Soviet diplomacy to lead many people to hope that perhaps things really had changed.

We have now had four years in which to study the political personality of this post-Stalin régime; and I am afraid that the time has come when we can no longer comfort ourselves with any of these illusions. Recent events, in particular, have left us no choice but to have a searching look at some of the peculiarities of the Russian Communist mind and to draw unsparingly the consequences of what we see.

From the time of their seizure of power, forty years ago, the Russian Communists have always been characterized by their extraordinary ability to cultivate falsehood as a deliberate weapon of policy. They began by adopting an attitude of complete cynicism about objective truth, denying its value, if not its existence, declaring the lie to be no less useful and respectable than the truth if only it served the purposes of the party. Departing from this premise, they have systematically employed falsehood not just as a means of deceiving others and exploiting their credulity, but also as a means of comforting and reassuring themselves. It has seemed to them at all times easier, and in no way improper, to operate a militant political movement on the basis of convenient falsehood than on the basis of awkward truth.

I think we have to recognize today, particularly on the example of Khrushchev's recent statements and policies, that the effects of this systematic abuse of the human intellect are more deep-seated and troublesome. Forty years of intellectual opportunism have wrought a strange corruption of the Communist mind, rendering it incapable of distinguishing sharply between fact and fiction in a single segment of its experience, namely in its relationship to any external competitive power. Let me stress that it is only in this one sector that the Communist mind is thus affected. In other respects, it is extremely shrewd and discerning.

I have been asked hundreds of times in recent years how it could be that men of such great native intelligence as the Soviet leaders, commanding so elaborate and costly a network of intelligence-gathering agencies, could be anything else but excellently informed about ourselves and everything having to do with us. I should like to suggest an answer to this question.

In everything that can be statistically expressed—expressed, that is, in such a way as not to imply any judgement on our motivation—I believe the Soviet Government to be excellently informed about us. I am sure that their information on the development of our economies, on the state of our military preparations, on our scientific progress, &c., is absolutely first-rate. But when it comes to the analysis of our motives, to the things that make our life tick as it does, I think this whole great system of intelligence-gathering breaks down seriously. It breaks down because over all these forty years the Communist Party has made it impossible for the people who collect the factual information to accompany that information with any really objective analysis of the nature of Western society. Some of the fictions dearest and most basic to Russian Communism's view of itself would be jeopardized at every turn by that sort of an analysis. The Soviet diplomatic representative or journalist abroad has no choice but to cast his analytical report in the terms of Marxist-Leninist ideology, whether this is applicable or not in the given instance. In this way the Soviet leaders find themselves committed to a badly distorted image of the outside world.

Being thus committed, they are able to apprehend everything about us but the main things. They view us as one might view the inhabitants of another planet through a very powerful telescope. Everything is visible; one sees in the greatest detail the strange beings of that other world going about their daily business; one can even discern the nature of their undertakings; but what one does not see and cannot see is the motivation that drives them on these various pursuits. This remains concealed; and thus the entire image, clear and intelligible in detail, becomes incomprehensible in its totality.

The fact is that the Soviet leaders are the first and leading victims of the abuse they have practised for so long on the freedom of the mind. I would not wish to maintain that they believe everything they say; I am sure they don't. But I would submit that their habitual carelessness about the truth has tended to obliterate in their minds the distinction between what they do believe and what they merely find it convenient to say.

It would be easier for us if they either believed things entirely or spoke them in utter cynicism. In either case, we would know where we stood. As it is, our problem is very difficult indeed; for we can never know, when we encounter their statements and reactions, whether we have to do with the substructure of sincerely held error which does indeed exist in their minds, or with the superstructure of contrived and deliberately cultivated untruth to which they are so committed.

Now, this, it seems to me, is what we are up against in the mentality of Mr. Khrushchev and his associates; and the implications for Western statesmanship are numerous and far-reaching. Let me mention only a few of those that seem to me of greatest importance.

We must accept, first of all, the fact that there is nothing anyone can do in any short space of time to alter this situation, to correct this corruption of thought, to make out of the Soviet leaders men capable of seeing world realities as we do. It is no good trying to argue them round to our point of view. On any one occasion they are men who can be directly influenced by situations, but not by words expressed in any terminology other than their own.

There is nothing that can be said to Mr. Khrushchev on any one occasion by any Western figures, however illustrious, that would suddenly dispel this obscurity of vision. What we are confronted with here is not just misunderstanding, not just honest error, but a habit of the mind, an induced state, a condition. Even assuming for the sake of argument that it were possible to explain away in some satisfactory manner all the sources of misunderstanding and suspicion that prevail today between the Kremlin and ourselves, and to start all over again with a fresh slate tomorrow morning, I would still hazard the guess that twenty-four hours would not elapse before that fresh slate would be fouled with new misunderstandings, and precisely as a consequence of the congenital inability of our Soviet friends to see themselves and us and our mutual relationship with any proper degree of realism.

In the face of this situation, I wonder about the wisdom of engaging the persons of the senior Western statesmen directly in the process of negotiation with the Soviet Government? With people whose state of mind is what I have just described no intimacy of understanding is really possible. There is only one sort of thing that can usefully be said to them and that is: what we would be prepared to do, and what we would not be prepared to do, in specific contingencies. This sort of thing they understand; but to say it, you do not need the physical presence of a President or a Prime Minister; and there are even reasons why it is better not to have it. I would not wish to say that there is never a time for summit meetings. There is a time for almost everything in the strange world of diplomacy. But surely, if the usefulness of these senior figures is to be protected and the raising of false hopes avoided, such meetings should occur, if at all, at the end of the negotiating process, and for the purpose of formalizing agreements already arrived at, rather than at the beginning and as a means of starting the wearisome process of accommodation.

However one strives to disclaim the intention, meetings at the summit will never fail to suggest to the public mind the possibility of early global solutions —sweeping and spectacular solutions—to outstanding problems.

But it is precisely this possibility of such solutions that is ruled out by what we know of the condition of mind of the Soviet leaders. The road to a safer and more hopeful state of world affairs is not to be traversed in any "giant strides." On the contrary, if the tension between Russia and the Western world is to be reduced, it must be broken down into its individual components— into a number of specific problems, that is; and each of these must be treated empirically and on its merits with a view to arriving at those compromises and accommodations that would be least unsettling to world peace. And for this, it is not the hectic encounters of senior statesmen under the spotlight of publicity which we need; it is the patient, quiet, orderly use of the regular channels of private communication between governments, as they have grown up and proved their worth over the course of the centuries.

This implies, it seems to me, that we must discard our recent fear of bilateral communication and our attachment to the idea of negotiating with Russia only as a coalition. There has recently been a good deal of talk about strengthening the decision-taking process in NATO. Certainly we need the maximum real political intimacy within NATO. But we will be creating difficulties for ourselves if we over-formalize in any way the processes for discussion and agreement among us. Apart from the fact that we do have real differences within the NATO family in fields aside from Russian policy —deep unavoidable differences, not to be bridged by creation of any new machinery—I fear for the effect of our relation to Russia if we make the procedures of NATO any more elaborate and more restricting than they are now. The delicate explorations and discussions which must precede accommodation in complex international questions cannot be conducted by a coalition, operating on the basis of sporadic, unanimous, and highly formalized decisions. For this, you need the privacy, the authority, and the day-to-day flexibility which only the sovereign government can provide. I would hazard the prediction that no solution to any serious problem of Soviet-Western relations is going to be discovered in meetings where a group of Western representatives, bound by prior understandings among themselves and limited by each other's inhibitions, confront the Soviet negotiators over a large green table, while the representatives of the world press wait in the next room to be briefed at once on all that has been said. We have urgent need to loosen up these rigidities of communication, to divest ourselves of the fear of all that is informal and exploratory, and to restore the element of privacy to the composition of differences.

In this same connexion, I find myself worried at the frequent sight of the United Nations being involved in the issues of our conflict with Soviet power, and particularly the United Nations Assembly. Some of the most important elements in the East-West conflict long pre-dated the foundation of the United Nations; they were part of the world into which it was born. It is not fair to the Organization today to ask it to resolve the predicaments of the past as well as of the present. No international organization can be stronger than the structure of relationships among the Great Powers that underlies it; and to look to such an organization to resolve deep-seated conflicts of interest among those Great Powers is to ignore its limitations and to jeopardize its usefulness in other fields.

When I said, as I said a moment ago, that the Soviet leaders can be influenced by situations, I had in mind real situations, not parliamentary ones. The Soviet Government is not insensitive to deeper trends of world opinion, but it cannot easily be shamed into doing things or not doing them by the votes of international majorities. Soviet power, always addressing itself to peoples over the heads of their rulers, grew great on the defiance of the opinions of other governments; and it is not afraid today of votes in its disfavour. Not only will international majorities not be effective in modifying Soviet behaviour but they may easily, as things now stand, be turned at any time against us in the West; and we, with our more legalistic tradition and our great moral commitment to the principle of international organization, will find it harder to defy them than the Soviets.

Many people, again, would like to by-pass the political issues entirely by agreements for general disarmament, and the effort to work something out along this line has recently preoccupied the attention of our governments and of the world public. I have great sympathy for the motives of those who have worked so hard to bring this dream to fruition; but I cannot agree that the approach is a very promising one.

It is true that armaments can and do constitute a source of tension in themselves. But they are not self-engendering. No one maintains them just for the love of it. They are conditioned at bottom by political differences and rivalries. To attempt to remove the armaments before removing these substantive conflicts of interest is to put the cart before the horse. At every turn we are confronted with the fact that there is no way of evading those specific political problems—for the main part territorial questions of who is to rule whom, and where and when—in which all this tension and trouble has its real origins. Only when these are alleviated will the prospects for disarmament become real; and only then will all this painstaking preparatory work yield its dividends.

Let me return for a moment, before I close, to the systematic Soviet distortion of the realities of our world and of the purposes to which we are dedicated. I should like to say that I think we cannot simply ignore this sort of thing. It is a serious error to dismiss Soviet falsehoods as "just propaganda" and to profess to find them too absurd and unimportant to answer. I am always startled at this phrase "just propaganda." Why "just"? What is the matter with propaganda? Is it not a serious and important force in world affairs? Let us not forget that these fantastic allegations are partially believed by those who say them, and they will be at least partially believed by many of those who listen. A wise Western policy will insist that no single falsehood or distortion from the Soviet side should ever go unanswered.

This will be tiresome. We don't like repetition. But we cannot afford to dispense with it. Truth does not win over error just on its merits. It, too, has to be assiduously propagated. I have asserted that there is nothing that could be said to the Soviet leaders in the space of a few days that would change their strangely corrupted mentality. But there are things which could be said to them every day over the course of several years which would exert a useful discipline upon them, would make it harder for them to ignore the distinction between the real and the unreal, and would place limitations—thus far not visible—on their use of falsehood as a weapon of political policy.

All in all, then, I fear it is a comfortless message with which I have come before you. One by one I have felt obliged to bring into question all those devices to which the minds of people here in the West have most hopefully turned in these recent years; summit meetings, global solutions, coalition diplomacy, the United Nations, disarmament. And in their place I have suggested only the unglamorous devices of an informational war of indefinite duration, and a quiet old-fashioned diplomatic attack on certain of the individual political problems that divide us from the Soviet world.

* * *

[18]

Epilogue: Western Values

$\mathcal{I}$t is almost a truism to say that Communist ideology, where it has abandoned the subtleties of the dialectic, has become most explicit about its values. On the other hand, as Professor Shepard Clough has written:

Although Western man may have a general notion as to what his basic values are, these ideas rest for the most part below the level of consciousness, or they are so much a part of our existence that they are taken for granted and statements about them seem commonplace, if not downright platitudinous. It is high time that our goals in life be made so explicit that there be no equivocation about them. It is important for all of us to be so clear regarding our values that we do not take a vague or uncritical attitude toward them nor by too great familiarity with them fail to realize their true worth.[1]

¶ The above considerations, combined with a commission from NATO and Professor Clough's own interest as a historian in the role ideologies and ideals play in shaping human behavior, led to his writing *Basic Values of Western Civilization,* a chapter from which is reprinted below.
¶ In this selection, Professor Clough examines our material values. Although basic to our value system, material values are the ones most often criticized outside of Western society and, indeed, questioned within it. Following a method he uses in other parts of his book, Professor Clough discusses the origin of our material values, traces their development, and assesses them as they now stand. He also pays particular attention to the instruments which further them and the degree to which these instruments are compatible with our basic values. In respect to this last consideration,

[1] Shepard B. Clough, *Basic Values of Western Civilization* (New York: Columbia, 1960), pp. 3–4.

Professor Clough concludes that "our culture has, in a manner inconsonant with its basic values, developed wants which are tyrannical."

This problem will have to be solved in the future. Professor Clough's conclusion strikes a somber note, especially if one thinks of the unfulfilled wants of the greater part of the non-Western world. But it need not be a note of despair. Elsewhere Professor Clough has suggested that, "In the West a firm conviction that while there is life there is hope for improvement means that the system (i.e. instruments or societal institutions furthering values) is perpetually stimulated to be better, to be more in conformity with our basic values." [2]

MATERIAL VALUES

Shepard B. Clough

CRITICS FROM other cultures, be they statesmen, politicians, scholars, social reformers, or cartoonists, delight in representing Westerners as excessively materialistic. Indeed, they have a marked penchant for portraying us as vulgar overweights, puffing big black cigars, and wearing vests upon which are emblazoned symbols of the dollar, the pound sterling, or the French franc.

Furthermore, these commentators from outside the West, particularly if they are from Communist societies, depict the capitalism of our culture as money slavery. The rich are described as living in extreme luxury, while the poor are pictured as living in squalor. Employers swagger about with enormous bull whips which they snap over the backs of their wage-receiving minions in order to force these creatures to keep the capitalist machine running. Yet, every so often and inevitably, this machine comes to a grinding halt with a business depression and those who live by wages are threatened with starvation.

Withal, these observers from other cultures condemn our capitalism most roundly. Yet their envy for our economic well-being is obvious, for they are now busy as can be trying to catch up with us in this very regard. They damn

[2] *Ibid.*, p. 47.

From Shepard B. Clough, *Basic Values of Western Civilization* (New York: Columbia University Press, 1960), pp. 48–65. Copyright © 1960 Columbia University Press, New York. Reprinted by permission.

the capitalist system with little knowledge of it as it is today and without stopping to think that they employ many of the devices of capitalism, including the wage system, for which they revile us.

In the Western view, the picture which others draw of our materialism is greatly overdone. Nevertheless, we recognize that we do place economic well-being high in our scale of values. Perhaps man does not live by bread alone, but obviously he cannot live without it. We hold not only that the satisfaction of material wants makes life safer and more agreeable, but also that stores of wealth are absolutely necessary if we are to realize our most basic values. Only if a society has economic resources and surpluses so that its members do not have to be continually employed at producing food, clothing, and shelter can it devote its energies and resources to learning ways to extend its control over its physical environment or to create or enjoy great artistic and intellectual works. And only when there is a degree of economic well-being within a society are tensions among groups relieved enough so that man may live in some semblance of peace with his fellows.

Furthermore, the West is of the opinion that the individual should receive special rewards for exceptional talent, for above-average industry, for risk-taking, and for self-deprivation in the present for greater rewards in the future. By means of opportunities for private profit, it is thought, are adequate incentives provided for man to strive to increase his material status.

This notion of rewards and incentives is at the very basis of the capitalist system. Capitalism, about which so much nonsense is uttered, is in essence an organization of production and distribution in which the individual or group of individuals combine their resources (capital) in order to acquire the means of production, to hire labor for wages, and to purchase materials for processing in order to produce goods and services. These goods and services are then sold in unknown markets at prices which will return sums in excess of the total costs of production, that is, which will result in a profit. It was by this system that the West was able to achieve the greatest degree of economic well-being which the world has ever known. Accordingly the West attaches a high value to the capitalist system as an instrument for attaining basic values. This is a judgment which, on the record, seems justified.

Yet, although the West has as a basic value a high degree of material well-being and believes that the capitalist system is the most efficacious manner for the organization of society for attaining a large supply of goods and services, it has certain reservations about both. Although it approves economic well-being, it condemns most heartily "miserly accumulations" or great concentrations of wealth if not employed for advancing basic values. Our literature is shot through with diatribes against the miser, as in George Eliot's *Silas Marner;* our religious leaders are forever reminding their faithful that it is more difficult for a rich man to enter the kingdom of heaven than it is for a camel to pass through the eye of a needle; and our socio-politico-economic planners keep telling us that holding hoards is antieconomic—that capital should be put to work—and they inform us also that purchasing power needs to be distributed widely enough to create mass markets so that capital will be encouraged to invest and there will be economic growth.

Even the very rich in our culture try to rationalize their wealth by contending either that they know best how to invest capital for future growth or that with wealth they can further our basic values through philanthropy.[1] Many have, indeed, established foundations to increase our control over some aspect of our physical world, such as conquering a disease, furthering education, aiding the poor, or encouraging the arts. Here is a kind of balancing of values to achieve multiple ends.

In much the same way the West has adjusted and altered the capitalist system in the search for the most effective instrument of production and distribution. Not only has it supplemented the wage system by all manner of welfare devices provided by the state or the firm, but also the collectivity has endeavored to curb excessive concentration of wealth by graduated taxes, to get the system back on the track when it has been thrown off by depressions, and to add to private initiative by investments in economic activity. In the United States in 1938 governmental loans and investments amounted to about 25 per cent of the total loans and investments of member banks of the Federal Reserve System. And at the present about 20 per cent of British industry is nationalized, about 30 per cent of national income in Italy comes from nationalized sectors of the economy, and from 1947 to 1951 30 per cent of new investments in France came from the state.[2] Although the West adheres to the doctrine of individual rewards for economic activity, it recognizes that the economy cannot under all circumstances be left to the free play of individual interests. The modification of "classical capitalism" by state action is consistent with the West's pragmatism —with an insistence that any existing organization or institution must be made to perform its appointed task and if necessary must be altered so that it will.

In the consideration of economic activity two questions inevitably arise. The first is: For whose eventual use are goods and services produced, that is, should economic well-being be limited to the few or extended to the many—should we rest blithely content with the Biblical consolation that "the poor, they are always with you"? The second question is: How much economic well-being is desirable and is there any way to gauge when there is too much wealth? These two questions may be considered simultaneously.

[1] Philanthropy amounts to about two per cent of national income in the United States. See Emerson Andrews, *Philanthropic Giving* (New York: Russell Sage Foundation, 1950).

[2] For a further discussion of these matters, consult Shepard B. Clough, *The American Way* (New York: Thomas Y. Crowell, 1953) and *The Economic Development of Western Civilization* (New York: McGraw-Hill, 1959).

From time immemorial the West has shown a concern for its poor. On the manor the lord assumed a responsibility for his people for humanitarian reasons as well as for the protection of his labor supply. Later, as towns grew, men of wealth and the Church provided for the poor through charities of various kinds. Then, with the formation of unified states, some kind of poor laws were adopted to furnish a minimum of care for those in very great need.

By the end of the eighteenth century or by the early nineteenth century Western man was demanding and getting the right to "life, liberty, and *property*." [3] This meant that all were free to engage in any economic activity which they might choose and that everyone, irrespective of status, could own property. To us such freedoms are taken as matters of course and accordingly are not given a second thought. To the people in the West who were first free to move about as they would and to engage in any calling of their choice, they were regarded as tremendous boons, somewhat equivalent to the throwing off of partial bonds of slavery. Even today Westerners find it difficult to believe that members of many cultures do not even now enjoy such privileges—they seldom stop to realize that in a Communist culture admissions to many professions are politically controlled and that ownership of private property for purposes of gain is taboo.

Then in the nineteenth century social legislation was developed, *pari passu* with the wage system and factory employment, to help protect the workers from abuse. Moreover, various forms of poor relief were used in times of depression to relieve suffering. And finally, the welfare state assumed the task, as we have seen, of preventing anyone from actual economic deprivation.

One of the most remarkable statements of recent times regarding a minimum of material well-being for everyone was included in the declaration of the Four Freedoms, a document drafted by Franklin D. Roosevelt and Winston Churchill shortly after America's entry into World War II. As presented to Congress, January 6, 1941, this declaration read:

In the future days, which we seek to make secure, we look forward to a world founded upon four essential human freedoms.

The first is freedom of speech and expression—everywhere in the world.

The second is freedom of every person to worship God in his own way—everywhere in the world.

The third is freedom from want—which, translated into world terms, means economic understanding which will secure to every nation a healthy, peaceful life for its inhabitants—everywhere in the world.

The fourth is freedom from fear—which translated into world terms, means a worldwide reduction of armaments to such a point and in such a thorough

[3] The Declaration of the Rights of Man and the Citizen (1789).

fashion that no nation will be in a position to commit an act of aggression against any neighbor—anywhere in the world.

The remarkable thing about the Four Freedoms was that *all* persons, irrespective of class, color, religion, or anything else "everywhere" in the world, were to be guaranteed freedom from want. Thus, expression was given once again to the West's high consideration for human life—for the sanctity of the human being—and to the intention of the state to assume as one of its obligations the material welfare of individuals.

Important as this statement of our minimum materialist position was, our wartime leaders would have come closer to expressing our ideal value in economic matters if they had propounded a doctrine for the "creation of abundance." As we have already explained, the attainment of our basic values has as a prerequisite the existence of considerable economic surplus. In fact, historical evidence supports the proposition that peaks of civilization have *followed* closely the attainment of heights of economic well-being per capita and that conversely declines in civilization have accompanied falls in abundance per capita.[4]

To explain how the ideal of abundance came to be established and how it attained such a high place in our value system as it now enjoys is exceedingly difficult, as in the case of most of our ideal values, for so many factors of imponderable weights are united in such intricate patterns and with such precise timing that a reconstruction of what has taken place in time is subject to some error. It is usually said by way of explanation, however, that one of the chief forces in developing a desire for economic surplus was that men living in regions with unproductive seasons had to store up goods to carry them through periods when nature was dormant. Unfortunately man, unlike hibernating animals, cannot live long on his own fat, although the size of some individuals might appear to belie this generalization. Accordingly Western man became accustomed to accumulating more goods than were needed for current consumption and in so doing achieved greater success than persons living in most other cultures. This is to be accounted for in part by the fact that rainfall was usually plentiful and the land fertile, in part because of ease of transportation along gently flowing rivers and on not very turbulent seas, in part because of the development of machines which supplemented the efforts of men, and in part because of such natural resources as timber, ferrous ores, and later on coal.

Inasmuch as surpluses provided leisure for pursuits which gave pleasure and permitted an exchange of goods with others for things which made life more agreeable, men came to place great importance on the creation of large stocks. Since the latter half of the Middle Ages, at least, stores of wealth have generally been great enough to permit relatively large segments of the

---

[4] This subject is the theme of Shepard B. Clough, *The Rise and Fall of Civilization* (New York: Columbia University Press, 1957).

population to take time to seek the riddles of the universe and to embellish life with works of art.

What is the West's formula for determining how much economic well-being is desirable? The optimum supply of goods and services is attained when it advances most effectively efforts to realize basic values for all members of our culture. If wealth leads to physical deterioration of the individual through overindulgence in things of the flesh, if it leads to tensions in society by the few impinging on the rights of others to life and happiness (an example would be motor scooters in Italy, which disturb the quiet of day and night and endanger life and limb because of the ostentatious cavorting of their owners), and if it detracts from the accomplishment of great works of art or the extension of man's control over his physical universe because those of wealth have no appreciation of the finer things of life, then society has more goods and services than it can properly absorb. Experience of the West has been that leadership in the use of wealth contrary to our values usually comes from those who are not educated in what the West believes is the proper function of wealth, whether these persons be *nouveaux riches* or the scions of old rich who have gone to seed. The culture here has obviously a major task of continual training.

If wealth used in accordance with and for the realization of the West's highest aims is a basic value, then it follows that those instruments which contribute to greater material well-being per capita of the population are given high value status, just as the family and the school are, because they train the young in the entire content of the culture. Inasmuch as Western man knows much about conditions of economic progress, he can isolate specific factors of growth and attach values to them according to their strategic roles.

The most important of these factors are (1) a large saving out of current income for investment in producer's goods; (2) a technology to extend the productive power of the individual by means of machines constructed of and driven by inorganic materials; (3) a supply of raw materials which can be increased by improving strains of plants and animals and by expanding areas devoted to them, by dipping more extensively into "nature's capital,'" that is, into the treasures stored in the world's crust or in the solar system, and by devising ways of substituting materials which are abundant for those which are becoming scarce; (4) a skilled labor force able and willing to man machines, to organize production, and to work for wages; (5) an extensive specialization in the performance of economic tasks, that is, what the economist calls a division of labor; and (6) an intense desire to achieve economic growth—such a high motivation that people are willing to forego present comforts for future gain.

Confirmation of the values attached to all of these factors can be found in the national economic plans of Western countries and in a vast body of Western economic literature.[5] In the first place, we value savings for investment. We recognize that a proportion of national income, somewhere in the neighborhood of 20 per cent of it, must be devoted annually to the construction of producer's goods if we are to have a desirable rate of growth. Indeed, we are very conscious of the fact that one of the recurring problems of statecraft is to determine what proportion of national income shall be devoted to consumer's goods to give us the kind of living which we want, what proportion shall go to defense, and what proportion shall go for renewing and expanding plant.

Furthermore, we realize that there must be an equitable enough distribution of goods and services so that those with great needs will have the purchasing power to acquire what they want, thus expanding the domestic market. We also acknowledge that adequate rewards go for economic achievements so that there will be incentives for continued accomplishments and that wealth be sufficiently concentrated to allow investment in large undertakings and the financing of the arts and sciences on a large scale.

In the second place, the role of technology is so great in the production of goods that a high value is attached to knowledge of the productive arts and to the methods of obtaining and increasing that knowledge. Thus additional support is given to "science," to that inquisitive spirit which leads Western man to be curious about everything, and for that optimism which makes him believe that if he applies himself assiduously enough he can "know" about everything that is empirically testable or observable in the entire universe.

In the third place, because of the expanding list of Western man's wants and because of the increasing number of humans in our culture, for whom a more equitable satisfaction of their wants is desirable, great value is placed on expanding supplies of raw materials. In the recent past we have increased our supplies by substituting for goods which are grown currently in nature materials which have been stored up in the earth's crust over eons of time. In part, however, the extension of supplies has been accomplished by drawing upon the more economically backward areas and by paying for the foodstuffs and raw materials thus obtained with finished goods. For this reason great value is attached to world trade, which is believed to benefit all parties concerned.[6]

[5] For the history of the economic growth of Western culture, see Shepard B. Clough, *The Economic Development of Western Civilization* (New York: McGraw-Hill, 1959). On the theory of economic growth, see W. Arthur Lewis, *The Theory of Economic Growth* (London: G. Allen, 1955) and Colin Clark, *Conditions of Economic Progress,* 3d ed. (London: Macmillan, 1957).

[6] Political imperialism was and economic imperialism is approved for the same general reasons. Whether or not all parties in trade benefit equally is open to question. Because of the relation between prices for finished goods and prices for raw materials and foodstuffs, the amount of human energy which goes to produce $1.00 worth of the former is generally less than that which goes into $1.00 worth of the latter. Hence producers of finished goods benefit in terms of human input at the expense of producers of raw materials. This has undoubtedly been true throughout all time.

In the fourth place, we place high value on an extreme division of labor, for it is clear that in every case throughout history in which people have attained a high standard of material well-being, specialization in the performing of tasks has been very great. Furthermore, in every instance where very high national incomes per capita are being realized at the present time the division of labor is carried to extraordinary lengths.

From the concept of division of labor additional support is given to the idea of interregional trade, for we hold that every district should turn out what it is best suited to produce—frigid zones timbers, furs, and fish, tropical zones fruits and vegetables, coal-mining areas coal, and so on. In this way, it is believed, output will be maximized and each region will get what it needs by an exchange of goods, just as in the specialization of work each individual will get what he wants through the market place.

Needless to say, the corollaries of these economic values are, in turn, numerous and far-reaching, and in studying them we obtain still more light on the most tantalizing of riddles—how patterns of human behavior come into being. They illustrate well how economic forces operate with factors from all other phases of societal existence to create "styles" or configurations of thought and action.

Among the first of these corollaries is the fact that trade under a system of division of labor has obviously to be both intensive and extensive. Hence commerce is highly valued, as are all things in the field of transportation and communication which make it possible. In fact, so important is trade, not only in the exchange of goods but also in the exchange of ideas, that it is frequently regarded by economic historians as the wellspring of development, both economic and intellectual.[7]

The second major corollary is that specialization in production requires a ready medium of exchange, a measure of value, and a store of wealth, which is the definition of money in all its various forms of cash and credit. Indeed, so important has money been in facilitating exchange that it is regarded as one of the most important inventions of all time. A monetary system in good working order is one of the most valued institutions of our culture.

The third corollary is that an extreme division of labor in society requires' that relations among individuals and regions be orderly and conducted on a basis of mutual respect and understanding. For this reason, in Western culture great value is placed upon so-called "responsible behavior," that is, on behavior designed to keep the economic system going without a breakdown because of excessively selfish demands.

This responsible way of life is further made possible by individuals abiding by what they have agreed to do. This explains why we attach so much impor-

[7] See, for example, the works of the Belgian medievalist, Henri Pirenne, notably his *Economic and Social History of Medieval Europe* (London: Paul Trench, 1936).

tance to the sanctity of contracts and why we have developed such an elaborate legal apparatus to give sanction to contractual arrangements.

Responsibility is also of crucial importance in our system because with economic specialization there is also specialization in other aspects of human existence—social, political, intellectual, and aesthetic. Perhaps it is not too much to say that one of the fundamental reasons for the "rises and falls" of civilization in cultures can be found in the degree to which people act responsibly one toward another. When mutual responsibility ceases to exist, it is not possible to have a high division of labor.

The ideal material value system outlined above began to take shape in the latter half of the Middle Ages and became more sharply delineated as greater economic opportunities presented themselves with the Renaissance and its emphasis on things of this world, with the expansion of Europe overseas, and with the growth of production by machines. Yet two major modifications of the ideal value should be noted in order to have a more realistic understanding of Western economic behavior patterns. These are the "tyranny of wealth" and the "tyranny of wants." By the former is meant such concentration of wealth and subsequently of power in society that a small number enjoy the material benefits of our productive system by the exploitation of the masses. By the "tyranny of wants" is meant a piling up of things to satisfy socially created wants to a point where they actually impede the individual in his efforts to realize those values which the West holds in highest esteem.

Without doubt there has been and is a considerable concentration of wealth in Western culture. It is said that in France of 1933 two per cent of the people owned some 35 per cent of the wealth and that two hundred families controlled the Bank of France and thereby much of the economic, social, and political life of the country. Indeed, the individual may well aspire to the accumulation of wealth in order, as we have seen, to accomplish purposes which are desirable from a social point of view or to effect greater economic growth through investment.

Although these values are undoubtedly the dominant ones in the West in the realm of things economic, sight should not be lost of a dissenting minority—a minority, if one may judge from the voting strength of socialist and communist parties in some regions, that is very sizable. Socialists question the fundamental assumption of capitalism—that private ownership and private profit are necessary to furnish incentives for economic betterment or to effect concentration of wealth for realizing basic values in our culture. They argue that society through its elected representatives can best and most equitably decide how accumulated surpluses can be used and that a desire for general economic welfare of the total collectivity will provide a more potent motivation for economic growth than will private profits. For the present, a working compromise between this position and that of completely unbridled private initiative has been effected in the welfare state and in the nationalization of certain branches of the various economies of the West. The aim has been to correct social and economic abuses, by mitigating actual hardships of the poor through state aid and by curbing great accumulations of the rich through progressive taxation. Capitalism has thus been modified, but it has not been abolished. How lasting such a compromise can be will depend on whether men make it work in conformity with the basic values of our culture.

Perhaps, however, a better compromise has been achieved in this regard than in the "tyranny of wants." Indeed, in Western culture such a strong desire for material things exists that we are using natural resources at a rate so rapid that we are bound to deprive future generations of much needed materials and are surfeiting ourselves with goods, in some instances, to our physical and social detriment. The plain fact is that we have become the slaves of our wants. Thus we crave automobiles and get them in such numbers that our legs are becoming useless, and cynics prophesy that we shall develop a race with extremely puny pedal extremeties, if with any at all. Again, automobiles so encumber our streets in the great metropolises that they have become well-nigh useless for local transportation. And we are so prone to ride just for the sake of "going" that we eat into our time and resources which might better be devoted to creative enterprises which we value highly. In a similar way we overuse and ill-use many socially desirable devices such as radio, television, and motion pictures. They tend to make passive observers of us and to take time, which is after all what life is measured by, from more desirable activities. Finally, we overindulge in food and drink. People eat to the point that they have to slenderize—a practice that has given rise to an important reducing industry—and they consume alcoholic beverages to such a degree that alcoholism is everywhere in the West a social-medical problem.

Then, too, we are gadget mad. We are becoming so accustomed to operating everything with push buttons that we fail to experience the thrill of achievement in the everyday business of living. Many of our young homemakers cannot get a meal without "ready mixes" or frozen foods—and if they were required to grow their food they would be at a loss as to how to proceed. Many of our young heads of families cannot mend a broken chair, to say nothing of making one in its entirety. And many young workers do not partake of the joy of achievement, for they perform such minute and mundane tasks that their main concern is how fast the boxes will flow on the assembly line and how soon the final whistle will blow.

Though the West has accomplished wonders in creating a system in which there is freedom from want for the vast majority and in which there is abundance enough to permit many individuals to devote themselves to creative enterprise and to controlling the physical universe, our culture has, in a manner inconsonant with its basic values, developed wants which are tyrannical.